T0189480

# Communications in Computer and Information Science 1499

More information about this series at http://www.springer.com/series/7899

Constantine Stephanidis ·
Margherita Antona · Stavroula Ntoa (Eds.)

# HCI International 2021 - Late Breaking Posters

23rd HCI International Conference, HCII 2021
Virtual Event, July 24–29, 2021
Proceedings, Part II

 Springer

*Editors*
Constantine Stephanidis
University of Crete and Foundation
for Research and Technology – Hellas
(FORTH)
Heraklion, Crete, Greece

Margherita Antona
Foundation for Research
and Technology – Hellas (FORTH)
Heraklion, Crete, Greece

Stavroula Ntoa
Foundation for Research
and Technology – Hellas (FORTH)
Heraklion, Crete, Greece

ISSN 1865-0929          ISSN 1865-0937  (electronic)
Communications in Computer and Information Science
ISBN 978-3-030-90178-3          ISBN 978-3-030-90179-0  (eBook)
https://doi.org/10.1007/978-3-030-90179-0

This Springer imprint is published by the registered company Springer Nature Switzerland AG
The registered company address is: Gewerbestrasse 11, 6330 Cham, Switzerland

# Foreword

Human-Computer Interaction (HCI) is acquiring an ever-increasing scientific and industrial importance, and having more impact on people's everyday life, as an ever-growing number of human activities are progressively moving from the physical to the digital world. This process, which has been ongoing for some time now, has been dramatically accelerated by the COVID-19 pandemic. The HCI International (HCII) conference series, held yearly, aims to respond to the compelling need to advance the exchange of knowledge and research and development efforts on the human aspects of design and use of computing systems.

The 23rd International Conference on Human-Computer Interaction, HCI International 2021 (HCII 2021), was planned to be held at the Washington Hilton Hotel, Washington DC, USA, during July 24–29, 2021. Due to the COVID-19 pandemic and with everyone's health and safety in mind, HCII 2021 was organized and run as a virtual conference. It incorporated the 21 thematic areas and affiliated conferences listed on the following page.

A total of 5222 individuals from academia, research institutes, industry, and governmental agencies from 81 countries submitted contributions, and 1276 papers and 241 posters were included in the volumes of the proceedings that were published before the start of the conference. Additionally, 174 papers and 146 posters are included in the volumes of the proceedings published after the conference, as "Late Breaking Work" (papers and posters). The contributions thoroughly cover the entire field of HCI, addressing major advances in knowledge and effective use of computers in a variety of application areas. These papers provide academics, researchers, engineers, scientists, practitioners, and students with state-of-the-art information on the most recent advances in HCI. The volumes constituting the full set of the HCII 2021 conference proceedings are listed in the following pages.

I would like to thank the Program Board Chairs and the members of the Program Boards of all thematic areas and affiliated conferences for their contribution towards the highest scientific quality and overall success of the HCI International 2021 conference.

This conference would not have been possible without the continuous and unwavering support and advice of Gavriel Salvendy, founder, General Chair Emeritus, and Scientific Advisor. For his outstanding efforts, I would like to express my appreciation to Abbas Moallem, Communications Chair and Editor of HCI International News.

July 2021                                                                   Constantine Stephanidis

# HCI International 2021 Thematic Areas and Affiliated Conferences

**Thematic Areas**

- HCI: Human-Computer Interaction
- HIMI: Human Interface and the Management of Information

**Affiliated Conferences**

- EPCE: 18th International Conference on Engineering Psychology and Cognitive Ergonomics
- UAHCI: 15th International Conference on Universal Access in Human-Computer Interaction
- VAMR: 13th International Conference on Virtual, Augmented and Mixed Reality
- CCD: 13th International Conference on Cross-Cultural Design
- SCSM: 13th International Conference on Social Computing and Social Media
- AC: 15th International Conference on Augmented Cognition
- DHM: 12th International Conference on Digital Human Modeling and Applications in Health, Safety, Ergonomics and Risk Management
- DUXU: 10th International Conference on Design, User Experience, and Usability
- DAPI: 9th International Conference on Distributed, Ambient and Pervasive Interactions
- HCIBGO: 8th International Conference on HCI in Business, Government and Organizations
- LCT: 8th International Conference on Learning and Collaboration Technologies
- ITAP: 7th International Conference on Human Aspects of IT for the Aged Population
- HCI-CPT: 3rd International Conference on HCI for Cybersecurity, Privacy and Trust
- HCI-Games: 3rd International Conference on HCI in Games
- MobiTAS: 3rd International Conference on HCI in Mobility, Transport and Automotive Systems
- AIS: 3rd International Conference on Adaptive Instructional Systems
- C&C: 9th International Conference on Culture and Computing
- MOBILE: 2nd International Conference on Design, Operation and Evaluation of Mobile Communications
- AI-HCI: 2nd International Conference on Artificial Intelligence in HCI

# Conference Proceedings – Full List of Volumes

1. LNCS 12762, Human-Computer Interaction: Theory, Methods and Tools (Part I), edited by Masaaki Kurosu
2. LNCS 12763, Human-Computer Interaction: Interaction Techniques and Novel Applications (Part II), edited by Masaaki Kurosu
3. LNCS 12764, Human-Computer Interaction: Design and User Experience Case Studies (Part III), edited by Masaaki Kurosu
4. LNCS 12765, Human Interface and the Management of Information: Information Presentation and Visualization (Part I), edited by Sakae Yamamoto and Hirohiko Mori
5. LNCS 12766, Human Interface and the Management of Information: Information-rich and Intelligent Environments (Part II), edited by Sakae Yamamoto and Hirohiko Mori
6. LNAI 12767, Engineering Psychology and Cognitive Ergonomics, edited by Don Harris and Wen-Chin Li
7. LNCS 12768, Universal Access in Human-Computer Interaction: Design Methods and User Experience (Part I), edited by Margherita Antona and Constantine Stephanidis
8. LNCS 12769, Universal Access in Human-Computer Interaction: Access to Media, Learning and Assistive Environments (Part II), edited by Margherita Antona and Constantine Stephanidis
9. LNCS 12770, Virtual, Augmented and Mixed Reality, edited by Jessie Y. C. Chen and Gino Fragomeni
10. LNCS 12771, Cross-Cultural Design: Experience and Product Design Across Cultures (Part I), edited by P. L. Patrick Rau
11. LNCS 12772, Cross-Cultural Design: Applications in Arts, Learning, Well-being, and Social Development (Part II), edited by P. L. Patrick Rau
12. LNCS 12773, Cross-Cultural Design: Applications in Cultural Heritage, Tourism, Autonomous Vehicles, and Intelligent Agents (Part III), edited by P. L. Patrick Rau
13. LNCS 12774, Social Computing and Social Media: Experience Design and Social Network Analysis (Part I), edited by Gabriele Meiselwitz
14. LNCS 12775, Social Computing and Social Media: Applications in Marketing, Learning, and Health (Part II), edited by Gabriele Meiselwitz
15. LNAI 12776, Augmented Cognition, edited by Dylan D. Schmorrow and Cali M. Fidopiastis
16. LNCS 12777, Digital Human Modeling and Applications in Health, Safety, Ergonomics and Risk Management: Human Body, Motion and Behavior (Part I), edited by Vincent G. Duffy
17. LNCS 12778, Digital Human Modeling and Applications in Health, Safety, Ergonomics and Risk Management: AI, Product and Service (Part II), edited by Vincent G. Duffy

**http://2021.hci.international/proceedings**

# HCI International 2021 (HCII 2021)

The full list with the Program Board Chairs and the members of the Program Boards of all thematic areas and affiliated conferences is available online:

**http://www.hci.international/board-members-2021.php**

# HCI International 2022

The 24th International Conference on Human-Computer Interaction, HCI International 2022, will be held jointly with the affiliated conferences at the Gothia Towers Hotel and Swedish Exhibition & Congress Centre, Gothenburg, Sweden, June 26 – July 1, 2022. It will cover a broad spectrum of themes related to Human-Computer Interaction, including theoretical issues, methods, tools, processes, and case studies in HCI design, as well as novel interaction techniques, interfaces, and applications. The proceedings will be published by Springer. More information will be available on the conference website: http://2022.hci.international/:

General Chair
Prof. Constantine Stephanidis
University of Crete and ICS-FORTH
Heraklion, Crete, Greece
Email: general_chair@hcii2022.org

**http://2022.hci.international/**

# Contents – Part II

## Physiology, Affect and Cognition

## HCI for Health and Wellbeing

## HCI in Learning, Teaching, and Education

**Culture and Computing**

**Social Computing**

## Design Case Studies

## User Experience Studies

# Contents – Part I

**UX Design and Research in Intelligent Environments**

### Interaction with Robots, Chatbots, and Agents

**Virtual, Augmented, and Mixed Reality**

## Games and Gamification

## HCI in Mobility, Transport and Aviation

# Design for All and Assistive Technologies

# Prototyping-Based Study of Designs for Eye-Tracking Interface in Augmentative and Alternative Communication Applications

Nayan Adhikari[1,2], Pedro G. Lind[1,2,3(✉)], and Gustavo B. Moreno e Mello[1,2,3]

[1] Department of Computer Science, OsloMet – Oslo Metropolitan University,
P.O. Box 4 St. Olavs plass, 0130 Oslo, Norway
[2] ORCA – OsloMet Research Center for AI, Pilestredet 52, 0166 Oslo, Norway
[3] NordSTAR – Nordic Center for Sustainable and Trustworthy AI Research,
Pilestredet 52, 0166 Oslo, Norway

**Abstract.** This establishes a basic template for the interface design of augmentative and alternative communication (AAC) software that use eye-gaze tracking technology as input. The main aim is to highlight desirable and undesirable characteristics in the user interface regarding usability. To do so, we conducted a systematic evaluation of the commercially available products and from that drawn design criteria, which combined with modern usability requirements, were used to develop an user interface prototype. This prototype was refined through evolutionary prototyping methodology. Several usability tests were performed to evaluate the design regarding: consistency, comprehensibility, clarity, flexibility, efficiency, consistency and potential for customization. The feedback from the users was integrated in subsequent iterations of the design. The prototyping process is used as the process for a critical analysis to address drawbacks in standard designs. As result, we provide a basic template that aggregate qualities of previous designs and minimizes drawbacks whenever possible, and that can be used as guideline for further development of tools for AAC.

**Keywords:** Augmented communication · Accessibility · Education

## 1 Introduction and Background

A segment of the world population is living with some form of speech disability, mainly caused by motion dysfunction. Since verbal communication is often the preferred mode of communication, non-verbal individuals face bigger challenges to perform bidirectional communication effectively, constraining their individual independence and life quality.

Augmentative and alternative communication (AAC) technologies can enable or supplement communication behavior in non-verbal individuals. There are

C. Stephanidis et al. (Eds.): HCII 2021, CCIS 1499, pp. 3–10, 2021.
https://doi.org/10.1007/978-3-030-90179-0_1

mainly two types of AAC. One is unaided AAC, which leverages the use of gestures, facial expressions or uses eye-gaze trajectories combined with images. The other is aided AAC, which uses pictures, pictographs, words or letters, focusing in alternatives to verbal or handwritten communication. The most common aided AAC technologies are eye-gaze communication technologies (EGCT) and they can be categorised into (i) non-electronic EGCT, that uses simple components such as E-tran (Swift 2012), which is a low-tech text-based communication board made of transparent plastic, and (ii) electronic EGCT, that uses different electronic components and software, such as *I-series* from *Tobii* company, which includes a communication device based in gaze control[1], and *EyeGaze Edge* a gaze-based communication device[2].

In this paper we will focus in the latter type of solutions. Electronic EGCT is a computer system, preferably a portable tablet personal computer, that leverages the use of eye gesture for pointing in the screen instead of using a mouse or hand. It has two main components: a camera component to track eye movement and an implemented software to drive the camera to track the eye-gaze on the computer screen and convert fixation periods of the eye-gaze trajectories into choices of images or words for communication. There are different software solutions for EGCT. They typically follow different design principles and strategies (Constable et al. 2017; Kumar and Krol, 1992) to convert the eye gaze gesture into communicable statements. Such solutions provide better chances for non-verbal individuals to communicate and consequently improve their life quality.

We will discuss the user interface design of existing symbol-based AAC softwares with the aim of identifying the elements in the screen and evaluate them with respect to their readability and usability. Moreover, we discuss how to establish prototype development processes to improve these solutions in the near future. We will focus in the following solutions: *Communicator 5*[3] (Gosmanova et al. 2017), *Text Talker*[4], *Gazetalk*[5], *Unidad*[6], *LAMP word for life*[7], and *Snap Core First*[8]. While the first three use alphanumeric virtual keyboard (Bates et al. 2007), the other use symbol keyboards (Van Donsel 2017).

We start in Sect. 2 by introducing the criteria for evaluating the existing solutions and describe them in detail. In Sect. 3, we design a prototype addressing the problems and explain the testing processes carried out till the final interface prototype. Section 4 we concludes the manuscript highlighting some limitations and possible futures directions to improve the prototype.

---

[1] https://www.tobiidynavox.com/products/i-series/.

[2] https://eyegaze.com/products/eyegaze-edge/.

[3] https://www.tobiidynavox.com/software/windows-software/communicator-5-gold-english-us/.

[4] https://thinksmartbox.com/product/text-talker/.

[5] https://wiki.cogain.org/index.php/Gazetalk.

[6] https://www.prentrom.com/prc_advantage/unidad-espanol-language-system.

[7] https://www.prentrom.com/prc_advantage/lamp-words-for-life-language-system.

[8] https://www.tobiidynavox.com/software/windows-software/snap-for-windows/.

## 2   Methods and Tools

In this study, we design and present a prototype for an AAC interface for easier and faster communication using EGCT. To that end, we followed the evolutionary prototyping approach. In doing so, we had the opportunity learn from previous interfaces without being encumbered by the lack of design specifications or rationale in them, and we could test some of the assumptions derived from previous designs. Through the different iterations of the prototype we aimed at addressing drawbacks and converging in a functional design that is informative about desirable qualities.

First, we characterised the targeted user group into personas. The primary user has sever motor but not cognitive impairment. The motor impairment often sets early in life, normally from birth, implying that the interface must support the acquisition of language. The primary user does not have defined nationality, so diverse language support must be provided. Finally the main user is likely to be financially dependent, which highlights the importance of cheap or open-source solutions.

Next, we evaluated the existing solutions for EGCT-based AAC through a comprehensive literature survey. The evaluation took into account the primary user, as well as features that are commonly used to compare these interfaces. We used the following criteria: (i) Literacy requirement; (ii) Cross-Platform support; (iii) Localisation and internalisation of application language as well as vocabulary in the communication application; (iv) Speed in the use of communication application; (v) Evaluation of communication features application; (vi) Cost factors; (vii) Autonomy while using and configuring the application.

We added few user interface accessibility requirements that are relevant for an AAC that must meet the demand of user navigating the application with their eyes (Bhaskar et al. 2001): (i) Comprehensibility, the design interface show enable to execute tasks—adequate information on the screen to understand and perform tasks in a meaningful order; (ii) Clarity, the information on the screen should be clear both in its content and layout; (iii) Configurable and control, the application should meet the users' specific needs, enabling anyone to configure it alone; (iv) Consistency and predictability, the interface should imply a predictable use, consistently following other similar interfaces, in order the users require less learning; (v) Efficiency, tasks should be completed within a number of interactions with the interface as small as possible; (vi) Familiarity, interface's components should follow a natural pattern and imitate users behaviour; (vii) Flexibility, the application should employ more than one way to carry out the communication. Following these requirements, we generated possible models for a minimum viable solution, containing the necessary features for a communication application and customisation features accessible to the user using EGCT as an input medium.

We designed the interface upholding the various user interface design concepts of universal design and usability principles, developed in an iterative way, interspersed with evaluation processes, mainly based in usability tests. We considered two iterations. In the first iteration, we developed a low-fidelity interface, to check the usability of the communication process. In the second iteration, we designed a high fidelity interface addressing the issues in the low fidelity design, and additionally we incorporate visually pleasing aesthetic and interaction animations.

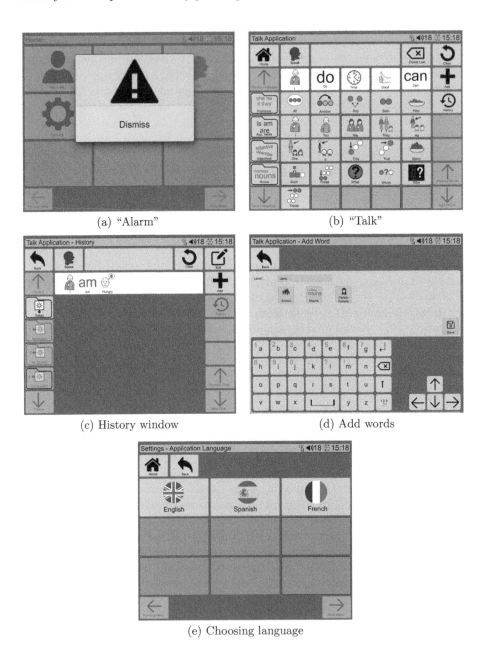

(a) "Alarm"                    (b) "Talk"

(c) History window             (d) Add words

(e) Choosing language

**Fig. 1.** Functionalities developed for EGCT interfaces.

For the usability testing, we recruited 14 participants with no specific background, all of them students from Oslo Metropolitan University and the University of Oslo. For the test we used a *MacBook Pro* laptop with 13-in screen and a mouse, together with a free user interface prototyping tool, namely the *InVision Studio*. No eye-tracking was used (see Discussion and Conclusions).

## 3 Iterative Development of the Interface Prototype

**Iteration 1: Low-Fidelity Prototype and Testing.** The initial design divides the software interface into several applications, which can be activated from the main screen. Each option is identified by an image-word pair. For the low-fidelity prototype we focused on the two most common functionalities: (i) Alarm; (ii) Talk application. Alarm is a quick access application that enables the user to quickly send an alert to request help in an emergency; since users often need assistance for care takers, this is an almost ubiquitous functionality. Talk application is what controls and gives access to the text or icon to speech interface; in other words, the core functionality. Once developed, the first prototype was tested by 14 participants. Which provided feedback about the prototype using the criteria previously described. Their feedback can be summarized in five remarks. First, ambient information in the form of symbols and colours increases the meaning to the interface. The ambient information, including distinguishing button groups based on colour, border colour and using icons like folders for representing similar information, increased the clarity of the interface.

Second, the application state information, title of the current window, time, language and volume, represented using text and symbols in the title bar, gave clear meaning. Similar symbols and test are common to other application making them more familiar to the participants. But the interaction mode symbol was less common to other applications making it hard to perceive.

Third, users tend to notice symbols and graphic representation of data rather than textual information more often. Information represented using icons and graphics tends to create ambiguity if the meaning of icons and text do not align.

Fourth, missing information like suffix in the volume level, symbols representing conflicting meaning for "Like" and "Love", and "Love" and "Health" icons create more confusion at first use.

Finally, some features were distracting to the users. For example, using sharp colours like red for the icons sometimes increase distraction. And there are higher chances of mistakes and confusion when using similar icons for different functions in the same interface. One participant was confused with a back arrow button used in the footer for pagination with the previous windows button in the navigation where we used a twisted back arrowhead. Similarly, the consistent representation of interface components with different functions increase confusion. Non-interactive information and interactive buttons, if represented using the same layout, creates confusion.

**Iteration 2: High-Fidelity Prototype.** The low-fidelity prototype was revised into a new version of the interface based on the previous feedback. Figure 1 illustrates the different parts of the interface at this stage.

The first functionality in our prototype was the "Alarm" (Fig. 1a), when user selects the button on the home screen it generates a ringing noise with a dialogue box to dismiss the alert to get attention of nearby caretaker. It is the fastest possible way of communicating with nearby people in an emergency. The button "Alarm" is accompanied by an icon making it easy to understand.

The second important functionality is the "Talk" application (see Fig. 1b), user navigates using category buttons, finds appropriate words, and constructs statement for communication. Selected words get populated in a text area at the top centre of the interface. With this, the user perceives the information of currently selected words. If the user finds something wrong with the statement, they can edit the statement before speaking using the remove and clear buttons. For faster communication, a row of suggested words is available to select anytime at their convenience. With this, the user can complete a statement with relatively fewer interactions.

Another functionality addressed in the study is the conversation history as shown in Fig. 1c. In the conversation history window, past conversation statements are arranged by date in descending order with the current date as default. To find conversation from previous days, the user can select a date or day buttons in the left column of the application. In this window, the user chooses a statement and press speak button to send feedback or press edit and edit the statement before sending feedback if the user finds something wrong. This process reduces a considerable amount of interaction and can contribute to a faster communication process.

We also include a function that enable user to add new words to the system without the intervention of caretaker. The user selects the add word button located at the right column of the talk application interface. On interaction with the "Add" button from the talk application, the application prompts the user to add a word window where the user enters a label for a new word and selects an icon, vocabulary and category. Icon gives a meaningful pictorial representation of the label, vocabulary is where the word resides, and category helps to search for the word quickly.

The "Conversation History" and "Add Word" features evolved from the phrase library feature for the previous iteration of the prototype design. Segregating the phrase library feature to conversation history and add word resulted in faster communication and adding custom words to the system.

The user customises the application using a different menu under settings. The user can access these settings with less interaction from the home screen because of the relatively flat menu hierarchy. Additionally, the consistency of layout and navigation buttons in the application makes it even more convenient for the user to navigate around.

Additionally, the user can find information on the current application configuration like sound, interaction mode, the application language, time and current window location from the title bar at the top of the application. With this, the user gets better insight into the application configuration from anywhere in the interface.

**Final Evaluation:** A qualitative evaluation of final version includes the following four remarks. First, the use of consistent navigation and a predictable menu decrease mistakes while navigating to reach the destination window. But the participants repeatedly navigated from one setting menu to another using the home button rather than using a back button. The certainty of the menu sometimes results in relatively more interactions for performing the task.

Second, one participant searched the setting button in the talk application rather than starting from the home screen. For such cases, it is better to add redundant buttons in the applications where applicable.

Third, tasks that take fewer interactions to complete are easier to understand with higher chances of success. A flat menu hierarchy decreases the number of interaction when executing a task. In the interface starting from the home screen, participants can reach anywhere in the application in less than three clicks. Additionally, the configurable application settings without the intervention of the caretaker added extra usability in the settings menu.

Finally, although the predictive next word suggestion feature has undoubtedly increased the number of interactions while constructing statements in the talk application, finding or predicting words was slower. Often participants were not sure of the location of words in the categories. For a symbol-based AAC software, usually, a language system plays determining role for a faster speed and better user experience.

## 4    Discussion and Conclusions

In this paper we introduce a prototype of an user interface for symbol-based AAC, developed to attend some of the drawbacks identified in existing commercial solutions. The prototype was tested with 14 university students. Two main overall remarks should be stressed. First, the consistency in the layout of the interface increased the speed of interaction, probably reflecting its high predictability. Second, through an iterative prototype development we were able to improve the navigation in the interface, which is also reflected in a faster task execution (Jiménez Iglesias et al. 2018), since we reduce the number of interactions to complete a task.

Before drawing general conclusion, we also need to emphasize some of the limitations or drawbacks which follow from these general remarks. For instance, concerning efficiency, speed is also influenced by other factors such as the number of interactions (Jiménez Iglesias et al. 2018) to complete a task. Thus, several factors are influencing the success of task completion, which may raise some issues with respect to limitations. Moreover, other remarks criticize the way the navigation was implemented in the interface. Users prefered the navigation buttons easier to locate when they were located at the left side of the interface.

This lead to a better navigation experience since participants found it hard to notice the buttons on the right side of the interface, which is expected in western readers that read from left to right. Finally, due to limitations imposed by the pandemic in 2020–2021 it was not possible to test the prototype with the target user group. It is highly relevant that the insights drawn in this study are extended with the opinion of end-users.

There are many commercially available and open source softwares for AAC, and they range from the crude and improvised to the well designed and tested. But to the best of our knowledge, there is no systematic study of what design features makes these interfaces usable and effective to the end user. We hope that this paper can shed light on some of the aspects that are relevant to make an usable User Interface for AAC and inspire open source developers around the world to create tools for their communities in different languages. Another way of understanding this paper, it sets a basic template for an interface for AAC that is properly tested and well grounded in design and usability principles.

## References

Bates, R., Donegan, M., Istance, H.O., Hansen, J.P., Räihä, K.-J.: Introducing cogain: communication by gaze interaction. Univ. Access Inf. Soc. **6**(2), 159–166 (2007)

Bhaskar, N.U., Naidu, P.P., Babu, S.R.C., Govindarajulu, P.: General principles of user interface design and websites. Int. J. Softw. Eng. (IJSE) **2**(3), 45–60 (2001)

Constable, P.A., Bach, M., Frishman, L.J., Jeffrey, B.G., Robson, A.G.: Iscev standard for clinical electro-oculograpghy (2017 update). Documenta Opthalmologica **134**(1), 1–9 (2017)

Gosmanova, K. A., et al.: Eeg-based brain-computer interface access to tobii dynavox communicator 5. Rehabilitation Engineering and Assistive Technology Society of North America (2017)

Jiménez Iglesias, L., Aguilar, C.A.P., Sánchez, L., Pérez-Montoro Gutiérrez, M.: User experience and the media: the three-click rule on newspaper websites for smartphones. Revista Latina de Communicación Social **76**, 595–613 (2018)

Kumar, A., Krol, G.: Binocular infrared oculography. Laryngoscope **102**(4), 367–378 (1992)

Swift, S.M.: Low-tech, eye-movement-accessible AAC and typical adults (2012)

Van Donsel, M.N.: Implementation of AAC (2017)

# Wearable Device to Aid Impaired Vision People Against Covid-19

Sandro Costa Mesquita[1]([✉]), Tiago Diógenes de Araújo[2],
and Victor Hazin da Rocha[1]

[1] CESAR School, Recife, Pernambuco, Brazil
scm@cesar.school
[2] IFCE, Fortaleza, Ceará, Brazil
https://www.cesar.school/
https://ifce.edu.br/

**Abstract.** The year of 2020 was greatly affected by COVID-19 pandemic, it was necessary to change the work routine, study and social life and adapt to the new world scenario that was suddenly established. The technology, and especially the software, contributed a lot for these changes to be managed and carried out efficiently, mainly in the scope of communication and information. To prevent the pandemic from advancing, protective measures were taken by the state and federal governments, including recommendations for social distancing, wearing masks in a public environment and avoiding people in a feverish state, so the world policed itself and tried to comply with the new guidelines. However, a visually impaired person would not be able to comply with these determinations, how could he know if the person in front of him is wearing a mask or not, or even far enough, not respecting the recommended minimum distance of 1.5 m, or even checking the temperature of someone entering the same environment as him. Motivated by this problem, this research was initiated, with the goal of the development of a case to be coupled to an eyeglass, with processors and sensors, that will detect if the person in front is wearing a face mask, is 1.5 m far and in a possible feverish state, being processed by an Artificial Intelligence software with 95% accuracy. The functional status of the project was successfully executed, the results were satisfactory, with improvements in terms of embedded technology and tests on the impaired resulted in hope and excitement for them.

**Keywords:** COVID-19 · Computer vision · Facial recognition

## 1 Introduction

Sars-cov-2 is the causative agent of a devastating pandemic in 2020 [1]. The outbreak began in December 2019 in Wuhan city, Hubei province, China [2]. As of November 1, 2020, according to Johns Hopkins University & Medicine [3], the number of confirmed COVID-19 cases worldwide was over 46 million, while the

© Springer Nature Switzerland AG 2021
C. Stephanidis et al. (Eds.): HCII 2021, CCIS 1499, pp. 11–16, 2021.
https://doi.org/10.1007/978-3-030-90179-0_2

number of global deaths was about 2 million people. Worldwide, a major effort by scientists is trying to reduce the spread of sars-cov-2. At the moment, there is no effective drug to treat the disease, not even a vaccine to prevent transmission, at the time of writing this thesis. The World Health Organization recommends three good practices to prevent human transmission [4]: wash your hands and keep them clean, keep a distance of at least 1 m between you and others, often as in shopping malls there are visual signs on the floor to guide the distance when there is a need to form lines or even when entering the elevator, where the sticker informs where the most distant positions between users should be. The last guideline is to always wear a mask when going out in public or being around other people.

In this context, it is necessary to care for the most vulnerable people, those who are susceptible to transmission due to their condition as elderly and physically disabled. Knowing this, this thesis focuses the research on developing glasses for the visually impaired with an embedded artificial intelligence system as it is noticeable that it is more difficult to maintain security for this niche of people because they are unable to maintain the recommended distance or avoid people who are not wearing mask in some situations due to their visual impairment. The World Health Organization (WHO) [5] estimates that, globally, 1 billion people have vision problems that could have been prevented or are not yet resolved. That 1 billion people includes those with moderate or severe visual impairment or blindness. In this thesis, an embedded system solution is proposed to help visually impaired people to maintain a safe distance, to measure the body temperature of the person ahead and to warn the user about people without a face mask.

## 2   Development

For the construction of this project, low-consumption components were necessary, as the final project should work at full capacity for prolonged periods, reaching up to 6 h of continuous operation. For this reason, the embedded system chosen was the Raspberry Pi4, which combines processing power with low consumption, reaching the goal of 6 h of continuous operation using a 10 Ah power bank.

For temperature measurement, the AMG8833 IR sensor was used, which has a 64 pixel resolution thermal camera and its communication works through the I2C protocol.

For the distance sensor, the VL53L0X was chosen, which has a compact size and excellent precision, being able to make accurate measurements from 2 m away, ideal for locating people who are not complying with social distance. This sensor also uses I2C protocol.

### 2.1   Mask Recognition Validation

The elevated points of our face are the references for locating the eyes, eyebrows, nose, ears, mouth and chin. For this, the Dlib package is used to estimate 68 coordinates to map the facial structure of the already trained model "shape_predictor_68_face_landmarks.dat" with open source license for academic and research use.

It was observed that the Convolutional Neural Network (CNN) method has obtained excellent efficacy in Deep Learning algorithms, achieving almost human precision [6]. Because of this, CNN was used in the development of this project.

Detection tests of facial landmarks were performed. The face detector used was developed using the classic Histogram of Oriented Gradients (HOG) [7], combined with a linear classifier, an image pyramid and a window detection scheme to mark the face. The pose estimator was developed using the Dlib implementation aligning the face with a set of regression trees, made by Vahid Kazemi and Josephine Sullivan [8] and with a face reference data set for training, iBUG 300-W [9].

In the case of this research, frame alignment is important for applying a PNG image of a mask on top of face photos to assemble a dataset, and with the dataset trained, the system will be prepared to be simulated on the computer, running the detection of masks, or the lack of them (Fig. 1).

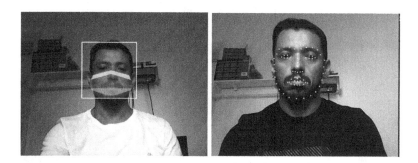

**Fig. 1.** Detection of facial landmarks and positioning of PNG image on top.

As the current situation in the world is unprecedented in this generation, it is very difficult to collect images of people wearing masks. For that reason, a dataset from a Software Engineer from India, Prajna Bhandary [10] was used. The technique used by her consists of facial marking to identify the related points in the region of the mouth, nose and chin, and in this way the software developed in Python would position an image of a mask in PNG format on the face.

1,376 images were downloaded from the dataset containing people without a mask, which 690 random images were separated to apply the software that would include the mask in these images, the rest of the 686 images would be original to be the training dataset without a mask. With these images, the recognition model was trained, applying a PNG image of a mask over the face images (Fig. 2).

**Fig. 2.** Result of mask recognition training.

## 2.2   First Version

In order to keep the glasses as portable as possible, an ESP32 with a camera installed on it was used to transmit the images of the glasses, with a built-in battery. However, it was reported a very high latency in sending images via Wi-Fi and the quality was not satisfactory.

Nevertheless, the convenience of having glasses completely detached from the computer is an important issue, having aroused interest in carrying out future tests with this premise again. The first version had a total cost of all components of $137 (USD), which can be reduced by $15 (USD) if the user already has a Bluetooth headset (Fig. 3).

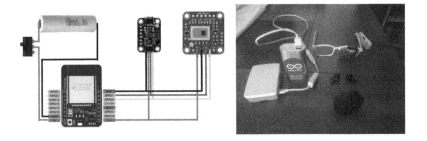

**Fig. 3.** First version of the glasses using ESP32 CAM.

## 2.3   Second Version

As the image transmission quality was not satisfactory in the first version using ESP32 as the image transmitter, a Logitech C270 USB camera was used in the second version, adding a cable that connects the glasses to the computer. The presence of this cable ruled out the need for a battery built into the glasses, reducing the complexity of the design and the weight of the system that will remain in the glasses for the impaired.

With the new camera, much more constant results and higher quality images were obtained, increasing the reliability of the project. The second version had a total cost, of all the components, of \$142 (USD) , also being able to reduce the cost if the user already has a Bluetooth headset (Fig. 4).

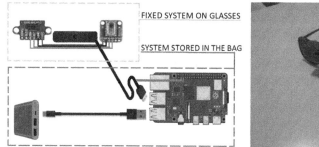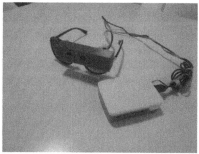

FIXED SYSTEM ON GLASSES

SYSTEM STORED IN THE BAG

**Fig. 4.** Second version of the glasses using an USB camera.

## 3    Conclusion

The Project obtained a satisfactory result in recognizing the non-use of the face mask with precise response at a distance up to 200 cm indoors and an average of 140 cm outdoors in the most varied lighting conditions with the user of the device standing still, as the purpose of this project is to detect who is without a mask in situations such as queues, shops, restaurants and buses, for example, giving the visually impaired the possibility of leaving the site to prevent contagion. The infrared distance sensor can be adjusted to respond up to 200 cm, as recommended by several countries. The body temperature sensor was only efficient in closed environments and with a maximum distance of 50 cm, acquiring readings much lower than the normal temperatures of a human being. With this result, a new search is being carried out to find models of thermal sensors that have precision over greater distances, the ideal being 150 cm.

Therefore the project proved to be feasible and with a total accessible cost of \$142 (USD) to help fight COVID-19 and other respiratory diseases that may arise in the world and can also be adapted for use in public for monitoring the use of PPE's, such as masks in the mining industry.

Future versions of this project are expected to meet new technology requirements. With the advent of 5G technology, it is possible that it will be necessary to completely reinvent the design of the assistance glasses for this project.

## References

1. Hu, B., Guo, H., Zhou, P., et al.: Characteristics of SARS-CoV-2 and COVID-19. Nat. Rev. Microbiol. **19**, 141–154 (2021). https://doi.org/10.1038/s41579-020-00459-7

2. Li, Q., et al.: Early transmission dynamics in Wuhan, China, of novel coronavirus-infected pneumonia. New Engl. J. Med. **382**(13), 1199–207 (2020). https://doi.org/10.1056/NEJMoa2001316

3. Johns Hopkins University & Medicine. https://coronavirus.jhu.edu/, Accessed 1 Nov 2020

4. WHO. https://www.who.int/emergencies/diseases/novel-coronavirus-2019/advice-for-public, Accessed 26 Mar 2021

5. ONU News. https://news.un.org/pt/story/2019/10/1690122, Accessed 5 Oct 2021

6. Feng, X., Jiang, Y., Yang, X., Ming, D., Li, H.: Computer vision algorithms and hardware implementations: a survey. Integr. VLSI J. **69**, 309–320 (2019). https://doi.org/10.1016/j.vlsi.2019.07.005

7. Dalal, N., Triggs, B.: Histograms of oriented gradients for human detection. In: 2005 IEEE Computer Society Conference on Computer Vision and Pattern Recognition, vol. 1, pp. 886–893 (2005). https://doi.org/10.1109/CVPR.2005.177

8. Kazemi, V., Sullivan, J.: One millisecond face alignment with an ensemble of regression trees. In: IEEE Conference on Computer Vision and Pattern Recognition (2014). https://doi.org/10.1109/CVPR.2014.241

9. Sagonas, C., Antonakos, E., Tzimiropoulos, G., Zafeiriou, S., Pantic, M.: 300 faces in-the-wild challenge: database and results. Image Vision Comput. **47**, 3–18 (2016). https://doi.org/10.1016/j.imavis.2016.01.002

10. GitHub Prajna Bhandary. https://github.com/prajnasb/observations, Accessed 9 Dec 2020

# An Evaluation of Foot Rowing Type Wheelchair for Elderly People by Using Questionnaire with Experiments

Naohisa Hashimoto[1]([✉]), Yusuke Takinami[1], and Nobuhito Kakuta[2]

[1] Human-Cantered Mobility Research Center, National Institute of Advanced Industrial Science and Technology, 1-1-1 Umezono, Tsukuba 3058568, Ibaraki, Japan
`naohisa-hashimoto@aist.go.jp`
[2] Aguri Kogyo Corporation, 17, Ichinomiya City 69121, Japan

**Abstract.** Providing useful and affordable mobility is one of the most important points for ideal aging society. Especially, mobility device for elderly, disabled and handicapped people should be provided. Current type of wheelchair is useful for those who can use their arms and hands. But, if their arms and hands are disabled or difficult to move, current type of wheelchair is not useful. In order to solve the problem, we developed the new type of wheelchair. The feature of the developed prototype wheelchair is foot rowing. We have developed the prototype considering elderly people and finally performed experiments for evaluation. In the experiments, the differences were evaluated between the developed wheelchairs and ordinary type of wheelchair, which is turned by user's hands. The contents of questionnaire are ease of movement, comfortability of riding and getting on and off, each movement including forward, backward, braking, right and left turning, traveling on bump road, slope and slalom. Also, comments about every content and indoor and outdoor locations to use this wheelchair were obtained. From the experimental results, interesting points were found and these points are valuable for the future developing.

**Keywords:** Wheelchair · Mobility for aging society

## 1 Introduction

Japan is facing aging society now and several countries will face the same situation [1]. In Japan, the annual number of fatality in traffic accidents has been decreasing, but elderly people occupy more than 50% [2, 3], shown in Fig. 1. Providing useful and affordable mobility is one of the most important points for ideal aging society [4–8]. Especially, mobility device for elderly people, disabled and handicapped people should be provided. Current type of wheelchair is useful for those who can use their arms and hands. But, if their arms and hands are disabled or difficult to move, current type of wheelchair is not useful especially in outdoor environment. In order to solve the problem we developed the new type of wheelchair. The feature of the developed prototype wheelchair is foot rowing.

C. Stephanidis et al. (Eds.): HCII 2021, CCIS 1499, pp. 17–22, 2021.
https://doi.org/10.1007/978-3-030-90179-0_3

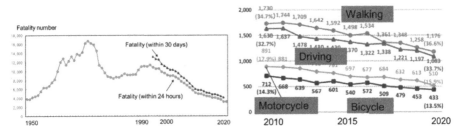

**Fig. 1.** Fatality number in traffic accidents [2, 3]

## 2 Prototype of New Wheelchair

We developed the new type of wheelchair, shown in Fig. 2. The design production process is shown from left-top to right-bottom in Fig. 2. The developed wheelchair was modified by using feedback from real users' opinions, discussion and trial, and it is evaluated by many real users with experiments. The modified points are follows;

- Optimization for load weight of wheels in order to better turning
- In order to improve the comfortability, comfortable tire and suspension were installed
- Driving mechanical mechanism for comfortable foot rowing type wheelchair

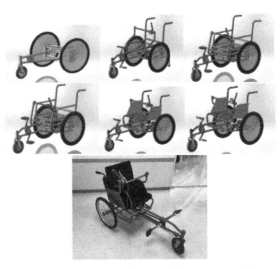

**Fig. 2.** Developed wheelchair (First: top-left, second: top-center, third: top-middle, fourth: middle-left, fifth: middle-center, sixed: middle-right, and final version: bottom)

# 3  Experiments with Subjects

## 3.1  Employed Subjects

We performed experiments for evaluation. The experiments were performed with 35 elderly people. The feature of subjects are as follows;

1. 35 subjects (18 men, 17 women)
2. Ages: from 65 to 80, average: 71.8
3. All subjects have driver's license
4. 82% subjects are first time to use wheelchair
5. All subjects can walk and ride a bicycle

## 3.2  Experimental Setup

In order to evaluate the difference between the proposed and normal wheelchairs, two kinds of wheelchairs, shown in Fig. 1 and Fig. 2 respectively, were employed. The used course for two kinds of wheelchairs was same and shown in Fig. 3. The experimental course consists of traveling slalom, on slope, on step and doing emergency brake. One assistant was accompanying each subject in the experiments for the safety reason. And, the experiments were applied to the committee in AIST for doing the experiments with subjects. The experimental scene is shown in Fig. 4. Two trials in one course were done, and they answered the following questionnaire after all trial.

Q1 Which is better between two wheelchairs?
1. Traveling, 2. Comfortable, 3. Getting on and off, 4. If you want to use, 5. If you want to buy, 6. About control, 6.1. Forward, 6.2. Braking, 6.3. Backward, 6.4. Right turning, 6.5. Left turning, 6.6. Climbing step, 6.7. Slope, 6.8. Slalom.
Q2 How much can you pay the proposed wheelchair?
Q3 Comments about each wheelchair on the above items from 1 to 6.8.
Q4 Where do you want to use the proposed wheelchair?

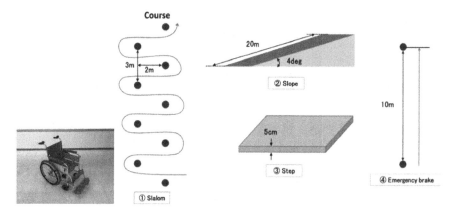

**Fig. 3.** Conventional wheelchair and experimental course

**Fig. 4.** Experimental scene

### 3.3 Result and Discussion

Figure 5 shows the questionnaire results about Q1 in Sect. 3.2. The result shows that the proposed wheelchair was better in 6.6 and 6.7 in Q1 question statistically at 5% significance level by using binominal test [11]. The feature of the proposed wheelchair is speed-controlled by foot, and the generated power is larger by foot than by hands. There are many places, where big torque is necessary outdoor environment, thus the proposed wheelchair is preferred. On the other hand, the result shows that the conventional wheelchair was better in 2 and 3 in Q1 question statistically at 5% significance level. These points should be improved for future development.

Figure 6 shows the result of Q2. This result shows that the price of proposed wheelchair should be near to the price of conventional wheelchair in average. But, some people like to use this wheelchair and they can pay more than about 1800$.

Figure 7 shows all comments in Q3. Especially, comments on left turning and get on and off are important to design this kind of wheelchair, and these comments are will be considered for the next wheelchair.

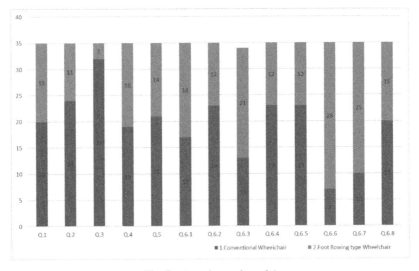

**Fig. 5.** Experimental result1

From the results of Q4, subjects want to use it in the park, to go shopping, to travel with friends, go to the hospital and station. Comparing to the conventional wheelchair, the proposed wheelchair was preferred in outdoor environment because this wheelchair is easy to handle outside.

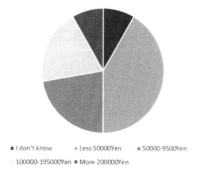

■ I don't know  ■ Less 50000Yen  ■ 50000-9500Yen
100000-195000Yen  ■ More 200000Yen

**Fig. 6.** Experimental result2 about price (110 Yen = about 1$)

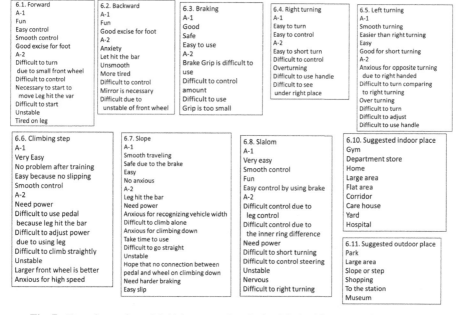

| 6.1. Forward | 6.2. Backward | 6.3. Braking | 6.4. Right turning | 6.5. Left turning |
|---|---|---|---|---|
| A-1 | A-1 | A-1 | A-1 | A-1 |
| Fun | Fun | Good | Easy to turn | Smooth turning |
| Easy control | Good excise for foot | Safe | Easy to control | Easier than right turning |
| Smooth control | A-2 | Easy to use | A-2 | Easy |
| Good excise for foot | Anxiety | A-2 | Easy to short turn | Good for short turning |
| A-2 | Let hit the bar | Brake Grip is difficult to | Difficult to control | A-2 |
| Difficult to turn | Unsmooth | use | Overturning | Anxious for opposite turning |
| due to small front wheel | More tired | Difficult to control | Difficult to use handle | due to right handed |
| Difficult to control | Difficult to control | amount | Difficult to see | Difficult to turn comparing |
| Necessary to start to | Mirror is necessary | Difficult to use | under right place | to right turning |
| move Leg hit the var | Difficult due to | Grip is too small | | Over turning |
| Difficult to start | unstable of front wheel | | | Difficult to turn |
| Unstable | | | | Difficult to adjust |
| Tired on leg | | | | Difficult to use handle |

| 6.6. Climbing step | 6.7. Slope | 6.8. Slalom | 6.10. Suggested indoor place |
|---|---|---|---|
| A-1 | A-1 | A-1 | Gym |
| Very Easy | Smooth traveling | Very easy | Department store |
| No problem after training | Safe due to the brake | Smooth control | Home |
| Easy because no slipping | Easy | Fun | Large area |
| Smooth control | No anxious | Easy control by using brake | Flat area |
| A-2 | A-2 | A-2 | Corridor |
| Need power | Leg hit the bar | Difficult control due to | Care house |
| Difficult to use pedal | Need power | leg control | Yard |
| because leg hit the bar | Anxious for recognizing vehicle width | Difficult control due to | Hospital |
| Difficult to adjust power | Difficult to climb alone | the inner ring difference | |
| due to using leg | Anxious for climbing down | Need power | **6.11. Suggested outdoor place** |
| Difficult to climb straightly | Take time to use | Difficult to short turning | Park |
| Unstable | Difficult to go straight | Difficult to control steering | Large area |
| Larger front wheel is better | Unstable | Unstable | Slope or step |
| Anxious for high speed | Hope that no connection between | Nervous | Shopping |
| | pedal and wheel on climbing down | Difficult to right turning | To the station |
| | Need harder braking | | Museum |
| | Easy slip | | |

**Fig. 7.** Experimental result3 (A1: conventional wheelchair, A2: proposed wheelchair)

## 4  Summary

In this paper, the protype of wheelchair was introduced and the design production process, and improvement process was explained as short paper. For the evaluation, the experiments were performed. The experimental results shows that the proposed wheelchair has advantage and disadvantage points comparing to the conventional wheelchair. From the experimental results, interesting points were found and these points are valuable for the future developing. The necessary points to improve the quality of the proposed wheelchair are follows:

1. Easy getting on and off
2. Price
3. Right turning when control interface is on right side
4. Function for Seat adjust

For future work, the assistance system, which assists foot rowing, will be considered. Also, we have a plan to use commercialized systems, which is already used in electric assist bicycle, because the commercialized systems are packaged, with high reliability and affordability. In addition, user interface for elderly people is important for the introduction of these kind of mobility. Acceptable user interface should be considered for using this prototype wheelchair.

**Acknowledgement.** This research was supported by Ibaraki prefecture fund for "Monozukuri" and Aguri Kogyo, Japan.

## References

1. United Nations (2019). World Population Prospects: The 2019 Revision
2. Fatality number. https://www.e-stat.go.jp/stat-search/files?page=1&layout=datalist&toukei= 00130002&tstat=000001032793&cycle=7&year=20190&month=0, Accessed 5 June 2021
3. Cabinet Office Japan. Annual Report on the Aging Society FY 2019 (2019)
4. ITF Research Reports. Cycling, Health and Safety, ITF (2013)
5. U.S. Department of Transportation. Beyond Traffic –trends and choices (2015)
6. European Commission. https://ec.europa.eu/transport/themes_en, Accessed Apr 2020
7. Leaman, H.M.L., Nguyen, L.: Development of a smart wheelchair for people with disabilities. In: 2016 IEEE International Conference on Multisensor Fusion and Integration for Intelligent Systems, pp. 279–284 (2016)
8. Hashimoto, N., Takinami, Y., Matsumoto, O.: An experimental study on vehicle behavior to wheelchairs and standing-type vehicles at intersection. In: Proceedings 13th International Conference on ITS Telecommunications, Finland (2013)
9. Cooper, R.A.: Stability of a wheelchair controlled by a human pilot. IEEE Trans. Rehabil. Eng. **1**(4), 193–206 (1993)
10. Hashimoto, N., Tomita, K., Boyali, A., Takinami, Y., Matsumoto, O.: Experimental study of the human factors when riding an automated wheelchair: supervision and acceptability of the automated system. IET Intel. Transp. Syst. **12**(3), 236–241 (2018)
11. Howell, D.: Statistical Methods for Psychology. Wadsworth Publishing Company, Belmont (2012)

# An Electronic Guide Dog for the Blind Based on Artificial Neural Networks

Sergej Lopatin$^{(\boxtimes)}$ ⓘ, Florian von Zabiensky ⓘ, Michael Kreutzer ⓘ,
Klaus Rinn ⓘ, and Diethelm Bienhaus ⓘ

Technische Hochschule Mittelhessen, Institute of Technology and Computer Science,
University of Applied Sciences, Giessen, Germany
{sergej.lopatin,florian.von.zabiensky,michael.kreutzer,
klaus.rinn,diethelm.bienhaus}@mni.thm.de

**Abstract.** This paper presents a feasibility study of an electronic assistance system to support blind and visually impaired people in finding their way in the area of public traffic. Optical recognition of walkways is implemented. For this purpose, a neural network for semantic segmentation is trained from scratch. In the practical test, an NVIDIA® Jetson Nano™ is used as the computing unit. A voice output gives the user feedback for orientation on the pavement.

**Keywords:** Electronic travel aid · Blind sidewalk detection · Portable eta system · Electronic travel aid technology · Computer vision · Convolutional neural network

## 1 Introduction

The goal of this work is to design a deep learning based *Electronic Guide Dog* to support visually impaired people in orientation and navigation tasks, especially in following unmarked side-walks and obstacle avoidance. It uses a camera to detect points of interests and obstacles in the environment and offers the blind user an intuitive human machine interface with audio feedback for safe navigation.

Typically, blind people use a white cane to scan their surroundings for obstacles and orientation marks. The cane covers an area up to about 1.5 m in front of the user from ground to about waist height. Due to this limitation, obstacles such as letterboxes or branches that protrude into the pavement can often not be detected and injuries occur. Because of the short range, moving obstacles are often detected too late, which leads to collisions with oncoming pedestrians. On footpaths that do not have a special guidance system for the blind and distinctive tactile edge markings, it often happens that the blind person strays from the path. Once the blind person is on the road, it is difficult to regain orientation because tactile markings are missing and there is a high risk of accidents with vehicles [8].

© Springer Nature Switzerland AG 2021
C. Stephanidis et al. (Eds.): HCII 2021, CCIS 1499, pp. 23–30, 2021.
https://doi.org/10.1007/978-3-030-90179-0_4

Technical devices to solve these problems are called Electronic Travel Aids (ETAs). Elmannai and Elleithy presented a comparative survey of the wearable and portable sensor-based assistive devices for visually-impaired people in order to show the progress in this field [4].

Some devices require the expansion of the infrastructure with electronic beacons or special markers. A Radio Frequency Identification Walking Stick (RFIWS) was designed in [7] in order to help blind people navigating on the sidewalk. This system helps detecting and calculating the approximate distance between the sidewalk border and the blind person. The system requires the preparation of pavements with RF-ID tags and is therefore costly and only available in a few locations.

A classic camera image-processing approach to side-walk tracking, is presented in [5]. The wearable system uses image segmentation, edge detection and boundary searching and is limited to recognize special markers (also called blind sidewalk) which are not always available.

A Deep Learning based approach to detect known obstacles or orientation points is shown in [1]. The framework employs transfer learning on a Single-Shot Detection (SSD) mechanism for object detection and classification using the Inception v3 convolutional neural network for object detection. Names of object-classes are presented to the visually impaired person in audio format. The main disadvantage of this approach is, that only learned (known) objects are recognized and localized in the camera-image, while unknown obstacles remain unidentified and therefore dangerous. So the system can only be used to identify orientation marks or other points of interest. Detecting the center of a sidewalk is also not possible in this way.

Core of this work is to use a state of the art segmenting neural network (SNN), which is able to perform a pixel by pixel segmentation of regions like pavement. While the pavement is recognized as a walkable region, unknown obstacles appear as holes in this region and can thus be localized. By analyzing the region map with classical methods of image processing, the position on the pavement can also be determined and safe guidance with voice commands can be realized. An NVIDIA® Jetson Nano™ provides the necessary computing power in mobile operation.

## 2   System Architecture

The Nano™ is a single board computer equipped with a GPU unit designed for deep learning tasks. One advantage is, that the computation of neural networks can be performed on the fly without internet connection. So latency problems can be avoided and data security is provided. Furthermore, the *Electronic Guide Dog* consists of a camera, a chest harness for the user to attach the camera, simple ear phones and a mobile battery. We use the Robot Operating System (ROS) version 2 for the systems software infrastructure. Figure 1 illustrates the image processing steps. Our system currently consists of five nodes as shown in Fig. 2.

1. The user's environment is captured frame by frame by a Camera Node.
2. The CNN Segmentation Node composes our trained neural network model to detect the environment's objects, at this stage merely sidewalk. The reason we use the segmentation task is to determine the shape of sidewalks. We train a convolutional neural network (CNN) model of BiSeNetV2 [9] with our handcrafted dataset labeled with sidewalks.
3. The Environment Node extracts some features of the sidewalk, for example, the computed width, edges, centroid and the intersection of the edges. These features provides a basis to compute the user's deviation from the center line of the sidewalk.
4. The Sidewalk Node of the system is used to compute the navigation feedback w.r.t the deviation.
5. The user receives the navigation feedback via voice output realized by the systems audio interface.

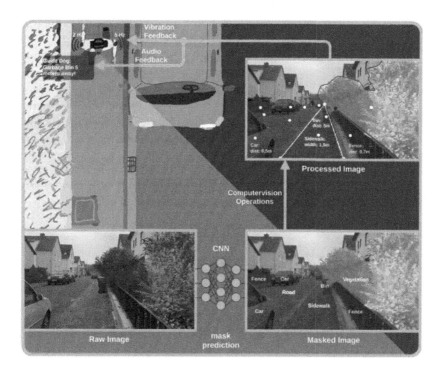

**Fig. 1.** Functional scheme of the *Electronic Guide Dog*

## 3  CNN Evaluation

The DeepLabV3 [2] network architecture was developed by Google in 2017. DeepLabV3 achieves a mean intersection over union (mIoU) score of 85.7% and

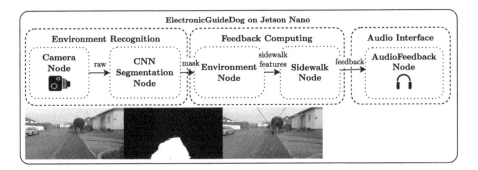

**Fig. 2.** System architecture of the *Electronic Guide Dog* . Doted border shapes represent ROS nodes. Dashed bordered shapes define a subsystem. Arrows describe the message-oriented data flow. The computation results of the single steps are shown in the bottom images.

81.3% on PASCAL VOC 2012 and Cityscapes, respectively. The averaged inference performance is 8 FPS on an NVidia Titan X GPU and 0.5 FPS on the CPU. The internal PyTorch implementation of DeepLabV3 with the backbone ResNet50 uses a model size of 321 MB. BiSeNetV2 is the newer architecture, published by Yu et al. [9]. A mIoU score of 72.6% was achieved and an inference performance of 156 FPS. Our trained model of CoinCheung's implementation of BiSeNetV2 has a model size of 58 MB [3]. BiSeNetV2 provides the better trade-off between speed and precision. The inference speed of 156 FPS is much higher than 8 FPS for the inference of DeepLabV3 and the specified precision of 72.6% mIoU is a sufficiently good value. Figure 3 shows the comparison between the architectures in terms of speed and precision. The smaller model size of BiSeNetV2 compared to DeepLabV3 is suited better for mobile devices.

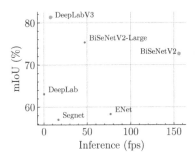

**Fig. 3.** Comparison of speed and precision of the architectures. Red dots indicate the architectures that are available for selection. Blue dots are other notable architectures. (Color figure online)

We develop a dataset with focus on sidewalks by taking pictures under different weather conditions. The images also contain different perspectives of the walkway to train a robust CNN that can be used in realistic conditions. As well known, the labeling task consumes a considerable amount of time. Hence, we first labeled only sidewalks. The dataset includes 850 verified images and is divided into 70% training, 15% testing and 15% validation subsets.

**Training Results.** New models of DeepLabV3 and BiSeNetV2 were trained with the sidewalk dataset from scratch. The loss of the DeeplabV3 converges quickly over 20 epochs to an approximate value of 0.1 and reaches an mIoU score of 78% on our testset. We train CoinCheung's implementation of the BiSeNetV2 for more than 1500 epochs [3,9]. The model achieves a mIoU score of 58%. Further, we measure the inference speed on the GPU of the Nano™ using PyTorch. The DeeplabV3 and BiSeNetV2 models reach an inference speed of 0.3 FPS and 4.2 FPS. Figure 4 shows one test sample for each model.

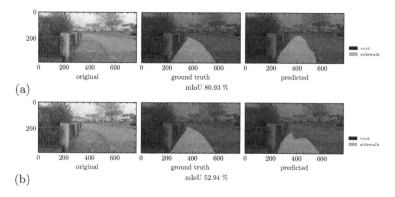

**Fig. 4.** The test result of a random sample for Deeplabv3 (a) and BiSeNetV2 (b) can be seen in the top and bottom row respectively.

The resulting prediction quality of 58% mIoU is 20% worse and the inference speed of 4.2 FPS is 14 times higher compared to the Deeplabv3 model. To achieve usable results in field tests, an inference speed of 1 FPS needs to be surpassed. Hence, the trained Deeplabv3 model doesn't fit this requirement for the current system setup and we decide to use BiSeNetV2 as the appropriate segmentation model for our system.

## 4   User Interface

In order to use the system as an assistance system, it must be able to inform the user about the sidewalk course. For this purpose, the *Electronic Guide Dog* starts with the idea of a virtual guide system for the blind. Grooves in the ground, that can be felt with a white cane signal the direction of a sidewalk. The ETA user should get feedback of the ideal path on the sidewalk in a similar way, especially if there is no guide system for the blind installed in the floor.

For this purpose, the *Electronic Guide Dog* uses results of the image processing and utilizes the walkway found in the image. As shown in Fig. 5, the edge of the sidewalk is detected and the preferred walking direction is calculated based on an image region close to the user. Using only a nearby image region is based on the idea that the sidewalk in 10 m distance is irrelevant for planning the next step. Due to the perspective in the image, the trajectories from the left and right edges of the sidewalk intersect. The horizontal difference of this intersection point to the center of the image represents the deviation from the center line of the walkway if the user plans to walk straight on. Under real conditions, the direction of the user's movement in relation to the image depends on the position and orientation of the camera. To simplify the problem, we assumed that the column of the center of the image corresponds to the direction of the user's gaze and movement.

The implemented user interface is separated from the underlying algorithm by means of using only the deviation from the walkway center line. Based on this value, audio commands are generated to guide the user to the center line. Text to speech is used to generate orientation commands. In case of deviations from the center instructions to go to the opposite direction are given. In addition, reaching and crossing the edges of the walkway is communicated.

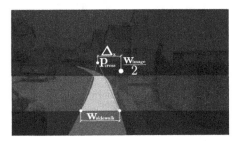

**Fig. 5.** Parameters for calculating the deviation from the optimal path

## 5   Experiments and Results

We have tested the system in good weather conditions. The test location is comparable to the dataset recordings. Figure 6 shows the experimental prototype.

During the test we record the processing steps as image files for later analysis. The Fig. 7 shows image frames overlayed with test results.

The output of the navigation instructions was responsive enough. On wide pavements the system navigated with the appropriate direction in about two-third of all cases.

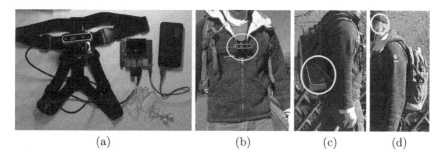

|    (a)    |    (b)    |    (c)    |    (d)    |

**Fig. 6. Experimental prototype.** (a) Assembly (b) Camera fixed on breast harness (c) The computing unit covered in a bag (d) Earphones.

**Fig. 7. Segmentation examples of field test.** Some good segmentation results.

The system has weaknesses in the classification of narrow sidewalks and if the terrain is unknown. This is caused by the small data base of only 850 samples. A generalization of the sidewalk segmentation is not yet achieved. Our dataset contains samples of sidewalk records with asphalt pavement, which is also a characteristic of roads. As a result, our system has problems distinguishing pavements from roads. Occasionally, the full width of a pavement is not segmented. Divergence of the camera position related to the user's path are caused by the user's walking movement which may cause a wrong audio instruction. Sometimes the system generates wrong instructions due to shaky recordings. Therefore, image stabilization algorithms must be implemented.

## 6   Conclusion

This work illustrates that convolutional neural networks (CNN) are appropriate for semantic segmentation of camera-captured environment images for ETAs to guide visually impaired users on the center line of a sidewalk.

In our approach a CNN performs a semantic segmentation of the camera-captured environment. The resulting masked images are processed using computer vision algorithms to detect an obstacle free and safe walkway. Finally, the user receives information about orientation on the walkway via voice output. Before deployment, the network was trained with 850 labeled samples from the pedestrian view. The implementation provides a classification at a frame rate of approximately 4 FPS on a NVIDIA® Jetson Nano™ using PyTorch for inference. A short demonstration of the *Electronic Guide Dog* is provided as video in [6].

Initial field tests show that the system delivers good results in the trained environment. The user is reliably kept in the middle of the walkway and unknown obstacles are mostly detected. In new environments, however, the error rate increases, which can be attributed to the currently too small base of training data.

Additional annotations of roads and other classes in the data set would lead to the network differentiating the objects of the environment better. A larger data set is required to train a network model to the point of generalization. An inertial measurement unit (IMU) or image correction by homography can be used for image stabilization. The use of a depth camera can improve obstacle detection by delivering distance information.

For the recognition of traffic signs or lights object detection CNN architectures can be used. In comparison to segmentation CNN architectures this enables an easier labeling process as well as faster processing of the image. A combination of different CNN architectures is promising to gain better results by simultaneous object recognition and semantically segmentation of the environment.

# References

1. Bhole, S., Dhok, A.: Deep learning based object detection and recognition framework for the visually-impaired. In: 2020 Fourth International Conference on Computing Methodologies and Communication (ICCMC), pp. 725–728. IEEE (2020)
2. Chen, L.C., Papandreou, G., Kokkinos, I., Murphy, K., Yuille, A.L.: DeepLab: Semantic image segmentation with deep convolutional nets, atrous convolution, and fully connected CRFs (2017). arXiv:1606.00915
3. CoinCheung: CoinCheung/BiSeNet. https://github.com/CoinCheung/BiSeNet, original-date: 2018–11–29T04:27:51Z
4. Elmannai, W., Elleithy, K.: Sensor-based assistive devices for visually-impaired people: current status, challenges, and future directions. Sensors **17**(3), 565 (2017). https://doi.org/10.3390/s17030565, http://www.mdpi.com/1424-8220/17/3/565
5. Jie, X., Xiaochi, W., Zhigang, F.: Research and implementation of blind sidewalk detection in portable eta system. In: 2010 International Forum on Information Technology and Applications, vol. 2, pp. 431–434 (2010). https://doi.org/10.1109/IFITA.2010.187
6. Lopatin, S.: Electronic Guide Dog - video of some tests. https://youtu.be/B0bz_o08990
7. Saaid, M.F., Ismail, I., Noor, M.Z.H.: Radio frequency identification walking stick (rfiws): A device for the blind. In: 2009 5th International Colloquium on Signal Processing & its Applications, pp. 250–253. IEEE (2009)
8. Sheth, R., Rajandekar, S., Laddha, S., Chaudhari, R.: Smart white cane-an elegant and economic walking aid. Am. J. Eng. Res. **3**(10), 84–89 (2014)
9. Yu, C., Gao, C., Wang, J., Yu, G., Shen, C., Sang, N.: BiSeNet v2: bilateral network with guided aggregation for real-time semantic segmentation (2020). arXiv:2004.02147

# Exploratory Study into the Disability Awareness Through an Inclusive Application Development Process Driven by Disabled Children

Kanako Nakamura[1] and Daisuke Kumagai[2(✉)]

[1] Non-Profit Organization Ubdobe Digi-Reha Division, 1-36-6-203, Sangenchaya, Setagaya-ku, Tokyo 154-0024, Japan
kanako@ubdobe.jp
[2] Tokyo University and Graduate School of Social Welfare, 4-23-1, Higashi-Ikebukuro, Toshima-ku, Tokyo 170-0013, Japan

**Abstract.** 【Background】

"Digital Interactive Rehabilitation System" (Digi-Reha), developed by Non-profit Organization Ubdobe, is a support tool for pediatric rehabilitation. Digi-Reha is a platform of applications which utilize several sensors to detect physical information such as acceleration and joint movements, and generate interactions of digital art and sound effects. The aim of this interaction is to improve children's motivation for rehabilitation.

【Objective】

One of the unique aspects of Digi-Reha is the Digi-Reha LAB (LAB), where children's ideas are used as a starting point for the application development process. As a new approach, a child with a diagnosis of Autism Spectrum Disorder (ASD) has been included as a participant in LAB. The aim of this report is to explore whether involving disabled children in the process of application development contribute to positive influence on the children as well as improving the quality of applications.

【Intervention】

A total of four sessions of LAB were carried out in a month. Three children, including a boy with ASD were recruited as participants. They learned to develop their original applications by using Scratch, a programming language. The participants' words and actions during the Lab were recorded and exploratively analysed.

【Result】

During LAB, the boy with ASD expressed his opinions about universal design ("I want to add some sound effects for blind people") and the awareness of his own symptoms through application development ("By creating applications that I enjoy, I can make people with the same disease enjoy too").

【Conclusion】

Joining LAB can be an opportunity for disabled children to learn about their impairments and reasonable accommodation for people with different needs in addition to improving Digi-Reha applications' quality, within the process of application development. In the coming years, its effectiveness will need to be further tested.

© Springer Nature Switzerland AG 2021
C. Stephanidis et al. (Eds.): HCII 2021, CCIS 1499, pp. 31–38, 2021.
https://doi.org/10.1007/978-3-030-90179-0_5

**Keywords:** Digi-Reha · Inclusive design · Inclusive education

## 1 Background

The Non-Profit Organisation Ubdobe is developing a supporting tool for paediatric rehabilitation, the "digital-interactive rehabilitation system" (Digi-Reha). The aim of Digi-
Reha is to motivate children with impairments to engage in rehabilitation by using digital
art with objects that they like. The interactions with digital art and sound are triggered by
the children's physical movements, detected through sensors (e.g. accelerometers and
laser-based sensors) (Fig. 1).

**Fig. 1.** The interactions with digital art and sound are triggered by the children's physical
movements, detected through sensors.

One of the features of Digi-Reha is that it is inspired by children's ideas and perspectives in the development process. Ubdobe has organised "Digi-Reha LAB", a workshop
where kids creators (children with skills or interests in computer programming, character design, etc.) design applications for rehabilitation by observing and interviewing
players (children who receive rehabilitation regularly). The purpose of Digi-Reha LAB
is to promote mutual understanding between non-disabled and disabled children, under
the slow progress in inclusive education in Japan, which is known to be lagging behind
internationally [1].

However, Digi-Reha LAB was previously a one-sided relationship, where children
without impairments invited disabled children to the workshop to observe as a subject.
This is an important opportunity for better application development, though, it can be
criticised for its similarity to the situation of *Koryu-gakkyu* (exchange class) in Japan. An

exchange class is an occasion where children in a special education school/class have a chance to interact with children in a mainstream class. In Japan, it is common that a few disabled children visit mainstream class [2]. It is a similar pattern to that of Digi-Reha LAB. According to the contact theory [3], interaction among children from different groups is useful for them to develop an understanding of each other. However, it has been reported that simple interaction is not enough; the effects are more likely to be felt by non-disabled children and have less benefit for disabled children [4]. Therefore, it was necessary for Digi-Reha LAB to shift the method of welcoming a disabled child as the main participant in order to improve the quality of the relationship.

## 2  Object

Taking into account the challenges mentioned above, the Digi-Reha LAB has chosen to include a child with a diagnosis of ASD as a participant. The aim of this paper is to explore whether involving children with impairments in the process of developing applications for pediatric rehabilitation, have a positive impact on the children themselves, not only improving the quality of the applications.

## 3  Methodology

### 3.1  Participants

The targets of this intervention are shown in the table below. Participants were recruited at Day-care centre N, where provides rehabilitation service training for disabled children. Participant A and B attended the Digi-Reha LAB at Centre N and participant C joined online via zoom. Consent to participate in this research has been given in both written and oral form from the participants and their parents.

Participant A has a diagnosis of ASD. His difficulties include: lack of confidence in communicating his thoughts and opinions, often giving up before even trying it. And he often asks for frequent feedback from others because he is not confident in his decisions (Table 1).

**Table 1.** Participants' list

| Participants | Age | Gender | Background |
|---|---|---|---|
| A | 9 | Male | Diagnosed as Autism spectrum syndrome |
| B | 11 | Female | Sibling of A |
| C | 12 | Male | Sibling of a child with physical and cognitive impairments |

### 3.2  Implementation

Four sessions of Digi-Reha LAB were carried out during one month. The participants' behaviour and statements during the LAB were recorded and exploratively analysed (Fig. 2).

**Fig. 2.** Participant A and B are attending Digi-Reha Lab and coding on Scratch

## 4   Result

As shown in Table 2, the statements of the three participants collected in the Digi-Reha LAB were grouped into five main categories: Competitive thinking arising from collaboration, Computational thinking, Encouragement, Universal design and Self-understanding.

**Table 2.**   Statements of participants

| Categories | Statements |
|---|---|
| A sense of competition arising from collaboration with others | • B has beat me to it (Participant A) |
| Computational thinking | • If you reduce the size (of an object). It's now 70%, you may reduce it to 40% (to make it harder). And to make it easier, you reduce it to 100% (Participant A)<br>• We made the alien and the robot bigger, so that the area against the robot was bigger and made the robot move slower. That way it would be easier to clear (Participant B)<br>• It would be nice if you could reset the thickness of the lines when you press the spacebar (Participant C) |

(*continued*)

**Table 2.** (*continued*)

| Categories | Statements |
|---|---|
| Encouragement | • I think it's a really good idea (Participant C)<br>• I hope we can make and publish the Digi-riha application together (Participant C) |
| Universal design | • So what about the blind people? (Participant A)<br>• If you put in a recorded sound, like"I got you!" (even blind people can hear) (Participant B) |
| Self-understanding | • I don't know that much (about my impairments), even though I know the word (Participant A)<br>• I just need to make a game that's fun for me (in order to make people with same disease fun)! (Participant A) |

In the following section, the differences in the tendency of each participant's statements in the Digi-Reha LAB is described. Firstly, participant A, who has a diagnosis of ASD, made more statements related to universal design and self-understanding than the other participants. For example, in relation to self-understanding, participant A stated that he was not sure about his own impairments. On the other hand, when the facilitator asked "What do you enjoy about Scratch?", he responded as;

I study alone at home, so I don't hear any sound. It is boring. But scratch is good, I don't know what's good about it. I don't know. (Participant A)

He identified computer programming as enjoyable in comparison to the general subjects. However, he is not able to clearly articulate the reasons for this. He also describes what is necessary to develop applications for people with similar impairments to himself as follows;

I just need to make a game that's fun for me. (Participant A)

In this way, it seems difficult for Participant A to fully understand his own personal traits. On the other hand, he expressed a willingness to contribute to others by understanding his own impairments. Second, in terms of participant B, who is A's sibling, she commented about computational thinking and universal design when discussing the applications with participant A. For example, when they were talking about sound effects in the application, she suggested that even visually impaired people could enjoy playing it by adding sound. In addition, participant C, who has programming skills, gave many words of encouragement to participants A and B. For example, he praised A's app idea as follows;

I hope we can make and publish the Digi-Reha application together. (Participant C).

# 5 Discussion

## 5.1 The Potential for Self-understanding Through Inclusive Design

Many approaches have been taken to support children with ASD through computer programming [5, 6]. These are mostly therapeutic and educational initiatives aimed at improving language and social skills through interaction with others. This suggests that computer programming is an accessible tool for children with ASD. In addition, this study employs an inclusive design approach in which collaborate with disabled users to develop the application. Inclusive design is a method of incorporating the user's point of view from the early stages of development [7]. This is expected to improve the quality of the products.

Furthermore, understanding one's own impairments and necessary reasonable accommodations is an important basis for self-advocacy for disabled children [8]. In this study, Participant A, who has a diagnosis of ASD, was unable to explain his own impairments and why he enjoys computer programming. This is consistent with reports that children with impairments such as ASD, especially younger children of primary school age, often find it very difficult to explain their impairments in words, and even when interviewed they are unable to give clear answers [9, 10]. Thus, it was very difficult for Participant A, a child with ASD, to face to his own personal traits.

However, with the clear aim of developing a more enjoyable application, the participants engaged in detailed and thoughtful discussions. In particular, Participant A expressed a willingness to contribute to children with similar conditions to him, by developing applications that he finds enjoyable. In order to achieve this, it is necessary to understand his own preferences and needs to translate it into the application more deeply. It is also important to explain them verbally to the team members. Therefore, it is expected that participating in the process of application development in the Digi-Reha LAB promotes children's self-understanding, especially children with impairments.

## 5.2 Limitation of This Research

Since the aim of this study is an exploratory analysis, a very small number of participants have been recruited. In addition, all the data analysed were collected through observation of behaviours and statements in Digi-Reha LAB, not through structured interviews with each participant. Therefore, it is highly difficult to generalise the findings of this paper. For example, the phenomena observed may be different if participants had other impairments (e.g., physical or intellectual impairments).

In further research, existing assessment methods like the Behavior Assessment System for Children [10] and the What I Am Like/Self-Perception Profile for Children (SPPC) [9] are needed to be adopted according to the impairments of the target groups as well as to verify the results in a larger number of children.

## 5.3 Challenges and Suggeations to Involve Disabled Children

As mentioned above, Digi-Reha LAB has the potential to promote a better understanding of children's impairments. However, there are significant challenges. For example, there is a risk of a child with a diagnosis may be required to disclose his or her impairments to other children. Disability is socially stigmatised in a strong way, so avoiding disclosure of one's own impairment may be a rational choice [11]. The content and purpose of the Digi-Reha LAB should be discussed and carefully agreed upon with the participating disabled children. Focusing too much on the name of the child's disorder may lead to promoting the individual model of disability [12]. It assumes that disability is caused by the individual's condition and that it is in the individual's best interest to resolve it. Instead, it is important to look at how the child's difficulties can be addressed through reasonable accommodations for conducting inclusive activities or/and studies.

## 6 Conclusion

Digi-Reha has developed applications with kids creators in order to address the gap between non-disabled and disabled children and disabled children. For this research, a disabled child was recruited as one of the main members of Digi-Reha LAB rather than a guest. The three participants worked together to develop an original application using the Scratch programming software. Throughout the process, it was observed that participant A, who is a child with impairments, deeply thought about his own impairments, preferences and other aspects that were difficult to understand. It is suggested that the willingness to contribute to oneself and to children with the same disease may promote self-understanding. Further research is needed to examine the practicality of this method, including the differences in impairments children have.

## References

1. Han, C., Ohara, A., Yano, N., Aoki, M.: The current situation and issues of inclusive education for special needs education in Japan. Bull. Fac. Educ. Univ. Ryukyus **83**, 113–120 (2013)
2. Hoshino, K., Sato, S.: Research on exchange and joint learning for pupils of special needs class. Bull. Uekusa Gakuen Junior Coll. **12**, 85–89 (2011)
3. Allport, G.: The Nature of Prejudice. 25th anniversary edn. Addison-Wesley, Boston (1979)
4. Edwards, B., Cameron, D., King, G., McPherson, A.: The potential impact of experiencing social inclusion in recreation for children with and without disabilities. Disabil. Rehabil. (2021). https://doi.org/10.1080/09638288.2020.1865465
5. Eiselt, K., Carter, P.: Integrating social skills practice with computer programming for students on the autism spectrum. In: 2018 IEEE Frontiers in Education Conference (FIE), vol. 1, pp. 1–5 (2018)
6. Munoz, R., Vilarroel, R., Barcelos, T., Riquelme, F., Quezada, A., Valenzuela, P.: Developing computational thinking skills in adolescents with autism spectrum disorder through digital game programming. IEEE **6**, 63880–63889 (2018). https://doi.org/10.1109/ACCESS.2018.2877417
7. Altay, B., Demirkan, H.: Inclusive design: developing students' knowledge and attitude through empathic modelling. Int. J. Incl. Educ. **18**, 196–217 (2014)
8. Pocock, A., Lambros, S., Karvonen, M., Algozzine, B., Wood, W., Martin, J.: Successful strategies for promoting self-advocacy among students with LD: the LEAD group. Interv. Sch. Clin. **37**(4), 209–216 (2002)
9. Cosden, M., Elliott, S., Noble, S., Kelemen, E.: Self-understanding and self-esteem in children with learning disabilities. Learn. Disabil. Q. **22**(4), 279–290 (1999)

10. Huang, A., et al.: Understanding the self in individuals with Autism Spectrum Disorders (ASD): a review of literature. Front. Psychol. **8**(8), 1–8 (2017)
11. Matthews, N.: Teaching the 'invisible' disabled students in the classroom: disclosure, inclusion and the social model of disability. Teach. High. Educ. **14**(3), 229–239 (2009)
12. Oliver, M.: The social model of disability: thirty years on. Disabil. Soc. **28**(7), 1024–1026 (2013)

# Evaluation and Classification of Dementia Using EEG Indicators During Brain–Computer Interface Tasks

Yuri Nishizawa[1]([✉]), Hisaya Tanaka[1], Raita Fukasawa[2], Kentaro Hirao[2], Akito Tsugawa[2], and Soichiro Shimizu[2]

[1] Kogakuin University, 1-24-2 Nishishinjuku, Shinjuku-ku, Tokyo 163-8677, Japan
`j117215@g.kogakuin.jp`, `hisaya@cc.kogakuin.ac.jp`
[2] Department of Geriatric Medicine, Tokyo Medical University, 6-1-1 Shinjuku, Shinjuku-ku, Tokyo 160-8402, Japan

**Abstract.** The rapid increase in the number of patients with dementia is currently a concern. According to a survey, the number of patients with dementia in Japan would exceed 10 million by 2060. Thus, there is a need to develop simple techniques for early diagnosis of dementia to suppress the increase in patients with dementia. In our laboratory, we are developing a dementia-screening tool using character input-type Brain–Computer Interface. In this study the electroencephalogram (EEG) data obtained using the tool were analyzed in the frequency band. The purpose is to find the difference in EEG between healthy people, patients with mild cognitive impairment (MCI), and patients with Alzheimer's disease (AD). The results show that the mean value of the ratio of $\beta$ to $\alpha$ wave ($\beta/\alpha$) significantly differs between healthy subjects and MCI patients. The mean value of $\beta/\alpha$ was lower in the MCI patients than in the healthy subjects. In addition, there was also a significant difference in the range of $\beta/\alpha$ between $\beta/\alpha$ for patients with MCI and that for the patients with AD; that of AD patients was higher. From the results, it is considered that the degree of concentration decreases, and its variation becomes remarkable as the cognitive function declines. With these indicators, the three states are expected to be classified. In future studies, we shall verify whether the classification accuracy can be improved by using these indicators in machine learning.

**Keywords:** Beta/Alpha · Dementia · Electroencephalogram

## 1 Introduction

The number of people having dementia is increasing rapidly, and this poses a serious problem in Japan. According to a survey conducted by the Ministry of Health, Labor, and Welfare [1], there were 4.62 million patients with dementia in Japan in 2012, and this number would rise above 11 million in 2060. In addition, there is a shortage of doctors that diagnose dementia. Black et al. reported a diagnostic route in Japan; from cognitive impairment to dementia [2]. It was found that specialists examine patients with

© Springer Nature Switzerland AG 2021
C. Stephanidis et al. (Eds.): HCII 2021, CCIS 1499, pp. 39–46, 2021.
https://doi.org/10.1007/978-3-030-90179-0_6

dementia at a rate of 81.2%. Also, 45.8% of people with dementia go to neurologists. Table 1 lists the available and the required number of doctors in Japan, as reported by the Ministry of Health, Labor, and Welfare, Japan [3]. As shown in the table, 1.2 times the current number of doctors is needed. Early detection of dementia can suppress the increase in dementia patients. Therefore, there is a need to develop simple tools for early diagnosis is expected of dementia.

Currently, we are developing a dementia-screening tool using the character input-type BCI [4, 5]. Kurihara et al. suggested that dementia can be diagnosed using the spelling-error distance value (SEDV) by character input-type BCI [6]. However, the technique shows no significant difference between healthy subjects and those with mild cognitive impairment (MCI). Obtaining the differences between healthy subjects and MCI patients is essential to enable early diagnoses. Hence, there is a need to develop new indicators other than SEDV. In this study, we focused on the frequency band of electroencephalogram (EEG).

This study clarifies the difference in EEG between healthy subjects, MCI patients, and Alzheimer's disease (AD) patients by introducing new indicators. We focused on differentiating healthy individuals from MCI patients as it directly aids the early detection of dementia. In our future studies, we shall employ these new indixators for classification in machine learning.

**Table 1.** Available and required number of doctors in Japan.

|  | Neurologists | Psychiatrists | Total |
|---|---|---|---|
| Current number doctors | 3528 | 10843 | 167063 |
| Number of doctors required | 712 | 1200 | 24033 |
| Magnification | 1.20 | 1.11 | 1.14 |

## 1.1  Dementia

Dementia is a disorder caused by a decrease in or loss of intelligence. It affects the daily life of the patients. It is of different types: AD, vascular dementia, and Lewy body dementia. Among others, AD is more common. In this study, the subjects were divided into healthy subjects, subjects with MCI, and subjects with AD, and they were analyzed and compared. MCI is a condition that precedes dementia. It is not completely normal but does not interfere with the daily life of the patients. It has been reported that cognitive function is generally within the normal range, but a third party observes the forgetfulness of the patients. AD is a type of dementia caused by unexplained brain degeneration, and it affects the daily activities of the patients. The main symptom of AD is memory impairment, where one loses the ability to learn new things and recall the existing ones.

## 2  Methods of Analysis

### 2.1  Previous Research

EEG analysis is considered an effective diagnostic tool for dementia, especially AD. In a study on EEG measurements in patients with dementia, Mori and Otomo revealed that β/α closely correlates with dementia [7]. In this study, EEG was measured during diagnosis by a specialist. Considering the shortage of doctors, it is desirable to make early diagnoses of dementia possible even when specialists are not directly involved. Therefore, it is necessary to confirm the relationship between β/α and dementia.

Simple EEG analyses by Hirai et al. revealed that β/α increases when one is subjected to a mental load. Therefore, the degree of mental stress and concentration could be measured by observing the β/α of an individual [8]. Haranaka et al. also measured the EEG activity of circuit racers [9]. They used α- and β-wave generation rates and β/α for their analyses.

### 2.2  Analysis Item

In this study, we measured the rate of generation of α and β wave and analyzed β/α as an index of concentration. Furthermore, the range of each subject was calculated by subtracting the minimum value from the maximum value of the average value of β/α. The formulas are presented below. In the equations, S denotes the total brain wave and Σ is the cumulative power spectrum. For β/α in (3), the average value was calculated for each subject's condition and used for the analyses. The conditions of the subjects include the healthy subjects, subjects with MCI, and subjects with AD.

$$\alpha\% = \frac{\Sigma\alpha}{\Sigma S} \times 100 \qquad (1)$$

$$\beta\% = \frac{\Sigma\beta}{\Sigma S} \times 100 \qquad (2)$$

$$\frac{\beta}{\alpha} = \frac{\Sigma\beta}{\Sigma\alpha} \qquad (3)$$

## 3  Experiment

### 3.1  Conditions

The experiment was performed using the character input-type BCI reported by Kurihara et al. [6]. The subjects wore an electroencephalograph on their heads to measure the EEG while they perform tasks. Electrodes were placed in 8 (Fz, Cz, P3, P4, Pz, Oz, O1, and O2) of the 10–20 electrode placement methods standardized by the International Electroencephalography Society.

The experiment was approved by the Ethics Research Committee of Tokyo Medical University (early diagnosis of dementia using Brain–Computer Interface (BCI) 2016–083). All subjects provided written informed consent.

## 3.2  Experimental Flow

First, the target characters were displayed in green on the screen and presented to the subjects. Figure 1 shows the actual displayed data and the setup for the experiment. The subjects gazed at the target character. The displayed table blinked in rows and columns, and when the row and column containing the target character blinked, the subjects were made to utter the character. Thereafter, the table put the lights out. This flow is for inputting one character. Then, the next target character was turned on in green and the process was repeated. This was repeated for five characters to complete one trial. The 5-character task was repeated once and a 6-character task was performed twice, making it a total of four trials. The data obtained by removing defects from the four EEG data were used for analyses.

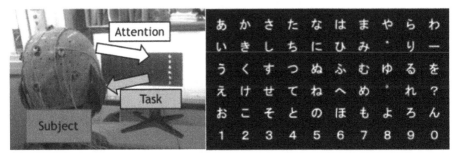

**Fig. 1.**  State of the experiment (left shows the setup; right is the displayed table).

## 3.3  Subject Information

This study was conducted using data from 55 people. Their average age was 79.62 ± 4.90 years. The subjects included those who visited the Tokyo Medical University outpatient department, and they were made up of 6 healthy subjects, 24 MCI patients, and 25 AD patients.

## 3.4  Hypothesis

The analysis performed is discussed in Sect. 2.2. We paid particular attention to the mean value of $\beta/\alpha$ and its range. The two hypotheses on which the study was based are shown in Fig. 2. The left is based on the average value of $\beta/\alpha$ and the right is based on the range of $\beta/\alpha$. NC denotes healthy subjects.

First, we hypothesized that the mean value of $\beta/\alpha$ for MCI patients is lower than that for healthy subjects. This is because the degree of concentration decreases as the cognitive function declines from healthy subjects to MCI patients; hence, the average value of $\beta/\alpha$, which is an index of the degree of concentration, would also decrease. Specifically, since healthy people can concentrate on a character-input task, their $\beta/\alpha$ is higher than that of people with MCI. On the other hand, it is more difficult for people with MCI to concentrate than it is for healthy subjects due to symptoms of MCI. As a result, β/α for subjects with MCI is lower than that for healthy subjects.

For the hypothesis based on the β/α range, the variation in the level of concentration is inferred to increase as cognitive function declines from MCI to AD. Therefore, the range of variation is larger in AD. Patients with AD find it difficult to concentrate due to the symptoms. Owing to this effect, it is expected that the level of concentration will not be uniform, including the time when concentration is possible and the times when it is not in all four measurements. In contrast, since MCI is a prestage of dementia, it is considered that such heterogeneity does not occur very often. It is inferred that the β/α range increases from MCI to AD due to the variation in concentration.

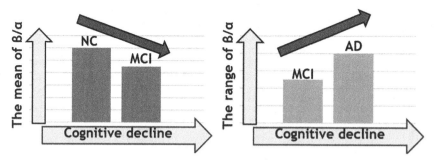

**Fig. 2.** Hypothesis about β/α (left is the mean value; right is the range).

## 4   Results

### 4.1   The Mean of β/α

The analysis results for the mean value of β/α are shown in Table 2 and Fig. 3 (where noncontributory (NC) refers to the healthy subjects). Table 2 summarizes the average β/α values obtained by extracting only two of the eight electrodes. The overall average was calculated for each subject's condition on the eight electrodes. From the overall average in Table 2, there was a decrease of about 0.1 from NC to MCI. Also, as shown in Fig. 3, the mean value of β/α decreased.

After performing a two-sample f-test on healthy subjects and MCI using the mean value of β/α, $p < 0.05$ was obtained for Fz, P3, and O2. In other words, the variances were equal, except for three sites. Then, we focused on the electrode part called Cz, which is also homoscedastic. In response to this, when the two-sample t-test was performed on a healthy subject and an MCI with Cz, a significant difference was observed because $p < 0.05$. Figure 3 is an excerpt of the Cz result.

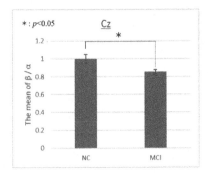

**Fig. 3.** The mean of β/α for NC and MCI (mean ± SD, N = 30).

**Table 2.** The mean of β/α for NC and MCI (N = 30).

| Electrode site | NC | MCI |
|---|---|---|
| Cz | 1.00 | 0.85 |
| Pz | 0.82 | 0.83 |
| Overall average | 1.08 | 0.95 |

## 4.2  The Range of β/α

The analysis results for the range of β/α are shown in Table 3 and Fig. 4. The range was calculated by subtracting the minimum value from the maximum value of all the measurement data for each subject. Some of the subject's data have only one total number of measured data (up to four) due to the exclusion of defects. We analyzed only subjects that had two or more measurement data per subject. Table 3 and Fig. 4 summarize the range for each subject obtained by calculating the overall average value for each state of MCI and AD. MCI originally had data for 24 people, but because there were two or more measurement data, we reduced it to 23 people and averaged the range values for the 23 people. The same was done for AD. We analyzed the data for Fz, Cz, and O2 among the eight electrodes.

Table 3 reveals that the value of AD was higher than that of MCI at all electrode sites. This is confirmed by Fig. 4. Then, when the two-sample f-test was performed for MCI and AD, $p < 0.05$ was obtained for Cz and O2. This indicates that the variances for the Cz and O2 ranges were not equal. Thus, we focused on Cz, as discussed in Sect. 4.1. Welch's t-test at Cz yielded $p$ of less than 0.05, indicating a significant difference. Thus, the result of Cz is extracted and depicted in Fig. 4.

**Table 3.** Mean of β/α rage for NC, MCI, and AD (N = 47).

| Electrode site | MCI | AD |
|---|---|---|
| Fz | 0.29 | 0.54 |
| Cz | 0.19 | 0.38 |
| O2 | 0.32 | 0.49 |

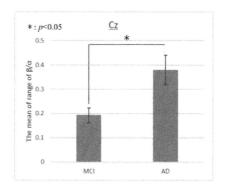

**Fig. 4.** Mean of β/α range for NC, MCI, and AD (mean ± SD, N = 47).

## 5  Discussion

First, we consider the average value of β/α. Comparing the hypothesis based on the average value of β/α (left of Fig. 2) with the result depicted in Fig. 3, we observe that the mean value of β/α decreases from NC to MCI in both cases. Since the obtained results agree with the hypothesis, it is considered that a decrease in the level of concentration can be measured by β/α. Table 2 validates the phenomenon as MCI is lower in all electrode sites other than Pz. The significant difference between NC and MCI suggests the possibility of classifying the two.

For the hypothesis based on the β/α range (right of Fig. 2), Fig. 4 shows that the obtained results agree well with the hypothesis. Table 3 shows that AD was higher at all three electrode sites, and it was about twice as high as MCI at Cz. From these results, it is inferred that the variation in the level of concentration ratio is larger in AD. In addition, we suggest that MCI and AD could be classified using the β/α range as a significant difference was obtained at Cz.

## 6  Conclusion

In this study, we measured the EEGs of different subjects using the character input-type BCI and analyzed them in the frequency band. The subjects were divided into three: healthy subjects, MCI, and AD. This study aimed to find the difference in EEG between healthy people and people with dementia by introducing a new index.

The results reveal a significant difference in the mean value of β/α between the healthy subjects and MCI and in the range of β/α between MCI and AD. Therefore, we infer that healthy subjects and MCI patients could be classified, as well as MCI and AD patients, by using these indicators. This is because β/α could determine a decrease in the level of concentration caused by the decline in cognitive function and the β/α range could measure an increase in the variation of the level of concentration caused by the onset of dementia.

Since significant differences were observed between healthy subjects and MCI patients, as well as between MCI and AD patients, the purpose of this study was achieved. In future studies, we shall introduce the indicators found so far [10] to machine learning and further develop tools that can classify dementia.

**Acknowledgments.** We express our sincere gratitude to the Department of Elderly Care, Tokyo Medical University, for their cooperation during this research. We also express our deep gratitude to all the collaborators that cooperated during the experiment. This research was partly supported by the fund for the development of minimally invasive treatment and diagnostic equipment, a joint research project by Tokyo Medical University and Kogakuin University. The research was also partly funded by JSPS KAKENHI, Grant Number JP19K12880.

# References

1. Ninomiya, T., Kiyohara, Y., Ohara, T., Yonemoto, K.: Research on future design of the elderly population with dementia in Japan, Ministry of Health, Labor and Welfare Science Research Grant Administrative Policy Research Field Ministry of Health, Labor and Welfare Special Research, H26–036 (2014)
2. Black, C.M., Ambegaonkar, B.M., Pike, J., Jones, E., Husbands, J., Khandker, R.K.: The diagnostic pathway from cognitive impairment to dementia in Japan: quantification using real-world data. Alzheimer Dis. Assoc. Disord. **33**(4), 346–353 (2019)
3. Ministry of Health, Labor and Welfare: Detailed results of the survey on the number of required doctors. https://www.mhlw.go.jp/bunya/iryou/other/dl/14.pdf. Accessed 10 Mar 2021
4. Morooka, R., Fukushima, A., Sato, A., et al.: Early diagnosis method of dementia using BCI and frontal lobe function test. Trans. Human Interf. Soc. **22**(2), 221–218 (2020)
5. Fukushima, A., Morooka, R., Tanaka, H., Hirao, K., Tsugawa, A., Hanyu, H.: Classification of dementia type using the brain–computer interface. J. Artif. Life Rob. **26**(2), 216–221 (2021). (in press)
6. Kurihara, R., Morooka, R., Tanaka, H., et al.: A new assessment method for the cognitive function in dementia using the spelling-BCI. Trans. Human Interf. Soc. **21**(1), 21–30 (2019)
7. Mori, A., Otomo, E.: Analysis of dementia by EEG. Jpn. J. Cogn. Neurosci. **3**(1), 45–48 (2001)
8. Hirai, F., Yoshida, K., Miyaji, I.: Comparison analysis of the thought and the memory at the learning time by the simple electroencephalograph. In: Transaction of Multimedia, Distributed, Cooperative, and Mobile Symposium, pp. 1441–1446 (2013)
9. Haranaka, Y., Ishida, Y., Kurihara, R.: An example of EEG activity of the prefrontal cortex during circuit driving. Trans. Soc. Autom. Eng. Jpn. **41**(2), 551–557 (2010)
10. Nishizawa, Y., Tanaka, H., Fukasawa, R., Hirano, K., Tsugawa, A., Shimizu, S.: Evaluation of cognitive decline using electroencephalograph beta/alpha ratio during brain–computer interface tasks. In: Proceedings of the 7th International Symposium on Affective Science and Engineering, no. 7A-05, pp. 1–4 (2021)

# Ideating for Co-designing with Blind and Visually Impaired Users:

## Exploring Possibilities for Designing User-Centered Healthcare Information in Pandemic Conditions

Sushil K. Oswal[1]([✉]) [iD] and Lohitvenkatesh M. Oswal[2] [iD]

[1] University of Washington, Seattle, WA 98195, USA
oswal@u.washington.edu
[2] University of Puget Sound, Tacoma, WA 98416, USA

**Abstract.** Access to information about the pandemic has been a major invisible barrier for people with visual impairments. As governments around the globe rush to distribute guidelines for the prevention of COVID-19 infections, the websites neglected to follow accessibility standards; thus, leaving out millions of users. Similar problems have been reported in acquiring information about medical help, such as locations for getting tested for COVID and even information about hospitals that accepted infected patients. On the other hand, digital-economy based rideshare services in many cases refused blind passengers, particularly if their destination was a medical facility. This problem has particularly been aggravated due to the absence of an easy-to-use, accessible reporting mechanism for the denial of such services by individual drivers. Those of us who have worked side by side with blind colleagues as participants in our design work, or as co-designers, are not unfamiliar with expressions of serious concern about the availability of information and reliability of technological infrastructure. Life for a majority of blind people, users, designers, academics, and citizens, was always unpredictable and it is definitely so in these pandemic times. This late-breaking poster paper presents the preliminary results of an in-progress survey of blind and low vision users in the United States which gauges the accessibility of healthcare information and related services during this pandemic. The results thus far reveal major identifiable access barriers to healthcare information on websites, HCI issues with telemedicine, information and reservation process about accessing COVID-19 vaccine sites, and digitally-dependent transportation.

**Keywords:** Accessibility to healthcare information for blind · Telehealth · Healthcare survey

## 1 Introduction

While the current pandemic offers some hope as medical providers have employed the tools of telemedicine so that medical professionals could make virtual visits with their patients using teleconferencing systems, not all patients have this access [1–3]. Likewise, medical economy supported by digital devices has also bestowed some autonomy on

© Springer Nature Switzerland AG 2021
C. Stephanidis et al. (Eds.): HCII 2021, CCIS 1499, pp. 47–55, 2021.
https://doi.org/10.1007/978-3-030-90179-0_7

patients for conducting basic medical tests to protect them from unnecessary exposure to infections in hospitals and clinics in these times of physical isolation and social distancing but again these affordances of technology did not reach a portion of disabled users. These pandemic concerns have been documented in public health literature in recent decades [4–6]. Those of us who have worked side by side with disabled colleagues as participants in our design work, or as co-designers, are not unfamiliar with expressions of serious concern about the availability of information and reliability of technological infrastructure because life for a majority of disabled people, users, designers, academics, and citizens, was always unpredictable but it is definitely so in these pandemic times [7]. Due to the ubiquitous presence of digital media in the operation of all these services and the embedding of digital interfaces in their delivery to patients, interaction designers with diverse expertise can play a central role in conceptualizing a more robust healthcare information infrastructure that does not fail disabled users.

## 2   Healthcare Information Access Issues for Blind and Visually Impaired Population During COVID-19

Accessibility has been defined as "all people, particularly disabled and older people, can use websites in a range of contexts of use, including mainstream and assistive technologies; to achieve this, websites need to be designed and developed to support usability across these contexts" [8]. A more comprehensive definition of accessibility comes from the perspective of web design which claims that "the ability to use, enjoy, perform, work on, avail of, and participate in a resource, technology, activity, opportunity, or product at an equal or comparable level with others. Separate is not equal and before or after the fact is also not equal" [9].

Access to information about the pandemic has been a major invisible barrier for people with visual impairments. As governments around the globe rush to distribute guidelines for the prevention of COVID-19 infections, the websites neglected to follow accessibility standards; thus, leaving out millions of users [10, 11]. Similar problems have been faced in acquiring information about medical help, such as locations for getting tested for COVID and even information about hospitals accepted infected patients.

On the other hand, many digital economy-based rideshare drivers refused disabled passengers, particularly if their destination is a medical facility. These transportation barriers themselves denied access to medical help because many disabled people do not drive and may not have a relative to give them a ride. This problem has particularly been aggravated due to the absence of an accessible reporting mechanism for the denial of such services by individual drivers. More carefully conceptualized digital interfaces and human computer interactions would have prevented such discriminatory actions on behalf of gig services that are otherwise considered a major achievement of the digital economy. Also, the transportation services support integrated in the EPIC System's MyChart for patients requiring help in reserving rides is not available to patients seeking medical assistance for suspected COVID infection.

Digital interfaces also have great potential for tackling with the accessibility barriers faced by disabled patients within the medical facilities. Social distancing and masking guidelines particularly restrict blind and deaf patients in communicating with medical professionals and few hospitals and clinics adopted existing digital technologies to accommodate the needs of these groups. Even during the virtual appointments, the medical providers have little understanding of how they could adopt their digital interfaces to meet the needs of blind and deaf patients.

While a pandemic like COVID-19 is a natural phenomenon beyond human control, public health policies, human ethics, and professional and social prejudices play a crucial role in how the relief efforts are targeted at certain population and ignore others. Disabled populations in such dire situations are often forgotten in logistical preparedness and as the society mobilizes its healthcare and other resources, the disabled are again overlooked in the frenzy of the moment [4]. This inequity became painfully obvious in March 2020 when countries imposed lengthy lockdowns on its populations and permitted limited movement of essential workers, or people travelling in private vehicles. More importantly, the general information about COVID-19, communications about the access to testing facilities, availability of hospital beds for infected people, and later vaccination related resources excluded the disabled and the elderly. Only users of up-to-date technology, such as, smartphones and other hand-held devices could acquire this information. State and private sector websites often expected speedy interactions with websites to make appointments for vaccine. Many department of health websites were not accessible to screen reader users [12].

In this late breaking paper, we present the preliminary results of a national survey with blind and low-vision users on the accessibility of healthcare information.

## 3 Brief Literature Review

Accessibility of healthcare information to blind and low vision people has not been studied extensively in the past; however, abundant research has taken place on the accessibility of websites, smartphone applications, health devices, telehealth, electronic health records, and digitally-dependent transportation [13–15]. Some of this research has primarily focused on the accessibility of technologies to blind or low vision people, or to the broader category of disabled people [10].

People with disabilities, including blind and low vision people, have lesser access to healthcare information on the Web, compared to people without disabilities [16, 17]. Healthcare information on the Web is not exempt from this issue. In fact, a study evaluating the accessibility of 697 Portuguese and Spanish healthcare institutions' websites found that none of them were WCAG 2.0 compliant [18]. In the same study, a specific analysis of 40 websites chosen from the larger list found that even the most accessible websites had several inaccessible elements. Meanwhile, others had hundreds of inaccessible elements. More specifically, a study on COVID-19 information found that blind and low vision users had lower exposure to graphical data on COVID-19 [10]. Automatically updating graphics and interactive graphics were reported to often lack alt text or descriptions, and even sources with some accessible graphics were inconsistent and unreliable. Similarly, in a study of COVID-19 information accessibility to blind users, data visualizations on the Web were found to be typically inaccessible [11]. This survey found that the majority of respondents reported inaccessible data-driven media, while the majority of respondents also rated access to data driven articles as very important or extremely important. Major issues reported were incompatibility with screen readers as well as missing alt text and tabular data. Respondents addressed these issues by looking for data in textual or auditory forms or relying on visual interpretation.

Healthcare information can also be accessed through smartphone apps by the blind; however, smartphone apps are often not fully accessible. One study found that usage speed was slower than sighted people even among expert, blind smartphone users [19]. Likewise, popular videoconferencing platforms, including Zoom, MS Teams, and Google Meet, have all been found inaccessible to varying levels [20]. Despite claiming compliance to standards, such as WCAG 2.1 AA, exceptions are noted in each platform, which indicates a lack of full accessibility [21].

## 4   Purpose and Design of This Study

This study avoids simply collecting reports from experts, or bystanders, and concentrates on identifiable access barriers to healthcare information and computer mediated interactions through a detailed survey with blind and low vision population in the United States. The second phase of the study will also include a set of focus groups with the survey participants available to speak to the researchers.

By the closing of this survey, we hope to involve up to 200 blind and low vision participants in this project—a significant number in the context of this population. The survey includes questions about the availability of relevant informational technology in the healthcare context, the barriers blind users experienced in using this technology, HCI issues experienced by adaptive and assistive technology users and the healthcare information infrastructure, and the technology gaps identified by these users.

## 5   Methods

This study employs a mixed method survey tool to collect data about accessibility barriers to healthcare information from blind and low vision users. The preliminary data from the participants is extensive which cannot be included in this poster paper. In the second phase of the study, we will employ an additional qualitative tool -several focus groups with select blind and low vision participants who might have volunteered to contribute.

## 6   Preliminary Quantitative Data

Based on the data collected thus far from the survey, this paper tries to portray the accessibility barriers experienced by blind and low vision users. These barriers range from difficulties in acquiring online information due to the accessibility problems with the state and federal government websites to inaccessible interaction design of online forms for making reservations for COVID-19 testing. The overall user experience with websites was patchy in general, even when participants were eventually able to obtain the healthcare information they needed about COVID-19. Although the users did not particularly complain about the accessibility of data visualization tools on the websites offering information about COVID-19 infection rates, they did not seem to have sufficient information about these rates. Similarly, the participants did not always point out the difficulties they faced with digital economy-based rideshare services; however, many disabled users of these services face accessibility barriers, even in non-COVID times, because Uber and Lyft drivers regularly refuse to take passengers with service animals on their vehicles. Later in the conclusion, we try to imagine how participatory interaction design approaches with the involvement of blind participants could produce ideas for creative and effective HCI solutions in healthcare information contexts. The preliminary qualitative data from our survey also suggests that the participants ideas from this survey could provide HCI community with some new avenues for conducting socially focused and inclusive research [22, 23]. The study's overall approach is to identify problems through participation of this population in this survey and focus groups to come up with ideas using participatory design-oriented ideation to overcome these access barriers. For example, researchers have proposed methodologies employing a knowledge engineering approach to data sharing to protect patient privacy while deriving necessary information from health records [24].

A total of $n = 71$ blind and low vision US residents responded to our survey at this preliminary stage of the study. All participants did not answer all questions; therefore, data may not always add up to these totals. Table 1 offers basic demographic data about the participants. In our final report on this survey, we will also have participant data on race and ethnicity.

**Table 1.** Demographic data from the survey.

|  | Disability Status | | Gender | | | Age | | | | | | |
|---|---|---|---|---|---|---|---|---|---|---|---|---|
|  | Blind | Low-vision | Male | Female | Other | 18–24 | 25–34 | 35–44 | 45–54 | 55–64 | 65–74 | 75–84 |
| Count | 52 | 19 | 18 | 52 | 1 | 7 | 11 | 12 | 11 | 14 | 15 | 1 |
| Percentage | 73.2 | 26.8 | 25.4 | 73.2 | 1.4 | 9.9 | 15.5 | 16.9 | 15.5 | 19.7 | 21.1 | 1.4 |

Table 2 presents survey results about the availability of information on COVID-19 prevention measures to the participants.

**Table 2.** Availability of preventative COVID-19 information.

|  | Masks (low vision) | Social Distancing (low vision) | Handwashing (low vision) | Masks (blind) | Social Distancing (blind) | Handwashing (blind) |
|---|---|---|---|---|---|---|
| Yes (count) | 18 | 17 | 17 | 43 | 42 | 48 |
| Yes (percent) | 94.7 | 89.5 | 89.5 | 84.3 | 82.4 | 94.1 |
| No (count) | 1 | 2 | 2 | 8 | 9 | 3 |
| No (percent) | 5.3 | 10.5 | 10.5 | 15.7 | 17.6 | 5.9 |

Table 3 includes data on the availability of various medical services and information about them to blind and low vision people. All participants did not answer every question.

**Table 3.** Availability of essential healthcare from medical providers during COVID-19 pandemic.

|  | Prescription for a medication | Telemedicine | Regular therapy | Rehabilitation for a recent injury/medical condition |
|---|---|---|---|---|
| Equal access (count) | 39 | 27 | 35 | 26 |
| Equal access (percent) | 56.5 | 39.1 | 50.7 | 37.7 |
| Somewhat equal access (count) | 22 | 21 | 10 | 6 |
| Somewhat equal access (percent) | 31.9 | 30.4 | 14.5 | 8.7 |
| No access (count) | 6 | 10 | 10 | 15 |
| No access (percent) | 8.7 | 14.5 | 14.5 | 21.7 |
| Not applicable (count) | 2 | 11 | 14 | 22 |
| Not applicable (percent) | 2.9 | 15.9 | 20.3 | 31.9 |

Table 4 offers findings about the availability of delivery services for prescription drugs to blind and low vision users. Many respondents did not answer all the questions in this section.

**Table 4.** Availability of pharmacy delivery services to blind and low vision patients.

|  | Free prescriptions delivery | Paid prescriptions delivery | Free prescriptions by mail | Paid prescriptions by mail | Family picking up prescriptions | Volunteer picking up prescriptions | Participant picked up prescriptions |
|---|---|---|---|---|---|---|---|
| Yes (count) | 26 | 15 | 27 | 15 | 46 | 18 | 35 |
| Yes (percent) | 37.7 | 21.7 | 39.1 | 21.7 | 66.7 | 26.1 | 50.7 |
| No (count) | 43 | 54 | 42 | 54 | 23 | 51 | 34 |
| No (percent) | 62.3 | 78.3 | 60.9 | 78.3 | 33.3 | 73.9 | 49.3 |

# 7   A Sampling of Qualitative Data

In the section below we share a summary of select qualitative responses due to space limitations. In our qualitative data, participants' responses varied not only by their blindness or low vision status, but also by the specific accessibility barriers they faced. In our discussion of these results, we maintain most of the differences that participants stated in their accessibility problems, unless the categories were either collapsible or were subcategories of a category, such as graphics and graphs.

Three (4.2%) participants also reported compounded accessibility issues due to their multiple disabilities.

When we asked if participants experienced equal healthcare information access as blind or low-vision consumers, 25 (48.1%) blind and 13 (68.4%) low vision participants reported equal access and another 25 (48.1%) of blind and 6 (31.6%) of low vision participants reported no equal access. In a follow-up answer, 11 (21.1%) blind and 1

(5.3%) low vision participants reported accessibility problems with charts, forms, graphs, and tables. Four (7.7%) blind participants also stressed problems accessing maps for locating vaccine centers.

Ten (14.5%) respondents reported no access to telemedicine during the pandemic.

When we asked participants which currently unavailable methods of providing healthcare information they would like to become available in the future, 6 (8.4%) respondents reported wanting more accessible telemedicine platforms.

When we asked if local or regional organizations had helped participants in acquiring health-related support and services, the National Federation of the Blind (NFB) was cited as a source of COVID information by 18 (34.6%) blind and 7 (36.8%) low-vision participants.

## 8   Discussion and Conclusion

Besides the results summarized above, some participant responses also raise more basic questions about HCI and touch. When a disease of the nature of COVID-19 makes physical surfaces prohibitive due to its transmission mechanisms and social distancing among human beings a necessity, a constant vigilance of touch and proximity becomes the new sociality [25]. Researchers will have to discover what this new sociality means for interaction design and disability. How does it disable the use of all those interaction designs which were previously deemed to be accessible and accommodating? Can we invent another embodied theory of design which can overcome these limitations [26]? How does touch suddenly debilitate and discard those who were just recently enabled by the affordances of touch and tactile designs? How does "social distancing" translate to this situation when COVID-19 can suddenly colonize any random surface and the touch of the erstwhile familiar takes a deadly turn? Nabil & Girouard write: "We believe that instead of a "killer app" for deformable interfaces and wearables, the key to their success resides in creating applications and devices for specialized users. So, what is most important is to work with a variety of users, such as people with visual impairments, people with mobility impairments, people living with repetitive-strain injuries, and everyday users, to co-design and evaluate prototypes that are useful for them." [27]. We endorse robust participatory approaches that lead to co-designing with our disabled colleague designers, developers, researchers, and users with disabilities [28].

**Acknowledgments.** This study has been approved by the Internal Review Board of the University of Washington.

We thank the program chairs for inviting us to present this poster paper in the Late Breaking session of the HCII 2021 Conference. Sushil Oswal thanks Hitender for his research assistance for this paper.

## References

1. Gubert, L.C., da Costa, C.A., Righi, R.: Context awareness in healthcare: a systematic literature review. Univ. Access Inf. Soc. **19**(2), 245–259 (2019). https://doi.org/10.1007/s10209-019-00664-z

2. Negrini, S., et al.: Telemedicine from research to practice during the pandemic. "Instant paper from the field" on rehabilitation answers to the Covid-19 emergency. Eur. J. Phys. Rehabil. Med. **56**(3), 327–330 (2020)

3. Jercich, K.: Telehealth may worsen digital divide for people with disabilities. https://www.hea lthcareitnews.com/news/telehealth-may-worsen-digital-divide-people-disabilities, Accessed 21 June 2021

4. Campbell, V.A., Gilyard, J.A., Sinclair, L., Sternberg, T., Kailes, J.I.: Preparing for and responding to pandemic influenza: Implications for people with disabilities. Am. J. Public Health **99**(2), 294–300 (2009). https://doi.org/10.2105/AJPH.2009.162677

5. Cameron, C. T.: Emergency planning for people with disabilities and other special needs. Washington, DC. Inclusion Incorporated, http://disabilitypreparedness.org/Planning% 20for%20People%20With%20Disabilities%20article.doc, Accessed 27 Sept 2008

6. White, G. W., Fox, M.H., Rooney, C., Cahill, A.: Assessing the impact of hurricane katrina on persons with disabilities. University of Kansas, Research and Training Center on Independent Living, Lawrence, KS (2007). http://www.rtcil.org/products/NIDRR_FinalKatrinaRep ort.pdf, Accessed 27 Sept 2008

7. Ehrenkranz, M.: Vital coronavirus information is failing the blind and visually impaired. https://www.vice.com/en/article/4ag9wb/vital-coronavirus-information-is-failing-the-blind-and-visually-impaired, Accessed 23 June 2021

8. Petrie, H., Savva, A., Power, C.: Towards a unified definition of web accessibility. In: Proceedings of the 12th International Web for All Conference (W4A '15), pp. 1–13. Association for Computing Machinery, New York (2015). https://doi.org/10.1145/2745555.2746653

9. Oswal, S.K., Kairos, A.: Ableism - multimodality in motion: disability and Kairotic Spaces. J. Rhetoric Technol. Pedagogy **18**(1) (2013). http://kairos.technorhetoric.net/18.1/coverweb/ yergeau-et-al.

10. Holloway, L., Butler, M., Reinders, S., Marriott, K.: Non-visual access to graphical information on COVID-19. In: The 22nd International ACM SIGACCESS Conference on Computers and Accessibility, pp. 1–3. Association for Computing Machinery, New York (2020)

11. Siu, A.F.,et al.: COVID-19 highlights the issues facing blind and visually impaired people in accessing data on the web. In: Proceedings of the 18th International Web for All Conference, pp. 1–15. Association for Computing Machinery, New York (2021)

12. Washington State Department of Health. https://www.doh.wa.gov/, Accessed 23 June 2021

13. Aiyegbusi, O.L.: Key methodological considerations for usability testing of electronic patient-reported outcome (ePRO) systems. Qual. Life Res. **29**(2), 325–333 (2019). https://doi.org/ 10.1007/s11136-019-02329-z

14. Brewer, R. N., Kameswaran, V.: Understanding trust, transportation, and accessibility through ridesharing. In: Proceedings of the 2019 CHI Conference on Human Factors in Computing Systems, pp. 1–11. Association for Computing Machinery, New York (2019)

15. Tavassoli, F., et al.: Towards an effective web-based virtual health intervention: the impact of media platform, visual framing, and race on social presence and transportation ratings. In: Duffy, V.G. (ed.) HCII 2021. LNCS, vol. 12778, pp. 165–181. Springer, Cham (2021). https:// doi.org/10.1007/978-3-030-77820-0_13

16. Dobransky, K., Hargittai, E.: Unrealized potential: Exploring the digital disability divide. Poetics **58**, 18–28 (2016)

17. Duplaga, M.: Digital divide among people with disabilities: analysis of data from a nationwide study for determinants of Internet use and activities performed online. PLoS ONE **12**(6), e0179825 (2017)

18. Martins, J., Gonçalves, R., Branco, F.: A full scope web accessibility evaluation procedure proposal based on Iberian eHealth accessibility compliance. Comput. Hum. Behav. **73**, 676–684 (2017)

19. Jain, M., Diwakar, N., Swaminathan, M.: Smartphone usage by expert blind users. In: Proceedings of the 2021 CHI Conference on Human Factors in Computing Systems, pp. 1–15. Association for Computing Machinery, New York (2021)
20. Leporini, B., Buzzi, M., Hersh, M.: Distance meetings during the covid-19 pandemic: are video conferencing tools accessible for blind people?. In: Proceedings of the 18th International Web for All Conference, pp. 1–10. Association for Computing Machinery, New York (2021)
21. Web Content Accessibility Guidelines 2.0. https://www.w3.org/TR/WCAG20/, Accessed 23 June 2021
22. Baker, P., Hanson, J., Hunsinger, J.: Unconnected: Social Justice, Participation, and Engagement in the Information Society. Peter Lang Publishing, New York (2013)
23. Oswal, S. K.: Participatory design: barriers and possibilities. Commun. Des. Q. Rev 2(3), 14–19 (2014). https://doi-org.offcampus.lib.washington.edu/, https://doi.org/10.1145/2644448.2644452
24. Morales Tirado, A.C., Daga, E., Motta, E.: Effective use of personal health records to support emergency services. In: Keet, C.M., Dumontier, M. (eds.) EKAW 2020. LNCS (LNAI), vol. 12387, pp. 54–70. Springer, Cham (2020). https://doi.org/10.1007/978-3-030-61244-3_4
25. Giudice, N. A.: Covid-19 and blindness: why the new touchless, physically-distant world sucks for people with visual impairment. https://medium.com/@nicholas.giudice/covid-19-and-blindness-why-the-new-touchless-physically-distant-world-sucks-for-people-with-2c8dbd21de63, Accessed 21 June 2021
26. Fogtmann, M.H., Fritsch, J., Kortbek, K.J.: Kinesthetic interaction: revealing the bodily potential in interaction design. In: Proceedings of the 20th Australasian Conference on Computer-Human Interaction: Designing for Habitus and Habitat, pp. 89–96. Association for Computing Machinery, New York (2008)
27. Nabil, S., Girouard, A.: Creative interactions lab@Carleton University. In: Interactions. Association for Computing Machinery, New York (2020). https://doi.org/10.1145/3389153
28. Oswal, S. K.: Breaking the exclusionary boundary between user experience and access: steps toward making UX inclusive of users with disabilities. In: Proceedings of the 37th ACM International Conference on the Design of Communication (SIGDOC '19), pp. 1–8. Association for Computing Machinery, New York (2019). https://doi-org.offcampus.lib.washington.edu/, https://doi.org/10.1145/3328020.3353957

# A Domain-Specific Language for Model-Driven Development of Networked Electronic Travel Aid Systems

Florian von Zabiensky$^{(\boxtimes)}$ , Christian Loosen , Michael Kreutzer ,
and Diethelm Bienhaus

Technische Hochschule Mittelhessen, Institute of Technology and Computer Science,
University of Applied Sciences, Giessen, Germany
{florian.von.zabiensky,christian.loosen,michael.kreutzer,
diethelm.bienhaus}@mni.thm.de

**Abstract.** This work introduces a domain specific language for the development of networked electronic travel aid systems (ETAs). ETAs help people who are visually impaired to move independently and safely in unfamiliar environments. They are usually developed as part of research projects or by small companies for specific tasks as a proprietary overall system. ETAs would benefit from a unified development process as well as interoperability between products. These systems usually consist of similar human-machine interfaces, but provide different information to the user. In order to focus more on this information presentation, new industrial or research projects should not have to re-engineer such systems. This problem can be solved by means of interoperability, interchangeability and a component-based development of ETAs. Hence components can be reused or even exchanged between products and prototypes. To keep the barriers of developing such systems low, a supporting framework was initiated [6]. This work presents a domain-specific modeling language as part of such a framework that supports component-based development of ETAs.

**Keywords:** Electronic travel aids · Domain specific language · Model driven development · Robot operating systen · ETA · ROS · ROS2

## 1 Introduction

Assistance systems can significantly support disabled people in their daily life. Electronic Travel Aids (ETAs) are special devices consisting of sensors and electronic components to assist and improve the mobility of visually impaired people in terms of safety and usability. Nowadays ETAs consist of proprietary isolated systems addressing often only one sensory channel – audible or haptic – to assist visually impaired people.

© Springer Nature Switzerland AG 2021
C. Stephanidis et al. (Eds.): HCII 2021, CCIS 1499, pp. 56–63, 2021.
https://doi.org/10.1007/978-3-030-90179-0_8

To facilitate the realization of heterogeneous, networked ETAs that can be combined in individual configurations, we are developing a Domain-Specific Language (DSL) to specify an ETA as a system of networked subsystems and software nodes.

An ETA specified in this DSL can, for example, be the combination of two systems. One that detects sidewalks and one that can display directions by means of voice instructions. In combination, a blind user can be guided along a walkway using voice instructions. In addition, splitting such a system into individual ETA components provides the possibility to reuse the voice instructions for other services as well.

Goal of our DSL is to foster reusability and to gain flexibility by means of a modular approach: ETA components encapsulate functionality independently of concrete hardware devices or platform dependent software like drivers. In general, reusability and interoperability are important quality criteria in software development. A well known technology in software engineering that addresses these aspects is the model-driven development (MDD) approach. The core of the MDD approach is a graphical or textual model describing both the software architecture and its behavior. Executable or compilable code is generated from these models. Thus, there is always an abstract description of the implementation, which is always synchronous to the model due to the development process.

In this work, we present a textual modeling language that supports the modeling of networked ETAs. The models can be compiled into C++ via code generation. The resulting software nodes use a common middleware for communication. Based on comprehensive research we chose the Robot Operating System 2 (ROS2) as the appropriate platform since it provides easy integration of networked components by means of clear interfaces. As a middleware ROS2 supports interchangeability and reusability of heterogeneous components.

In contrast to graphical modeling solutions like *Papyrus4Robotics*[4] or *UML/MARTE*[5] our DSL addresses developers, who are familiar with a textual description. Textual modeling languages that provide code generation to ROS or ROS2 have already been implemented with the use of the *Architecture Analysis and Design Language* (AADL) [1,2,7] or Rebeca [3]. However, our experience with AADL revealed that the language itself is very powerful and offers many possibilities that are rarely used in the development of assistance systems. As a result, the necessary effort for familiarization is significantly higher than the benefits that can be reached. Rebeca is a language and framework that does not address the topic of embedded systems. However, this is important in the area of ETA Systems, since many ETA components are implemented on resource-constrained hardware due to their portability requirements.

In the following sections, ROS2 is discussed, since this is used as middleware in the generated code. The proposed *Framework for Electronic Travel Aids - Modeling Language* (FETA-ML) is then described, followed by a discussion of the current project status. Finally, since this is an ongoing development, current limitations and future work are described.

## 2   Robot Operating System 2

ROS2 is an open source framework created for the development of networked mobile robots, but it has also many advantages for use in ETAs. The framework consists e.g. of tools that support development, a unified development process, and middleware that enables communication between network participants. A robot is constructed by dividing its components into different network nodes. Each node has concrete tasks and responsibilities that can be used by other nodes via clearly specified interfaces. As a result, a robot consists of many nodes, which in their entirety can solve complex tasks. The individual nodes are, for example, device drivers or algorithms for data processing.

Due to the possibilities offered by the ROS paradigm, a large community has formed sharing nodes and devices. For standard robotics problems, such as the detection of obstacles in a 3D point cloud, or the self-localization of a robot, there are already various solutions that are also interchangeable on the basis of uniform interfaces. This ROS paradigm is to be applied to ETAs using FETA.

Furthermore, ROS2 has other advantages like a completely decentralized network that also takes security aspects into account for communication, since the Data Distribution Service is used as communication protocol. In addition, ROS2 is designed to allow resource-constrained embedded systems to be integrated into such a network.

In summary, ROS2 is chosen as the middleware for our ETAs, because it allows to integrate existing algorithms and sensors or actuators from the robotics domain easily to build ETAs. Hence the development of new ETAs does not have to start from scratch. Moreover, it is possible to divide the system into ETA components, which together form a complete ETA system, as shown in the example above with the sidewalk guidance system.

## 3   FETA-ML as a DSL for Networked ETAs

As explained in the introduction, our goal is to define a unified development process across ETA components. The main aim of such a process is to ensure that these components can also communicate with each other in a uniform manner. To support this, an initial proposal for a new language for developing networked ETA components is presented here.

The FETA-ML and the associated development process is shown in Fig. 1. The color-coded hexagonal arrows correspond to language components of the FETA-ML that describe different aspects of an ETA component. The FETA-ML is a textual modeling language which is divided into four categories: System-level software architecture (blue), behavioral description (green), hardware-related software (yellow), and deployment (orange).

Listing 1.1 shows an example excerpt of the textual notation of a system description. This may be the audio instruction ETA component that was mentioned before. It describes a system with one input data port and two node instances. Each node exist separately as a node description.

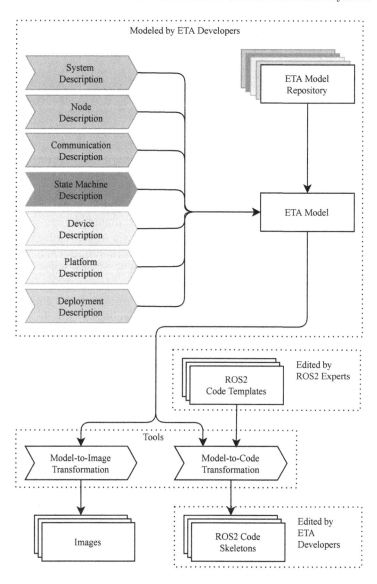

**Fig. 1.** Functional Scheme of the Model-Driven Development of an ETA based on ROS2. Blue hexagon arrows contain the models of the software architecture illustrating the nodes and the communication between them. The green hexagon arrow provides the behavior model of a node. The yellow hexagon arrows represent the hardware model of a platform comprising the available sensors and actuators. The orange hexagon arrow describes the combination of the software and hardware descriptions to model the deployment of each node in the distributed ETA. (Color figure online)

Both also have data ports for communication connected to each other or to the system boundary. For example, the input data port named command is connected to the input data port of the *TextToSpeechNode* instance.

**Listing 1.1.** Example system.

```
system  AudioInstructionInterface:
  data  ports:
    in  String        command;
  node instances:
    TextToSpeechNode    tts;
    AudioNode           output;
  connections:
    command    ->  tts.command;
    tts.pcm    ->  output.pcm;
end  AudioInstructionInterface;
```

The notation is consistent across the language components. The language components for describing the system-level software includes three descriptions: The system description, the node description and the communication description. A system description is used to describe a network of nodes and subsystems that communicate and cooperate with each other. It is a hierarchical description, which in turn can use or integrate other systems (e.g. further ETA components). For this purpose, it describes the nodes and system instances belonging to the system and the communication links between these components. In addition, a system itself can define communication ports to the outside world, so that it can also be used as a subsystem and used as a communication partner.

Another part of the language is the description of a node. A node has concrete, related tasks and is used to perform complex tasks collectively with other nodes. For example, the processing of an image with the extraction of sidewalk information can be considered as a node that receives an image and computes sidewalk information. The node makes this data available to others. The description of a node contains its communication ports as well as declarations of functions, which will be discussed in more detail in the deployment description. In order to also describe the behavior of a node, a state machine is linked to the node which can be seen in Fig. 2. Thus, a clear separation exists between the Architectural Description and the Behavioral Description. Additionally, attributes of the node can be described as variables.

The last language component of the system-level software architecture is the description of the communicated data. It defines the data structures that are exchanged via communication ports. For communication ports, and thus also for the data description, a distinction must be made between data and services.

The behavior of a node is described in terms of a hierarchical state machine. States can store a function list for the Enter, Always, Leave activity. Events are associated with transition to switch between states. These transitions can also be conditioned by guard expressions. All functions used in the state machine must be described in the node that uses this state machine as a behavior description. This allows the state machine to call the functions of the node at runtime. In the same way, events can be generated for the state machine from other node functions in order to control its behavior.

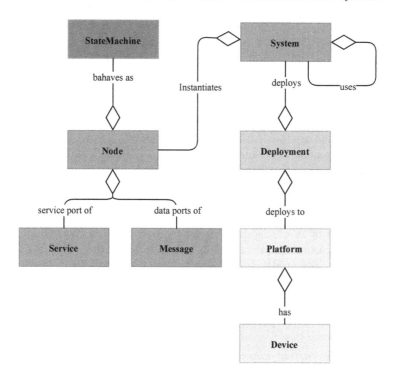

**Fig. 2.** Overview of the relation between FETA-ML language components.

By combining the system-level software architecture and the behavior description by the state machine, the fundamental software is described. A special feature of FETA-ML is, however, that not only the software is modeled at higher levels, but also the hardware-related software. This enables a clean and efficient integration and development of embedded devices. For this area, FETA-ML provides a description facility for platforms that model a runtime environment. A platform holds the information about the operating system used (if one exists), the existing bus systems to which sensors or actuators are connected and the instantiations of these sensors or actuators as a device.

A device, in turn, describes the interface of, for example, a sensor with functions that can be called, such as the configuration of a sensor. In addition, functions that can be called from the sensor are also described, such as a function that informs that the sensor has new data ready to be read out.

Via the deployment description all these descriptions can be connected to an overall construct. The deployment describes processes and binds them to the runtime environment, which is described by a platform. Nodes of a system are assigned to these processes, to be executed within. In addition, a connection of functions of the node description with functions of the device description takes place, so that a device can call functions of a node and vice versa, without both models explicitly knowing about each other.

An ETA component can be described with these language components. Multiple of such descriptions will form the basis of an ETA Model Repository, which is illustrated in the upper right corner in Fig. 1. Thus, when developing a new ETA component, descriptions from the ETA Model Repository can be reused (e.g. State Machines or Devices). In addition, other node or system descriptions can be used to connect other ETA components to the own. This enables the development of collaborative, networked ETA systems.

An ETA model can be transformed into code via model-to-code transformation, or code generation, which in turn uses a network communication middleware. For the reasons explained before, ROS2 is used here. The generation creates a code skeleton basis for further development of the component. This variant offers the advantage that the developers of the ETA component do not have to be ROS2 experts to develop it and integrate it into a network of components. The use of ROS2 as middleware is abstracted to the extent that all communication links are implemented by the code generation. Just as the transformation to code, the model can likewise be generated into diagrams that serve as a basis for communication between stakeholders.

## 4   Conclusion and Future Work

In this work, the current status of FETA-ML is presented. FETA-ML is a domain-specific textual modeling language to develop networked ETA components and consistently generate code that uses ROS2 as communication middleware. The language provides various components to describe systems at the architecture level describing the communication between nodes as well as the software interfaces of nodes. FETA-ML offers also the possibility to specify the behavior of nodes by means of state machines.

This DSL supports modeling of execution platforms as well as sensors and actuators. FETA-ML enables the modeling of embedded systems as appropriate target platforms to implement ETA components. A deployment description can be used to relate these model components to each other. From a FETA-ML model description of an ETA component a ROS2 project can be generated via code generation tools. The resulting code encapsulates ROS2 specific implementation details so that no in-depth knowledge of ROS2 is required to prototype a system. The code generation tool chains are still under development and will be completed step by step.

At the moment, a migration from the existing implementation, which was developed from scratch, to a Xtext[1] based implementation is taking place. The project is expected to be released at the end of the year to evaluate and improve the language as well as the opportunities through the tools according to suggestions. Initial findings are that node extensibility is a missing feature so that a node type can extend an existing node type. This would make the reusability of node descriptions for similar systems much more convenient. In the upcoming

---

[1] https://www.eclipse.org/Xtext/.

year, prototype of a complete assistance system is planned which will be specified using FETA-ML and code will be generated automatically. Hence a MDD approach will be applied comprehensively in the domain of ETAs.

# References

1. Bardaro, G., Matteucci, M.: Using AADL to model and develop ROS-based robotic application. In: 2017 First IEEE International Conference on Robotic Computing (IRC), pp. 204–207. IEEE (2017). https://doi.org/10.1109/IRC.2017.59
2. Bardaro, G., Semprebon, A., Matteucci, M.: A use case in model-based robot development using AADL and ROS. In: Proceedings of the 1st International Workshop on Robotics Software Engineering, RoSE '18, pp. 9–16. ACM (2018). https://doi.org/10.1145/3196558.3196560
3. Dehnavi, S., Sedaghatbaf, A., Salmani, B., Sirjani, M., Kargahi, M., Khamespanah, E.: Towards an actor-based approach to design verified ROS-based robotic programs using rebeca. Procedia Comput. Sci. **155**, 59–68 (2019). https://doi.org/10.1016/j.procs.2019.08.012
4. Radermacher, A., Morelli, M., Hussein, M., Nouacer, R.: Designing drone systems with papyrus for robotics. In: Proceedings of the 2021 Drone Systems Engineering and Rapid Simulation and Performance Evaluation: Methods and Tools Proceedings, pp. 29–35. ACM (2021). https://doi.org/10.1145/3444950.3444956
5. Wehrmeister, M.A.: Generating ROS-based software for industrial cyber-physical systems from UML/MARTE. In: 2020 25th IEEE International Conference on Emerging Technologies and Factory Automation (ETFA), pp. 313–320. IEEE (2020). https://doi.org/10.1109/ETFA46521.2020.9212077
6. von Zabiensky, F., Bienhaus, D.: A framework for electronic travel aids. In: Proceedings of the International Conference on Computer-Human Interaction Research and Applications, pp. 172–177. SCITEPRESS - Science and Technology Publications (2017). https://doi.org/10.5220/0006514701720177
7. von Zabiensky, F., Kreutzer, M., Bienhaus, D.: AADL zur Modellierung, Analyse und Code-Generierung für ROS2-Architekturen. In: Bauer, B., Wittenberg, C. (eds.) AALE 2019 Autonome Und Intelligente Systeme in Der Automatisierungstechnik 16, Fachkonferenz, Heilbronn, 28 Februar–1 März 2019, pp. 373–380. VDE Verlag (2019)

# The Packaging Design of Braille Beverage Bottle Based on Universal Design Thinking

Zhou Yang, Shuyi Chen, Tianhong Fang[✉], and Yifei Zhu

School of Art Design and Media, East China University of Science and Technology,
Shanghai, China
thfang@ecust.edu.cn

**Abstract.** In 2018, the number of visually impaired people in China reached 17.31 million. With the development of universal design thinking, a series of design works have greatly improved the quality of life of blind people. However, in more life scenes, the convenience of blind people's life is still far from the level of normal people. Therefore, this study focuses on the packaging design of Braille beverage bottles, based on the universal design thinking, with the analysis of the principles of Braille composition and experimental research, to ensure the readability and decoration of Braille. In this way, both ordinary consumers and blind consumers can directly understand the main information related to the product, and help blind consumers to improve their shopping convenience and initiative, reduce the "specialization" treatment, so as to help the blind group better integrate into social life.

**Keywords:** Braille · Beverage bottles design · Universal design

## 1 Introduction

In the field of design, the theories of humanistic care, design for special groups and universal design have been hot topics for decades. A series of design works based on the above theories have greatly improved the quality of life of the blind group, and indirectly enhanced the attention to the blind group of the society through awards and government publicity. However, this has not helped blind people achieve the standard of living of normal people. For example, due to the lack of Braille information in most commodity packages, the shopping process for blind consumers is cumbersome and inconvenient. The Braille on some packages has some defects such as small Braille area and secret location. In addition, the mental health of the blind is also worthy of attention. Feeling difficult to integrate into society as a result of being single out is more common. Therefore, this study suggests that in the design process, with the exception of some special products only for the blind, such "specialization" should be avoided in other design works to ensure that the blind will not feel special. Among all kinds of packaging, the shape and material of beverage bottle packaging are more special, and more common at the same time. How to properly to apply Braille information to the packaging of beverage bottle is an urgent problem to study.

C. Stephanidis et al. (Eds.): HCII 2021, CCIS 1499, pp. 64–70, 2021.
https://doi.org/10.1007/978-3-030-90179-0_9

## 2   Literature Review

### 2.1   Universal Design

With the development of society, the drawbacks of barrier-free design, which separates ordinary people from vulnerable groups, gradually appear. Universal design originated from accessible design emphasizes design for all. Originals from the United States, it is based on "no discrimination, equal opportunities and individual rights" [1]. Its core idea is to try to meet the needs of users with different abilities, and emphasizes that cognitive responses and physical characteristics of all users should be considered without distinction [2]. Universal design requires that the particularity of each individual should be emphasized, while the individual should not feel special as much as possible [3]. The fundamental purpose of it is that design should meet the needs of both special groups and the general public.

In the 1990s, Ron Mace and ten other advocates of universal design put forward the seven principles of universal design [4], including the principle of fairness, to meet the needs of users with different physical conditions, to avoid special treatment; adjustable, to provide a variety of use; simple intuitive, easy to understand the use of the way; information clear, effectively to the user to convey the necessary information; fault-tolerant, as far as possible to reduce the negative impact of misoperation; labor-saving, the use of appropriate movement labor-saving and reduce repeated movement; the size of the operating space is suitable, the scale of the operating space satisfies all users.

One of the important functions of beverage bottle packaging is to convey accurate and effective information. However, the existing beverage bottle packaging is difficult to convey product information to blind consumers effectively without Braille. Therefore, this study combined with the seven principles of universal design, through the reasonable use of Braille, so that the beverage bottle packaging can meet the information identification needs of both blind people and ordinary consumers.

### 2.2   Design Related to the Blind

Design works related to the blind can be roughly divided into two categories according to the users. One is products only for the blind, such as blind sticks, Braille writing tools, etc., which are usually aimed at meeting the special needs of the blind. The other category is universal design works that blind people can use, such as smart phones with blind mode, electrical buttons with Braille, etc., usually by incorporating special functions or Braille into the product. Such a product could reduce the emotional damage that blind people suffered from being single out [5].

However, this type of design works are still rare and have not yet covered all aspects of the life of the blind community. Taking packaging as an example, the lack of Braille in commodity packaging obviously presents a series of difficulties for blind people to identify commodity information. At present, only a few countries and regions have issued standard specifications to ensure that Braille printed on drug packaging meets the specifications, and some of them do not have the mandatory requirement that drug packaging must be printed in Braille [6]. Braille is even more difficult to see in other categories of goods. Even if there are some commodity packages printed with Braille, the Braille still has some problems such as small Braille area, partial location and less information. The extensive use of Braille will take up too much space on the packaging surface, which will cause some confusion for ordinary consumers in information identification. Therefore, this study suggests that the decorative use of Braille is a way to solve this dilemma, which will be discussed in Sect. 3.

### 2.3 Braille

Braille, a tactile form of writing, was first created in 1824 by Louis Braille, a French teacher [7]. The basic unit of it is square. Each square consists of six dots arranged in two columns and three rows in a rectangle, and the different information represented by each square is represented by controlling the protruding of each dot. This form of representation is also known as Braille, and most of the world's Braille systems are based on it. In order to promote the development of education, cultural development and living standards of the blind in China, China officially adopted the National General Braille Program in December 2017.On the basis of the previous Braille scheme, this scheme abandons the principle of "general non-standard tone" in the past, avoids the misreading caused by the confusion of tone of the use of Braille, and ensures the efficiency of Braille reading as far as possible, which marks that Braille in China has stepped into a new stage [8].

In practical application, the size of Braille should be suitable for the tactile psychological and physiological characteristics of the blind to avoid reading difficulties. Common Braille convex dot bottom diameter of 1.0–1.6 mm, dot height of 0.2–0.5 mm, dot distance of 2.2–2.8 mm. In addition, there are many printing methods of Braille, including die embossing, ink printing, thermoplastic molding, three-dimensional imitation and foaming printing. In the actual printing process, the appropriate printing mode should be selected according to the printing materials and the application [9]. Considering the special material of beverage bottle packaging, this study intends to adopt the foaming printing method, which is the mainstream method of Braille printing at present.

## 3    Analysis of the Aesthetic Characteristics of Braille

### 3.1    Analysis of the Aesthetic Characteristics of Braille "Dots"

Braille is a special form of writing. To consumers who do not understand Braille, Braille is a pattern of raised dots in a specific arrangement. Considering the related characteristics of Braille and the application scenarios of Braille in this study, the three-dimensional attribute of Braille itself has been weakened. Therefore, in this section, we regard Braille "dot" as a plane "point", and mainly discuss the principle of the composition of "point" and the possibility of "point" in its decorative application.

Generally speaking, the "composition" in design is a combination of forms or materials based on visual effects and psychological principles. It is a combination of vision and reasoning, rationality and sensibility. In plane composition, materials used for composition are not only abstract elements such as points, lines and planes, but also irregular shapes such as graphics [10]. In this section, we only discuss the principle of "point" composition: A single point has the function of concentrating or condensing the sight; More than two points can produce a visual dynamic effect; point has the function of interruption or rest; the continuity of points produces rhythm, and direction, that is, the visual effect of lines; the centralized arrangement of points can produce the visual effect of the surface; the same point in different background will produce different area of optical illusion effect; a specific arrangement of points of different sizes can produce a sense of space at different depths.

Therefore, for designers, the visual nature of the "point" leads to a lot of possibilities for its use. The good use of "point" can bring consumers more in line with the visual feeling of the packaging product itself, increase the desire of consumers to buy [11].

### 3.2 Study on the Design and Application of the Basic Unit "Square" in Braille

"Square" is the most basic unit of information in Braille, and its special form also brings it rich decorative application possibilities. Specifically, it can be divided into the following points: The subform of "square" is "dot". As for the composition and application of "dot", the previous section has analyzed its application possibility in detail. Plenty of squares are piled up to produce the effect of facets. With the reasonable arrangement of "square", on the premise of ensuring the information legibility, a large number of "square" can produce a variety of graphics, so as to bring different visual beauty to the decoration. The "square" constituted by the "dot" in a specific arrangement has a unique aesthetic sense of order. The aesthetic sense of order, as a way of expression of formal aesthetic sense, usually appears to be heavy, dull and boring. But this aesthetic sense of order is also indispensable. It can bring a scientific and delicate visual feeling, and can also integrate other relevant elements to enhance the overall effect of decoration. Therefore, no matter it is a single "square" or the orderly arrangement and repetition of "square", the aesthetic sense of order brought by them cannot be ignored. The specific arrangement of a large number of "squares" has a unique aesthetic sense of muscular rationality. In the packaging decoration design, the application of different textures to strengthen the picture effect, highlighting the theme so as to attract consumers' cases are everywhere. It is worth noting that the muscular aesthetic of "square" discussed here not only includes the visual effect of the plane, but also the tactile feeling brought by the texture generated in this way can bring consumers a more comprehensive shopping experience.

## 4    Experimental Study on the Optimal Arrangement of Braille

At present, in order to be unified with visual characters, the reading method of Braille in China is touching with the abdomen of the index finger from left to right. Common books and Braille writing tools all conform to this law, so the use of Braille on the body of beverage bottles should also conform to this law of reading. However, considering that most beverage packaging bottles on the market are cylindrical, and due to the three-dimensional nature of cylindrical bottles, the legibility of the Braille printed on the surface of the bottle is bound to be affected. When the Braille is arranged along the perimeter of the bottle body, it may be difficult to read because of the excessive curvature.

When the Braille is arranged along the height of the bottle, the position of holding the bottle is uncomfortable. Therefore, experiments were conducted to determine the best arrangement of Braille for the blind.

## 4.1 Experiment Design

In this study, a cylinder beverage packaging bottle with a capacity with 500 ml, a height of 20 cm and a bottom diameter of 5 cm of a certain brand was selected. Braille paper with different arrangement of writing was wrapped on the bottle body to simulate the real Braille printing situation. Three different Braille arrangement methods were provided in the experiment: A: vertical arrangement (along the length of the bottle), B: horizontal arrangement (along the circumference of the cross section of the bottle) and C: oblique arrangement (along the spirally upward direction of the bottle). Considering the advantages and disadvantages of vertical arrangement and horizontal arrangement, an intermediate scheme for inclined direction arrangement is added in the experiment. 33 blind volunteers with good Braille reading ability were invited to participate in the experiment. The participants ranged between age from 27 to 53 and included seven women and 26 men. Volunteers need to touch in turn three bottles of different Braille arrangement. The five Likert subscales were used to score the bottle packages with different Braille arrangement from two aspects: information identification (speed and accuracy in identifying Braille information) and reading comfort (comfortable posture when holding the bottle). The score range of 1 to 5 points, the higher the score, the better the recognition or comfort.

## 4.2 Data Analysis

In this study, SPSS 25.0 was used to calculate Cronbach $\alpha$ coefficient, a reliability index widely used in the academic circle. In general, the $\alpha$ coefficient should be at least greater than 0.7, and greater than 0.8 is the ideal reliability. The results showed that the $\alpha$ coefficient of the scale was 0.834, which suggested that the questionnaire had good reliability. Then, SPSS 25.0 ANOVA was used to test whether there were significant differences in the information identification and reading comfort among all the arrangement methods. The results (Table 1) showed that beverage bottles of different Braille arrangement had difference in reading comfort ($P < 0.05$), while there was no significant difference in information identification. According to the LSD (Least Significant Difference) post-comparison results, the reading comfort of horizontal arrangement is significantly better than that of vertical arrangement and spiral arrangement. Therefore, the horizontal Braille arrangement is chosen as the arrangement for application.

**Table 1.** Experimental data

| Data analysis | | Mean | | ANOVA | | |
|---|---|---|---|---|---|---|
| Project | | Identification | Comfort | | Identification | Comfort |
| Arrangement | Vertical | 4.241 | 4.366 | F | 1.340 | 3.248 |
| | Horizontal | 4.337 | 3.739 | | | |
| | | | | P | 0.249 | 0.041 |
| | Oblique | 3.966 | 3.654 | | | |

## 5  Design Practice

Soda sparkling water was selected from popular drink types and two flavors were identified: strawberry watermelon and cherry blossom peach. In terms of visual decoration style, aiming at the young consumer group of soda sparkling water, this study adopt a young and energetic illustration style combined with the corresponding taste. The overall shape adopts simple cylinder shape, which is easy for users to hold. As shown on the left side of Fig. 1, the Braille on the bottle body is arranged horizontally and divided into three areas (marked 1, 2, and 3 for easy identification). Zone 1 is the brand name, Zone 2 is the product taste information, and Zone 3 is the production date, price, capacity and other information of the product. Transparent foaming printing process is adopted. The Braille is concentrated in the middle of the bottle, which is normally held in the hand area, allowing the blind consumer to touch the Braille very quickly, also providing a certain anti-skid effect. Some of the transparent Braille are combined with a specific pattern to bring a certain aesthetic texture to the pattern. On the right of Fig. 1 is another flavor package.

**Fig. 1.** Packaging effect drawing

## 6  Summary

In order to ensure the readability and adornment of Braille, this study combined with the principles of composition to analyze the aesthetic characteristics of Braille elements. The analysis of the aesthetic features of Braille elements shows that the Braille arranged by "dots" has a unique sense of order. The basic Braille unit "square" can be formed into different figures to produce the effect of "face"; The arrangement of "square" can produce a unique aesthetic feeling of texture. In order to determine the best Braille information identification and reading comfort between the three arrangements, the researchers designed an experiment. The experimental data shows that there was no significant difference in the information identification among the three arrangements but the reading comfort of horizontal arrangement is significantly higher than the other two types of arrangement. Finally, based on the above analysis, this study designed two different flavors of beverage bottle packaging, the combination of Braille patterns of the packaging to increase the beauty of the packaging, while ensuring its readability.

This study only explores the application of Braille in beverage bottle packaging. In the future, the application of Braille in machines, packaging, public facilities and so on is still worth further exploration. The application specifications related to Braille will greatly improve the efficiency of Braille application. The standardized application of Braille on packaging is a possible future direction.

## References

1. Liu, Y., Zhu, Z.: General Design and Application. China Machine Press, Beijing (2010)
2. Chen, X.: Return to the origin of creation -- comment on the concept, goal and practice of universal design. New Art (02), 63–66 (2004)
3. Huang, Q.: Accessibility and Universal Design. Machinery Industry Press, Beijing (2009)
4. Fan, J., Li, K.: Analysis of universal design and accessibility design. Pack. Des. Eng. (04), 223–225 (2006)
5. Chen, L., Zhang, H.: Research progress on mental health of visually impaired people in China in recent 30 years. J. Guizhou Inst. Eng. Technol. **33**(06), 104–108 (2015)
6. GB/T 37105–2018, Braille on packaged drug packaging
7. Huang, J.: On the history, present situation and future of Chinese Braille. Educ. Res. (05), 77–78 (1994)
8. Zhong, J.: Research on national universal Braille program. China Spec. Educ. (06), 42–46+41 (2018)
9. Wang, C.: Braille and Braille printing. Screen Print. (01), 13–15 (2007)
10. Xin, H.: Morphological Tectonics. China Academy of Art Press, Hangzhou (1999)
11. Hou, W.: Application of point, line, plane and body elements in packaging design. Electron. Manuf. (07), 242 (2014)
12. Gao, Y.: Research on the function and decoration of braille in commercial packaging. Art Sci. Technol. **30**(01), 276–277 (2017)

# Physiology, Affect and Cognition

# Obtaining External Motivation from Strangers: A Study on Customer-to-Customer Interaction in Gymnasiums

Ying-Yu Chiang[1] , Hsien-Hui Tang[1]([⊠]) , and Shu-Yi Chen[2]

[1] National Taiwan University of Science and Technology, Taipei 106335, Taiwan
`drhhtang@gapps.ntust.edu.tw`
[2] Ming Chuan University, Taipei 111, Taiwan

**Abstract.** Many government-owned gyms in Taiwan consider coaches' conflicts of interest and often the communication between customers is not encouraged. However, from the perspective of gym users, exercisers have expectations for interaction. Through a service design case study, the research explored how the customer-to-customer interaction service in the gymnasium can fulfill users' needs and have a positive impact on the atmosphere of the gyms.

The objectives of this research are as follows. (1) To propose digital and physical on-site services that help initiate the interaction between strange customers smoothly, and services that continue the connection between strange customers after exercise. (2) From the perspective of social exchange theory, to review the case and propose service suggestions that promote positive customer-to-customer interaction services.

There are three findings in this research: (1) When providing customer-to-customer interaction service, gyms need to consider the familiarity of customers and help customers to establish trust relationships; (2) Services that trigger internal motivation of exercisers to interact helps to maintain a long-term and positive cycle of customer-to-customer interaction services in gyms; (3) Providing a medium to trigger interaction and heating an interactive atmosphere help to improve the quality of customer-to-customer interaction service.

**Keywords:** Customer-to-customer interaction · Service design · Gym

## 1 Introduction

Many services have the phenomenon of customer-to-customer interaction (CCI). In addition to CCI in physical spaces, such as co-working spaces, hotels and other interactions for different purposes, services also promote CCI in digital ways. Many studies have pointed out the commercial benefits that can be achieved by CCI interaction. For example, good CCI can increase customer satisfaction and customers' willingness to return, and even make customers spontaneously invite others to join.

This research explores the CCI services in the physical field, and choose the gymnasiums in National Sports Centers as a research case. As a public service entity, the

© Springer Nature Switzerland AG 2021
C. Stephanidis et al. (Eds.): HCII 2021, CCIS 1499, pp. 73–79, 2021.
https://doi.org/10.1007/978-3-030-90179-0_10

gymnasiums of the National Sports Center are open to the public, welcoming all types of customers, but their service staff is limited. On the other hand, due to the in-depth understanding of fitness exercises, there are certain thresholds, and long-term regular habits are required to achieve fitness effects. Therefore, it is possible and necessary to develop CCI in this case. The research of CCI provides a good insight to improve the fitness habit formation process of the gym customers of the National Sports Center.

## 2   Method

In order to clarify this relatively unexplored topic, this study refers to the Double Diamond design model invented by the Design Council [1]. This iterative process includes four stages: Discovery, Definition, Development and Delivery. This process is performed in a continuous and iterative manner. In the design process, we engage users through multiple in-depth interviews, co-creation workshops and evaluation tests to ensure that the solution meets user needs.

### 2.1   Discovery and Definition

In the Discovery stage, since the service is established in the physical field, this research conducts field observation and contextual inquiry. The AEIOU observation framework can be used to initially explore the current status of the service and serve as the basis for user interview. Then, in-depth interviews were conducted to understand the problems and expectations the interviewee faced when interacting with others. The work activity affinity diagram is used to organize and summarize the interview data, so that we can define different types of personas and the five CCI topics, and sort out the stages of the customer journey map of CCI in the gyms.

### 2.2   Development

In order to understand gym customers' expectations for the service, we invites gym customers who have expectations for interacting with others to participate in co-creation workshops. The purpose is to make exercisers of different natures have a dialogue about the five CCI topics, and try to find the balance between the two sides, and explore the possibility of new services. After the co-creation workshop, researcher analyzed the ideas proposed by the participants during the ideation stage, as well as the content of the dialogue during the workshop, and developed the service design concepts for the interaction among exercisers. Adhering to service design thinking, the case properly provides online services to extend the touchpoints from on-site service to the process before and after the entry, thereby developing omni-channel services. A more complete service process can be close to the life of the exerciser and enhance customer engagement, so as to increase the frequency of return visits.

## 2.3  Delivery

In the evaluation stage, the case evaluates ten service concepts that promote CCI among exercisers from three perspectives, that is, value, feasibility and experience. It also conducts evaluation interviews with target exercisers, and considers how to balance the overall customer experience and implementation constraints. During the evaluation, physical and digital prototypes enable exercisers to emerge specific ideas about the new CCI service model, so as to obtain feedback from exercisers and propose service suggestions to the gymnasiums of the National Sports Center (Table 1).

**Table 1.**  CCI topics and their corresponding design concepts.

| CCI topic | Design concept |
| --- | --- |
| 1. Creating an environment suitable for interaction | Happy Hour |
|  | Truth Message Board |
| 2. Triggering discussion on fitness topics | Target Planning Wall |
|  | Three-Level Equipment Guide |
| 3. Finding interaction partners | Ask Me Wristband |
|  | Training Arrangement Cards in different colors |
| 4. Continuing the interaction | Real-Time Feed |
|  | Nutrition Map |
|  | Weekly Plan |

# 3  Results and Initial Findings

## 3.1  Creating an Environment Suitable for Interaction

Two design concepts for the first CCI topic, creating an interactive environment, are Happy Hour and Truth Message Board. The case found that exercisers had positive feedback on the concept of "happy hour". Before customers fully accept the CCI services in the gyms, dividing the specific time period of the CCI service allows customers to have the correct expectations for visiting the gym in advance. If the exerciser wants to pursue his/her personal record without disturbed this time, he/she can avoid a specific time period. On the contrary, if the exerciser wants to exercise casually and is willing to interact with others more, he/she can arrive during "Happy Hour". In this way, every customer comes to the gym has a consensus that they will have the opportunity to interact more with others. At the same time, they do not have to worry about others unwilling to be disturbed. 3–1 Create an interactive environment.

On the other hand, the more authentic and personal experience the customers share through the "message board", the easier it is for the exercisers to imagine the situation when communicating with others, thus reducing worries about interaction. It is also important to provide a lively fitness environment. The gym can provide CCI services to break the barriers between customers due to everyone focusing on their own training. Through the evaluation interviews, we also found that if the customers can stay in a relaxing area for a while after working out and put aside the things at hand, they can easily join the group conversation. It is recommended that the gym provide equipment such as bar tables to allow exercisers to join and form a circle at any time to promote dialogue with each other.

### 3.2  Triggering Discussion on Fitness Topics

Two design concepts for the second CCI topic, triggering discussion on fitness topics, are Target Planning Wall and Three-Level Equipment Guide. One is for mid-term fitness planning, and the other is for learning the use of equipment immediately. The interview found that setting the Target Planning Wall in an area that does not charge fees can prompt exercisers to discuss without time pressure.

The Three-Level Equipment Guide meets the needs of both parties in equipment teaching. Those who ask questions have relatively lack of fitness knowledge, and this guide can help them know how to ask questions appropriately. On the other hand, the party providing instructions usually makes good use of the training time and is concerned about whether the fitness process has been interrupted for too long. This guide also allows them to answer questions with light prompts.

### 3.3  Finding Interaction Partners

There are two concepts for the third CCI topic, namely Ask Me Wristband and Training Arrangement Cards in different colors. After testing, it is found that understanding the interaction willingness of others through objects is indeed helpful for interaction and dialogue. However, exercisers care about the form of this object. Exercisers believe that the form of "Training Arrangement Cards" does not fit the fitness scenario, because it is troublesome to bring a piece of paper card during training. Although there is a chance to wear a wristband, the lack of recognition is a problem that needs to be improved.

In addition, some exercisers believe that once the interaction is quantified, it may destroy the purity of sharing. When providing rewards, they will consider aspects such as the effectiveness of learning, the degree of other's intentions and the other's fitness qualifications. In this way, those who ask questions is worried that the rewards he/she gives cannot satisfy the other. And the questioned person may interact with others with an expectation of receiving rewards. If the rewards received do not meet expectations, it may cause negative feeling and may even no longer be willing to help in the future.

### 3.4  Continuing the Interaction

There are three design concepts for the fourth CCI topic, continuing the interactive relationship. Real-Time Feed provides digital service during fitness; Nutrition Map provides physical on-site service after fitness; Weekly Plan provides digital off-site service before the next workout. We found that these three design concepts are applicable to interactive objects with different levels of familiarity.

First, Real-Time Feed can be used as an opportunity to initiate interaction between familiar strangers, especially those who have had several conversations. They can express their concerns for each other in a light manner without causing misunderstandings. Second, the Nutrition Map makes exercisers find strangers on the spot to order meals and dine together after exercising. Unfamiliar customers will not feel embarrassed or uncomfortable when casually chatting and eating in the same place. Third, this Weekly Plan is related to the personal schedule, so this service is more suitable for exercisers to interact with partners they are already familiar with. Because customers in the same gym are likely to meet again, they will be more concerned about privacy issues.

## 4  Discussions and Suggestions

### 4.1  Consider Familiarity and Help Build Trust

From the perspective of social exchange theory, the more familiar the two parties have interacted many times in the past and established trusting relationship. The trust relationship plays an important role in the process of social exchange. Both parties are willing to pay their own value first, and do not care about immediately exchanging the value provided by the other party. Because they believe that they will be able to obtain value from each other in the future, the barriers to initiating interaction are lowered.

Therefore, the gym should provide services to help bodybuilders who have not yet established a trust relationship find homogeneous interaction objects and initiate interaction. For instance, the "Nutrition Map" and the "Real-Time Feed" services help customers find exercisers who often visit at the same time. Also, providing services that can continue the interaction with each other can gradually transform the exerciser from a stranger relationship to a partnership. For example, the "Weekly Plan" can help exercisers and people with the same training goals to visit at the same time, thereby improving their relationship.

### 4.2  Initiate Spontaneous Motivation to Maintain a Virtuous Circle of Exerciser Interaction

Many interviewees who have had positive interactions with other gym customers believe that they do not need to provide rewards after interaction. Even if offering incentives increases motivation, it usually results in customers interacting with others with complex motivations. Once the other stop providing feedback, gym customers may be reluctant to interact with others. On the contrary, the interactive behavior derived from intrinsic motivation does not immediately get substantial benefits, but it helps the gym to form a long-term and sustainable interactive system. The reason is that the exerciser's trust in the gym community has been established, and they do not necessarily have to get rewards from specific interactive objects. On the one hand, exercisers had social exchanges with others and obtained value from others in the past; on the other hand, they also believed that they would have the opportunity to obtain value from others in the future, even if they did not think of it every time they interacted. This case study suggests that keeping the fitness environment in a healthy interactive cycle is the long-term solution. Therefore, the gym should provide services that can prompt exercisers to actively interact with others, rather than indirectly requiring exercisers to passively interact with others by establishing a mechanism for external incentives.

### 4.3  Provide Catalyst and Heat Interaction

The first CCI topic, creating an environment suitable for interaction, is like heating chemical reactions, providing a warmer atmosphere for existing interactions. And the second topic, triggering discussion on fitness topics, provides an interactive medium that, like a catalyst for a chemical reaction, can help initiate a dialogue between two participants who do not want to interact. Providing a medium to cause interaction and heating an interactive atmosphere complement each other, which can enable better interaction between customers and even increase the enthusiasm of the overall sports environment. In this study, the discussion on this topic is mostly aimed at providing physical objects. However, from the perspective of service design, it is recommended to further explore the CCI service touchpoints with service personnel and service environment.

## 5  Conclusions and Future Work

Through contextual inquiry, user interviews, prototyping, evaluations and other service design methods, this research explored the possibility of CCI services, and proposed five design aspects of CCI services in gyms: creating an interactive environment, triggering discussion on fitness topics, finding interaction partners, continuing the interaction, and prevent exercisers from affecting each other. In addition, social exchange theory was used to explore service suggestions for the gyms of the National Sports Center when providing CCI services.

So far this research has mainly focused on the interaction between individuals. In the future, the relationship between individuals and communities can be considered to help individuals integrate into the existing communities in the gyms. In addition, it is suggested that future researchers can conduct more complete evaluation interviews with service providers to understand the constraints encountered when implementing CCI services, as well as the values and challenges that may emerge after long-term implementation.

## References

1. Cook, K., Cheshire, C., Rice, E., Nakagawa, S.: Social exchange theory. In: DeLamater, John, Ward, Amanda (eds.) Handbook of social psychology, pp. 61–88. Springer, Dordrecht (2013). https://doi.org/10.1007/978-94-007-6772-0_3
2. Heinonen, K., Jaakkola, E., Neganova, I.: Drivers, types and value outcomes of customer-to-customer interaction: An integrative review and research agenda. J. Serv. Theory Pract. **028**, 71–732 (2018)

3. Kim, H., Choi, B.: The effects of three customer-to-customer interaction quality types on customer experience quality and citizenship behavior in mass service settings. J. Serv. Mark. **30**(4), 384–397 (2016)
4. Lawler, E.J.: An affect theory of social exchange. Am. J. Sociol. **107**(2), 321–352 (2011)
5. Martin, C., Pranter, C.: Compatibility management: customer-to-customer relationships in service environments. J. Serv. Mark. **3**(3), 5–15 (1989)
6. Martin, C.L.: Consumer-to-consumer relationships: satisfaction with other consumers' public behavior. J. Consum. Aff. **30**(1), 146–169 (1996)
7. Molm, L.D., Collett, J.L., Schaefer, D.R.: Conflict and fairness in social exchange. Soc. Forces **84**(4), 2331–2352 (2006)
8. Tschimmel, K.: Design thinking as an effective toolkit for innovation. In: ISPIM Conference Proceedings, p. 1. The International Society for Professional Innovation Management (ISPIM) (2012)

# Real-Time Feedback of Subjective Affect and Working Memory Load Based on Neurophysiological Activity

Sabrina Gado[1]([⊠]) ⓘ, Katharina Lingelbach[1,2]([⊠]) ⓘ, Michael Bui[1], Jochem W. Rieger[2], and Mathias Vukelić[1]

[1] Fraunhofer Institute for Industrial Engineering IAO, Stuttgart, Germany
{sabrina.gado,katharina.lingelbach,michael.bui,
mathias.vukelic}@iao.fraunhofer.de
[2] Department of Psychology, Carl Von Ossietzky University, Oldenburg, Germany
jochem.rieger@uol.de

**Abstract.** We investigated the effects of feedback on users' performance during a cognitive task with concurrent emotional distraction. Our aim was to provide participants with insights into their current affective and cognitive state by measuring and decoding brain activity. Therefore, a real-time preprocessing, analyzing, and visualization routine was developed based on electroencephalographic (EEG) data measured during a primary study. To explore users' behavioral and neurophysiological reactions, error-tolerance as well as possibilities to improve feedback accuracy by the means of feedback-based event-related potentials (ERPs), we provided either legit or inappropriate sham feedback in a second study. The kind of feedback (legit or inappropriate) had only marginal influence on participants' subsequent performance. On a neuronal level, we did not observe differences in the ERPs evoked by the legit and inappropriate feedback. In qualitative interviews, participants evaluated the feedback as interesting but also sometimes irritating due to odd feedback trials. Our study emphasizes the importance of performance accuracy and transparency towards users regarding the underlying feedback computations.

**Keywords:** Brain-computer interfaces · Electroencephalography (EEG) · Feedback · Adaptive systems · State monitoring · Affect · Working memory load

## 1 Introduction

Identifying users' mental states is a decisive task for many human-machine applications like in industrial production, semi-autonomous vehicles, medical surgery, or in the context of learning. Providing users with insights on their current affective and cognitive state by measuring and decoding brain activity allows to foster self-regulation and stress-management [1]. It might even enhance cognitive performance via neurofeedback [2]. Especially affective states are known to be significant predictors of work performance

---

S. Gado and K. Lingelbach—The Authors contributed equally to this research.

C. Stephanidis et al. (Eds.): HCII 2021, CCIS 1499, pp. 80–87, 2021.
https://doi.org/10.1007/978-3-030-90179-0_11

[3] and satisfaction [4]. Whereby, workload is related to occupational exhaustion, stress, and fatigue [5]. Research simultaneously investigating interdependencies of the two constructs [6] and their decoding for adaptive application is, unfortunately, scarce [7]. For the application of (neuro-)adaptive systems, the feedback about the recognized states, its perceived appropriateness, and reliability of the system are essential factors. How users perceive and evaluate closed-loop human-machine systems, is significantly mediated by trust: Previous research revealed that trust in an agent or system is strongly influenced by its reliability in task performance and negatively correlated with perceived errors of the automated system [8, 9]. Consequently, users' acceptance and trust regarding a system is interrelated with the perceived accuracy of the system's feedback and subjective error tolerance of the user. In their research on performance monitoring feedback loops, Alder and Ambrose [10] highlighted the influence of perceived feedback accuracy and fairness as well as perceived control over the feedback (e.g., its frequency) on attitudinal reactions like satisfaction and commitment as well as behavioral outcomes. Hence, the perceived feedback appropriateness and accuracy are suggested to be critical, since these factors seem to affect the feedback's impact on users' performance, their attitude towards the system, and the perceived usefulness of the system application. To investigate how precise respective applications should be, one has to explore the error tolerance of users with respect to feedback on their current affective and cognitive states. With electroencephalographic (EEG) recordings, event-related potential (ERP) responses evoked by the feedback can be used for an automatic error correction to improve subsequent feedback cycles [11, 12]. The ERP responses differ depending on whether a feedback is appropriate or not. The feedback-related negativity (FRN), a negative deflection around 250 ms after feedback-onset (comparable with the error-related negativity), and the P300, an indicator for mismatch between internal and external representations, are sensitive to erroneous feedback [13].

Here, we investigate whether we can continuously monitor users' current states and provide an intuitive feedback of recognized states. Therefore, a real-time preprocessing, analyzing, and visualization routine was developed based on an experimental dataset of a preliminary study. In the second feedback study, on which we mainly focus here, we were interested in two aspects: 1) the effectiveness and evaluation of non-reliable feedback by investigating users' reactions to a sham feedback that was either legit (consistent with the task condition) or inappropriate (inconsistent with the task condition) [cf. 14, 15] and 2) the detection of neuronal correlates associated with erroneous feedback to improve the accuracy. Both studies were realized via a wireless, easy-to-use EEG with dry electrodes [cf. 16].

## 2 Preliminary Study

### 2.1 Participants Declaration

Eight participants (three female) took part in the preliminary study (mean age 23 years, $SD = 1.12$) and seven participants (four female) in the second feedback study (mean age 25.48 years, $SD = 2.66$). All participants had normal or corrected-to-normal vision, no psychiatric history, and were free of neurological diseases. They signed an informed consent according to the recommendations of the declaration of Helsinki. The study was approved by the ethics committee of the Medical Faculty of the University of Tuebingen, Germany (ID: 827/2020BO1).

## 2.2  Experimental Procedure

The real-time preprocessing, analyzing, and visualization routine of the feedback was developed based on the dataset acquired in the preliminary study where participants performed elementary and complex arithmetic tasks with concurrent auditory emotional distractions (negatively, neutrally, and positively associated sounds). After each mathematical task, we asked them to rate their subjectively perceived affect and effort. We investigated neurophysiological correlates and behavioral outcomes in a 2 (low working memory load vs. high working memory load) × 3 (low valence, neutral valence, and high valence) design resulting in six experimental conditions. The experimental framework was similar for the following feedback study. The experimental setup can be seen in Fig. 1A.

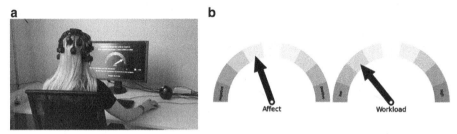

**Fig. 1. A)** Experimental setup. **B)** Visualization of the recognized affective and cognitive state based on the frontal alpha asymmetry score (left) and workload index (right).

## 2.3  Data Acquisition, Preprocessing and Analysis

EEG data was recorded according to the international 10–20 system using a wireless, easy-to-use EEG headset well-suited for the application in naturalistic settings with 20 electrodes and dry sensor technology. The EEG was grounded to the left mastoid, which was also used as common reference. The impedance was kept below 2,500 kΩ at the onset of the experiment. Data was acquired at a sampling rate of 500 Hz and saved via LabStreaming Layer. Data analysis was performed with custom written scripts in python™. For the online analysis, the signal was re-referenced to the Cz-electrode, detrended, and filtered with a second order zero-phase lag infinite impulse response (IIR) filter using a narrow frequency band of 0.5 to 14 Hz. During the task, the affective and cognitive states of the preceding 2 s were estimated every 0.5 s using power spectral measures computed via a modified version of the Fast Fourier Transformation (FFT), the so-called Welch's method. For the estimation of affect, the frontal alpha asymmetry coefficient was calculated [17], while working memory load estimates were derived from frontal theta and parietal alpha power [18]. A 3-min resting state measurement served as baseline for the subsequent estimation of the online scores. Substantial changes in these scores that exceeded one standard deviation of the baseline scores were concurrently translated to visual feedback. The feedback was presented on a gauge dial (see Fig. 1B).

## 3 Feedback Study

In the second study, we investigate neuronal and behavioral effects (i.e., response time and accuracy) of either appropriate or erroneous sham visual feedback [cf. 14, 15]. We further explore how participants accept and experience the real-time feedback. As ERP responses evoked by feedback allow to continuously improve the system's accuracy, we were interested whether we can identify neuronal correlates distinguishing appropriate and erroneous feedback [11, 12]. After each trial, we showed participants a sham feedback allegedly based on their brain activity during the task and asked them to potentially correct the score according to their own perception by clicking in the respective field. In 80% of the trials, the feedbacked score corresponded to the working memory load or emotional valence condition; in 20%, we presented an odd feedback, e.g., high cognitive load score during a rather simple task. After the experiment, we asked participants in a semi-structured qualitative interview how they perceived the feedback and whether they used it to adapt their behavior.

To analyze the neurophysiological data offline, EEG signals were de-trended, band-pass filtered between 0.5 to 23 Hz using a zero-phase lag finite impulse response (FIR) filter and cut into epochs starting 200 ms before to 1 s after feedback onset. We rejected epochs containing a maximum deviation above 250 $\mu$V in any frontal EEG channels (Fp1, Fp2). Afterwards, an independent component analysis (ICA) using the extended infomax ICA algorithm [19] as implemented in the MNE-Python toolbox [20] was used to remove cardiac-related and muscular artefacts as well as ocular movement by careful visual inspection of the topography, time course, and power spectral intensity [21]. The epochs were baseline corrected by subtracting the mean amplitude of the time interval before feedback onset. For identifying differences in the ERPs between the feedback conditions (odd vs. legit for affect and workload), we used a cluster-based, non-parametric randomization approach [22]. Clusters were identified as adjacent points in space (EEG channels) and time (samples in the epoch) using a $T$-value based cluster-level threshold of $p < .01$ and group-level threshold of $p < .05$ (two-sided).

To investigate behavioral effects of the feedback, we performed one-way repeated measures analyses of variance (rANOVAs) with feedback (legit vs. inappropriate) as main effect and perceived correctness reflected in probability that users correct the feedbacked score as well as response time and accuracy in the subsequent trial as dependent variables. Additionally, we explored interaction effects on performance regarding the kind of feedback (legit vs. inappropriate) and experimental condition.

## 4 Results

### 4.1 Effects on Perceived Correctness

Participants were significantly more likely to correct an odd feedback compared to a reasonable one regarding the cognitive effort, $F(1, 6) = 30.82$, $p < .001$, partial $\eta^2 = .84$. Similarly, participants tended to be more likely to correct an odd feedback compared to a reasonable one regarding the affective state, $F(1, 6) = 5.14$, $p = .064$, partial $\eta^2 = .46$.

## 4.2  Effects on Performance

No significant effects were found of inappropriate, odd feedback on participants' performance in the subsequent trial. Interestingly, there was neither a difference between trials with previous odd or appropriate feedback for affect nor working memory load (see Fig. 2). Further, we observed no interactions between feedback and experimental condition for affect and effort. Increased working memory load did not change the perceived correctness of and probability to adjust an inappropriate feedback score.

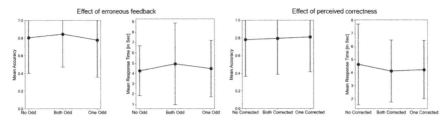

**Fig. 2.** Effects of odd feedback (left) and perceived correctness of the scores (right) on performance (accuracy and response time) in the subsequent trial. Error bars = standard deviation.

## 4.3  Results of the ERP Analysis

The cluster-based, non-parametric randomization test revealed no significant spatio-temporal cluster for the difference between the appropriated and odd feedback. Figure 3 depicts the grand average response over epochs and participants per condition and region of interest (frontal, central, and parietal).

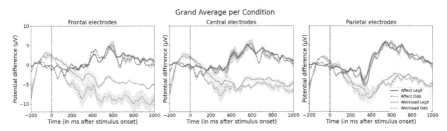

**Fig. 3.** Grand average over epochs and participants per condition. Dashed lines: odd feedback, solid lines: legit feedback. Shaded area: standard deviation.

## 4.4  Insights Gained in the Interviews

Most participants evaluated the feedbacked scores positively and as interesting. However, some participants also characterized the feedback as irritating. The design and feedback format were perceived as suitable and engaging. Some participants recommended to provide detailed explanation on the underlying computations, the used data (components of the data), and recommendations for the score interpretation. About half of the participants reported that they rather did not use the provided feedback scores intentionally to change their behavior in the subsequent trial. One reported a higher intrinsic motivation to increase focus and concentration. Two responded that they had memorized the feedback-sound combination for particularly irritating sounds to suppress them more efficiently in upcoming trials. Most of the participants could not imagine using the technology in realistic environments. Especially, because some of them perceived the dry-electrode EEG device as uncomfortable over the course of time. Nevertheless, they stated that monitoring of current or potentially only critical affective and cognitive states might be interesting in safety-relevant applications, e.g., when maneuvering a car or airplane. They reported further potentials of adaptive feedback systems to enhance effectiveness in learning and training scenarios.

## 5  Discussion and Conclusion

Our real-time EEG-based feedback approach contributes to the development of closed-loop human-machine systems allowing to recognize users' state, provide feedback, and adapt the system parameters to individual capabilities and demands. Our study revealed two main challenges for adaptive feedback systems: 1) We observed no significant positive effect on participants' performance for appropriate compared to erroneous feedback. Since participants reported irritation in response to the inaccurate feedback and the wish to get more information regarding the score computation, it is likely that they had limited trust in the feedback system. Although, they evaluated the system in general positively, their (involuntary) trust evaluation might have mediated the feedback's impact. Probably only systems perceived as reliable and consistent, are able to induce effects on a behavioral and neuronal level [23]. Therefore, participants in our study might have ignored or suppressed the feedback without considering it as a significant cue to change behavioral strategies. An alternative explanation why participants did not actively use the feedback, might be that they did not perceive it as relevant for solving the arithmetic task. In addition, we did not provide any explicit instruction to use the feedback during the task. 2) On the neuronal level, we observed no difference in feedback-related potentials between the conditions. This absence of distinct neuronal correlates associated with erroneous feedback (FRN, P300) might be explained by either the inconsistent feedback performance or the lower signal to noise ratio due to an insufficient number of trials or the dry-electrode EEG device [16].

With this study, we investigated an approach to provide real-time insights into users' cognitive and affective states during a cognitively demanding task and the neuronal and behavioral effects of the given feedback. The described research contributed to the development of closed-loop human-machine systems and understanding of associated challenges in performance-oriented contexts.

# References

1. Yu, B., Funk, M., Hu, J., Wang, Q., Feijs, L.: Biofeedback for everyday stress management: a systematic review. Front. ICT **5**(23), 1–22 (2018). https://doi.org/10.3389/fict.2018.00023
2. Dessy, E., Van Puyvelde, M., Mairesse, O., Neyt, X., Pattyn, N.: Cognitive performance enhancement: do biofeedback and neurofeedback work? J. Cogn. Enhancement **2**(1), 12–42 (2017). https://doi.org/10.1007/s41465-017-0039-y
3. Shockley, K.M., Ispas, D., Rossi, M.E., Levine, E.L.: A meta-analytic investigation of the relationship between state affect, discrete emotions, and job performance. Hum. Perform. **25**(5), 377–411 (2012). https://doi.org/10.1080/08959285.2012.721832
4. Niklas, C.D., Dormann, C.: The impact of state affect on job satisfaction. Eur. J. Work Organ. Psychol. **14**(4), 367–388 (2005). https://doi.org/10.1080/13594320500348880
5. Bowling, N.A., Alarcon, G.M., Bragg, C.B., Hartman, M.J.: A meta-analytic examination of the potential correlates and consequences of workload. Work Stress **29**(2), 95–113 (2015). https://doi.org/10.1080/02678373.2015.1033037
6. Moore, M., Shafer, A.T., Bakhtiari, R., Dolcos, F., Singhal, A.: Integration of spatio-temporal dynamics in emotion-cognition interactions: a simultaneous fMRI-ERP investigation using the emotional oddball task. NeuroImage **202**, 116078 (2019). https://doi.org/10.1016/j.neuroimage.2019.116078
7. Maior, H.A., Wilson, M.L., Sharples, S.: Workload alerts - using physiological measures of mental workload to provide feedback during tasks. ACM Trans. Comput.-Hum. Interact. **25**(2), 1–25 (2018). https://doi.org/10.1145/3173380
8. Chen, M., Nikolaidis, S., Soh, H., Hsu, D., Srinivasa, S.: Planning with trust for human-robot collaboration. In: Proceedings of the Anual ACM/IEEE International Conference on Human-Robot Interaction, Chicago, IL, USA 2018, pp. 307–315. Association for Computing Machinery (2018). https://doi.org/10.1145/3171221.3171264
9. Master, R., et al.: Measurement of trust over time in hybrid inspection systems. Hum. Factors Ergon. Manuf. Serv. Ind. **15**(2), 177–196 (2005). https://doi.org/10.1002/hfm.20021
10. Alder, G.S., Ambrose, M.L.: Towards understanding fairness judgments associated with computer performance monitoring: an integration of the feedback, justice, and monitoring research. Hum. Resour. Manag. Rev. **15**(1), 43–67 (2005). https://doi.org/10.1016/j.hrmr.2005.01.001
11. Ferrez, P.W., Millan, J.d.R.: Error-related EEG potentials generated during simulated brain-computer interaction. IEEE Trans. Biomed. Eng. **55**(3), 923–929 (2008). https://doi.org/10.1109/TBME.2007.908083
12. Mattout, J., Perrin, M., Bertrand, O., Maby, E.: Improving BCI performance through co-adaptation: applications to the P300-speller. Ann. Phys. Rehabil. Med. **58**(1), 23–28 (2015). https://doi.org/10.1016/j.rehab.2014.10.006
13. Pfabigan, D.M., Alexopoulos, J., Bauer, H., Sailer, U.: Manipulation of feedback expectancy and valence induces negative and positive reward prediction error signals manifest in event-related brain potentials. Psychophysiology **48**(5), 656–664 (2011). https://doi.org/10.1111/j.1469-8986.2010.01136.x
14. Enriquez-Geppert, S., Huster, R.J., Herrmann, C.S.: EEG-neurofeedback as a tool to modulate cognition and behaviour: a review tutorial. Front. Hum. Neurosci. **11**(51), 1–19 (2017). https://doi.org/10.3389/fnhum.2017.00051
15. Logemann, H.N.A., Lansbergen, M.M., Van Os, T.W.D.P., Böcker, K.B.E., Kenemans, J.L.: The Effectiveness of EEG-feedback on attention, impulsivity and EEG: a sham feedback controlled study. Neurosci. Lett. **479**(1), 49–53 (2010). https://doi.org/10.1016/j.neulet.2010.05.026

16. Guger, C., Krausz, G., Allison, B., Edlinger, G.: Comparison of dry and gel based electrodes for P300 brain-computer interfaces. Front. Neurosci. **6**(60), 1–7 (2012). https://doi.org/10.3389/fnins.2012.00060

17. Smith, E.E., Reznik, S.J., Stewart, J.L., Allen, J.J.B.: Assessing and conceptualizing frontal EEG asymmetry: an updated primer on recording, processing, analyzing, and interpreting frontal alpha asymmetry. Int. J. Psychophysiol. **111**, 98–114 (2017). https://doi.org/10.1016/j.ijpsycho.2016.11.005

18. Käthner, I., Wriessnegger, S.C., Müller-Putz, G.R., Kübler, A., Halder, S.: Effects of mental workload and fatigue on the P300, alpha and theta band power during operation of an ERP (P300) brain-computer interface. Biol. Psychol. **102**, 118–129 (2014). https://doi.org/10.1016/j.biopsycho.2014.07.014

19. Lee, T.-W., Girolami, M., Sejnowski, T.J.: Independent component analysis using an extended infomax algorithm for mixed Subgaussian and Supergaussian sources. Neural Comput. **11**(2), 417–441 (1999). https://doi.org/10.1162/089976699300016719

20. Gramfort, A., et al.: MNE software for processing MEG and EEG data. NeuroImage **86**, 446–460 (2014). https://doi.org/10.1016/j.neuroimage.2013.10.027

21. Chaumon, M., Bishop, D.V.M., Busch, N.A.: A practical guide to the selection of independent components of the electroencephalogram for artifact correction. J. Neurosci. Methods **250**, 47–63 (2015). https://doi.org/10.1016/j.jneumeth.2015.02.025

22. Maris, E., Oostenveld, R.: Nonparametric statistical testing of EEG- and MEG-data. J. Neurosci. Methods **164**(1), 177–190 (2007). https://doi.org/10.1016/j.jneumeth.2007.03.024

23. Kluger, A.N., DeNisi, A.: The effects of feedback interventions on performance: a historical review, a meta-analysis, and a preliminary feedback intervention theory. Psychol. Bull. **119**(2), 254–284 (1996). https://doi.org/10.1037/0033-2909.119.2.254

# A Hierarchical Classification Scheme for Efficient Speech Emotion Recognition

Panikos Heracleous[1(✉)], Kohichi Takai[1], Keiji Yasuda[2], and Akio Yoneyama[1]

[1] KDDI Research, Inc., 2-1-15 Ohara, Fujimino-shi, Saitama 356-8502, Japan
{pa-heracleous,wa-yanan,ko-takai,yoneyama}@kddi-research.jp
[2] Nara Institute of Science and Technology,
8916-5 Takayama-cho, Ikoma, Nara 630-0192, Japan
ke-yasuda@dsc.naist.jp

**Abstract.** The current study focuses on speech emotion recognition based on a hierarchical classification scheme. The study aims at overcoming the problem of low accuracy in the case of a large number of emotions that are considered in a specific task. In the proposed method, the emotions are classified based on the valence-arousal 2-dimensional map, and models are trained for each group. In a second pass, with-in group recognition is performed for the group selected in the previous stage.

**Keywords:** Speech emotion recognition · Hierarchical classification · Valance-arousal mapping

## 1 Introduction

Speech emotion recognition plays an important role in human-computer interaction and its real-world applications [1]. Speech emotion recognition can be applied in robotics, call centers, education, and health care. Due to the high importance of speech emotion recognition and its applications, a large number of studies have investigated and reported methods and results in this research area [2–8]. Studies in emotion recognition using visual modality have also been reported [9,10]. However, the majority of available studies focus on detecting a small number of emotions. For practical applications a larger number of emotions is often required. The current study addresses this problem by introducing a novel hierarchical method based on valence-arousal space clustering. The current method was evaluated on the IEMOCAP English emotional corpus [11] for the recognition of six and seven emotions.

---

Dr. Panikos Heracleous is currently with Artificial Intelligence Research Center (AIRC), AIST, Japan.

© Springer Nature Switzerland AG 2021
C. Stephanidis et al. (Eds.): HCII 2021, CCIS 1499, pp. 88–92, 2021.
https://doi.org/10.1007/978-3-030-90179-0_12

## 2    Methods

### 2.1    Classification of Emotions Based on the 2-Dimensional Valence-Arousal Map

The 2-D valence-arousal space is a universal and accurate mapping of emotions. Valence shows the affectivity, and arousal represents how calming or exciting the information is. Clustering similar emotions together aims at reducing the number of classes in the first pass in order to deal with a larger number of emotions. Figure 1 shows a valence-arousal 2-D dimensional map and the locations of specific emotions.

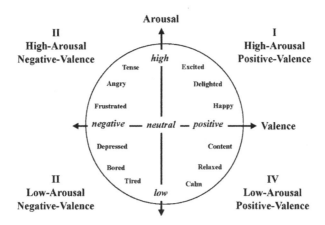

**Fig. 1.** Valence-arousal 2-dimensional map.

### 2.2    Data and Acoustic Features

In the current study, the English state-of-the-art IEMOCAP database was used. The basic acoustic features used were 12 mel-frequency cepstral coefficients (MFCC) [12] concatenated with shifted delta cepstral (SDC) coefficients [13], pitch, and energy. Following MFCC extraction, i-vectors of 150 dimensions were constructed [14]. The i-vectors have been previously used in speaker recognition and language identification. Using i-vectors, each sentence can be represented by a vector of dimension 100–400. To further improve the discrimination ability of the emotion models, supervised linear discriminant analysis (LDA) [15] was also performed on the extracted i-vectors, which resulted in a lysis (LDA) [15] was also performed on the extracted i-vectors, which resulted in a $Class - 1$-dimension final emotion vectors. The six emotions considered were happy, excited, sad, angry, frustration, and neutral. In the case of seven emotions, the *other* emotion was also added. For training and testing, 476 and 119 utterances for each emotion were used, respectively. For classification in this preliminary experiments, the very popular support vector machine (SVM) [16] classifier was used.

## 2.3   The Proposed Method for Emotion Recognition

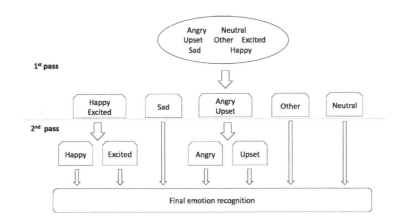

**Fig. 2.** The proposed hierarchical classification scheme for emotion recognition.

Figure 2 shows the proposed method. Based on valence-arousal space [17], the emotions were clustered into four clusters. In the first pass, a cluster is detected, followed by with-in cluster classification. When a single-member cluster is selected, no additional classification is conducted in the second pass. Combining the results of the two passes, an input emotional utterance can be classified into one of the emotions being considered.

## 3   Results

Table 1 shows the results obtained using the proposed method compared with a conventional method when all emotions are considered together in a single pass. As shown, using the proposed hierarchical scheme, higher accuracies were achieved in both cases with six and seven emotions.

**Table 1.** Unweighted average recall (UAR) [%] using the proposed method compared to conventional method.

| Method | 6 emotions | 7 emotions |
|---|---|---|
| Conventional | 46.8 | 41.5 |
| Proposed | 53.9 | 47.1 |
| Relative improvement | 12% | 10% |

# 4    Conclusions

In the current study, we presented a hierarchical classification scheme based on valence-arousal clustering for effective speech emotion recognition. Experimental results shows significant improvements as compared to conventional methods. Currently, similar experiments using deep neural networks (DNNs) are being conducted.

# References

1. Busso, C., Bulut, M., Narayanan, S.: Toward effective automatic recognition systems of emotion in speech. In: Gratch, J., Marsella, S. (eds.) Social emotions in nature and artifact: emotions in human and human-computer interaction, pp. 110–127. Oxford University Press, New York, NY, USA (November (2013)
2. Feng, H., Ueno, S., Kawahara, T.: End-to-end speech emotion recognition combined with acoustic-to-word ASR model. In: Proceedings of Interspeech, pp. 501–505 (2020)
3. Huang, J., Tao, J., Liu, B., Lian, Z.: Learning utterance-level representations with label smoothing for speech emotion recognition. In: Proceedings of Interspeech, pp. 4079–4083 (2020)
4. Jalal, M.A., Milner, R., Hain, T., Moore, R.K.: Proceedings of Interspeech, pp. 4084–4088 (2020)
5. Jalal, M.A., Milner, R., Hain, T.: Empirical interpretation of speech emotion perception with attention based model for speech emotion recognition. In: Proceedings of Interspeech, pp. 4113–4117 (2020)
6. Stuhlsatz, A., Meyer, C., Eyben, F., Zielkel, T., Meier, G., Schuller, B.: Deep neural networks for acoustic emotion recognition: raising the benchmarks. In: Proceedings of ICASSP, pp. 5688–5691 (2011)
7. Han, K., Yu, D., Tashev, I.: Speech emotion recognition using deep neural network and extreme learning machine. In: Proceedings of Interspeech, pp. 2023–2027 (2014)
8. Lim, W., Jang, D., Lee, T.: Speech emotion recognition using convolutional and recurrent neural networks. In: Proceedings of Signal and Information Processing Association Annual Summit and Conference (APSIPA) (2016)
9. Rawat, W., Wang, Z.: Deep convolutional neural networks for image classification: a comprehensive review. Neural Commun. **29**, 2352–2449 (2017)
10. Huynh, X.-P., Tran, T.-D., Kim, Y.-G.: Convolutional neural network models for facial expression recognition using BU-3DFE database. In: Information Science and Applications (ICISA) 2016. LNEE, vol. 376, pp. 441–450. Springer, Singapore (2016). https://doi.org/10.1007/978-981-10-0557-2_44
11. Busso, C., et al.: IEMOCAP: interactive emotional dyadic motion capture database. J. Lang. Resour. Eval. 335–359 (2008). https://doi.org/10.1007/s10579-008-9076-6
12. Sahidullah, M., Saha, G.: Design, analysis and experimental evaluation of block based transformation in MFCC computation for speaker recognition. Speech Commun. **54**(4), 543–565 (2012)
13. Bielefeld, B.: Language identification using shifted delta cepstrum. In: Fourteenth Annual Speech Research Symposium (1994)

14. Dehak, N., Kenny, P.J., Dehak, R., Dumouchel, P., Ouellet, P.: Front-End Factor Analysis for Speaker Verification. IEEE Trans. Audio, Speech Language Process. **19**(4), 788–798 (2011)
15. Fukunaga, K.: Introduction to Statistical Pattern Recognition, 2nd ed. New York. Academic Press, Cambridge, ch. 10 (1990)
16. Cristianini, N., Taylor, J.S.: Support Vector Machines. Cambridge University Press, Cambridge (2000)
17. Lubis, N., Sakti, S., Yoshino, K., Nakamura, S.: Positive emotion elicitation in chat-based dialogue systems. IEEE/ACM Trans. Audio, Speech Lang. Process. **27**(4), 866–877 (2019)

# Research on the Finger Contact Force of Persons of Different Gender as Grasping Bottles

Ru Ji[1], Zhellin Li[1,2], Jiaxu Fan[1], Yongyi Zhu[1], and Lijun Jiang[1,2(✉)]

[1] School of Design, South China University of Technology, Guangzhou 510006, China
{zhelinli,ljjiang}@scut.edu.cn
[2] Guangdong Engineering Research Center of Human-Computer Interaction Design, Guangzhou 510006, China

**Abstract.** In order to explore the contact force characteristics of fingers in grasping objects, this paper invited persons of different gender and studied their finger contact force distribution when they grasped bottles with 500 g water and 4 different surface materials. Experiment data of 54 subjects (27 male, 27 female) were collected by a thin film pressure sensor. Analysis indicated that the mean value of contact force (MVCF) of the thumb and middle finger was significantly higher than that of the index and ring finger, and the MVCF of the four fingers of male was higher than that of the female. And the independent samples t-tests and variance analysis results showed that the MVCF of thumb, index and middle finger was affected by the bottle material ($p < 0.01$). The MVCF of the ring finger was not affected by the material of bottles since its result was not significant ($P = 0.258 > 0.01$).

**Keywords:** Grasping · Interactive behavior · Finger contact force · Surface material

## 1 Introduction

Hands have played a vital role in daily life. studying the grasping laws of human hands will contribute greatly in the fields of human-computer interaction, hand rehabilitation, and service robots [1, 2].

Luo etc. [3] has designed a 4-finger dynamic grasp force experiment without thumb participation to analyze the function of each finger in grasping process. Results showed that the four fingers have different motion mechanisms in the stable and changing grasping force. The index and ring finger played a very important role in grasping control and adjustment, and there was a complementary relationship between them. Amis [4] used a measuring instrument to measure the normal force and tangential shear forces exerted by each finger knuckle of 17 subjects when grasping a cylinder with a diameter of 31–116 mm. The results showed that the force exerted by the distal knuckles of each finger was significantly greater than that of the middle and proximal knuckles. The average contribution of the fingers from the index finger to the little finger was 30%, 30%, 22%, and 18% respectively. Mohammed Shurrab [5] used a special measuring tool

© Springer Nature Switzerland AG 2021
C. Stephanidis et al. (Eds.): HCII 2021, CCIS 1499, pp. 93–100, 2021.
https://doi.org/10.1007/978-3-030-90179-0_13

to conduct two-hand experiments, in order to explore the influence of pinch and grasp style, width, gender, lean body mass (LBM), t-body mass index (BMI), and hand size on the grasp force. He found that the pinch and grasp style, width, gender and hand size have significant effects on the pinch and grasp strength, and there was no significant difference between the lateral and the chuck grip. Hussain [6] analyzed how food's type and tableware affect human hand motion and force in the eating process, proposing that the bending motion of the index finger and thumb was affected by the food characteristics and the type of tableware, while that of the middle finger has not been affected. The contact force of the fingertips of the thumb and index finger was not influenced by the type of food and tableware.

Above researches show that there have been related studies on the hand contact force in grasping objects. These studies mainly focus on the static grasping scenes, which cannot reflect the corresponding movements in the real state. There's little research till now concerning the grasping behavior of human hands in dynamic grasping scenarios. This paper aims to conduct research on the grasping law of fingers in the scenario of drinking water, the most frequent daily activity, and discuss the effect of gender and bottle surface material on the contact force of fingertip. This study will enrich relevant researches on hand contact force.

## 2  Experimental Method

### 2.1  Experimental Device

A pressure data acquisition system was used to collect the contact force of each fingertip. The system consists of data acquisition instrument RFP-CJ8 (China Yubo Intelligent Technology Co., Ltd.), RFP thin film pressure sensor (model RFP-602, thickness 0.25 mm, accuracy ±3%) and Labview, a data display software. In the experiment, four bottles with different surface materials were selected: hard plastic, soft plastic, soft silicone, and soft cloth surface. And four RFP film pressure sensors were fixed on fingertips of the thumb, index finger, middle and ring finger to measure the contact force exerted by fingers in the process of grasping the bottle.

### 2.2  Experimental Design

The focus of this study is investigating the effect of bottle material and gender on the contact force of the fingertips of each finger in drinking motion. Subjects were asked to use only 4 fingertips (the thumb, index finger, middle finger and ring finger) to touch the bottle. The little finger and palm could not touch the bottle during the whole drinking process. The diameter of the bottles of 4 different materials is basically the same (64.42 ± 2.54 mm). The mass after filling the water is 500 g.

Subjects were asked to sit on a chair with adjustable height, keep their sitting posture in the whole experiment and move their hand smoothly. On hearing the instructions, they proceeded to the next step. At the end of each experiment, subjects rested for 30 s to rule out the effects of muscle fatigue. They grabbed four bottles of different surface materials in turn to drink and drunk two times with a cup. The drinking behavior of grasping a bottle includes the following 5 steps, as shown in Fig. 1:

Step 1. The subject wears the thin film pressure sensor on the right hand, sits with fixed posture in front of a table on which there are with four bottles of different surface materials, and naturally puts their hand on the tabletop.

Step 2. The subject grasps the bottle with fingers wearing the sensor, and keeps the bottle vertical to the desktop for about 3 s until the sensor value stabilizes.

Step 3. The subject raises the bottle and drinks. The bottle is rotated from a vertical state to a nearly horizontal state at a constant speed, making the cup level with the subject's mouth. The subject maintains this state for about 3 s until the sensor value stabilizes.

Step 4. The subject puts down the bottle to restore it to the state in step 2, and maintains this state for about 3 s until the sensor value stabilizes.

Step 5. The subject puts down the bottle to the table, and completely separates the hand from the bottle, returning to the state at step 1.

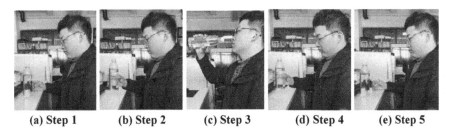

(a) Step 1      (b) Step 2      (c) Step 3      (d) Step 4      (e) Step 5

**Fig. 1.** 5 steps of grasping the cup and drinking

## 2.3  Data Collection

A total of 54 healthy right-handed subjects (27 young male and 27 young female), aged $20.37 \pm 0.83$, participated in the experiment. They were able to independently complete the experimental tasks. Subjects grasped 4 kinds of bottles, each cup was grasped two times. Each subject had 8 sets of data. The validity of the data was screened, and the data of 45 subjects (23 males and 22 females) were used. There are a total of 360 valid fingertip contact force data.

# 3   Data Analysis and Results

The analysis of the four fingertips' contact force data indicates that all the subjects' fingertips contact force have the same change trend in the eight complete drinking processes. Considering step 3 is the main step of drinking and subjects at the step has performed stable grasping posture, the study selected this stage to analyze the contact force of 4 fingertips.

## 3.1   The Influence of Gender on Fingertip Contact Force

In order to analyze the difference in fingertip contact force between men and women, the study controlled the material variables of the cup, performed independent sample t-tests on the fingertip contact force data, and applied SPSS (SPSS Statistics 24) software for data processing.

**Table 1.** Finger contact force of different genders when grabbing water glasses

| Contact force of fingertips | | Surface material of bottle | | | | |
|---|---|---|---|---|---|---|
| | | Hard plastic | Soft plastic | Soft silicone | Soft cloth | The average |
| Thumb (N) | Male | 5.07 ± 1.60 | 4.07 ± 0.91 | 4.66 ± 1.74 | 4.81 ± 1.49 | 4.65 ± 1.50 |
| | Female | 4.50 ± 1.70 | 3.58 ± 1.22 | 3.74 ± 1.78 | 4.53 ± 1.46 | 4.09 ± 1.60 |
| Index finger (N) | Male | 1.62 ± 0.78 | 1.27 ± 0.73 | 1.59 ± 0.85 | 1.47 ± 0.73 | 1.49 ± 0.78 |
| | Female | 1.39 ± 0.85 | 0.99 ± 0.62 | 1.32 ± 0.69 | 1.07 ± 0.83 | 1.19 ± 0.77 |
| Middle finger (N) | Male | 3.51 ± 0.91 | 3.08 ± 0.90 | 3.48 ± 0.87 | 3.55 ± 0.79 | 3.41 ± 0.88 |
| | Female | 2.85 ± 0.93 | 2.40 ± 0.94 | 2.91 ± 0.78 | 2.84 ± 0.76 | 2.75 ± 0.87 |
| Ring finger (N) | Male | 1.76 ± 0.64 | 1.63 ± 0.44 | 1.81 ± 0.52 | 1.74 ± 0.42 | 1.73 ± 0.51 |
| | Female | 1.51 ± 0.68 | 1.27 ± 0.59 | 1.20 ± 0.65 | 1.30 ± 0.67 | 1.32 ± 0.66 |

It can be seen from Table 1 that in the process of drinking water, the four fingertip contact force of both male and female shows the same trend. The contact force of the fingertips of the thumb and the middle finger is significantly greater than that of the index and middle finger. The fingertip of thumb has performed the largest contact force, followed by the index finger. There is no significant difference between the contact force of the index and ring finger.

Figure 2 indicate that no matter what material of the bottle has been held for drinking, the average value of fingertips' contact force of male is greater than that of the female. While drinking water, male tend to exert more contact force on the fingertips than the corresponding fingers of women. The independent sample t-tests was performed on the data. Results are shown in Table 2.

It can be seen from Table 2 that (1) When holding a hard plastic bottle for drinking, only the mean value of the middle finger's fingertip contact force was affected by gender (p = 0.001 < 0.01). The average fingertip contact force of the thumb, index, and ring finger was not affected by gender. (2) In grasping a soft plastic bottle, the average fingertip contact force of the remaining 4 fingers except for the index finger was affected by gender. The mean value of fingertip contact force of the middle and ring finger shows significant statistical difference (p = 0.001 < 0.01). (3) The mean value of fingertip contact force of thumb, middle finger, and ring finger was affected by gender when grasping the silicone surface bottle. Among them, the mean value of the middle finger and the ring finger's fingertip contact force shows extremely significant statistical difference, while that of the index finger is not affected by gender. (4) When grasping the cloth surface bottle for

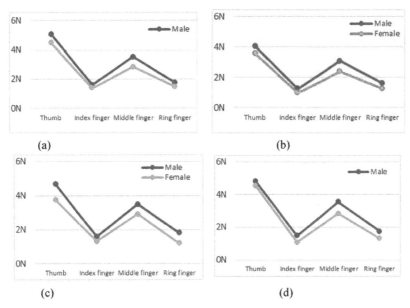

**Fig. 2.** (a) The average value of contact force in grasping the hard plastic bottle (b) The average value of contact force in grasping the soft plastic bottle (c) The average value of contact force in grasping the soft silicone bottle (d) The average value of contact force in grasping the soft cloth bottle

**Table 2.** Independent sample t-tests of the mean value of each fingertip contact force

| | Group | Hard plastic bottle | | Soft plastic bottle | | Soft silicone bottle | | Soft cloth bottle | |
|---|---|---|---|---|---|---|---|---|---|
| | | t | Sig./p value | t | Sig./p value | t | Sig./p value | t | Sig./p value |
| Thumb | Male | 1.65 | 0.103 | 2.15 | 0.034* | 2.47 | 0.015* | 0.92 | 0.363 |
| | **Female** | | | | | | | | |
| **Index** finger | Male | 1.34 | 0.184 | 1.96 | 0.054 | 1.67 | 0.099 | 2.43 | 0.017* |
| | Female | | | | | | | | |
| Middle finger | Male | 3.37 | 0.001** | 3.53 | 0.001** | 3.29 | 0.001** | 4.3 | 0.000** |
| | Female | | | | | | | | |
| Ring finger | Male | 1.82 | 0.072 | 3.30 | 0.001** | 4.9 | 0.000** | 3.7 | 0.000** |
| | Female | | | | | | | | |

drinking, there is a significant difference in the mean value of fingertip contact force of the index, middle and ring finger, which was affected by gender. Among them, the mean value of fingertip contact force of the middle finger and the ring finger have extremely significant statistical differences ($p = 0.000 < 0.01$).

## 3.2 The Influence of Different Cup Materials on Fingertip Contact Force

In order to analyze the influence of material on the fingertip's contact force, the one-way analysis of variance was performed on the fingertip contact force of each finger when holding cups with different surface materials. The analysis results are shown in Table 3.

**Table 3.** Summary table of analysis of variance

| The contact force of fingertips | The surface material of bottle | | | | F | Sig./p value |
|---|---|---|---|---|---|---|
| | Hard plastic | Soft plastic | Soft silicone | Soft cloth | | |
| Thumb (N) | 4.79 ± 1.67 | 3.83 ± 1.09 | 4.21 ± 1.81 | 4.67 ± 1.47 | 7.41 | 0.000** |
| Index finger (N) | 1.51 ± 0.82 | 1.14 ± 0.69 | 1.46 ± 0.78 | 1.27 ± 0.80 | 4.43 | 0.004** |
| Middle finger (N) | 3.19 ± 0.98 | 2.75 ± 0.97 | 3.20 ± 0.87 | 3.20 ± 0.85 | 5.45 | 0.001** |
| Ring finger (N) | 1.63 ± 0.67 | 1.45 ± 0.55 | 1.51 ± 0.66 | 1.53 ± 0.60 | 1.35 | 0.258 |

It can be seen from Table 3 that in the grasping process of stage 3, the material of the cup has significantly affected the average value of the fingertip contact force of the thumb, index finger, and middle finger, with the p value all less than 0.01. There is no statistically significant difference in the mean value of the fingertip contact force of the ring finger when using cups of different materials. Based on the results of the variance analysis, it can be concluded that the average value of the fingertip contact force of the thumb, index finger, and middle finger is affected by the material of the cup, while that of the ring finger is not affected by the cup material.

## 4   Discussion

During the research, four RFP thin film pressure sensors (model RFP-602, thickness 0.25 mm, accuracy ±3%) were fixed on the fingertips of the thumb, index finger, middle finger and ring finger to measure the fingertip contact force during the whole process. This measurement method makes the grasping motion more natural, and the collected data more realistic. Luo [3] created a 45 mm cylindrical handle whose finger side consisted of four independent finger pads. Each finger pad had an independent groove. Subjects were asked to put their four fingers in the groove during the entire experiment, which caused them unable to grasp the handle in a natural way. Hussain [6] and Ju [7] used data gloves to measure finger pressure in their experiments. The constraints of the data gloves had a certain impact on the grasping behavior of the human hand, causing the bias of the measured data. The RFP thin film pressure sensor used in this study has good flexibility. It fits the fingertips well during the experiment without affecting the normal grasping actions of subjects, which greatly alleviates the impact of experimental equipment on human hands.

This study also shows that the average fingertip contact force is affected by gender. It is in consistent with the conclusions of McDowell TW [8] who has pointed out that gender differences have a significant impact on grasp strength. This study also found that during the entire drinking process, the average value of the fingertip contact force of the male subjects was greater than that of the female counterparts. This may be caused by the cognition difference in gender, which needs to be further explored.

In addition, this research has some problems. The hand size (i.e. length, width, thickness) was not considered during the experiment. In related studies of McDowell TW [8], D. Welcome [9], and Yong-Ku Kong [10], the size of the hand has been described, and they have pointed out that the size of the hand has a significant effect on the grasp force. Therefore, the relationship between hand size and fingertip contact force will be further discussed and improved in subsequent research.

## 5  Conclusion

In this study, the hand motion of 45 subjects in the drinking process has been collected and 360 copies of effective fingertip contact force data were obtained. In analyzing the collected data, the changes in the fingertip contact force of the four fingers, and the influence of gender and bottles' materials on the fingertip contact force have been discussed. Below are some conclusions:

(1) In drinking activities, the average fingertip contact force of the thumb and middle finger was significantly greater than that of the index and ring finger. The thumb performs the largest fingertip force, up to 5.07N.
(2) The independent sample t-test analysis shows that the mean value of the fingertip contact force of the 4 fingers in drinking water were affected by gender. And the average value of the male 4-point fingertip contact force is greater than that of the female.
(3) Variance analysis shows that the average fingertip contact force of the thumb, index, and middle finger were affected by the material of the bottle during drinking, while that of the ring finger has not been affected.

The research results of this paper will further supplement the motion law of human hands grasping objects, enrich the research on human grasping behavior, and have reference significance for human hand rehabilitation research, the precise control of bionic hands and other related fields.

**Acknowledgments.** We express our gratitude to all the subjects who participated in this work. The research is supported by the Natural Science Foundation of Guangdong Province (grant 2020A1515010397 and 2021A1515010934).

## References

1. Ergen, E.H.I., Oksuz, C.: Evaluation of load distributions and contact areas in 4 common grip types used in daily living activities. J. Hand Surg. **45**(3), 251.e1–251.e8 (2020)

2. Mühldorfer-Fodor, M., Ziegler, S., Harms, C., et al.: Load distribution of the hand during cylinder grip analyzed by Manugraphy. J. Hand Ther. **30**(4), 529–537 (2017)
3. Luo, S.J., Shu, G., Gong, Y.: Real time relationship between individual finger force and grip exertion on distal phalanges in linear force following tasks. Appl. Ergon. **69**, 25–31 (2018)
4. Amis, A.A.: Variation of finger forces in maximal isometric grasp tests on a range of cylinder diameters. J. Biomed. Eng. **9**(4), 313–320 (1987)
5. Shurrab, M., Mandahawi, N., Sarder, M.D.: The assessment of a two-handed pinch force: quantifying different anthropometric pinch grasp patterns for males and females. Int. J. Ind. Ergon. **58**, 38–46 (2017)
6. Hussain, Z., Azlan, N.Z., Yusof, A.Z.B.: Human hand motion analysis during different eating activities. Appl. Bionics Biomech. 8567648 (2018)
7. Ju, Z., Liu, H.: Human hand motion analysis with multisensory information. IEEE/ASME Trans. Mechatron. **19**(2), 456–466 (2014)
8. McDowell, T.W., Wimer, B.M., Welcome, D.E., et al.: Effects of handle size and shape on measured grip strength. Int. J. Ind. Ergon. **42**(2), 199–205 (2012)
9. Welcome, D., Rakheja, S., Dong, R., Wu, J.Z., Schopper, A.W.: An investigation on the relationship between grip, push and contact forces applied to a tool handle. Int. J. Ind. Ergon. **34** (6), 507–518 (2001)
10. Kong, Y.-K., Lowe, B.D.: Optimal cylindrical handle diameter for grip force tasks. Int. J. Ind. Ergon. **35**(6), 495–507 (2005)

# Sensorimotor EEG Rhythms During Action Observation and Passive Mirror-Box Illusion

Nikolay Syrov[1,2](✉), Anatoly Vasilyev[1,3](✉), and Alexander Kaplan[1,2](✉)

[1] Lomonosov Moscow State University, Moscow, Russia
kolascoco@gmail.com, a.vasilyev@anvmail.com, akaplan@mail.ru
[2] Immanuel Kant Baltic Federal University, Kaliningrad, Russia
[3] Center for Neurocognitive Research (MEG Center), Moscow State University of Psychology and Education, Moscow, Russia

**Abstract.** The mirror therapy and the action observation therapy are widely used post-stroke rehabilitation techniques. Both action observation (AO) and the mirror feedback (MF) lead to the activation of the motor and sensorimotor areas, but differences in the mechanisms of their impact on the motor cortex remain unknown. To investigate that the EEG was used to study the sensorimotor rhythms dynamic of 25 healthy participants during AO and mirror illusion with the passive right-hand movement. Functional electrical stimulation was used to perform involuntary movements. We found a significant increase in beta-desynchronization during the third-person AO in both hemispheres, whereas mirror illusion observation led to the beta-synchronization decrease. Our results suggest that AO and MF lead to the motor-cortex activation through different neural networks. Beta-desynchronization is likely to reflect the sensorimotor cortex activity, while the MF, in contrast to AO, affects the motor and premotor cortices.

**Keywords:** Mirror therapy · Action observation · Desynchronization · Functional electrical stimulation · Post movement beta rebound

## 1 Introduction

Mirror therapy (MT) is one of the promising approaches for rehabilitation after a stroke or neurotrauma. A mirror placed in a sagittal plane between two hands provides both the illusion of kinesthetic sensation and the visual illusion of the impaired limb movement [1]. Many studies have reported that mirror therapy could be a beneficial strategy for enhancing motor skills of after-stroke patients. Observation of the mirror illusion leads to the activation of primary motor cortex and sensorimotor cortex, which was shown in TMS [2] and EEG [3] studies. The mirror neuron (MN) system is one of the proposed reasons for such visuo-motor integration. The mirror neurons are activated both while a person is observing a movement performed by another person and while a person is executing the same movement. Also, this phenomenon underlies the action observation therapy

© Springer Nature Switzerland AG 2021
C. Stephanidis et al. (Eds.): HCII 2021, CCIS 1499, pp. 101–106, 2021.
https://doi.org/10.1007/978-3-030-90179-0_14

(AOT). During the AOT, the participants are asked to observe healthy actions from a third-person perspective. EEG studies have reported sustainable mu and beta rhythms desynchronization during AO. Despite the popularity of AO and MT as rehabilitation methods, differences in the mechanisms of their impact on the motor cortex remain unknown [4].

Traditionally sensorimotor mu and beta desynchronization (decrease in power in the frequency ranges of ~10 and ~20 Hz, respectively) is used as the EEG correlate of motor and sensorimotor cortex activation. There are several reasons for associating mu/beta event-related desynchronization (ERD) with mirror neurons activity. Many studies show increased ERD both during action execution and movement observation. Moreover, the sensorimotor rhythms are sensitive to goal-directedness of actions. Thus, ERD value can reflect the effectiveness of a post-stroke rehabilitation technique.

Another event-related oscillatory phenomenon registered over the sensorimotor cortex is beta-synchronization (beta-ERS) or beta rebound. Specifically, it is reflected in the EEG power increase in the beta frequency range following somatosensory afferent stimulation, motion execution or motor imagery [5]. Importantly, voluntary movements are associated with mu and beta ERD. Following the movement termination, amplitudes of the rhythms return to baseline. It is proposed that for beta ERD this process is consistently followed by synchronization [6]. Beta ERS may reflect processes of 'active inhibition' of the primary motor cortex (M1) during movement termination, thus, to avoid excessive movements [7]. But plenty studies demonstrated that afferent nerves stimulation can induce the same beta-rebound even without preliminary ERD [8]. Thus, beta ERS may be related to sensory information integration and can reflect the inhibitory effect of sensorimotor cortex on M1.

Since beta-ERS value reflects the motor cortex deactivation, this EEG phenomenon can be a new informative correlate of the post-stroke rehabilitation effectiveness. The main goal of both AOT and MT is stimulation of the motor cortex circuits to provide neuronal plasticity processes. The events of mu/beta desynchronization are rather related to the sensorimotor cortex activity, and ERD value cannot reflect M1 excitability directly [9].

Thus, changes in the sensorimotor EEG amplitude can characterize processes of the movement implementation and the movement perception. ERD and ERS can be used to monitor post-stroke therapy. The aim of this work was to study the sensitivity of individual EEG components (beta-ERD and beta-ERS) to mirror illusion and to action observation. The mirror therapy is suitable for hemiplegic patients because it requires voluntary movements of at least one limb, while AOT has no such limitations. Therefore, we access the effectiveness of mirror illusion with passive performance of movements, triggered by functional electrical stimulation (FES). We assume that the combination of MT and FES will make the mirror-box therapy available for patients with bilateral paresis and therefore will increase the efficiency of motor recovery.

## 2 Methods

25 healthy right-handed subjects (11 females, all the participants signed an informed consent approved by the Lomonosov Moscow State University Ethical Committee) aged 18–31 performed the voluntary right-hand grasping movements. In the other conditions, movement was triggered by functional electrical stimulation (FES). During the execution of the movement, the subjects observed in front of them a motionless left hand or a mirror reflection of a moving right hand. The mirror was placed along the sagittal plane in between the two hands of participants (the left-hand was covered behind the mirror-box), such that the reflection of the moving right-hand provided the illusion of bimanual movements.

In the action-observation condition subjects performed the right-hand movements (the same as in previous sessions) and observed online-streamed video of their own moving hand on the screen (non-mirrored). Participants sat 50 cm away from a monitor, on which stimuli appeared on a grey background. The visual cues with hand image instructed participants to perform movement (or FES was activated). The pictures with abstract symbols (lines and dots) denoted the state of motor rest and visual attention, during which the subject was asked to count elements of that picture. The motor rest and the motor execution cues ($60 + 60$ cues for each experimental condition) were presented for 6 s in a semi-random sequence with 1 s intervals.

Functional electrical stimulation («Neuro-MEP-4», Neurosoft, Russia) was used to perform the passive involuntary grasping movement of the right-hand. Two stimulating electrodes was placed on the forearm over the m.flexor digitorum superficialis (FDS), and current parametres was finely tuned to induce natural voluntary-like movement (amplitude: 30–65 mA, frequency: 45–60 Hz, duration: 1 s). The electromyography was used to control the movement onset.

During the experiment, the EEG signal recorded (EEG was sampled at 500 Hz, with a bandpass filter at 0–200 Hz). Data were collected from 30 Ag+/AgCl electrodes embedded in a cap, at the following scalp positions: F3, F4, FC5, FC3, FC1, FCz, FC2, FC4, FC6, C5, C3, C1, Cz, C2, C4, C6, CP5, CP3, CP1, CPZ, CP2, CP4, CP6, P5, P3, P1, PZ, P2, P4, P6, using the international 10–10 method of electrode placement. The impedances on all electrodes were measured and confirmed to be less than 10 KΩ.

We used the common localizer task to construct sensitive spatial filters to identify the sources of sensorimotor spectral events: movement related beta ERD, post-movement beta-ERS. After applying the target filters with central sensorimotor ipsi- and contralateral to the active limb localization to the signal we used a set of complex Morlet wavelets with a variable number of cycles for different frequencies (the geometric mean was calculated according to [10]). The values of the time-frequency matrix for the epochs of each experimental condition were normalized by the median value of the same matrix for the motor rest state. Resulted values were transformed in decibels. Positive values were interpreted as synchronization, and negative values as desynchronization (relative to the motor rest). To evaluate effects of mirror feedback and action observation on ERD/ERS-value, paired Wilcoxon tests (with Bonferroni p-values correction) were applied.

## 3  Results

We observed stable mu and beta-ERD during the right-hand movement, and slow mu/beta amplitude recovering after movement termination (see Fig. 1). Beta-ERS appears in 1–2 s both after the FES-triggered movements and after the voluntary movements. We found that beta-ERD and beta-ERS occur in different frequency ranges: beta-ERD had a frequency in range of 21–26 Hz and typical parietal-central localization (bilaterally relative to the active arm with contralateral dominance), while beta-ERS was observed in the lower frequency range (14–22 Hz) with a frontal-medial location. Differences in the frequency range and the sources localisation confirm the hypothesis that beta-ERD and beta-rebound reflects independent processes.

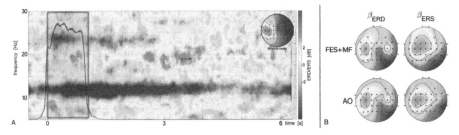

**Fig. 1.** The spatio-temporal beta-ERD/ERS patterns. A - time-frequency dynamic of spectral power in one of beta-ERD spatial sources of one subject during FES-triggered right-hand movement (without mirror). A blue shade defines ERD, a red indicates ERS. The grey line in the red rectangle is EMG signal RMS transformation (beta-rebound appears after action termination). B - Averaged sources of the ERD/ERS patterns for all subjects (N = 25, averaged values are weighted by ERD/ERS amplitude). (Color figure online)

The effect of mirror illusion provided by passive FES-triggered movements and by voluntary movements were the same (Fig. 2 shows the results only for FES-condition). We found a statistically significant decrease of the post-movement beta-ERS in mirror-feedback conditions and this effect was observed in both hemispheres (see Fig. 2B). No effect of the mirror illusion on ERD-reaction was found. At the same time, the action observation induced the significant increase of beta-desynchronization during action execution (in both ipsi- and contralateral sources, see Fig. 2A), but the decrease of beta-rebound in the AO-condition was observed only in the contralateral area.

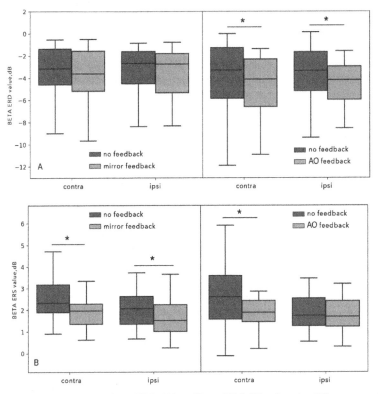

**Fig. 2.** The averaged (N = 25) beta-ERD (A) and beta-ERS (B) values in different experimental conditions. Note: paired comparisons - *p < 0,05 (Wilcoxon test, p-values were adjusted by Bonferroni correction).

## 4 Discussion

The synchronizing beta-activity was investigated in numerous studies as a consequence of beta-ERD restoration. In present study we extracted fronto-central beta-ERS activity without any lacking precursory ERD in the same frequency band. This synchronization appears to occur in 1–2 s after voluntary and passive movements termination. This fact suggests that beta-ERS was rather induced by the proprioceptive afferentation than by a voluntary intention to move the hand. The inhibitory effect of the peripheral afferentation on motor cortex excitability depends on neural interactions between the sensorimotor cortex and M1. Fronto-central localization of ERS-patterns suggests possible relation between the beta-rebound and M1 excitability. Here, we have shown a decrease of beta-ERS via mirror feedback observation and this pattern can be used in post-stroke rehabilitation as an EEG-marker of M1 activation and AOT/MT effects. At the same time beta ERD was not changed by MF and we observed ERD increase only in the AO-condition. Rossiter et al. described the beta-ERD increase during the mirror illusion observation only in post-stroke patients. They showed that the effect of MT on cortex function differs in stroke patients compared to healthy participants. We also observed the absence of MT effect on the sensorimotor-beta ERD.

In the present study we have shown that AO and MF affect central EEG-rhythms differently. In particular, sensorimotor-beta ERD with the centro-parietal sources localization was increased while patients were observing online video-feedback of their own action. Our results suggest that AO and MF lead to the activation of separate neural networks. Specifically, ERD reflects the sensorimotor cortex activity, whereas the mirror feedback, in contrast to AO, affects predominantly M1.

## 5 Conclusions

We found that the effects of the mirror illusion with active movements and with FES-induced movements are similar. This suggests that visual feedback, but not voluntary intention, plays an important role in therapy. This makes MT therapy potentially effective for people with the bilateral paresis, since movement can be triggered by FES controlled in the motor-imagery BCI loop. Our findings confirm that despite the fact that both MO and MF activate sensorimotor and motor area, they do it in different ways.

**Acknowledgments.** This work was prepared as part of a state assignment FZWM-2020–0013 and was partially funded by the Russian Foundation for Basic Research (Grant № 19–315-60011).

## References

1. Rothgangel, A.S., Braun, S.M., Beurskens, A.J.: The clinical aspects of mirror therapy in rehabilitation: a systematic review of the literature. Int. J. Rehabil. Res. **34**(1), 1–13 (2011)
2. Läppchen, C.H., Ringer, T., Blessin, J.: Optical illusion alters M1 excitability after mirror therapy: a TMS study. J. Neurophysiol. **108**(10), 2857–2861 (2012)
3. Lee, H.M., Li, P.C., Fan, S.C.: Delayed mirror visual feedback presented using a novel mirror therapy system enhances cortical activation in healthy adults. J. Neuroeng. Rehabil. **12**(1), 1–11 (2015)
4. Hsieh, Y.W., Lin, Y.H., Zhu, J.D.: Treatment effects of upper limb action observation therapy and mirror therapy on rehabilitation outcomes after subacute stroke: a pilot study. Behav. Neurol. **2020**, 6250524 (2020). https://doi.org/10.1155/2020/6250524. Article ID 6250524
5. Pfurtscheller, G., Stancak, A., Jr., Neuper, C.: Event-related synchronization (ERS) in the alpha band—an electrophysiological correlate of cortical idling: a review. Int. J. Psychophysiol. **24**(1–2), 39–46 (1996)
6. Torrecillos, F., Alayrangues, J., Kilavik, B.E.: Distinct modulations in sensorimotor postmovement and foreperiod β-band activities related to error salience processing and sensorimotor adaptation. J. Neurosci. **35**(37), 12753–12765 (2015)
7. Salmelin, R., Hámáaláinen, M., Kajola, M.: Functional segregation of movement-related rhythmic activity in the human brain. Neuroimage **2**(4), 237–243 (1995)
8. Houdayer, E., Labyt, E., Cassim, F.: Relationship between event-related beta synchronization and afferent inputs: analysis of finger movement and peripheral nerve stimulations. Clin. Neurophysiol. **117**(3), 628–636 (2006)
9. Vasilyev, A., Liburkina, S., Yakovlev, L.: Assessing motor imagery in brain-computer interface training: psychological and neurophysiological correlates. Neuropsychologia **97**, 56–65 (2017)
10. Moca, V.V., Bârzan, H., Nagy-Dăbâcan, A.: Time-frequency super-resolution with super-lets. Nature Commun. **12**(1), 1–18 (2021)

# Multiple Regression Model for Cognitive Function Evaluation Using P300 Based Spelling-Brain–Computer Interface

Kohei Yoshida[1](✉), Hisaya Tanaka[1], Raita Fukasawa[2], Kentaro Hirao[2], Akito Tsugawa[2], and Soichiro Shimizu[2]

[1] Kogakuin University, 2665-1 Nakanomachi, Hachioji-shi, Tokyo 192-0015, Japan
j117298@g.kogakuin.jp
[2] Department of Geriatric Medicine, Tokyo Medical University, 6-1-1 Shinjuku, Shinjuku-ku, Tokyo 160-8402, Japan

**Abstract.** Early diagnosis is important in the treatment of dementia; however, many dementia patients are resist seeking medical attention. In our laboratory, we are developing a dementia-screening device using a P300 based spelling-brain–computer interface (spelling-BCI) for early diagnosis of dementia. We believe that by estimating the results of neuropsychological examinations through measurements using the spelling-BCI, it would be possible to realize tests similar to those performed by medical specialists. According to a previous study, a multiple regression equation with Mini-Mental State Examination (MMSE), the Japanese version of the Montreal Cognitive Assessment (MoCA-J), and Frontal Assessment Battery (FAB) scores are objective variables, and the features obtained using the BCI and age are explanatory variables. In multiple regression analysis, variable selection was performed via the forward–backward stepwise selection method and the data exceeding the 95% confidence interval of the estimation error were excluded. As a result, the measurement data were removed using 95% confidence intervals for the estimation errors so that the multiple regression equation was identified using only about 30 of the more than 200 measurement data. In this study, we evaluated the estimation model of neuropsychological examinations using errors and investigated the effect of excluding outliers. As a result, in the estimation model of each neuropsychological examination, there was little change in the root mean squared errors before and after outlier removal. Therefore, the effect of outlier removal on the estimation model was insignificant.

**Keywords:** Dementia · BCI · P300

## 1 Introduction

Number of patients with dementia in Japan is projected to increase to approximately 6.5–7 and 8.5–11.5 million in 2025 and 2060, respectively [1]. Early detection is important in the treatment of dementia; however, according to Black et al., the mean time from initial symptoms to the first consultation is 7.4 years ± 6.9 months, and the mean time from

C. Stephanidis et al. (Eds.): HCII 2021, CCIS 1499, pp. 107–112, 2021.
https://doi.org/10.1007/978-3-030-90179-0_15

the first consultation to formal diagnosis is 2.9 years ± 11.0 months [2]. Thus, early diagnosis of dementia is difficult. Therefore, a testing device that can easily identify patients with dementia at home or in public facilities without the need to visit a hospital is required.

In our laboratory, we are developing a cost-effective and simple dementia-screening device that uses a P300 based spelling-brain–computer interface (spelling-BCI). Morooka et al. estimated the frontal lobe function, and Fukushima et al. classified the symptoms of dementia using the spelling-BCI [3, 4]. In addition, Yoshida et al. estimated neuropsychological examination scores using the spelling-BCI, and the coefficient of determination of the estimation models exceeded 0.95 [5]. However, as these estimation models excluded many outliers, the evaluation of these estimation models was an issue.

In this study, we evaluate an estimation model of neuropsychological examinations using errors and investigate the effect of excluding outliers.

## 2  Experiment

### 2.1  Experimental Method

This study was conducted on 78 patients in their 60s to 90s (average age: 79.3 ± 5.43 years) who visited the outpatient department of the Department of Elderly Care, Tokyo Medical University. This experiment was conducted based on the research ethics examination, "New cognitive function test method for early diagnosis of dementia 2019-B-18," for humans at Kogakuin University. All subjects provided written consent prior to participating in the experiment.

A 6 × 10 letter matrix was presented to each subject, and each subject was given a specific character to gaze at. Figure 1 shows the display of the P300 based spelling-BCI. While the subject gazed at the character, the rows or columns of the matrix blinked in a random sequence as a stimulus. The P300 component of the subject was averaged in

**Fig. 1.** Display of the P300 based spelling-brain–computer interface

each row and column, and the character at the intersection of the row and column, where the P300 component was detected the most, was estimated as the character being gazed at. The characters that prompted the subjects were defined as task characters and those estimated by the spelling-BCI were defined as estimated characters. After the subjects were given instructions, five or six characters were input alternately for 60 or 120 s and four inputs were made. The first input was treated as learning data for the linear discriminant analysis, and other three inputs were used as analysis target data.

## 2.2  BCI System

Figure 2 shows the diagram of the P300 based spelling-BCI system. Electroencephalograms (EEGs) were measured and collected using an active electrode (LADY bird electrode manufactured by g.tec) and an electrode box (g.SAHARAbox manufactured by g.tec), respectively, and the signal was amplified using a bioamplifier (g.USBamp manufactured by g.tec). In addition, MATLAB 2012a was used for EEG recording, stimulus presentation, and analysis processing. The electrodes were placed at eight locations, as defined by the International 10–20 system: Fz, Cz, P3, P4, Pz, O1, O2, and Oz.

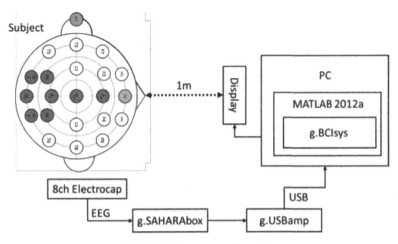

**Fig. 2.**  BCI system configuration

# 3  Analysis

## 3.1  Estimation of the Neuropsychological Examination

A multiple regression analysis was performed using the BCI measurement data and subject age to create an estimation model for neuropsychological examinations. Variable selection in a multiple regression analysis is based on forward–backward stepwise selection. Estimation models were created for Mini-Mental State Examination (MMSE), the Japanese version of the Montreal Cognitive Assessment (MoCA-J), and the Frontal

Assessment Battery (FAB) and then recreated after outlier removal, as described in Sect. 3.2. Table 1 shows the amount of data included in the estimation model before and after removing the outliers.

**Table 1.** Amount of data in the estimation models

|  | Before outlier removal | After outlier removal |
|---|---|---|
| Mini-Mental State Examination (MMSE) | 211 | 30 |
| the Japanese version of the Montreal Cognitive Assessment (MoCA-J) | 211 | 26 |
| Frontal Assessment Battery (FAB) | 209 | 30 |

### 3.2 Confidence Interval for an Estimation Error

The error between the estimated value and subject's score of the neuropsychological examination was used as the estimation error. Herein, the 95% confidence interval was calculated based on the standard deviation of the estimation error. In addition, the data with errors exceeding the 95% confidence interval were excluded to avoid the loss of estimation accuracy.

### 3.3 Root Mean Squared Error

While previous studies have evaluated the estimation model of neuropsychological tests using the coefficient of determination, this study evaluates the estimation model using the root mean squared error (RMSE) [5]. RMSE is calculated using Eq. (1).

$$RMSE = \sqrt{\frac{\sum_{i=1}^{n} (y_i - \hat{y}_i)^2}{n}} \tag{1}$$

where $y_i$ and $\hat{y}_i$ represent a subject's actual score during neuropsychological examination and the predicted score using the estimation model, respectively.

## 4 Results

For the MMSE, the RMSE of the estimation model before and after outlier removal were 3.386 and 3.387, respectively. For the MoCA-J, the RMSE of the estimated model before and after outlier removal were 3.778 and 3.779, respectively. For the FAB, the RMSE of the estimated model before and after outlier removal were 2.005 and 2.010, respectively. The results are summarized in Table 2.

**Table 2.** RMSE of estimation models

|        | Before outlier removal | After outlier removal |
|--------|------------------------|-----------------------|
| MMSE   | 3.386                  | 3.387                 |
| MoCA-J | 3.778                  | 3.779                 |
| FAB    | 2.005                  | 2.010                 |

## 5  Discussion

In the estimation model of each neuropsychological examination, there was little change in the RMSE before and after outlier removal even though many outliers were removed. Thus, the outlier removal using the confidence interval for the estimation error described in Sect. 3.2 may not have a significant effect on the estimation of neuropsychological examination scores.

In addition, the estimation models for all neuropsychological examinations resulted in larger RMSEs after outlier removal than before removal. The error of an estimation model increases with increasing RMSE. This suggests that outlier removal using confidence intervals may not be appropriate to improve the accuracy of an estimation model for neuropsychological examination.

## 6  Conclusion

In this study, we investigated the effect of outlier removal using confidence intervals through a multiple regression analysis on the estimation model of neuropsychological examination. Results showed that the RMSE of the estimation model did not change significantly before and after the outlier removal. Therefore, the effect of outlier removal on the estimation model is considered to be small. In the future, we will improve the accuracy of the estimation model by removing outliers from the data in which the predicted score varies widely from the subject's score.

**Acknowledgments.** We would like to thank all the collaborators who participated in our experiment. We also thank everyone at the Department of Elderly Care, Tokyo Medical University, for their cooperation. This research was supported in part by a research fund for the development of minimally invasive treatment and diagnostic equipment, a joint research project of the Tokyo Medical University and Kogakuin University. In addition, this research was supported in part by research funding from JSPS KAKENHI (Grant Number JP19K12880).

## References

1. Ninomiya, T., et al.: Research on Future Design of the Elderly Population with Dementia in Japan. Ministry of Health, Labor and Welfare Science Research Grant Administrative Policy Research Field Ministry of Health, Labor and Welfare Special Research, H26–036 (2014)

2. Black, C.M., Ambegaonkar, B.M., Pike, J., Jones, E., Husbands, J., Khandker, R.K.: The Diagnostic Pathway From Cognitive Impairment to Dementia in Japan: Quantification Using Real-World Data, Alzheimer disease and associated disorders, vol. 2019, 22 May (2019)
3. Morooka, R., et al: Early diagnosis method of dementia using BCI and frontal lobe function test. J. Hum. Interface Soc. **22**(2), 211–218 (2020)
4. Fukushima, A., Morooka, R., Tanaka, H., Hirao, K., Tsugawa, A., Hanyu, H.: Classification of dementia type using the brain-computer interface. J. Artif. Life Robot. **26**(2), 216–221 (2021). (in press)
5. Yoshida, K., Tanaka, H., Fukasawa, R., Hirano, K., Tsugawa, A., Shimizu, S.: Estimating cognitive decline using P300-based spelling-brain-computer interfaces. In: Proceedings of the 7th International Symposium on Affective Science and Engineering, No. 7A-06, pp. 1–4 (2021)

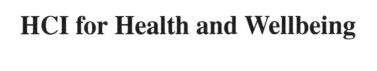

# HCI for Health and Wellbeing

# Co-Designing M-Healer: Supporting Lay Practitioner Mental Health Workers in Ghana

Liam Albright[1]([📧]), Hoa Le[1]([📧]), Suzanne Meller[2]([📧]), Angela Ofori Atta[3]([📧]),
Dzifa A. Attah[3]([📧]), Seth M. Asafo[3]([📧]), Pamela Y. Collins[2]([📧]),
Dror Ben Zeev[2]([📧]), and Jaime Snyder[1]([📧])

[1] Information School, University of Washington, Seattle, WA, USA
{liamaw,lnqhoa,jas1208}@uw.edu
[2] School of Medicine, Department of Psychiatry,
University of Washington, Seattle, WA, USA
{smeller,pyc1,dbenzeev}@uw.edu
[3] University of Ghana, Accra, Ghana
{daattah,smasafo}@ug.edu.gh

**Abstract.** Mental health is a vast problem around the globe and is one of the key population health issues in the world today. At any given time, up to 6.8% of the world's population suffers from a serious mental illness (SMI) such as schizophrenia or bipolar disorder. The impacts of SMI on a population are especially challenging in low and middle-income countries (LMIC). Mobile healthcare application research is a growing area of research aiming to ameliorate these challenging impacts. In Ghana, a LMIC in West Africa, mental healthcare systems are severely under-resourced and people with SMI often receive care from lay practitioners such as traditional and faith healers rather than trained mental health clinicians. These challenges exist alongside developed wireless infrastructure. In these contexts, mobile applications can substantially increase access to health information. This is the basis for our work developing a mobile health (mHealth) application to support mental health lay practitioners in Ghana. We describe the ways that our principled design research practice is intersecting with local faith-based practices, vernacular expertise and values, and the practicalities of technology adoption in Ghana.

**Keywords:** Mobile health · Mental health · Ghana

## 1 Introduction

By leveraging wireless infrastructure and available technologies, mobile applications can substantially increase access to health information, especially in under-resourced communities [7,19]. In particular, in many low- and middle-income countries (LMIC), challenges related to health care equity exist alongside strong

C. Stephanidis et al. (Eds.): HCII 2021, CCIS 1499, pp. 115–124, 2021.
https://doi.org/10.1007/978-3-030-90179-0_16

wireless infrastructure. HCI work in the area of information and communication in developing contexts (ICT4D) advocates for (1) the critical importance of establishing strong collaborations with local stakeholders and (2) avoiding a "one size fits all" approach to technology design [26]. In describing our ongoing work designing and implementing a mobile app to support non-clinically trained spiritual healers in Ghana, we highlight ways that our principled design research practice intersected with local faith-based practices, vernacular expertise and values, and the practicalities of technology adoption in West Africa.

Mental illness is a significant global health problem. At any given time, up to 6.8% of the world's population suffers from a serious mental illness (SMI) such as schizophrenia or bipolar disorder [14]. These psychiatric conditions result in particularly devastating long-term impacts in LMIC [29]. In West Africa, hardships associated with SMI are compounded by pervasive societal stigma, scarce treatment options, and systematic neglect and abuse [20,21,23]. West African mental healthcare systems are severely under-resourced leading to substantial unmet mental health needs [10,12,13,25]. People with SMI often receive care from traditional and faith healers rather than trained mental health clinicians [11,18,22]. Previous research in Ghana found that stakeholders from all sectors (patients, providers, government officials, and faith healers) were open to exploring mobile health approaches to improve the clinical outcomes of those in need [3].

To address this gap, we are developing a smartphone intervention, M-Healer, to provide local healers with educational content and practical tutorials for techniques such as de-escalation, deep breathing, and re-framing anxious thoughts. Our goals are two-fold: (1) to reduce human rights violations commonly associated with the care of people with SMI in LMIC [8,28] by providing information about more humane alternatives and (2) to evaluate the impacts of a mobile app on treatment outcomes for individuals with SMI in West Africa.

## 2   Related Work

Health information and interventions delivered via mobile systems (mHealth) have the ability to improve mental health-care outcomes [5,9,15]. A systemic review and meta-analysis of randomized controlled trials that used smartphone applications to treat symptoms of anxiety found that the most successful programs combined mobile content with the delivery of face-to-face interventions [9]. A team of researchers responding to a large treatment gap in mental health in Zimbabwe (approximately 10 psychiatrists for a population of 13 million) investigated if lay health workers delivering psychological interventions using a form of cognitive-behavioral therapy (CBT) could improve symptoms of depression and anxiety. Participants were taught a structured approach to identifying problems and finding workable solutions through 4 individual sessions, first with lay health workers then in peer-led groups. The study concluded that primary care administered by lay health worker combined with education and support resulted in improved symptoms at 6 months [6].

Our approach involves local stakeholders in the app design process. Related work uses similar co-design methodology. Two case studies in Mozambique and in Romania [27] document procedures, successes, and hurdles of community-based participatory design. In Romania, hierarchy in social interaction and decision-making led to some participants not feeling empowered to engage fully in the design process [27]. In contrast to the intended impact, participatory and co-design methods highlighted lack of agency experienced by people the process was meant to empower. However, a co-design study in rural South Africa focused on a billing system for voice services provided by a community network shows that the co-design process can result in an intervention that is usable and integrated with local culture [24]. Another group of researchers used co-design methods to enhance communication between mothers and Neonatal Intensive Care Unit (NICU) staff in South Africa [16]. While researchers noted that co-design sessions seemed to make participants feel more comfortable about contributing substantively, they also observed that junior nurses did not feel free to critique ideas of more senior members of the healthcare system [16]. In response, researchers introduced a card-sorting method to encourage group cohesion.

## 3   Methodology

During fall 2019, members of our team traveled to Ghana to (1) learn more about the context in which our intervention would be implemented and (2) conduct co-design sessions with local stakeholders. As a result, we were able to compile a set of system, interface, and content requirements for a fully functional prototype. User feedback sessions with target users were conducted during summer 2020. User feedback sessions were conducted on-site by collaborators from the University of Ghana, in accordance with WHO recommended COVID-19 preventative practices. This work was approved by the Institutional Review Boards of the University of Washington and the University of Ghana.

### 3.1   Design Research and Requirements Gathering

Prior to field work, We conducted survey of digital infrastructure requirements, focusing on the likelihood of certain technologies being readily used, data and storage constraints, and other factors that would constrain the future application development. Our team also completed a series of design research activities aimed at better understanding Ghanaian culture, care and treatment of people with mental health issues in West Africa, common practices of faith healers that provide care to individuals with SMI, and the nature of relationships among clinicians, religious leaders, and policymakers. Interview protocols and elicitation materials drew on the team's previous work in Ghana [3], mHealth literature, and user-centered technology design best practices.

In Ghana, interviews and verbal prototyping sessions with 18 faith healers took place at three prayer camps located just outside the capital of Accra. Field work culminated with a half day co-design focus group with 12 healers representing each of the three camps. During these activities, the research team met daily to discuss findings and to reflect on qualitative and design methods as they unfolded. These discussions were documented in field notes and serve as the primary source of data for the emergent themes we highlight here.

## 3.2  System Design

In response to design research insights, emergent co-design concepts, and requirements gathered on site, we developed the M-Healer prototype to be a stable and self-contained Android platform. The android platform was chosen because it is estimated to have 84% of the mobile operating system market share in Ghana [17]. Due to low broadband support and costs associated with data plans in West Africa, the application was built to be self-contained with content delivered via optimized and light-weight animated videos downloaded with install files. This means that M-Healer has no backend functionality, API integration, or database connections. The user interface was also designed dark mode first as dark mode has shown to be more efficient in battery consumption [1]. See Fig. 1.

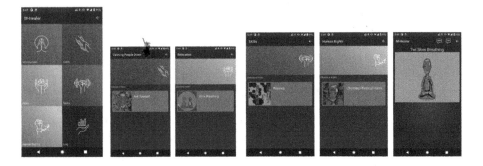

**Fig. 1.** Functional prototype

The application was written in Kotlin, the official android platform development language. A benefit of Kotlin, as opposed to Flutter or React Native, is that it is optimized for performance across all android phones. It scores better on performance metrics such as CPU usage, memory use, battery efficiency, all vital for an app operating in environments with limited access to power and data connectivity. Additionally, Kotlin typically leads to a codebase that is more compact and concise than traditional java android applications [2]. Kotlin has also shown the ability to reduce the frequency of Null Pointer Exceptions [2] which is often a hurdle in Java Android development. The application's user interface design was built using a modified version of Google's Material Design language. The app uses Material Design system icons and square buttons in a grid-like layout with flat lateral navigation flows. The main navigation buttons are also relatively larger than the traditional Material Design button size with the six of them each evenly taking up 16.67% of the screen for ease of clicking.

The M-Healer application itself consists of a home screen where users have the option to click on six buttons that each correspond to a content bucket. Content areas, established in collaboration with stakeholders, include de-escalation and relaxation techniques, tutorials on alternatives to problematic practices such as physical restraints and forced fasting, and general education regarding human rights in the care of people with SMI. Original content was aligned with, but did not explicitly refer to, religious messaging and language discussed during interviews and co-design sessions. From content landing pages, users can choose from a list of videos, accessed through a video player integrated in the application. Users also have the option to switch video language between Twi (a common spoken language in the southern region of Ghana) and English.

Documentation, including (1) key path information architecture, (2) style guide for implementing preliminary M-Healer branding, (3) examples of animated video and text content, and (4) specifications for loading the free-standing app onto smart phones, was written for non-technical audiences and tested with clinical research colleagues at the University of Ghana.

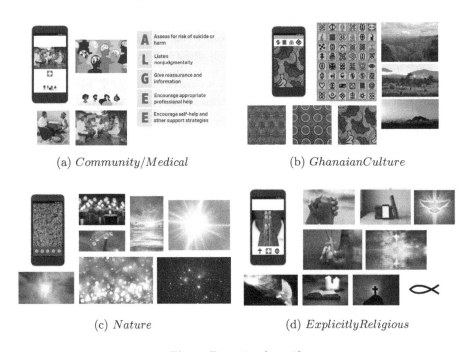

(a) *Community/Medical*    (b) *GhanaianCulture*

(c) *Nature*    (d) *ExplicitlyReligious*

**Fig. 2.** Four visual motifs

## 4    Preliminary User Feedback

An initial set of user feedback findings emerged from our fieldwork. While still in Ghana, we created a series of five visual design directions for the look and feel of the app, ranging from highly medicalized to explicitly religious, as shown in Figs. [2a, 2b, 2c, 2d]. The explicitly Christian imagery (e.g., a bible, a dove, and a wooden cross) was very popular with focus group participants. However, several of the faith healers argued that the design concept that drew on images of nature (e.g., water droplets on grass blades, sun beams bursting from behind clouds, glowing candle flames) would be the most accessible option for prayer camp leaders of different faiths, such as Islam and traditional religions, who are also intended users of the app.

Once we had a functional prototype of the app, our colleagues in Ghana took it to our primary stakeholders to gather feedback. The protocol focused on assessing the interface and content for usability issues. Several users mentioned being excited about the application and could envision themselves using the application on a daily basis. Users were mostly able to navigate through the application, access the video content, and summarize the video content [4]. However, the testing sessions took place on phones not owned by the participants which caused minor hurdles for some. The video content was found to be broadly acceptable and useful for the participants. Participant feedback on how to improve the design of the application was focused on the meaning of icons and the dark background. The previously cited paper also found some of the participants had trouble understand the connection between specific icons and content areas. Additionally, one participant mentioned that the main application icon was blurry. Some participants also mentioned the colors in the application being a bit dark, noting that a brighter interface could be easier to see for users with vision problems. Finally, when participants were asked about future features in the application, they mentioned wanting more spoken voice cues describing different modules of the application. Participants described future iterations of the application that might include these features as intriguing and exciting.

### 4.1   Influence of Technical Constraints on Design Process

One of the major technical constraints on our application development process was the need to balance infrastructure requirements with design of an engaging user experience. For complex interventions that require having access to dynamic data or more extensive software architecture designs, balancing these types of design requirements can be challenging. This project forced our mobile app development team to rethink assumptions, both implicit and explicit, about the ubiquity of reliable data connections and power sources. Thinking about workflows and processes to easily incorporate people and environments that do not have access to traditional development tools is valuable for future endeavors.

In the case of M-Healer, the environment in which our application operates lacks consistent access to a mobile grid and power. Therefore, content was integrated into the application itself and loaded at startup. Because we identified this limitation early in our development process, we were proactive about considering implications in all aspects of our design. Application file size became a primary design requirement throughout the development process, playing a role in decisions from color to length of scripted animations.

Building the application with these design constraints also meant having to go without some of the usual tools associated with Android development. With no backend to the project, the application had to be manually loaded onto phones. Without typical manual processes used with Google Developer Console tools, the application was shared in APK form and installed directly on devices by colleagues in Ghana. Tracking usage data such as clicks without using Google Analytics or another user data tracking API was also a challenge. For applications that operate in resource-constrained environments like ours, devising extensible tracking methods that do not require connectivity is particularly challenging. This continues to be a major focus of our work as we prepare to roll out a large-scale field trial of the M-Healer intervention.

## 4.2   Code-Sharing and Workflow

In future stages of the app development, we will prioritize introducing concrete code-sharing plans and workflows that are both accessible to non-technical team members and in line with traditional software development tools (i.e., Git Hub). Two factors made it necessary for the code base to be more available to the full team than perhaps is typical for app development projects like this: (1) close coordination across design activities (i.e., platform, interface, brand/identity, content) resulted in an iterative process involving multiple cycles of code updates and evaluation by the team and (2) user feedback sessions run by local collaborators who are trained as clinicians rather than technologists made it necessary to package a preliminary release of the app in a format that was easy to extract and install. From an application development standpoint, a key hurdle was sharing code. With only one member of our team experienced in the Git environment, a lot of code was shared over email, making version control very challenging.

Gathering and responding to software bug fixes also presented challenges. The team members tasked with installing the preliminary version of the application on phones in Ghana mainly used WhatsApp for communication among themselves and with other international team members. This meant issues, fixes, and eventually updated software were frequently shared over WhatsApp. During this process, we noticed that as a chat and messaging platform WhatsApp was not quite as optimized for developer communication as is a platform like Slack. For instance, Slack has a feature called Share Code Snippets that allows users to share code snippets and have the code appear very similar if not the same as it does in the development environment it was copied from. An interesting solution for this issue would be for WhatsApp to add more features to support software developers and create an identity for itself as the communicating platform of choice for international software development.

## 4.3   Innovation and Broadening Impacts of User Centered Design

Initial user feedback was elicited and gathered by Ghanaian members of our team who are clinical psychologists familiar with the contexts of the prayer camps but with limited exposure to user centered design practice. Members of our team trained in usability studies attempted to craft a protocol that was clear, concise, and easily understood by both the clinicians eliciting feedback and the participants providing it. While these questions did provide some insights into what was working and what was not in the preliminary version of the app, we recognize that mastering techniques for follow-up questions and clarifications can be challenging, even for very experienced designers. Additionally, questions were written in English and translated to Twi in the moment. For the most part, responses were given in Twi, and were then translated by researchers, sometimes at that time and sometimes later, when notes were compiled on standardized data sheets to send to colleagues in the U.S. As we have reported, participants in this initial round of user feedback interviews found the application usable and feasible. We are confident that this feedback is reliable, while at the same time looking forward to larger scale field tests where we will have the opportunity to refine our approach so that participants can give us more pointed feedback regarding alternatives to navigation, graphic design, and visual identity.

For example, we used a modified fusion of Microsoft's Metro and Google Material Design. While a current design trend in mobile development is bottom navigation using a carousel of selectable icons, our application differs quite a bit from this trend and uses large evenly space squares for navigation through the main content. Future testing could compare both navigation methods in terms the accessibility issues most commonly experienced in this content. Further, future rounds of user feedback will include training in user centered design to local colleagues, and ideally direct observations of the app being used in situ. From a software engineering standpoint, this project can be used as an example of thinking about innovation and accessibility in different ways. To make this intervention feasible it required thinking about innovation from the standpoint of resource-constrained environments, users with low literacy and experiences with technology distinct from Western user groups . In this context, our innovation focused on permanence, longevity, and cultural competence rather than speed, accuracy, or monetization. This app development project has been a platform for our design team to explore the ways that constraints can enable us to shift the focus of innovation from "the next new feature" to broadening the impacts of user centered design insights.

## 5    Conclusion

Our methods were selected for their capacity to (1) avoid a "one size fits all" approach to mHealth technology design and (2) support strong collaborations with local stakeholders. However, we also recognize that our work exists and relies on the global mobile telecommunications industry, including its endemic inequities. Preliminary user feedback and emergent themes resulting from our design research approach signal potential for this work to contribute a method-ological resource for HCI researchers working in the areas of ICT4D, mHealth for mental health, and supporting personal informatics for vulnerable populations. We offer them here as a signal of the value we see in case studies of DEI efforts.

# References

1. URL. https://www.cnet.com/news/using-androids-dark-mode-improves-battery-life-google-confirms-p/
2. Ardito, L., et al.: Effectiveness of Kotlin vs. Java in android app development Tasks.. Inf. Softw. Technol. **127**, 106374 (2020). https://doi.org/10.1016/j.infsof.2020.106374.
3. Ben-Zeev, D.: Mobile health for mental health in west Africa: the case for Ghana. Psychiatr. Serv. **69**(7), 741–743 (2018). https://doi.org/10.1176/appi.ps.201700555.
4. Ben-Zeev, D., et al.: Development of M-Healer: a digital toolkit to improve care and reduce human rights abuses against people with mental illness in West Africa. JMIR Mental Health **8**(7), e28526 (2021)
5. Ben-Zeev, D., et al.: Feasibility, acceptability, and preliminary efficacy of a smartphone intervention for schizophrenia. Schizophrenia Bull. **40**(6), 1244–1253 (2014)
6. Chibanda, D., Weiss, H.A., Verhey, R.: Effect of a primary care–based psychological intervention on symptoms of common mental disorders in Zimbabwe: a randomized clinical trial. JAMA **316**(24), 2618–2626 (2016). https://doi.org/10.1001/jama.2016.19102
7. Donker, T., et al.: Smartphones for smarter delivery of mental health programs: a systematic review. J. Med. Internet Res. **15**(11), 247 (2013). https://doi.org/10.2196/jmir.2791
8. Esan, O., et al.: A survey of traditional and faith healers providing mental health care in three sub-Saharan African countries. Soc. Psychiatry Psychiatr. Epidemiol. **54**, 395–403 (2019). https://doi.org/10.1007/s00127-018-1630-y, PMID: 30456425
9. Firth, J., et al.: Can smartphone mental health interventions reduce symptoms of anxiety? A meta-analysis of randomized controlled trials. J. Affective Disord. **218**, 15–22 (2017). https://doi.org/10.1016/j.jad.2017.04.046
10. Gureje, O., Lasebikan, V.: Use of mental health services in a developing country: results from the Nigerian survey of mental health and well-being. Soc. Psychiatr. Psychiatr. Epidemiol. **41**(1), 44–49 (2006)
11. Gureje, O., et al.: The role of global traditional and complementary systems of medicine in the treatment of mental health disorders. Lancet Psychiatr. **2**(2), 168–77 (2015)
12. Samba, D.: Ibadan, Nigeria, University College Hospital, Department of Psychiatry, Mental Health Leadership and Advocacy Programme (mhLAP). http://www.mhlap.org/country-of-activities/gambia (2012)
13. Johnson, K., et al.: Association of combatant status and sexual violence with health and mental health outcomes in postconflict Liberia. JAMA **300**(6), 676–690 (2008)
14. Kessler, R.C., et al.: The global burden of mental disorders: an update from the WHO World Mental Health (WMH) surveys. Epidemiol. Psychiatr. Sci. **18**(1), 23–33 (2009)
15. Kola, L., Abiona, D., Adefolarin, A., Ben-Zeev, D.: Mobile phone use and acceptability for the delivery of mental health information among perinatal adolescents in Nigeria: survey study JMIR Ment. Health **8**(1) (2021). https://doi.org/10.2196/20314
16. Mburu, C.W., et al.: Co-designing with mothers and neonatal unit staff: use of technology to support mothers of preterm infants. In: Proceedings of the Second African Conference for Human Computer Interaction: Thriving Communities (AfriCHI 2018). Association for Computing Machinery, vol. Article 12. New York, NY, USA, pp. 1–10 (2018). https://doi.org/10.1145/3283458.3283487

17. Mobile Operating System Market Share Ghana. Accessed 25 Nov 2020. https://gs.statcounter.com/os-market-share/mobile/ghana

18. Ae-Ngibise, K., et al.: Whether you like it or not people with mental problems are going to go to them: a qualitative exploration into the widespread use of traditional and faith healers in the provision of mental health care in Ghana. Int. Rev. Psychiatr. **22**(6), 558–567 (2010)

19. Norris, L., Swartz, L., Tomlinson, M.: Mobile phone technology for improved mental health care in South Africa: possibilities and challenges. South African J. Psychol. **43**(3), 379–388 (2013). https://doi.org/10.1177/0081246313493376

20. Esan, O., et al.: Mental health care in Anglophone West Africa. Psychiatr. Serv. **65**, 1084–1087 (2014)

21. Ofori-Atta, A., et al.: A situation analysis of mental health services and legislation in Ghana: challenges for transformation. African J. Psychiatr. **13**(2), 99–108 (2010)

22. Read, U.: I want the one that will heal me completely so it won't come back again: the limits of antipsychotic medication in rural Ghana. Transcultural Psychiatr. **49**(3–4), 438–460 (2012)

23. Read, U.M., Adiibokah, E., Nyame, S.: Local suffering and the global discourse of mental health and human rights: an ethnographic study of responses to mental illness in rural Ghana. Globalization Health **5**(1), 13 (2009)

24. Rey-Moreno, C., et al.: Co-designing a billing system for voice services in Rural-South Africa: lessons Learned. In: Proceedings of the Fifth ACM Symposium on Computing for Development (ACM DEV-5 2014). New York, NY, USA: Association for Computing Machinery, pp. 83–92 (2014). https://doi.org/10.1145/2674377.2674389

25. Roberts, H.: A way forward for mental health care in Ghana? Lancet**357**, 1859 (2001)

26. Rusatira, J., et al.: Enabling access to medical and health education in Rwanda using mobile technology. Needs Assessment Dev. Mob. Med. Educator Apps JMIR Med. Educ. **2**(1), e7 (2016). https://doi.org/10.2196/mededu.5336.. https://mededu.jmir.org/2016/1/e7

27. Sabiescu, A.G., et al.: Emerging spaces in community-based participatory design: reflections from two case studies. In: Proceedings of the 13th Participatory Design Conference: Research Papers 1. PDC 2014, pp. 1–10 (2014). https://doi.org/10.1145/2661435.2661446

28. Human Rights Watch. Living in chains: Shackling of people with psychosocial disabilities worldwide. ISBN: 978-1-62313-8653, 6 October 2020

29. Whiteford, H.A., et al.: Global burden of disease attributable to mental and substance use disorders: findings from the Global Burden of Disease Study 2010. Lancet **382**(9904), 1575–1586 (2013)

.

# Using Experience-Based Co-design to Develop mHealth App for Digital Pulmonary Rehabilitation Management of Patients with Chronic Obstructive Pulmonary Disease (COPD)

Qingfan An[1]([📧]) [iD], Marjorie M. Kelley[2] [iD], and Po-Yin Yen[3] [iD]

[1] Royal College of Art, Kensington Gore, South Kensington, London, UK
qingfan.an@network.rca.ac.uk
[2] The Ohio State University, 281 W Lane Avenue, Columbus, OH 43210, USA
kelley.415@osu.edu
[3] Washington University in St. Louis, 1 Brookings Dr, St. Louis, MO 63130, USA
yenp@wustl.edu

**Abstract.** Chronic obstructive pulmonary disease (COPD) is a progressive life-threatening lung disease that causes breathlessness, chronic cough, and overall decrease in patients' quality of life. Pulmonary rehabilitation (PR) slows COPD progression and reduces the overall economic burden of the disease. However, only a small portion of patients participate in conventional face-to-face PR due to a lack of resources, or motivation. Digital PR interventions may reduce these barriers, but only a few digital PR interventions available are rigorously designed and tested. The purposes of this study were to (1) develop a high-fidelity prototype app for digital PR using an experience-based co-design (EBCD) approach, and (2) conduct a usability testing of the PR prototype app. We engaged 15 COPD patients and 11 healthcare providers in the EBCD process. Following the development, 7 patients participated in the usability testing and a semi-structured interview to provide their feedback on the prototype app. The EBCD approach resulted in a prototype of a digital PR intervention – COPDTrack, with features suggested from patients and providers. These features include: digital PR exercise courses, real-time health monitoring, digital 6-min walk test, visualization of progress, patient reported outcomes, and the ability to communicate with healthcare providers. The usability testing results indicated that most participants completed tasks successfully and were able to navigate smoothly throughout the app. Our study demonstrates the feasibility of integrating EBCD into the HCD process to facilitate the design and development of the digital PR intervention for COPD patients.

**Keywords:** Human centered design · Digital health intervention · Rehabilitation exercise · Pulmonary Rehabilitation · Chronic obstructive pulmonary disease

© Springer Nature Switzerland AG 2021
C. Stephanidis et al. (Eds.): HCII 2021, CCIS 1499, pp. 125–133, 2021.
https://doi.org/10.1007/978-3-030-90179-0_17

# 1    Introduction

The disease burden of chronic obstructive pulmonary disease (COPD) is increasing globally due to aging populations and the increasing prevalence of smoking [1]. COPD is associated with abnormalities of the airway which are predominantly caused by exposure to noxious gases and particulates over a long period of time [2]. As a progressive life-threatening lung disease that causes breathlessness, COPD has a negative impact on patients' physical health, mental health and social well-being [1, 2].

Pulmonary Rehabilitation (PR) plays an essential role in the management of patients with COPD [3]. PR involves exercise training and self-management education to improve physical and psychological well-being [4]. The National Institute for Health and Care Excellence (NICE) supports PR as the core management intervention for COPD [5] because it helps to relieve dyspnea, increasing exercise tolerance, and improving health-related quality of life for patients with COPD [6]. However, resource limitations, geographical distance from treatment centres, and availability of PR services in addition to low motivation and poor adherence to traditional programs limit PR uptake and efficacy [6, 7]. Consequently, attendance at PR is uniformly low and completion of courses similarly suboptimal with only 69% of patients referred attending for assessment [6]. Furthermore, due to the limited resources, greater than 37% of patients wait over 3 months to access PR classes [6]. Digital PR interventions may offer hope in ameliorating these concerns. But rigorous design and testing are necessary. However, patient and healthcare provider perspectives towards using digital interventions or mobile health (mHealth) remain relatively unexplored [8]. Experience-based co-design (EBCD) is an approach that engages patients and healthcare provider in partnership to develop and improve healthcare services [9].

# 2    Objectives

The purposes of this study were to (Aim 1) develop a prototype app focused on PR for patients with COPD, and (Aim 2) conduct a usability test of the prototype.

# 3    Methods

Human-centred design(HCD) focuses on designers' empathy of users, and is a proven method that optimizes the usability and acceptance of the digital health intervention [8, 10–12]. In Aim 1, we integrated EBCD into the HCD process with six phases: diagnostic, gathering, locating, prototyping and upgrading, and developed an interactive prototype app called COPDTrack. In Aim 2, we conducted a usability test consisting of seven use-based tasks specific to COPDTrack. In addition, we interviewed patients for their feedback and acceptance of COPDTrack. Interview questions were informed by the Technology Acceptance Model [13]. The study was approved by the Institutional Review Board (IRB) of a metropolitan medical center in northeast China.

### 3.1 Aim1: EBCD-Based HCD to Develop a Prototype App

**Setting and Sample.** COPD patients and healthcare providers were recruited via a written invitation by the researcher. Patients with early to moderate stage COPD and with at least one episode of COPD exacerbation requiring hospitalization were eligible as PR is most effective during these two stages of the disease process [14].

**Study Design.** We integrated EBCD [15] into the HCD process. The process consists of six phases: Diagnostic, Gathering, Locating, Prototyping, and Upgrading (Fig. 1).

| Phases | Diagnostic | Gathering | Locating | Prototyping | Upgrading |
|---|---|---|---|---|---|
| Objectives | To gain the concerns from COPD patients and healthcare providers separately. | To enable patients and healthcae providers share their concerns and generate the desired features | To transfer the desired features into design solutions | Use prototye to address the desired features and conduct the pilot evaluation | To upgrade the prototype after the pilot evaluation |
| Methods | Interview<br>Zaltman metaphor elicitation technique<br>Thematic analysis | Co-creation session<br>Thematic analysis | Design meeting<br>Thematic analysis | Experience prototyping<br>Think aloud protocol | Usability test<br>Semi-structured interview<br>Think aloud protocol |

**Fig. 1.** Design process

*Diagnostic Phase.* We interviewed participants to understand their concerns while using a digital health intervention for PR.

*Gathering Phase.* We used co-creation sessions to collect data and descriptive thematic analysis [16] to generate their needs.

*Locating Phase.* Participants and designers worked together to design solutions to address the desired features generated from the *Diagnostic* and *Gathering* phases.

*Prototyping Phase.* We adopt the experience prototyping approach [17] to enable practical solutions for users through their active engagement. Patients and healthcare providers provided their feedbacks on the prototype via the thinking aloud method.

*Upgrading.* We finalized the prototype after a pilot evaluation with participants.

### 3.2 Aim2: User Testing to Evaluate the Prototype App

We used a mixed-methods approach to assess the usability of the prototype. Usability is the extent to which a product can be used by users to achieve specified goals [18].

**Setting and Sample.** A convenience sample of COPD patients who participated in Aim 1 were invited to participate in the usability testing of COPDTrack.

**Usability Testing.** We created seven interactive tasks (Table1) representing the features in COPDTrack. We asked participants to complete the seven tasks and thinking aloud [19] when performing the task. Usability was measured by task completion and users' operational error. Table 1 outlines the tasks and the evaluation goal of each task. A task was considered completed if the participant was able to achieve the task (0 = not achieve; 1 = achieve). The operational errors was considered as any steps or expression not associated or contributing to the task completion, such as pushing the wrong button, and expressing words like "don't know", "confused", etc. The completion rate was measured by the average number of tasks achieved by the participants; The error rate was measured by the average of errors per tasks and per participant.

**Table 1.** Mapping table of tasks and purpose of tasks

| Task | Evaluation goal |
| --- | --- |
| Task 1: Find the running map and choose your preferred path | The accessibility and navigation in the running map |
| Task 2: Find your body data and send it to your physician | The navigation to and within real-time body data function |
| Task 3: Find your peak flow report and send it to your physician | Patients' ability to create peak flow reports accurately and without problems |
| Task 4: Complete the 6-min walk test(6MWT) | The clearness of the audio/written self-help instructions |
| Task 5: Find a hint on the homepage to help navigate to another page | Patients' ability to find help in the app |
| Task 6: Send a question to your physician | Patients' ability to use the chat channel to communicate with their provider |
| Task 7: Quit out of the walk test page and enter your body data page | System error tolerance and users ability to navigate errors |

**Semi-structured Interview.** Following the usability test, participants were interviewed about their experience and their acceptance of COPDTrack. The semi-structured interview included questions about ease of use, usefulness, and satisfaction, guided by the Technology Acceptance Model [13].

## 4   Results

### 4.1   Aim1: EBCD-Based HCD to Develop a Prototype App

**Diagnostic Phase**
*Patients.* Six themes were identified by patients during the diagnostic phase: Privacy, Accessibility, Visible progress, Schedule, Cost and Online physician.

Privacy: Some patients reported that privacy is an important concern for them when doing rehabilitation exercise. One said: *"I don't want others to watch what I do when I exercise, it is kind of embarrassing."*

Accessibility: Participants expressed concern about access to PR tools and ability to do PR exercises, with one patient stating, *"I am not sure I'll make it. I prefer the tools are cheap and easy to get."*

Visible Progress: Visualizing progress toward a goal is an important motivator for patients. One of the patients *said "I don't know how to tell if the PR exercise is effective or not. Everyone's physical condition is different. I think I will quit the PR exercise once the disease worsens again."*

Schedule: Patients also discussed scheduling difficulties. One patients commented, *"It is kind of different for me to spare time for PR exercise."*

Cost: Patients expressed concerns over the cost of PR. One patient said *"I won't spend too much money on the PR exercise. I am not sure if it's useful."*

Online Physician: Effective and real-time communication between patients and physicians is vital for patients. One patient stated, *"It will be more convinced if there is a real-time doctor monitoring my exercise and track my body condition."*

*Healthcare providers.* Providers' needs emerged into three themes: Self-assessment, Knowledge, and Trust.

Self-Assessment: Healthcare providers thought patient self-assessment was important to help patients track their condition over time, using a standardized, valid and reliable measure – six-minute walk test (6MWT). One healthcare provider said *"Six-minute walk test is widely used in assessment of patients' condition. It would help if they can conduct the assessment themselves".*

Knowledge: Patients need basic knowledge to self-manage. One provider said *"Most patients don't want to exercise because they don't understand their disease."*

Trust: Compliance is essential to effective self-management, and the patient-provider trust is the key to compliance. One provider said *"Patients won't follow you when their condition gets worse again during the treatment because they don't trust you."*

**Gathering Phase.** During the co-creation sessions, patients and providers consolidated their ideas and generated 8 needs: 1) cost-effectiveness; 2) accessibility; 3) transparency; 4) privacy; 5) education; 6) visible progress; 7) real-time monitoring; 8) flexibility. These 8 needs informed the Locating phase and were used for the prototype design development.

**Locating Phase.** The design team developed six solutions/features to address the needs: 1) digital PR exercise courses; 2) real-time body monitoring; 3) digital 6MWT; 4) visualization of progress;5) patient reported outcomes 6); communication with healthcare providers (Table 2).

**Table 2.** Solutions/features to address the needs

| Solutions | Needs |
| --- | --- |
| Digital PR exercise courses | Cost-effectiveness; accessibility; transparency; privacy; education |
| Real-time body monitoring | Visible progress; real-time monitoring |
| Digital 6MWT | Cost-effectiveness; visible progress; flexibility |
| Visualization of progress | Visible progress; accessibility |
| Patient reported outcomes | Cost-effectiveness; accessibility |
| Communication with healthcare providers | Cost-effectiveness; flexibility; transparency; education; |

**Prototyping Phase and Upgrading Phase.** We developed the prototype based on the needs and design solutions. After the pilot evaluation of the prototype with patients and healthcare providers (Aim 2), we updated the prototype and ultimately finalized it into a high-fidelity prototype, COPDTrack. We demonstrated the user interface of three features patients feel most willing to use (Fig. 2).

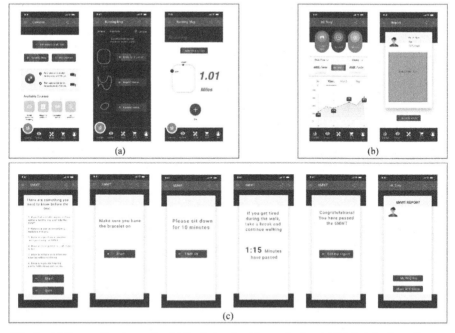

**Fig. 2.** (a) Personalized exercise (b) Real-time health monitoring (c) Digital 6-min walk test

## 4.2   Aim2: User Testing to Evaluate the Prototype App

**Usability Testing.** 7 COPD patients who participated in Aim 1 agreed to participated in the user testing of COPDTrack. We reported that participants were able to navigate the app smoothly and complete a set of assigned tasks successfully. The average completion rate of the tasks is 95.9%; the average error rate of the tasks is 16.3%.

**Interview Results.** Participants confirmed that COPDTrack has good affordance and is useful for encouraging them to do PR exercise. One patient commented *"The operation is quite clear, it is not difficult for me to use it. COPDTrack can remind me to exercise and show me the actual improvement of my body by providing the comparison value of non-exercise."* Overall, they were satisfied with COPDTrack and have intention to use it in the future. One patient commented *"I think the functions of COPDTrack are what I need. I would like to use COPDTrack to manage my disease."*

## 5   Discussion

The key of HCD is empathy creation for designers, and we applied EBCD to help to find the empathy more efficiently. In our study, there are two features constantly emphasized and appreciated by patients and healthcare providers, were the digital 6MWT and the visualization of progress. Unlike glucose, which can be easily measured using a portable glucose meter [20], there is no easy to measure biomarker to determine the condition of the COPD patient. Most COPD patients only go to see physicians when the exacerbation is evident and serious. Thus, the digital 6MWT provided COPD patients with a self-assessment opportunity which helps in encouraging COPD patients to perform PR continuously. Current studies focus more on proving the short-term impact of digital PR on patients [7, 21, 22]. Our study designed a high-fidelity app for COPD patients to maintain their PR self-management. In the future, we plan to conduct a study to understand the long-term impact of COPDTrack on patient outcomes.

## 6   Conclusion

Our study demonstrates the feasibility of integrating EBCD into the UCD process to facilitates a more transparent and effective approach to the design and development of a user-friendly mHealth application-COPDTrack for COPD patients.

**Acknowledgments.** I would like to acknowledge the COPD patients and healthcare providers who participated in the study and thank them for their support.

# References

1. Chronic obstructive pulmonary disease (COPD). https://www.who.int/news-room/fact-she ets/detail/chronic-obstructive-pulmonary-disease-(copd)
2. Alqahtani, J.S., et al.: Prevalence, severity and mortality associated with COPD and smoking in patients with COVID-19: a rapid systematic review and meta-analysis. PLoS ONE **15**, e0233147 (2020). https://doi.org/10.1371/journal.pone.0233147
3. Bourbeau, J.: Making pulmonary rehabilitation a success in COPD. Swiss Med. Wkly. (2010). https://doi.org/10.4414/smw.2010.13067
4. Lindenauer, P.K., et al.: Association between initiation of pulmonary rehabilitation after hospitalization for COPD and 1-year survival among Medicare beneficiaries. JAMA **323**, 1813–1823 (2020). https://doi.org/10.1001/jama.2020.4437
5. Chronic obstructive pulmonary disease. https://www.nice.org.uk/guidance/conditions-and-diseases/respiratory-conditions/chronic-obstructive-pulmonary-disease
6. Bourne, S., et al.: Online versus face-to-face pulmonary rehabilitation for patients with chronic obstructive pulmonary disease: randomised controlled trial. BMJ Open **7**, e014580 (2017)
7. Rassouli, F., Boutellier, D., Duss, J., Huber, S., Brutsche, M.H.: Digitalizing multidisciplinary pulmonary rehabilitation in COPD with a smartphone application: an international observational pilot study. Int. J. Chron. Obstruct. Pulmon. Dis. **13**, 3831–3836 (2018)
8. Korpershoek, Y.J.G., Vervoort, S.C.J.M., Trappenburg, J.C.A., Schuurmans, M.J.: Perceptions of patients with chronic obstructive pulmonary disease and their health care providers towards using mHealth for self-management of exacerbations: a qualitative study. BMC Health Serv. Res. **18**, 757 (2018). https://doi.org/10.1186/s12913-018-3545-4
9. Green, T., et al.: Use and reporting of experience-based codesign studies in the healthcare setting: a systematic review. BMJ Qual. Saf. **29**, 64–76 (2020)
10. IDEO's human centered design process: How to make things people love. https://www.userte sting.com/blog/how-ideo-uses-customer-insights-to-design-innovative-products-users-love
11. Altman, M., Huang, T.T.K., Breland, J.Y.: Design thinking in health care. Prev. Chronic Dis. **15**, E117 (2018). https://doi.org/10.5888/pcd15.180128
12. Yardley, L., Morrison, L., Bradbury, K., Muller, I.: The person-based approach to intervention development: application to digital health-related behavior change interventions. J. Med. Internet Res. **17**, e30 (2015). https://doi.org/10.2196/jmir.4055
13. Venkatesh, V., Davis, F.D.: A theoretical extension of the technology acceptance model: four longitudinal field studies. Manag. Sci. **46**, 186–204 (2000)
14. COPD Stages and the Gold Criteria (2019). https://www.webmd.com/lung/copd/gold-cri teria-for-copd
15. Donetto, S., Pierri, P., Tsianakas, V., Robert, G.: Experience-based co-design and healthcare improvement: realizing participatory design in the public sector. Des. J. **18**, 227–248 (2015)
16. Miles, M.B., Huberman, A.M.: Qualitative Data Analysis: An Expanded Sourcebook. SAGE Publications, Thousand Oaks (1994)
17. Buchenau, M., Suri, J.F.: Experience prototyping. In: Proceedings of the Conference on Designing Interactive Systems Processes, Practices, Methods, and Techniques - DIS 2000. ACM Press, New York (2000)
18. Usability of consumer products and products for public use - Part 2: Summative test method. https://www.iso.org/obp/ui/#iso:std:iso:ts:20282:-2:ed-2:v1:en
19. Güss, C.D.: What is going through your mind? Thinking aloud as a method in cross-cultural psychology. Front. Psychol. **9**, 1292 (2018). https://doi.org/10.3389/fpsyg.2018.01292
20. Brzan, P.P., Rotman, E., Pajnkihar, M., Klanjsek, P.: Mobile applications for control and self management of diabetes: a systematic review. J. Med. Syst. **40**(9), 1 (2016). https://doi.org/10.1007/s10916-016-0564-8

21. Burkow, T.M., et al.: Internet-enabled pulmonary rehabilitation and diabetes education in group settings at home: a preliminary study of patient acceptability. BMC Med. Inform. Decis. Mak. **13**, 33 (2013). https://doi.org/10.1186/1472-6947-13-33

22. Jackson, E.R., Bulbeck, V., Evans, T.: P85 virtual pulmonary rehabilitation: a worthwhile intervention? In: Virtually Systematic: Current Interventions and Digital Delivery in Pulmonary Rehabilitation. BMJ Publishing Group Ltd and British Thoracic Society (2021)

# A Speech-Based Data Collection Interface for Contact Tracing

Tamara Babaian[✉]

Bentley University, Waltham, MA 02452, USA
tbabaian@bentley.edu

**Abstract.** In this paper we present the design of an innovative contact tracing application, with an interface that intends to meet several goals: automatic capture of speech and its transcription into text, enabled playback capability, entity recognition and entity visualization on a timeline. We present the overall design as well as a review of the implemented components of the interface, discuss challenges and future work.

**Keywords:** Interface design · Speech-based interface · Visualization · Timeline

## 1  Introduction and Motivation

Contact tracing is an epidemiological method of identifying persons who have been exposed to infection through contact with an individual who is a suspected or confirmed carrier of the infection (patient) [3]. The first stage of contact tracing is called contact elicitation; it involves a trained professional interviewing the patient about the personal history of the days leading to the diagnosis, when the patient may have been contagious. The purpose of the interview is to identify people that have interacted with the patient, in order to notify them of the possible exposure to the disease. Contact tracing has been used for decades, in particular, in relationship to tuberculosis cases, and it became a prominent component on of the US public health system's response to the COVID-19 pandemic. Several approaches have been developed so far [1].

In this paper we present the design of an innovative contact tracing application, with an interface intends to meet several goals:

1. Automate the process of recording contact data interview from a patient, conducted with or without an interviewer, based on the published CDC questionnaires and guidebooks, using automatic speech recording and transcription.
2. Identify the key relevant components of the patient's reported contact history, such as (per CDC guidelines) people, exposure settings, locations and dates, and symptoms.
3. Enable easy semi-automatic recording of contact data, such as phone and email address, with the system identifying candidate information from the interviewee's available contact lists.

© Springer Nature Switzerland AG 2021
C. Stephanidis et al. (Eds.): HCII 2021, CCIS 1499, pp. 134–138, 2021.
https://doi.org/10.1007/978-3-030-90179-0_18

4. Enhance patient's capabilities for recall of temporal and other details using a timeline visualization of the collected data in real time simultaneously with the interviewing, aiding in obtaining a more complete history of contacts. Personal geolocation and photo data may also be used to increase recall.
5. Enable easy audio playback, review and editing of the contact interview by a patient and/or the interviewer.
6. Maintain a non-invasive from the privacy standpoint nature of the data collection process, which would rely on the patient's provided information, rather than automatically collected geolocation or other smartphone data.

A proof-of-concept prototype with partial implementation of the above features is built using Python Dash, Google Speech and Natural Language APIs. Figures 1, 2 and 3 present the design of the prototype screen and its implemented components. After presenting a simple use case, we discuss the overall design and the functionality of components implemented so far.

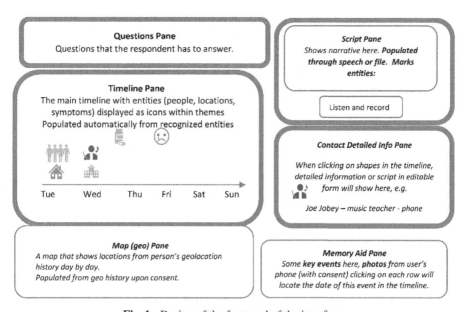

**Fig. 1.** Design of the front end of the interface.

## 2 A Sample Usage Scenario

Joe has recently received a positive COVID test result and was asked to self-quarantine on campus. He has been given a URL he can use to enter his contact tracing information for the past several days. When he opens the URL, he sees a set of Questions and a Timeline going several days prior to the current date. Joe presses on a button to start recording his answers to the questions. The recording gets captured and its text is displayed in the Script pane of the interface. The words identifying locations, people, dates and symptoms (entities) are automatically identified and highlighted. Icons corresponding to the identified entities automatically appear on the Timeline based on the application's best guess of the date that the narrative refers to.

References to people in Joe's narrative also automatically appear in the Contact Detailed Info Pane. Upon finishing a segment of his narrative, Joe is able to adjust the icons on the Timeline to match the correct dates. He provides more complete description of the contacts in the Contact pane. When the information is completed, he sends it to the contact tracing authorities, who may contact Joe again, upon reviewing the information, to check on him and ask for any additional details.

## 3   Implementation

We have implemented three components of the above design:

a. Script pane enabling the recording, speech-to-text capture and display and audio playback capabilities.
b. Timeline Pane, and
c. Detailed Info Pane

We present an overview of these components, displayed in Figs. 2 and 3.

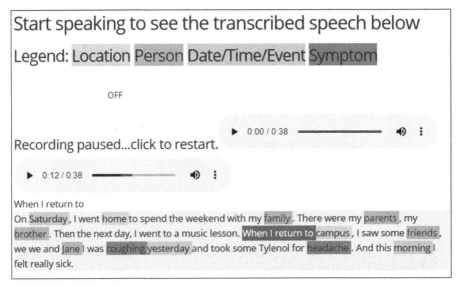

**Fig. 2.** Script Pane interface for recording the interview automatically transcribes the audio of the speech into text and highlights entities of interest identified in real-time. (Color figure online)

## 3.1  Script Pane

A screenshot of the component is shown in Fig. 2.

This component provides a way to start, pause and resume recording of audio input. The audio is simultaneously transcribed into text and passed to entity recognition engine, which recognizes four types of entities of interest in contact tracing: Location, Person, Date/Time/Event, and Symptom. Those entities are highlighted in the text according to the legend.

In addition to recording, the interface enables playback of the entire audio as well as playback of a selected sentence. Figure 2 shows the user having selected a portion of the text, which is highlighted in blue. The second playback control bar is automatically set to play the selected sentence. The top playback control bar enables to replay the entire captured audio from any point. This capability is essential for a tool that uses speech-to-text, due to the inevitable mistakes associated with using an automated transcription tool.

## 3.2  Timeline and Detailed Info Pane

The Timeline and Detailed Info panes (also, henceforth, the Details table) are integrated into one component, depicted in Fig. 3. Information that is displayed in each of the panes comes from the entities of interest detected in the speech. Those entities are categorized via four different entity types: symptom, event, location and person. The timeline contains four horizontal lanes corresponding to the entity types, onto which rectangles are placed to indicate the start and the end of a specific occurrence that was identified in the speech. For example, the pink rectangle in the top lane – symptom – corresponds to the reported *Coughing* between Jan 4th and Jan 16th. The same information is also accessible through the Details table on the right, in which the user can easily edit the information associated with each entity.

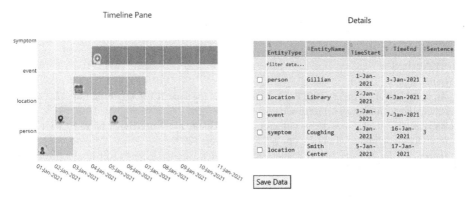

**Fig. 3.** Timeline and Detailed Info Panes are implemented in one component that displays entities in two different formats, and enables editing of the information on the Timeline as well as in the Details table,

The Details table allows for sorting the entries, adding, removing rows and editing of the data. The Timeline pane is scrollable and enables creation of new entity rectangles, which are simultaneously added to the Details table. All of the entities and their associated timing and duration are adjustable on the Timeline or in the Details table, as the automatic transcription and identification of the associated dates will likely be faulty and must therefore be easily editable.

## 4 Future Work

One of the greatest challenges for the usefulness of this application is dealing with the inherent presence of errors of the machine-learning-based automatic transcription, entity identification and temporal references. The audio playback capability mitigates the concerns by providing a way to hear the original source of the information. In addition to playback, we are working on providing editing facilities to the transcript, in addition to the editing that is already available within the Timeline and the Detailed Info Panes. Quick and seamless editing of the transcript and the associated Timeline are important for the effectiveness of the tool and the associated user satisfaction, and we are planning on testing and validating our implemented approach to the editing in pilot and field user studies.

Another challenge lies in the accuracy of the automatic identification of the dates associated with the specific entities as well as recognizing colloquial references to symptoms. While terms like "headache", "fever", and "loss of smell" are easy to recognize, it is harder to identify "feeling lungs are clogged up" as a symptom. Machine learning-based approaches [5] combined with a user-system collaboration-based design [2, 4] can be explored to create an effective and efficient mechanism for more precise recording of the dates from user speech and other input. We are also working on developing a trained model for recognizing colloquial references to medical symptoms to improve their identification from speech and informal writing.

Finally, we note that the approach described here can be extended to handling not only contact tracing, but any form of interview data collection, which would benefit from a temporal or other kind of just-in-time visualization.

## References

1. Ahmed, N., et al.: A survey of COVID-19 contact tracing apps. IEEE Access. **8**, 134577–134601 (2020). https://doi.org/10.1109/ACCESS.2020.3010226
2. Babaian, T., et al.: A writer's collaborative assistant. In: Proceedings of Intelligent User Interfaces Conference (IUI-02), pp. 7–14 ACM Press (2002)
3. Eames, K.T.D., Keeling, M.J.: Contact tracing and disease control. In: Proceedings of the Royal Society of London. Series B: Biological Sciences, vol. 270(1533), pp. 2565–2571 (2003). https://doi.org/10.1098/rspb.2003.2554
4. Lucas, W., Babaian, T.: The collaborative critique: an inspection method for expert evaluation of user interfaces. Int. J. Hum.-Comput. Interact. **31**(11), 843–859 (2015)
5. Roberts, K., et al.: A flexible framework for recognizing events, temporal expressions, and temporal relations in clinical text. J. Am. Med. Inform. Assoc. **20**(5), 867–875 (2013). https://doi.org/10.1136/amiajnl-2013-001619

# A Feasibility Study of an ICT Based Training for Older People with Mild Cognitive Impairment: Future Perspective for Designers and Health Professionals

Roberta Bevilacqua[1]($\boxtimes$), Elena Gambella[2], Elisa Felici[1], Patrizia Civerchia[2], Giovanni R. Riccardi[3], Susi Paolini[2], Sara Pasquini[2], Giuseppe Pelliccioni[2], and Elvira Maranesi[1,3]

[1] Scientific Direction, IRCCS INRCA, Ancona, Italy
r.bevilacqua@inrca.it
[2] Neurology Unit, IRCCS INRCA, Ancona, Italy
[3] Clinical Unit of Physical Rehabilitation, IRCCS INRCA, Ancona, Italy

**Abstract.** The aim of this study was to investigate the feasibility of a cognitive training for older people with MCI, performed through a easy-to-use platform, Myro. A 3-week study was made to test the feasibility of the cognitive training, involving three older people. A mixed-method approach, including neuropsychological tests and structured interviews was used for data collection. The effect of training was assessed by comparing outcome measures in pre- and post-test. Overall, the device was easy to use and accepted by outpatients. Use of technology in cognitive training of older outpatients with MCI was feasible and well accepted.

**Keywords:** Mild cognitive impairment · Robot technology · Cognitive training

## 1 Introduction

Mild Cognitive Impairment (MCI) represents a grey zone along the continuum between normal aging and early dementia [1–3]. MCI is characterized by a slightly impaired performance in one or more cognitive domains (i.e. memory, executive function, attention, language, and visuospatial skills), which does not interfere with psychosocial functioning and does not meet the criteria for dementia [4]. Accumulating evidence indicates that cognitive training may act on the preserved cognitive plasticity of subjects affected by MCI [5], preserving cognitive functioning and enhancing compensatory strategies to support those already affected by the neurodegenerative process [5, 6]. Although executive functions and attentional control are involved both in the execution of memory tasks [7] and in daily life activities [8], there are a few studies focused on their training in MCI [9]. Cognitive technology-based interventions appear to be useful in promoting significant improvements in executive functions in MCI subjects [10, 11]. Indeed, computerized cognitive training is effective on global cognition, select cognitive domains, and psychosocial functioning in people with MCI [10, 12]. The types of technology used

C. Stephanidis et al. (Eds.): HCII 2021, CCIS 1499, pp. 139–146, 2021.
https://doi.org/10.1007/978-3-030-90179-0_19

may vary across studies including computers, tablets, virtual reality (VR), and gaming consoles [10]. In this study, we evaluate the feasibility of a cognitive training based on the application of a technological platform for neurocognitive recovery (Myro-Therapy Desk) of MCI subjects. The input from the present case study will inform future and extended interventions in the field.

## 2   Materials and Methods

### 2.1   Study Design

This study was an open pilot aims to examine the feasibility and acceptability of a technological cognitive training in the older adults with MCI. Investigators, psychologists, and participants were aware of the study intervention and a control group was not included.

### 2.2   Participant

Three participants were recruited in the IRCCS INRCA Neurology Unit. To be eligible, subjects must meet the following inclusion criteria: (1) age > 65 years; (2) diagnosis of MCI according to NIA-AA criteria [15], clinical dementia rating scale (CDR) equal to 0.5 and Mini Mental State Examination (MMSE) $\geq$ 24; (3) slight deficits in Executive Functions; (4) no evidence of anxious depressive state; (5) absence of any physical condition that could preclude regular attendance at the intervention program; (6) adequate visual and auditory acuity to complete training; a comprehensive ophthalmological examination was performed in all cases. Baseline patients' characteristics are reported in Table 1.

**Table 1.** Baseline patient demographic characteristics.

| Participant | Age (years) | Gender | Education (years) | MMSE |
|---|---|---|---|---|
| 1 | 80 | M | 8 | 26 |
| 2 | 70 | M | 13 | 29 |
| 3 | 77 | F | 5 | 25 |

M = male; F = female; MMSE = Mini Mental State Examination [16].

Subject 1: A 80-year-old retired mechanic with good problem-solving skills. He was not familiar with technology and he didn't routinely use the computer or surf the Internet. At the first session, he was motivated to prevent a deterioration of the mild cognitive difficulties. He was confident on his memory. The global cognitive state was good enough (Table 2) there were occasional alterations of attention and episodic tremors of the hand. During the training, however, a generalized cognitive slowing was clear and required extending the default times of the exercises.

Subject 2: A 70-year-old retired bookkeeper who had a strong motivation for personal growth. He loved literature and philosophy, he was very familiar with technology and usually surfed the internet. He was concerned for his recent cognitive changes. However, he was still confident on his memory and problem-solving skills in everyday life. At the first session, he was motivated to try to do all that he could to prevent a deterioration of his difficulties. Cognitive evaluation showed deficits in long-term verbal memory, attention, executive functions and visual-spatial skills (Table 2). Furthermore, a speech disorder characterized by anomia and circumlocutions was clear.

Subject 3: This 77-year-old woman is a retired head department of a children's clothing factory. She was not familiar with technology and that she was unable to use the computer or surf the internet. The pain in her hand impeded her from writing and performing manual work. She was confident on her memory but, at the same time, she reported a state of anxiety that made it difficult to solve the problems of daily life. At the beginning, she was not confident in using technology for training; however, she was motivated to get involved in new situations, despite the age. Neuropsychological evaluation showed deficits in attention, executive functions and visual-spatial skills, with a potential constructive apraxia in the copying of figures.

## 2.3  Procedure

The study took place at the IRCCS INRCA Hospital, Ancona, Italy. The feasibility study was performed from December 2, 2019, to January 13, 2020. All enrolled outpatients participated in 6 individual sessions, 2 times a week over 3 weeks, consisting of 45-min sessions per day using Myro system. Myro is a sensor-based platform designed to support patients with deficits in motor function, concentration, selective attention, visual-spatial perception, and spatial-perceptive ability [13]. It consists in a table, adjustable in height and inclination, with the entirely touch surface (similar to a smartphone or tablet) with which the subject interacts by touching the screen with his hand or with various objects supplied (Fig. 1).

**Fig. 1.** Myro system.

Myro also offers a multitude of neurocognitive modules, which can be completed either alone or in multiplayer mode and the bilateral work enables a better rewiring of the hemispheres. Each training session was divided into three parts: introduction and discussion of homework, cognitive exercises with Myro, conclusions and assignment of tasks for the next session.

### 2.4  Myro-Therapy Desk Intervention

The training was conducted by two psychologists who took care of starting the tool and choosing and preparing the exercises, as well as explaining the cognitive functions involved in performing the specific task. Among all the cognitive exercises proposed by Myro, those most suitable for the type and age of participants were selected. The exercises chosen aimed to stimulate primarily the executive functions, the attentive control, the visual-spatial skills such as spatial perception, spatial visualization and in some cases mental rotation. The activities can therefore be grouped into two categories: introductory and preparatory games and cognitive therapy games.

### 2.5  Data Collection

In order to evaluate the feasibility and usefulness of the Myro-Therapy Desk Intervention, a pre - post training evaluation was carried out. The outcome measurements of the study focused on the training sessions, verifying time consumption and number of completers; the management, assessing the work environment, workflow, and technical challenges; the experience of the cognitive rehabilitation through an innovative device such as Myro from the view of the patients. A series of standardized neuropsychological tests were used: Mini Mental State Examination (MMSE) [14], Copy of Rey's Figure (ROCF) [15], Poppelreuter-Ghent's Overlapping Figures Test (PGT) [16], Trail Making Test (TMT A and B) [17], Free and Cued Selective Reminding Test (FCSRT) [18], Digit Span forward (SPAN F) and backward (SPAN B) [19, 20], Semantic/Category Subtest of verbal fluency test (VFT) [21, 22] and Stroop test [23].

### 2.6  Statistical Analysis

Descriptive statistics were computed for participant characteristics, feasibility and acceptability. The Student's T test for paired samples was performed to assess the presence of significant differences between the pre- and post-test in the neuropsychological outcomes.

## 3  Results

A total of 3 people (one woman and two men) were admitted to the feasibility study. The mean age of the subjects was $75.7 \pm 5.13$ years, the duration of education was $8.66 \pm 4.04$ years and the initial MMSE score was $27.33 \pm 1.53$. The values of the neuropsychological test scores, pre and post intervention are reported in Table 2.

Comparing the pre and post test scores, a significant improvement ($p < 0.05$) both in semantic fluence and in the free delayed recall of the FCSRT was observed (Table 2). Moreover, two subjects reported an improvement in the Poppelreuter-Ghent's Overlapping Figures Test although not significant (Table 2). An improvement ($p = 0.057$) for the backward component of the Digit Span Test was also observed (Table 2).

**Table 2.** Values of the neuropsychological test scores, pre and post intervention.

| Subject | Pre | | | | Post | | | | p (T Test) |
|---|---|---|---|---|---|---|---|---|---|
| | 1 | 2 | 3 | Mean (sd) | 1 | 2 | 3 | Mean (sd) | |
| MMSE | 26 | 29 | 27 | 27.3 (1.5) | 27 | 29 | 28 | 28 (1) | 0.18 |
| ROCF | 31 | 33 | 22 | 28.7 (5.9) | 29 | 36 | 32 | 32.3 (3.5) | 0.40 |
| TMT-A | 74 | 66 | 60 | 66.7 (7.0) | 85 | 65 | 72 | 74 (10.1) | 0.22 |
| TMT-B | 234 | 348 | 375 | 319.0 (74.8) | 269 | 447 | 284 | 333.3 (98.7) | 0.82 |
| TMT B-A | 160 | 282 | 315 | 252.3 (81.6) | 184 | 382 | 212 | 259,3 (107.2) | 0.92 |
| FCSRT-IFR | 27 | 27 | 32 | 28.7 (2.9) | 29 | 31 | 33 | 31 (2) | 0.12 |
| FCSRT-ITR | 35 | 35 | 36 | 35.3 (0.6) | 36 | 36 | 36 | 36 (0) | 0.18 |
| FCSRT-DFR | 6 | 8 | 10 | 8 (2) | 10 | 11 | 12 | 11 (1) | 0.035 |
| FCSRT-DTR | 11 | 12 | 12 | 11.7 (0.6) | 12 | 12 | 12 | 12 (0) | 0.42 |
| FCSRT-ISC | 0.9 | 0.9 | 1 | 0.9 (0.1) | 1 | 1 | 1 | 1 (0) | 0.18 |
| PGT-MF | 29.7 | 27 | 29.9 | 28.9 (1.6) | 29.6 | 36 | 34 | 33.2 (3.3) | 0.24 |
| PGT-ML | 28.3 | 19 | 22.3 | 23.2 (4.7) | 23.7 | 31 | 25.2 | 26.6 (3.9) | 0.55 |
| PGT | 58 | 46 | 52.2 | 52.1 (6) | 53.3 | 67 | 59.2 | 59.8 (6.9) | 0.41 |
| Semantic VFT | 31 | 28 | 18 | 25.7 (6.8) | 41 | 37 | 26 | 34.7 (7.8) | 0.0041 |
| Stroop-TI | 27.5 | 194.5 | 100 | 107.3 (83.7) | 33 | 139.5 | 90.5 | 87.7 (53.3) | 0.39 |
| Stroop-EI | 1 | 7 | 17.5 | 8.5 (8.4) | -0.5 | 21 | 2 | 7.5 (11.8) | 0.92 |
| Span F | 4 | 5 | 6 | 5 (1) | 5 | 4 | 4 | 4.3 (0.6) | 0.53 |
| Span B | 3 | 3 | 3 | 3 (0) | 5 | 4 | 4 | 4.3 (0.6) | 0.057 |

*FCSRT immediate free recall (FIR), total immediate recall (ITR), delayed free recall (DFR), delayed total recall (DTR) and Sensitivity Index (ISC); abstract figures (PGT-ML) and common objects (PGT-MF); Stroop Time Interference Index (TI) and Error Interference Index (EI); Span forward (F) and backward (B).

## 4  Discussion

Participants was completers and showed high adherence to training session and homework. The duration of the sessions was adequate; as longer sessions would have been too tiring. It made also possible to adapt the default time of cognitive exercises according to the needs of each participant. The duration of the training was also adequate, allowed the participants to repeat the exercises sufficiently, gradually increasing the level of difficulty. The scalability of the exercises made it possible to create a tailored training program for each, both in content and difficulty making a linear workflow. Consistent with previous study the possibility to personalize the training and the exercises differentiating the stimuli favored engagement [6]. The presence of the psychologists was a key factor in determining ICT-based treatment adherence, consistent with previous studies [24, 25]. Whereas software for cognitive training programs often focused only on the domains of memory and attention [10, 11], the technology-based training in this study attempted to fill the gap by stimulating executive functions, the attention control and visuospatial skills. According to literature, healthy older people who underwent cognitive training on processing speed had a reduction in the risk of dementia compared to the untreated control group, therefore it is extremely important to work on executive functions [26]. Although the study involved only three participants, were investigated the neuropsychological outcomes of the intervention to inform future studies. Consistent with previous studies an improved performance in tasks that required divided attention and discrimination of visual stimuli (i.e. PGT and TMT test) was observed [11]. Only one subject showed an improved executive function ability to tune out irrelevant stimuli keeping attention focused on the main task (Stroop Test). Interestingly, one participant showed the subjective perception of an improvement in the speed of stimulus processing, although this is not detectable by tests. As expected, it was difficult to achieve significant improvement in executive functions and visuospatial abilities because these cognitive functions are more sensitive to age-related changes [9, 27]. Although the direct effects of training on executive functions was scarce, it was possible to observe interesting transfer effects on other functions, consistent with previous studies [10]. Indeed, although memory was not directly stimulated during the training a significant improvement in the delayed free recall of visual stimuli was observed. Probably, the subjects were facilitated in visuospatial analysis and retention of visual material in memory after an extensively work with visual stimuli during the training. According to literature executive functions and attentional control were involved in carrying out memory tasks [7]. Therefore, this could be an interesting transfer effect of the training. In the same way the improvement in the Backward Digit Span Test could be an example of transfer effect about working memory because it recruits central executive resources for successful task performance [28]. Finally, according to literature the observed improvement in category fluency task could be linked to the executive component of verbal fluency which determine the strategic search and retrieval processes of stimuli [29]. This executive component was trained during the sessions, although through visual not verbal stimulus. In addition, semantic fluency was directly stimulated through the training homework. However, the small sample represents a sever limitation to this study, that could only be the basis for future larger-scale clinical trials.

## 5   Conclusion

This study showed that use of the Myro system as a technologic-based training for person with MCI is acceptable and feasible. Use of technology in cognitive training of executive functions, attentional control and visual-spatial skills of older outpatients with MCI holds promise as a non-pharmacological preventive intervention.

## References

1. Reisberg, B., Ferris, S.H., de Leon, M.J., et al.: Stage-specific behavioral, cognitive, and in vivo changes in community residing subjects with age-associated memory impairment and primary degenerative dementia of the Alzheimer type. Drug. Dev. Res. 15(2–3), 101–114 (1988)
2. Petersen, R.C., Smith, G.E., Waring, S.C., et al.: Mild cognitive impairment: clinical characterization and outcome. Arch. Neurol. 56(3), 303–308 (1999)
3. Petersen, R.C., Caracciolo, B., Brayne, C., et al.: Mild cognitive impairment: a concept in evolution. J. Intern. Med. 275(3), 214–228 (2014)

4. Petersen, R.C.: Mild cognitive impairment. Continuum (Minneap Minn) **22**, 404–418 (2016)
5. Olchik, M.R., Farina, J., Steibel, N., Teixeira, A.R., Yassuda, M.S.: Memory training (MT) in mild cognitive impairment (MCI) generates change in cognitive performance. Arch. Gerontol. Geriatr. **56**(3), 442–447 (2013)
6. Simon, S.S., Yokomizo, J.E., Bottino, C.M.C.: Cognitive intervention in amnestic Mild Cognitive Impairment: a systematic review. Neurosci. Biobehav. Rev. **36**, 1163–1178 (2012)
7. Buckner, R.L.: Memory and executive function in aging and AD: multiple factors that cause decline and reserve factors that compensate. Neuron **44**, 195–208 (2004)
8. Aretouli, E., Brandt, J.: Everyday functioning in mild cognitive impairment and its relationship with executive cognition. Int. J. Geriatr. Psychiatry **25**, 224–233 (2010)
9. Zhang, H., et al.: A randomized controlled trial of combined executive function and memory training on the cognitive and noncognitive function of individuals with mild cognitive impairment: study rationale and protocol design. Alzheimer's Dement. Transl. Res. Clin. Interv. **4**, 556–564 (2018)
10. Ge, S., Zhu, Z., Wu, B., McConnell, E.S.: Technology-based cognitive training and rehabilitation interventions for individuals with mild cognitive impairment: a systematic review. BMC Geriatr. **18**, 213 (2018)
11. Lin, F., et al.: Cognitive and neural effects of vision-based speed-of-processing training in older adults with amnestic mild cognitive impairment: a pilot study. J. Am. Geriatr. Soc. **64**, 1293–1298 (2016)
12. Hill, N.T.M., Mowszowski, L., Naismith, S.L., Chadwick, V.L., Valenzuela, M., Lampit, A.: Computerized cognitive training in older adults with mild cognitive impairment or dementia: a systematic review and meta-analysis. Am. J. Psychiatry **174**(4), 329–340 (2017)
13. ECTRON Homepage. https://www.ectron.co.uk/myro-far-reaching-therapy. Accessed 18 Mar 2021
14. Folstein, M.F., Folstein, S.E., McHugh, P.R.: "Mini-mental state". A practical method for grading the cognitive state of patients for the clinician. J. Psychiatr. Res. **12**(3), 189–198 (1975)
15. Caffarra, P., Vezzadini, G., Dieci, F., Zonato, F., Venneri, A.: Rey-Osterrieth complex figure: normative values in an Italian population sample. Neurol. Sci. Official J. Ital. Neurol. Soc. Ital. Soc. Clin. Neurophysiol. **22**, 443–447 (2002)
16. Della Sala, S., Laiacona, M., Spinnler, H., Trivelli, C.: Poppelreuter-Ghent's overlapping figures test: its sensitivity to age, and its clinical use. Arch. Clin. Neuropsychol. Official J. Natl. Acad. Neuropsychologists **10**, 511–534 (1995)
17. Giovagnoli, A.R., Del Pesce, M., Mascheroni, S., Simoncelli, M., Laiacona, M., Capitani, E.: Trail making test: normative values from 287 normal adult controls. Ital. J. Neurol. Sci. **17**(4), 305–309 (1996)
18. Frasson, P., et al.: Free and cued selective reminding test: an Italian normative study. Neurol. Sci. **32**(6), 1057–1062 (2011). https://doi.org/10.1007/s10072-011-0607-3
19. Wechsler, D.: The Measurement of Adult Intelligence, p. 229. Williams & Witkins, Baltimore (1939)
20. Mondini, S., Mapelli, D., Vestri, A., Bisiacchi, P.S.: Esame Neuropsicologico Breve (ENB) Una batteria di test per lo screening neuropsicologico. Raffello Cortina Editore, Milano (2003)
21. Novelli, G., Papagno, C., Capitani, E., Laiacona, M., Vallar, G., Cappa, S.: Tre test clinici di ricerca e produzione lessicale. Taratura su soggetti normali. Arch. Psicol. Neurol. Psichiatr. **47** (1986)
22. Barletta-Rodolfi, C., Gasparini, F., Ghidoni, E.: Kit del Neuropsicologo Italiano. Società Italiana di Neuropsicologia (2011)
23. Caffarra, P., Vezzadini, G., Dieci, F., Zonato, F., Venneri, A.: Una versione abbreviata del test di Stroop: Dati normativi nella popolazione Italiana. Nuova Riv. Neurol. **12**(4), 111–115 (2002)

24. Salthouse, T.A.: General and specific speed mediation of adult age differences in memory. J. Gerontol. B Psychol. Sci. Soc. Sci. **51B**, 30-P42 (1996)
25. Ben-Sadoun, G., Sacco, G., Manera, V., Bourgeois, J., König, A., Foulon, P., et al.: Physical and cognitive stimulation using an exergame in subjects with normal aging, mild and moderate cognitive impairment. JAD **53**(4), 1299–1314 (2016)
26. Edwards, J.D., Xu, H., Clark, D.O., Guey, L.T., Ross, L.A., Unverzagt, F.W.: Speed of processing training results in lower risk of dementia. Alzheimer's Dement. Transl. Res. Clin. Interv. **3**, 603–611 (2017)
27. Borella, E., Carretti, B., Cantarella, A., Riboldi, F., Zavagnin, M., De Beni, R.: Benefits of training visuospatial working memory in young–old and old–old. Develop. Psychol. **50**(3), 714–727 (2014)
28. Hester, R.L., Kinsella, G.J., Ong, B.: Effect of age on forward and backward span tasks. J. Int. Neuropsychol. Soc. **10**, 475–481 (2004)
29. Peter, J., et al.: Category and design fluency in mild cognitive impairment: performance, strategy use, and neural correlates. Neuropsychologia **93**, 21–29 (2016)

# Usability Optimization of National Health Insurance Express App

Li-Hsin Chen and Meng-Cong Zheng[⊠]

Department of Industrial Design, National Taipei University of Technology, 1 Sec. 3, Chung-hsiao E. Rd, Taipei 10608, Taiwan

**Abstract.** In Taiwan, the National Health Insurance Department has promoted the PHR " National Health Insurance Express App, "downloaded 7.3 million times widely used by the public. However, with the mass demand of the public, the interface design and operability seem not good. To understand the experience and problems encountered by the first-time users of the National Health Insurance Express APP. We used the semi-structured interview method and usability scale to know the ranking of preference for functions and the evaluation of interfaces. We found that the most favorite function of the NHIE APP was medical records and medication records, followed by the location query of medical institutions. The core of SUS belonged to the scope of the unacceptable. Through this study, the operation behavior of the APP is understood, summarized, and quantified. "Word narrative", "operation", "functional classification", and "consistent visual style" all need to be optimized. The suggestions are given to help with subsequent development optimization.

**Keywords:** PHR · Interface design · Usability

## 1 Introduction

With the rapid development of the Internet, more and more industries are becoming more real-time, global, and personalized, including the medical application industry, which is closely related to the quality of people's lives. In 1995, the World Health Organization (WHO) suggested that we should change patients' care in medical institutions from passive medicine to active prevention. It intended that patients should actively participate in the creation and maintenance of medical records [5]. American Health Information Management Association (AHIMA) defines PHR as electronic. Users can obtain health Information from any place for individuals to make relevant Health decisions. PHR Information sources include Healthcare providers and patients themselves, and individuals can own and manage PHR Information [1]. Since 2013, National Health Insurance Administration(NHIA) The "Health Care Cloud Enquiry System" and "Health Passbook" have been successively developed by the Health Insurance Department to provide real-time, interactive, and transparent application service systems for Big Data sets. In the same year, the Developer adopted the Hybrid App method to develop the " National Health Insurance Express App " (NHIE APP) on Android and iOS operating platforms

C. Stephanidis et al. (Eds.): HCII 2021, CCIS 1499, pp. 147–154, 2021.
https://doi.org/10.1007/978-3-030-90179-0_20

[2]. Since the launch of the " My Health Bank " system until 2015/03/18, 18,630 people have downloaded it [3]. By the end of December 2018, it had accumulated over 1,000,000 downloads, However, it was clear from the tens of thousands of reviews and feedback on the two major download platforms, Google Play and AppStore, that users had a negative view of the application and found it lacking usability. Therefore, this study will conduct on the mobile interface of the existing NHIE APP, understand the operational problems of the APP, summarize and give optimization suggestions to the subsequent developers.

## 2  Method

This study used NHIE App, downloaded 7.3 million times. Meanwhile, the Health Care category ranked No.1 in Google Play, downloaded and ranked No.1 in App Store in Taiwan 2020. Analyze the online comments of App Store with the Content analysis method. Select 800 comments (about 1/10) from 8059 comments in 2019–2020 and randomly select them. Regardless of the number of stars, involving political issues, meaningless, and simple criticism, research will not accept any substantive function content, Finally, 296 valid comments were adopted for content analysis. Analyze and filter meaningful feedback that users write in free form on App Sore. It is classified according to the major function categories released by the Ministry of Health and Welfare. (Hospitals, My Health Bank, E-Counter, Search, Service, Spots, NHI Acts, ER Beds, First Aids, FAQs,Add the Verify and Login category; exclude outside the chain web pages. A total of 16 categories of functions were analyzed by statistical feedback, and we screened out six functions for which more users gave negative feedback. Also, the test project of Verify and Login is added. Because of entering My Health Bank, e-counter... And other functions need to go through this process, above a total of seven operations of the experiment.

We asked participants to complete seven experimental tasks, and the condition was no experience with NHIE App. The experiment includes the following items: 1. "Complete verification and login": Login function test; 2. "Inform the examiner. of the names of the two drugs used on the specified treatment date": My Health Bank functional test; 3. "Binding designated dependents": My Health Bank function test; 4. "Find the amount of health insurance coverage at the specified time": E-Counter functional test; 5. "Find the designated dental clinic within a radius of one kilometer from your location": inquire about the Search; 6. "Find the price of specified drugs: medical quick search function test"; 7. "Find the designated hospital and inform the examiner if the bed is full.: ER Beds function test" The selected participants, who had not used the National Health Care Initiative Express, recruited 30 subjects, half male and half female, ranging in age from 21 to 32, with no medical background. PHR = 8 for women and PHR = 2 for men; Their behaviors were recorded by the video camera. Their ranking of function and interface features was evaluated using a semi-structured interview and usability scale. The experiment is divided into the following stages: 1. Participants will sign an Informed Consent Form and be given a set of accounts and passwords for the experiment. 2. The participants completed the assigned interface operation tasks and recorded the process by video. 3. Semi-structured interviews were conducted at the end of the tasks to understand their difficulties. 4. Let the subjects complete the System Usability Scale (SUS), the ATTrack-Diff questionnaire and ranked the NHIE APP function preferences.

## 3   Results

All subjects completed the Usability Scale(SUS)。(Table 1. System Usability Scale) An unacceptable score ranges from 0 to 50, 51 to 70 is an acceptable score, and a score above 71 is acceptable. A SUS average score above 68 is an above-average score. John Brooke describes the SUS score in terms of acceptability [4]. The average score for SUS in the NHIE App study was 26.06, Belonging to the scope of the unacceptable.; There were 27 participants with a score of 0 to 50, 3 with a score of 51 to 70, and no participants with a score higher than 71. 90% of the participants gave an evaluation of less than 50.

**Table 1.**  System usability scale (2013)

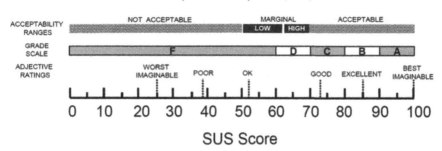

In the task operation, no user can complete all tasks in the shortest path.(see Fig. 1. Pages schematic problem). Below is the completion time of the task: Only in task one (complete verification and login), subjects underestimated the predicted time. This task requires proof that the user is a natural person and must be completed in order to proceed with other charges. The average actual time for users to complete task 1 was 21 s longer than the estimated time, and 93% of respondents said that verification and login should be more visible. (see Fig. 1-a) And that the current placement is not appropriate. Almost every participant mistakenly clicked on an external link while performing a task. Fifty-three percent of respondents said they did not understand the term "device verification" and could not find the login button because they ignored it. The other tasks' actual operation time was shorter than the estimated time. The participants in task 6 (to find the specified drug price) counted an extra 4 min and 17 s on average, which was the highest. Fifty-six percent reviewed that the feature title (Search) and the feature title (History) caused confusion and made it difficult to find a specific drug price (Table 2).

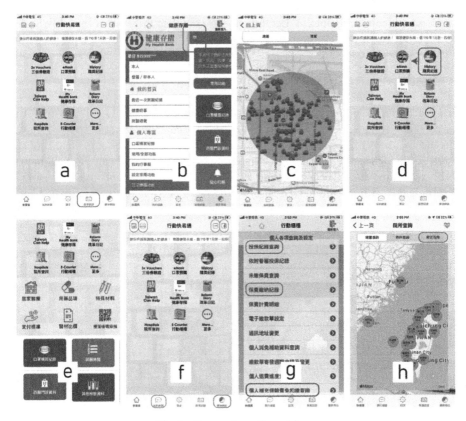

**Fig. 1.** Pages schematic problem.

**Table 2.** Completion time of the task.

|          | Estimated average | Actual completion average | The time difference |
|----------|-------------------|---------------------------|---------------------|
| Task1    | 3min24s           | 3min45s                   | -21s                |
| Task2    | 5min              | 2min23s                   | 2min37s             |
| Task3    | 5min48s           | 3min39s                   | 2min9s              |
| Task4    | 4min42s           | 3min5s                    | 1min37s             |
| Task5    | 4min54s           | 3min1s                    | 1min53s             |
| Task6    | 5min30s           | 1min13s                   | 4min17s             |
| Task7    | 5min10s           | 2min53s                   | 2min17s             |

After completion of the task, we provided subjects to fill in the Attrakdiff-Short Scale. Each of the ten questions contains positive and negative adjectives, and each pair of adjectives is divided into seven equal parts (−3, −2, −1, 0, 1, 2, 3). 5 items are positive fractions, and five items are negative fractions. The results showed that the score of the negative question "Confusing/Structure-2.3" and the positive question "Simple/Complicated" was 2.1, (Table 3. AttrakDiff-Short Average scores.)both of which were higher than the average. Both results could correspond to the interface problems encountered by the subjects.

Table 3. AttrakDiff-Short average scores.

|  | Positive and negative adjectives | Average score |
|---|---|---|
| Positive1 | Simple/Complicated | 2.1 |
| Positive2 | Practical/Impractical | 0.8 |
| Positive3 | Stylish/Tacky | 1.3 |
| Positive4 | Predictable/Unpredictable | 1.2 |
| Positive5 | Good/Bad | 1.1 |
| Negative1 | Ugly/Beautiful | −1.2 |
| Negative2 | Cheap/Premium | −1.4 |
| Negative3 | Unimaginative/Creative | −1.2 |
| Negative4 | Confusing/Structured | −2.3 |
| Negative5 | Dull/Captivating | −1.1 |

After completing the six tasks, the participants were given an explanation of each function and then asked to rank the 16 functions in the NHIE App according to their preference. (Table 4. Average of the liking scores) 60% of the respondents said that their favorite function was "My Health Bank" (medical records and medication records, etc.), 93% of the respondents said that they liked the function of consulting medical records, but 83% thought the information content was too complicated. For example, there was another Menu Button in this function to display more functions. (see Fig. 1-b) The second favorite feature for 43% of respondents was "Hospitals. "50% of respondents liked the ability to search Hospitals near them. Still, most felt that the medical terminology in the hospital category option was incomprehensible and would be deemed unnecessary by users. And most people think that hospitals within a radius on the map cannot be pressed. (see Fig. 1-c),This caused a lack of further access to hospital information. The third was "eMask" (pre-ordered surgical masks online), with 90% of respondents saying they would prioritize this function because of the global epidemic. Besides, most respondents thought that the function of "history" (the record of pre-purchased masks) should be classified within the eMask, rather than separate into a separate function. (see Fig. 1-d).

**Table 4.** Average of the liking scores.

| Name of the function | Rank | Average of the liking scores |
| --- | --- | --- |
| My health bank | 1 | 1393.7 |
| Hospitals | 2 | 1234.3 |
| eMask | 3 | 1106.2 |
| ER beds | 4 | 1100 |
| First aids | 5 | 1021.8 |
| Mask map, E-Counter | 6 | 993.7 |
| History | 7 | 912.5 |
| Search | 8 | 896.8 |
| Taiwan can help | 9 | 609.3 |
| FAQs | 10 | 556.2 |
| 3x vouchers | 11 | 496.8 |
| Virtual NHI card | 12 | 456.2 |
| Service spots | 13 | 437.5 |
| NHI acts | 14 | 381.2 |
| Reform diary | 15 | 159.3 |

After the task, the participants were interviewed to explain the problems or opinions they encountered during the operation without limitation. If necessary, the interviewees were asked in-depth questions. During the interview, the interviewees gave many feedbacks, further sorted into the following situations:

1. 95% of respondents believe that word statements in the APP will cause misjudgment in operation. For example, the name of the E-counter is challenging to be associated with the related query of health insurance.
2. 90% of the respondents think that the visual style of APP content is inconsistent. For example, the Icon style on the Home page is different from the type of Icon within the function (see Fig. 1-e).
3. Eighty-two percent of respondents said they encountered buttons that didn't seem to be able to be pressed—for example, the medical hospital symbol in the map in the hospital inquiry.
4. 66% of the interviewees expressed that they had similar words for different functions. For example, the names of service sites and hospital inquiries will cause confusion.
5. 66% of the respondents thought that the APP was too professional in medical terms for them to understand. For example, the medical institution classification term inquired by the hospital.
6. 56% of the subjects thought that the functional classification was illogical. For example, the purchase record should be classified in the mask pre-order.

7.  All the subjects indicated that there were too many external links in the APP, which would cause difficulties in operation. For example, the marked position on the page will lead to the outer chain (see Fig. 1-f).

# 4   Discussion

A In the login function test, most people said that the process was too complicated, except that the subjects reported that the function should be in the upper right corner and left corner or classified to the set function. 40% of the subjects would doubt the path they were operating and return to the original screen due to too many levels, only to find that they had to go through these processes the second time. This may increase the actual average operation time because most subjects expect verification logins to be fast and smooth. In the functional test of "My Health Bank," we can find that the page content is composed of forms and texts after clicking the main project icon. Some forms can be connected to the next page, while others can't. When clicking on the "medical overview" function, there will be two classified sections: "number of medical treatment" and "medical history," the first item that shows out is number of medical treatment, must do the second click to see the medical history, 80% of the participants thought the page should first appear "medical history" because is an issue they are more concern about. Despite the operational problems, the function ranking still showed that subjects preferred this function the most. We can see that subjects pay the most attention to knowing their medical records, but many poor operation conditions still make users feel confused and frustrated. In the test of the "e-counter" function, most people said that there were too many content options and many words were repeated. For example, there are 15 buttons on the same page, among which three "Insurance Record Enquiry," "Premium Payment Record," and "Individual Supplementary Premium Enquiry" have similar meanings (Fig. 1-g). The correct step was tap (insurance record query), but 56% of respondents repeated the last two functions and said the text was too similar to find the correct option. In addition, the word "e-counter" also confused many subjects in the task test of "Binding Design-Dependents ", who usually believed that "e-counter" represented the function of handling the Binding of family members: In the "Hospitals" test, which ranked second. When clicking the first screen, there are three fields from left to right: "map search," "condition search" (department, type, etc.), and "nearby institutes." The first thing the user will see is how many institutions there are in different administrative regions of Taiwan. (Fig. 1-h) After this task, most of the subjects expressed that (how many hospitals there are in each administrative area) was not the first thing they wanted to see. Instead, the first they wanted to see was the nearby hospitals listed in the third column. Most of the subjects wanted to see their location and the map of the surrounding hospitals. In the "Search" function test, there are many situations. Some people think that the word "Search" is about searching hospitals or searching medical records, but in fact, this function is mainly about the cost of medicinal materials and so on. Most of the feedback mentioned above is due to the fact that the meaning of the function name is too wide to be better and accurate, which is also the main reason that 95% of the respondents believe that the text description in the APP will cause misjudgment in operation. In the experiments, we found that the main interface design problems were unclear text description, illogical function classification, and important information placement in hidden places.

## 5  Conclusion

This study enumerates the operational behaviors and problems of inexperienced users in operating the NHIE APP interface. To understand the ranking of users' preferences for various functions, "My Health Bank" was the top three preferred by users to check their medical records, followed by "Hospitals": to check nearby Hospitals and "Emask": to pre-order masks online and select convenience stores from which to pick up the masks. There are many improvements to be made in terms of the interface's operation, such as more accurate text description and more consistent visual planning of the overall App. The image button should be more prominent and can be clicked. Different functions should be used in terms that better distinguish their use. Over-professional academic language is not helpful to users, so we should use it to make the general public understand the language or use advanced functions to hide it. Functions should have a logical architectural placement. External URL should be placed where they are not easily touched but can still be found. These suggestions will be the direction for future designers to redesign or improve the NHIE App.

## References

1. AHIMA e-HIM Personal Health Record Work Group: Defining Personal Health Record. AHIMA **76**(6), 24-25 (2005)
2. Government Offices Information Notices; no. 318,2014 April. https://www.ndc.gov.tw/default.aspx
3. Government Offices Information Notices; no. 331, May 2015. https://www.ndc.gov.tw/default.aspx
4. Brooke, J.: SUS: a retrospective. J. Usability Stud. **8**(2), 29–40 (2013)
5. World Health Organization (2016) mHealth: use of mobile wireless technologies for public health (2016)

# Preliminary Study on the Multi-person Cooperative Training Module in the Application of Virtual Reality Technology to the Advanced Cardiac Life Support

Hsu-Wen Hung and I.-Jui Lee[(✉)]

Department of Industrial Design, National Taipei University of Technology, Taipei, Taiwan
t108588006@ntut.org.tw, ericlee@ntut.edu.tw

**Abstract.** Advanced cardiac life support (ACLS) is a first-aid procedure that is implemented by multiple individuals through collaboration within a limited time, and it is a necessary first-aid procedure in hospitals. According to the statistics, the number of patients with prehospital cardiac arrest is as high as 20000 per year in Taiwan, but no more than 3% of patients recover and leave the hospital. Hence, it could be seen that cardiopulmonary resuscitation is a first-aid procedure that should be urgently enhanced in emergency medical services, and the training of first-aid members in ACLS is very important. Those ACLS team members also need high communication, tacit understanding and cooperation abilities, in the team besides the professional ability in first-aid.

Besides traditional training, this study hoped to integrate the two different VR immersion technologies into ACLS clinical first-aid training, including: (1) fully immersive virtual reality technology; and (2) semi-immersive virtual reality cave technology (VR-CAVE).

Finally, it could be seen from the interview results that the incorporation of the VR and VR Cave training structures into ACLS clinical first-aid training could make up for the defects of current ACLS first-aid teaching methods and reach the object of multi-person ACLS training. It could be a new multi-person cooperative training method for ACLS teams in clinical first-aid treatment.

**Keywords:** ACLS · Virtual reality · Virtual reality cave · Clinical medical service · First-aid procedure · Multi-person cooperative training

## 1 Introduction

### 1.1 Research Background

**Danger of Sudden Cardiac Arrest**

Sudden cardiac arrest is one of the main reasons for high mortality in the world. It is defined as when the heart stops beating suddenly, causing organs including the brain and heart to lose their functions and fail due to the lack of oxygen. Hence, the mortality

C. Stephanidis et al. (Eds.): HCII 2021, CCIS 1499, pp. 155–162, 2021.
https://doi.org/10.1007/978-3-030-90179-0_21

of patients will be extremely high if they cannot get timely medical aid. Therefore, the American Heart Association (AHA) released the first version of the principle of cardiopulmonary resuscitation, with the emphasis on the importance of medical workers knowing the procedure well. However, most clinical medical workers working on the front line should be supported by advanced cardiac life support (ACLS) to allow the return of spontaneous circulation (ROSC) for patients at the highest probability to reach the objective of first-aid treatment besides being proficient in a completed first-aid procedure, mastering the operation of the first-aid device, the interpretation of vital signs of patients and proper use of all kinds of medicines.

## 1.2  Research Motivations

### The Weakness of the Current ACLS Training Methods

There are a number of common weaknesses in current teaching methods: (1) current evaluation methods focus on the performance of clinical technology, so the feelings of patients and the importance of communication among members will be ignored for simulated patients having no real response [1]; (2) there is no timely correction feedback for the operation of clinical techniques, so they cannot judge whether their operations are right or not; and (3) they do not understand the importance of ACLS procedures, since there is one-way interaction only with simulated patients and they know nothing about the differences in the vital signs of patients if the treatment procedure is wrong [2]. Therefore, as students will be unable to improve their sense of success and will have less learning motivation, ACLS learning is not ideal.

## 1.3  Research Objectives

This study hoped to design a new ACLS training mechanism by integrating with the advantage of VR and VR Cave to improve the ability of emergency medical workers in regards to first-aid procedures and multi-person cooperation. In the training mechanism, this study paid more attention to the features of multi-person cooperation training to enhance the emergency medical workers' ability to master the first-aid procedures. Through multi-person training, the students were encouraged to finish difficult cooperative first-aid treatment and correct operation tasks through communication, teamwork and professional ability exploration in a limited time, so as to improve their ability to be more familiar with clinical operations and quickly organize teams according to the system and complete process. Therefore, the purposes of this study were as follows:

1. To conclude the strength and weaknesses of the present ACLS in traditional teaching methods from interviews with experts and to find out the key points that ACLS should focus on.
2. To explore the advantages of VR and VR Cave, as well as how to master the technology and apply it to ACLS first-aid training.
3. To suggest a set of ACLS clinical first-aid training procedure meeting the needs of multi-person cooperation training.

4. According to the interview result, to verify that the ACLS clinical first-aid education training procedure was an improvement to the traditional teaching method and
   implementation on feasibility evaluation.

## 2   Related Work

### 2.1   First-Aid Procedures of ACLS

Advanced cardiac life support (ACLS) is used mainly to provide emergent treatment for
patients losing their cardiopulmonary function and help them recover so that patients
can return to spontaneous circulation and stay alive. According to the guidelines of
the American Heart Association, there are usually four to six members on the ACLS
team, and they are given different tasks according to their specific roles in the team
during the training of ACLS first-aid procedures. Besides, there will be supervision and
evaluation in the training. ACLS is a first-aid procedure that is used to rescue patients
who are losing their cardiopulmonary function and is based on teamwork, coordination
and communication [3]. Since it is time sensitive, team members should apply their
medical knowledge within a short time (in areas such as medication processes and rapid
patient diagnosis) and clinical skills (such as CPR and airway) to reach the first-aid
objective effectively [2].

### 2.2   Current ACLS Training Methods

The present ACLS training methods for the medical workers are: (1) reading training
manuals and learning about procedures; (2) teaching case references; (3) watching films
to simulate and study; (4) using paper-based tests; and (5) learning from clinical situations
[4]. However, except for the clinical situation teaching, most of these procedures cannot
be directly used during first-aid treatment.

   Finally, it can be seen that students might learn the theoretical basis of ACLS, but it
is hard to improve the proficiency of their clinical skills and their communication skills
with members. Therefore, how to provide a team with practical training is the main
target of ACLS training, as current training modes lack teamwork and on-site practice
mechanisms that result in the high human resource cost of clinical situation teaching.

### 2.3   Application of Virtual Reality

There are a number of practical aspects to virtual reality, such as intuitive operation,
multi-layer sensory stimulations and interactive experiences, which provide a fully-
immersive 3D virtual environment. Through the performance of head-mounted displays
(HMD), multiple situations can be reached, and users can have much more outdoor
experiences with virtual objects [5].

### 2.4  Application of Virtual Reality Cave

Compared with the individual immersion of a head-mounted display, the environment of virtual reality cave puts emphasis on cooperative study, so as to provide a virtual environment with multi-people situational simulation that promotes increased participation. Users can reach the effect of integration between reality and virtuality in the CAVE [6]. The VR Cave environment can maintain the advantage of virtual reality under different multi-person cooperation modes. Cave provides a highly simulated virtual environment and maintains the virtual-reality feedback and interaction of the virtual environment among users [7].

### 2.5  Summary

This study used ACLS team training with VR and VR Cave as the principal axis. The literature review of the advantages of VR and VR Cave in ACLS emphasized that an immersive environment can maintain the interaction with the real world, so as to reach an interactive balance in team cooperation. With the target improving team cooperation and communication ability, it could increase the ACLS clinical first-aid treatment and build up the ACLS Team Dynamic VR clinical first-aid education training procedure. The procedure was classified to sort out a level of composition and questionnaire evaluation indicator. The modified Delphi method was used to hold discussions with experts to verify that the advantages of VR and VR Cave could be incorporated into the ACLS clinical first-aid treatment education training and improve the defects of the traditional ACLS education method.

## 3  Methods

### 3.1  Recruitment of Experts

This study adopted the modified Delphi method [8] and made use of interviews with experts. The interview objects in this study were five medical workers with an ACLS license and at least one year of clinical experience, three engineers with VR project experience, and two educators with experience in using VR media. There were a total of 10 experts in the interview. Before the interview, this study presented a complete explanation of the advantages of VR and VR Cave and an introduction to the whole study object and process. Through the assistance of the 10 cross-filed experts, the researcher planned a suitable ACLS team dynamic VR system procedure, as a reference for system development in the future.

### 3.2  Experimental Procedure of the System

In the implementation, the researcher divided the study content into four different levels (1) stereoscopic intuitive spatial operability; (2) interactive immersion; (3) remote application; and (4) team cooperation promotion. The system procedure was then sorted to be questionnaire evaluation indicator according to the four different levels, after which the modified Delphi method was used to test the VR ACLS clinical first-aid education system procedure.

The experimental procedure consisted of a two-phased investigation. In phase one, there was a full introduction to the advantages of VR and VR Cave through the present videos on VR ACLS training [9] and VR Cave cooperation contents, which allowed the 10 cross-field experts to make suggestions on incorporating the advantages of VR and VR Cave into the ACLS first-aid operation procedure. In addition, the ACLS Team Dynamic VR system procedures designed by this study were evaluated by the experts in the form of a questionnaire evaluation, so as to compare the pros-and-cons of traditional VR and ACLS Team Dynamic VR.

In phase two, there was a modification of the questionnaire according to the professional opinions given by the experts in the first phase, and the feasibility of the ACLS Team Dynamic VR training system procedure was further verified in the questionnaire interviews so as to explore how to help students understand the interpretation of ACLS, get familiar with the first aid process, and improve their communication skills and teamwork through the system, which was deemed as a new ACLS education training method. If the interview results showed there were still incomprehensible items, in-depth interviews would be held, so as to objectively sort out the interview result and test the ACLS Team Dynamic VR system procedure.

### 3.3  System Structure

According to the literature review of VR and VR Cave, this study divided the ACLS Team Dynamic VR system procedure into three phases, as described below.

Phase one: Creation of a highly simulated ACLS clinical first-aid situational simulation with a VR system.

Phase one was based on creating a highly simulated ACLS clinical first-aid simulation with a VR system, including the use of first-aid tools, judging the patient's heart rhythm, and undertaking cardiopulmonary resuscitation, electric shock and other first-aid operation simulations.

Phase two: Synchronous picture output in VR Cave.

After the first-aid situation through the VR system, the VR first-aid procedure picture was output synchronously to VR Cave as the training material for the ACLS team's first-aid operation with VR Cave. The ACLS members in the VR Cave then engaged in a multi-person cooperation procedure with VR Cave according to the teaching materials to engage in ACLS clinical first-aid operation training.

Phase three: Remote guidance operation.

At the same time, the ACLS Team Dynamic VR system presented a teleguidance operation through VR and a dynamic capture system, so that a remote clinical guidance physician could engage in real-time guidance of the ACLS members to rectify their operations in clinical first-aid operations and provide timely feedback through remote cooperation methods.

### 3.4  Evaluation Tools

The modified Delphi method was evaluated with a Likert 7-point scale, which was used to quantify the feedback of the experts. The scores ranged from 1 (disagree the most) to 7 (agree the most), and the measurement standards were as follows:

The mean was used to indicate the concentration of the statistical data. When the mean (M) was not less than 5.5, it meant that the experts felt the indicator was very important; the mean of the indicator would then be compared with the mode to judge whether the indicator was consistent with the opinion of the experts.

The quartile deviation was mainly based on the quartile deviation of the opinion distribution of each questionnaire index to judge the consensus. When the quartile deviation was no more than 0.6, it meant that the experts had reached high consent on the indicator; when it ranged from 0.6 to 1.0, it meant that medium consensus had been reached. When the quartile deviation was greater than 1.0, it meant that the experts could not reach the consent. If 75% of all indicators reached the high consent, it meant that the experts had reached the high consistency and the questionnaire investigation could be completed.

## 4  Results

In the study, two phases of questionnaire investigations are carried in the experts' interview with the Modified Delphi method. The total number of questionnaires in phase one is 10, and the recovery rate is 100%; while that in phase two is 8 and the recovery rate is 80%.

### 4.1  Result of the First Questionnaire with Modified Delphi Method

After the ACLS Team Dynamic VR System Procedure – First Questionnaire Investigation for Expert was recovered, the results of checking the evaluation value answered by statistical experts and scholars are calculated. The mean of the four indicators was no more than 5.5, which indicated the importance of the evaluation indicators could not reach the satisfaction of the experts. There were five indicators with quartile deviations that were no more than 0.6, indicating that the experts only reached high consent on only 50% of the indicators. Hence, based on the suggestions made by the experts, the content and the ACLS Team Dynamic VR system procedures were rectified to undertake the second questionnaire investigation based on the modified Delphi method.

**Rectifying of First Questionnaire with Modified Delphi Method**
This study rectified the ACLS Team Dynamic VR system procedures according to the result of the first questionnaire based on the modified Delphi method. First, there was an in-depth interview with the experts about the evaluation indicators that could not reach the mean so as to gain their feedback. The experts showed that the evaluation indicators should be more intuitive and that indicators should be added with correspondent application case to add students' comprehension and mastery of ACLS operation, such as the specific ability of VR in the application of clinical ACLS teaching or the existence of student anxiety during the learning procedure.

After rectifying the first questionnaire with the modified Delphi method and the ACLS Team Dynamic VR system procedure in stage three, the second interview questionnaire investigation based on the modified Delphi method was implemented.

**Rectifying of Second Questionnaire with Modified Delphi Method**
This study recovered the ACLS Team Dynamic VR System Procedure Second Experts Questionnaire Investigation. The investigation result indicated that there is no project that the mean is no more than 5.5 in all levels of composition, meaning that all indicators were highly important. However, there is a total of 12 quartile deviations of all indicators after rectifying no more than 0.6, meaning the experts reached high consent on all indicators. Hence, the interviews using the modified Delphi method of this study were completed.

**Suggesting Rectifying to Rectify the Second Questionnaire with Modified Delphi Method**
This study performed in-depth interviews with experts according to the data result of the second questionnaire using the modified Delphi method. The experts provided feedback after the interviews. The experts showed how the evaluation indicators should be clarified using situational diagrams. Hence, this study rectified the ACLS Team Dynamic VR system procedures according to the in-depth interviews with the experts. The rectified and newly-added situational diagrams are shown below.

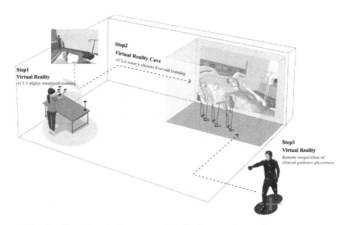

**Fig. 1.** Situational diagrams of ACLS team dynamic VR system

### 4.2   Conclusion-Result Analysis of ACLS Team Dynamic VR System

This study verified the ACLS Team Dynamics VR system procedure through the questionnaire data using the modified Delphi method in two phases. In addition to describing the standard ACLS first-aid working procedure, it also focused on multi-person cooperation. The advantages of the VR and VR Cave systems were combined and input into the ACLS clinical first-aid training, so as to enhance the team members' ACLS clinical cooperation operation. There were high advantages in all levels of composition, and the experts had high consent. Thus, the results verified that the ACLS Team Dynamic VR system procedure in this study was an improvement of the present ACLS clinical first-aid training.

## 5  Future Development

This study applied the VR and VR Cave systems to ACLS clinical first-aid education. The feasibility and satisfaction of the teaching procedures were verified through the expert interviews and data analysis. In the future, there will be a buildup of the actual system according to the verification procedure in the system, so as to introduce the system procedure of this study into the first-aid operations in other medical fields for further development.

## References

1. Moore, N., Yoo, S., Poronnik, P., Brown, M., Ahmadpour, N.: Exploring user needs in the development of a virtual reality-based advanced life support training platform: exploratory usability study. JMIR Serious Games 8(3), e20797 (2020)
2. Khanal, P., et al.: Collaborative virtual reality based advanced cardiac life support training simulator using virtual reality principles. J. Biomed. Inform. 51, 49–59 (2014)
3. Neumar, R.W., et al.: Part 8: adult advanced cardiovascular life support: 2010 American heart association guidelines for cardiopulmonary resuscitation and emergency cardiovascular care. Circulation 122(18_suppl_3), S729–S767 (2010)
4. Jafarizadeh, H., Moradi, Y., Rasouli, J., Zeinalzadeh, S.: The effect of scenario-based and participatory method of cardiopulmonary resuscitation (CPR) training on the knowledge of basic and advanced life support (BLS and ACLS) in emergency medical technicians. Medico Legal Update 20(2), 245–249 (2020)
5. Chun, H.W., Han, M.K., Jang, J.H.: Application trends in virtual reality. Electron. Telecommun. Trends 32(1), 93–101 (2017)
6. DeFanti, T.A., et al.: The StarCAVE, a third-generation CAVE and virtual reality OptIPortal. Future Gener. Comput. Syst. 25(2), 169–178 (2009)
7. Peters, E., et al.: Design for collaboration in mixed reality: technical challenges and solutions. In: 2016 8th International Conference on Games and Virtual Worlds for Serious Applications (VS-GAMES), pp. 1–7. IEEE, September 2016
8. Delbecq, A.L., Van de Ven, A.H., Gustafson, D.H.: Group Techniques for Program Planning: A Guide to Nominal Group and Delphi Processes. Scott, Foresman (1975)
9. Katz, D., et al.: Utilization of a voice-based virtual reality advanced cardiac life support team leader refresher: prospective observational study. J. Med. Internet Res. 22(3), e17425 (2020)

# Study on the Step-By-Step Service Design and Service Strategy of CoVID-19 Prevention and Control Medical Products

Jinze Li[1,2(✉)], Mingming Zong[1(✉)], and Kamolmal Chaisirithanya[2(✉)]

[1] School of Design and Art, Zhuhai College, Beijing Institute of
Technology, Zhuhai, People's Republic of China
[2] School of Education, Bangkok Thonburi University, Bangkok, Thailand

**Abstract.** Purpose: Through service design concepts, explore the system operation and service experience of medical prevention and control products and services in large-scale public infectious diseases, and analyze service design touch points based on the principles of ease of use, satisfaction, and effectiveness, so as to achieve product service design and strategy Optimization and collaboration. Method: Taking service design as the concept, adopting "distributed service design" as the method from users to service products to user feedback, deconstructing product design in a way of analysis and comparison, realizing the re-empowerment of the product, and breaking through the recognition of the product itself Know the barriers and improve the service value of products. Result: Constructing a modern medical product service model based on service design and service strategy, combining intelligent design and interactive design experience model, analyzing the user experience and usage needs of medical products in large-scale public infectious diseases from both internal and external service ends. To achieve the optimization of products and services. Conclusion: Describe the service ecology and service blueprint of medical products based on large-scale public infectious diseases, combine service touch points, optimize the service experience from "user" to "design" itself, and improve the overall service design.

**Keywords:** Service design · Service strategy · Design thinking · Cognitive barriers · Service ecology

Phase research results of provincial key platforms and major scientific research projects in Guangdong universities "Welfare, People's Livelihood and Design Services-Guangdong Rural Future Lifestyle System Research" Project Number: 2019KZDZX2029.
In 2021, the research project of party building in colleges and universities in Guangdong Province "Research on the Social Service Mechanism of Colleges and Universities in the Context of Promoting the Party's Innovative Theory in the New Era" Phased Research Results Project Number: 2020MB075.

C. Stephanidis et al. (Eds.): HCII 2021, CCIS 1499, pp. 163–175, 2021.
https://doi.org/10.1007/978-3-030-90179-0_22

## 1   Introduction

Since the outbreak of new coronary pneumonia, many countries and regions around the world have been affected, and the number of patients has continued to increase, resulting in a shortage of medical products and anti-epidemic products. The product quality and product services of anti-epidemic products are very important to the protected groups, which directly leads to In order to determine whether medical care and users can work and live more comfortably and securely in a dangerous environment, the design of medical products and the service experience of the product itself need to be combined with the use of the environment to further deepen and improve, which requires designers to While designing with all our heart, we deeply explore user pain points, needs, etc., and continuously optimize products to assist in design positioning, so that various parts of the link can effectively collaborate, and avoid isolation and separation of these contacts. It is even more necessary for designers to have a global vision, in-depth exploration of user experience combined with intelligent design for future-oriented design and thinking. This article takes the new coronary pneumonia prevention and control medical disposable or reusable wearable products and medical equipment products as the research object to deeply analyze product services and user experience, and provide strategic services to products and services from the perspective of service design and design services. Guide, adjust and summarize, hoping to provide design positioning and design reference for the design and service of medical products.

## 2   New Coronary Pneumonia and Prevention and Control Products

### 2.1   New Crown Pneumonia and Epidemic Prevention and Control

(Corona Virus Disease 2019, COVID-19), referred to as "new coronary pneumonia", since the outbreak of new coronavirus pneumonia in December 2019, the virus has a strong spread and the speed of transmission is fast. In some areas, it has been found that a small number of patients can be infected without symptoms. This has increased the difficulty of preventing and controlling the epidemic. At present, confirmed cases have been discovered in many countries around the world. With the continuous increase in global infection cases, medical prevention and control products are in short supply and are in great demand, such as masks, goggles, gloves, protective clothing, virus detection equipment and kits. Taking medical protective products as an example, in the process of fully guaranteeing the quality and quantity of medical products in the production process, it is necessary to consider the comfort and experience of the product, the use environment of the product and the working environment of the doctor. For example, because some medical staff have been in a closed and isolated working environment for a long time, they need to wear disposable protective equipment such as goggles, protective clothing and medical masks for a long time when they are in contact with patients. People have strangulations and allergies on their faces. Due to the shortage of some products, the unified model is based on the principle of versatility. As a result, some protective clothing is designed to be too lenient after meeting different work actions, which gives medical workers a shuttle It is difficult to walk in an emergency situation in laboratories, laboratories or emergency wards with many equipment. Therefore, it is necessary to comprehensively analyze the practicability, applicability and usability of the product.

## 2.2  Medical Protection Products and Composition

In the process of participating in the treatment and protection of patients with large infectious diseases, in order to stop the virus and fully protect their own safety so that they can perform their work better, they need to wear medical protection products. Common medical personal protective equipment is generally divided into protective masks, protective clothing, isolation clothing and hats, hand protection products, foot isolation products, isolation shields, etc., and their material composition, process, production and use are shown in Table 1 Classification of healthcare products.

## 2.3  Medical Product and Service Logic

From the perspective of use, medical wearable products are mainly divided into disposable and reusable related products. Disposable products such as disposable sterile gloves, sterile gowns, etc., can be used repeatedly, such as doctor's white coat Wait. From the perspective of shape and function, it is divided into conventional type and equipment type. Conventional type such as: auxiliary products for routine testing: equipment type such as: first aid equipment, etc.

From the perspective of design and product service, medical products must first use shape and function as a means of expression, try to hide the mechanical parts inside the product, chamfer the appearance, reduce sharp corners, use curved surfaces and pay attention to the non-slip of the handheld device. The surface can be frosted and so on. Pay attention to the psychological feelings of users, the overall appearance is soft, and the color design does not use irritating pure color design to make the product warm and moist. Secondly, we must take the applicability and ease of use of the product as the design principle, make the product have a sense of relatives and temperature, and comprehensively consider the use environment of the product, the user's various needs and technical conditions, so that the doctor can work together. The patient resonates psychologically and eliminates the patient's anxiety and fear. See the service logic diagram Fig. 1 of the medical product.

**Table 1.** Common medical care product classification (Drawed by the author)

| Name | Protective mask | Protective clothing | Isolation coat | Hand protection | Foot isolation | Isolation shield |
|---|---|---|---|---|---|---|
| **Description** | Consists of one or more masks that have an isolation and barrier effect on virus aerosols, virus-containing liquids, etc. under the action of breathing and other air currents. | It is processed from one or more fabrics that have an isolation effect on virus aerosols, virus-containing liquids, etc. | Most of them are tailored and sewn from non-woven fabrics as the main raw material. One-time use. | It is usually made of materials such as polyvinyl chloride and rubber. Single use | It is generally made of suitable materials, possessing certain strength and blocking viruses. | Usually made of polymer material, composed of foam strips and fixing devices |
| **Common constituent materials** | Composite production of fiber materials and non-woven fabrics | High-density fabrics, coated fabrics, laminated fabrics, fiber materials, etc. | Non-woven fabrics, synthetic materials, fiber materials, etc. | Made of polyethylene (PE), ethylene-vinyl acetate copolymer (EVA) | Commonly environmentally friendly EVE materials, etc. | Optical glass, other combined materials. |
| **Common process** | Meltblown, spunbond, hot air or needle punch, etc. | Woven and non-woven products are sewn by hand or machine. | Manual or machine sewing of woven and non-woven products. | Ingredients, defoaming storage, mixing materials into the trough, dipping PU, lip curling, demoulding, packaging, etc. | High-density environmentally friendly materials are integrated injection molding or synthesis, etc. | A common process is to add some metal oxides, such as iron, chromium, manganese, etc., to optical glass. |
| **Use** | It is used on the face of doctors and patients to block the spread of viruses. It has the effect of Tecan liquid, filtering particles and bacteria, etc. | Protective clothing used for medical protection is used to block the spread of viruses with air or liquids to medical care, etc. | Used in outpatient clinics, inspection rooms, operating rooms, etc. to block viruses, etc. | Used to protect the user's fingers, avoid exposure to the air, prevent infection, etc. | Prevent medical staff from contacting patients' blood, body fluids, secretions, etc. during work | It can block the splash or splash of liquid and blood. |
| **Style** | Disposal, duplex half-face, comprehensive, etc. | Full body pose and so on. | Head cover/half-length (white coat), etc. | Hand wraps etc. | Foot wraps etc. | Eye coverage, etc. |

(continued)

**Table 1.** (*continued*)

| Name | Protective mask | Protective clothing | Isolation coat | Hand protection | Foot isolation | Isolation shield |
|---|---|---|---|---|---|---|
| **Common products** | Medical masks, KN100, KN95 and KN90, etc. | Medical protective clothing, disposable protective clothing, surgical gowns, etc. | Isolation gowns, medical caps, etc. | Medical rubber gloves, sterile film gloves, etc. | Medical isolation shoes, shoe covers, etc. | Medical isolation masks, eye masks, goggles, etc. |
| **Image** | | | | | | |

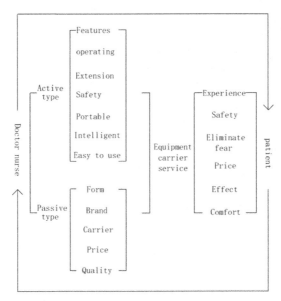

**Fig. 1.** Medical product demand service logic (author self-drawn)

## 3   Service Awareness and Service System

### 3.1   Differences in User Experience and Services

User Experience (UE/UX for short) is a purely subjective feeling established by users in the process of using the product [User Experience-quoted from Baidu Encyclopedia. 2 Service design-quoted from Baidu Encyclopedia.]. From the perspective of the experience of most users after using the product, the product must be safe enough to not be harmed during use. The appearance of the product must be able to impress users and attract people. The function of the product should be perfect, easy to use, able to please users, and be able to resonate well in the process of use and experience. Medical products have stricter requirements for safety and operability due to their special product attributes. The safety of the product is equally important for medical care and users. If there is a problem with safety, all the good experiences that have been established before will collapse instantly. If there is a problem with the product or the operation is cumbersome when the doctor is working, it will bring difficulty to the rescue of the patient, and may also lose valuable rescue time. Therefore, when developing products and researching user groups, it is necessary to deeply analyze the serviceability, difference and particularity of products and user groups based on the needs of special groups.

### 3.2   Service Demand and Service System

The service demand of medical products refers to the empowerment experience of medical equipment based on the operation, experience, function, utility and service of the medical equipment itself, and the feedback and demand after the use of the product. Medical equipment is divided into active demand and passive demand from the perspective of product demand and service for doctors, nurses and patients. Active requirements include requirements for the functionality, intelligence, operability, extended function addition, safety, ease of use, and portability of the equipment when doctors and nurses use the equipment. Passive demand includes product form, brand, carrier, price and quality, etc. The patient's requirements for equipment experience, safety, elimination of fear, price, use effect, and comfort [2].

### 3.3 Design Service and Service Ecology

"Design" is divided into plane, space, animation, interaction, service, industry, architecture and other directions and design fields. Design service refers to the use of design methods to provide customers with problems and related needs from a professional and achievable perspective solution. Medical product design service refers to a project or an all-round activity for the development and design of medical products, covering the whole process of design activities from product planning to design to development, production, and market feedback. After the medical products are put into use, it is necessary to focus on further following up the service effects of the products and the feedback of the users to ensure that the products can be used normally and safely, and to improve the unreasonable operation and poor experience in a timely manner. The product's life cycle from design to mass production to scrap is a product's life cycle [3]. Design itself should be a service activity in the whole process, an experience activity that involves creating and improving with people. Medical product designers are ensuring that products are easy to use., Under the premise of application, the life cycle of the product and the ecological and environmental protection of the service should be fully considered.

### 3.4 Service Design and Service Awareness

Service design is a design activity that effectively plans and organizes the people, basic equipment, communication, materials and other related factors involved in a service to improve user experience and service quality [5]. Service design covers multiple areas. In the public medical system, the experience of service is more needed. When the hospital is saturated with patients and faces most of the medical treatment, how to divert patients to reduce the pressure on the guidance desk, and how to quickly shorten the time when patients are queuing for medical treatment Waiting time has avoided the patient's anxiety and so on. This requires systematic service design and design activities. After entering the 21st century, people's living standards will gradually improve, and the quality and experience of services will gradually improve. We need to have services in the information society. Awareness to promote patient satisfaction, to increase work efficiency to win time for rescue patients.

## 4 Front-End Data and Cognitive Barriers

### 4.1 Technology-Oriented and Design-Oriented

The information and technology of the Internet are massive and constantly updated at all times. This is a challenge for non-intelligent and non-automated medical products themselves. The smart product has a smart terminal, which can obtain information in time by connecting to the Internet, and obtain software updates of the equipment through the terminal program, and online analysis of the detection data to assist the doctor in the self-examination of the patient. At the same time, the updated system data can also be used. Make the equipment have continuous stability, functionality and ease of use. However, non-intelligent devices must have excellent product quality, product functions, and product appearance to ensure their usefulness and irreplaceability. The design of wearable disposable medical protective clothing should be more ergonomic, and the working conditions of medical staff in different environments should be considered. For example, when performing first aid in the field, the toughness of the clothing and the fit during running should be considered., When working in a humid environment, you need to consider the water permeability of the clothing. Medical products in the new era must be technology-oriented and design-oriented at the same time [1].

### 4.2 Data Information and User Research

The birth and continuous development of the Internet has brought new development opportunities for data detection and user research of medical products [6]. Most wearable devices have emerged at the historic moment, and are widely welcomed due to their lightweight appearance and the immediacy of detection data. The use of the equipment by different patients can obtain personalized use plan and crisis response through user analysis and feedback after use. Most medical wearable products in the form of "link" are both versatile. By connecting to different smart terminals, the patient's test data is compared and analyzed through the standard data of the big data cloud, so as to quickly obtain physical signs and information, So as to facilitate users to make timely response to their own situation.

### 4.3 Front-End Service and Terminal Feedback

The design activity of the service front-end refers to the preliminary investigation and preparation work in the whole design process [7]. Understanding from the perspective of design services refers to the data collection, demand investigation and data accumulation before the design service, including the investigation of theoretical data, so that the subsequent design service can be accurately positioned during the design service, and also for the design The program provides theoretical support. The most important thing in the process of medical device design services is the preliminary basic research and medical data collection and subsequent use feedback, which will greatly optimize the design and improvement of medical products in order to maintain a long life. cycle [4].

# 5   Design Thinking and Product Empowerment

## 5.1   Problem Analysis and Design Orientation

**Operability and Experience.** The design of medical products requires special attention in terms of operability and experience. The use of medical equipment faces doctors and nurses on the one hand and patients on the other. When the medical staff is operating the equipment, due to the continuous updating of patients with the same type of disease, it may be necessary to perform multiple repetitive operations on the equipment within a day. If the equipment operation is too complicated, the treatment time will be shortened, and the value may be delayed in critical situations. Golden time for treatment. In addition, when using the equipment, patients may use the same product for a long time due to special diseases in order to recover as soon as possible. If the experience of the product is not good, it will greatly restrict the use of the product, increase the patient's worry or cause serious illness. When designing, it is necessary to fully consider the use characteristics of different applicable people and integrate experience, operability and use environment to design and consider the system.

**Color Sense and Temperature Sense.** When doctors are operating medical devices for a long time, patients may be treated in a awake or non-awake state. Doctors and patients may sometimes be in contact with the equipment and the environment in which the equipment is located for a long time. This is very easy to cause visual fatigue. If the color contains irritation, it will easily lead to fear and irritability of the patient. Therefore, you can design such products. Try to use colors that can relieve visual fatigue to design the appearance of the product, such as light blue and light green to keep the product mild.

**Portability and Safety.** When doctors are in the process of treating patients and the patient's life is in critical condition, the portability, versatility and safety of medical testing equipment are particularly important. Of course, the portability of the equipment requires comprehensive consideration of the integration and integration of the internal components of the equipment. Reduction, which greatly increases the added value of the product, but the portability of the product can shorten the treatment time to a certain extent, so that the doctor can carry it with him, and it is convenient for timely first aid and testing. This requires designers to always pay attention to new technologies and core components, and complete the internal component matching and external modeling design of the equipment.

**Pertinence and Effectiveness.** During the design process of medical rehabilitation and health care equipment products, the target user population should be fully investigated, and the design should be combined with the corresponding diseases to achieve pertinence and effectiveness. Do not use a machine to advertise that it can cure more without basis. A kind of disease, covering multiple functions, it is necessary to fit the actual and internal chips and functions to seek truth from facts.

**Comfort and After-Sales Service.** Medical disposable products and multiple-use products require special attention during use. The user's comfort experience is often worn for a long time in special environments when medical workers are working, such as laboratories and infected ones. Wards, isolation areas, etc. If the design of the product itself is unreasonable, it will bring bad user experience or allergic reactions to users, and even increase the chance of infection. Therefore, the design process of wearable medical products should conform to the physical characteristics of different groups of people. Design appropriately, and at the same time fully consider the after-sales service of the product and the feedback information of users, and continuously improve and improve the product.

### 5.2  Target Feedback and Product Empowerment

Another important link after perfecting the design orientation is the user experience after completing the product use. After analyzing the feedback of the target and the target needs, combined with the "design" itself, it is necessary to understand the entire ecological chain of medical product design based on scientific and technological means to give the product practical functions and improve the product's use value system, which mainly reflects In the product empowerment system, it can be integrated into product design from two aspects. One is to create an Internet + model to realize the ecological link of data experience, and to provide network interconnection and data communication with equipment under the premise of guarantee functions, and further improve the life cycle of equipment, Equipped with interactive experience, constantly updating and maintaining equipment to keep it stable on the operating system. The second is to combine artificial intelligence technology to realize a data analysis and data intelligent identification system, and to develop a cloud intelligent management and operation platform to give products more use value.

## 6  Product Perception and Service Strategy

### 6.1  Demand Pain Points and Process Experience

The user's pain points for product needs can be roughly divided into the need for product functions, out of their own liking and liking, specific needs to achieve their wishes, the value of the product itself, the degree of satisfaction during the use of the product, and the quality of the product. A comprehensive analysis of the user's demand and pain points based on the use of the product helps to accurately solve the user's difficulties and problems during product design, maximize the advantages of the product, and benefit the user. In the process of trial and simulation of product use, the process of product experience is improved, the details are well done, and the continuous improvement and improvement of the program will help users to obtain a good experience in the process of use.

### 6.2  Distributed Service Design Process

**Before Service-Information, Consensus, Insight.** Products are for people. first, we need to design and service around the "people" used. We need to gain insight into user needs and understand the objective facts behind the needs. How to design, improve and analyze medical products needs factual basis, and further explore the functions of the products. Take medical products as an example. Before a medical product is designed to mass production, the product itself and the target user group need to be analyzed in detail. At the same time, it needs to be compared with similar products to analyze the value and mass production of the product. The possibility of this contains two levels of information. The first level of information refers to the information level: based on the relevant needs of the target user group for similar products, the facts, opinions, attitudes and various extension possibilities after use. The second level is based on the user's understanding or understanding of the product after the first level, including the adoption of new technologies, new usage methods, new functions, or new perspectives.

**In Service-Simulation, Use, and Deliberation.** In the product design process, or in the pre-promotion process of a service, the design plan or service plan needs to be repeatedly scrutinized and simulated. Look at product design and users' feelings from multiple angles and consider the various possibilities and problems that will be encountered after product promotion, in order to deepen user characteristics and product use conditions in specific scenarios, and secondly, the same as the target group keep in touch, update user needs, and build user empathy.

**After Service-Feedback, Improvement, Perfection.** After using the product, most users need not only the product function and the product itself, but gradually begin to pay attention to the service experience of the product's full life cycle. This service experience includes the functions and operational services of the product in use and the product purchase after-sale protection. The service of the product itself has transitioned from functionality such as modeling, color, material, and interface to emotionality, that is, the transition of the value that can be created, from tangible experience to intangible activity. Therefore, before the product is designed, it is necessary to accurately position the product's full life cycle, continuously follow up the service experience, and receive service and use feedback to continuously improve and improve the product.

### 6.3 Service Links and Social Responsibility

When many products are connected through the Internet as a link, the interconnection between products and products is formed. When the service of the product itself radiates from a single directional type to multiple demand connections based on the function of the product, the interconnection of product services is opened up. Products and product services themselves are a "use" chain, and the people served are users. Designers need to accurately find the various chains between products and services, so that the chains can be interconnected and lubricated. The 21st century is an era of "links". The continuous updating of products encourages users to obtain more and more superior services and user experience. Designers who design products need to shoulder the responsibility of designing while continuously improving the functions and services of products in combination with modern technology Responsibility, especially for some particularly important medical products, under the improvement and optimization of product functions and precursors, repeated trials and verifications are required, because this may be related to the lives of users and recipients.

# 7   Iterative Services and the Intelligent Era

## 7.1   Intelligent Interaction and Somatosensory Design

Design and technology are inseparable. Intelligent interactive design and somatosensory design refer to systems that use human, machine dialogue or interactive gestures to recognize information. They use language or gesture recognition to complete machine language instruction input and comparison, and integrate smart chips to collect data And analysis to obtain feedback and communication as a way of communication and interactive operation, which replaces the traditional contact operating system. The interactive system and somatosensory design will greatly improve the working conditions and use requirements of medical care under special conditions. During the operation and acute rescue, it can effectively prevent indirect infection caused by active contact with objects. This will also improve the traditional physical sign monitoring methods of patients. The detection of physical sign data can be completed in real time through smart chips and detection chips using smart bracelets or wearable devices.

## 7.2   Additional Lightweight Products and Services

Lightweight products refer to products that are easy to operate, convenient to carry, and have no redundant functions. The portability of medical auxiliary products will greatly improve the rescue efficiency of doctors for patients. After the weight of the equipment is lightened, it will not be restricted by region, get rid of the heavy volume, and be applied to different usage scenarios anytime and anywhere. In the medical system, older professors generally have more clinical experience, but the continuous updating of equipment and the complexity of operating procedures often make some older professors intimidated by the operation, and the lightweight of the operating system will make the older professors more Use the equipment quickly to win rescue time for the patient.

## 7.3   The Future of Product Intelligence and Service

The advancement of technology and information technology promotes the continuous upgrading and evolution of products, and new technologies represented by artificial intelligence, Internet of Things, big data and cloud computing are constantly being integrated into our lives. As an important factor in the value creation of smart products, information data is gradually replacing traditional single-function auxiliary medical equipment. The simulation application of AI equipment for intelligent scenes in the medical field enables doctors to perform high-level simulation simulations of the surgical environment. While exercising medical capabilities, it also provides personalized diagnosis and treatment plans and customized scene simulation services.

As the core driving force of the new industrial transformation, smart products have also played an important role in the development and promotion of the medical industry. This improves work efficiency during medical and nursing operations and also provides patients with a comfortable service experience.

# 8  Summary

The rapid development of science and technology promotes the continuous upgrading of products. More and more new technologies and new designs are applied to the internal and external of the products, so that the quality of the products is improved, the functions are becoming more and more powerful, and they are getting closer to people's lives.. Under the premise of combining operability and ease of use in future medical auxiliary products, the equipment itself will also realize more product interconnection, data exchange, and development in the direction of multi-type equipment product collaboration through the network. Patients with critical symptoms are in medical care. The rescue time is very urgent during the rescue process. This method will effectively save the time of equipment treatment and physical sign detection, but the premise is to strictly guarantee the accuracy, reliability and error probability of the product, and set up two emergency treatment methods, namely traditional Treatment and equipment networking assistance to ensure the safety of patients' lives.

From the perspective of product design, it is necessary to fully consider the use environment of the product and the versatility and popularity of the product. For example, in a space isolated from large-scale public infectious diseases, medical workers need to perform repetitive tasks in internal operations for a long time. The comfort of the product and the cumbersome degree of operation will directly lead to whether medical workers can reduce fatigue in the process of work. One-time or reusable medical products used for medical equipment and wearables need to pay special attention to the applicable people of the product in the process of research and development and design, and pay attention to the applicability and practicability of the product under the premise of different operating actions. And usability.

With the continuous application and innovation of new technologies and the continuous accumulation of technical experience, future medical products will also become more intelligent, experiential and service-oriented. At the same time, they will also give birth to new industrial models and technological changes. The medical field brings more innovation and development.

# References

1. Li, J., Zong, M.: The design and thinking of medical portable equipment based on the concept of user experience. Ind. Des. **06**, 81–83 (2015)
2. Han, T., Yang, Y.: Medical product service design in the Internet + era. Art Obs. **10**, 20–21 (2016)
3. Yang, Y.: Research on the design of product service system aiming at sustainable development, pp. 1–52. Jiangnan University (2009)
4. Cai, K.: Analysis of building elements in product system design, pp. 1–46. Wuhan University of Technology (2008)
5. Lv, C.: Research on the Application of Service Design in Medical Service Management. Industrial Design Research (Third Series) (2015)
6. Wang, J.: Research on home medical product design based on service design concept, pp. 1–64. Qingdao Technological University (2017)
7. Li, D., Ming, X., Kong, F., et al.: Research on service design. Mech. Des. Res. **6**, 6–10 (2008)

# Exploring the Role of Cognitive Empathy and Emotional Empathy in Medical Crowdfunding

Lili Liu, Qianyi Tao$^{(\boxtimes)}$, and Shanjiao Ren

College of Economics and Management, Nanjing University of Aeronautics and Astronautics, Nanjing, China
{llili85,joy9971}@nuaa.edu.cn

**Abstract.** Medical crowdfunding is booming in recent years, especially as patients with little or no health insurance turn to appeal for help online in covering medical costs. However, most of medical crowdfunding campaigns fail to reach their goals, and we rarely know the reason. Therefore, this study seeks to explore what determines users' donation behavior in medical crowdfunding. Drawing on the S-O-R model, this study explores how certain stimulus (altruism, trust, and strength of social relationships) induce individuals' cognitive empathy and emotional empathy (organism), which in turn affect their donation behavior (response) in medical crowdfunding. Data was collect from 142 respondents and analyzed with SmartPLS 3.2.9. Findings indicate that individuals' donation behavior is positively influenced by their cognitive empathy and emotional empathy, which are positively related to altruism, trust, and strength of social relationships. The potential theoretical and practical contributions are discussed.

**Keywords:** Medical crowdfunding · S-O-R model · Cognitive empathy · Emotional empathy · Donation behavior

## 1 Introduction

Medical crowdfunding is booming in recent years, especially as patients with little or no health insurance turn to appeal for help online in covering medical costs [9]. For millions of Americans, any serious illness comes with a potentially crippling burden or a financial shock (e.g., the average cost of hospital stays for cancer patients in 2015 was $31,390 – about half that year's median household income according to government report), forcing them to either leave their illness untreated or look for alternative ways to pay for the bills [18]. In that pursuit, medical crowdfunding that is effective to alleviate patients' financial pressure has grown significantly, thus becomes a major sector of the crowdfunding marketplace. For instance, the largest medical crowdfunding platform "GoFundMe", reports that all campaigns have raised $9 billion by 2019. However, the reality is that 90% of medical crowdfunding campaigns fail to reach their goal, and patients have to compete for funds from potential donors [25]. Therefore, it is important for us to explore what determines users' donation behavior in medical crowdfunding.

© Springer Nature Switzerland AG 2021
C. Stephanidis et al. (Eds.): HCII 2021, CCIS 1499, pp. 176–183, 2021.
https://doi.org/10.1007/978-3-030-90179-0_23

Despite crowdfunding has been demonstrated to have significant success outside the medical field [21], its use in the medical realm is relatively new [20] and empirical research on user participation is scarce [5, 11]. To fill this gap, this study draws on the stimulus-organism-response (S-O-R) model and synthesizes various antecedents that influence user participation in medical crowdfunding. The S-O-R framework posits that environmental cues act as stimuli that affect a user's cognitive and affective reactions, which in turn affect behavior [17]. Referring to existing literature on crowdfunding, we operationalize "stimulus" as a potential donor's personal characteristics (including Altruism [13, 26], Trust [14], and Strength of Social Relationships [7]), "organism" as cognitive and emotional empathy [3], and "response" as users' donation behavior. In short, this study aims to investigate how donors' personal characteristics affect their donation behavior, through the mediation of cognitive empathy and emotional empathy.

## 2 Theoretical Background

### 2.1 Medical Crowdfunding

Crowdfunding is a particularly effective and popular tool for supporting charities, among which, medical crowdfunding is increasingly popular [26]. Medical crowdfunding is a crowdfunding method that enables non-professionals to raise designated amount of money for medical purposes (e.g., treatment expenses) within a fixd period of time, by creating a sharable web page on crowdfunding platforms [10]. In China, the successive emergence of platforms such as "qingsongchou"and "shuidichou" is an important manifestation of the development of crowdfunding platforms for serious diseases. These platforms integrate the information of initiator, and connect initiator and donors, while creating channels for information diffusion for initiator, it can shorten the information search time of donors' intention.

### 2.2 S-O-R Model

This study draws on the Stimulus-Organism-Response (S-O-R) model to integrate the various factors that influence individual donation behavior in medical crowdfunding [14]. S-O-R model suggests that when a user is exposed to certain environmental stimuli, he/she responds through his/her organism accordingly.

Research has shown that individuals are able to share others' happy feeling when they donate, thus they donate for altruistic motives [3]. In addition, trust towards the project and the strength of the social relationship can also affect an individual's intention to donate [22, 27]. To sum up, altruism, trust and social relationship strength that represenets potential donors' personal characteristics are identified as the stimuli of S-O-R model. Empirical research indicates that empathy is a key factor that encourages donation behavior [13]. Besides, empathy has been further divided as cognitive empathy and emotional empathy, in which cognitive empathy is described as an individual cognitively adopt the others' viewpoint and enter into their role, while emotional empathy means an individual is able to share others' emotional feelings such as happiness or sadness [7]. Accordingly, cognitive empathy and emotional empathy have been identified as individuals' internalized organism that predicts donation behavior.

In conclusion, drawing on S-O-R model, we develop a model that explores how certain stimuli (altruism, trust, strength of social relationships) induce individuals' organism (cognitive empathy and emotional empathy), which in turn affect their donation behavior (response) in medical crowdfunding.

## 3   Research Model and Hypotheses

Our research model is depicted in Fig. 1. Hypotheses are discussed respectively in following section.

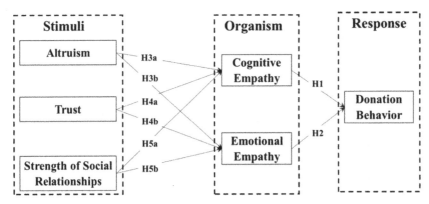

**Fig. 1.**  Research model

### 3.1   Cognitive Empathy, Emotional Empathy, and Donation Behavior

Cognitive empathy refers to the understanding of others' reasoning and cognitive process of participation, similar to the mind theory or perspective taking [7]. In real life, being able to recognize, understand and think from the perspective of others, could generate a willingness to help others, then motivate prosocial behavior. Therefore, cognitive empathy is an important factor that determines the willingness to donate. Emotional empathy is defined as "an observer's emotional response to another person's emotional state" [2]. When people shares similar emotional feelings (e.g., happiness, sadness) of others, they will unconsciously have emotional empathy. This emotion will deepen with the deepening of understanding others' emotional states, further motivating people's specific aid behavior. Therefore, emotional empathy could be considered as another predictor of donation behavior. Accordingly, we propose:

**H1.** Cognitive empathy is positively related to donation behavior.

**H2.** Emotional empathy is positively related to donation behavior.

## 3.2   Altruism, Trust, and Strength of Social Relationships

Altruism is defined as "the willingness of individuals to sacrifice their own interests for the welfare of others" [23]. Researchers state that under the influence of Altruism, people expect their actions to effectively assist those in need. Altruism has been demonstrated as an important factor that determines individuals' empathy and behavior [15]. For instance, previous study indicates that altruistic motivation is directed toward the ultimate goal of increasing another person's welfare, empathy-induced altruism is likely to motivate help that is more sensitive to that person's need. Because of the person's altruistic nature, they are more likely to develop empathy under certain situation. When people move from cognitive empathy and emotional empathy to empathetic behavior, they will sacrifice their own interests in exchange for the interests of others. We thus hypothesize:

**H3a.**  Altruism is positively related to cognitive empathy.

**H3b.**  Altruism is positively related to emotional empathy.

Trust is defined as "assured reliance on the character, ability, strength, or truth of someone or something", including particular trust towards the crowdfunding sites and project initators [15]. Before posting a project online, information of the project and help seekers need to be verified by the crowdfunding platform to ensure the authenticity. Research shows that when more information of a charitable campaign (e.g., pictures, videos) is provided, audiences trust it more. In charitable crowdfunding, people's trust towards projects and the platforms, inspires greater empathy, which makes them more likely to donate, and donate greater amount of money [27]. Therefore, we propose:

**H4a.**  Trust is positively related to cognitive empathy.

**H4b.**  Trust is positively related to emotional empathy.

Strength of social relationship refers to the closeness of people's social relationships [22]. Social relationships with different strengths affect people's attitude and behavior differently. For instance, Friedkin argues that people with weak social relationships can help to spread information faster among different groups and attract greater social attention from others [6]. Besides, Lin et al. prove that strong social relationships play an important role in alleviating stress in all aspects [12]. In existing crowdfunding platforms, audiences who develop strong social relationships with help seekers are familiar with their situation, thus have strong empathy towards them, and more willing to donate money as well as forward the project to more potential donors, their participation can help to enhance the credibility of the project and stimulate other's empathy. Therefore, we propose:

**H5a.**  Strength of social relationships is positively related to cognitive empathy.

**H5b.**  Strength of social relationships is positively related to emotional empathy.

# 4   Research Methodology

## 4.1   Measurements

Measurement items for all constructs in the research model were adapted from existing research. More particularly, altruism was assessed with items adapted from Hartmann et al. [8]. Items for Trust were adapted from Schwienbacher [19], while items of strength of social relationships were derived from Stanko et al. [22]. Furthermore, items of cognitive empathy and emotional empathy were adapted from the work of Reniers et al. [16]. Finally, items of donate behavior were adapted from Ajzen [1], which defines participation as the subjective probability that a donor volunteers to participate in a crowdfunding project. Seven-point Likert scale were used to measure the items, rangeing from 1 (strongly disagree) to 7 (strongly agree).

## 4.2   Data Collection

Data was collected by releasing an online survey on Sojump.com, a platform functionalized as Amazon Mechanical Turk. Individuals who had forwarded or donated to crowdfunding for serious diseases were invited to fill out the questionnaire. Eventually, 142 valid responses were received.

Table 1 shows the demographic information of the respondents. In general, 58.5% of the respondents were female while 41.5% of them were male. 45.7% of the samples were between 18 and 25 years old. More than 65% of the respondents had Bachelor's degree. 43.67% of the samples' monthly income was between 1000 and 3000 CNY. Therefore, most of our respondents were young and middle-aged females with good educational background and upper middle income.

**Table 1.** Respondent demographics.

| Item | Category | Frequency | Percentage (%) |
|---|---|---|---|
| Gender | Male | 59 | 41.5 |
|  | Female | 83 | 58.5 |
| Age | Under 18 | 1 | 0.71 |
|  | 18–25 | 64 | 45.07 |
|  | 26–35 | 25 | 17.60 |
|  | 36–45 | 23 | 16.20 |
|  | 46–55 | 25 | 17.60 |
|  | 56 and above | 4 | 2.82 |
| Education | High school and below | 14 | 9.86 |
|  | Associate degree | 23 | 16.20 |

(*continued*)

**Table 1.** (*continued*)

| Item | Category | Frequency | Percentage (%) |
|------|----------|-----------|----------------|
| | Bachelor's degree | 96 | 67.60 |
| | Master's degree and above | 9 | 6.34 |
| Monthly Income | Below 1000 yuan | 18 | 12.68 |
| | 1000–3000 yuan | 62 | 43.67 |
| | 3001–5000 yuan | 25 | 17.61 |
| | 5001–8000 yuan | 20 | 14.08 |
| | Above 8000 yuan | 17 | 11.96 |

### 4.3 Data Analyses and Results

SmartPLS 3.2.9 was used to analyse the data. We tested the measurement model and structural model respectively. The reliability and validity of the measurement model were verified via checking Cronbach's Alpha values ($>0.7$), factor loadings ($>0.7$), and composite reliability ($>0.7$). Moreover, average variance extracted (AVE) values were all greater than 0.50, indicating good convergent validity [4, 24].

Results of the regression analysis of the structural model were shown in Fig. 2, in which altruism to cognitive empathy ($\beta = 0.317$, $p < 0.01$), altruism to emotional empathy ($\beta = 0.401$, $p < 0.001$), trust to cognitive empathy ($\beta = 0.235$, $p < 0.01$), trust to emotional empathy ($\beta = 442$, $p < 0.01$), strength of social relationships to cognitive empathy ($\beta = 0.179$, $p < 0.05$), strength of social relationships to emotional empathy ($\beta = 0.238$, $p < 0.01$), cognitive empathy to donation behavior ($\beta = 0.191$, $p < 0.01$), emotional empathy to donation behavior ($\beta = 0.806$, $p < 0.001$). Hence, H1, H2, H3a, H3b, H4a, H4b, H5a, and H5b were supported. Altruism, trust, and strength of social relationships jointly explained 34.2% variance of cognitive empathy and 75.8% variance of emotional empathy, which in turn explained 73.1% variance of donation behavior.

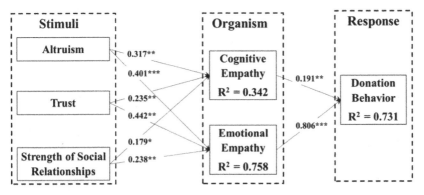

**Fig. 2.** Structural model

## 5   Contribution

This study seeks to explore the determinants of user donation behavior in medical crowd-funding. In light of Stimulus-Organism-Response (S-O-R) model, we developed and empirically tested a research model. Findings confirmed that altruism, trust, and strength of social relationships positively affected potential donors' cognitive and emotional empathy, which in turn positively encouraged their donation behavior. Audiences who were altruistic, who had developed strong relationships with crowdfunding founders, and who believed crowdfunding platforms and projects were trustworthy, were more likely to generate cognitive and emotional empathy towards the projects, thus were more likely to donate money.

It is worth noting that, this study pioneeringly verifies the key role of cognitive and emotional empathy in medical crowdfunding, thus extends our knowledge on empathy and crowdfunding. Practically, findings of this study provide beneficial enlightenment for managers. First, managers should improve the quality of crowdfunding service to quickly and effectively response to the initiator's request for help. Second, in order to maintain a trustworthy crowdfunding platform, managers should on one hand strictly examine the personally identifiable information and medical information provided by the initiators, on the other hand punish those who publish false information and return money to the donors. Third, at the early stage of a medical crowdfunding project, it is important to encourage friends and acquaintances to donate money, as well as persuade those who build weak relationships with project initators to forward the project to their social circle.

**Acknowledgement.** This study was supported by the Fundamental Research Funds for the Central Universities No. NR2021003 awarded to the first author; this study was also supported by the Fundamental Research Funds for the Central Universities: No. 2019EC07 awarded to the second author and the Creative Studio of Electronic Commerce in Nanjing University of Aeronautics and Astronautics.

## References

1. Ajzen, I.: From intentions to actions: a theory of planned behavior. In: Kuhl, J., Beckmann, J. (eds.) Action control. SSSSP, pp. 11–39. Springer, Heidelberg (1985). https://doi.org/10.1007/978-3-642-69746-3_2
2. Blair, R.J.R.: Responding to the emotions of others: dissociating forms of empathy through the study of typical and psychiatric populations. Conscious. Cogn. **14**(4), 698–718 (2005)
3. Chilton, S.M., Hutchinson, W.G.: Some further implications of incorporating the warm glow of giving into welfare measures: a comment on the use of donation mechanisms by Champet al. J. Environ. Econ. Manag. **37**(2), 202–209 (1999)
4. Chin, W.W.: The partial least squares approach to structural equation modelling. In: Marcoulides, G.A. (ed.) Modern Business Research Methods, pp. 295–336 (1998)
5. Durand, W.M., Johnson, J.R., Eltorai, A.E., Daniels, A.H.: Medical crowdfunding for patients undergoing orthopedic surgery. Orthopedics **41**(1), e58–e63 (2018)
6. Friedkin, N.: A test of structural features of Granovetter's strength of weak ties theory. Soc. Netw. **2**(4), 411–422 (1980)

7. Gladstein, G.A.: Understanding empathy: Integrating counseling, developmental, and social psychology perspectives. J. Couns. Psychol. **30**(4), 467–482 (1983)
8. Hartmann, P., Eisend, M., Apaolaza, V., D'Souza, C.: Warm glow vs. altruistic values: how important is intrinsic emotional reward in proenvironmental behavior? J. Environ. Psychol. **52**, 43–55 (2017)
9. Jopson, B.: Why are so many Americans crowdfunding their healthcare. Financ. Times (2018). https://www.ft.com/content/b99a81be-f591-11e7-88f7-5465a6ce1a00
10. Kim, J.G., Kong, H.K., Karahalios, K., Fu, W.T., Hong, H.: The power of collective endorsements: credibility factors in medical crowdfunding campaigns. In: Proceedings of the 2016 CHI Conference on Human Factors in Computing Systems, pp. 4538–4549, May 2016
11. Krittanawong, C., Zhang, H.J., Aydar, M., Wang, Z., Sun, T.: Crowdfunding for cardiovascular research. Int. J. Cardiol. **250**, 268–269 (2018)
12. Lin, N., Woelfel, M.W., Light, S.C.: The buffering effect of social support subsequent to an important life event. J. Health Soc. Behav. **26**(3), 247–263 (1985)
13. Liu, L., Suh, A., Wagner, C.: Empathy or perceived credibility? An empirical study on individual donation behavior in charitable crowdfunding. Internet Res. **28**(3), 623–651 (2018)
14. Mummalaneni, V.: An empirical investigation of web site characteristics, consumer emotional states and on-line shopping behaviors. J. Bus. Res. **58**(4), 526–532 (2005)
15. Panasiti, M.S., Violani, C., Grano, C.: Exploring the relationship between umbilical blood cord donation and the impact of social distance on altruism and trust. Int. J. Psychol. **55**(6), 1003–1010 (2020)
16. Reniers, R.L., Corcoran, R., Drake, R., Shryane, N.M., Völlm, B.A.: The QCAE: a questionnaire of cognitive and affective empathy. J. Pers. Assess. **93**(1), 84–95 (2011)
17. Russell, J.A., Mehrabian, A.: The mediating role of emotions in alcohol use. J. Stud. Alcohol **36**(11), 1508–1536 (1975)
18. Sara, H.: Can medical crowdfunding address patient financial responsibility? Patient Engag. Hit (2018). https://patientengagementhit.com/news/can-medical-crowdfunding-address-patient-financial-responsibility
19. Schwienbacher, A., Larralde, B.: Crowdfunding of small entrepreneurial ventures. Handbook of Entrepreneurial Finance. Oxford University Press (2010). Forthcoming
20. Snyder, J., Chow-White, P., Crooks, V.A., Mathers, A.: Widening the gap: additional concerns with crowdfunding in health care. Lancet Oncol. **18**(5), e240 (2017)
21. Sorenson, O., Assenova, V., Li, G.C., Boada, J., Fleming, L.: Expand innovation finance via crowdfunding. Science **354**(6319), 1526–1528 (2016)
22. Stanko, M.A., Bonner, J.M., Calantone, R.J.: Building commitment in buyer–seller relationships: a tie strength perspective. Ind. Mark. Manag. **36**(8), 1094–1103 (2007)
23. Steele, W.R., et al.: The role of altruistic behavior, empathetic concern, and social responsibility motivation in blood donation behavior. Transfusion **48**(1), 43–54 (2008)
24. Tenenhaus, M., Vinzi, V.E., Chatelin, Y.-M., Lauro, C.: PLS path modelling. Comput. Stat. Data Anal. **48**(1), 159–205 (2005)
25. Vox, F., Folkers, K.M., Caplan, A.: Medical crowdfunding's dark side. Health Affairs (2018)
26. Young, M.J., Scheinberg, E.: The rise of crowdfunding for medical care: promises and perils. JAMA **317**(16), 1623–1624 (2017)
27. Zheng, H., Hung, J.L., Qi, Z., Xu, B.: The role of trust management in reward-based crowdfunding. Online Inf. Rev. **40**(1), 97–118 (2016)

# Advancing Reminiscence Therapy Using Virtual Reality Applications for Persons with Dementia

Daniel Presas[1], Rob Shewaga[1], Alvaro Uribe-Quevedo[1], Winnie Sun[1(✉)], and Sheri Horsburgh[2]

[1] Ontario Tech University, Oshawa, ON, Canada
daniel.presas@ontariotechu.net,
{alvaro.quevedo,winnie.sun}@ontariotechu.ca
[2] Ontario Shores, Whitby, ON, Canada
horsburghs@ontarioshores.ca

**Abstract.** Reminiscence therapy relies on pictures, images, and videos organized and presented by the caregiver. However, such traditional media may be lack of immersion and engagement to help with reducing anxiety and improving recollection of events. Virtual Reality (VR) has seen a surge in applications related to elderly care associated with social connectedness, physical and mental stimulation. This paper presents the development of a VR framework that presents immersive and non-immersive VR environments for reminiscence therapy employing facial and head tracking to ease navigation and visualization of content. We have developed two non-immersive and one immersive VR prototypes based on feedback collected during the stress test sessions with the end-users.

**Keywords:** Immersion · Reminiscence therapy · Virtual reality

## 1 Introduction

Dementia is a syndrome that affects memory, thinking, and behavior that affects around 50 million people worldwide. While dementia affects people differently, the symptoms can be classified under three stages: i) early, ii) middle and iii) advanced [8]. Although a cure for dementia does not exist, there are a number of treatments including reminiscence therapy (RT) to improve the quality of life [9]. RT Treatments can focus on physical and/or mental well-being, and in our case, RT targets behavioral aspects associated with memory and the progression of forgetfulness through the stages of dementia [2]. Traditionally, RT relies on graphical media employing pictures, illustrations, and videos to help the patients remember events from their past. The narrative is controlled by

Supported by Ontario Shores, Ontario Tech University, Canadian Aging and Brain Health Innovation (CABHI).

C. Stephanidis et al. (Eds.): HCII 2021, CCIS 1499, pp. 184–188, 2021.
https://doi.org/10.1007/978-3-030-90179-0_24

the caregiver who presents the materials based on selections provided by family members or by familiarity with the patient's history [1]. However, these media lack the immersion that VR can offer. Most recently, RT therapy applications in VR include those pertaining to the reconstruction of known locations to the patient combined with 360 pictures and videos replacing traditional content [7], the assessment of impacts on cognitive function and morale with noticeable differences in morale [6], and the reduction of anxiety [3].

This paper presents a novel approach to VR RT by taking a framework approach to offer customized scenarios offering the experience in immersive VR, non-immersive VR without depth perception, and non-immersive VR with depth perception. This approach is unique and responds to the need to design accessible experiences as VR is traditionally and primarily targeted toward the healthy users. The work presented here builds on previous research conducted developing social connectedness for RT [4], and non-immersive storytelling for RT [5].

## 2   Materials and Methods

The development of the RT VR framework followed a systemic approach where the user needs were identified through co-design sessions in partnership with Ontario Shores Centre for Mental Health Sciences in Ontario, Canada. The user case scenario was built by analyzing the current flow of actions when conducting RT sessions to best capture its virtualization. For this purpose, a storytelling module was created to enable caregivers to upload content to enrich the virtual experience and define for the patient to follow. For the development, we used the Unity game engine and a web camera for the non-immersive VR with depth perception, and an Oculus Quest for the immersive VR scene. This particular set-up allows the VR RT to take place on consumer-level devices, meaning that it can be adopted very easily by others who would like to leverage this kind of immersive RT.

### 2.1   Non-Immersive VR

We considered employing non-immersive VR as this approach may be more suitable for persons with advanced stage of dementia because VR headsets may have the risks of triggering responsive behaviors. Our initial approach adopted the development of a system employing a holographic display that [5]. However, we decided to employ OpenCV, an open-source computer vision library and a regular web camera and the FaceTrackNoir plugin for Unity to capture head movements and mapping them onto the virtual camera using a regular web camera to lower any entry barriers. Figure 1 shows head tracking information changing the camera position and orientation.

## 2.2    Immersive VR

Regarding immersive VR, an Oculus Quest is used to navigate the RT virtual room presenting memories embedded onto 3D objects, such as photo frames, monitors, and the television as shown in Fig. 2. In this scenario hand tracking and head tracking allow users to visualize and interact with the content.

(a) Center view          (b) Looking to the left          (c) Strafing to the right

**Fig. 1.** Web camera head tracking controlling a virtual camera to increase immersion in non-immersive VR.

(a) Third person view of a    (b) VR media manipula-    (c) Hand tracking interac-
VR room with embedded tra-    tion                              tion
ditional content

**Fig. 2.** Immersive VR room with objects embedding RT media.

## 2.3    Facial Tracking

The facial tracking portion of the software employed the open-source OpenCV computer vision library, which has been packaged into a plugin for the Unity game engine. Additionally, a face tracker made by Enox Software leverages the plugin for improved tracking. This solution allows us to access a distributed model for points on a human face to identify where the face is in a given frame. Additionally, the facial points can be stored with timestamps and replayed for later assessment as shown in Fig. 3. Capturing the facial mesh allows the therapists to see facial expressions to better understand reactions such as surprise, happiness, disgust or anger in response to media being presented.

(a) Facial tracking overlay

(b) Facial mesh

(c) Playback graphical user interface

**Fig. 3.** Current facial tracking software features.

## 3 Discussion

VR remains an open field of research with respect to RT. RT can be implemented by porting traditional content into VR or by capturing 3D representation that may help the patients with their reminiscence experiences. Here, we presented a more inclusive approach that acknowledges immersive and non-immersive solutions that can be better adapted to those in different stages of dementia. Additionally, our solution can be more inclusive for those with visual impairment or those who cannot wear a VR headset to promote accessibility. While no formal testing has been conducted at this stage, the co-design has provided us with an understanding of user interactions and content display strategies aiming at maintaining the patients' engagement with a low cognitive load. From a technical point of view, the use of head and facial tracking using a web camera posed challenges associated with proper detection as a result of lighting conditions, hair, and eyeglasses. The next phase of our project is to assess the usability, engagement, and cognitive load from a caregiver and patient point of view, as well as comparing our systems against traditional RT methods to understand their effectiveness, ease of use, and user's intention for adoption.

## References

1. Cotelli, M., Manenti, R., Zanetti, O.: Reminiscence therapy in dementia: a review. Maturitas **72**(3), 203–205 (2012)
2. Klein, P., Uhlig, M., Will, H.: The touch and feel of the past–using haptic and VR artefacts to enrich reminiscence therapy for people with dementia. Technologies **6**(4), 104 (2018)
3. Niki, K., et al.: Immersive virtual reality reminiscence reduces anxiety in the oldest-old without causing serious side effects: a single-center, pilot, and randomized crossover study. Front. Hum. Neurosci. **14**, 598161 (2021). https://doi.org/10.3389/fnhum.2020.598161. PMID: 33536887; PMCID: PMC7849024
4. Sun, W., et al.: Advancing reminiscence therapy through virtual reality application to promote social connectedness of persons with dementia. J. Int. Soc. Gerontechnology **19**(Suppl. 1) (2020)

5. Tabafunda, A., et al.: Development of a non-immersive VR reminiscence therapy experience for patients with dementia. In: Stephanidis, C., Antona, M., Ntoa, S. (eds.) HCII 2020. CCIS, vol. 1294, pp. 509–517. Springer, Cham (2020). https://doi.org/10.1007/978-3-030-60703-6_66

6. Tominari, M., Uozumi, R., Becker, C., Kinoshita, A.: Reminiscence therapy using virtual reality technology affects cognitive function and morale of elderly with dementia: developing topics. Alzheimer's Dementia **16**, e047538 (2020)

7. Tsao, Y.C., Shu, C.C., Lan, T.S.: Development of a reminiscence therapy system for the elderly using the integration of virtual reality and augmented reality. Sustainability **11**(17), 4792 (2019)

8. WHO: Dementia, September 2020. https://www.who.int/news-room/fact-sheets/detail/dementia

9. Woods, B., O'Philbin, L., Farrell, E.M., Spector, A.E., Orrell, M.: Reminiscence therapy for dementia. Cochrane Database Syst. Rev. **3**(3), CD001120 (2018). https://doi.org/10.1002/14651858.CD001120.pub3. PMID: 29493789; PMCID: PMC6494367

# Information Chaos in the Electronic Health Record as a Threat to Patient Safety

Emily Schaefer[1]([✉]), Nicole Werner[2], and Matthew Scanlon[1]

[1] Medical College of Wisconsin, Milwaukee, WI 53226, USA
emschaefer@mcw.edu
[2] University of Wisconsin, Madison, WI 53706, USA

**Abstract.** *Information chaos* refers to the chaotic presentation and subsequent suboptimal reception of information in the electronic health record (EHR). Prior work in ambulatory settings identified a group of hazards that were described collectively as information chaos. These hazards include *information overload, information underload, information conflict, information scatter,* and *erroneous information.* This pilot project examined four inpatient EHR records in a pediatric intensive care unit (PICU) to investigate whether information chaos was present. All four patient charts revealed numerous information hazards, suggesting the presence of *information chaos* within PICU patient charts. All charts demonstrated *information chaos and information overload.* We also identified three novel hazards: *non-intuitive abbreviations, non-intuitive access of information,* and *copy & paste.* Information chaos may confound information intake and processing, which raises mental workload and lowers situation awareness. Thus, PICU physicians may be at heightened risk for impaired performance of clinical tasks, which may jeopardize the safety of critically ill pediatric patients.

**Keywords:** UX (User Experience) · Electronic health record · Chaos

## 1 Introduction

### 1.1 Background

Safe, quality health care requires information intake and processing. Anything that interrupts information intake and processing may confound patient diagnosis, management, and overall safe care. Information chaos refers to the chaotic presentation and suboptimal reception of information in the electronic health record (EHR) [2]. Information chaos can be identified by the presence of various information hazards. These have been previously described as information overload, information underload, information scatter, information conflict, and erroneous information [2]. The presence of information chaos likely disrupts cognition through increased mental workload and decreased situation awareness [2]. Information chaos has been described in a limited manner within an adult ambulatory care [2] and a pharmacy [4] setting. It is unknown whether this phenomenon exists in other healthcare settings such as the inpatient environment.

© Springer Nature Switzerland AG 2021
C. Stephanidis et al. (Eds.): HCII 2021, CCIS 1499, pp. 189–196, 2021.
https://doi.org/10.1007/978-3-030-90179-0_25

Diagnostic errors, medication errors, and inadequate communication are three ubiquitous problems in the current healthcare system that have been previously described in the pediatric intensive care unit (PICU) [1, 3, 5, 6, 15, 16, 20]. The interactions that lead to potential errors are influenced by a multitude of factors and processes, one of which is cognitive capacity. Therefore, anything that poses a threat to cognitive capacity may affect patient safety outcomes. One example of this is information chaos. The reach of information chaos may also extend beyond outpatient settings to inpatient settings such as the PICU. Therefore, the purpose of this pilot study was to investigate whether information chaos was present in EHRs of PICU patients.

## 2    Methods

Two members of the research team (ES, MS) selected a convenience sample of four patients randomly from among a cohort of patients recently discharged from the PICU. The PICU is a 72-bed care unit located in a Midwest Free-Standing Children's Hospital. Each of the four charts were reviewed looking for evidence of any of the five known types of information hazards previously identified by Beasley et al. Additionally, chart review sought evidence of any new types of information hazards. Identified issues in the charts were categorized by primary type of information hazard. When issues did not fit into one of the previously identified types of information hazards, a new category was identified.

## 3    Results

A total of 22 information hazards were identified in the four reviewed charts (Mean of $5.5 \pm 1.29$ hazards per chart). Information overload and information conflict were most prevalent (Table 1). Among three of the four reviewed charts, a total of eight hazards were identified that did not fit into previously identified categories. As a result, three new types of information hazards were identified: non-intuitive information hazards were identified: *non-intuitive abbreviations, non-intuitive access of information*, and *copy & paste*-related hazards.

### 3.1    Results by Specific Hazard Type

**Information Overload.** Information overload occurs when there is too much data (e.g., written, verbal and nonverbal, physician's memory) for the clinician to organize, synthesize, draw conclusions from, or act on [2]. All four charts suffered from this. An example of information overload is that the initial History and Physical (H&P) landing page (Fig. 1) is overwhelming and contains many tabs, dialogue boxes, and drop-down menus. Other examples of information overload included one chart in which the patient's entire past medical history was pulled into both the ED note and the H&P, the majority of which was not relevant to the encounter. In another patient's chart, clicking on the most recent PICU encounter also yielded notes from separate hospital encounters with non-PICU departments.

**Information Underload.** Information underload is when important information is lacking from the EHR [2]. Two of four reviewed patient charts showed evidence of information underload. One example was an H&P for an asthmatic patient that had no documented respiratory exam. The same chart also had a note pertaining to the patient's Total Parenteral Nutrition (TPN) and jejunostomy tube feedings. The plan was to continue feeding to replicate their TPN glucose infusion rate (GIR), but no GIR was specified. The plan also failed to mention what kind of TPN was used or how much. In this case information underload could have led to errors in executing the feeding plan, jeopardizing the patient's nutrition.

**Information Scatter.** Information Scatter is defined as information that is in multiple places. The EHR utilized in this study has three main modules of accessing patient information. These are (1) Patient Station – used for admissions, (2) Chart Review – used for internal health system encounters, and (3) Care Everywhere – used for external encounters in health systems that operate with the same EHR. Each module contains unique information, as well as some of the same information. The information in the "Patient Station" and "Chart Review" modules is not standardized with respect to accessibility or presentation. When a user flips between the two modules, they mentally negotiate the differences to process and use the information. Two of the four charts we examined contained information scatter. One of the reviewed patient charts had critical notes in "Care Everywhere", which required more mouse clicks, interrupted the flow of chart review, and might have been missed if this EHR section was not reviewed. The second chart with information scatter included notes that were scattered across separate hospital encounters for no apparent reason.

**Information Conflict.** Information conflict occurs when the user cannot determine which data are correct [2]. All four charts contained information conflict. In one instance, a transfer note showed a discrepancy between the EHR date of the note and the stated date of service within the body of the note. A second example was a progress note that listed a numerical value for the patient's urinary output, but the progress note stated that no urinary output was measured.

**Erroneous Information.** Erroneous information is when information is wrong within the EHR [2]. Two of four patient charts contained erroneous information. For example, we found a statement in a progress note claiming a patient's hyponatremia had resolved, but the patient's lab results were still significant for hyponatremia. A second example was an erroneous diagnosis of respiratory failure when the patient had respiratory insufficiency. This error may alter future clinical assessment and decision making if this patient is ever seen again for respiratory concerns.

**Non-intuitive Abbreviations.** Non-intuitive abbreviations refer to the use of non-standard or specialty-specific abbreviations without context to sufficiently infer the meaning of the abbreviation. Three of four charts contained this hazard. Our evaluation of pediatric ICU patient notes revealed many abbreviations that were deemed non-intuitive to a pediatric intensivist. These included: "OSH" (outside hospital), "BMA/bx" (bone marrow aspiration and biopsy), "FBOA" (foreign body obstructed airway), "IST" (inappropriate sinus tachycardia), "PNH clones" (paroxysmal nocturnal hemoglobinuria clones), "EBNa" (Ebstein Barr Virus Nuclear Antigen), "EDTC" (Emergency department trauma center), "SAA" (severe aplastic anemia), and "mIVF" (maintenance intravenous fluid). The implications of non-intuitive abbreviations are that they require extra consideration and time to determine their meaning, or their meaning could be inferred incorrectly.

**Non-intuitive Access of Information.** This study defines non-intuitive access of information as when the method of accessing needed information within the EHR cannot be reasonably inferred by the user. We chose to describe this novel information hazard after experiencing non-intuitive access challenges with two of the four charts. First is the chart previously described in the information overload and information scatter sections where notes were populated across multiple encounters. Determining the patient's accurate medical timeline required a uniquely strong understanding of the EHR that not all users could reasonably be expected to have. In the second chart we had difficulty accessing an intraoperative anesthesia record that required logging into an anesthesia module to which many PICU providers at the hospital lack access. It would not be intuitive for a physician to go searching in a portal for information to which they do not have access. It is also one extra obstacle in the way of obtaining pertinent information.

**Copy and Paste.** "Copy and Paste" is the practice of duplicating pre-written text from one document into another and is commonly done to save time when charting. This study identified copy and paste in three of four charts using a built-in EHR function that determines if text was copied and pasted, and where it was copied from. We identified a 52-word run-on sentence in an admission note that was copied and pasted from an emergency department note, which copied and pasted the same language from a prior ICU admission H&P. We also identified a hospital note where the problem list was copied and pasted from the ED note problem list, which was originally copied and pasted from the patient's entire past medical history in the EHR. Furthermore, the same hospital note also copied the History of Present Illness (HPI) from the ED note, but used it for the HPI *and* the assessment. This practice can contribute to note bloat and propagate errors over time [13].

## 4   Discussion

Our analysis of the EHR of four patient PICU encounters revealed multiple information hazards in all previously known categories. In addition, we identified evidence for three new types of information hazards. Collectively, these hazards represent forms of information chaos. The presence of information chaos within the EHR is more than a frustration; it is also likely a patient safety issue. Specifically, the potential impact of information chaos on Mental Workload (MW) and Situation Awareness (SA), two well-described concepts in the field of Human Factors/Ergonomics, might be used to connect information chaos to patient safety.

High MW occurs when a physician's coping resources are exhausted by the mental demands of their tasks [10, 12]. Information chaos increases these mental demands contributing to a high MW. For example, having to process a large amount of information within a short time makes it more likely to miss key details. Piecing together scattered, non-intuitively accessible information, and non-intuitive abbreviations exhausts time and patience, using cognitive resources that could have been devoted to patient care. Situation Awareness (SA) is a person's awareness and understanding of their task-oriented situation [8, 9]. SA may be important for healthcare providers to provide safe, high-quality care in the ever-changing environment of patient care [23–25]. There is an intake and processing of information from the environment and an effector phase where decisions are made, actions are taken, communication occurs, and new informatic stimuli are fed back into the environment. However, disruptions to this system at any level can lower a physician's SA. Information chaos is one of these disruptions that can confound information intake and processing, effectively lowering a physician's SA. High MW may also lower SA, though the relationship between them is complex [2, 11, 21, 22].

While the relationship between MW and SA is complex, literature suggests that high mental workload and low situation awareness impair physician performance of cognitive work tasks [2, 10, 12, 18, 19]. Examples of these tasks are diagnosis, decision making, treatment, communication, problem identification, and problem solving [2, 7]. Since information chaos contributes to high MW and low SA, it can be argued through syllogism that information chaos is likely to adversely affect the performance of cognitive tasks. The consequence is that these tasks are part of a larger network of processes that produce observable outcomes, such as patient safety. While we can now connect the dots from information chaos to patient safety, this is just one line amidst a massive web of interconnected variables that link structures, processes, and outcomes in a healthcare work system.

The Systems Engineering Initiative for Patient Safety 2.0 (SEIPS 2.0) model is useful for articulating this point [14]. SEIPS 2.0 suggests that there are six groups of factors in a work system: person factors, internal environment factors, task factors, organization factors, tools & technology factors, and external environment factors. These factors impact the physical, cognitive, and social processes through which work is conducted, determining the outcomes of the system like patient safety [14]. We can classify elements of the present study according to the SEIPS 2.0 model to illustrate their connectedness. Information chaos in the EHR (Tool & Technology factor) can increase MW and detract from SA (Person). Time pressure, interruptions (Task factors), and the PICU environment (Internal environment factors) interact to influence the levels of MW and SA (Person factors). These are also influenced by PICU staffing, the number of junior doctors on the unit (Organization factors), and the toll from caring for sick children [6, 17] The strain of a global pandemic (External environment factor) would arguably impact all of the factors. Together these factors influence system processes, e.g., the cognitive work performed by physicians. Processes subsequently produce outcomes. Thus, if these processes are impaired, this can have negative consequences on patient safety outcomes [19].

This pilot study is limited in that it only examined the medical records of four patients. Additional study in the PICU setting is necessary to determine whether information chaos as a hazard is a pervasive problem. Additionally, the findings are limited as the presence of hazards were not linked to any harm events, nor was the risk associated with the hazards quantified.

## 5  Conclusion

As has been described in outpatient settings including both the primary care setting and in pharmacies, the presence of information chaos in the PICU represents both a potential threat to patient safety and an opportunity for facilitating safer patient care by improving MW and SA. Future work should focus on characterizing the direct impact of information chaos on MW and SA, as well as using iterative design to reduce the information chaos designed into commercially available EHRs.

**Table 1.** Distribution of information hazards by patient chart

| Distribution of Information Hazards by Patient Chart | | | | |
|---|---|---|---|---|
| | Patient 1 | Patient 2 | Patient 3 | Patient 4 |
| Information Overload | X | X | X | X |
| Information Underload | X | | X | |
| Information Scatter | X | | | X |
| Information Conflict | X | X | X | X |
| Erroneous Information | X | | | X |
| Non-Intuitive Abbreviations | | X | X | X |
| Non-Intuitive Access of Information | | | X | X |
| Copy & Paste | | X | X | X |

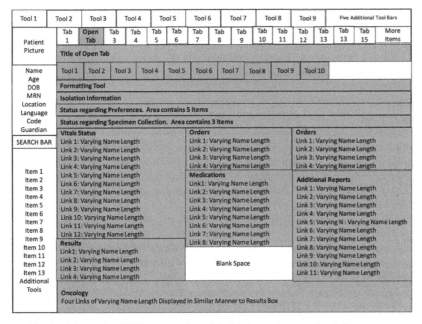

**Fig. 1.** Schematic of EHR conveying global information overload phenomenon

# References

1. Alali, H., Antar, M., AlShehri, A., AlHamouieh, O., Al-Surimi, K., Kazzaz, Y.: Improving physician handover documentation process for patient transfer from pediatric intensive care unit to general ward. BMJ Open Qual. **9**(4), e001020 (2020)
2. Beasley, J.W., et al.: Information chaos in primary care: implications for physician performance and patient safety. J. Am. Board Family Med. **24**(6), 745–751 (2011)
3. Cardoso, M.P., Bourguignon da Silva, D.C., Gomes, M.M., Saldiva, P.H.N., Pereira, C.R., Troster, E.J.: Comparison between clinical diagnoses and autopsy findings in a pediatric intensive care unit in Sao Paulo, Brazil*. Pediatric Crit. Care Med. **7**(5), 423–427 (2006)
4. Chui, M.A., Stone, J.A.: Exploring information chaos in community pharmacy handoffs. Res. Soc. Adm. Pharm. **10**(1), 195–203 (2014)
5. Cifra, C.L., et al.: Diagnostic errors in a PICU. Pediatric Crit. Care Med. **16**(5), 468–476 (2015)
6. Crowe, S.: Disenfranchised grief in the PICU. Pediatric Crit. Care Med. **18**(8), e367–e369 (2017)
7. Custer, J.W., et al.: Diagnostic errors in the pediatric and neonatal ICU. Pediatric Crit. Care Med. **16**(1), 29–36 (2015)
8. Endsley, M.R.: Toward a theory of situation awareness in dynamic systems. Hum. Factors J. Hum. Factors Ergon. Soc. **37**(1), 32–64 (1995)
9. Endsley, M.R., Garland, D.J.: Situation Awareness Analysis and Measurement. [E-book]. Taylor & Francis Group (2000). https://doi.org/10.1201/b12461
10. Hancock, P.A.: A dynamic model of stress and sustained attention. Hum. Factors J. Hum. Factors Ergon. Soc. **31**(5), 519–537 (1989)
11. Hancock, P.A., Desmond, P.A.: Stress, Workload, and Fatigue (1st ed.) [E-book]. CRC Press (2000). https://doi.org/10.1201/b12791

12. Hancock, P.A., Hoffman, J.E.: Tactical Display for Soldiers: Human Factors Considerations, pp. 129–162. National Academy Press, Washington DC (1997)
13. Haugen, H.: Overcoming the risks of copy and paste in EHRs. J. AHIMA **85**(6), 54–55 (2014)
14. Holden, R.J., Carayon, P., Gurses, A.P., et al.: SEIPS 2.0: a human factors framework for studying and improving the work of healthcare professionals and patients. Ergonomics **56**(11), 1669–1686 (2013)
15. Janjua, K.J., Sugrue, M., Deane, S.A.: Prospective evaluation of early missed injuries and the role of tertiary Trauma survey. J. Trauma Injury Infect. Crit. Care **44**(6), 1000–1007 (1998)
16. Johnson, E.M., et al.: An intensive, simulation-based communication course for pediatric critical care medicine fellows. Pediatric Crit. Care Med. **18**(8), e348–e355 (2017)
17. Montgomery, V.L.: Effect of fatigue, workload, and environment on patient safety in the pediatric intensive care unit. Pediatric Crit. Care Med. **8**(Suppl), S11–S16 (2007)
18. Smith, K., Hancock, P.A.: Situation awareness is adaptive, externally directed consciousness. Hum. Factors J. Hum. Factors Ergon. Soc. **37**(1), 137–148 (1995)
19. Stanton, N.A., Chambers, P.R.G., Piggott, J.: Situational awareness and safety. Saf. Sci. **39**(3), 189–204 (2001)
20. Sutherland, A., Ashcroft, D.M., Phipps, D.L.: Exploring the human factors of prescribing errors in paediatric intensive care units. Arch. Dis. Child. **104**(6), 588–595 (2019)
21. Vidulich, M.A.: The relationship between mental workload and situation awareness. In: Proceedings of the Human Factors and Ergonomics Society Annual Meeting, vol. 44, no. 21, pp. 3–460. Sage CA, SAGE Publications, Los Angeles, July 2000
22. Vidulich, M.A., Tsang, P.S.: The confluence of situation awareness and mental workload for adaptable human–machine systems. J. Cogn. Eng. Decis. Mak. **9**(1), 95–97 (2015)
23. Wright, M.C., Endsley, M.R.: Building shared situation awareness in healthcare settings. In: Improving Healthcare Team Communication, pp. 97–114. CRC Press (2017)
24. Schulz, C.M., Endsley, M.R., Kochs, E.F., Gelb, A.W., Wagner, K.J.: Situation awareness in anesthesia: concept and research. J. Am. Soc. Anesthesiologists **118**(3), 729–742 (2013)
25. Brady, P.W., Goldenhar, L.M.: A qualitative study examining the influences on situation awareness and the identification, mitigation and escalation of recognised patient risk. BMJ Qual. Saf. **23**(2), 153–161 (2014)

# Rewards in Mental Health Applications for Aiding with Depression: A Meta-analysis

Stephanie Six⬤, Maggie Harris, Emma Winterlind, and Kaileigh Byrne$^{(\boxtimes)}$⬤

Clemson University, Clemson, SC 29634, USA
{ssix,kaileib}@clemson.edu

**Abstract.** The combination of technology and therapeutic techniques has shown promise of providing people relief through mental health applications (MHapps). Previous research shows that computerized cognitive behavioral therapy can effectively reduce depressive symptoms. Anhedonia, a common symptom of depression, often leads to blunted sensitivity to reward. However, technology-based reward elements have been suggested as a way of increasing motivation and adherence towards treatment and app usage, yet it is unclear whether reward elements also help reduce depressive symptoms. We hypothesize that MHapps with reward elements will provide a greater reduction in depressive symptoms than MHapps without reward elements. Utilizing the PRISMA guidelines, a total of 5,597 articles were collected from 5 different databases. After duplicate removal, 2,741 articles remained to be manually screened by two independent researchers based on their titles and abstract. Once the screening phase concluded, 2,640 articles were excluded for failing to meet inclusion criteria or engaging in one or more of the exclusion criteria with an inter-rater reliability k-value of 0.85. Ultimately, 41 articles remained for data extraction. From these articles, 58 total comparisons between post-intervention MHapp interventions groups and control groups were included in the meta-analysis. We conducted three random effects models to compare the results of all studies (n = 58), the studies which included reward elements (n = 14), and the studies which did not include reward elements (n = 44). Results showed a small to moderate effect size across all MHapps in which the MHapp intervention effectively reduced depressive symptoms compared to controls (Hedge's $g = -.28$). While reward-based MHapps ($g = -.32$) elicited a numerically larger effect size than MHapps without rewards ($g = -.27$), there was no significant difference in effectiveness between MHappps with and without rewards. This research has important clinical implications for understanding how reward elements influence the effectiveness of MHapps on depressive symptoms.

**Keywords:** Depression · Reward · Mental health applications

## 1 Introduction

Depression is a common mental disorder that affects around 17.3 million Americans per year; around 7% of Americans experienced a major depressive episode in 2017 [1]. According to DSM-5, characteristic symptoms include a persistent feeling of sadness on

© Springer Nature Switzerland AG 2021
C. Stephanidis et al. (Eds.): HCII 2021, CCIS 1499, pp. 197–206, 2021.
https://doi.org/10.1007/978-3-030-90179-0_26

most days, fatigue, loss of appetite, trouble making decisions and concentrating, feelings of worthlessness, and potential suicidal ideation [2]. People with depression often find daily activities and responsibilities more difficult and energy inducing [2]. Common treatments often include medication and therapy, like cognitive behavioral therapy or interpersonal therapy [3]. However, there are widespread challenges to treatment, such as problems of consistent adherence, access to mental healthcare resources, and cost [4–6]. As of 2019, 81% of all Americans own a smartphone [7], which suggests that the ready availability of technology could help increase the availability of treatment by providing individuals with cost-efficient tools and applications to aid them between sessions.

One hallmark symptom of depression is anhedonia, which is characterized by loss of excitement, pleasure, motivation, or joy about things that previously motivated or intrigued them [2]. A key cognitive correlate of anhedonia is blunted sensitivity to reward [8–10]; people view rewards, like money or social encouragement, as less motivating than individuals without depressive symptoms [11–13]. Providing an active, playable game element increased activation in the reward center of the brain, specifically the ventral striatum [14]. Additionally, the enjoyability of video games shares a strong connection and activation in the reward processing center of the brain, specifically the ventral striatum [15, 16]. Work has shown that individuals who performed an action video game where the participants operated a tank with the objective of collecting white flags and destroying enemy tanks experienced extended dopamine release, and therefore greater feelings of pleasure [16]. With this discovery, video games containing a goal that provides motivation to receive a prize, like the opportunity to win or feelings of success, represent a potential tool that can be leveraged to increase reward experiences.

The purpose of our analysis is to succinctly pool evidence to determine whether the addition of a reward or gamification element influences the effectiveness of MHapps on depressive symptoms. Based on the success of previous literature in discovering that video games can provide high levels of reward motivation and pleasure [15, 16], we predict that MHapps will have a positive effect and do indeed lessen the symptoms of depression and increase reward motivation. Additionally, we hypothesize that MHapps which include reward or gamification elements will prove more effective in reducing depressive symptoms than those which do not.

## 2   Methods

### 2.1   Search Strategy

Five databases were identified as containing potentially relevant articles on the topic of MHapps aiding with depression: PubMed, PsychInfo, Cochrane Clinical Trials Registry, Web of Science, and PsyArXiv, which was used to address publication bias. The search and overall structures followed the Prisma guidelines. Search terms were divided into three categories: application based, depression, and reward. Then, two categories were combined at a time to form three concepts with 129 search combinations (application based + depression: 12; application based + reward: 108; depression + reward: 9).

## 2.2 Eligibility Criteria

Five inclusion criteria were identified: *(1)* randomized control trials published from 2005 to 2020, *(2)* studies involving human participants, *(3)* MHapps targeting depression as a primary, secondary, or tertiary concern, *(4)* data on the outcomes of MHapps or usability of those apps, and *(5)* pre and post measures of depression that include mean, standard error, and standard deviation.

Twelve exclusion criteria were identified: *(1)* studies not written and originally published in English, *(2)* articles not related to mental health, *(3)* any duplicates discovered in the process, *(4)* any studies lacking a complete set of data, *(5)* any studies published prior to 2005 or after 2020, *(6)* any studies not related to the research question, *(7)* studies with participants who had a terminal or life threatening disorder or disease, *(8)* studies containing participants younger than 18, *(9)* studies which did not include CBT or ACT intervention or elements of meditation, mindfulness, and relaxation *(10)* studies lacking a control group or experimental/quasi-experimental design, and *(11)* meta-analyses, books, reviews, care studies, opinion pieces, or replies.

## 2.3 Study Selection and Screening Procedure

During the identification phase, articles were identified and collected based on the search terms combinations from the five databases. The result of this phase led to 5,597 identified

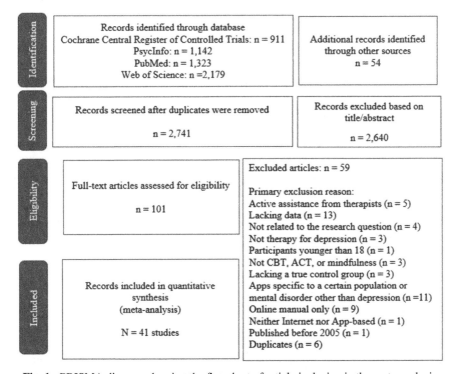

**Fig. 1.** PRISMA diagram showing the flowchart of article inclusion in the meta-analysis.

articles. Duplicates are removed to reveal 2,741 articles eligible for title and abstract screening. Two independent researchers (S. Six & K. Byrne) began the first screening phase by reading through the titles and abstracts to decide whether they met the inclusion criteria or included any of the exclusion criteria. Screeners had an agreement rate of 98.94%, (inter-rater reliability Cohen's $k = 0.85$). After independent article screening was completed, the two independent researchers resolved differences in ratings through discussion. A total of 101 articles were deemed eligible for full-text screening. After the second phase of screening, 41 studies [17–56] containing 40 different apps were deemed eligible for data extraction. See Fig. 1 for more details.

### 2.4  Data Extraction and Analysis

This study compared post-intervention results for the intervention and control groups. A data extraction sheet was developed, and group means and standard deviations for the respective depression measure used in each study were extracted. If a study compared more than one MHapp intervention to a control group, or if more than one independent sample was examined in an article, then both were included as separate comparisons in the analysis. This led to a resulting total of 58 comparisons in the meta-analysis. From this data, the pooled standard deviation, Hedge's $g$, t-value, p-value, degrees of freedom, and standard error were calculated in Microsoft Excel. The depression questionnaire data taken from the articles were analyzed in RStudio to determine if any between-group differences were detected and significant. The depression questionnaires included in the analyzed studies were as follows: PHQ-9, BDI-II, CES-D, DASS-21 Depression Subscale, HADS, QIDS-SR, IDS-SR, PROMIS Depression, CCAPS 34 Depression Scale, and GDS. If the articles met any of the exclusion criteria, specifically missing data, they were excluded from data analysis (n = 12). To test the hypotheses, a random effects model was utilized to determine if any between-group differences for the magnitude of depressive symptomology exists between those MHapps with reward elements and those without reward elements. The random effects model assumes that differences in effect sizes can be attributed to true variation between studies and not random error. The $I^2$ statistic was also computed to provide an index of heterogeneity of effect sizes; higher values indicate greater heterogeneity. While some articles provided follow-up timepoint data, only data from the post-intervention period (i.e., the end of the intervention period) or data that was specified as the primary endpoint was analyzed. When determining which apps included reward elements, the definition for reward in MHapps included badges, achievements, points, and/or virtual rewards [57]. A coding sheet was developed and used to classify MHapps as reward-based *(n = 14)* or non-reward-based *(n = 44)*.

## 3  Results

A forest plot for the post-intervention differences between the MHapp intervention group and control are shown in Fig. 2. Across all eligible studies, the total sample size was 9,729 participants (4,938 in the app intervention group and 4,791 in the control group). The random effects model for all eligible studies (*n* = 58) revealed a small effect size to medium effect of mental health apps in reducing depressive symptoms compared to

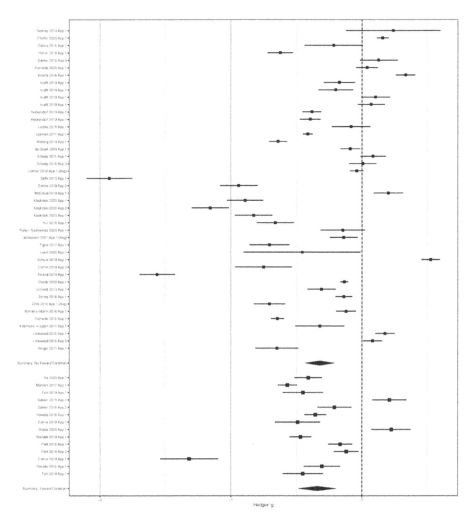

**Fig. 2.** Forest plot for post-intervention differences between the MHapp intervention group and control group.

controls, $g = -0.28$ (95% CI: $-0.38$ to $-0.18$). Significant heterogeneity in the results were observed, however ($I^2 = 76\%, p < .01$).Next, subgroup analyses were performed for apps that included reward-based elements compared to those that did not contain reward-based elements. Results for the non-reward-based apps ($n = 44$) also revealed a small to medium effect size, $g = -0.27$ (95% CI: $-0.39$ to $-0.15$), with significant heterogeneity ($I^2 = 80\%, p < .01$).Effect of the app intervention compared to control for the reward-based apps ($n = 14$) showed a small to medium effect size, $g = -0.32$ (95% CI: $-0.46$ to $-0.17$), with minimal heterogeneity ($I^2 = 39\%, p = .07$). Although the effect size was larger for the reward-based apps than non-reward-based apps, the overlapping confidence intervals suggest that there is no significant difference between apps with reward elements compared to those without reward elements on reduction in depressive symptoms.

## 4  Discussion

This meta-analysis sought to evaluate the effectiveness of MHapps with and without reward elements on changes in depressive symptoms between intervention and control groups. While we predicted that reward elements would augment the therapeutic properties of MHapps, the result of this meta-analysis suggest that reward elements do not seem to significantly reduce depressive symptoms more than MHapps which do not contain reward elements. However, the results replicate prior meta-analyses showing that MHapps are effective in reducing depressive symptoms. Thus, this work provides further evidence of the benefits of MHapps for alleviating or helping to manage depressive symptoms [58].

All of the MHapps included in the meta-analysis utilized strong, evidence-based therapeutic interventions, including cognitive behavioral therapy, acceptance and commitment therapy, and mindfulness. The inclusion of rewards may not provide sufficient mental health benefits over and above these evidence-based psychological interventions. Instead, rewards may increase the use, likeability, and sustained adherence to using MHapps. Prior research hints at the idea that reward elements may be popularized by developers as a way of improving adherence to apps [59, 60]. Future research is needed to better identify the usability benefits and user preferences of MHapps with and without rewards. Moreover, in future research, the authors will examine the follow-up timepoints for studies that assessed the long-term effects of a given MHapp on depressive symptoms. It is possible that, if MHapps with reward elements are more enjoyable or likeable than MHapps without reward elements, then users may be more willing to continue using those MHapps beyond a given intervention period. Longer MHapp use duration may lead to longer-lasting reductions in depressive symptoms, which would produce a clear therapeutic benefit. Furthermore, it is possible that gamification, instead of or in addition to, may be beneficial. Additionally, in future research, the authors will also examine whether MHapp gamification elements, including stories, themes, games, challenges, and level progressions, influence depressive symptoms compared to MHapps without gamification.

Alternatively, individuals with depressive symptoms may experience hyposensitivity to rewards due to a reduction in their neural reward pathway [8–13], so rewards combined with computerized therapeutic techniques may not be sufficient to further greatly reduce the symptoms. We note that, while this meta-analysis focused on depressive symptoms, given the strong ties between altered reward processing and depression, it is possible the MHapps with reward and/or gamification elements may influence anxiety or stress symptoms, and future research should consider examining the effectiveness of MHapp reward and gamification on other mental health conditions or psychological well-being.

In conclusion, MHapps have proven to be a useful tool in reducing depressive symptoms with or without the inclusion of rewards. Additional elements, like gamification, aesthetics, and usability need to be investigated as to whether these could lead to a further reduction of not only depressive symptoms but symptoms of anxiety and stress.

With millions of people having ready access to technology, MHapps may provide a readily available option for global psychological care; however, supplementary research is needed on their effectiveness before true implementation into the health care system can occur.

# References

1. National Institute of Mental Health page on Major Depression (2017). https://www.nimh.nih.gov/health/statistics/major-depression. Accessed 01 June 2021
2. American Psychological Association: Diagnostic and Statistical Manual of Mental Disorders, 5th edn. American Psychological Association Publishing, Washington, DC (2018)
3. Weir, K.: APA offers new guidance for treating depression (2019). https://www.apa.org/monitor/2019/09/ce-corner-depression. Accessed 01 June 2021
4. Cartwright, C., Gibson, K., Read, J., Cowan, O., Dehar, T.: Long-term antidepressant use: patient perspectives of benefits and adverse effects. Patient Prefer. Adherence 10, 1401 (2016)
5. Stein-Shvachman, I., Karpas, D.S., Werner, P.: Depression treatment non-adherence and its psychosocial predictors: differences between young and older adults? Aging Dis. 4(6), 329 (2013)
6. Wood, P., Burwell, J., Rawlett, K.: New study reveals lack of access as root cause for mental health crisis in America (2018). https://www.thenationalcouncil.org/press-releases/new-study-reveals-lack-of-access-as-root-cause-for-mental-health-crisis-in-america/. Accessed 01 June 2021
7. Pew Research Center. Demographics of Mobile Device Ownership and Adoption in the United States (2019). https://www.pewresearch.org/internet/factsheet/mobile/. Accessed 01 June 2021
8. Admon, R., Pizzagalli, D.A.: Dysfunctional reward processing in depression. Curr. Opin. Psychol. 4, 114–118 (2015)
9. Chen, C., Takahashi, T., Nakagawa, S., Inoue, T., Kusumi, I.: Reinforcement learning in depression: a review of computational research. Neurosci. Biobehav. Rev. 55, 247–267 (2015)
10. Eshel, N., Roiser, J.P.: Reward and punishment processing in depression. Biol. Psychiat. 68(2), 118–124 (2010)
11. Foti, D., Hajcak, G.: Depression and reduced sensitivity to non-rewards versus rewards: evidence from event-related potentials. Biol. Psychol. 81(1), 1–8 (2009)
12. Yang, X.H., et al.: Motivational deficits in effort-based decision making in individuals with subsyndromal depression, first-episode and remitted depression patients. Psychiatry Res. 220(3), 874–882 (2014)
13. Liu, W., et al.: Deficits in sustaining reward responses in subsyndromal and syndromal major depression. Prog. Neuro-Psychopharmacol. Biol. Psychiatry 35(4), 1045–1052 (2011)
14. Cole, S.W., Yoo, D.J., Knutson, B.: Interactivity and reward-related neural activation during a serious videogame. PLoS One 7(3), e33909 (2012)
15. Lorenz, R.C., Gleich, T., Gallinat, J., Kühn, S.: Video game training and the reward system. Front. Hum. Neurosci. 9, 40 (2015)
16. Koepp, M., et al.: Evidence for striatal dopamine release during a video game. Nature 393, 266–268 (1998)
17. Ha, S.W., Kim, J.: Designing a scalable, accessible, and effective mobile app based solution for common mental health problems. Int. J. Hum.-Comput. Interact. 36, 1354–1367 (2020)
18. Twomey, C., et al.: A randomized controlled trial of the computerized CBT programme, MoodGYM, for public mental health service users waiting for interventions. Br. J. Clin. Psychol. 53, 433–450 (2014)

19. Pfeiffer, P.N., et al.: Effectiveness of peer-supported computer-based CBT for depression among veterans in primary care. Psychiatric Serv. **71**, 256–262 (2020)
20. Collins, S., et al.: Evaluation of a computerized cognitive behavioural therapy programme, MindWise (2.0), for adults with mild-to-moderate depression and anxiety. Br. J. Clin. Psychol. **57**, 255–269 (2018)
21. Mantani, A., et al.: Smartphone cognitive behavioral therapy as an adjunct to pharmacotherapy for refractory depression: randomized controlled trial. J. Med. Internet Res. **19**, e373 (2017)
22. Fish, M.T., Saul, A.D.: The gamification of meditation: a randomized-controlled study of a prescribed mobile mindfulness meditation application in reducing college students' depression. Simul. Gaming **50**, 419–435 (2019)
23. Bakker, D., et al.: A randomized controlled trial of three smartphone apps for enhancing public mental health. Behav. Res. Ther. **109**, 75–83 (2018)
24. Richards, D., et al.: A pragmatic randomized waitlist-controlled effectiveness and cost-effectiveness trial of digital interventions for depression and anxiety. NPJ Digit. Med. **3**, 1–10 (2020)
25. Howells, A., Ivtzan, I., Eiroa-Orosa, F.J.: Putting the 'app' in happiness: a randomised controlled trial of a smartphone-based mindfulness intervention to enhance wellbeing. J. Happiness Stud. **17**, 163–185 (2016). https://doi.org/10.1007/s10902-014-9589-1
26. Botella, C., et al.: An Internet-based program for depression using activity and physiological sensors: efficacy, expectations, satisfaction, and ease of use. Neuropsychiatric Dis. Treat. **12**, 393 (2016)
27. Krafft, J., et al.: A randomized controlled trial of multiple versions of an acceptance and commitment therapy matrix app for well-being. Behav. Modif. **43**, 246–272 (2019)
28. Levin, M.E., et al.: Comparing in-the-moment skill coaching effects from tailored versus non-tailored acceptance and commitment therapy mobile apps in a non-clinical sample. Cogn. Behav. Ther. **48**, 200–216 (2019)
29. Lüdtke, T., et al.: A randomized controlled trial on a smartphone self-help application (Be Good to Yourself) to reduce depressive symptoms. Psychiatry Res. **269**, 753–762 (2018)
30. Lokman, S., et al.: Complaint-directed mini-interventions for depressive complaints: a randomized controlled trial of unguided web-based self-help interventions. J. Med. Internet Res. **19**, e4 (2017)
31. Moberg, C., Niles, A., Beermann, D.: Guided self-help works: randomized waitlist controlled trial of Pacifica, a mobile app integrating cognitive behavioral therapy and mindfulness for stress, anxiety, and depression. J. Med. Internet Res. **21**, e12556 (2019)
32. De Graaf, L.E., et al.: Clinical effectiveness of online computerised cognitive–behavioural therapy without support for depression in primary care: randomised trial. Br. J. Psychiatry **195**, 73–80 (2009)
33. Gilbody, S., et al.: Computerised cognitive behaviour therapy (cCBT) as treatment for depression in primary care (REEACT trial): large scale pragmatic randomised controlled trial. BMJ **351**, 1–13 (2015)
34. Löbner, M., et al.: Computerized cognitive behavior therapy for patients with mild to moderately severe depression in primary care: a pragmatic cluster randomized controlled trial (@ktiv). J. Affect. Disord. **238**, 317–326 (2018)
35. Sethi, S.: Treating youth depression and anxiety: a randomised controlled trial examining the efficacy of computerised versus face-to-face cognitive behaviour therapy. Aust. Psychol. **48**, 249–257 (2013)
36. Dahne, J., et al.: Pilot randomized controlled trial of a Spanish-language Behavioral Activation mobile app (¡Aptívate!) for the treatment of depressive symptoms among united states Latinx adults with limited English proficiency. J. Affect. Disord. **250**, 210–217 (2019)
37. Bosso, K.B.: The effects of mindfulness training on BDNF levels, depression, anxiety, and stress levels of college students. Dissertation, Florida Atlantic University (2020)

38. Bostock, S., et al.: Mindfulness on-the-go: effects of a mindfulness meditation app on work stress and well-being. J. Occup. Health Psychol. **24**, 127 (2019)
39. Flett, J.A.M., et al.: Mobile mindfulness meditation: a randomised controlled trial of the effect of two popular apps on mental health. Mindfulness **10**, 863–876 (2019)
40. McCloud, T., et al.: Effectiveness of a mobile app intervention for anxiety and depression symptoms in university students: randomized controlled trial. JMIR mHealth uHealth **8**, e15418 (2020)
41. Kladnitski, N., et al.: Transdiagnostic internet-delivered CBT and mindfulness-based treatment for depression and anxiety: a randomised controlled trial. Internet Interv. **20**, 100310 (2020)
42. Hur, J.-W., et al.: A scenario-based cognitive behavioral therapy mobile app to reduce dysfunctional beliefs in individuals with depression: a randomized controlled trial. Telemed. e-Health **24**, 710–716 (2018)
43. Fuller-Tyszkiewicz, M., et al.: Efficacy of a smartphone app intervention for reducing caregiver stress: randomized controlled trial. JMIR Mental Health **7**, e17541 (2020)
44. Tighe, J., et al.: Ibobbly mobile health intervention for suicide prevention in Australian Indigenous youth: a pilot randomised controlled trial. BMJ Open **7**, e013518 (2017)
45. Levin, M.E., Hicks, E.T., Krafft, J.: Pilot evaluation of the stop, breathe & think mindfulness app for student clients on a college counseling center waitlist. J. Am. Coll. Health 1–9 (2020)
46. Schure, M.B., et al.: Use of a fully automated internet-based cognitive behavior therapy intervention in a community population of adults with depression symptoms: randomized controlled trial. J. Med. Internet Res. **21**, e14754 (2019)
47. Dahne, J., et al.: Pilot randomized trial of a self-help behavioral activation mobile app for utilization in primary care. Behav. Ther. **50**, 817–827 (2019)
48. Deady, M., et al.: Preventing depression using a smartphone app: a randomized controlled trial. Psychol. Med. **8**, 1–10 (2020)
49. McMurchie, W., et al.: Computerised cognitive behavioural therapy for depression and anxiety with older people: a pilot study to examine patient acceptability and treatment outcome. Int. J. Geriatr. Psychiatry **28**, 1147–1156 (2013)
50. Lintvedt, O.K., et al.: Evaluating the effectiveness and efficacy of unguided internet-based self-help intervention for the prevention of depression: a randomized controlled trial. Clin. Psychol. Psychother. **20**, 10–27 (2013)
51. Birney, A.J., et al.: MoodHacker mobile web app with email for adults to self-manage mild-to-moderate depression: randomized controlled trial. JMIR mHealth uHealth **4**, e8 (2016)
52. Roepke, A.M., et al.: Randomized controlled trial of SuperBetter, a smartphone-based/internet-based self-help tool to reduce depressive symptoms. Games Health J. **4**, 235–246 (2015)
53. Choi, I., et al.: Culturally attuned Internet treatment for depression amongst Chinese Australians: a randomised controlled trial. J. Affect. Disord. **136**, 459–468 (2012)
54. Montero-Marín, J., et al.: An internet-based intervention for depression in primary care in Spain: a randomized controlled trial. J. Med. Internet Res. **18**, e231 (2016)
55. Richards, D., et al.: A randomized controlled trial of an internet-delivered treatment: its potential as a low-intensity community intervention for adults with symptoms of depression. Behav. Res. Ther. **75**, 20–31 (2015)
56. Berger, T., et al.: Internet-based treatment of depression: a randomized controlled trial comparing guided with unguided self-help. Cogn. Behav. Ther. **40**, 251–266 (2011)
57. Hoffmann, A., Christmann, C.A., Bleser, G.: Gamification in stress management apps: a critical app review. JMIR Serious Games **5**, e13 (2017)
58. Li, J., et al.: Game-based digital interventions for depression therapy: a systematic review and meta-analysis. Cyberpsychol. Behav. Soc. Netw. **7**, 519–533 (2014)

59. Saric, K., et al.: Increasing health care adherence through gamification, video feedback, and real-world rewards. Paper presented at the 40th Annual International Conference of the IEEE Engineering in Medicine and Biology Society (EMBC), Honolulu, HI, 18 July 2018
60. Ali, Z., et al.: High adherence and low dropout rate in a virtual clinical study of atopic dermatitis through weekly reward-based personalized genetic lifestyle reports. PloS One **15**, e0235500 (2020)

# Discussions About Covid-19 in Indonesia. Bibliometric Analysis and Visualization Article Indexed in Scopus by Indonesian Authors

M. Syamsurrijal[1]([⊠]), Achmad Nurmandi[2], Misran[3], Hasse Jubba[1], Mega Hidayati[1], and Zuly Qodir[1]

[1] Islamic Politics - Political Science, Government Affairs and Administration, Jusuf Kalla School of Government, Universitas Muhammadiyah Yogyakarta, Bantul, Indonesia
[2] Government Affairs and Administration, Jusuf Kalla School of Government, Universitas Muhammadiyah Yogyakarta, Bantul, Indonesia
nurmandi_achmad@umy.ac.id
[3] Government Affairs and Administration, Universitas Muhammadiyah Yogyakarta, Bantul, Indonesia
misran.psc20@mail.umy.ac.id

**Abstract.** The Covid-19 pandemic has become a trending topic among researchers in the publication of article journals indexed in Scopus. This study aims to explain the trends and characteristics of Scopus indexed journal articles by Indonesian authors and map Scopus indexed journal articles' topics about the Covid-19 pandemic in Indonesia. In this study, the bibliometric analysis approach was used with two analysis models: analyzing search results and VOSviewer. This study found that the trends and characteristics of the Scopus indexed journal articles published by Indonesian authors have developed quite rapidly since 2020, which is because the issue of the Covid-19 pandemic is the most prevalent in Indonesia. This study also found that the theme and subject of Covid-19 in Indonesia were not based on increasing literacy and education for the public but were more focused on topics and issues that tended to be threatening and sporadic and not substantive. The issues and topics built not based on increasing literacy and education will create new problems in society.

**Keywords:** Covid-19 · Bibliometric analysis · Visualization · Cluster · Indonesian

## 1 Introduction

The Covid-19 pandemic has become a prevalent issue among academics around the world, including Indonesia (Qodir et al. 2020; Airlangga and Akrim 2020). In addition to conducting research, academics also have a strong interest in publishing articles indexed in Scopus. However, the publication article indexed in Scopus by Indonesian authors tends to look at three main issues; First, that the Covid-19 pandemic has brought about traumatic consequences, psychological pressure, health, and medical problems,

C. Stephanidis et al. (Eds.): HCII 2021, CCIS 1499, pp. 207–214, 2021.
https://doi.org/10.1007/978-3-030-90179-0_27

and even resulted in death (Abdullah 2020; Ing et al. 2020; Yuliana 2020; Aldila et al. 2020; Angeline et al. 2020; Ansori et al. 2020). Second; The Covid 19 pandemic has an immediate impact on the weakening of the global economy (Azikin et al. 2020; Susilawati et al. 2020; Caraka et al. 2020). Third; The Covid-19 pandemic has resulted in changes in communication patterns in the government system and education system through limited learning activities (Salahudin et al. 2020). From the three trends above, there has been no research that has looked at the Covid-19 pandemic in terms of narrative issues built through research topics in articles indexed in Scopus by Indonesian authors.

This paper seeks to complement the shortcomings of previous studies by conducting research based on a bibliometric approach to the analysis of Covid-19 in Indonesia, which is accelerated using two analysis models, namely search results analysis in the Scopus and VOSviewer. In line with that, three questions can be formulated in this paper: (a) what are the trends and characteristics of journal articles written by Indonesian authors; (b) how the topics (narratives) are developed in journal articles by Indonesian authors about the Covid-19 pandemic. Thus, based on these two questions, it is possible to find a solution in tackling Covid-19 to run well, ensure the general good, and seek new and better policy directions.

This paper is based on an argument that the themes and issues developed about Covid-19 in Indonesia by most writers (experts) are more aimed at problems that lead to sporadic and not substantive issues. The study of Covid-19 by the author (expert) also did not focus on values that have the essence of a narrative that educates the public. Themes and issues constructed in the form of written articles determine society's social attitudes and behavior in government policies. Topics and problems in writing articles that are limited to studies oriented to emotional problems by ignoring substantive studies will directly influence people's attitudes and behavior. Lessons based on narratives that have educational value for the community will positively impact community submission and compliance with various government policies.

## 2   Methodology

This study uses a bibliometric review of analysis based on journal articles indexed by Indonesian authors and quantitative. Data collection was based on the keyword "Covid-19 in Indonesia" and found 210 journal articles. Then the researchers narrowed down the words on "Covid-19 AND Indonesian authors" and found 88 journals after a selection of published years starting from 2019, 2020, 2021, the election in English. The articles selected from the Scopus database are saved in the form of a CSV file. Furthermore, it was analyzed using two forms of analysis: search results analysis in the Scopus menu and analysis using VOSviewer software. To provide a clear picture of the steps carried out in this study, it is described in Fig. 1 below.

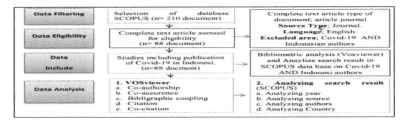

**Fig. 1.** Bibliometric analysis working steps using VOSviewer.

## 3 Results

### 3.1 Trend Article Journal and Publication on Covid-19 in Indonesia

Based on data obtained from the Scopus database, using analyzing search results, it was found that the trend in the number of journal articles written by Indonesian authors on topics related to the published Covid-19 pandemic at Scopus in 2020 experienced a surge in article publication with the number of documents reaching 52 articles. From January to March 2021 alone, it has compared 36 pieces, as shown in Fig. 2. The number of published articles published in 2020, maybe because in March, Indonesia has started to be exposed to Covid-19. Scholars feel interested in publications related to issues that are trending topics in 2020. The trend that occurs in 2020 continues until March 2021, so there will likely be an increase in publications until the end of 2021.

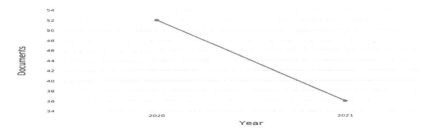

**Fig. 2.** Analysis yearly trend article Covid-19 by Indonesian authors in Scopus

Based on the VOSviewer analysis, it was found that the computation of the number of articles related to the Covid-19 pandemic indexed by Scopus by Indonesian authors was based on a minimum frequency of 2 (two) document articles, so that 15 popular journals were obtained with quite various citation numbers and total link strength which is shown in Table 1. Whereas Fig. 3 shows a visualization of the authors who have at least 1 article document that has been published in the Scopus indexed journal by Indonesian authors. Panulis Indonesia often collaborates with writers from abroad such as Malaysia, Australia, Taiwan, Thailand, United Kingdom, Brazil, China, United States, Netherland, New Zealand, and Turkey, as shown in Fig. 4 and Table 2 below.

**Table 1.** Top 15 journal and their publication in Scopus

| No | Journal | Dokument | Citation | Link strength |
|----|---------|----------|----------|---------------|
| 1 | International journal of public health | 6 | 2 | 17 |
| 2 | Frontiers in public helalth | 2 | 1 | 11 |
| 3 | Frontiers in Pshyarty | 2 | 2 | 9 |
| 4 | Studies and English language and education | 3 | 2 | 5 |
| 5 | Universal Journal of education research | 3 | 0 | 4 |
| 6 | Asia-pasific journal of public health | 2 | 4 | 3 |
| 7 | International Journal of learning teaching | 2 | 10 | 2 |
| 8 | Journal of social studies education research | 2 | 2 | 1 |
| 9 | Acta medica Indonesia | 2 | 0 | 0 |
| 10 | Annal of medicine and surgery | 2 | 0 | 0 |
| 11 | Bali medical journal | 2 | 0 | 0 |
| 12 | Medical journal of criminology | 2 | 10 | 0 |
| 13 | Journal of sustainability science | 2 | 0 | 0 |
| 14 | Cesmas | 4 | 4 | 0 |
| 15 | Open acces macedonian journal | 4 | 0 | 0 |

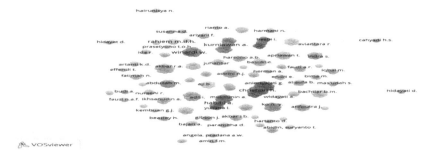

**Fig. 3.** analysis co-authorship network visualization of author

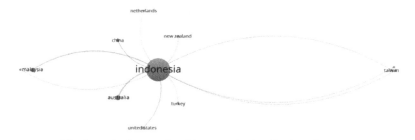

**Fig. 4.** analysis co-authorship network visualization of country

**Table 2.** Analysis co-authorship of countries on Covid-19 in Indonesia

| No | Country | Document | Citation | Link strength |
|----|---------|----------|----------|---------------|
| 1 | Indonesia | 88 | 64 | 20 |
| 2 | Australia | 5 | 0 | 5 |
| 3 | Malaysia | 4 | 1 | 5 |
| 4 | Taiwan | 1 | 5 | 3 |
| 5 | Thailand | 1 | 5 | 3 |
| 6 | United Kingdom | 1 | 5 | 3 |
| 7 | Brazil | 1 | 0 | 2 |
| 8 | China, | 2 | 1 | 2 |
| 9 | United States | 2 | 0 | 2 |
| 10 | Netherland | 1 | 0 | 1 |
| 11 | New Zeland | 1 | 2 | 1 |
| 12 | Turkey | 1 | 3 | 1 |

### 3.2 Topic Article Journal on Covid-19 by Indonesian Authors

Based on the VOS viewer analysis, 2,812 keywords were obtained. If filtered with a minimum number of 6 terms, then 128 keywords have met the threshold of the data analysis set of 88 Scopus indexed journal articles published from 2020 to 2021. Of the 128 existing keywords, filtering is carried out. And selected 83 keywords that have a relationship between one node and another node; The closer the distance between one node and another node, the higher the connection level of the node. VOSviewer is used for bibliometric mapping of the Covid-19 topic in Indonesia which is grouped into 8 clusters; each cluster has a different color namely; first; red cluster with 26 keywords such as Coronavirus disease 2019 keywords, cough, dizziness, fever, hypertension, fatigue, headache, diabetes mellitus, mixed infection. Second, green clusters, as psychology, epidemiology says. Third, the blue cluster is a word of anxiety, attitude, attitude towards health, awareness. Fourth, yellow clusters as said beta coronavirus, epidemic, neuro-surgery. Fifth, the purple cluster, as said Covid-19, is a new routine, social distancing. Sixth, the light blue cluster, as stated by the public administration, is approaching the government approach. Seventh, the Gold color cluster is like the word health literate, young adults. Eighth, the Tosca color group, such as the word online learning and higher education (Fig. 5).

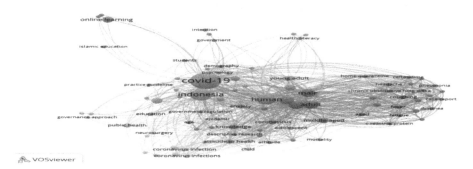

**Fig. 5.**  Analysis co-assurance network visualization of Covid-19 in Indonesia

## 4   Discussion

This study found that the trends and characteristics of the Scopus indexed journal articles published by Indonesian authors have developed quite rapidly since 2020. This development is more due to the increasing popularity of the Covid-19 pandemic issue in Indonesia since March 2020, which is of concern. Can threaten the safety of human life. The results of this study found that the scientific community around the world has widely accepted published journal articles related to Covid-19 by Indonesian authors, as evidenced by the level of journal article citation and the level of collaboration in publication of Scopus indexed articles between Indonesian authors and authors from countries of the world. In line with that, besides this research finds that the topics and issues narrated by Indonesian writers tend to be sporadic, impacting psychological distress and death threats. This research has also seen a research model that ensures the prevention of the pandemic runs well and that the public benefit can be achieved by conducting research that is oriented not only to novelty but more importantly, to increase knowledge literacy about the Covid-19 pandemic in Indonesia so that people are made aware of all forms. Policies in dealing with a pandemic.

The results showed two different sides, namely, (a) on the one hand. There has been a segmentation of the publication of Scopus indexed journal articles written by Indonesian writers, which tend to be subjective and ignore substantive matters; (b) the results of this study serve as the basis for seeing that there has been a disturbing condition that has had a fundamental impact on the narrative built through the publication of journal articles indexed by Indonesian authors on the fragility of government mobility in the community in carrying out the policy of handling the Covid-19 pandemic in Indonesia.. The emotional bond between people as consumers and the narrative that is built through the writing of the article has legitimized the resistance in society to government policies; (c) the results of this research provide a more substantive research model by ignoring emotional issues and topics.

These results also provide an overview of the trends and characteristics of articles published in Scopus indexed journals, no longer a narrative that is built solely based on a lot of research and published journal articles, but it is more important to consider various aspects that can have an impact on people's understanding. About the Covid-19 pandemic (Halim et al. 2020), especially by authors in Indonesia. This kind of publication condition shows that the narrative built through research and articles published in Scopus indexed journals by Indonesian authors has resulted in the slow handling of the COVID-19 pandemic in Indonesia.

This study is different from other studies that discuss Covid-19 in Indonesia which have so far confirmed that the Covid-19 pandemic is a latent threat that endangers humankind both in physical, psychological, economic, social health, and even death (Hafiz et al. 2020; Handoko 2020; Murad et al. 2020; Hendarwan et al. 2020). Some consider that the Covid-19 pandemic is one of the viruses that have a high level of spread and is spread throughout the world and has held humans from various kinds of activities, and narrowed the space for conducting social, religious, political, and economic relations (Handoko 2020). This study confirms that the slow handling of the Covid-19 pandemic in Indonesia is more due to a narrative that tends to be subjective, resulting in the rejection of various policies related to the Covid-19 pandemic in Indonesia.

In line with the fundamental changes in the relations between the Covid-19 pandemic and the policy for handling the Covid-19 pandemic, a research action plan and publication of Scopus indexed journal articles are needed that lead to research based on issues and topics that provide direction for the creation of increased literacy by providing an understanding through narratives that educate and give knowledge to the public about the Covid-19 pandemic. Good socialization and expertise through writing journal articles to the public need to be started by organizations and higher education institutions concerned with handling the Covid-19 pandemic in Indonesia.

## 5  Conclusion

The topic of the Covid-19 pandemic published by Indonesian authors is not based on research topics and issues that lead to increased literacy but instead based on research that tends to be subjective and sporadic. Topics and issues built on subjectivity legitimize the occurrence of resistance in society. On the other hand, research topics and issues based on something substantive to increase literacy for the community will create public awareness and compliance with government policies. This research has made it possible to find the causes of neglect of government policies related to handling the Covid-19 pandemic. New policy directions can be found for tackling Covid-19 to run well for the public benefit to be guaranteed.

This research is limited to analyzing trends and characteristics of journal articles that are only indexed by Scopus and written by Indonesian authors so that they do not have the authority to generalize. Simultaneously, the bibliometric analysis approach used has limitations to see how broad the coverage of topics and issues regarding the Covid-19 pandemic in Indonesia. Thus, this paper suggests the need for further studies that accommodate articles from both google scholar, crosref, Web of science and using a combined method in addition to getting more comprehensive results and more targeted policies.

## References

Abdullah, I.: COVID-19: threat and fear in Indonesia. Psychol. Trauma Theory Res. Pract. Policy 12(5), 488–490 (2020). https://doi.org/10.1037/tra0000878

Halim, A., et al.: Understanding of young people about COVID-19 during early outbreak in Indonesia. Asia Pac. J. Public Health 32(6–7), 363–365 (2020). https://doi.org/10.1177/1010539520940933

Airlangga, E., Akrim, A.: Learning from COVID-19, will this pandemic reappear: a reflection for Indonesian children future. Syst. Rev. Pharm. 11(6), 1008–1015 (2020). https://doi.org/10.31838/srp.2020.6.144

Aldila, D., Ndii, M.Z., Samiadji, B.M.: Optimal control on COVID-19 eradication program in Indonesia under the effect of community awareness. Math. Biosci. Eng. 17(6), 6355–6389 (2020). https://doi.org/10.3934/mbe.2020335

Angeline, M., Safitri, Y., Luthfia, A.: Can the damage be undone? Analyzing misinformation during COVID-19 outbreak in Indonesia. In: Proceedings of 2020 International Conference on Information Management and Technology, ICIMTech 2020, October, pp. 360–64 (2020). https://doi.org/10.1109/ICIMTech50083.2020.9211124

Ansori, A.N.M., Kharisma, V.D., Muttaqin, S.S., Antonius, Y., Parikesit, A.A.: Genetic variant of SARS-CoV-2 isolates in Indonesia: spike glycoprotein gene. J. Pure Appl. Microbiol. 14(Suppl1), 971–978 (2020). https://doi.org/10.22207/JPAM.14.SPL1.35

Azikin, A., Karno, P.N., Fitriani, S., Cahyono, Y.: Indonesian government dilematics in Covid-19 pandemic handling. Eur. J. Mol. Clin. Med. 7(7), 125–133 (2020)

Caraka, R.E., et al.: Impact of COVID-19 large-scale restriction on environment and economy in Indonesia. Global J. Environ. Sci. Manag. 6(Special Issue), 65–84 (2020). https://doi.org/10.22034/GJESM.2019.06.SI.07

Hafiz, M., Icksan, A.G., Harlivasari, A.D., Aulia, R., Susanti, F., Eldinia, L.: Clinical, radiological features and outcome of COVID-19 patients in a secondary hospital in Jakarta, Indonesia. J. Infect. Dev. Countries 14(7), 750–757 (2020). https://doi.org/10.3855/jidc.12911

Handoko, L.H.: Bibliometric analysis and visualization of islamic economics and finance articles indexed in scopus by Indonesian authors. Sci. Editing **7**(2), 169–176 (2020). https://doi.org/10.6087/KCSE.213

Hendarwan, H., et al.: Assessing the COVID-19 diagnostic laboratory capacity in Indonesia in the early phase of the pandemic. WHO South-East Asia J. Public Health **9**(2), 134–40 (2020). https://doi.org/10.4103/2224-3151.294307

Ing, E.B., Xu, Q.A., Salimi, A., Torun, N.: Physician deaths from coronavirus (COVID-19) disease. Occup. Med. **70**(5), 370–374 (2020). https://doi.org/10.1093/occmed/kqaa088

Murad, D.F., Hassan, R., Heryadi, Y., Wijanarko, B.D., Titan: The impact of the COVID-19 pandemic in Indonesia (face to face versus online learning). In: Proceeding - 2020 3rd International Conference on Vocational Education and Electrical Engineering: Strengthening the Framework of Society 5.0 through Innovations in Education, Electrical, Engineering and Informatics Engineering, ICVEE 2020, pp. 4–7 (2020). https://doi.org/10.1109/ICVEE50212.2020.9243202

Qodir, Z., et al.: Covid-19 and chaos in Indonesia social-political. Int. Res. Assoc. Talent Dev. Excellence **12**(1), 4629–4642 (2020)

Salahudin, Nurmandi, A., Sulistyaningsih, T., Lutfi, M., Sihidi, I.T.: Analysis of government official Twitters during Covid-19 crisis in Indonesia analysis of government official Twitters during Covid-19 crisis in Indonesia. Talent Dev. Excellence **12**(1), 3899–3915 (2020)

Susilawati, S., Falefi, R., Purwoko, A.: Impact of COVID-19's pandemic on the economy of Indonesia. Budapest Int. Res. Critics Inst. (BIRCI-J.) Humanities Soc. Sci. **3**(2), 1147–1156 (2020). https://doi.org/10.33258/birci.v3i2.954

Yuliana: Corona virus diseases (Covid -19); Sebuah tinjauan literatur. Wellness Healthy Mag. **2**(1), 187–192 (2020)

# UI/UX Design of Portable Simulation Pet 'KEDAMA' Hairball for Relieving Pressure

Jiang Wu[1,2(✉)], Yihang Dai[1,3], Jiawei Li[1], and Yuan Yuan[1]

[1] Kakuchi Academy, Kakuchi Co., Ltd., 3-2-17 Shimoochiai, Shinjuku-ku,
Tokyo 161-0033, Japan
`riverwu@gzac.net.cn`
[2] The University of Tokyo, 7-3-1 Hongo, Bunkyo-ku, Tokyo 113-8656, Japan
[3] Graduate School of Bionics, Computer and Media Sciences, Tokyo University of Technology,
1404-1 Katakuramachi, Hachioji City, Tokyo 192-0982, Japan

**Abstract.** Nowadays, the number of people who keep pets is increasing, and keeping pets is entertaining and relieves the stress of life. However, since the owner has less time to meet his pet on business trips or overtime, we would like to make a hairball which is called 'KEDAMA' in Japanese that can be near the owner instead of the pet at such times. This research is a UI/UX design aimed at relieving stress that acts on the five senses. We would like to select the effect of pets on the five senses of people and reduce the stress of people of the present generation. This KEDAMA system in addition to allowing users to choose existing options, can also be customized in the hair length, color, curl and other aspects. After the practical application of the system to the target people and the customized use of the KEDAMA, through our subjective questionnaire survey, the results show that 85% of the people would relieve the pressure to a certain extent after using it.

**Keywords:** UI/UX design · Relieving stress · Five senses · Hairball · Customization

## 1 Introduction

More and more global trends see pets as part of the family. In fact, millions of people around the world love their pets, enjoy their company, walk, play and even talk to them. Attachment to pets is beneficial to human health and relieves all kinds of pressure [1, 2]. Especially under the COVID-19 influence, most families have acquired pets. New pet owners under the age of 35 accounted for 59%, and among those who bought a pet for the first time, 56% had children at home [3].

On the contrary, the situation of abandoning pets also happens correspondingly. Except the extremely bad man-made injury and abandonment of pets, as well as pet loss and other accidents, most of the elderly cannot keep pets with the increase of age or special circumstances [4, 5]. Furthermore, because of studying abroad, business trip, travel and other factors, or the death of the pet itself, it will lead to long-term or short-term separation from the pet [6, 7]. In this process, the owner's yearning for the pet is inevitable.

© Springer Nature Switzerland AG 2021
C. Stephanidis et al. (Eds.): HCII 2021, CCIS 1499, pp. 215–223, 2021.
https://doi.org/10.1007/978-3-030-90179-0_28

In recent years, the development of virtual pets has become more and more diversified. People hope to realize it through virtual pets, which is not only convenient to carry, but also can achieve the same effect as keeping pets, so as to seek comfort and relieve pressure [8]. For example, by letting children exercise, play and train virtual pets with their own physical activities as input, to reduce children's obesity rate [9]. In addition, in view of the fact that it may be difficult for the elderly to keep real pets, they are allergic to pets, unable to control the behavior of pets and their own living conditions. Therefore, as an alternative solution, many pet robots have been developed as partners for the elderly and provide them with emotional care [10]. Therefore, we aim to design a portable simulation pet through UI/UX to relieve the pressure. We hope that the selection or customization of pets will have an impact on the five senses of human beings, to reduce the pressure of contemporary people. In this study, through the UI/UX design, we'd like to make a hairball called "KEDAMA" in Japanese and use it to replace the real pet.

## 2   Related Works

### 2.1   Analysis of Users' Pain Points and Resolution

To analyze the needs and difficulties of users and put them into design. We conducted a predesign questionnaire survey on 300 people (Fig. 1).

**Fig. 1.** Results of questionnaire survey before design were analyzed for 300 people. From left to right, they are as follows:

Q1: How long do you want to touch your pet after parting from it? (Level 5 is the strongest)
Q2: Do you feel comfortable touching your pet? (Level 5 is the strongest)
Q3: Do you remember your child when you hear someone else's pet's voice?
Q4: Does keeping a pet help relieve stress? (Level 5 is the strongest)
Q5: Can you relax by listening to your pet's voice? (Level 5 is the strongest)

### 2.2   Persona-User Positioning in User Portrait and Usage Scenario

Alan Cooper, the father of interaction design, first proposed the concept of user portrait: Personas are a concrete representation of target users [11, 12]. User portrait is a tagged user model abstracted based on information such as users' social attributes, living habits, and consumption behavior. Based on the differences in the three user portraits (Fig. 2), users' experience of raising pets, types and breeds of pets, personal characteristics and related backgrounds (different from the pet experience due to business trips, study abroad, travel, etc.), in terms of color, appearance, sound, texture, etc. to customize different products. Based on the usage scenario (Fig. 3), the blindness of product design and production can be avoided, and design errors and investment risks can be reduced. By constructing two usage scenarios for three users at different time periods, users can understand whether they can customize products through our app when they want to touch their pets to reduce stress in the context of business trips or study abroad to achieve the purpose of reducing stress.

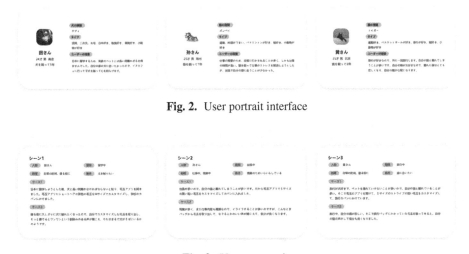

**Fig. 2.** User portrait interface

**Fig. 3.** Usage scenario

## 3   Method

### 3.1   Product Positioning and Architecture

We specifically targeted KEDAMA from the following five aspects.

Customization of KEDAMA, ordering KEDAMA, purchasing KEDAMA, change the sound of KEDAMA and KEDAMA management.

The specific product architecture is shown in Fig. 4. In the personal page of the app, we can perform basic personal information design and software updates. Among more, we can generate personal QR codes or scan other people's QR codes. In addition, FAQs and logout of the app itself can also be achieved. The originality of this research is that it is based on the individual's different breeding experience, or the long-term and short-term separation from the pet to personalize the KEDAMA, not only in appearance, but also in terms of hair length, color, taste, etc. settings. In addition, the most healing thing for the owner, the choice of pet sounds and the recording of personalized pet sounds are also considered in this design.

The interactive prototype is shown in Fig. 5, which satisfies the above five aspects of the product positioning and has also been reasonably designed in specific details.

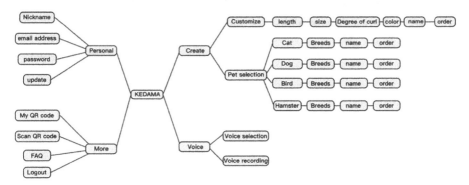

**Fig. 4.** Product architecture

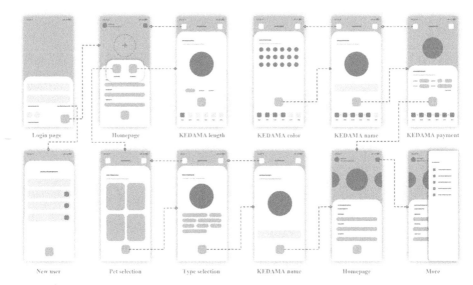

**Fig. 5.** Interactive prototype

## 3.2  Visual Image

**App Appearance Design (Fig. 6).** We adopted four types of animals that are well bred, visualized them, unified them into a circle, and matched them with a circular KEDAMA. In terms of color, the pale warm colors used just like the pages of the entire app. The overall design style is mainly flat illustrations, and you can feel comfortable and relaxed by matching the illustrations with warm colors.

**Color Selection.** HSB, also known as HSV, represents a color mode: in HSB mode, H (hues) represents hue, s (saturation) represents saturation, and B (brightness) represents brightness. In hue, warm colors are often used; Low saturation is selected for saturation; Select high brightness on brightness [13].

**Fig. 6.** Appearance design of KEDAMA app

**Hairball Appearance (Fig. 7).** Randomly selected 7 different types of hair for comparative analysis, the main differences between hair are as follows: 1) Length of hair 2) Thickness of hair 3) Density of hair 4) Curl of hair 5) Color of hair. Through these 5 differences, the first of the two ways of making KEDAMA in the app is "Customize".

According to the American Veterinary Association (AVMA), 38.4% of families have dogs, 25.4% have cats and 2.8% have birds. Therefore, these common pets and their detailed types are regarded as the second way of making hair ball "Pet selection". When you directly select a kind of pet, the effect of KEDAMA will be automatically generated in the app.

**Fig. 7.** Appearance design of hairball appearance

## 4   UI/UX Design

### 4.1   Initial Page Design and Home Page Design

Figure 8 shows the landing interface of KEDAMA app, which is also the cover of the work. A flat illustration is used to describe the scene of a traveler using KEDAMA. In addition, all the graphics and buttons in the screen are rounded.

The home page (Fig. 9) has 2 functions. Click the '+' button in the screen to create the KEDAMA. There are two ways to customize and select pets. Click the horn button in the screen to recruit or import the sound of KEDAMAs. When a KEDAMA is customized, the name, birthday and shape attributes of it will be displayed in the screen.

**Fig. 8.** Initial page design          **Fig. 9.** Home page design

### 4.2   Customization Page Design and Pet Selection Page Design

**Customization Page Design.** In the customization page, size of the KEDAMA, the length of the hair, the curl of the hair and the color of the hair can be customized. In first step to choose the size of the KEDAMA there are three options: large, medium and small. In second step to choose the length of the hair, there are three options: long, medium and short. In third step to choose the curl degree of the hair, there are three options: straight hair, micro curl and curl. At the bottom of the screen, it shows which step of the customization process is in progress. There is a return key in the upper left corner of the screen to reverse the previous operation. The fourth step is to customize the color, it has three options: monochrome, spot and stripe. When the spot or stripe is selected, multiple colors can be given to the hair ball. After customizing the first four steps, KEDAMA would be rendered in the fifth step. If there is any dissatisfaction, go back to the previous steps and select again. In fifth step, named KEDAMA. The sixth step is to place an order, to fill in the receiving information and make payment. When the payment is completed, the customized KEDAMA can be delivered to the door.

**Pet Selection Page Design.** Figure 10 is the second way to make KEDAMAs – Pet selection. Four kinds of pets with the largest number of people were selected. They are cat, dog, bird and hamster. After selecting the pet type in first step, enter the second step to select the pet variety. For example, Samoye, husky, Chihuahua, Teddy, Chaigou and so on are among the dog options. Cat options include British short tail cat, American short tail cat, Persian cat, puppet cat, Garfield cat, etc. Bird options include parrot, oriole, magpie, etc. Hamster options include Golden Bear, silver fox hamster, Xishi bear and so on.

**Fig. 10.** Pet selection page design

## 5   Results and Conclusions

Figure 11 describes the overall use scenario process of KEDAMA. When users feel great pressure in the workplace/study and want to feel their pets to release the pressure, they have no conditions to contact pets because they are separated from their pets on business or because they are not allowed to keep pets. At this time, you can make your own KEDAMA on the KEDAMA app, and you can input your pet's voice or pet's call you like into the KEDAMA. When you touch it, it would make a lovely call. The pressure mood can get some relaxation.

**Fig. 11.** Usage scene

After a series of personalized customization of pet selection, hair, color, sound, etc., our customized KEDAMA can arrive in our hands for actual use (Fig. 12).

**Fig. 12.** Pet selection page design

We randomly selected 20 overseas students from China to study in Japan as experience users, explained to them how to use the KEDAMA app, and let them personally practice the operation, customize KEDAMA, and have a 10 day experience. After the experience, we sent out questionnaires and conducted a 10 min subjective interview hearing for each user. The results showed that 17 of the 20 subjects (85%) said that after 10 days of experience, they were in a better mood, which could reduce the missing of their real pets and reduce the pressure. Among them, 13 subjects (65%) said that compared with raising real pets, the use of KEDAMAs is more convenient, and they can enjoy the real experience of raising pets without the cost of feeding and purchasing pet food.

However, the subjects we selected this time are more restricted to international students than the elderly and the workplace. In addition, there is no evaluation on the fragrance and smell of KEDAMA. Therefore, in the future study, we plan to expand the scope of the experimental subjects, increase the experience time (for example, from 10 days to 30 days), and increase the objective evaluation of the fragrance of KEDAMA, to verify whether the different smell of hair plays a decisive role in relieving stress, and use saliva detection to quantitatively verify the degree of pressure reduction.

## References

1. Households 'buy 3.2 million pets in lockdown'. https://www.bbc.com/news/business-563 62987. Accessed 10 June 2021
2. The Healing Power of Pets for Seniors. https://www.agingcare.com/articles/benefits-of-eld erly-owning-pets-113294.htm. Accessed 10 June 2021
3. When pets are family, the benefits extend into society. https://theconversation.com/when-pets-are-family-the-benefits-extend-into-society-109179. Accessed 10 June 2021
4. Fatjó, J., Calvo, P.: Affinity Foundation study on the abandonment, loss and adoption of pets in. https://www.fundacion-affinity.org/sites/default/files/white-paper-estudio-fundac ion-affinity-abandono-adopcion-2016-en.pdf. Accessed 18 Oct 2021
5. Lu, C.-p., Fei, R.-m., Lu, Y.: The welfare and caring of pets. Chin. J. Comp. Med. **20**(11,12), 43–45 (2010)

6. Mills, E., Akers, K.: "Who gets the cats... you or me?" Analyzing contact and residence issues regarding pets upon divorce or separation. Family Law Q. **36**(2), 283–301 (2002)
7. Rynearson, E.K.: Humans and pets and attachment. Br. J. Psychiatry **133**(6), 550–555 (1978)
8. Long, J.: Portable pets: live and apparently live animals in fashion, 1880–1925. Costume **43**(1), 109–126 (2009)
9. Johnsen, K., et al.: Mixed reality virtual pets to reduce childhood obesity. IEEE Trans. Visual. Comput. Graph. **20**(4), 523–530 (2014)
10. Huang, H.-Y., et al.: Design of robotic pets to help the elderly with social interactions (2020)
11. Cooper, A.: The inmates are running the asylum. In: Arend, U., Eberleh, E., Pitschke, K. (eds.) Software-Ergonomie 1999. BGCACM, vol. 53, p. 17. Vieweg+Teubner Verlag, Wiesbaden (1999). https://doi.org/10.1007/978-3-322-99786-9_1
12. Wang, X.: Personas in the user interface design. University of Calgary, Alberta, Canada (2014)
13. Soma, I.: Psychological effects of color. J. Japan Soc. Color Mater. **58**(9), 548–557 (1985)

# A Usability Testing of COVID-19 Vaccine Appointment Websites

John Xie[✉]

Great Neck South High School, Great Neck, NY 11020, USA
jxie1@student.gn.k12.ny.us

**Abstract.** While COVID-19 caused a huge number of casualties, many people rushed to register for a vaccine appointment when the vaccines were available. However, the existing vaccination appointment websites were confusing and hard to use. To help alleviate this problem, this usability study was conducted to understand the major challenges users faced in order to provide possible design solutions. Three U.S. government vaccine appointment websites were chosen: one state government, and two local government websites. In order to properly evaluate the usability of these three websites, a triangular approach with Heuristic Evaluation, Persona Design, and Cognitive Walkthrough was used. The study revealed many usability problems for each chosen site. 1) For the New York State (NYS) site, the clustering of information was not organized well. Vaccine status was displayed inconsistently between parent and child pages. 2) For the New York City (NYC) site, there was a major lack of error prevention in many different aspects. Vaccine brands were not attached to vaccine sites, which can lead to people who have conflicting medical issues with one vaccine but not another. 3) For the Nassau County site, there was a poor organization of information, as everything was linearly displayed with a lack of visual organizations to facilitate navigation. The most fatal problem was there was no local vaccine system to book an appointment at Nassau County site. Corresponding design solutions were discussed based on these findings.

**Keywords:** COVID-19 · Usability · Heuristic evaluation · Cognitive walkthrough · Persona design

## 1 Background and Aim

COVID-19 has caused a huge number of casualties and disrupted people's daily life [1]. It has had many devastating effects on our society (e.g. the economy and people's mental health) [1, 2]. Throughout these crucial times, the official government agencies and public health organizations were considered the most reliable source of information [2]. When people searched for information about viruses on the Internet, they mainly went to the official sources (websites of government agencies or professional organizations) [3]. This led them to various governmental agencies at all different levels including federal, state, and local level websites.

C. Stephanidis et al. (Eds.): HCII 2021, CCIS 1499, pp. 224–230, 2021.
https://doi.org/10.1007/978-3-030-90179-0_29

After the first emergency user authorization for the COVID-19 vaccine was officially released on December 11, 2020, in the U.S. [4], the U.S. Centers for Disease Control and Prevention (CDC) recommended phased allocation of vaccines and provided guidance for federal, state, and local jurisdictions while vaccine supply was limited. Various government agencies and private pharmacies were all tasked with providing vaccines to the public. They provided vaccine registration through their respective websites to ensure contact-free registration, and to minimize the possible spread of COVID-19. However, online registration raised many usability issues.

Understanding that vaccinations are extremely important in that they help keep everyone safe, people rushed to register for a vaccine appointment. With a limited supply of vaccines and a desperate need for them, it is crucial for citizens to easily get vaccine information and register for appointments. However, the diverse vaccination appointment websites at the time were confusing in terms of how to search available slots and make appointments. Thus, the objective of this usability study was to understand the major challenges users were facing in order to provide possible design solutions.

## 2 Method

Three government vaccine registration websites were chosen based on the fact that users were most likely to go to governmental resources to register for vaccines and get COVID-19 information.

- New York State Official: https://covid19vaccine.health.ny.gov (state level)
- New York City (NYC): https://vax4nyc.nyc.gov/patient/s/ (local level)
- Nassau County: https://www.nassaucountyny.gov/vaccine (local level)

In order to properly evaluate the usability of these three websites, three evaluation techniques were used to identify usability problems: Heuristic Evaluation, Persona Design, and Cognitive Walkthrough.

Heuristic evaluation assesses the design of the user interface, according to accepted principles, called heuristics. A heuristic is a guideline, rule of thumb, or general principle that can be used to critique a design. Table 1 lists all 8 heuristic principles and corresponding 12 heuristic questions which were drawn from *An Interactive Heuristic Evaluation Toolkit* developed from HCI Design Interface Golden Rules [5]. Heuristic evaluation was conducted on all three websites, meaning that all 12 questions were asked for every single website, and results were recorded for every question for every website. The heuristic evaluation went through two passes. Two experts conducted an individual inspection in the first pass, and a group inspection was followed to discuss the identified usability problem, and to assess the severity of the problem in the second pass. For each identified usability problem, severity was rated on the scale of 1–4 (4 = Catastrophic problem, 3 = Major problem, 2 = Minor problem, 1 = Cosmetic problem).

Persona design includes the creation of personas of possible users and to set a task or scenario for the possible user to complete. Personas are usually representative users. In this study, a total of 4 personas (Sicky Sally, Regular Ready, Curious Cary, and Helpful Holly) were created. Sally, Randy, and Cary each has two scenarios to complete while

**Table 1.** Heuristic principles used for the study

|   | Heuristic principles |   | Suggested questions |
|---|---|---|---|
| 1 | Visibility of system status | 1.1 | Is status feedback provided continuously (eg progress indicators or messages)? |
| 2 | Match between system and real world | 2.1 | Does the task sequence parallel the user's work processes? |
|   |   | 2.2 | Is information presented in a simple, natural and logical order? |
|   |   | 2.3 | Does the system cater for users with no prior experience of electronic devices? |
| 3 | User control and freedom | 3.1 | Are facilities provided to "undo" (or "cancel") and "redo" actions? |
| 4 | Consistency and standards | 4.1 | Is there consistency between data entry and data display? |
| 5 | Error prevention | 5.1 | Does the system prevent calls being accidentally made? |
| 6 | Flexibility and efficiency of use | 6.1 | Is it possible to access and re-use a recent history of instructions? |
| 7 | Structure of information | 7.1 | Are related pieces of information clustered together? |
|   |   | 7.2 | Are the URLs, page titles and headlines straightforward, short and descriptive? |
|   |   | 7.3 | Incomplete information |
| 8 | Navigation | 8.1 | Are any navigational aids provided? |

Holly only has one scenario. Table 2 list all 4 personas and their corresponding scenarios and websites.

**Table 2.** Persona and corresponding scenarios for three websites

| Persona | Scenario | Site |
|---|---|---|
| Sick Sally | S1: Compare different vaccines<br>S2: Make an appointment | New York City |
| Regular Randy | S3: Make an appointment | New York City |
| Curious Cary | S4: Learn about vaccine<br>S5: Check availability | Nassau County |
| Helpful Holly | S6: Make an appointment for others | New York State |

Cognitive Walkthrough [6–8] evaluates the design of the user interface, especially for "first-time" use. Cognitive walkthrough is based on the theory of explanatory learning, which summarizes user interactions in a total of 4 steps. These four steps are:

Step 1: The user sets a goal to be accomplished with the system (for example, "make a vaccine appointment").
Step 2: The user searches the interface for currently available actions (menu items, buttons, command-line inputs, etc.).
Step 3: The user selects the action that seems likely to make progress toward the goal.
Step 4: The user performs the selected action and evaluates the system's feedback for evidence that progress is being made toward the current goal.

Evaluators inspect the following three questions for each step during cognitive walkthrough.

Q1:  Is the correct action available in the interface?
Q2:  How well does that action's description match the user's goal?
Q3:  Does the system's response to the action show progress toward the user's goal?

This technique is used to discover task-specific usability issues while heuristic evaluation identifies usability problems across different tasks.

## 3   Results

Heuristic evaluation revealed many usability problems. Table 3 reports the total number of heuristic evaluation problems for each site. The New York City (NYC) site had the least number of issues, which indicated that it was the most usable. The Nassau County site had the second most issues, but this also includes a catastrophic issue, which makes it the least usable of the 3 websites. Finally, the New York State (NYS) site had the most issues, but these were mostly of severity 2, which are only minor problems.

Table 3. The number of heuristic problems for each vaccine appointment site

|   |   | New York city | Nassau county | New York state |
|---|---|---|---|---|
| 4 | Catastrophic problem | 0 | 1 | 0 |
| 3 | Major problem | 3 | 3 | 5 |
| 2 | Minor problem | 0 | 2 | 5 |
| 1 | Cosmetic problem | 1 | 0 | 1 |
|   | **Total** | **4** | **6** | **11** |

Cognitive Walkthrough revealed additional problems for each persona.
    The first persona had 2 scenarios, and these were all for the NYC website. This persona was Sick Sally, who had underlying medical conditions, which made her ineligible

**Table 4.** Usability problems identified from heuristic evaluation

| Severity of the problems | Descriptions of problems | Principles violated |
|---|---|---|
| Catastrophic problem | Nassau County:<br>• In the tab of "Where to get the Vaccine information", there were no hyperlinks to vaccine sites. There was also no additional specific information on where a vaccine could be provided | 2.1 |
| Major problem | NYC:<br>• Problem 1: On the homepage, the information is not displayed in a logical way. There is also an overload of information which makes it very not simple<br>• Problem 2: Verification for the 1st dosage is not accurate. Location verification was not valid. No review was provided before submission of the appointment confirmation<br>• Problem 3: No user profile is allowed to be created to reuse the information<br>Nassau County:<br>• Problem 1: Links for vaccine appointments and where to get vaccine info is not listed together. In the where to get the vaccine section in the homepage, the information is in a list rather than in an efficient table. General information about the vaccine and second dosage information can be placed together<br>• Problem 2: There are no dates as to updates about the vaccine supply updates. There are no additional sites listed other than Jones Beach. There is no list of where to get vaccination sites or even hyperlinks as to places where you could get the information<br>• Problem 3: There are no navigation aids provided<br>NY State:<br>• Problem 1: On Eligibility Page, instead of showing the eligibility criteria, it shows the availability of vaccine sites. In addition, instead of providing screening questions, personal names were asked first<br>• Problem 2: The homepage was dis-organized with no clear navigation guide/menu; no make an appointment link was on the homepage<br>• Problem 3: On selection time process, there is no undo button for four steps<br>• Problem 4: On schedule appointment page & locate provider page, availability is not consistently provided on the following page<br>• Problem 5: No user profile is allowed to be created to reuse the information | NYC:<br>• 2.2<br>• 5.1<br>• 6.1<br>Nassau County:<br>• 7.1<br>• 7.3<br>• 8.3<br>NY State:<br>• 2.1<br>• 2.2<br>• 3.1<br>• 4.1<br>• 6.1 |
| Minor problem | Nassau County:<br>• Problem 1: After clicking the pre-registration link on the homepage, you are redirected to a page with information about appointments that has a huge appointment heading<br>• Problem 2: The URL of the website is long and difficult to remember<br>NY State:<br>• Problem 1: On Provider results page, a map will add clarity to where the locations are<br>• Problem 2: On the Schedule process "Prescreen" Page, a progress indicator was missing at the beginning<br>• Problem 3: On state homepage, Knowledge information (such as Education, Distribution Plan, FAQ) could all go to "What you need to know" section. On date choice page of a chosen site, multiple available dates are not grouped together<br>• Problem 4: On Eligibility page, "additional information" should be "eligibility for phase 1a and 1b"<br>• Problem 5: On the homepage, there are a lot of different ways to get to different pages, and the bottom of the homepage has extra navigation tabs | Nassau County:<br>• 4.1<br>• 7.2<br>NY State:<br>• 2.1<br>• 4.1<br>• 7.1<br>• 7.2<br>• 8.1 |

(*continued*)

**Table 4.** (*continued*)

| Severity of the problems | Descriptions of problems | Principles violated |
|---|---|---|
| Cosmetic problem | NYC:<br>• Bottom information on the home page can be better displayed by using proximity principle<br>NY State:<br>• On the prescreening page, feedback indicator appears until multiple pages into the process | NYC:<br>• 7.1<br>NY State:<br>• 1.1 |

for certain vaccines, but eligible for others. Her first scenario was to compare different vaccines. The NYC website lacked this information on all the pages she searched for it on. This was a major issue because Sally needed to find out which vaccines she was not eligible for. Her second scenario was to make a vaccine appointment based on the type of vaccine she can get. The NYC website did not display the vaccine that was being used at each appointment, and therefore, Sally faced another major issue, as she was unable to register for an appointment based on which vaccine she wished for.

The second persona had just 1 scenario, and this was tested on the NYC website again. This persona was Regular Randy, who was a normal citizen, eligible for vaccination, who wanted to get vaccinated in order to be safe. His one scenario was simple: register for an appointment. He faced no major issues, but a minor issue was that no map was displayed for the locations of vaccination sites, so it was hard for Randy to make a choice of which location to get his vaccine shot at.

The third persona had 2 scenarios, and this was tested on the Nassau County website. The persona was Curious Cary, who was somebody that was not yet eligible for vaccination, but wanted more information on vaccinations. His first scenario was to learn about the vaccine, and his second scenario was to check appointment availability. In both of these, he faced a major issue with the extreme lack of visual organization and navigation guide. Thus, Cary was unable to get the information that he required.

The fourth and final person had 1 scenario, and this was tested on the NYS website. This persona was Helpful Holly, who was not actually registering for an appointment for herself, but was actually helping her grandma register. Her one scenario was to make an appointment for others. She faced the issue of a lack of continuity between pages. A parent and child page stated conflicting availability, so she often had to try multiple locations before finding a location that actually had available vaccination spots. Corresponding design solutions are provided based on these findings.

## 4  Conclusion

For the NYC site, there was a major lack of error prevention in many different aspects. For the Nassau site, there was a poor organization of information, as everything was linearly displayed with a lack of visual organizations to facilitate visual navigation. In addition, similar information was not clustered together, and so the website did not parallel the natural workflow of the user. Finally, the catastrophic issue was the lack of a registration system for a vaccine. You had to use other websites to register for a vaccine when visiting the Nassau County vaccine registration website. For the NYS site, the clustering of information was not organized well. Furthermore, a progress bar only appeared later on in the appointment process and for the first few steps, no feedback was given to the user on the progress that they have made.

In summary, our results concluded that following natural user mental model, providing good organization of information, and being consistent in providing feedback are the key to a successful vaccine appointment site.

## References

1. Nicola, M., et al.: The socio-economic implications of the coronavirus pandemic (Covid-19): a review. Int. J. Surg. (London Engl.) **78**, 185 (2020)
2. Ko, N.Y., et al.: COVID-19-related information sources and psychological well-being: An online survey study in Taiwan. Brain Behav. Immun. **87**, 153–154 (2020)
3. Hernández-García, I., Giménez-Júlvez, T.: Assessment of health information about COVID-19 prevention on the internet: infodemiological study. JMIR Public Health Surveill. **6**(2), e18717 (2020)
4. Office of the Commissioner (n.d.). Pfizer-BioNTech COVID-19 Vaccine. U.S. Food and Drug Administration. https://www.fda.gov/emergency-preparedness-and-response/coronavirus-dis ease-2019-covid-19/pfizer-biontech-covid-19-vaccine#:~:text=On%20December%2011% 2C%202020,of%20age%20and%20older
5. Preece, J., Rogers, Y., Sharp, H.: Interaction Design: Beyond Human-Computer Interaction. Wiley, Hoboken (2002)
6. Barnum, C.M.: Usability Testing Essentials: Ready, Set... Test!. Morgan Kaufmann, Burlington (2020)
7. Nielsen, J.: 10 Usability Heuristics for User Interface Design (2020). https://www.nngroup. com/articles/ten-usability-heuristics/
8. Nielsen, J.: Usability inspection methods. In: Conference Companion on Human Factors in Computing Systems, pp. 413–414, April 1994

# HCI in Learning, Teaching, and Education

# Student eXperience: A Survey in Argentinian Universities About Education in the Pandemic Context

Iván Balmaceda Castro[1,2(✉)] ⓘ, Cristian Rusu[3] ⓘ, and Silvana Aciar[1,4] ⓘ

[1] Consejo Nacional de Investigaciones Científicas y Técnicas (CONICET),
Buenos Aires, Argentina
ibalmaceda@unlar.edu.ar
[2] Universidad Nacional de La Rioja, La Rioja, Argentina
[3] Pontificia Universidad Católica de Valparaíso, Av. Brasil, 2241, 2340000 Valparaíso, Chile
cristian.rusu@pucv.cl
[4] Universidad Nacional de San Juan, San Juan, Argentina
saciar@unsj-cuim.edu.ar

**Abstract.** The spread of the coronavirus (COVID-19) caused institutions to adapt to virtuality around the world. With the social changes brought by new technologies, universities must adapt and get to know their students. Student eXperience (SX) refers to the totality of experiences that students live in higher education, incorporating academic and pedagogical resources, research, information systems, libraries, study rooms, as well as extracurricular activities such as social, recreational, cultural activities, among others. Therefore, SX is associated with the institution's sense of identity. Our exploratory comparative study was conducted to know the experiences of students in the context of pandemic in several Argentinian universities. The survey includes students from different universities, both public and private. The aim is to know what kind of experiences students had in 2020 with virtual learning environments. The results indicate that students show a rather significant satisfaction with online learning.

**Keywords:** Student experience · Customer experience · e-Learning · Higher education · COVID-19

## 1 Introduction

The Covid-19 has impacted our lives, producing change, including in education. In 2020 therefore, educational establishments, involving students and professors, have had to take on new forms of learning and teaching. e-Learning became the most efficient and sometimes the only available form to continue education.

e-Learning is defined as a teaching and learning modality, which may represent all or part of the educational model in which it is applied, which exploits electronic media and devices to facilitate access, evolution, and improvement of the quality of education [1]. In recent years, it evolved in relation to educational content, technological resources,

© Springer Nature Switzerland AG 2021
C. Stephanidis et al. (Eds.): HCII 2021, CCIS 1499, pp. 233–241, 2021.
https://doi.org/10.1007/978-3-030-90179-0_30

interaction possibilities, and offers multiple advantages, some of them are that it can help to better organize the agenda of each day and to categorize the activities, needs and responsibilities. In order for meaningful learning to take place, students need to be involved in the learning process. The role of professors is to facilitate learning and to ensure students are actively engaged in the learning process.

Student eXperience (SX) is built through all interactions that students have throughout their relationship with a university. In 2020, the learning mode was shifted from mostly face to face learning to fully online learning. It gives different experience to everyone involved, specially to the students as e-learning was not yet a form of education in the universities, and many professors had no previous experience in online teaching.

The research question of our study is as follows: What kind of experiences have students when using virtual learning environment? The paper presents a diagnostic of the SX in the National University of La Rioja (UNLAR) and, for comparison, we collected some data from other public and private universities of Argentina.

This document is organized as follows: Sect. 2 presents the background; Sect. 3 describes the survey and the participants; Sect. 4 discusses quantitative results. Finally, we present preliminary conclusions and future work in Sect. 5.

## 2   Student eXperience as a Customer eXperience

Rusu et al. [2] consider that "CX examines the whole customer journey and experiences with several systems, products or services that a company offers, instead of focusing on a single one." CX, emphasizes the extent to which the customer has met their needs, about the emotions and physical experience when interaction with a product or service, through to the post-consumption [3, 4].

CX in the education involve the student participation at different levels, such as emotional, sensory, and physical of the total of the products, systems and/or services offered [5, 6].

The Student eXperience (SX) is a particular case of the CX, where each student is involved in a different way. Today's students are more demanding customers in relation to the quality of teaching and are more liable to evaluate the experience of higher education as part of the broader context of their networks. Students' feeling of ownership to the institution that offers educational products or services is a vital factor in a positive experience [7].

## 3   The Survey

We made an exploratory comparative study that it aims to know about the conditions and experiences related to the virtual learning by students. We designed a specific questionnaire, where we invited the students to participate in our survey by email or Whatsapp.

Questions are related to the experience in the virtual campus, including, general aspects (questions 1 to 3), aspects related to the content (questions 4 to 14), aspects related to the communication (questions 15 to 17), aspects related to the usability (questions

18 to 23), aspects related to the accessibility (questions 24 to 29), and aspects related communication between the professor and the student (questions 30 to 33).

Finally, questions 34 refer to the overall experience of studying in 2020.

To obtain the answers, we used binary alternatives (Yes/No), options and selection tables, and Likert scales from 1 to 5, where 5 is Totally Satisfied, and 1 is Unsatisfied.

The survey involved 169 students, 113 of them from the National University of La Rioja (UNLAR) and the other 56 from different universities of Argentina. In the Table 1, it is shown to which university are enrolled and which type of management. There are 158 students studying in public universities (93%) and 11 students (7%) in private universities.

**Table 1.** Distribution of students by university and type of management

| Public university | | Private university | |
|---|---|---|---|
| National University or La Rioja | 113 | 21st Century Business University | 4 |
| National University of San Juan | 12 | University Catholic Argentine | 3 |
| National University of Misiones | 9 | University Blas Pascal | 2 |
| National University of Cuyo | 5 | Argentine University of Enterprise | 1 |
| National University of La Plata | 3 | University Catholic of Córdoba | 1 |
| National University of Quilmes | 3 | | |
| National University of Santiago del Estero | 3 | | |
| National University of General Sarmiento | 3 | | |
| National University of Mar del Plata | 2 | | |
| National University of Sur | 2 | | |
| National University of Buenos Aires | 1 | | |
| National University of Cordoba | 1 | | |
| Balseiro Institute | 1 | | |

Of these, there are 156 students at the grade and 13 students at the post-graduate level. Most of the students of grade were enrolled in Veterinary (20%), followed by Public Accountant (15%), Computer Science (13%), Human Resources (7%), History (5%). Law, Biology, Nursing, and Electronic Engineering with 4% each. Medicine and Physical Education with 3% each. Visual Arts, Educational Sciences and Philosophy with 2% each. Criminalistics, Industrial Design, Civil Engineering, Natural Resources Engineering, Anthropology, Geosciences, and Tourism with 1% each.

Postgraduate students, 6 are studying for a doctorate (1 Public Health, 1 Biology, 3 Education Sciences, 1 Communication), 5 students in masters (1 Exact Sciences, 2 Ambient, 1 Physics and 1 Accounting) and 2 students in specializations (1 Business Management and 1 Human Sciences).

The distribution by gender is 95 females (56%); 64 males (38%) and 10 did not identified a binary gender (6%).

The age of students varied from 18 to more than 40 years. Most of the respondents belonged to the age group between 21 and 29 years (51%), followed by the age group between 30 - 39 years (21%), group between 18 and 20 years (20%). and more than 40 year (8%).

With respect to the internet connection, the students surveyed said that 53% have a good connection, 17% say that the connection is very good, and 17% say that it is bad. 6% say it is very bad and 4% say it is excellent. While 3% have no connection at home.

The 6% of the students expressed some specific need, mostly visual, followed by hearing and, to a lesser measure, cognitive and motor needs.

In relation to the academic year, 27% are in their 1st year, 30% in their 2nd year, 18% in 3rd year, 15% in their 4th year, 9% in their 5th year and 1% in their 6th year. Also, the number of subjects enrolled is between 1 and 14. The highest number of subjects is 7 and 9, with 16.6% each. Together, these data show proportionate and relatively representative situations of the students.

## 4   Results and Discussion

The Table 2, shown general aspects of campus virtual, for P1, the 31% qualified as moderately satisfied the facility to access the virtual campus and the enrollment procedure. The 18% qualified it as an exceptionally good experience and 51% qualified it as a bad experience. Although, in P1, 51% said they had a bad experience in the enrollment, in P2, 69% said that there are user manuals that explain the procedure, and, in P3 the 55% said that the technical requirements for its use are specified.

**Table 2.** General aspects

| Question | | Mean | SD | Mode |
|---|---|---|---|---|
| P1 | Access and registration to the virtual campus | 3.54 | 1.205 | 3 |
| P2 | Users' manual about the use of the virtual campus | 3.19 | 1.263 | 3 |
| P3 | Technical requirements of the learning action | 2.71 | 1.255 | 3 |

With respect to content, described in Table 3, (questions 4 to 14), concern the structure of the courses, the resources and materials that support the content, the access to the bibliography, the activities, and the evaluation procedures. The 56% qualified the experience as satisfied and totally satisfied, 24% as moderately satisfied, 13% as little satisfied and the 7% as unsatisfied.

**Table 3.** Aspect related to content.

| | Question | Mean | SD | Mode |
|---|---|---|---|---|
| P4 | Structure of course | 3.66 | 0.75 | 4 |
| P5 | Abstracts or introductory of each topic | 3.54 | 1.22 | 5 |
| P6 | Relevant resources and materials | 3.53 | 1.25 | 5 |
| P7 | Diverse and actualized bibliographic | 3.59 | 1.29 | 5 |
| P8 | Access to these bibliographic | 3.35 | 1.34 | 3 |
| P9 | Different types of activities at the virtual campus | 3.83 | 1.23 | 5 |
| P10 | In the proposed activities, it is clear the procedure to it out | 3.91 | 1.12 | 5 |
| P11 | The activities included the studies of real cases | 3.59 | 1.21 | 4 |
| P12 | The evaluation techniques used have remained with the aims of the course | 3.53 | 1.13 | 4 |
| P13 | The activities and the resources used have been helpful | 3.57 | 1.14 | 4 |
| P14 | The topics were in line with your expectations as a student | 3.45 | 1.11 | 3 |

Correlations between the eleven variables that were measured to determine the learning were calculated respect with content (Table 4), we conclude that there is a significant lineal correlation between variables (sig = 0,01).

**Table 4.** Spearman correlations of the variables that determine the learning path.

| Question | P4 | P5 | P6 | P7 | P8 | P9 | P10 | P11 | P12 | P13 | P14 |
|---|---|---|---|---|---|---|---|---|---|---|---|
| P4 | 1 | ,434 | ,458 | ,404 | ,411 | ,410 | ,461 | ,397 | ,597 | ,611 | ,665 |
| P5 | | 1 | ,619 | ,505 | ,421 | ,346 | ,427 | ,431 | ,431 | ,529 | ,444 |
| P6 | | | 1 | ,635 | ,391 | ,422 | ,399 | ,406 | ,462 | ,552 | ,401 |
| P7 | | | | 1 | ,548 | ,303 | ,361 | ,365 | ,471 | ,541 | ,316 |
| P8 | | | | | 1 | ,232 | ,425 | ,343 | ,441 | ,479 | ,360 |
| P9 | | | | | | 1 | ,426 | ,334 | ,436 | ,524 | ,502 |
| P10 | | | | | | | 1 | ,414 | ,486 | ,477 | ,470 |
| P11 | | | | | | | | 1 | ,534 | ,546 | ,489 |
| P12 | | | | | | | | | 1 | ,681 | ,622 |
| P13 | | | | | | | | | | 1 | ,698 |
| P14 | | | | | | | | | | | 1 |

P15 and P16 are related to communication. The first one (P15) is related to communication with the professor where 46% are satisfied, while 28% are moderately satisfied.

For the second (P16) related to communication among students where they showed similar results to P15. 48% are satisfied, 26% are moderately satisfied, and 22% are not very satisfied.

Likewise, with respect to the communication tools used (P17), 33% of the students are moderately satisfied, 22% are satisfied, 18% are totally satisfied, 14% are not very satisfied and 13% are dissatisfied.

Questions P18 to P23 (Table 5) are related to usability: the navigation in the virtual campus, the links functionality, the language used, and the visualization of images. In this regard, 58% are satisfied, 26% are moderately satisfied, and 16% are not satisfied.

Students (82%) said that the virtual campus interface is intuitive (P18), and 58% are satisfied with the comfort of navigation (P19).

The 57% said they do easily recognize the links (P20) and 60% that these links do work (P21). Also, 70% report that the language used is clear (P22) and 53% that the images do look good (P23). Therefore, it is a good experience in the overall use of the Virtual Campus.

**Table 5.** Aspect related to usability.

| Question | | Mean | SD | Mode |
|---|---|---|---|---|
| P18 | Interface is intuitive | 3.43 | 1.13 | 3 |
| P19 | Navigation is comfortable | 3.69 | 1.21 | 5 |
| P20 | The links are recognized easily | 3.65 | 1.13 | 5 |
| P21 | The links work | 3.76 | 1.10 | 5 |
| P22 | The Language used is clearly and concise | 3.88 | 1.02 | 4 |
| P23 | The images included looking good | 3.60 | 1.12 | 3 |

Table 6 described the aspect related the accessibility. In P24, 70% report a good experience with the font size, font type, alignment, and typographical effects used. In addition, 37% respond to a good experience in that the same content are provided in different formats (P25), while 33% say they have a bad experience and 30% respond to moderately satisfactory.

**Table 6.** Aspect related to accessibility.

| Question | | Mean | SD | Mode |
|---|---|---|---|---|
| P24 | Font size, font type, alignment, typographical effects used, makes reading easy | 3.89 | 1.11 | 4 |
| P25 | Contents are provided in different formats | 3.05 | 1.32 | 3 |

Table 7 shows questions P26 and P28. Of those who said "YES" to question P26, in P27, the 39% are totally satisfied because the browser used does show the content of the courses well, followed by 36% that are satisfied, 16% that are moderately satisfied, and 9% that had a bad experience.

**Table 7.** Description of connection device(s)

| Question | | Yes | No |
|---|---|---|---|
| P26 | Do you use a desktop/notebook/netbook to connect? | 149 | 20 |
| P28 | Do you use Cell Phone or Tablet to connect? | 130 | 39 |

If the answer in P28 was "YES", In P29, asked, if has the content of the course been shown well, the 32% of students were satisfied with the way the content is shown, 27% moderately satisfied, 24% totally satisfied, 13% little satisfied and 4% unsatisfied.

Table 8 presents the correlation between usability and accessibility so that a positive correlation can be concluded, which shows that there is some relationship between them.

**Table 8.** Spearman correlations of the variable's usability and accessibility.

| Question | P18 | P19 | P20 | P21 | P22 | P23 | P24 | P25 | P27 | P29 |
|---|---|---|---|---|---|---|---|---|---|---|
| P18 | 1 | ,617 | ,376 | ,146 | ,434 | ,292 | ,453 | ,050 | ,468 | ,442 |
| P19 | | 1 | ,479 | ,319 | ,438 | ,336 | ,423 | ,474 | ,421 | ,416 |
| P20 | | | 1 | ,603 | ,493 | ,504 | ,487 | ,281 | ,316 | ,370 |
| P21 | | | | 1 | ,472 | ,642 | ,316 | ,348 | ,325 | ,416 |
| P22 | | | | | 1 | ,515 | ,511 | ,246 | ,367 | ,453 |
| P23 | | | | | | 1 | ,492 | ,412 | ,435 | ,464 |
| P24 | | | | | | | 1 | ,226 | ,501 | ,414 |
| P25 | | | | | | | | 1 | ,095 | ,329 |
| P27 | | | | | | | | | 1 | ,575 |
| P29 | | | | | | | | | | 1 |

P30, ask how the student communicated with the teacher. The student could choose between different options. Whatsapp groups were the most used with 31%, followed by e-mail with 25%, virtual campus forum with 18%, internal message in Campus Virtual with 16% and 10% by facebook groups.

Students expressed that 46% are satisfied, while 29% are moderately satisfied and 25% did not have a good experience with respect to answers provided by the professors in case of doubts (P31), to interactions with the professors (P32), and to the motivation towards the course (P33). The motivation and communication have been crucial in the pandemic context, and experience has been good in this respect.

Finally, in P34, students are asked how they the experience of studying online during the year 2020. 42.6% of the students qualify as a very good experience. Then, 30.2% had a good experience. Followed by 13% with an unbelievably bad experience and 7.1% with a bad experience. Also, the 7.1% students qualify the experience as excellent.

## 5  Conclusion and Future Work

The Argentinian higher education system has an extensive territorial distribution and is characterized by its institutional heterogeneity. It is composed of public and private institutions. It has a total of 57 public universities, and a total of 51 private universities. In this study, a participation included students from a total of 13 public universities and 5 private universities, 66.9% of students from the National University of La Rioja.

The COVID-19 pandemic has affected all higher education institutions in Argentina, which had to resort to new virtual education technologies in order to begin classes in 2020. At the same time, social inequality emerged, expressed in the equipment and connectivity problems reported by a significant number of students, evidencing that the conditions of opportunity are not equal for all. In our study, 43 students have bad or no Internet access, while 90 students have a good connection but at non-peak times (9 pm to 8 am), which means that during the course, generally between 8am and 8pm, the connection is unstable. Only 36 of a total 169 students have a very good connection during the day.

The study shows that the main difficulties that students found were the technical problems in registration to the virtual campus, though there are manuals, and the technical requirements are specified, therefore we consider that the revision of these manuals is necessary to increase the percentage of good experience in enrollment.

Although the connection was bad, the students expressed that they are very satisfied with the Virtual Campus, the good result is based on the usability and accessibility, as the students express that there is a good navigability and facility access to the resources provided. Especially, students were very satisfied with the adaptability of the virtual campus to different devices (desktop, laptop, netbook, cell phone or tablet), so we can conclude that the design is responsive.

The students are satisfied with the communication with the professors and other students. This high degree of satisfaction is given by the time of response to doubts and the communication tools used.

The pandemic in university education has generated opportunities to discuss the role of digital tools in higher education. Students' satisfaction was high; 79.9% were satisfied with online learning.

The present work allowed us to explore the student experience in 2020. From the above, the challenge is to give this study its continuity in other universities through the elaboration of a new instrument that includes some of the issues that are already studied, but that also allows us to think further than the exceptionality and start to explore the effects, learnings, and transformations in the pedagogical relationships.

**Acknowledgment.** We would like to thank to all the participants in the survey.

Iván Balmaceda Castro is a beneficiary of one CONICET (Argentina) doctoral scholarship since 2019 at 2024 at Informatics Institute of the Faculty of Exact, Physical and Natural Sciences of the National University of San Juan.

The authors are participating in the HCI-Collab Project – The Collaborative Network to Support HCI Teaching and Learning Processes in IberoAmerica (http://hci-collab.com/).

# References

1. Adam, M.R., Vallés, R.S., Rodríguez, G.I.M.: E-learning: características y evaluación. Ensayos de economía **23**(43), 143–159 (2013)
2. Rusu, C., et al.: Forming customer eXperience professionals: a comparative study on students' perception. In: Ahram, T., Karwowski, W., Pickl, S., Taiar, R. (eds.) IHSED 2019. AISC, vol. 1026, pp. 391–396. Springer, Cham (2020). https://doi.org/10.1007/978-3-030-27928-8_60
3. Laming, C., Mason, K.: Customer experience – an analysis of the concept and its performance in airline brands. Res. Transp. Bus. Manag. **10**(2014), 15–25 (2014). https://doi.org/10.1016/j.rtbm.2014.05.004
4. Hill, N., Roche, G., Allen, L.: Customer Satisfaction. The Customer Experience Through the Customer's Eye. Congent Publishing, London (2007)
5. Frow, P., Payne, A.: Towards the "perfect" customer experience. J. Brand Manag. **15**(2), 89–101 (2007). https://doi.org/10.1057/palgrave.bm.2550120
6. Balmaceda Castro, I., Rusu, C., Aciar, S.: Customer eXperience in e-learning: a systematic mapping study. In: Meiselwitz, G. (ed.) HCII 2020. LNCS, vol. 12195, pp. 158–170. Springer, Cham (2020). https://doi.org/10.1007/978-3-030-49576-3_11
7. Hayes, A., O'Neil, E., Nemetz, F., Oliver, L.: Building an Enhanced Student Experience: Reflections from the Department of Computer Science at the University of Bath. Durham, Reino Unido (2020)

# Development of a Digital Collaborative Whiteboard

Armin Beckmann, Marc Bollmann, Tim Buchholz, Rafael Geiser, Daniel Kerpen[(✉)], and Jan Conrad

Faculty of Computer Science and Micro Systems Technology, Hochschule Kaiserslautern – University of Applied Sciences, Zweibruecken, Germany
mabo0032@stud.hs-kl.de, daniel.kerpen@hs-kl.de

**Abstract.** Nowadays, products and services are commonly developed by cross-functional teams in collaborative approaches. In course of these, individual team members bring expertise in various areas, e.g., product management, UX design, implementation, testing, marketing, to the table. Hence, collaboration in projects is more important than ever and design thinking or design processes cannot be done without collaboration.

But since the outbreak of the COVID-19 pandemic, many institutions from the academic and the business sector are still facing the challenge of converting the usual on-site workday to remote work settings. This challenge includes issues such as finding appropriate tools, which are capable of replacing or replicating the on-site workflow. The problem with such tools is mainly that they are often too expensive or come with issues regarding data privacy. Our proposed approach aims to solve these challenges especially for one activity: working together on a whiteboard. The resulting solution is Whitebird, a collaborative, digital whiteboard built with Nest.js, Nuxt.js, Fabric.js and MongoDB.

Our poster presentation discusses the pros and cons of embracing the principle of web-based skeuomorphism, i.e. mimicking real-world objects and applying them to the whiteboard in order to foster a sense of familiarity in users. From the web development perspective, we discuss the use of free and open-source web application/front-end development web frameworks such as Nest.js and Nuxt.js along with illustrating the implementation of JavaScript library Fabric.js which provides an object model on top of HTML5 canvas methods.

We conclude by showing how the results obtained within the scope of this project can be used for further open-source web service development.

**Keywords:** Remote work · Digital whiteboards · Free and open-source development frameworks · Skeuomorphism

## 1 Motivation

In recent years, products and services are increasingly developed using collaborative approaches [1]. It is more important than ever to use tools that can facilitate this work. However, collaboration has to overcome some obstacles in everyday life. For instance,

© Springer Nature Switzerland AG 2021
C. Stephanidis et al. (Eds.): HCII 2021, CCIS 1499, pp. 242–248, 2021.
https://doi.org/10.1007/978-3-030-90179-0_31

team members might have to work from different locations. The COVID-19 pandemic serves as prime example, because ongoing from March 2020 – when the World Health Organization declared a pandemic status – many people could no longer work on-site but instead had to work remotely from their homes ("home office"). This resulted in the urgent need to find the right software to work collaboratively.

One of the most important tools for collaborative remote work settings is a digital (i.e. virtual) whiteboard. Currently, there is a multitude of digital whiteboards available; however, most products comprise of proprietary software, come along with restrictive price models, and issues in legal information privacy. This last point serves as a major problem for privacy-oriented customers regarding data protection. Whitebird [2] tries to address this issue by providing a self-hosted, open-source solution. It is a collaborative digital whiteboard built with Nest.js [3], Nuxt.js [4], Fabric.js [5] and MongoDB [6]. Whitebird has been released as a minimum viable product (MVP) which includes all the essential features to create collaborative ideas and work together on them in online settings. It stems from a graduate student course (Master of Science, M.Sc.) in computer science education at Kaiserslautern University of Applied Sciences, Germany.

## 2    Architecture

### 2.1    Frontend

The frontend is mainly built on-top of two bigger frameworks. NuxtJs – a framework on-top of VueJs [7] – is used for the general structure of the frontend and its view. FabricJs is used as canvas-framework on-top of the HTML5-canvas. We just shortly discuss some examples to illustrate what these frameworks are capable of.

One of VueJs' key-features is the concept of SFCs (Single File Components), which encapsulate the principle of easily reusable UI-components by making each vue-file a standalone component, which can have its own structure, functionality and design.

NuxtJs extends the tools provided by VueJs by taking the concepts of Vue and making them more accessible for developers. It simplifies several tasks, for example routing by changing the place where a page is contained within the directory-structure of the project instead of having to manually implement such routing.

FabricJs provides a not-so-intuitive but powerful way to work on the HTML5-canvas. It makes tasks such as rendering text and changing its content afterwards way simpler than just working with the canvas itself. It is a powerful framework but lacks a good documentation which makes working with it somewhat challenging.

There are other frameworks that could be utilized, such as NextJs [8] instead of NuxtJs or Konva [9] instead of FabricJs. NuxtJS was chosen due to prior development-experience by team members, and FabricJs is capable of doing more out of the box in a simpler way than Konva. For instance, FabricJs comes with an option to rotate objects out of the box, while this functionality must be explicitly implemented in Konva. Also, FabricJs is backed up by larger community support.

### 2.2    Backend

The backend is built on NestJs which is a typescript framework on-top of ExpressJs [10], which is one of the go-to webservers for NodeJs. It provides a very clean way to set up a webserver by introducing the concepts of modules and dependency injection into the usually unstructured nature of ExpressJs.

Also due to the fac, that NestJS is somewhat popular in the world of NodeJs-development, it comes with the benefit of deep integration with other industry-standard tools. For example, NestJS provides a direct integration with socket.io, so that it just works out of the box without the usual setup which would be necessary in an application built on pure ExpressJs.

Furthermore, the backend communicates with a MongoDB to store the content and state of a given whiteboard. MongoDB was chosen due to its relatively easy way of interacting with data of which the structure is not known prior to its creation.

### 2.3 Communication

The communication between back- and frontend is split into two separate areas. On the one hand, there is a REST-API for tasks which do not require real-time-synchronization between clients. On the other hand, there is a websocket which tackles the task of keeping the whiteboards of clients synchronized.

**The REST-API** is only used for two distinct tasks. The first is the actual initial creation of a whiteboard. This API-Request takes all the necessary steps in the backend to prepare the corresponding canvas-reference in the mongoDB while replying to the user with a reference to it. The other task is to reply with an existing canvas when a user decides to join a session or reloads the page.

**The Websocket** is built on-top of socket.io [11] which provides an intuitive way to interact with websockets. Each client, who joins a whiteboard, will be automatically connected to its corresponding websocket by the unique ID given to each whiteboard. Over this connection, the client's actions on the whiteboard are synchronized between all clients. By using a socket, the overhead that would come with each request over a REST-API is avoided. This is very similar to 'fire-and-forget'-approach, which is a common way to achieve speed in web-applications. But it comes with the drawback of some inconsistency which manifests itself in our case when one client might be moving an object while another client is deleting this actual object being moved. Then it will reappear once the first client finishes moving, as the last action that is executed on an object is the one that will be synchronized to all clients. This is however a minor inconvenience on a whiteboard, where speed is a crucial metric.

**An example workflow of creating an object** is illustrated in Fig. 1. The process is initiated by *Client A* who creates an object on the canvas with the tools provided by FabricJs. NuxtJs communicates this creation over socket.io to the websocket running in the backend. The backend checks if the update is valid and persists it in the connected database. After this, the socket in the backend notifies all connected clients, except the sender itself, about the change. Each client listening on the connection then reflects the change in its local canvas by using the tools provided by FabricJs.

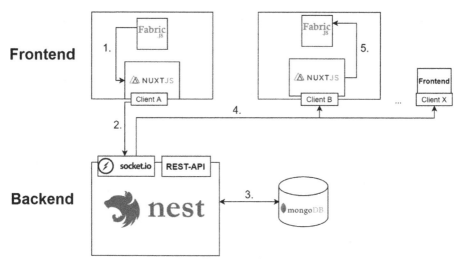

**Fig. 1.** Workflow of creating an object and synchronizing the clients.

## 3   UX/UI

### 3.1   Web-based Skeuomorphism

Skeuomorphism is a term most often used in graphical user interface design to describe interface objects that mimic their real-world counterparts in how they appear or how the user can interact with them. Whitebird adapts these counterparts and tries to create an environment that is already familiar to the user, in which he feels comfortable and knows instantly how to interact with the objects.

Whitebird mimics its real-world counterpart and provides basic tools that you can find in the real-world. These tools include sticky notes, pencils, basic geometric objects or shapes and editing actions.

### 3.2   Designing Whitebird

Focusing on anticipating what the user needs was the key of designing the application. Interface elements should provide a clear context on how the user can interact with them. Starting with the landing page, the content had to be on-point, highlighting our unique value proposition. Thus, the content should depend on the type of product. Our landing page was created for one purpose: convince people. Unlike a homepage, which has multiple conversion goals and encourages general exploration, a landing page should only have one conversion goal and one clear call to action. We wanted the user to use our collaborative whiteboard. The design is very dependent on our corporate identity. From a heuristic point of view, when a user visits a web page, we have only a short period of time to convince them to continue reading. A term which is most often associated with this approach is called goldfish memory. It refers to the approximately timespan we have to convince the user to stay and make an impression on them that allows for curiosity reading.

To keep the users focused we provided simple call to action buttons, so the user knows immediately how to interact with the application. We promise in our call to action that the content reflects what we have promised – working on a whiteboard and collaborating as a team.

### 3.3  The Whiteboard

The consistency in the design-elements is extremely important, as this is how recognition and familiarity are created for the user.

The repetition of a shape, color or feature in the design also creates harmony in the eye of the user. Because of the similar shapes, colors or features, it can be quickly perceived what kind of pattern is in the design. In other words, the user understands the design and can comprehend what is dominant in the design. A design with constantly changing characteristics would be overwhelming in the long run, as viewers would have to continually relearn it. Imagine having to read a text in which every letter is unique, rather than repetitive - you would get tired very quickly.

Following this design principle, the whiteboard provides a clear context on how the user can interact with it without the need of providing a lot of context.

Another important principle is to note spacing and leave white space. White spaces in our whiteboard support the primary elements, surrounding the main form of our design – the canvas.

Figure 2 shall demonstrate how the toolset of Whitebird (especially the Sticky Notes) can be used to work collaboratively on a problem statement for instance.

## 4  Feedback

After completion of the minimum viable product (MVP) the next important step is to gather feedback. With quick feedback, it is possible to detect design faults or misconceptions in the architecture of our whiteboard and take them into account in future development iterations, without the need of doing enormous changes the whole application. To gather feedback, Whitebird was promoted on several open-source developer communities.

On one platform the application got a lot of attention, which will be further considered. It was on a subreddit called "selfhosted". The subreddit is, in its own words, "A place to share alternatives to popular online services that can be self-hosted without giving up privacy or locking you into a service you don't control". The promotion [12] received a lot of feedback from casual consumers up to software developers from companies. By directly addressing the subreddit 'selfhosted' it was possible to target a specific user-group: developers who want to host free and useful applications secure on their own hardware. With that target group it is possible to get useful feedback. The condensed key takeaways of the feedback are explained as follows.

### 4.1  Different Expectations

In the community, there were basically two different point of views which functionality a whiteboard should contain. One group had the expectations that the whiteboard should

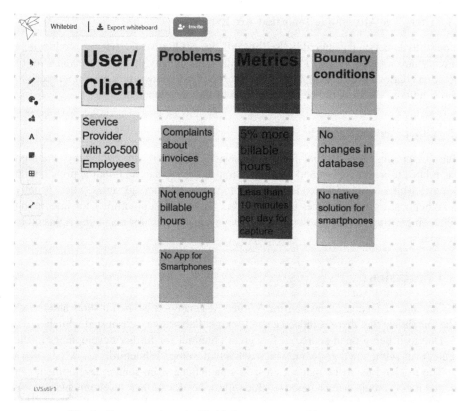

**Fig. 2.** Demonstration of whitebird – use case: problem-statement [14]

be a tool for artists with the main focus on drawing. This user group almost expected the application to be a photoshop-esque tool with different layers and brushing functionality (e.g.: Aggie [13]). The other group expected the tool to be a flowchart tool in which you have predefined objects like shapes, rectangles, squares and sticky notes which you can connect with each other.

## 4.2 Different End-User Devices

Some members in the community asked questions about the compatibility of the application regarding specific end-devices. With such feedback, it was possible to ensure that there is a wider range of devices than initially expected. It is very important to know for further development that there are users which expect the whiteboard application to be touch- and pencil-optimized.

## 4.3 Alternative Tools Do not Fulfill the Expectations of Users

Some users explained that other current open-source applications do not fulfill their needs and expectations. The considered alternatives seem to be less polished than our approach.

### 4.4  There Are Alternative Tools that Are Expensive

In our initial post on the subreddit "selfhosted", we explicitly said that our product is in an early development phase. This is one of the reasons why the post received a lot of recommendations how our application could look like. Many users gave references to paid solutions which should be considered in further development.

### 4.5  Other Feature Requests

Many comments were special feature requests. One feature that got more attention was related to authorization and authentication. It seems that the initial approach with joining a whiteboard by join-code seems not to be enough for companies, where usually an authentication server comes into play. Users asked for a possibility for integrating with their existing LDAP/AD Servers, and they want a system for managing rights more granularly.

## 5  Conclusion

The amount of feedback and traction Whitebird generated in such a short amount of time has shown that there is indeed a need for a collaborative, self-hosted whiteboard.

Due to it being open-source, it has great potential for further development in the future, even without a core-team, which actively develops Whitebird.

The received feedback made it clear how beneficial open-source development can be, and it helps to determine next possible milestones for further development.

However, one of the biggest realizations made possible through feedback was that there must be a clear vision about what Whitebird tries to accomplish in the long-term growth.

## References

1. Steimle, T., Wallach, D.: Collaborative UX design. dpunkt, New York (2018). ISBN: 978-3-86490-532-2
2. Whitebird Repository. https://github.com/BuchholzTim/Whitebird. Accessed 27 Feb 2021
3. NestJS. https://nestjs.com/. Accessed 27 Feb 2021
4. Nuxt.js. https://nuxtjs.org/. Accessed 27 Feb 2021
5. Fabric.js. http://fabricjs.com/. Accessed 27 Feb 2021
6. mongoDB. https://www.mongodb.com/. Accessed 27 Feb 2021
7. Vue.js. https://vuejs.org/. Accessed 27 Feb 2021
8. Next.js. https://nextjs.org/. Accessed 27 Feb 2021
9. Konva. https://konvajs.org/. Accessed 27 Feb 2021
10. ExpressJs. https://expressjs.com/. Accessed 27 Feb 2021
11. socket.io. https://socket.io/. Accessed 27 Feb 2021
12. Whitebird Post. https://www.reddit.com/r/selfhosted/comments/lnddc7/whitebird_a_opensource_webbased_collaborative/. Accessed 27 Feb 2021
13. Aggie.io. https://aggie.io/. Accessed 27 Feb 2021
14. Problem Statement, Ergosign. https://www.ergosign.de/ch/insights/2019/article-collaborative-workshops-part2.html. Accessed 10 Mar 2021

# Computational Thinking and Language Immersion with Umwelt

Zeynep Büyükyazgan, Demir Alp, Elif Selin Kozanoğlu, Rana Taki, Arda Eren[✉],
and Sedat Yalçın

Hisar School Istanbul, Istanbul, Turkey
{arda.eren,sedat.yalcin}@hisarschool.k12.tr

**Abstract.** To improve computational thinking skills and second language acquisition in primary schoolers whose learning has been impacted by COVID-19, Umwelt presents a game that simulates real-life interactions and simple tasks (e.g., collecting several items given in the form of a computation problem, selecting an object with an identified color) to demonstrate the place of computation and language in everyday life through an XR system. The game consists of challenges that test the abilities of kids to break problems down into smaller parts, recognize patterns and important details amongst them, and develop step-by-step strategies to solve these challenges. These problems will require sizable amounts of interaction where kids will gain language learning skills in addition to computational thinking skills. Umwelt is built on the fundamentals of Krashen's Theory of Second Language Acquisition (SLA) and Natural Language Processing (NLP) systems. Noting the portability of Umwelt, children will have the opportunity to tackle problem sets and immerse themselves in new languages wherever they feel most comfortable and confident. The implemented Interactive Voice Response (IVR) system will guide users as they continue to understand the given questions, solve the tasks and familiarize themselves with these applications. Children will be able to enhance their computational abilities through these interactive activities. This method of gamification takes advantage of XR technology to provide all the necessary grounds for learning through games, a channel common amongst children. These principles, coupled with creative problem sets, prepare students for the immediate future based on Computer-Human Interaction while simultaneously raising them as world citizens. Considering the impact of COVID-19, houses have become the new learning environments of primary schoolers, and Umwelt's XR based structure builds on this by bringing the world to these children.

**Keywords:** Computational thinking · Computation · XR system · Natural Language Processing (NLP) · Interactive Voice Response (IVR) · Krashen's Theory of Second Language Acquisition (SLA)

## 1 Introduction

Only in the United States, the COVID-19 pandemic forced schools to close in spring 2020 and over 50 million students were asked to continue their education remotely [8].

© Springer Nature Switzerland AG 2021
C. Stephanidis et al. (Eds.): HCII 2021, CCIS 1499, pp. 249–257, 2021.
https://doi.org/10.1007/978-3-030-90179-0_32

According to a survey conducted by Youth Truth Student Survey, an American nonprofit occupied within "The Center for Effective Philanthropy" (CEP), although students state that they understand the benefits of online learning (flexibility, closure to family members), however, distractions at home, stress, and anxiety [3], and lack of social connections underscores the importance of modifications in online learning curriculums [8]. According to UNESCO's data, the extent of COVID's impact on learning has significantly increased during the April-May period due to localized and national lockdowns in low-income and high-income countries, resulting in a consequential decrease in the accessibility of face-to-face education. Combining the aforementioned consequences of school curriculums being taught and learned remotely, the weighted impact of COVID in learning and education arises as a major issue [5].

### 1.1 Learning During Covid

The negative effects of the pandemic particularly in language learning and the development of math and problem-solving skills of children is a great issue. Second language learning and teaching, alongside many other fields, were significantly influenced during the pandemic era. B.W. Sarnecka's studies show that social interaction is a key component to accelerating proficiency, fluency, and speaking skills in a second language, especially for children [7]. Temporary school closures and mitigation policies due to COVID resulted in the restriction of such interactions among children and teachers, directly affecting the learning efficiency of second languages. Supporting this fact, research conducted for English learning speakers shows that learners of the second language showed less development in speaking skills [14], which used to include social interactions, than in other areas.

## 2 2D and 3D Learning Environments

A study on "Student performance and appreciation using 3D vs. 2D vision in a virtual learning environment," aimed to investigate the differences in the performance and appreciation of students that worked in 2D and 3D virtual learning environments. It was seen that students were more appreciative of and better at performing tasks in 3D learning environments [13], which validates Umwelt's use of 3D visuals to engage with the learners.

### 2.1 XR Systems in Learning

Extended reality (XR) is a term that refers to all the combined real and virtual environments and human-machine interactions. The most common XR technologies are Virtual Reality (VR), Mixed Reality (MR), and Augmented Reality (AR). Virtual Technologies are found to be capable of improving students' academic performance and motivation by taking advantage of the students' free and secure environment and intriguing designs [9]. These immersive and interactive tools have the potential to increase learner motivation through gamification and engagement through their 3D field while promoting a student-centered learning experience [4], supporting collaborative learning, and enabling learners to concretely and tangibly access previously physically inaccessible/invisible or abstract content [9].

During times of isolation, XR systems provide an interactive environment with the virtual outer world. Umwelt's proposed VR system's aim is to create the interactive world middle schoolers are lacking during online learning.

In addition to providing immersive and interactive learning experiences, VR, and XR systems in general, motivate students to explore new academic or nonacademic fields [2]. For instance, to help people grasp 3D concepts (e.g. geometry), studies have shown that through AR and VR, people can check out 3D geometric forms from multiple perspectives; they can rotate a shape to see it from different angles including looking from an internal point of view and external point of view [15] (Kaufmann). Umwelt aims to take advantage of this free space. Umwelt's 3D world creates an environment specific to the selected culture of the language the player wishes to immerse themselves in. The images of the game are from a Spanish perspective, the market contains objects indigenous to Spain and the actions of the characters represent the widely accepted courtesy displays. Taking advantage of the freedom provided by VR, Umwelt also aims to set different goals at different levels- or even different steps in a given level. The supermarket level aims to familiarize the player with cultural elements and their names. The player is then expected to break down the task (explained in detail at 3.1) and perform simple computation while also developing simple financial literacy through calculating for change.

## 2.2 Related Works

XR has only recently started being utilized in SLA. However, attributes of VR systems strongly complement that of SLA [10] As a result XR technology has been utilized by various applications designed to teach language. An example of this is Mondly. Mondly is an XR-based SLA application. Mondly also utilizes speech recognition systems to test pronunciation [11]. Speech recognition allows Mondly to also increase the amount of interaction, much like our goal with Umwelt. However, Umwelt follows a more rewarding and game-based approach to this concept, effectively combining it with computational skills, to allow higher acquisition rates.

Moreover, a system designed for SLA called Ogma also utilizes VR technology [12]. Ogma uses virtual reality to create an immersive experience in an environment representing a place related to the desired language. The system functions similarly to Umwelt, with a focal point on cultural immersion. On the other hand, Umwelt utilizes both cultural immersion and social interaction. In Ogma's pilot study "the effectiveness and enjoyability ratings given by users were significantly higher for the VR method." [12] This positive result provides insight into the expected research results from Umwelt's pilot test.

## 3   Game Design

### 3.1  Gameplay

The VR environment is assembled in Unity. The prototype consists of two main scenes: the start scene and the supermarket scene, labeled as Figs. 1 and 2. The start screen only serves the purpose of an introduction to the supermarket scene. The demo only consists of one scene which is the supermarket. Once the character enters the supermarket, a notebook is displayed to greet the player and explain the task as seen in Fig. 3. The greeting is given in both English and Spanish but the rest is only in Spanish.

**Fig. 1.** Start scene                    **Fig. 2.** Supermarket scene

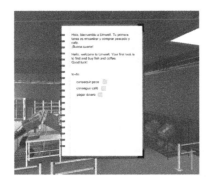

**Fig. 3.** Notebook with greeting and to-do list

The player is told to find certain items that are shown after the instructions: The desired objects are allocated through the aisles in the supermarket in a pre-arranged order. The player will have to rely on their common sense to locate the necessary aisles and examine the products on shelves to find required objects. To eliminate the chance of players finding the objects by chance, it is required that they are next to the object to pick it up. The game instructs the player to select a fish and a bag of coffee. The coffee aisle is the second aisle from the entrance and the fish aisle is located at the very end of the supermarket. When the player reaches the necessary sections and interacts with the containers, the required item is handed over to the player. Around the fish section, three NPCs can be found; a fish seller, a lady buying fish, and a coffee enthusiast. When the player approaches the NPCs, a dialogue is played. The coffee enthusiast expresses his love for coffee and the lady is buying fish in a conversation with the seller, as seen in Fig. 4. All of the dialogues are in simple grammar so as not to overwhelm the player. After acquiring the items, the player then has to go to the cashier to pay for the fish. When the player faces the cashier that says: "A fish and some coffee. Is there anything else?" in Spanish. The player thereafter has to give an appropriate response to advance the conversation. The same dialogue is repeated until the player informs the cashier that's all. Through IBM Watson's voice recognition system the communication between the player and non-player characters (NPCs) is established. IBM Watson's Castilian Spanish model ("es-ES_BroadbandModel") is implemented. After informing the cashier, the cashier says "That will be 7 (monetary units) for a fish and some coffee". Then, the player has to utter a payment in the form of a sentence. To do this, the player must listen to other NPCs (non-player characters) to figure out the words they need, to form sentences. The conversation between the lady and the fish seller is especially informative in this regard. This develops the player's computational skills and improves their second language acquisition as the player needs to compartmentalize speech given by NPCs and recognize patterns to learn the language. Subtitles are provided to more easily understand the contents and the meaning of the spoken dialogue. After the player forms a sentence that indicates that they are paying the required amount of money for a fish and some coffee through speech, the cashier thanks the player. This is where the demo concludes.

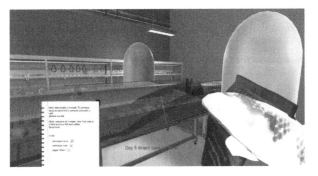

**Fig. 4.** The lady and fishmonger's conversation

## 3.2 Krashen's Theory of Second Language Acquisition (SLA)

One of Umwelt's aims is to provide a means of Second Language Acquisition. The foundations of Umwelt were built on Krashen's Theory of Second Language Acquisition (SLA), which consists of 5 fundamental parts. The Acquisition-Learning hypothesis, the Monitor hypothesis, the Input hypothesis, the Affective Filter hypothesis, and the Natural Order hypothesis [6] The initial step states that acquisition, the process children go through when learning their first language, should be prioritized in SLA as it differs from "formal" learning [17], which is based on conscious "knowledge" typically seen in student-teacher interactions. Concordantly, Umwelt focuses on highlighting acquisition instead of being taught an additional language. The player acquires language through interacting with NPCs, listening to them, and repeating the words and word order they use under similar circumstances. The game's levels replicate a student-centered environment utilizing acquisition to enable players to fully benefit from the available input. Even though traditional learning methods play a minuscule role in SLA, it still functions as a monitor to police the utterances of a language learner as given in the Monitor Hypothesis

[]. Umwelt accomplishes this through "monitoring" reactions of NPCs to the player's speeches. These can be in the form of facial expressions, gestures, or questions such as "Did you mean …?" Moreover, Umwelt's game design aids players in acquisition per the Input Hypothesis. The NLP system in Umwelt recognizes the level of the player in terms of language, and then provides input of a reasonably higher level. As a result, the acquisition process of players is guided according to their current level, allowing learners to go at their own pace. Throughout this entire process, the game allows the user to stay motivated by adjusting the level of difficulty and not discouraging the player, as well as establishing a simple reward system. When the player performs exceptionally well on a level, they receive a gift from the level's NPCs that allow them to unlock additional levels and locations throughout the game. This is in line with the Affective Filter hypothesis.

### 3.3    Simple Computation and Computational Thinking

Computational thinking (CT) entails four main processes. Decomposition, abstraction, pattern recognition, and algorithms. Decomposition is the breaking down of a problem into smaller parts, while abstraction is removing unnecessary details [16]. Pattern recognition is realizing a pattern between those parts, and algorithmic thinking is when we use those patterns to form a comprehensive step by step, set of rules [16]. All of which are expressed thoroughly in Umwelt's design, as will be mentioned later on. Umwelt transfers this type of thinking through two main methods, both of which are ingrained into the very function of the game. First is our method of language education provides a great means of CT education as well. A player has to break spoken language down in parts, recognize patterns of words and gestures or objects and then connect these to form their own sentences, essentially making an algorithm of their own. This method of SLA strongly integrates CT into acquisition. Additionally, Umwelt's gameplay involves a sizable amount of puzzles where players will need to follow the methods of CT in order to progress in the game (See Sect. 2.1 aisles for an example). As a result, players' CT skills are highly stimulated through every aspect of the gameplay. Simple computation, however, is a process of performing basic numeric and algebraic operations differing from the CT process. Umwelt also works to improve the computational skills of player's since, as seen in Dr. Rahmah Apen's study [1], while developing computational skills, retention of aspects of grammar increased drastically. Since Umwelt does not directly focus on grammar teaching, computation was integrated into its gameplay to increase retention from monitoring systems detailed in Sect. 2.2. Umwelt -in its demo- achieves computation based task implementation by the means of financial literacy. An example of this can be seen in the scenario given in Sect. 2.1. In this scenario, players are tasked with making the optimal choice, as a result the player uses computation to determine how much money to give the cashier, and how much change to ask for. This method was used for Umwelt's demo as financial literacy provides a tangible and objective method of measurement to look for any correlations between computational improvements and language acquisition.

# 4  Expected Research Plan

Through research, Umwelt aims to develop its content and format as well as enlightening theoretical information with empirical data. At Umwelt's development stage, the main research concept is testing the effects of implementing a language teaching approach via XR systems, 3D visualization, in an environment of cultural elements, supported by Krahsen's SLA, and the features of Umwelt as presented above rather than standardized digital language learning methods and products on learners' efficiency in learning and proficiency in the language. An additional aim is testing the effects of personalized learning approaches in language learning and teaching for Umwelt and different frequencies of exposure to the language via Umwelt on the proficiency of the learner for future improvements. It is expected that Umwelt, with its engaging features, helps learners of its target audience gain practice with Spanish grammar, speaking, and listening with comparably higher efficiency and productivity and resulting in a learner more proficient in the language than a learner trained with standardized methods, where "standardized methods" refers to popularized language teaching methodologies in digital apps.

Through this research, Umwelt can be proven or disproven of its effectiveness and be improved in various places, particularly on personalized learning, the optimal frequency of use, reconsideration of the implementation of SLA, and engagingness from students' test scores and feedback.

As Umwelt's target audience, 5th-grade students, with Turkish as their mother language, that voluntarily participates will be a part of the research. The following steps show the research process:

Students will be separated into two groups: Group A, which includes those who have had no formal education in Spanish, and Group B, which includes those who have. Students involved from each group will be sent a survey highlighting their interest in learning a new language, their interest in learning Spanish, their previous knowledge of any language, languages spoken and native speakers in their households, their familiarity with languages, and their specific familiarity with Spanish. After the survey, students will be grouped once again according to their involvement and previously shown interest in Spanish and other languages. This is required since familiarity with the language and exposure has a direct and significant impact on proficiency as concluded from Brière's studies. Then, students will be introduced to their working schedule and product. A group of students from Group A and Group B that contain students from all different subgroups will use standard digital language teaching apps, as the rest use Umwelt, whilst exposure to Spanish being kept the same for each student. The research will go on for one month. Students will follow this program with proper controlling periods to track their exposure time and progress. This part of the research will require the researchers to be highly engaged with the students to check their progress. After one month, students will take a test that tests only the topics covered on both of the platforms. The date of this test will not be announced to the students to make sure no intentional studying was present and to extract data with higher accuracy. This test will be based on speaking skills and pronunciation. Speaking skills will be valued particularly due to COVID-19's effects on children's proficiency in speaking and to test how our product can cope with this way of teaching. Afterward, points gained from the test will be analyzed to determine the effectiveness of our product and to improve its features based on that.

## 5 Conclusion and Future Works

Umwelt, though in its prototype stage, aims to provide a gamified environment to enhance learning. Currently, Umwelt only focuses on second language acquisition and includes some computational thinking elements but hopes to expand and cover a wide range of other supplementary options to aid other course contents and include more computational thinking in the process. The game warrants computational thinking-based approaches to SLA in a manner tailored to kids. Thus strengthening both simultaneously. Umwelt does not follow a certain curriculum; therefore, anyone can access the game without feeling alienated. Additionally, more complex sentence structures and an expanded set of vocabulary are soon to be introduced. The current gameplay of Umwelt is simple and easy to understand. Once the game is tested, Umwelt hopes to introduce a more personalized experience for students and implement visual feedback loops within its gameplay. It is true that the characters in the gameplay only accept certain phrases even though students may come up with sentences with different words that mean the same thing. This is why Umwelt hopes to enlarge its library and randomize the plot for future players. Umwelt also aims to implement Machine Learning systems to customize the game according to the player's level, increasing the efficiency of learning of individuals by letting them go at their own pace.

## References

1. Apen, R.M.: The applicative use of problem solving technique in teaching grammar. In: Proceedings of the Fourth International Seminar on English Language and Teaching (ISELT-4), State University of Padang (2016). https://ejournal.unp.ac.id/index.php/selt/article/viewFile/6975/5509
2. Augmented Reality, Virtual Reality, and Mixed Reality.: 7 things you should know about augmented reality, virtual reality, and mixed reality, EDUCAUSE (2017). https://library.edu cause.edu/-/media/files/library/2017/10/eli7149.pdf
3. Burgess, S., Sievertsen. H.H.: The Impact of COVID-19 on education. VOX, CEPR Policy Portal, 1 Apr 2020. https://voxeu.org/article/impact-covid-19-education
4. Georgieva, M., Craig, E., Pfaff, D., Neville, D., Burchett, B.: 7 Things You Should Know About AR/VR/MR, 3 Oct 2017. https://library.educause.edu/resources/2017/10/7-things-you-should-know-about-ar-vr-mr
5. Education: From Disruption to Recovery. UNESCO, 2 June 2021. https://en.unesco.org/cov id19/educationresponse.
6. Gülay, E.R.: The input hypothesis and second-language acquisition theory. Dergipark, f!Dr.,Ondokuz Mayıs University. https://dergipark.org.tr/en/download/article-file/188335
7. Sarnecka, B.W.: Language development across childhood and adolescence. Research-gate, Sept 2006. www.researchgate.net/publication/248670881_LANGUAGE_DEVELO PMENT_ACROSS_CHILDHOOD_AND_ADOLESCENCE
8. Students weigh in: learning and well-being during COVID-19.: YouthTruth. https://youthtrut hsurvey.org/student-weigh-in/
9. Yang, K., et al.: XR-Ed framework: designing instruction-driven and. XR-Ed framework: designing instruction-driven and learner-centered extended reality systems for education. 24 Oct 2020. https://arxiv.org/pdf/2010.13779.pdf

10. Schwienhorst, K.: Why virtual, why environments? Implementing virtual reality concepts in computer-assisted language learning - Klaus Schwienhorst. SAGE J. (2002). https://journals.sagepub.com/doi/abs/https://doi.org/10.1177/1046878102332008
11. Mondly, A.R.: Augmented reality language learning. www.mondly.com/ar
12. Dylan Ebert University of Texas at Arlington, et al.: Ogma: a virtual reality language acquisition system. In: Ogma I Proceedings of the 9th ACM International Conference on PErvasive Technologies Related to Assistive Environments, 1 June 2016. dlnext.acm.org/doi/abs/https://doi.org/10.1145/2910674.2910681
13. de Boer, I.R., Wesselink, P.R., Vervoorn, J.M.: Student performance and appreciation using 3D vs. 2D vision in a virtual learning environment. Eur. J. Dental Educ. Official J. Assoc. Dental Educ. Eur., U.S. National Library of Medicine. https://pubmed.ncbi.nlm.nih.gov/26072997/
14. Hartshorn, K.J., McMurry, B.J.: The effects of the COVID-19 pandemic on ESL learners and TESOL practitioners in the United States. Int. J. TESOL Stud. 2(2), 140+. Gale Academic OneFile (2020)
15. Kaufmann, H.: Construct3D: an augmented reality application for mathematics and geometry education. ResearchGate. Institute of Software Technology and Interactive Systems, Mar 2003. www.researchgate.net/publication/2570081_Construct3D_An_Augmented_Reality_Application_for_Mathematics_And_Geometry_Education
16. Labusch, A., et al.: Computational thinking processes and their congruence with problem-solving and information processing. Springer, Springer Open, 3 May 2019. https://doi.org/10.1007/978-981-13-6528-7_5
17. Krashen, S.D.: Principles and Practice in Second language acquisition /Stephen D. Krashen. Prentice-Hall Internat (1987)

# Usability of Digital Numeration Training for Students at Primary School

Ningxi Chen[1], Adrian Roussel-Fayard[1], Nadine Vigouroux[1], Jean-François Camps[2], Charlotte Tabarant[3], and Frédéric Vella[1(✉)]

[1] IRIT, CNRS, UPS, 118 Route de Narbonne, 31062 CEDEX 9 Toulouse, France
{Nadine.Vigouroux,Frederic.Vella}@irit.fr
[2] URI Octogone-Lordat, UT2J, 5, allée Antonio Machado, 31058 CEDEX 9 Toulouse, France
jcamps@univ-tlse2.fr
[3] Academic's Direction, French National's Education, Toulouse, France
charlotte.artus@ac-toulouse.fr

**Abstract.** This article report the principles and the design of usability method used on HMK-Learning application. It is a digital tool for students at primary schools in France based on Mounier's numeracy work in didactics. Firstly, the design method of HMK-Learning is described. Then, we describe the survey design method to study the usability of HMK-Learning. This questionnaire is based on Nielsen's and Alsumait's heuristics. Next, we present the survey results answered by four teachers of primary schools. We mainly report them from the point of view of the design interface elements. The study underlines the importance of offering interaction and feedback techniques adapted to the motor and cognitive abilities of elementary school students.

**Keywords:** Usability · Primary school · Mathematics digital numeration

## 1 Context

Trends in International Mathematics and Science Study survey (2019) ranks France last in the European Union countries for the level of knowledge in arithmetics compared to statistics, probability and geometry. In France, the mathematics Villani-Torossian report notes learning difficulties (sense of numbers, counting, transcoding between oral and written numeration, etc.) in mathematics from primary school. A recommendation of the report concerns the meaning of the four operations (addition, subtraction, multiplication and division) and the teaching of the quantities and measures in primary school that should support number and operation sense. Moreover, [1] and [2] demonstrated the good influence of digital tools on student's development of skills and mathematical knowledge. [2] highlighted the fact that "the success of digital technology in mathematics education include the design of the digital tool and corresponding tasks exploiting the tool's pedagogical potential, the role of the teacher and the educational context". Based on these findings, our hypothesis is that the design of HMK-L application integrating Mounier's [3] numeracy work could be more efficient for students at primary schools

C. Stephanidis et al. (Eds.): HCII 2021, CCIS 1499, pp. 258–265, 2021.
https://doi.org/10.1007/978-3-030-90179-0_33

in France. More precisely, Mounier worked on acquisition of the "sense of numbers", the organization of collections, oral-written transcoding of numeration information, the concept of numeration of position. In HMK-L, we will experiment the comparison of collections with an analysis of the numerical manipulation of tokens. The observation is focused on strategies of moving tokens, to group tokens or not in order to study the efficiency of installing the need to group by 10.

The aim of this paper is to describe the design method of the application HMK-Learning for pupils at primary school. Then, we will focus on the survey design method to study the usability of HMK-Learning. Finally, we will present mainly the results of the usability study on the interface elements and they will be used in the design method of HMK-L.

## 2   Design Methodology of HMK-L

Together with a mathematics Villani-Torossian-65 (France) group, we designed the HandiMathKey Learning (HMK-L) through a participatory design approach. The particularity of our approach concerns the involvement of the ecosystem in the sense of Guffroy et al. [4]. This ecosystem is composed of 5 primary school teachers, an Expert in Mathematical Didactic and pedagogy, 3 researchers in Human Computer Interaction (HCI) and 1 cognitive psychology researcher. A first activity developed was the comparison of numbers. The constraints of use were that primary school children did not have a sufficient reading level for instructions, and that the interface should be simple to use and fun. The other constraint concerns the running of the application on any operating system. We chose the choice of a web application (https://www.irit.fr/HandiMathKey-Learning/). We describe below the design method of the student interface of HMK_L.

Firstly, the mathematics Villani-Torossian-65 (France) group has written the specifications of the comparison of numbers application (case study scenario, interface for configuring interaction techniques and token colors). Then, the HCI researchers has designed a first low fidelity prototype with the following interactive components (see Fig. 1) the button to return to the home page; 2) the help button for handling the tokens; 3) the textual instructions 6) the 2 classes of tokens to be compared; 7) the button to be selected for the choice of the correct answer; an animation and audio feedback are given according the answer 8) the digital tape to help the pupils visualize the quantity of tokens. Representation of the tokens, modality of the instructions, animated help; feedback on evaluation of the student's response; interface design (simple, aesthetic and fun aspects) have been discussed with the mathematics referent regarding their design for children. The teachers' group has then expressed two new needs (see Fig. 1): 4) the level of the exercise; 5) the pictogram representing the child's progress in the exercise. This representation has allowed the pupil to monitor his/her advances. The second high-fidelity prototype takes into account the decisions of the focus group (see Fig. 1)

Another strong demand is the ease of interaction in manipulating collection tokens for students with motor disabilities so that cognitive processes are primarily dedicated to the task of learning and reasoning and not to solving token manipulation problems.

The HCI team has designed three interaction techniques: (Drag and Drop (DD), Click to Click (CC) and Magnetization by Click (MC)). The pupil with or without

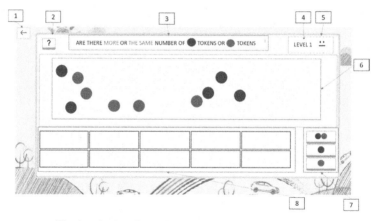

**Fig. 1.** The interface of the number comparison exercise

motor disabilities has thus the option to select the one that is most appropriate for him after manipulation trials.. [5] have studied these techniques for object manipulation for patients with cognitive disorders. The interaction device has been evaluated as a usability indicator and will be evaluated in the future with users directly.

## 3   Usability Questionnaire

### 3.1   Several Approaches

Two main types of methods can be used to evaluate usability of interactive system: heuristic and standardized survey. Heuristic evaluations are mainly done by human computer experts during the different phases of the design. User experience, on the other hand, involve users (final or secondary) who are not experts in human computer interaction but who can identify concrete problems when using the application to be evaluated. The most well-known questionnaires are: SUS (System Usability System) [6] and USE (Usefulness, Satisfaction and Ease of Use) [7].

Nielsen [9] is the reference for usability heuristics. [8] have proposed 21 Heuristic Evaluation for Child E-learning based on Nielsen's heuristics and adapted to children and e-learning applications. Ssemugabi and De Villiers [10] proposed in 2007 a comparative study between a set of 20 heuristic evaluation and a user survey. They concluded that heuristic evaluation is cheaper, more efficient and easier to implement than user survey. On the other hand, the problems found using heuristics, although more numerous, are less important and less related to the context of use of the evaluated application.

The output from using the heuristic evaluation method is a list of usability problems in the interface with references to those usability principles that were violated by the design in each case in the opinion of the evaluator. We have chosen the heuristic evaluation because firstly, we want to identify the problems during the design phase and secondly, 75% usability problems in an interface are found by heuristic evaluation using five of evaluators.

## 3.2   The Design of the Usability Method

In the health context of COVID in March 2020, our approach was to design a remote evaluation. This makes it possible to overcome the heavy constraints associated with face-to-face work (social distancing, cleaning of experimental equipment, etc.).

A multidisciplinary team (1 cognitive psychology researcher, 2 researchers, a student in human-computer interaction and an expert in mathematical didactic and pedagogy) has designed the questionnaire. We used the set of 21 heuristics proposed by Alsumait and Al-Osaimi [8]. These heuristics are highly relevant for the usability study of HMK-L because they are based on Nielsen's heuristics (see Fig. 1), adapted to children and e-learning applications. The Table 1 gives the distribution of the 47 criteria to the ten Nielsen's Heuristics as illustrated below.

While this approach allows for the respect of health conditions, it does raise some adaptations in its implementation. Indeed, it is necessary to ensure: 1) that the questions are understandable by the evaluators since the experimenter is not present and 2) that the evaluator has discovered all the functionalities of the interactive system. To meet objective 1, the comprehension of the questionnaire was presented to two teachers of primary school and a representative member of the mathematics Villani group who checked the comprehension (objective of the question, meaning of words) of version 1 of the questionnaire. After this focus group, we corrected ambiguous questions. The questionnaire contains 65 questions using 76.6% of the criteria of Alsumait and Al-Osaimi. The Table 1 gives the distribution of criteria according the Nielsen's Heuristics as Table 2 gives the links between of the question, the Nielsen's Heuristic and Alsumait's criteria.

**Table 1.** Distribution of criteria used according the Nielsen's Heuristics used (extracted from [11]).

| Nielsen's Heuristics | Number of criteria used | Number of criteria by category | Percentage use of criteria |
|---|---|---|---|
| Visibility of System Status | 6 | 8 | 75% |
| Match between system and the real world | 4 | 5 | 80% |
| User Control freedom | 3 | 4 | 75% |
| Consistency and standards | 4 | 6 | 66,67% |
| Error prevention | 3 | 4 | 75% |
| Recognition rather than recall | 3 | 4 | 75% |

**Table 2.** Links between the questions, the Nielsen's Heuristic and Alsumait's criteria.

| Tasks | Nielsen's Heuristics | Alsumait's criteria | Question |
|---|---|---|---|
| Choice of the interaction technique | Consistency and standards | Control keys are intuitive, convenient, consistent, and follow standard conventions | Is the interaction technique useful for picking and moving the ball? |
| | Flexibility and efficiency of use | Input/output devices are used for their own purposes and are suitable for the specific age group of the child | Do you feel these interaction techniques are appropriate for use with students? |
| | Help and documentation | The child does not need to use a manual to use the application | Is the interaction technique easy to understand? There is no need to explain how to use it |

A scenario of tasks and subtasks is associated with the questionnaire. The evaluator must perform a sequence of actions with the HMK-L application and then answer questions about these actions. We will illustrate the principle on manipulation tests with the two interaction techniques (DD and CC) described in Sect. 2.

Task: Choice of the interaction technique.

Action: Click on "interaction technique" to open the menu for the selection of an interaction technique.

Sub task 1.1: Drag and Drop.

Action: Select the "drag and drop" interaction technique.

**Table 3.** Examples of question for the task "Choice of the interaction technique".

| Questions | Answers |
|---|---|
| Is the interaction technique useful for picking and moving the ball? | Likert scale: Absolutely not convenient (0), Not convenient (1), Somewhat not convenient (2), Somewhat convenient (3), Convenient (4), Perfectly convenient (5) |
| Is the interaction technique user-friendly? There is no need to explain how to use it | Likert scale: Very difficult (0), Difficult (1), Rather not difficult (2), Rather not easy (3), Easy(4), Very easy(5) |
| Is the interaction technique easy to understand? There is no need to explain how to use it | Verbatims |

Action: Put the football ball at various locations in the test area to test the interaction technique.

Subtask 1 will be duplicated for the CC interactions.

Table 3 shows three questions and the type of response expected for each of them.

The questionnaire consists of 65 questions (37 closed questions, 11 questions with a Likert scale and 17 open questions).

## 4   Results of the Usability Questionnaire

An expert in mathematical didactic and pedagogy presented the objectives and principles of the HMK_L application to 5 teachers of primary school. During health confinement in November 2020 in France, the document containing task scenarios and questions was sent to them. 4 of them responded. On the overall, according to users' feedback, the HMK-L digital application is identified as an interactive, useful and practical tool to develop skills in numbers' comparison and overall in numeration. Table 4 summarizes the evaluation on interface elements.

**Table 4.** Evaluation on interface elements

| Interface elements | Evaluation report |
|---|---|
| Visual aspect of the interface | Pleasant, airy, understandable, playful and well-structured; |
| Textual instructions | Understandable, presentation in sound modality required |
| Spatial layout of tokens | Good distribution, token overlapping to be avoided, no need of audio feedback |
| Feedback Interaction techniques (DD and CC) | Progress scale for exercises is suitable, feedback of success or failure is also appropriate Ease to use, Ease to understanding |

The textual instructions (button 3 in Fig. 1) is considered readable (4.75 on a 5-point Likert scale) and the application combine aesthetics and ergonomics design (4.25 out of 5). The scale of progression in the exercises (change of color of the smiley and the level label: button 4 and 5 in Fig. 1) is concerned as encouraging and understandable for 3 primary school teachers. The two verbatims confirm this point of view: "Related to what is used in class". "It is motivating". The last suggests improving the smiley representation to distinguish better the levels of exercise: To questions, -- "Why not keep the same smiley face with a progression of colors? " What do you think of the animations (image, sound and animation of the tokens) linked to the expected correct answer or the erroneous answer? Do you think they are suitable for students? Do they encourage further use of the application?--. The animations broadcast according to the student's results are very playful and fun for 4 of the teachers for a correct answer and only 3 for an incorrect answer (verbatim: "Very good, these animations are very playful and visual: the children will perfectly associate each pictogram and the sound, either to a success or error; they are very motivating. Be careful with the animation of the tokens a little too fast according to the level and a little clutter (several tokens are arranged at the same time)". However, the teachers also suggested that in the case of an incorrect answer, it would be preferable to put a picture a little more encouraging for the child. The role of the digital tape is also understandable for the students according to the 4 teachers. The arrows for navigation through the exercise (go to the next exercise, repeat the exercise, go to the next level of difficulty) are affordable.

We compare the ease of understanding and use of the two interaction techniques (DD and CC). For these variables, we used a 0–5 point Likert scale. The DD technique is considered slightly easier (5 vs. 3.66) and (4.66 vs. 4.33) by the teachers (see Table 3 for scale values). Feedback from selecting (4.66 out of 5), moving (4.33) and releasing (4.66) a token was perceived as visible. The teachers validated these two dimensions of the interaction (modes of control of token movement and feedback of the student's action in the interface). However, studies of use by students with motor and/or attentional disorders should confirm these results. At this stage of the design of HMK_L, this postulates to allow the choice of the interaction technique as a parameter of the HMK-L application.

The implementation of the usability method linking controlled scenario and questionnaire provided relevant input for the redesign of HMK-L. Indeed, the results of this usability study are currently being taken into account for the development of the 2nd iteration of the HMK-L application before usage studies are performed by children.

## 5    Conclusion and Perspective

A multidisciplinary team has designed a questionnaire based on Alsumait's criteria and Nielsen's heuristics to evaluate the HMK-L design. However, the health constraints due to the COVID 19 pandemic have affected the usability method implemented. We initially measured the understanding of the questionnaire with 4 teachers. On the overall, according to primary teacher's usability test, the HMK-L is identified as an interactive, useful and practical tool to learn and to develop skills in numbers' comparison and overall in numeration. The questionnaire analysis is very rich and usable to redesign interaction components (instruction, progress feedback, etc.) to improve ergonomics and accessibility of HMK-Learning by students. It also demonstrated the relevance of the application's feedback and the interaction techniques implemented.

The main limitation of our study is the insufficient number of evaluators. The next steps are: 1) usability and utility test for primary school students with the release of HMK- following the consideration of the usability study by the teachers; 2) the analysis of the movement of the tokens with or without a specific method, the modalities of grouping will allow us to deepen our knowledge in particular of the relations between space and number and of the numeration of position.

**Acknowledgment.** This project was partly funded by the MSHS-T in Toulouse (France). The authors would like to thank the teachers from the primary schools who participated in the HMK-Learning specifications and who answered the questionnaires.

# References

1. Drijvers, P.: Digital technology in mathematics education: why it works (Or Doesn't). In: Cho, S.J. (ed.) Selected Regular Lectures from the 12th International Congress on Mathematical Education, pp. 135–151. Springer International Publishing, Cham (2015). https://doi.org/10.1007/978-3-319-17187-6_8
2. Geiger, V., Goos, M., Dole, S.: The role of digital technologies in numeracy teaching and learning. Int. J. Sci. Math. Educ. **13**(5), 1115–1137 (2014). https://doi.org/10.1007/s10763-014-9530-4
3. Mounier, E.: Nouveaux outils d'analyse des procédures de dénombrement pour explorer leur lien avec la numération écrite chiffrée et la numération parlée. Recherches en didactique des mathématiques **36**(3), 347–396 (2017)
4. Guffroy, M., Vigouroux, N., Kolski, C., Vella, F., Teutsch, P.H.: From human-centered design to disabled user and ecosystem centered design in case of assistive interactive systems. Int. J. Sociotechnology Knowl. Dev. (IJSKD) **9**(4), 28–42 (2017)
5. Vella F., Vigouroux N., Rumeau P.: Investigating drag and drop techniques for older people with cognitive impairment. In: Jacko J.A. (eds.) Human-Computer Interaction. Users and Applications. HCI 2011. Lecture Notes in Computer Science, vol. 6764, pp, 530-538. Springer, Heidelberg (2011). https://doi.org/10.1007/978-3-642-21619-0_65
6. Brooke, J.: SUS: a "quick and dirty" usability scale. In: Jordan, P.W., Thomas, B., Weerdmeester, B.A., McClelland, A.L. (eds.) Usability Evaluation in Industry. Taylor and Francis, London (1986)
7. Lund, A.M.: Measuring usability with the use questionnaire12. Usability interface **8**(2), 3–6 (2001)
8. Alsumait, A., Al-Osaimi, A.: Usability heuristics evaluation for child e-learning applications. In: Proceedings of the 11th International Conference on Information Integration and Web-Based Applications and Services, pp. 425–430 (2009)
9. Nielsen, J.: 10 usability heuristics for user interface design. Nielsen Norman Group **1**(1) (1995). http://www.useit.com/papers/heuristic/heuristic_list.html
10. Ssemugabi, S., De Villiers, R.: A comparative study of two usability evaluation methods using a web-based e-learning application. In: Proceedings of the 2007 Annual Research Conference of the South African Institute of Computer Scientists and Information Technologists on IT Research in Developing Countries, pp. 132–142 (2007)
11. Roussel-Fayard, A., Vigouroux, N., Vella, F., Camps, J.-F., Tabarant, C.: Design approach of digital numeration training for students in a primary school. In: 12th International Conference on Applied Human Factors and Ergonomics, AHFE 2021, pp. 25–29 (July 2021)

# LABS ONLINE – An Opportunity to Access High Quality Laboratory During COVID Breakout

Romi Dey[✉] and Kailash Manjhi[✉]

Solved By Design, Kolkata, India

**Abstract.** Context: Students and job seekers are not getting any labs or practical experience using machines to be industry ready during the lockdown. Expensive machines are not accessible to these in general resulting in missed opportunities. Holistic remote learning of theory and lab is the need of the hour. With no proper remote training, their entire career will be at stake possibly causing damage to the machine or personal safety.

How can a great lab experience be offered remotely? The skills that Aarush has to acquire is challenging without good lab experiences.

Solution Approach:

- OpenGL on the web browser provides a 3D lab like experience to users from the comfort of their home.
- Using open source technology makes the solution cost effective. Technologies like Blender to create 3D models, A-frame for web framework for VR, Skectchfab for 3D marketplace, WebAR, Coffeescript etc.
- Users who are students and job seekers get an effective lab experience and worry less about burdening parents financially.
- Using Google cardboard can be an alternate solution for development in the future.

Viability:

- Futuristic technology that is not too expensive.
- The solution is viable for any time, however the lockdown has accelerated the urgency of such learning platforms.
- Collaborative and team learning features in the product stresses the fact *"during lockdown, remote learning need not be learning alone, it can be learning along"*
- It is the design for the new normal.
- The product is driven "by the community - for the community" to reach the masses in general. For example, 3D modellers develop the models, The teachers use the solution to enhance experience, students benefit with the viable solution and be confidently career ready.

**Keywords:** Labs online · Lab experience · Remote learning · Collaboration technology

© Springer Nature Switzerland AG 2021
C. Stephanidis et al. (Eds.): HCII 2021, CCIS 1499, pp. 266–271, 2021.
https://doi.org/10.1007/978-3-030-90179-0_34

# 1  Introduction

## 1.1  Background

Learning becomes easier and understandable due to the access of the practical experiences and the great quality laboratories that the students and researchers get. Practical experience is greatly important as the theoretical knowledge for any domain. Also, virtual laboratories might assist the students in overcoming the problems faced by them in a conventional laboratory. As the global pandemic almost crippled the entire world, various sub domains of education, such as, access to high quality laboratories for the purpose of practical and hand on experience, got hit.

Study carried out in Slovenia shows that virtual laboratories help in better understanding of knowledge acquisition [1]. The virtual learning can improve student's understanding and also enrich their knowledge as per the outcome of the study carried out in Taiwan [2].

## 1.2  Problem Statement

Access to laboratories, that demands availability of high-quality machines, devices and other relevant instruments, got almost impossible for the students and professionals, mainly during pandemic.

# 2  Methodology

## 2.1  Design Thinking

During the entire period of research, we followed the Design Thinking Methodology [3]. Design Thinking refers to the cognitive, strategic and practical process by which design concepts (proposals for products, buildings, machines, communications, etc.) are developed (Fig. 1).

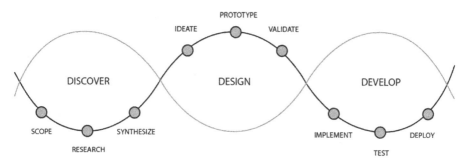

**Fig. 1.** Diagram showing the design led development process [4]

**Research (Primary and Secondary).** Observing and interviewing the users will provide many insights that will help in making educated decisions while building a product [5]. We interviewed 10+ users and conducted a detailed study on the various usages of laboratories, pain points faced, roles and responsibilities etc.

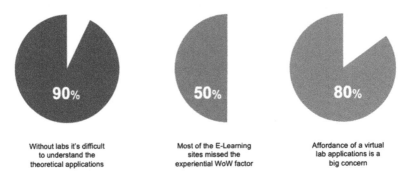

| | | |
|---|---|---|
| Without labs it's difficult to understand the theoretical applications | Most of the E-Learning sites missed the experiential WoW factor | Affordance of a virtual lab applications is a big concern |

**Ideate.** This phase helps us to move from the problem to the solution, converge on the best approach, assess the viability and feasibility and visualize the experience through story boarding. [4]. Creating a detailed story board, empathy map, flow chart and mood board, logo design for the prospective solution helped us in visualizing the skeleton of the product more vividly.

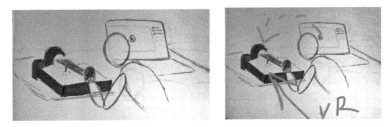

**Prototype.** The goal of the prototyping phase is to provide a low fidelity version of the design. Creating an actionable prototype with the appropriate data, charts, actions and controls gives an understanding of the prototype and its probable usage.

**Validate.** Verifying the focus of research and synthesis, evaluating the effectiveness of the design are few of the main goals of user testing/ validation. After the completion of the working prototype, we tested the product with 5+ users to validate the usability of the product created.

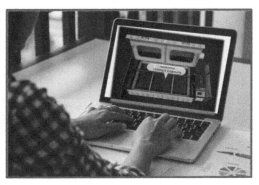

## 3  Impact and Result

### 3.1  Execution and Viability

LABSONLINE provides the following:

- Inexpensive futuristic technology.
- The solution is viable at any point in time, irrespective of the pandemic situation.
- Features related to collaboration and team building activities would ensure the mental health of the individuals as well, promoting "Not learning alone, but learning along".
- The product is driven "by the community - for the community" where the 3D modellers would develop the models, teachers would use the solution to enhance the experience, and the students would benefit with the viable solution and be confidently career ready.

### 3.2  Impact

Learning psychologists, after studies [6] compared traditional teaching methods and virtual labs, it was tested that there was a 76% higher learning effectiveness with virtual labs over traditional teaching methods.

As for the teachers, combining virtual and theoretical knowledge along with a teacher mentoring resulted in a total of 101% increase in learning effectiveness.

- Revolutionary and effective distance learning
- Teachers twice as effective
- Improves the quality of lab education
- Students can perform on the machines almost like in the real world

- Remote learning need not mean learning alone, it can be learning along with options to collaborate
- Engages students with stories and quizzes in the video

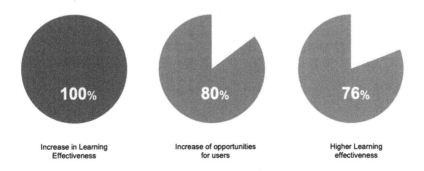

| | | |
|---|---|---|
| **100%** | **80%** | **76%** |
| Increase in Learning Effectiveness | Increase of opportunities for users | Higher Learning effectiveness |

## References

1. Herga, N.R., Čagran, B., Dinevski, D.: Virtual laboratory in the role of dynamic visualization for better understanding of chemistry in primary school. Eurasia J. Math. Sci. Technol. Educ. **12**(3), 593–608 (2016)
2. Shyr, W.-J.: Multiprog virtual laboratory applied to PLC programming learning. Eur. J. Eng. Educ. **35**(5), 573–583 (2010)
3. https://en.wikipedia.org/wiki/Design_thinking
4. https://www.build.me/learning
5. https://www.build.me/learningDetail/647
6. https://go.ted.com/CyGv

# Conversational Agents in Language Education: Where They Fit and Their Research Challenges

Rahul R. Divekar$^{(\boxtimes)}$, Haley Lepp, Pravin Chopade, Aaron Albin,
Daniel Brenner, and Vikram Ramanarayanan

Educational Testing Service, Princeton, USA
{rdivekar,hlepp,pchopade,aalbin,dsbrenner,vramanarayanan}@ets.org

**Abstract.** Conversational agents (or dialogue agents or Artificial Intelligent AI agents or chatbots) can provide a foreign language learner with otherwise hard-to-find conversational exposure to a new language. Such agents that teach languages differ significantly from their general-purpose counterparts in their goals, their approach, and their users' characteristics, thereby effectively creating a new interaction paradigm for which little literature exists in the HCI of Conversational Interfaces community. The difference from general-purpose agents comes from two themes highlighted in this work: the user is not expected to know the language of interaction, and the purpose of the conversation is language education through task completion rather than task completion itself. This paper highlights the role and the research challenges of interactions with dialogue agents that allow people to learn and practice new languages.

**Keywords:** Spoken dialogue systems · Language learning ·
Conversational agents · Conversational user interfaces · Immersion ·
Multimodal interfaces

## 1  Introduction and Literature

### 1.1  Introduction

Foreign language learners often lack access to native speaking partners. Dialogue agents within TOEFL MOOC, Duolingo, Mondly, Cleverbot, and Busuu, [11,27, 31,32] address this gap by mimicking conversational interactions with a human [35]. However, the HCI community has not given much attention to language-teaching agents which come with unique challenges.

The uniqueness arises from two broad differences between ordinary agents and language teaching agents: user characteristics and conversation goals. Ordinarily, agent designers can assume that the user is proficient in the language of interaction, whereas language learners are seeking to build that proficiency. Secondly, while most agents are designed to assist a user with completing a task

C. Stephanidis et al. (Eds.): HCII 2021, CCIS 1499, pp. 272–279, 2021.
https://doi.org/10.1007/978-3-030-90179-0_35

in the easiest possible way (e.g., booking a flight), in a language learning application task-completion is mostly a means to the end of language acquisition. The difference in goals of the conversation along with differences in user characteristics create a new paradigm of interaction and consequently new research challenges; as detailed in this paper.

## 1.2  Literature

Language learning requires repeated conversational practice [16]. Dialogue agents can facilitate this and expose students to natural language, culture, and pragmatics of communication by playing different interaction roles. [24] show a Question-Answer (QA) based teaching agent, [28]'s chatbot can make small talk, converse in a QA format, and give hints to a learner. [34]'s agents role play scenarios and give feedback. [35] use conversational agents to tell a story and ask follow-up questions to the learner; it adjusts questions based on a learner's ability to answer, and focuses on encouragement in dialogue. [17] presented the use of conversational agents in e-learning environments with examples for supporting self-assessment. [7]'s agents in an Extended Reality (XR) street market allow role-play opportunities to practice conversation and colloquial negotiation skills. [2,27] have done a systematic review. From above, we derive that designers use a combination of text or speech/audio as the interaction medium and situate their agents on platforms ranging from smart speakers to high-fidelity extended reality virtual environments in order to teach various aspects of language such as grammar, vocabulary, culture, pragmatics, interactive dialogue, etc.

## 2  Research Challenges of Language-Teaching Dialogue Agents

[29] highlight the need to move away from transactional request-response-like interactions to a colloquial conversation with a user that demonstrates pragmatics, personality, turn-taking, and enthusiastic verbal and non-verbal conversational overlap without the need of an invasive wake-up word. This is in line with creating social presence and rapport [3]. The importance of these complex research challenges apply to all agents and cannot be overstated in the case of language education. However, in this text we contextualize broad challenges to language-education agents and articulate new ones.

We do so from four perspectives seen in Fig. 1 which map to subsections below. The intersectional perspectives in the figure delineate the bases of situated learning [4], a widely-recognized theory in foreign language acquisition that promotes learning by doing.

### 2.1  Language Learning, Teaching, and Assessment

Well established learning theories like situated learning and task-based language teaching [20] advocate for learning by doing. For language acquisition, this means

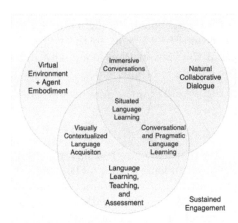

**Fig. 1.** Illustration of the domain space for an effective language learning solution

not only learning vocabulary and grammar but also applying them to communicate in real-life scenarios. Learners are best able to conceptualize the target language by being visually, culturally, and linguistically immersed in it, i.e. participating in interactions with context and feedback as opposed to only learning translations [20]. Such opportunities are scarce for most language learners due to a lack of fluent conversation partners and appropriate situations in which to practice. Dialogue agents can bring natural conversational opportunities. Combined with virtual environments and educational elements like targeted feedback, situated language learning can be enabled as seen in Fig. 1. Details of their challenges are discussed next.

## 2.2   Virtual Environments (VEs) with Embodied Agents

**Contextual Learning in VEs:** Creating a visual context for a educational dialogue agent has many advantages: it sets up the conversational and learning expectations, enhances social and cultural immersion, and increases the chances of incidental learning among others. A wide range of platforms differing in levels of immersiveness and presence (i.e. feeling of "being there") are available in which VEs can be implemented varying in their fidelity, availability, costs, ubiquity, etc. Each medium has different effect on different subsets of populations [15]. [26] have done a systematic review of VEs in language education. We observe that few studies have explored VEs with dialogue agents.

**Embodiment:** In addition to increasing presence, agents that use human-like gestures are more effective in teaching [23]. An embodied dialogue agent can produce gestures and expressions consistent with the target culture and give students an exposure to appropriate non-verbal communication. Further, they can ease communication by letting students make sense of the conversation through multimodal cues and mouth movements [5].

Creating a holistic cultural-rich visual environment with dialogue agents is important as learning communication without cultural pragmatics sets students up to appear as "fluent fools" [1]. Further, VEs can teach students how to bring visual, contextual information into their conversations. For example, a role-play of ordering food in a virtual restaurant would teach a learner how to use a menu, which is present outside the spoken context and is only present in the visual context. We will explore dialogue agents next.

## 2.3   Natural Collaborative Dialogue

While VEs can create virtual presence (i.e. feeling of "being there"), dialogue agents can add social presence (i.e. feeling of talking to an "intelligent entity" [3]) thereby completing the picture of an immersive virtual world [6]. This section focuses on role of agents in language education with and without VEs.

**Naturalness in Dialogue:** Dialogue agents can enable realistic interactions in a VE, improving spoken proficiency and willingness to communicate in a foreign language [18]. However, [27] note that some language-education agents' dialogues have a scripted quality. Probabilistic methods can counter this perception but afford less control over teaching materials and responses.

In a speech-enabled dialogue, synthetic voice output can create the impression of artificiality. [23] shows that a human voice is preferable and has a better effect on learning than synthetic voices. Being able to easily synthesize speech that sounds natural is an existing research challenge, amplified in a code-switched language (native and target language) environment. However, the artificialness may lower the stakes of the interaction and lead to more comfortable learning [7,15].

**Role of Dialogue Agents:**   Agents can play three roles: an interaction medium itself used to navigate through the environment, instructor (e.g., teaching language constructs and giving targeted feedback), or a roleplay partner (e.g., a server in a virtual restaurant).

Conversation exercises can either be focused on a specific construct or general exposure to conversation. E.g., [9]'s game allows learners to play a conversational guessing game where they are shown several avatars, one of which is the "target avatar". The learners can ask yes/no questions to the agent to guess the target avatar. Meanwhile, [7]'s agent provides scenario role-play where a student may learn the language, culture, and pragmatics of shopping at a street market.

The interaction with the agent can range from *exploratory* to *guided*. The former relies on students' initiation of dialogue and provides more autonomy while the latter relies on agent-initiated conversations guiding the student through a conversational experience. Each student may benefit from a different level of autonomy, targeted feedback, and scaffolding in their learning journey.

**Speech Recognition:** Dialogue agents in language learning tend to be text-based partially because building automatic speech recognition (ASR) systems for language learners is a hard task. Compared to regular speakers, learners make more mistakes, code-switch with their native language, thus requiring more complex modeling with large data sets [30].

**Natural Language Understanding (NLU):** [25] show that even though ASRs have a high word-error rate with non-native speech, non-native speakers can still successfully communicate with agents; likely because of the NLU's probabilistic intent mapping. Probabilistic NLUs rely on intelligibility rather than accuracy. For example, "I want to go *at* school" is inaccurate but intelligible and would likely map to the same intent as the accurate phrase. The focus of NLUs on intelligibility provides a smooth interaction in ordinary conversations. However, in language learning, such inaccuracies must not be ignored, and errors must be brought to attention. This calls for a different approach to NLUs that can separate accurate from inaccurate speech yet move the dialogue forward.

**Multiple Agents and Users:** Exposure to non-dyadic conversations furthers students' glimpse into the target language and culture. Further, learning with others or cooperative learning is an effective language learning mechanism. An experience where students can learn together can give a sense of accomplishment, encourage students further, and add richness to the interactions. An interesting concept would be a learning space where human teachers, AI agents, and humans cooperatively learn together [7].

**Multimodal Understanding:** Non-verbal cues can help interpret a user's affective state to which the dialogue agent can respond empathetically to nurture a learning progression [14]. Further, it can help communication move forward as it is common for learners to substitute unknown words or elaborate abstract meanings with actions/gestures [8]. Recognizing gestures can allow the dialogue agent to administer Total Physical Response (TPR) exercises to pair new information along with a physical response and improve retention [33].

**Repair and Grounding:** Foundational research [21] has explored how learners converse with native speakers and learn from them in linguistically immersive settings. Native and non-native speakers modify their language and use a variety of strategies and tactics to communicate with each other such as repair, grounding, and negotiating meaning; all formidable challenges in HCI. Few agents today could cogently respond to a request like "What do you mean?". It remains a research task to identify what kinds of repair and negotiation strategies students use while talking to AI agents while learning a language and how agents can respond. [8] show simple ways like pre-defined translations, explanations, and hints as a start but much of the work in this direction remains.

**Personalization in Dialogue:** Scaffolding helps learners build new knowledge and skills. A conversational agent thus could identify a learner's language level and provide additional dialogue-based tasks for a student to learn. Such dialogue-based tasks could be a new exercise or the same dialogue but a different parse of the dialogue tree. The agent would have to personalize the amount of user autonomy, generate appropriate hints, etc.

**Dialogue-Based Assessment and Feedback:** Identifying errors made while speaking at many linguistic levels (e.g., phoneme, syllable, vocabulary, grammar, semantic, dialogue) and then communicating it effectively and encouragingly to the learner in an actionable way while having a dialogue is another hard research challenge from NLP/HCI perspective.

Surprising learning patterns with agents and who-knews await discovery. For example, [8] showed that users in a dialogue with embodied agents found it helpful to see something as simple as live transcriptions of their speech as it ended up being a proxy for pronunciation feedback that signaled errors.

### 2.4   Sustained Engagement

As opposed to ordinary chatbots that help humans with a relatively short task, language learning is a prolonged cognitive effort that spans over months and years thus needing agents to sustain learners' engagement. Solutions commonly used in Computer-assisted language learning to bring engagement are gamification [10], serious games, immersion, humor, etc. [27]. It remains a research question to find how these elements can be executed in dialogue-based language learning and in a longitudinal manner [12].

### 2.5   Accessibility

Finally, two missing aspects in designing and evaluating agents are accessibility and special needs. [19] discuss how conversational interactions can be designed for the visually impaired, [13] show conversational interactions for deaf and hard of hearing users. In the domain of education, [22] demonstrate using embodied conversational agents to support spoken language development in children with hearing loss by making use of the visual modality. We note that literature in accessibility for conversational interfaces is limited, which provides a further research opportunity to address this gap.

## 3   Conclusion

The language learning community has rarely seen applications where all the above perspectives have come together. The technical challenges to make it happen are significant and acknowledged but rarely in the context of education which provides a new motivation. We have articulated the motivation for dialogue interfaces that can create unique opportunities for language learners by bringing to them AI-enabled situated learning. We have articulated the progress in the field and highlighted the many inter-disciplinary research challenges of HCI of foreign/second/other language education. New interaction paradigms are waiting to be discovered in the intersection of multiple users, multiple agents, communicating with multiple modalities, and learning together in virtual worlds.

# References

1. Bennett, M.J.: How not to be a fluent fool: understanding the cultural dimension of language. New Ways Teach. Cult. 16–21 (1997)
2. Bibauw, S., François, T., Desmet, P.: Discussing with a computer to practice a foreign language: research synthesis and conceptual framework of dialogue-based call. Comput. Assist. Lang. Learn. **32**(8), 827–877 (2019)
3. Biocca, F., Harms, C.: Defining and measuring social presence: contribution to the networked minds theory and measure. Proc. PRESENCE **2002**, 1–36 (2002)
4. Brown, J.S., Collins, A., Duguid, P.: Situated cognition and the culture of learning. Educ. Res. **18**(1), 32–42 (1989)
5. Burnham, D., Lau, S.: The integration of auditory and visual speech information with foreign speakers: the role of expectancy. In: AVSP 1999-International Conference on Auditory-Visual Speech Processing (1999)
6. Divekar, R.R.: AI Enabled Foreign Language Immersion: Technology and Method to Acquire Foreign Languages with AI in Immersive Virtual Worlds. Ph.D. thesis, Rensselaer Polytechnic Institute (2020)
7. Divekar, R.R., et al.: Foreign language acquisition via artificial intelligence and extended reality: design and evaluation. Comput. Assis. Lang. Learn. 1–29 (2021)
8. Divekar, R.R., et al.: Interaction challenges in ai equipped environments built to teach foreign languages through dialogue and task-completion. In: Proceedings of the 2018 Designing Interactive Systems Conference, pp. 597–609 (2018)
9. Evanini, K., et al.: Game-based spoken dialog language learning applications for young students. In: INTERSPEECH, pp. 548–549 (2018)
10. Flores, J.F.F.: Using gamification to enhance second language learning. Digital Educ. Rev. **27**, 32–54 (2015)
11. Fryer, L., Coniam, D., Carpenter, R., Lăpusneanu, D.: Bots for language learning now: Current and future directions (2020)
12. Fryer, L.K., Ainley, M., Thompson, A., Gibson, A., Sherlock, Z.: Stimulating and sustaining interest in a language course: an experimental comparison of chatbot and human task partners. Comput. Hum. Behav. **75**, 461–468 (2017)
13. Glasser, A., Mande, V., Huenerfauth, M.: Accessibility for deaf and hard of hearing users: Sign language conversational user interfaces. In: Proceedings of the 2nd Conference on Conversational User Interfaces, pp. 1–3 (2020)
14. Grafsgaard, J., Wiggins, J., Boyer, K.E., Wiebe, E., Lester, J.: Predicting learning and affect from multimodal data streams in task-oriented tutorial dialogue. In: Educational Data Mining 2014 (2014)
15. Hsu, L.: To call or not to call: empirical evidence from neuroscience. Comput. Assist. Lang. Learn. 1–24 (2020)
16. Ismail, J.: Language exposure and second language learning. The English Teacher, p. 11 (2017)
17. Kerry, A., Ellis, R., Bull, S.: Conversational agents in e-learning. In: Allen, T., Ellis, R., Petridis, M. (eds.) Applications and Innovations in Intelligent Systems XVI, pp. 169–182, Springer, London (2009). https://doi.org/10.1007/978-1-84882-215-3_13 ISBN 978-1-84882-215-3
18. Lee, J.S., Lee, K.: Affective factors, virtual intercultural experiences, and l2 willingness to communicate in in-class, out-of-class, and digital settings. Language Teaching Research **24**(6), 813–833 (2020)
19. Loddo, I., Martini, D.: The cocktail party effect. an inclusive vision of conversational interactions. Des. J. **20**(sup1), S4076–S4086 (2017)

20. Long, M.: Second Language Acquisition and Task-Based Language Teaching. Wiley, Hoboken (2014)
21. Long, M.H.: Native speaker/non-native speaker conversation and the negotiation of comprehensible input1. Appl. Linguist. **4**(2), 126–141 (1983)
22. Massaro, D., Liu, Y., Chen, T., Perfetti, C.: A multilingual embodied conversational agent for tutoring speech and language learning, vol. 2 (01 2006)
23. Mayer, R.E.: Using multimedia for e-learning. J. Comput. Assist. Learn. **33**(5), 403–423 (2017)
24. Molnár, G., Szüts, Z.: The role of chatbots in formal education. In: 2018 IEEE 16th International Symposium on Intelligent Systems and Informatics (SISY), pp. 000197–000202, IEEE (2018)
25. Moussalli, S., Cardoso, W.: Intelligent personal assistants: can they understand and be understood by accented l2 learners? Comput. Assist. Lang. Learn. **33**(8), 865–890 (2020)
26. Peixoto, B., Pinto, R., Melo, M., Cabral, L., Bessa, M.: Immersive virtual reality for foreign language education: a prisma systematic review. IEEE Access 1 (2021)
27. Petrovic, J., Jovanovic, M.: Conversational agents for learning foreign languages-a survey. arXiv preprint arXiv:2011.07901 (2020)
28. Pham, X.L., Pham, T., Nguyen, Q.M., Nguyen, T.H., Cao, T.T.H.: Chatbot as an intelligent personal assistant for mobile language learning. In: Proceedings of the 2018 2nd International Conference on Education and E-Learning, pp. 16–21 (2018)
29. Pinhanez, C.S.: HCI research challenges for the next generation of conversational systems. In: Proceedings of the 2nd Conference on Conversational User Interfaces, pp. 1–4 (2020)
30. Qian, Y., Ubale, R., Lange, P., Evanini, K., Ramanarayanan, V., Soong, F.K.: Spoken language understanding of human-machine conversations for language learning applications. J. Sig. Process. Syst. 1–13 (2019)
31. Ramanarayanan, V., et al.: Toward scalable dialog technology for conversational language learning: Case study of the toefl® mooc. In: INTERSPEECH, pp. 1960–1961 (2018)
32. Rosell-Aguilar, F.: Autonomous language learning through a mobile application: a user evaluation of the busuu app. Comput. Assist. Lang. Learn. **31**(8), 854–881 (2018)
33. Si, M.: A virtual space for children to meet and practice Chinese. Int. J. Artif. Intell. Educ. **25**(2), 271–290 (2015)
34. Wik, P., Hjalmarsson, A.: Embodied conversational agents in computer assisted language learning. Speech Commun. **51**(10), 1024–1037 (2009). ISSN 0167–6393, spoken Language Technology for Education
35. Xu, Y., Wang, D., Collins, P., Lee, H., Warschauer, M.: Same benefits, different communication patterns: comparing children's reading with a conversational agent vs. a human partner. Comput. Educ. **161**, 104059 (2021)

# Digital Tool to Detect the State of Languishing of Students During the Covid-19 Pandemic

M. Guzmán$^{(\boxtimes)}$, P. Manzanilla$^{(\boxtimes)}$, J. Martínez$^{(\boxtimes)}$, T. Tapia$^{(\boxtimes)}$, A. Núñez$^{(\boxtimes)}$, and S. Zepeda$^{(\boxtimes)}$

Universidad Autónoma Metropolitana, Vasco de Quiroga 4871, México City, Mexico
{albanunez,sergioz}@dccd.mx

**Abstract.** This paper presents a mobile application prototype that pretends to identify the state of languishing in postgraduate students, who have been dealing with social distancing due COVID-19 pandemic. In order to make visible the social significance of tools that encourage students and other users to understand their emotions and to look for a good mental health accompanied by specialists, with the knowledge that no one is spare of suffering from an emotional problem. In addition, the data obtained may be used to take appropriate measures by the corresponding authorities by the hand of mental health specialized. The presented prototype development process in this paper responds to an interface design based on human-computer interaction methods and tools and shows some suggested improvements after the evaluating phase.

**Keywords:** Context-dependent system · Creativity · Design Thinking · Emotions in HCI and design · Heuristics and guidelines for design

## 1 Introduction

The effects of social distancing on mental health due COVID-19 pandemic started to be studied a few months ago, most of the results obtained by researches conducted by specialists have reported emotional disturbances, depression, stress, apathy, irritability, insomnia, post-traumatic stress disorder, anger, and emotional exhaustion [1–4]. Having said that, efforts to generate research on mental health care have acquired special relevance in this context of confinement [5], in order to generate reliable health measures to face the COVID-19 pandemic, it is a reality that after social distancing other problems, associated with mental health, can emerge. Languishing it is conceived of as emptiness and stagnation, constituting a life of quiet despair that parallels accounts of individuals who describe themselves and life as 'hollow', 'empty', 'a shell' and 'a void' [6]. During confinement time, this state is difficult to identify, because it could be confused with boredom state or sadness related with the monotony provoked by confinement. As indicated by the foregoing, it could be claim that students who present a languishing state cannot easily identify this condition, because they have been faced with extraordinary routines caused by Covid-19 pandemic. All of this may mean that students are socially disconnected and maybe they have a poor self-care routine. Therefore, it is important to

C. Stephanidis et al. (Eds.): HCII 2021, CCIS 1499, pp. 280–285, 2021.
https://doi.org/10.1007/978-3-030-90179-0_36

highlight that mental health diagnostic measures and criteria can be useful as monitoring and clinic evaluation tools [7].

In contrast, as stated in [8], people with emotional granularity can recognize their emotions, name them, and choose the most relevant care measures to cope with a complex emotional situation. In this context, the proposition of students capable to identify, understand, and attend to their emotional state and personal health during extraordinary periods, like the confinement during the Covid-19 pandemic, thanks to the recognition of their emotions, help to validate the proposal of generate tools for students to gain better relationships with their environment through the granularity emotional development. Furthermore, it is clear that the COVID-19 pandemic has affected lots of our daily activities [9], this is the case of technology and the confinement, given that, presential classes were suspended in Mexico since March, 2020, most of the students have used technology as a major connecting tool, to study, to work, to communicate, etc. However, even when it was thought that this would help to have a greater connectivity, the reality is that it has generated an alienation effect between people and their daily life. Inevitably, it is necessary a link between technology and daily activities but with social responsibility [10] since these tools can help to reduce a sense of being social distancing [11].

Therefore, it is a reality that current conditions may generate other kind of problems associated with mental health or violence. This is why it is highly important to recognize and create useful technology that allows us to overcome obstacles such as location or time and in this case, to identify a possible languishing state. Based on Design Thinking methodology our approach aims to create an emphatic proposal to generate an effective user-computer relationship.

## 2  Background

It is essential to mention that Keyes in [6] describes two important characteristics about emotional health: the presence of mental health described as flourishing and the absence of mental health, languishing. He mentions that when a person is on a languishing state, they have six times more probability to experience a depressive episode, compared to people who are flourishing. Besides, to understand the real affections generated by the confinement the paper [12] investigated the state of flow[1] in people who are subjected to a high-stress con-text. They survey to citizens of Wuhan, China during the period quarantine by means of an online test, their main goal was evaluated the citizen's experiences when they were in flow state. It was found that people who experienced a state of flow during the quarantine had few emotional diseases. Also, it was determined that to achieve the flow state people must maintain a challenging and rewarding activity, which provides them clear goals [12]. Additionally, the concept of emotional granularity by Lisa Feldman Barret, who defined it as the capability to have large vocabulary to express the different emotion that a person might feel, thus to be aware of them [8], sustain the proposal of integrate a map of emotions, based on Plutchik's wheel of emotions [14], which provides a way to make sense of feelings, it is formed by a set of primary emotions: fear, surprise, sadness, disgust, anger, hope, joy and acceptance. Accordingly, to

---

[1] Flow is a psychological state in which individuals concentrate on a task, this allows them to reach a state of well-being without thinking about time and space [13].

Plutchik the other emotions are combinations of the primary emotions and are dimmed according to the degrees of intensity. In this perspective, the design process of the digital prototype to help to the identification of a possible state of languishing in Mexican students, contemplates the mentioned terms besides the context of social distancing due to the pandemic.

## 3  Mobile Application Prototype Development

With respect to the prototype development process, the subsequent section describes it briefly. In the first phase, was carried out a brainstorming that allowed us to have the first draft of the system, as a result of this process were detected the next needs: to have an introduction window to describe how the application works, the insertion of an emotion map to provide a tool that allows users to gain emotional granularity and to include a mental health status test to help them to identify a possible state of languishing, as well as a link to address the mental health unit of the University, which will be enabled only for users with a state of languishing detected.

Then, the design prototype considerer the inclusion of the next elements: an avatar to allows users to empathize with emotional issues, descriptions about three mental health states (flourishing, languishing and mental illness), an emotion map and a test that allows them to identify their mental status health. Regarding the first part of the ideation phase, it was decided that the avatar would be a lemon, due to this fruit is related to an acid taste, which is an accurate description for people who is living a languishing state.

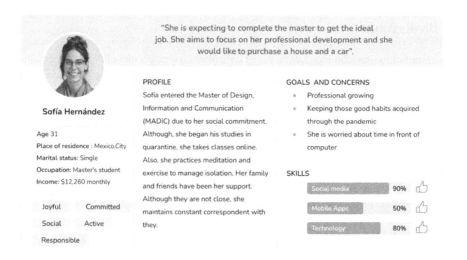

**Fig. 1.** Shows profile/Person of students.

In addition, it is proposed that the test will be work by means of to Complete State Model of Health by Keyes [15], which have been used for another Italian study [16], the paper analyzed worker mental health during the first part of the pandemic. This model is relevant because of its findings which declare although don't exist illness, it doesn't mean to exist health and vice versa, furthermore, mentioned that the presence of mental health assumes a psychosocial positive operation.

Continuing with the process, we defined users' interests, their activities, their emotions after confinement and their future plans, in order to create the profile/Person, Fig. 1 presents an example of it. Finally, during the evaluation phase, three usability tests were carried out with students, the targets of the test were to collect usability and interaction data for its subsequent analysis. Table 1 shows some of the results centered on aesthetic aspects, and the images (Fig. 2) correspond to the prototype interfaces.

**Table 1.** Findings after evaluation phase.

| User | Finding | Suggestion |
|---|---|---|
| User 1, User 2, User 3 | Users do not understand which is the meaning of the lemon avatar | Use of a suitable avatar |
| User 1, User 3 | They were trying to comprehend the meaning of certain words | Avoid technical/specialized language |
| User 2, User 3 | Users refer the use of this kind of applications by night | Use of light colors |
| User 1, User 2, User 3 | The prototype seems unreliable | Improve icons definition |

**Fig. 2.** The prototype of the application, from left to right: principal menu, languishing's description and emotions map.

In general, users who tested the system, during the evaluation tests, considered that this prototype is a relevant and helpful tool, especially for those who are not convinced to request psychological therapy.

## 4  Discussion

In a broader context, the presence of COVID-19 cases affected people all over the world, in February 2020 the first patient with COVID-19 was detected in Mexico and with it a series of health measures that had a strong impact on the lives of millions of Mexicans. The prevention protocols established in the country to detain the mass infections invited citizens to use masks, and to maintain social distancing between citizens.

In consequence, students of all levels were confined to their homes to receive classes through internet or television, by various technological devices and with a limited social interaction. It is worth noting that, prior to people developing severe stress conditions, people may present a languishing state, characterized by experiencing relative emotional stability, but there is no joy and there is a sense of being aimless [6]. However, we can ensure that if students are able to recognize this state, through the development of emotional granularity using tools such as the one presented here, it is possible to react in time and take measures, this must be always guided by university authorities, whom will be able to help students to achieve an emotional health balanced, thus avoid the development of serious psychological illnesses such as depression or anxiety.

## 5  Conclusions

The proposed system allows students to generate emotional granularity [8] to avoid serious mental problems such as depression or anxiety. All of this due to the mapping of emotions and the collaboration with specialized psychological care units within the University. This application is conceived within the framework of social distancing conditions established in Mexico on March, 2020, as a measure to prevent massive contagion by COVID-19. The project invites us to think on developments user centered for emotional categorization in an extraordinary period such as the one we are living, it may be the basis to provide useful information with high impact for the reality of our society in a post-COVID-19 moment.

## References

1. Dong, L., Bouey, J.: Public mental health crisis during COVID-19 Pandemic. China. Emerg. Infect. Dis. **26**(7), 1616–1618 (2020)
2. YaMei, B., Chao, L., Chih, L., Jen, C., Ching, C., Pesus, C.: Survey of stress reactions among health care workers involved with the SARS outbreak. Psychiatr. Serv. **55**(9), 1055–1057 (2004)
3. Brooks, S., et al.: The psychological impact of quarantine and how to reduce it: rapid review of the evidence. The Lancet **395**(10227), 912–920 (2020)
4. Broche, P., Fernández, C., Reyes, D.: Psychological consequences of quarantine and social isolation during COVID-19 pandemic. Revista Cubana de Salud Pública. **46**(Suppl 1), 1–14 (2020)
5. Pan America Health Organization: COVID-19 Recommended Interventions in Mental Health and Psychosocial Support (MHPSS) during the Pandemic, June 2020. https://iris.paho.org/handle/10665.2/52485. Accessed 11 June 2021

6. Keyes, C.: The mental health continuum: from languishing to flourishing in life. J. Health Soc. Behav. **43**(2), 207–222 (2002)
7. Dhingra, S., Simoes, E., Keyes, C.: Change in level of positive mental health as a predictor of future risk of mental illness. Am. J. Publ. Health **100**(12), 2366–2371 (2010)
8. Feldman, L., Bliss-Moreau, E.: Affect as a psychological primitive. In: Advances in Experimental Social Psychology, pp. 167–218. Elsevier Inc., London (2009)
9. Karasmanaki, E., Tsantopoulos, G.: Impacts of social distancing during COVID-19 pandemic on the daily life of forestry students. Child Youth Serv. Rev. **120**, 1–7 (2021)
10. Livingstone, S., Helsper, E.: Gradations in digital inclusion: children, young people and the digital divide. New Media Soc. **9**(4), 671–696 (2007)
11. Mariën, I., Prodnik, J.K.: Digital inclusion and user (dis)empowerment: a critical perspective. Info. J. Policy, Regul. Strategy Telecommun. Inf. Media **16**(6), 35–47 (2014)
12. Sweeny, K., et al.: Flow in the time of COVID-19: findings from China. PLoS ONE **15**(11), 1–12 (2020)
13. Csikszentmihalyi, M.: Flow. HarperCollins e-books, The Psychology of Optimal Experience (1990)
14. Plutchik, R.: The nature of emotions. Am. Sci. **89**(4), 344–350 (2001)
15. Keyes, C.: Mental illness and/or mental health? Investigating axioms of the complete state model of health. J. Consult. Clin. Psychol. **73**(3), 539–548 (2005)
16. Berinato, S. https://hbr.org/2020/03/that-discomfort-youre-feeling-is-grief. Accessed 11 June 2021

# Use of Virtual Resources as a Tool for Teaching Language Skills at the Colombian Caribbean Region Primary Basic Level

Maria Moreno[1](✉), Sonia Duran[2], Margel Parra[3], Irmina Hernández-Sánchez[4], and Javier Ramírez[5]

[1] Universidad Rafael Belloso Chacín, Guajira Avenue 2th Highway, Maracaibo, Venezuela
[2] Universidad Libre, 46 Street # 48-170, Barranquilla, Colombia
[3] Corposucre, 21 Street #25-59, Sincelejo, Colombia
[4] Universidad de la Costa, 58 Street #55 66, Barranquilla, Colombia
[5] Corporación Universitaria Latinoamericana, 58 Street #55 66, Barranquilla, Colombia

**Abstract.** In recent times, education in general faces great challenges due the constant changes in the economic, social, and political spheres, as a product of globalization; therefore, it is essential to improve education and interaction during the teaching and learning processes. However, as a consequence of technological and scientific development, every aspect of human life has been transformed, immersed, and influenced by it; the individual's learning must be attached to the revolutionary changes brought by new technologies, Constant updating is essential, for the best use of technological applications and tools in educational institutions. In order to analyze JueduLand software, for teaching language skills in elementary educational institutions in the Colombian Caribbean, the results of a study with descriptive statistical analysis of variables are shown. The results allowed respondents to recognize each of the components that make up the variable, having a high presence in the use of JueduLand as a tool for teaching linguistics skills.

**Keywords:** Technological tool · JueduLand · Linguistics skills

## 1 Introduction

Adapting to new times is critical for elementary educational institutions because they have a responsibility to convey basic knowledge, to move into the field of secondary studies, characterized by presenting in its evolution the most important social phenomena, decisive in the emotional and social stability of the individual [1]. The teacher, as responsible for the academic process, must define how to manage a planning based on the development of the cognitive, procedural, and affective areas of the student; in addition, the teacher must ensure the active participation for the construction of the students' self-learning [2].

Globally, the open education movement or the use of Open Educational Resources (OER) is growing from different perspectives, as expressed by UNESCO [3]. This generational evolution is produced by electronic means and digitization, from there that

C. Stephanidis et al. (Eds.): HCII 2021, CCIS 1499, pp. 286–293, 2021.
https://doi.org/10.1007/978-3-030-90179-0_37

interactive games like the JueduLand have generated a new more abstract, and artificial code of representation of information for class activities.

In view of these considerations, UNESCO states that the educational systems in Latin American countries have not been able to take advantage of technological advances and principles by expressing the budgetary advantage of adopting public policies on interactive tools in the educational field [4]. Colombia does not escape from this reality, although strong public policies have been implemented in the region for both the distribution of IT resources and the adoption of OER, the attempts have been unflattering in relation to the imposed expectations. In this regard Murillo, states that the student population in Colombian elementary educational institutions have low levels of diverse competences recognized as fundamental to life both socially and professionally [5]; like reading and writing language skills, that come from "concrete problems in speech management, difficulties in arguing, oral expression poverty and limitations in the handling of textual references" [6].

When emphasizing in using JueduLand within the classroom requires teachers to explicitly include it in the planning as a key element to develop language skills, using for this purpose the previous ideas that the student has on the subject. In this order of ideas, Ausubel points out that the development of language skills occurs when new information "connects" with a relevant pre-existing concept in the cognitive structure, this implies that new ideas, concepts, and propositions are integrated into the system under construction [7].

On the integration of Computer and Communication Technologies, the Colombian National Education Ministry or MEN (Ministerio de Educación Nacional) expresses in the document "Competencias TIC para el Desarrollo Profesional Docente", that the 21st century faces social challenges regarding educational methods pointing at their quality [8], for which better preparation of educators is required, supported by the conception of new skills, abilities and knowledge, where JueduLand as a technological tool will be a great help in achieving these goals.

However, multimedia applications according to the MEN are: "computer materials that represent knowledge, and their purpose is to facilitate self-learning for the user" [9]. These applications integrate various textual elements (sequential and hypertextual) and audiovisual elements (graphics, sound, video, animations) which characterized by their high interactivity, or in other words, by the control that the user can have over the learning object. Multimedia applications are seen as means for joining different meanings, allowing interactive communication between students, that is why they become innovative learning strategies towards traditional education, enabling personal discovery and permanently developing the cognitive process.

Considering, the above considerations multimedia educational resources are an attractive method that helps in the development of different language skills in elementary school students in a significant way leading to flexible and engaging learning that allows the participation of all its senses, from the point of view of education, it is a means that allows the student to maintain motivation, arouse interest and generate significant learning. JueduLand is an open educational resource recognized for its high interactivity, which is possible for its multimedia support. For this reason, it is part of the multimedia applications that make up certain types of open educational resources, elaborated by

Antonio Ángel Ruiz Molino in 2007 [10]. In this sense, its application has on its horizon the constructivist teaching to achieve participants able to learn by themselves.

Considering what was formulated, even though teachers mostly maintain their traditional teaching schemes, by opening up their range of possibilities, they can verify the effects of multimedia resources use on classroom environments, which tends to improve, as does the interest in learning increases, so it benefits the acquisition of new knowledge. Under the interpretations above, there is a need for elementary school teachers to incorporate multimedia elements into their activities in order to attract the students' attention, encouraging stimulus that allow to increase their motivation and understanding, in order to develop all the knowledge acquired, besides abilities and skills that involve the development in the linguistics area.

As a result, by using jueduLand for teaching language skills, it is necessary to incorporate visual images, which helps the elementary school student to understand even better the proposed content in the different subjects. In addition, this software presents an alternative, when the learning style leans towards the auditory, it favors the students' listening, allowing information to be assimilated in a more orderly and sequential manner, this gives them the possibility to be able to explain and transmit orally to others the information that they have captured; likewise, it must be recognized that auditory sense is relevant in the school sphere because it allows to follow orders, acquire concepts, develop thought, etc.

In relation to this multimedia element, it can be said that animations are part of the motivating elements that strengthen students' learning processes, because this allows a sequence of motions to be displayed in the images that are presented, getting students' attention and awake their interest in knowing. In this order of ideas, it can be interpreted that developing linguistics skills through jueduLand as an interactive strategy, generates greater motivation in students. In this sense, Moreno-Hernández, et al. state that this leads to a fast and effective assimilation of the information, creating new experiences for students by becoming the protagonists of their own learning [11].

## 2 Method

This document aimed to evaluate using JeduLand software as a tool for teaching linguistics skills in elementary institutions from the Colombian Caribbean, with an epistemological approach and quantitative design, focused on a descriptive non-experimental research; the variable: jueduLand use for linguistics skills teaching is given and the researcher does not condition it, nor manipulates it deliberately; that is, it assumes the facts as they arise in reality by the time of conducting the study. In addition, it is framed in the descriptive context by measuring a group of people to analyze jueduLand use for linguistics skills teaching in elementary educational institutions from the Colombian Caribbean.

This study is described as a descriptive study. The population consisted of 14 elementary teachers from educational institutions in the Colombian Caribbean. For the development of the investigation's data collection, a questionnaire which consisted on 42 questions was developed using a Likert measurement scale. In order to determine reliability, the Alpha Cronbach Coefficient method was used, achieving a reliability of

0.82 which reveals a high degree of consistency. A summary of the data collected, and its statistical processing will be presented through statistical analysis.

## 3   Results and Discussion

The following tables details the results of applying the instrument to the first-grade teachers of the elementary educational institutions of the Colombian Caribbean. These tables show the results for each dimension with their indicators corresponding to the variable under study in this research (Table 1).

**Table 1.** JueduLand multimedia elements

| Indicator | Images | Sounds | Animations | Interactivity |
|---|---|---|---|---|
| Indicator mean | 4,33 | 4,19 | 4,43 | 3,83 |
| Interpretation | Very high presence | High presence | Very high presence | High presence |
| Indicator mean | 4,20 | | | |
| Interpretation | High presence | | | |

**Source:** Own elaboration (2021)

In general, this dimension entitled Multimedia Elements reached an average of 4.20 positioning it in the category: High presence, so it is clear that these results coincide with the theory exposed by Segovia, and later by Pinto [12, 13]. The position posed by these authors is aimed at describing the most commonly used multimedia elements in the educational field, that come to be visual and auditory elements, since they create a more pleasant environment within classrooms. Likewise, they manage to arouse interest, stimulate the senses and motivation of students, allowing them to acquire new knowledge.

As can be seen, both theoretically and in practice, multimedia elements grab all the students' attention, exerting in this a stimulus that allows them to assimilate, understand and can develop all the knowledge acquired; likewise, it will develop in them abilities and skills that will allow them a further development of language skills.

Multimedia tools provide a variety of methodological means and strategies that are considered important in the educational field, because it allows students to adapt to their learning pace where the teacher goes on to play a mediator role by assisting in the process, using technology as an instrument.

Similarly, following the guidelines set out above, multimedia tools also allow the teacher to attend in the same classroom the wide variety of learning styles presented by students. On the other hand, multimedia tools provide within their characteristics the transparency, and the branching that facilitate self-learning as evidenced by the results of this investigation (Table 2).

**Table 2.** Linguistics skills

| Indicator | Speaking | Reading | Writing | Listening |
|---|---|---|---|---|
| Indicator mean | 3,93 | 4,38 | 4,02 | 4,05 |
| Interpretation | High presence | Very high presence | High presence | High presence |
| Indicator mean | 4,10 | | | |
| Interpretation | High presence | | | |

Overall, this dimension entitled Linguistic Skills reached an average of 4.10 positioning it in the category: High Presence, so it is clear that these results coincide with the theory exposed by: Ramírez, Ortiz or Amaya [14–16]. These positions coincide in arguing that in school age it is necessary to provide the greatest number of elements for the improvement of each of the communicative skills.

As evidenced, Jueduland encourages the development of linguistic skills, reading, writing, speaking, and listening as a set of skills that individuals develop because of their good development in activities. These by themselves are a group of qualities that can be overestimated in children, teenagers, and adults because when these have been acquired, and are well used, professionals demonstrate their skills in any of their communicative acts.

**Table 3.** JueduL and use for linguistics skills teaching

| Indicator | Jueduland multimedia elements | Linguistics skills |
|---|---|---|
| Indicator mean | 4,20 | 4,10 |
| Interpretation | High presence | High presence |
| Indicator mean | 4,15 | |
| Interpretation | High presence | |

Table 3 shows the arithmetic mean of the variable, using jueduland as a tool for teaching linguistics skills, as a product of the mean average of its dimensions, it has a value of 4.15 placing itself in the High presence category according to the comparison scale of this research; This makes it possible to infer that respondents recognize each of the components that make up the variable.

Likewise, following the guidelines proposed above, multimedia tools also allow to attend in the same classroom a great diversity of learning styles that students present. On the other hand, multimedia tools provide within their characteristics the transparency and the ramification that facilitate self-learning as evidenced by the results of this investigation.

Based on the findings obtained by Moreno-Hernández, et al., itis important to note that humanist educational processes emphasize not so much in educating but in learning, students therefore become active subjects of their own development. Students are people who have interests, previous concepts and through them interact with external perceptions and social environments to generate new concepts, visions, aptitudes, motivations, and ways of acting [17]. Certainly, the linkage of new technologies has brought significant changes within the global environment, going through all kinds of organizations, which range from private organizational entities to educational institutions at their various levels [1, 18].

## 4 Conclusions

Finally, the latest considerations are presented; participating teachers recognize the importance and benefits of JueduLand's multimedia elements: image, sound, animation, and interactivity; facilitating self-learning through these, reaching the high presence category, for the characteristics of the JueduLand software in its teaching practice. In addition, it promotes the development of linguistics skills: reading, writing, speaking, and listening as a skill set, being this tool the adequate for this objective, therefore in school age it is necessary to provide the greatest number of elements for the improvement of each of the linguistics skills.

Other evidence comes from the adequacy of the participants to the work guidelines proposed by the tool, strengthening the training process, thus enabling a pedagogical and innovative method for teachers in education. In this way it is formalized as a methodological strategy that is considered important in the field of education, because it allows students to be helped at their learning pace where the teacher becomes a mediator by supporting the process, through technology as an instrument. Following these guidelines, the same strategies also allow to observe in the classroom different levels of demand that students present, providing within its characteristics: transparency, branching, navigation, and interaction that facilitate self-learning.

In relation to this multimedia element, it can be said that animations are part of the motivating elements that strengthen students' learning processes, because this allows a sequence of movements to develop in the images that are presented, getting students' attention and awake their interest in knowing.

Language skills are a set of skills developed by individuals through their successful use of speaking, listening, reading, and writing activities; These are intrinsic to the person, developing them better with stimulus from the school, the family environment and society. In this order of ideas, it can be interpreted that for the development of linguistics skills through jueduLand as an interactive strategy, greater motivation is generated in students, which leads to a quick and effective assimilation of information, creating new experiences and becoming the protagonist of their own learning.

In accordance with what is described, the act of listening complements the activities carried out in the use of JueduLand, because students need to follow the instructions given by the teacher in order to reach the end of the task entrusted. Considering what is established, speaking constitutes an act of verbal production which is important for JueduLand's use, where the teacher discloses his ideas, thoughts and positions in front of any subject just like the student, reflecting the real context where it unfolds, as well as the intentionality of the message, that is, when the subjects speak it is possible to analyze the structure of their thinking, their knowledge degree, and in some cases their training and production level.

In this way, the act of reading has to be understood as a process of interaction that is analyzed through jueduLand's use, between the teacher and the students, where interests, wishes, tastes are shared, with a meaning of a cultural, political, ideological, and aesthetic perspective in which interests play an important role, where the ideology and cultural assessments of a given social group are present. It is one of the greatest sources of knowledge, perfecting both writing and speaking. To promote reading in the schoolthrough the use of thejueduLand, is to print on the student, an act of apprehension of knowledge continuously.

## References

1. Parra, M., Marambio, C., Ramírez, J., Suárez, D., Herrera, H.: Educational convergence with digital technology: integrating a global society. In: Stephanidis, C., Antona, M., Ntoa, S. (eds.) HCII 2020. CCIS, vol. 1294, pp. 303–310. Springer, Cham (2020). https://doi.org/10.1007/978-3-030-60703-6_39
2. Parra, M., Hernández-Sánchez, I., Maussa, E., Fernández, M.: Elementos que definen una estrategia pedagógica en la escuela de padres del ICBF del sur-occidente de Barranquilla. Hexágono Pedagógico **9**(1), 1–14 (2018)
3. UNESCO OER Community. https://en.unesco.org/themes/building-knowledge-societies/oer. Accessed 02 Mar 2021
4. Gasto público en la educación de América Latina ¿Puede servir a los propósitos de la Declaración de Paris sobre Recursos Educativos Abiertos? http://www.unesco.org/new/fileadmin/MULTIMEDIA/FIELD/Montevideo/pdf/CDCI1-Karisma-ES.pdf. Accessed 02 Mar 2021
5. Lay, N., Ramírez, J., Parra, M.: Desarrollo de conductas ciudadanas en estudiantes del octavo grado de una institución educativa de Barranquilla. In: Memorias del I congreso internacional en educación e innovación en educación superior. Caracas, Venezuela (2019)
6. Murillo, J.: La universidad y los procesos de lecto-escritura: centro de apoyo para la lectura, la oralidad y la escritura DIGA. Revista Panorama **6**(10), 87–97 (2013)
7. Ausubel, D.: Psicología educativa: un punto de vista cognoscitivo. México, Editorial Trillas (1976).
8. Competencias TIC para el Desarrollo Profesional Docente. https://www.mineducacion.gov.co/1759/w3-article-339097.html?_noredirect=1. Accessed 07 Feb 2021
9. Ministerio de Educación Nacional. Competencias Comunicativas. Programa de transformación de la Calidad Educativa. Bogotá, Educar editores S.A. (2012)
10. Juedu, L.: http://roble.pntic.mec.es/arum0010/. Accessed 07 Mar 2021
11. Moreno-Hernández, M., Tezón, M., Rivera, M., Duran, S., Parra, M.: Autoestima: Desarrollo de la autonomía personal en estudiantes del área técnica. Revista Espacios **39**(46), 6–11 (2018)
12. Segovia, N.: Aplicación Didáctica de las Actividades de Cineforum. Editorial Ideas Propias, Spain (2007)
13. Elementos multimedia. http://www.mariapinto.es/alfamedia/cultura/mapa_elementos.htm. Accessed 03 Feb 2021
14. Ramírez, M., Mortera F.: Implementación y desarrollo del portal académico de Recursos Educativos Abiertos (REA): KnowledgeHub para educación básica. México, Editorial Red de Posgrados en Educación (2010)
15. Ortiz, A.: Educación infantil pensamiento, inteligencia, creatividad, competencias, valores y actitudes intelectuales. Spain, Edición litoral (2009)
16. Amaya, J.: El docente de lenguaje. Editorial Limusa, Bogota (2006)

17. Moreno-Hernández, M., Rivera, J., Rivera, T.: Competencias y aprendizajes del docente: Un reto de la globalización. Hexágono Pedagógico **8**(1), 180–197 (2017)
18. Lay, N., et al.: Uso de las herramientas de comunicación asincrónicas y sincrónicas en la banca privada del municipio Maracaibo (Venezuela). Revista Espacios **40**(4) (2019)

# Establishing Cyberpsychology at Universities in the Area of Cyber Security

Paulina Ruh[1]([envelope]) [ORCID] and Holger Morgenstern[2] [ORCID]

[1] Independent Researcher, Lindau, Germany
[2] Albstadt-Sigmaringen University, Albstadt, Germany
morgenstern@hs-albsig.de

**Abstract.** Cyberpsychology deals with the question of the extent to which people interact with technologies, such as computers, and how this can lead to different types of behavior. It also investigates the extent to which behavior and one's own identity can change, depending on the current sphere of activity - either online or offline. Therefore, Cyberpsychology can be a powerful addition to the currently technical oriented Cyber Security. In addition, an overview is provided of what other universities and colleges in and outside Europe offer in the field of cyberpsychology in terms of modules.

To the end of the methodology module contents, learning outcomes and the final implementation are discussed. This includes a model with different phases like call for lecturers, preparing transcripts and presentations. Additionally, the European ECTS to hour ratio will be used to determine an appropriate number of working hours.

In conclusion, the design of the branch of cyberpsychology at universities is described as future-oriented and promising, while the development at other colleges and universities is undergoing similar changes. Although not necessarily in the field of cyberpsychology, the technical courses of study, and especially computer science, are increasingly oriented towards cyber security and the like.

**Keywords:** Cyberpsychology · Module development · Information security

## 1 Introduction

Anyone who uses the Internet without being able to object to personal data being collected and processed. And all this without being able to know about it or requiring a declaration of consent. But how can you protect yourself from this to a certain extent? What can an individual do to hide his or her assets, personal rights and private data from unauthorized access in the vast jungle of cyberspace?

The field of cyberpsychology deals with human behavior on the internet and its effects. But others are not always to blame if a computer becomes infected or data is lost.

The more people are concerned about security on the Internet, the more frightening it becomes to realize that the majority of people who move around in cyberspace have

C. Stephanidis et al. (Eds.): HCII 2021, CCIS 1499, pp. 294–301, 2021.
https://doi.org/10.1007/978-3-030-90179-0_38

no idea what kind of data they are sharing with companies, third parties and strangers - consciously or unconsciously. Yet the trade in personal data is "currently the backbone of the Internet economy" [1] and almost 100% of the annual turnover of, for example, Google and Facebook is linked to advertising or similar based on the personal data analyzed above. But why do people handle their data so carelessly? Or do they not even know what happens to it and what is shared? If you were to approach individual people on the street and ask them for their address or credit card details, most of them would probably not answer, because they would have reservations about sharing this information. But what is different about the internet that it is suddenly no longer a problem? Because there is no direct counterpart to write down the data? Because it serves a purpose online, such as placing an order, and you can benefit from it? Of course, this does not only refer to online orders, but also to daily actions that are carried out, for example, via apps on smartphones. According to a survey, only 31% of respondents always pay attention to what personal data an app wants to access. 7% don't care at all what information is collected while the app is running (and sometimes even outside of it [2].

In the course of time the question arises why people make it so easy for attackers. Be it like in the example above by "naively" clicking on attachments, or by using simple passwords that are easy to guess. The aim of this paper is to develop a concept for universities, which involves the development of a module where the topic of cyberpsychology is brought closer to the students in order to cover a large area of cyber security. After all, it is not always just the defense or attack on networks that counts, but also the further training of a company's employees, for example, because, as most people are probably aware, people are still the biggest weak point in a system.

## 2 Methodology

The following methodology offers insights on the basics of cyberpsychology, as well as current programs with a share of the topic in a certain subject. It is finished with a short approach on how to establish a program within a university.

### 2.1 Basics of Cyberpsychology

The area of cyberpsychology is a new phenomenon in the field of psychology, as it could only develop over time, based on the evolution of technology. As a result, it is difficult today to establish a single definition or scope, but Alison Attrill [3] hits the nail on the head with the statement "[...] cyberpsychology considers the psychological processes, motivations, intentions, behavioral outcomes, and effects on both our online and offline worlds, associated with any form of technology". In summary, the statement means as much as: Cyberpsychology deals with human behavior and its effects on any form of technology, which leads to the conclusion that this type of research will always evolve as technology changes.

The topic is of great relevance for today's world, as over the years more and more people have acquired at least one internet-enabled device (laptop, smartphone, desktop computer, tablet,...), which has led to an increased number of users on the internet [4].

This behavior and, above all, the actual type of use is relevant for the developers of end devices, since, among other things, the new devices are developed on the basis of this knowledge.

The question now arises to what extent the increased number of Internet users and, above all, Internet-capable end devices have an impact on criminal activities in cyberspace. On the one hand, the Darknet has formed, which is a non-indexed and only partially accessible area of the Deep Web. The actual use of this part of the Internet was anonymous communication when the communication partners were afraid of persecution and the resulting dangers [5]. So, if more people now have access to anonymous places on the Internet, it can be concluded that the chances of increasing criminal activity in these areas may also increase. As a result, the need for new investigative methods and approaches is growing, since the offline hunt for criminals on the WWW does not work as investigators have been used to up to now. Gráinne Kirwan [6] describes in the chapter "Forensic cyberpsychology" how this new way of fighting crime on the internet can be used, as the focus is on victimology, profiling of offenders, rehabilitation of offenders and the strategy for fighting crime.

What the future of cyberpsychology looks like cannot be said with certainty. Andrew Power and Gráinne Kirwan give a brief insight into how it might behave in the last chapter of their book "Cyberpsychology and New Media" [7]: Due to the ever-changing world of technology, for example new apps, academic publications in this field have a hard time to be timely and up to date. As a result, despite the increasing amount of research, there are still some gaps in the knowledge of human behavior in the online world. In addition, anonymity and identity play an important role, which can influence online behavior. A better understanding is needed, not specifically in the field of applications, but mainly in a general context. What happens if anonymity should no longer exist on the Internet? How would this affect the behavior and information we share?

Human behavior has a certain continuity on the one hand, but in other areas it changes permanently. Future scientists in the cyberpsychology context could, for example, work with the same phenomena that already exist today, or with completely new circumstances that are still beyond imagination today.

## 2.2    Current Programs Worldwide

Despite the new topic of cyberpsychology, there are already degree programs in Germany and internationally that deal with and impart knowledge in this field. However, the extent to which the topic is established in its entirety or whether it is only touched upon will be examined below.

The programs with a focus on IT security or forensics in Germany are not yet as advanced in the field of cyberpsychology as, for example, those offered by universities from abroad. Only a fraction of the universities and colleges offer a module in which the subject of cyberpsychology is addressed, as shown in Table 1.

This does not mean, however, that the subjects deal exclusively with cyberpsychology, only a certain contingent of this topic is found in the respective module.

In the international environment, especially in other European countries, the positioning around the topic of cyberpsychology is different compared to the German area. In Great Britain alone, there are some degree programs that focus purely on the area under

**Table 1.** Modules at German universities with cyberpsychology share

| University | Course of studies | Degree | Module |
|---|---|---|---|
| Wismar | IT-Forensic | Bachelor | - Ethical Hacking |
| Wismar | IT-Security and Forensic | Master | - Criminal Psychology |
| Ruhr-University Bochum | IT-Security/Information technology | Bachelor | - Introduction to Usable Security and Privacy<br>- Web-Security |
| Ruhr-University Bochum | IT-Security/Networks and Systems | Master | -Introduction to Usable Security and Privacy<br>- Web-Security<br>- Human Centred Security and Privacy<br>- Usable Security and Privacy<br>- Web-Security |
| Ruhr-University Bochum | IT-Security/Information technology | Master | - Introduction to Usable Security and Privacy<br>- Web-Security |
| SRH Berlin | Computer Sciences – Cyber Security | Master | - Security Technologies |

investigation. Table 2 shows some of the international programs that were available in 2019, again, only an extract of some programmes:

**Table 2.** Modules at international universities with cyberpsychology share

| University | Course of studies | Degree |
|---|---|---|
| University of North Dakota (US) | Cyberpsychology | Certificate |
| Bournemouth University (GB) | Cyberpsychology | Bachelor |
| Nottingham Trent University (GB) | Cyberpsychology | Master |
| University of Central Lancashire (GB) | Cyberpsychology | Bachelor |
| University of Wolverhampton (GB) | Cyberpsychology | Master |
| Dún Laoghaire Institute of Art, Design and Technology (IE) | Cyberpsychology | Master |
| IDC Herzliya (IL) | Psychology | Bachelor |
| IDC Herzliya (IL) | Government, Diplomacy & Strategy | Master |

## 2.3  Target Audience

The target group for the module series Cyberpsychology are interested students who would like to get closer to the topic of psychology in relation to technologies instead of continuing to orientate themselves in a purely technical direction. They may wish to act as consultants and interfaces in a technical environment, as there is often a strict separation between "social" and "technical" people, which can lead to communication problems. Therefore, it makes sense if there are employees who understand both areas and can therefore mediate between the two fronts.

Another reason for choosing cyberpsychology could be that during their very technical studies, students have realized that although they are fundamentally interested in it, it is not the area in which they want to work. A change of focus at a late stage in their studies offers students the opportunity to reorient themselves without having to start a completely new course of study. The big advantage here is that there is still the possibility of working in a technical profession, as the basics are all there and, if necessary, only further education courses need to be taken instead of a completely new orientation. And finally, integration of both areas, the technical cyber security and the cyberpsychology has a large potential to improve both areas and enables both to cope with the increasing challenges of cybercrime.

One of the final arguments in favor of the new module series is that students are taught a subject that is only rarely represented, but which is of great topicality and necessity on the labor market. Not only police departments or state employers are looking for specialists in this field, but also private companies are increasingly recognizing the value of employees who are positioned in both the social and technical fields.

## 2.4  Structure and Contents of a Cyberpsychology Module in a European Country

The general composition of a module is left to each college and university to decide for itself, which means that "the content, ECTS (European Credit Transfer and Accumulation System) distribution and scope" can be determined by the institutions themselves.

A total of 180–240 ECTS is required for a Bachelor degree in countries that follow the "Bologna process", which can be earned over a time between six and eight semesters (standard period of study) by passing examinations and eventually completing internships. This results in a quota of 30 ECTS for each individual semester, divided into different subjects with different weightings. One ECTS point is awarded for 25–30 h of study time [8]. For example, 60 h of attendance and 90 h of self-study, each distributed over the entire semester, result in a total of 150 working hours for a subject. Dividing 150 h by 30 h yields a result of five, which in turn would be the number of ECTS for this module.

In terms of structure, each module has a supervising professor or lecturer, in some cases even an additional person for practicals. These groups of people are then responsible for ensuring that students' performance is assessed at the end of the semester or at the appropriate time in order to check what they have learned. The teaching staff can be either professors, partners with relevant knowledge from companies or guest lecturers. However, there may be exceptions within the above-mentioned groups of persons.

Depending on the semester the cyberpsychology module will be taught in, it can be necessary to formulate pre-requisites for the students that must be fulfilled before advancing in higher semesters and more elevated subjects. These requirements can include the completion of certain semesters or modules, as well as gaining a specific amount of ECTS.

Due to the constantly changing requirements and especially the constantly changing technology, the contents should be checked at regular intervals and adapted if necessary. The following list is a compact summary of a possible, individual module "Cyberpsychology", which could be introduced at universities together with other focal points.

*Module Goals/Desired Learning Outcomes*
The aim of the course Cyberpsychology is to impart knowledge in the field of human behavior in relation to technologies, as well as possible dangers and problems. Contents and desired outcomes are only an example and don't cover other possible areas.

*Contents*
Students learn the basic knowledge in the field of cyberpsychology which includes, inter alia, computer-assisted communication and the forensic side after crimes. In addition, privacy and trustworthiness are a big issue in the online world - this is where the students find out what possibilities there are to protect themselves and others.

### 2.5  Establishing the Program

Before a Cyberpsychology module can be chosen by students, a number of points must be achieved and clarified, such as who will teach the respective subject, what materials will be used and how a transcript might look like. Accreditation should also be considered.

In addition to the lecturers or professors, it can be interesting to find experienced guest speakers for the respective subject, who take over in a lecture instead of the actual speaker and illustrate their point of view. This is not only advantageous for the students, as they are given variety and new perspectives, but also for the usual teaching staff, as they too gain new views. Such guest speakers do not necessarily have to come from the native-speaking country. Lectures in English are also good for language development on the one hand, and on the other hand it offers a wider range of possible candidates. Cooperation with partner universities can be advantageous in this respect, as appropriate guest speakers can be found there and the network between subject representatives is expanded.

In the second stage, the relevant points can be summarized under the heading "Lecture Preparation". A script or a presentation should be prepared according to how the lecture will be structured. In addition, the important contents must first be extracted from relevant literature. This can include books, journal articles or specialist lectures. If necessary, practical exercises can be integrated into the lectures, which contributes to a better understanding of the teaching material. Furthermore, advertisement inside and outside the university is important, as it can draw the attention of new students and give already enrolled students the opportunity to reconsider their choices and, if they like it, to take a new path. Advertising in this sense can include flyers describing the direction of choice, information events at high schools, and lectures at events at the university itself. Another way of dissemination would be through social media channels, on Facebook and Instagram, or through the public website on the Internet.

In the last stage, the actual implementation of the module series begins. To this end, the new module must be integrated into the lecture plan without overlap for professors, lecturers and students. Due to tight schedules, it often happens that lectures are entered in blocks on Saturdays, especially for lecturers who are still working elsewhere during the week, which makes the teaching units on the corresponding days longer and more intensive. This has the advantage that the material can be studied more quickly and potential working lecturers are not affected in their work during the week. After the new modules have been integrated into the lecture plan, suitable rooms must be allocated. This must also function without overlap in all semesters and programs. In addition to the possible rooms, group sizes must be estimated. Furthermore, care must be taken to ensure that some lectures only take place on certain dates, i.e. possible rooms must be occupied twice if no such lecture is currently taking place.

The final consideration in the third stage is the procurement of literature for the student library. It is important, especially at the beginning of a new module series with new subjects, that sufficient literature is available so that students not only have to search for sources on the Internet, but also have the opportunity to read the books recommended by the professors and lecturers.

## 3    Conclusion

We found that the integration of Cyberpsychology in the academic education of technical Cybersecurity and Digital Forensics offers a large potential to improve both sides.With the shift of criminal activities from the physical to the cyberspace, not only new technical skills but also social/cyber-psychological skills are needed to cope with the emerging challenges. Also for psychology it's important to better understand some of the technical aspects of cyberspace. So the integration into a mixed university program is very promising.

As mentioned above, there are some German and international degree programs with more or less cyberpsychology-oriented content, but the national modules in particular perform poorly in comparison to the international.

Although efforts are being made to counteract the shortage of skilled workers as best as possible, it is still astonishing how many vacancies there are in the end in the field of computer science or natural sciences [9]. By adapting the study programs to current and future topics, like the integration of cyberpsychology into technical cybersecurity, high school graduates and other prospective students can be picked up early on and the change in the labor market can possibly be supported by this. In any case, it is essential to always address technical, economic and social changes.

The field of cyberpsychology itself and especially the integration of it in technical cybersecurity education is currently at the very beginning but very much needed. The demand for highly educated specialists in cybersecurity is very high in Germany and worldwide and will grow further with the advancement of digitalization and cyber physical systems in industry, smart home, cities and personal medicine. Therefore, increasing numbers of students in Germany [10] offer the best opportunities to provide innovative courses that are adapted to today's requirements. Also, it is very challenging to call psychologists in a technical computer science faculty and vice versa, Albstadt-Sigmaringen University, as an example, is currently establishing such a program in its cybersecurity education and we are looking forward to evaluate it in future work.

# References

1. Palmetshofer, W., Semsrott, A., Alberts, A.: Der Wert persönlicher Daten. Ist Datenhandel der bessere Datenschutz? Hg. v. Sachverständigenrat für Verbraucherfragen beim Bundesministerium der Justiz und für Verbraucherschutz (2017)
2. Statista - Das Statistik-Portal: Achten Sie darauf, auf welche Informationen die von Ihnen genutzen Apps zugreifen? Hg. v. Statista - Das Statistik-Portal (2017)
3. Attrill, A.: Cyberpsychology. Oxford University Press, Oxford (2015)
4. ITU: Anzahl der Internetnutzer weltweit in den Jahren 2005 bis 2017 sowie eine Schätzung für das Jahr 2018 (in Millionen). Hg. v. Statista - Das Statistik-Portal (2018)
5. Görmer, J.: Anonmyität im Darknet. Nutzer und Usability im Vergleich der drei Hauptvertreter. Bachlorarbeit. Hochschule Anhalt (2018)
6. Kirwan, G.: Forensic Cyberpsychology. In: Irene Connolly, Marion Palmer, Hannah Barton, Gráinne Kirwan (Hg.): An Introduction to Cyberpsychology, Routledge, S. pp. 139–152 (2016)
7. Power, A., Kirwan, G.: Cyberpsychology and New Media, Psychology (2014)
8. Komenda, T., Malisa, V.: Summarized evaluation of optimizing workload by implementing an ECTS-barometer. In: 2013 IEEE Global Engineering Education Conference (EDUCON), pp. 906–909 (2013) https://doi.org/10.1109/EduCon.2013.6530214
9. Nier, H.: In Deutschland fehlen immer mehr MINT-Kräfte. Hg. v. Statista Das Statistik-Portal (2017)
10. Rudnicka, J.: Anzahl der Studierenden an Hochschulen in Deutschland in den Wintersemestern von 2002/2003 bis 2018/2019. Hg. v. Statista - Das Statistik-Portal (2019)

# Using a Mobile Augmented Reality APP on Mathematics Word Problems for Children

Mengping Tsuei[✉] and Jen-I Chiu

Graduate School of Curriculum and Instructional Communications Technology, National Taipei University of Education, Taipei, Taiwan
mptsuei@mail.ntue.edu.tw

**Abstract.** Augmented reality provides students a presence and an immersive learning environment. The purposes of this study were to develop an augmented-reality mathematics word-problem (AR-MW) learning system and to explore its effects on students' learning. The study had a pre-test–post-test quasi-experimental design. It was conducted with 37 fourth-grade students in Taiwan. Nineteen students used the AR-MW system and 18 students used the traditional approach to learn mathematics word problems about decimal concepts. Overall mathematics achievement scores did not differ between groups. On the post-test, students in the experimental group, but not those in the control group, showed improvement in the word problem score. The overall number of errors decreased significantly in both groups. The number of misunderstood sentence errors decreased significantly in both groups, and the number of computing errors decreased significantly in the experimental group. These findings demonstrate that the AR-MW system effectively enhances students learning of mathematics word problems.

**Keywords:** Augmented reality · Mathematics word problems · Problem-solving strategies

## 1 Introduction

The importance of mathematics literacy and problem solving is emphasised in the National Council of Teachers of Mathematics standards [1]. This emphasis has significant implications for classroom practice focused on higher-order skills, such as reasoning and problem solving [2]. Parmar et al. [3] indicated that word problems may pose a challenge for students with learning difficulties because their solution requires numerous steps and skills. Mathematical problem solving requires students to apply knowledge, skills and strategies [4]. Many students who have learning difficulties in mathematics and reading, especially those in primary school, struggle to comprehend problem descriptions [5, 6]. Without being presented with their contexts, many students fail to understand mathematics word problems.

Augmented reality (AR) technology interactively connects real-world and virtual contexts. Its use has many advantages for learning and facilitates educational gains. In education, the use of AR for science has been explored most thoroughly [7]. In

C. Stephanidis et al. (Eds.): HCII 2021, CCIS 1499, pp. 302–306, 2021.
https://doi.org/10.1007/978-3-030-90179-0_39

mathematics domain, AR has been used with elementary-school students to successfully teach basic matching skills [8, 9], geometry [9], spatial abilities [10] and probability [11]. However, research on the use of AR interventions for children involving mathematics word problems is limited. In the current study, an augmented-reality mathematics word-problem (AR-MW) learning system was developed and its effects on students' learning were explored.

## 2 Related Works

Recent research has examined mobile AR technology applications in mathematics. Cai, Liu, Shen, Li and Shen [11] developed three such applications to teach probability to junior high-school students. Probability concepts were explored in lessons entitled 'experience the likelihood', 'sample space' and 'empirical probability and theoretical probability', which facilitated students' learning gains on this topic. The students had positive attitudes toward the AR applications [11]. Muhimmah and Pritami [8] developed a digital game-based AR mathematics learning system that they tested with 60 third–sixth-grade students. In this first-person shooter game, the player must answer questions by finding and shooting balloons appearing on a mobile screen. They reported that the students felt challenged and enthusiastic about learning mathematics using this game [8]. Chen [9] developed a mobile AR system to teach algebra and geometry to elementary-school students, which they tested with a total of 82 students in experimental and control groups. The system recognised the real object and trigger images to display the video or three-dimensional (3D) objects. Students using the AR system had significantly better algebra and geometry performance than did the control students. In the AR group, high-anxiety learners had significantly higher scores than did low-anxiety learners [9].

## 3 Method

### 3.1 Design, Participants and Procedure

This study had a pre-test–post-test quasi-experimental design. Thirty-seven fourth-grade students (21 boys and 17 girls) of two classes in a primary school in Taipei City, Taiwan, participated in it. Nineteen students were allocated to the experimental group and used the AR-MW system, and 18 students were allocated to the control group used paper worksheets to learn mathematics word problems about decimal concepts for two weeks. Each student in the experiment group was provided with an Android tablet.

### 3.2 The AR-MW System

An image-based AR-MW system was developed base on Unity game engine with Vuforia. SDK The AR-MW system was designed according to Pólya's problem-solving strategies [12]. In the 'understanding the problem' step, the students viewed the augmented 3D animation. In the subsequent 'devise a plan' step, the system highlights the keywords of the word problems. In the 'carry out the plan' step, the system shows the prototype of the equation. In the final 'look back' step, students enter answers and receive feedback from the system.

The students scanned the trigger images to follow the steps required to solve problems about decimals, which were aligned with the fourth-grade mathematics curriculum in Taiwan. Figure 1 presented the 3D animation for presenting the context of the word problem question on the AR-MW system ("A bottle of apple juice is 0.6 *l*. Mary drank six bottles. How many *l* she drank?"). When the student pressed the button for highlighting the keywords in the 'devise a plan' step, the system showed the highlighted keywords on the question.

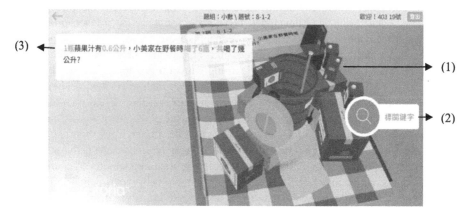

**Fig. 1.** The augmented-reality mathematics word problem system: (1) 3D animation (2) button for highlighting the keywords (3) question of word problem

### 3.3 Curriculum-Based Assessment Testing

The mathematics achievement pre- and post-test was designed to align with curriculum-based assessments. The pre-test was implemented a week before the experiment. The post-test was administered after the experiment. It consisted of four computational problems and five word problems. Each computational problem was scored by dividing the number of correct digits (correct numerals in the correct places) in the answer by the total number of digits in that answer and multiplying by 10 (total possible score, 10 points) [13]. Each word problem was scored by summing scores for the equation (total possible score, 5 points), calculation (total possible score, 5 points), numerical value of the answer (total possible score, 1 point) and unit of the answer (total possible score, 1 point; overall possible score, 12 points).

## 4   Results

### 4.1   Mathematics Achievement

Analysis of covariance (ANCOVA) was used to compare mathematics achievement in the experimental and control groups. The overall, computational problems and word problems scores did not violate the assumption of homogeneity of regression slopes ($F_{(2,34)} = 0.62$, 0.91 and 1.82, respectively), confirming that ANCOVA could be used to analyse them. Overall and computational problems scores did not differ significantly between groups ($M^a = 95.23$ and 90.50 [experimental and control groups, respectively], $F_{(1,34)} = 2.33$, $\eta^2 = 0.32$ and $M^a = 38.3$ and 39.45, $F_{(1,34)} = 1.43$, $\eta^2 = 0.21$, respectively). Word problems scores were significantly higher in the experimental group than in the control group ($M^a = 56.65$ and 51.29, respectively; $F_{(1,34)} = 4.18$, $\eta^2 = 0.51$, $p < .05$; Table 1).

**Table 1.** Mean scores and differences between groups

| Score | EG ($n = 19$) | | | CG ($n = 18$) | | | $F$ | $\eta^2$ |
|---|---|---|---|---|---|---|---|---|
| | Pre-test M (SD) | Post-test M (SD) | $M^a$ | Pre-test M (SD) | Post-test M (SD) | $M^a$ | | |
| Overall | 72.12 (20.94) | 95.11 (6.35) | 95.23 | 75.00 (12.33) | 86.71 (22.61) | 90.50 | 2.33 | 0.32 |
| Computational problems | 31.47 (11.47) | 38.4 (3.38) | 38.36 | 35.46 (4.57) | 39.43 (1.29) | 39.45 | 1.43 | 0.21 |
| Word problems | 40.65 (10.76) | 56.65 (4.75) | 56.65 | 39.54 (9.93) | 51.05 (10.56) | 51.29 | 4.18* | 0.51 |

* $p < .05$, $M^a$: Adjusted Means

## 4.2 Word Problem Error Patterns

The patterns of errors on word problems were analysed using four categories: misunderstood sentences, computing errors, omission errors and others. The number of misunderstood sentence errors decreased significantly in both groups ($EG_{pre} = 19$, $EG_{post} = 3$; $CG_{pre} = 24$, $CG_{post} = 11$), and the number of computing errors decreased in the experimental group ($EG_{pre} = 23$, $EG_{post} = 4$) (Table 2).

**Table 2.** Mathematics word problem errors

| Error pattern | Pre-Test (numbers) | | Post-Test (numbers) | |
|---|---|---|---|---|
| | EG ($n = 19$) | CG ($n = 18$) | EG($n = 19$) | CG ($n = 18$) |
| Misunderstand sentences | 19 | 24 | 3 | 11 |
| Computing | 23 | 9 | 4 | 6 |
| Omission | 2 | 5 | 0 | 2 |
| Others | 1 | 5 | 3 | 3 |

## 5   Conclusions

The purpose of this study was to compare the mathematics achievement obtained with AR-MW and traditional approaches. Students using the AR-MW system showed significant improvement on mathematics word problems relative to the control group. The number of misunderstood sentence errors decreased significantly in both groups, and the number of computing errors decreased significantly in the experimental group. These findings provide evidence of the effectiveness of AR-MW interventions for elementary-school students. Additional research is needed to replicate the findings of this study and to examine the effects of AR applications for other mathematics concepts (i.e. fractions) for children.

**Acknowledgments.** This work was supported by funding from the Ministry of Science and Technology of Taiwan (MOST-108–2511-H-152–011).

## References

1. Maccini, P., Gagnon, J.C.: Perceptions and application of NCTM standards by special and general education teachers. Except. Child. **68**, 325–344 (2002)
2. Cawley, J.F., Parmar, R.S., Yan, W., Miller, J.H.: Arithmetic computation performance of students with learning disabilities: implications for curriculum. Learn. Disabil. Res. Pract. **13**(2), 68–74 (1998)
3. Parmar, R.S., Cawley, J.F., Frazita, R.R.: Word problem-solving by students with and without mild disabilities. Except. Child. **62**, 415–429 (1996)
4. Mayer, R.E., Quilici, J.L., Moreno, R.: What is learned in an after-school computer club? J. Educ. Comput. Res. **20**(3), 223–235 (1999)
5. Vukovic, R.K.: Mathematics difficulty with and without reading difficulty: findings and implications from a four-year longitudinal study. Except. Child. **78**, 280–300 (2012)
6. Durnin, J.H., Perrone, A.E., MacKay, L.: Teaching problem solving processes in elementary school mathematics. J. Struct. Learn. Intell. Syst. **13**(1), 53–69 (1997)
7. Yilmaz, R. M.: Augmented reality trends in education between 2016 and 2017 Years. https://www.intechopen.com/books/state-of-the-art-virtual-reality-and-augmented-reality-knowhow/augmented-reality-trends-in-education-between-2016-and-2017-years. Accessed 02 Jun 2021
8. Muhimmah, I., Pritami, F.A.: Digital game based learning using augmented reality for mathematics learning. In: Proceedings of the 7th International Conference on Software and Computer Applications (ICSCA 2018), pp. 254–258. Association for Computing Machinery, New York (2018)
9. Chen, Y.C.: Effect of mobile augmented reality on learning performance, motivation, and nath anxiety in a math course. J. Educ. Comput. Res. **57**(7), 1695–1722 (2019)
10. Gün, E.T., Atasoy, B.: The effects of augmented reality on elementary school students' spatial ability and academic achievement. Egitim ve Bilim **42**, 191 (2017)
11. Cai, S., Liu, E., Shen, Y., Li, S., Shen, Y.: Probability learning in mathematics using augmented reality: impact on student's learning gains and attitudes. Interact. Learn. Environ. **28**(5), 560–573 (2020)
12. Pólya, G.: How to Solve It: A New Aspect of Mathematical Method. Princeton University Press, New York (1945)
13. Tsuei, M.: A web-based curriculum-based measurement system for class-wide ongoing assessment. J. Comput. Assist. Learn. **24**(1), 47–60 (2008)

# Implementation of ICTs in a University Curriculum for the Development of Math and Critical Reading Skills During COVID-19 Pandemic

Derlis Aminta Villadiego Rincón[1]([envelope]), Alex Alberto Castellar Rodríguez[1], Harold Gamero Rodríguez[2], and Adriana del Rosario Pineda Robayo[3]

[1] Universidad de La Costa, 58 street #55 66, Barranquilla, Colombia
`{dvilla3,acaste116}@cuc.edu.co`
[2] Universidad del Atlántico, 30 street # 8-49, Puerto Colombia-Atlántico, Colombia
`haroldgamero@mail.uniatlantico.edu.co`
[3] Universidad Manuela Beltrán, Bogotá, Colombia
`adripineda10@hotmail.com`

**Abstract.** This research was developed to determine the effectiveness of using ICT as part of the curriculum of Colombian university students in the areas of mathematics and critical reading during the COVID-19 pandemic. The University Academic Accompaniment Plan (AAP) was aimed at freshmen students whose ICFES test results were below the national average. The study's approach was quantitative, where two semesters were analyzed 2020-I and 2020-II consisting in 189 and 146 surveyed students, respectively. The SPSS version 22 statistical program and the Academic Valuation Software were used, and results were parameterized by two tests a pre-test and post-test. Mann Whitney's U-test was applied to contrast the two semesters, to analyze the effectiveness of each semester, the T-Student test was used for related samples and the Wilcoxon test in cases where there was no normality; finally, an exploratory factorial and reliability analysis was carried out through the Cronbach's alpha statistic to determine how related the questionnaire questions were in terms of quality of service and methodologies. According to the results of this study, it was found that the AAP in the two semesters managed to be statistically effective and the methodologies implemented for the approach and development of skills through ICT in both semesters resulted to be statistically significative, reliable, and adequate. These findings lead to the conclusion that the AAP in mathematics and critical reading was effective for skills development, through the working process in remote access during the COVID-19 pandemic.

**Keywords:** COVID-19 · Mathematics skills · Critical reading skills

## 1 Introduction

World Health Organization in 2020 stated that COVID-19 can be characterized as a pandemic [1], this led to changes in education systems worldwide, affecting all levels

© Springer Nature Switzerland AG 2021
C. Stephanidis et al. (Eds.): HCII 2021, CCIS 1499, pp. 307–314, 2021.
https://doi.org/10.1007/978-3-030-90179-0_40

of education and thereby hundreds of millions of students [2], forcing educational institutions to turn their sights to methodologies associated with the remote access modality to meet the objectives of education.

In this sense, Information and Communication Technologies (ICT) became an indispensable tool in the teaching and learning processes of students and teachers [3], and in this way meet the proposed objectives set out by higher education, as mentioned by UNESCO at one of its conferences [4], recognizing the formative value that universities provide within society towards advancement and development [5]. That is the reason why several universities around the world have opted for competency-based learning within their educational model, since it has been proven that, by developing math skills in university students in areas of calculus and other disciplines, incorporating ICT positively favors students in their training processes [6]. Likewise, the development of reading skills allows the student in higher education to improve their skills in their writings and reading by integrating ICT into the teaching process [7].

In line with the above, the Universidad de la Costa, through the Academic Vice-Chancellor's office offers an academic accompaniment plan (AAP) for freshmen students whose ICFES (which stands for Instituto Colombiano para el Fomento de la Educación Superior) "saber 11°" test results were below the national average, in order to develop skills in critical reading and math and in this way level them as envisaged in the definitions of the basic standards of language, mathematics, science and civic skills of the Colombian Education Ministry (Ministerio de Educación Nacional or MEN) [8]. Mathematical competencees give the individual thoughtful thinking with a deep understanding and the reading competition allows to develop the knowledge and personal potential to participate in society [9].

In this sense, the purpose of this research was to analyze the effectiveness of the AAP during the global preventive isolation due to COVID-19 in order to develop math and critical reading skills in freshmen students, for the 2020-I and 2020-II academic periods with classes in remote access mode with proper use of ICT, highlighting in this research Microsoft Teams, Moodle platform and Geneally. To this end, a pre-experimental design was made with two parameterized tests; an online pre-test through the Academic Valuation Software, developed to estimate skills levels in math and critical reading, after ten remote access intervention sessions with interactive workshops and guides to help improve skills development; finally, the online post-test was applied with the same Academic Valuation Software version 2.5. The analysis of the data was carried out with the SPSS statistical program version 22.

## 2  Method

### 2.1  Population and Sample

The 2020-I and 2020-II semesters were represented by 189 and 146 students respectively, of which 116 were part of the AAP in mathematics and 73 in critical reading from the period 2020-I, meanwhile, 96 in mathematics and 50 in critical reading from the period 2020-II.

## 2.2 Procedure

The academic accompaniment plan was applied to the population of students identified with performances below the national average in math and critical reading skills in the "Saber 11" test, which is applied by the National Education Ministry. When conducting the interview and registration process, students sign an agreement and enroll the assigned plan on the university's institutional platform. The study was conducted in the following phases:

**PHASE 1.** An academic assessment test was applied to all students through a software that allows to identify the skills with which students register, not only was the overall score analyzed but the percentage in each math competence and the reading level were checked; this, in addition to the performance level at which students were placed based on their overall test result. This pre-test consisted of 25 mathematical questions with generic elements (quantitative reasoning) and non-generic elements (mathematical elements), and 25 critical reading questions; the test was multiple choice question with only one answer per question. The test was two hours long and measures freshmen students' abilities according to their competences with scores from zero to one hundred and performance levels defined by ICFES [10], who provides theoretical reliability in terms of evaluation. These performance levels bring students together into 4 levels (1, 2, 3 and 4) (Table 1).

**Table 1.** Scores of performance levels according to ICFES

| Performance level | Math test scores | Critical reading test scores |
| --- | --- | --- |
| 1 | 0 to 35 | 0 to 35 |
| 2 | 36 to 50 | 36 to 50 |
| 3 | 51 to 70 | 51 to 65 |
| 4 | 71 to 100 | 66 to 100 |

**PHASE 2.** Students were socialized with the results and based on them a series of interventions were developed, through guides and infographics as another learning resource, which were designed by the AAP teachers; a total of ten guides taking into account math and critical reading skills with interactive, dynamic and engaging content using the tool Geneally for this purpose, and for each session, introductory problems and multiple-selection questionnaires were designed with only one answer focused on the competences development and uploaded to the Moodle platform. Classes and meetings were developed through the Microsoft Teams platform that enables real-time interaction between the teacher and the student and using the prepared guides in Moodle.

**PHASE 3.** A post-test was applied to assess progress in each competence and performance level according to the results obtained with the same characteristics described in phase 1 for the pre-test.

**PHASE 4.** A perception survey was applied in course satisfaction and ICT use and mediation in the learning process and strengthening of the evaluated skills. Twelve questions were asked from which four of them were associated to the platforms and focused on students' perception of these digital resources and the methodologies associated with their use, and which answers were established with a Likert scale, with five answer choices: 1 (Strongly disagree), 2 (Disagree), 3 (Neither agree nor disagree), 4 (Agree) and 5 (Strongly agree).

**PHASE 5.** Results were analyzed and a group performance report was organized to show significant student progress in their competencies. For the analysis for each academic period: 2020-I and 2020-II, it was analyzed whether the differences between pre-test and post-test came from a normal distribution taking as a reference the scores of students, which are quantitative variables, this is why and according to the size of the samples, that for both academic periods (2020-I and 2020-II) the Kolmogorov-Smirnov test is used. In this regard, Wilcoxon's non-parametric signed rank test was used for non-normality in critical reading for the period 2020-I and the T-Student test to the paired differences for the case of normality in the math 2020-I, math 2020-II, and critical reading 2020-II groups.

Mann Whitney's non-parametric U-test allowed to contrast the post-tests of the semesters 2020-I and 2020-II, which led to an assessment of whether the pedagogical strategies and tools used for the development of competences were the same, with performance levels understood to be random ordinal variables.

The perception of methodology, management, resources, use of digital tools and quality of service was determined by a survey, where its reliability was assessed through the Cronbach's alpha statistic and an exploratory factor analysis to determine how related the questions were. Sand used the IBM SPSS (Statistical Product and Service Solutions) version 22 statistical package for information analysis.

## 3 Results

Through the Kolmogorov-Smirnov test, with a significance level of $\alpha = 0.05$, it was determined that the differences between the pre-test and the post-test of the groups: Math 2020-I, Math 2020-II and Critical Reading 2020-II, are distributed normally with p-values equal to: 0.139, 0.2 and 0.2, respectively; on the contrary, the differences between the pre-test and the post-test of the Critical Reading 2020-I group, where the data is not normally distributed with a p-value $= 0.033$.

Data analyses show in both semesters better results in critical reading and math post-tests (Table 2) and their differences are statistically significant (Table 3 and 4).

To contrast methodologies in both semesters, student performance levels were considered (Table 1), so the procedure was to determine if the data came from a normal distribution through the Kolmogorov-Smirnov test with a significance $\alpha = 0.05$, in this sense, it was obtained that post-tests in the 2020-I and 2020-II semesters in mathematics and critical reading do not come from a normal distribution with p-values-0.000 $\leq 05$. In addition, the results of the Mann-Whitney U test determined that there are no significant differences between the 2020-I and 2020-II post-tests, so students received the same

**Table 2.** Mean, Median and standard deviation of the grades.

|  | Math 2020-I Pre-test | Math 2020-I Post-test | Critical Reading 2020-I Pre-test | Critical Reading 2020-I Post-test | Math 2020-II Pre-test | Math 2020-II Pos-test | Critical Reading 2020-II Pre-test | Critical Reading 2020-II Post-test |
|---|---|---|---|---|---|---|---|---|
| Mean | 30.9 | 59 | 36.55 | 47.73 | 43.71 | 61.96 | 37.85 | 52.5 |
| Median | 32 | 60 | 36 | 48 | 44 | 64 | 38 | 47.6 |
| Standard deviation | 10.676 | 14.445 | 9.691 | 11.913 | 11.68 | 15.012 | 12.288 | 22.823 |

**Table 3.** Paired samples T Test results pre-test vs post-test scores

|  | 95% Confidence interval of the difference | | t | Sig. (2 tailed) |
|---|---|---|---|---|
|  | Lower | Upper |  |  |
| Pre-test vs Post-test Math 2020-I | −31.172 | −25.035 | −18.141 | *0.000 |
| Pre-test vs Post-test Math 2020-II | −21.948 | −14.552 | −9.798 | *0.000 |
| Pre-test vs Post-test Critical Reading 2020-II | −21.143 | −8.169 | −4.54 | *0.000 |

* Value of p indicates significant difference between the compared data ($p \leq 0.05$)

**Table 4.** Wilcoxon signed ranks test

| Pre-test vs Post-test Critical Reading 2020-I | Z | Asymp. Sig.(2 tailed) |
|---|---|---|
|  | −5.454 | *0.000 |

*Value of p indicates significant difference between the compared data ($p \leq 0.05$).

study materials and the same treatment in both academic periods, there were no changes or alterations in the process, this means that the same methodologies were implemented in terms of the development of the classes (Table 5).

**Table 5.** Statistics Test ($\alpha = 0.05$)

|  | Mann-Whitney U | Z | Asymp. Sig.(2 tailed) |
|---|---|---|---|
| Post-tests levels Math (2020-I and 2020-II) | 5303.500 | −0.645 | *0.519 |
| Post-tests levels Critical Reading (2020-I and 2020-II) | 1786.000 | −0.212 | *0.832 |

* Value of p indicates no significant difference between the compared data ($p > 0.05$)

Exploratory factorial analysis with KMO $= 0.94 > 0.5$ and Bartlett's test of sphericity with p-value $= 0.000$ confirm the correlation of questionnaire questions and their reliability using Cronbach's alpha coefficient with the value of 0.95. Figure 1 represents the questions about the results of students' perception of digital resources used and associated methodologies versus their use.

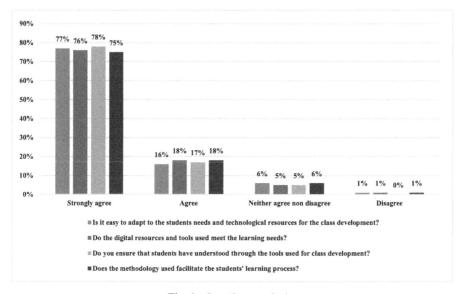

**Fig. 1.** Questions analysis.

Below are the questions asked in the survey regarding students' perception of methodologies, management, resources, use of digital tools and quality of service (Table 6).

**Table 6.** Survey results

| Questions asked in the survey | Mean | Variance |
| --- | --- | --- |
| Q1: Assess quality of service received | 4.63 | s |
| Q2: Is the teacher punctual in the development of the sections? | 4.75 | .272 |
| Q3: Does the teacher have good conceptual and theoretical management of the topics taught? | 4.69 | .353 |
| Q4: Does the teacher easily adapt to the students' needs and technological resources for class development? | 4.67 | .468 |
| Q5: Does the dynamics used enable the active participation of students? | 4.68 | .356 |

*(continued)*

**Table 6.** (*continued*)

| Questions asked in the survey | Mean | Variance |
|---|---|---|
| Q6: Do the digital resources and tools used meet the learning needs? | 4.69 | .395 |
| Q7: Do teachers ensure that students have understood through the tools used for class development? | 4.73 | .292 |
| Q8: Does the methodology used facilitate the students' learning process? | 4.67 | .386 |
| Q9: Does the teacher consider the ideas, opinions and suggestions given? | 4.73 | .251 |
| Q10: Does the teacher establish together with the students, rules that create a stable, safe environment that promotes the proper functioning of the sessions? | 4.69 | .282 |
| Q11: Do you consider that the Academic Accompaniment Plan contributed significantly to the development of your generic competences? | 4.77 | .248 |
| P12: Does the teacher care about those students who are frequently absent? | 4.63 | .535 |

# 4   Conclusion

This research showed that the academic accompaniment plan AAP is an effective university strategy for skills development in math and critical reading, in the midst of the process of working in remote access in pandemic (Table 2, 3 and 4), studies show that developing high school competences allows students to perform better in their college careers [11], and it is for this reason that the university as a strategy proposes to the community this mandatory service for freshmen students, although if we add to this teaching experience the remote access modality with the complexity of the COVID-19 pandemic, this process does not always turn out to be effective and impactful in students [12].

The results of this study show that there was assertiveness in the methodologies applied and the digital tools implemented, so it was statistically proven that in the two academic semesters the same strategies were used in the skills development process and this was significant (Table 5); similar studies show that such treatments help improve students' grades [13].

In addition, it was found that the implemented questionnaire to find out the effectiveness of strategies, methodologies, and quality in the process, turned out to be reliable with a Cronbach's alpha coefficient of 0.95; then students' acceptance of digital resources for ICT learning development is evident (Fig. 1) and the same goes for their quality of service satisfaction (Table 6), studies reaffirm that the use of these resources and methodological strategies in this research, are effective and interesting by students for their learning [14, 15]. Certainly, the new teaching trends demonstrate the direction that the educational system is taking towards achieving a true cohesion between education and technology at all levels [16].

# References

1. Archived: Who Timeline-COVID-19. https://www.who.int/news/item/27-04-2020-who-tim eline---covid-19. Accessed 15 Mar 2021
2. From COVID-19 learning disruption to recovery: A snapshot of UNESCO's work in education 2020. https://en.unesco.org/news/covid-19-learning-disruption-recovery-snapshot-une scos-work-education-2020. Accessed 13 Mar 2021
3. El profesorado y las tecnologías en tiempos de confinamiento por la pandemia Covid-19. Creencias sobre actitudes, formación, competencia digital e importancia de las TIC en educación. http://hdl.handle.net/10366/143691. Accessed 9 Mar 2021
4. Declaración mundial sobre la educación superior en el siglo XXI: visión y acción. https:// www.iesalc.unesco.org/ess/index.php/ess3/issue/view/21. Accessed 14 Mar 2021
5. Hernández-Sánchez, I., Mata, K., Tovar, M., Ramírez J.: Variables organizacionales como predictores de las conductas de ciudadanía en el ámbito universitario. In Creatividad e innovación: ejes de la economía naranja para el desarrollo sostenible. Colombia, Fundación Colombo Internacional (2018)
6. Martínez-Palmera, O., Combita-Niño, H., De La Hoz, E.: Mediación de los Objetos Virtuales de Aprendizaje en el Desarrollo de Competencias Matemáticas en Estudiantes de Ingeniería. Formación universitaria 11(6), 63–74 (2018)
7. Gómez, D., Carranza, Y., Ramos, C.: revisión documental, una herramienta para el mejoramiento de las competencias de lectura y escritura en estudiantes universitarios. Revista Chakiñan de Ciencias Sociales y Humanidades 1, 46–56 (2017)
8. Estándares básicos de competencias en Lenguaje, Matemáticas, Ciencias y Ciudadanas. https://www.mineducacion.gov.co/1621/article-340021.html. Accessed 13 Mar 2021
9. PISA: Marcos Teóricos de Pisa. [Versión electrónica], Instituto Nacional de Evaluación y Calidad del Sistema Educativo. Spain, Ministerio de Educación y Ciencia
10. Guía de orientación Saber 11° para instituciones educativas. http://www.icfes.gov.co. Accessed 15 Mar 2021
11. Shin, D., Shim, J.: Competencia del profesor de matemáticas percibidas por los estudiantes: asociaciones longitudinales con resultados de aprendizaje y elección de carrera universitaria. Ciencias de la Educación 11(1), 18 (2021)
12. Nesenbergs, K., Abolins, V., Ormanis, J., Mednis, A.: Uso de la realidad virtual y aumentada en la educación superior remota: una revisión sistemática de paraguas. Educ. Sci. 11, 8 (2021). https://doi.org/10.3390/educsci11010008
13. Moradi, M., Liu, L., Luchies, C., Patterson, M., Darban, B.: Enhancing teaching-learning effectiveness by creating online interactive instructional modules for fundamental concepts of physics and mathematics. Educ. Sci. 8(3), 109 (2018)
14. Abou-Khalil, V., Helou, S., Khalifé, E., Chen, M., Majumdar, R., Ogata, H.: Emergency online learning in low-resource settings: effective student engagement strategies. Educ. Sci. 11(1), 24 (2020)
15. Sidpra, J., Gaier, C., Reddy, N., Kumar, N., Mirsky, D., Mankad, K.: Sustaining education in the age of COVID-19: a survey of synchronous web platforms. Quant. Imaging Med. Surg. 10, 1422 (2020)
16. Parra, M., Marambio, C., Ramírez, J., Suárez, D., Herrera, H.: Educational convergence with digital technology: integrating a global society. In: Stephanidis, C., Antona, M., Ntoa, S. (eds.) HCII 2020. CCIS, vol. 1294, pp. 303–310. Springer, Cham (2020). https://doi.org/10. 1007/978-3-030-60703-6_39

# Culture and Computing

# An Exploratory Study of the Business Strategies for Virtual Idols in the Era of Phygitalization—Analysis in the Perspective of Cases in China

Han Han[1], Minling Lin[1(✉)], and Francesco Zurlo[2]

[1] Shenzhen University, Shenzhen, China
`han.han@szu.edu.cn`
[2] Politecnico di Milano, Milan, Italy
`francesco.zurlo@polimi.it`

**Abstract.** With the breakthrough of technologies such as VR and AR, the virtual idol has become an emerging topic in the idol industry in the digital age. Comparing to Japan where acquires more-industrialized models of the virtual idol, nowadays, there has less-strict definition of the term in the field of virtual idols in China, the notion of the virtual idols in the Chinese market has been extended, and the industry is gradually changing from classical artist-pattern-oriented to internet-celebrity-pattern-oriented, which brings out larger complexities for business strategies. Regarding this issue, this paper analyzes three major types of virtual idol in China combining with relevant cases, explores and sorts out their corresponding commercial approaches. It is expected to summarize some innovative suggestions of relevant business patterns, and to provide the feasible strategies for the future development of virtual idol industry in China.

**Keywords:** Virtual idol · Phygitalization · Business strategy

## 1 Introduction

### 1.1 Research Background

**Phygitalization—A Design Tool for the Innovative Experience for Business.** With the development of extended reality technologies (e.g. AR/VR/MR, etc.), users in the market is no longer satisfied with the basic presentation and interaction of virtual scenarios, instead, they increasingly expect to be able to connect the virtual scenarios directly to their real-life experiences, whether it is to obtain physical commodities with virtual payment methods or to get emotional attachment to the virtual objects. As a result, demand for the designs of phygital experiences and tools/models arises at this remarkable moment.

Phygitalization, as originally suggested by Australian Agency Momentum in 2013, is becoming an emerging concept in both marketing and design disciplines, which refers

© Springer Nature Switzerland AG 2021
C. Stephanidis et al. (Eds.): HCII 2021, CCIS 1499, pp. 317–324, 2021.
https://doi.org/10.1007/978-3-030-90179-0_41

to the integration of physical presence and digital space to create an ecosystem between brands and consumers, in order to maximize the impact of integrated brand communication. In recent years, the designs of phygital models are stepping out to the market from the innovative retail industries, unlocking varieties of applications for O2O business, such as the QR code that can be seen everywhere on books and product packaging, the online shopping channels on Instagram and YouTube, and the digital runway show of Milan Men's Fashion Week under the epidemic situation. All of these indicate that phygitalization has gradually become a basic business tool of most industries due to the development directions of the Internet environment.

It can be seen that in the current virtual age of the Internet, people are constantly shuttling between the physical space and the digital world, and enjoying diversified contents created by extended reality technologies for their life experiences and mundane practices, and among which, virtual idol is extracted as one of the hottest outputs of the content production in the era of phygitalization.

**Virtual Idol—A New Commercial Outlet of Idol Market.** According to the relevant research on virtual idols, the concept 'virtual idols' was proposed by Japanese industry since 1990s, while the topic that is most discussed within this field of the academia mainly focuses on Hatsune Miku during the past decade. Analyses were based on the logic that Hatsune Miku belongs to the category of 'idol' to the extent of economic considerations, meanwhile is carried by a virtual figure when discussing the methodological issues [1, 2]. Therefore, from the perspective of phygitalization, virtual idols can be divided into dual aspects in terms of digital and physical elements. The digital elements mainly refer to the carrier of virtual idols themselves, while physical elements are related to real-life contents generated through this digital carrier, such as physical music performance, live broadcast for commodity selling, and even any consumption practice that forms fan economy. Although virtual idols have no living body, they possess developed fan groups just like real idols, and also have a great appeal among their fans. Compared with real idols, virtual idols have obvious advantages—features such as permanence, strong self-management ability that is more able to satisfy fans' fantasies about their idols to a stable extent, and even interactivity by which fans can directly participate in the construction of content related to virtual idols [3].

In China, 2017 was a year of explosion for virtual idols, with 14 virtual idols stepped out in the market in the same year, which presents a larger number than even all the ones accumulated in the previous years. At the same time, rising demand appeared in the market driven by the young consumers who are into the ACGN (animation, comics, games, & novel) subculture group. With the support of phygitalization methods and relative technologies, the industrial chain of virtual idols is gradually revealed. Especially due to the explosive growth of live streaming e-commerce, short video and other content industries, virtual idols are rapidly dragged from the ACGN subculture group to the general public in a larger scale. Things even jumped since the beginning of 2020, as the global outbreak of the epidemic situation, which limited the activities of real idols and made the giant internet corporations move their focus and increase their resource tilt to the virtual idol industry. Going with such trend, virtual idols have gradually shed the label of otaku culture and stand out as an emerging concept of mass culture.

## 2  Research Objective

As introduced above, virtual idol is becoming a hot topic to both industries and academic research in China. From the explosion of Hatsune Miku in Japan, to the concert held by Luo Tianyi—the virtual idols who started out in the form of groups, and even to the appearance of virtual idol in some popular talent shows in China, the commercial market of virtual idol is progressively showing a state of blossom.

In this case, as artificial intelligence and technologies for extended reality is steadily dominating people's real-life experiences and mundane practices, this study is trying to understand the logic of the business strategies behind the diversified virtual idols in China, and to summarize a basic structure to develop the virtual idols in a more industrialized method with the support of relative technologies, which is expected to provide possible advice for the industry.

## 3  Research Method

As it has been more than 30 years since the birth of virtual idol concept, distribution of the figures could be found in various fields, such as fashion, music, games and even live broadcasting. Every step in the development is accompanied by the evolution of technology and the innovation of business strategies. Virtual idols in different fields are formed by varied types of business entities and business models, and their production team who create the virtual images also adopts different operating strategies according to the driving forces and market conditions behind them to seek differentiated market presence [4].

Within the context described, the case study is conducted qualitatively as the main research strategy with both theoretical and empirical support to achieve the proposed research objective of this study. Theoretically, literature about virtual idol industries provides this research the basic perspectives for case sampling [5–7]; while advanced discussions on phygital experience design in the recent years together with business strategies in the 'internet celebrity economy' support the case analysis and interpretation of the empirical data collected [8–12]. Being nurtured by the theoretical exploration,

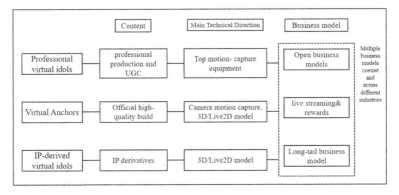

**Fig. 1.** Categorization structure of the virtual idol business strategies

empirical studies are conducted with the cases categorized in three basic types—① professional virtual idols, ② virtual anchors, and ③ IP-derived virtual idols (Fig. 1).

To further explain, the first type (the professional virtual idols) are those who are created by professional productions and UGC productions, such as Luo Tianyi (similar to Hatsune Miku in Japan), which are in an open business pattern to generate related derivative contents similar to traditional real idols. The technologies this type of virtual idols adopt, including 3D modeling and holographic projection, are all supported by the top-tier motion capture equipment in the industry, in order to better actualize the immersive experience under rich content (Fig. 2).

The second type (the virtual anchors, or called the 'authorized virtual uploaders') are those who are created by the official account of brands or merchants. This type requires relatively lower technical conditions rather than the first one, while the main technical tools are aiming to support the regular performance of virtual idols (e.g. the AI algorithm through video motion capture technology), which can save a lot of production costs and risks for instant interaction compared to a real-person anchor. At the same time, it is required to make immediate switch between 3D and Live2D models, so as to assist to the essential business pattern of this type of virtual anchor that relies on the rewarded live streaming and/or instant consumption (Fig. 3).

The third type refers to the virtual idols derived from animation and Intellectual Properties (IP) of games, of which the business strategy is similar to the long-tail model that is based on existing games and fans circles of the animation. 3D and Live2D model technology is mainly conducted to make the virtual idols alive in different scenarios out from the original pictures of the games and animations, and enable them to build up stronger emotional attachment with fans like in real life (Fig. 4).

**Fig. 2.** Concert of Luo Tianyi     **Fig. 3.** Live broadcast of Caicaizi     **Fig. 4.** Photo shared by K/DA

Based on these categories, analysis of the respective strategies will be elaborated in the following parts of the paper with detailed evidence from cases so as to summarize the business patterns with deeper exploration of the impacts.

## 4    The Main Business Patterns of Virtual Idols

### 4.1    Professional Virtual Idols—An Open Scenario

Among the business patterns of virtual idol industry, the business model of professional virtual idols in Japan is relatively mature. Luo Tianyi, one of the most representative professional virtual idols in China, has followed a similar pathway as Hatsune Miku in Japan, from appearing on the TV screen, to collaborating with various brands and even holding live concert with millions of audiences. In the past, professional virtual idols' concerts are mainly organized online to interact with their fans. When stepping to the era of phygitalization, professional virtual idols are also be able to perform with the transformation and interaction across physical and digital spaces. The audience can participate to the live performance of virtual idols in real-life occasion without wearing glasses and also interact with them at the same time (Fig. 2). In 2016, Luo Tianyi has already attended the Hunan TV New Year's Eve concert; In 2020, she even cooperated with famous musician Fang Jinlong to perform the music "Jasmine Flower", and applied four times of consecutive costume changing, bringing the audience a brand new experience with a cross-over collaboration between ACGN culture and Chinese classical music. In 2021, it was also the first time that a virtual singer appeared in the CCTV (China Central Television) Spring Festival Gala in the history. Thousands of fans in the physical world shouted their idol's name, while the object of their passion was actually a digital "image". With the efficient technical support (e.g. 3D modeling and holographic projection), Luo Tianyi has been capable to follow almost all the same business strategies as what real idols do, making profit transformation by holding concerts and birthday parties, developing peripheral products, and endorsing commercial brands, which forms an open business model.

From the success of Luo Tianyi, it can be realized that the essential business strategy of professional virtual idols is creating cross-border intervention among realities and scenarios to obtain traffic and its monetization, such as advertising endorsement and crossover collaboration with different creative cultural industries, to integrate virtual idols with internet economy. With such strategy, the digital value of virtual idols is outputted placing on the real content, for instance, the derived tangible products and live concert collaborating with real-life celebrities, so as to effectively connect the ACGN culture with fan economy and cultivate larger offline commercial potentials.

## 4.2   Virtual Anchors—A 'Live + Reward' Scenario

With the rise of live streaming e-commerce and new trend for the production of video content, a subdivision in the commercial industry chain of virtual idols is emerging, which is hosted by virtual anchors. Virtual anchors can be well-designed from their images of outfit to personal talents according to the preferences of the users, in order to better meet the expectations of their target consumers. Unlike the professional virtual idols (in the first category) who are lack of timely interaction with their fans, the virtual anchors function more to provide instant response to their audience. Behind each virtual anchor, there are real actors to pre-produce the samples of the movements for the figure so as to convey the realistic tone and body movements that can build up a vivid character to the audience. Compared to real anchors, the biggest advantage of virtual anchors lies in that they can better replace physical bodies and directly launch 24-h live broadcasting without interruption, which efficiently support the commodity promotion and product recommendation during their air roadshow for the brands/merchants. Yet, in essence, the business model of virtual anchors is as same as that of real anchors, which is based on the tip reward and instant consumption of the recommended commodities during their live broadcasts.

Virtual anchor requires a very basic level of motion capture technology nowadays that does not need to rely on high-demanding resources of the developers, as there have already been a lot open resources to generate the figures with universal tools provided to the mass public. A large number of local virtual anchors are pumping out in the Chinese virtual idol market one after another (Lingyuan Yousa, Hanser, Aggressive Rock Candy and New Ke Niang, etc.), serving for commercial outlets.

As selling commodities in live-stream broadcast is an essential path for the virtual anchors to transfer the traffic of views to considerable profit, the precondition is to build up stable user base as loyal customers meanwhile keep producing creative content for live broadcast to attract newcomers to the base. This to some extent in current situation in China, relies on the demographic dividend. For example, the visit popularity of a Chinese virtual anchor called CaiCaiZi (Fig. 3) reached 6 million traffic number within one hour in her first broadcast, and it only took 25 min for her to obtain '100 ships' as tip reward (1 ship as reward currency equals to around 780 US dollars). And it is also important for the anchors to find ways producing new content constantly, for instance, Lingyuan Yousa who is a popular anchor on Bilibili website keep collaborating with real anchors and presenting various personal talents, which gained almost 80 million video views of its live broadcast for one single time.

In sum, the commercial value of virtual anchors is being well developed in the phygital era with the support of relative technologies, which provide great possibilities for the 'content e-commerce industry' by improving the instant interactivity between the anchor and its audience, and cultivating the creativity to produce varieties of content that enable the transformation of traffic to commercial profits.

### 4.3  IP-Derived Virtual Idol—A Long Tail Commercial Scenario

There is another development trend in the business model of virtual idols, which are derived from available images of the characters in the existing works like animations and games. This kind of virtual idols has already gained a certain degree of awareness regarding the recognition among fans of the IP of the existing works. The K/DA virtual idol girl group (Fig. 4) who were officially debuted on the stage of the 2018 League of Legends Global Finals can be taken as a significant case in this category. K/DA is a virtual idol group derived from the character's IP from the original online game called League of Legends with one of the largest player base in China, and the MV of their first EP hit over 100 million view counts on YouTube within a month after its release. The popularity of K/DA is driven by the factors in mainly two dimensions—firstly, the loyal fans of League of Legends are all over the world, which lays a certain traffic foundation for the virtual idol group transformed from the game and facilitates significant consumption potential for any derived products developed from the original IP; in the meantime, the rapid-developing technologies enable K/DA to attain fashionable art modeling and exquisite three-dimensional images, to leap them into the 'top stream' in the global virtual idol market for its enhanced image and reputation as a fashion icon, and even materialized on the fashion magazine "Dazed" as more commercial applications of phygital scenarios.

Moreover, thanks to the development of technology that promotes more phygital applications, the long-tail business model is able to be implemented for the IP-derived virtual idols, similar to the blockchain economy. The business model of this type of virtual idol is mainly to cultivate diverse and even marginalized commercial values of an original IP by developing derived varieties of products and scenarios of content, and in this way, the strategic effort is put to the integrative marketing of the brand image (e.g. the game and its derived virtual idol relatives) among its existing fan base to consolidate the consumer loyalty so as to enhance the brand equity of the IP as a whole concept.

To summarize, IP-derived virtual idols make the characters come to the audience's real-life scenarios from their original animation/game work, and it is more direct to transfer the audience's emotional attachment to the characters from the original work to the derived virtual idols, which provides more advantages as stable precondition for the commercial transformation, being compared to creating a new professional virtual idols or virtual anchors. In addition, phygitalization breaks the entertainment attribute of the game itself, which further expands the commercial value of its IP, helps the breakthrough of the virtual idols derived from IP to achieve more possibilities, and points out a path for the development of the brand integrally in the future.

## 5   Conclusion: The Future of Virtual Idol Business Strategies

As the result of the analysis, the business strategies of the virtual idols based on the above structure reveal the transformation of its business value into the impact of a larger scale in terms of economic, cultural, and social dimensions. The economic impact is mainly constructed by the competitive market environment promoted by the traffic performance of the virtual idols. Also, the cultural brands which are seeking for innovative development are trying to apply the traffic value of their IP into virtual idols that are more capable to build up constant social interactions with their audience by diverse phygital methods, so as to co-create the cultural value with the public. Moreover, it is important to note that whatever types virtual idols they are, virtual idols surely have the potential to interfere and empower the social production practices with its radical impact from Internet in a larger scale with more possible real-life scenarios.

On the other hand, phygitalization method has effectively assisted virtual idols to upgrade their business models with the commercial increase in terms of 'quantity', more qualitative breakthroughs are still to be explored, for instance, how to connect the unique fans' emotion of individuals to their virtual idols and shape the fan economy in long term, and how to ethically monetize the traffic of idols into profits. These are the potential directions that needs to be further studied and developed in the near future, so that virtual idols would truly integrate into our lives and play their meaningful part in different fields with more possible impact not only economically, but also with more sustainable cultural and social influence.

**Acknowledgments.** The corresponding author Minling Lin and the other authors would like to express sincere appreciation to all the participants who contribute advise and data to this study.

## References

1. Rahma, S., Black, D.: The virtual ideal: virtual idols, cute technology and unclean biology. Continuum J. Media Cult. Stud. **22**(1), 37–50 (2008)

2. Guga, J.: Virtual idol Hatsune Miku. In: Brooks, A.L., Ayiter, E., Yazicigil, O. (eds.) Arts and Technology, pp. 36–44. Springer, Cham (2015). https://doi.org/10.1007/978-3-319-188 36-2_5

3. Thunderstorm: Research on the production and consumption of virtual idols. Nanjing Normal University (2019)

4. Guoming, Y., Yang, M.: Virtual idol: a new type of communication media with its own relational attributes. Journalism Writ. **10**, 68–73 (2020)

5. Galbraith, P.W., Karlin, J.G.: Idols and celebrity in Japanese media culture. Soc. Sci. Jpn. J. **16** (2013)

6. Kobayashi, H., Taguchi, T.: Virtual idol Hatsune Miku: case study of new production/consumption phenomena generated by network effects in Japan's online environment. Markets Globalization Dev. Rev. **3**(4), 3 (2019)

7. Liu, J.: Research of the business potentials of the AI virtual idols. Pub. Commun. Sci. Technol. **11**(249(24)), 124–125 (2019)

8. Osterwalder, A., Pigneur, Y.: Clarifying business models: origins, present, and future of the concept. Commun. Assoc. Inf. Syst. **16**, 1–28 (2005)

9. Belghiti, S., Ochs, A., Lemoine, J.F., Ba Dot, O.: The Phygital shopping experience: an attempt at conceptualization and empirical investigation. Academy of Marketing Science World Marketing Congress (2018)

10. Zurlo, F., Arquilla, V., Carella, G., Tamburello, M.C.: Designing acculturated phygital experiences. In: Diffused Transition & Design Opportunities, NAEMURA, vol. 11, no. 4, pp. 153–164 (2018)

11. Laura, Davis-Taylor: Let's get phygital. Sound Commun. **63**(1), 50–51 (2017)

12. Melekhova, A.S.: Phygital-technologies as a tool for developing efficient communication with today's customer. Vestnik Plekhanov Russ. Univ. Econ. **2**, 158–167 (2020)

# Mobile Application to Disseminate the History of Historical Buildings

A. Méndez[✉], C. Borja[✉], D. González[✉], A. Núñez[✉], and S. Zepeda[✉]

Metropolitan Autonomous University, Vasco de Quiroga 4871, Mexico City, Mexico
`{albanunez,sergioz}@dccd.mx`

**Abstract.** Most of the cities around the world have historical buildings, some of them are usually constituted as tourist places that people can visit; however, many others are not so well known and the inhabitants themselves tend to be unaware of their historical value and significance to the heritage of the city or the country. This paper presents the process of development of a mobile application prototype that pretend to help to disseminate the history of places or buildings with historical value. In this first case, the prototype was designed for an old building that used to be a cinema. The prototype aims to use Augmented Reality to disseminate the history of buildings, and at the same time preserve the history of the city through a mobile application that shows various audiovisual materials, like a timeline and a photo gallery and videos, which allow people to know the historical context of the building when it was in splendor.

**Keywords:** Adaptive and personalized interfaces · Heuristics and guidelines for design · Augmented reality

## 1 Introduction

The Historic Center of Mexico City was declared a World Heritage Site in 1987 by UNESCO [1]. It has approximately 1,500 buildings with historical relevance; however, only some have been classified as immovable historical monuments[1], these few concentrate the efforts of dissemination and preservation [3]. Consequently, some of the buildings considered as historical heritage go unnoticed, and their past and importance to the city are unknown by the inhabitants. Many of those buildings have been occupied as shopping centers, hotels, government agencies or to many other uses, making its relevance diffuse in the history of the city. For this reason, this research focuses on the important task of giving access to the history of historical sites little known.

It is considered that based on knowledge, the inhabitants could appropriate such spaces and reinforce their identity [4], this work seeks to help citizens to get involved with

---

[1] According to the Norms on Typical or Picturesque Zones of the Council of National Monuments, a Pro-perty of Historic Artistic Interest has formal and spatial architectural characteristics that stand out In Me-xico, the naming of historic buildings and monuments is in charge of the National Institute of Anthropology and History [2].

C. Stephanidis et al. (Eds.): HCII 2021, CCIS 1499, pp. 325–330, 2021.
https://doi.org/10.1007/978-3-030-90179-0_42

these sites that represent learning spaces, whose historical value cannot be articulated by the mere fact of being in front of them without knowing what they were or how they looked. In some cases, people have no idea of what was the meaning of "ruins and relics" of a bygone era that hardly resemble their original form [5].

Since some years ago, most developers are really interested in improve user experience and personalize interaction through different interaction design methods. As a result of it, different paradigm interaction has emerged, like Augmented Reality (AR). Alkhamisi defines AR as an emerging practice through which the real world is enhanced with computer-generated content, that is connected to particular places and/or events [6]. The AR "complements the users' sensory perception of the real world by adding computer-generated content to the user's environment and offers a new form of interactivity between the real and virtual worlds" [7], as a consequence, the Augmented Reality technology can be used to many purposes.

So, if we considered that the exhibition, recreation, observation and discovery of the historical and cultural content of an area through AR can promote commitment and participation [8], it could be possible to disseminate information of historical buildings through AR to increase the interest of the inhabitants in the historical past of the place, in consequence they could generate a new form of interaction with the city.

## 2 Mobile Application Prototype Development

As shown above, the use of Augmented Reality is an attractive and valuable way to show the attributes of those historical buildings that can not be visualized as in their original appearance, the uses that were given to them, their importance in the past, among other aspects. Sometimes only ruins remain of the historical buildings, but in other cases the physical space remains; however, its history has been forgotten. This project pretends to spread the history of historical building through Augmented Reality.

As a result, the selected space to start the project was part of the architectural program of the theaters-cinemas at the beginning of the twenties in Mexico City, it was the Olimpia Cinema. At the beginning, its characteristics made it a modern space, this place had one of the first projection rooms with sound in films; actually, the first sound film was screened there: The jazz singer [9]. Unfortunately, as a consequence of the affectations that Olimpia Cinema suffered after the 1985 earthquake it was closed and reopened ten years later. At the beginning of the XXI century, the site was adapted to be suitable for a new purpose, a commercial plaza with more than 300 commercial premises dedicated exclusively to the sale of computer equipment [10]. Nowadays, it is a commercial plaza called Olimpia, in honor of the old cinema.

Specifically, the methods used to develop the project were direct observation, structured observation and experimentation. These included the ideation and prototyping phases, as well as the application of usability tests and a heuristic evaluation. Additionally, it was through structured observation and from the opinions shared by users, that it was possible to identify failures and successes in interface designs, which were taken up again in the prototyping stage. Therefore, the first version was a low-fidelity prototype, it was designed based on the navigation map and on proposals generated in the ideation phase.

Hence, once the prototype was finished, it was subjected to a heuristic evaluation, in which the navigability of the interface was positively assessed, since it uses icons and graphic elements that are familiar to users; in addition, the memorability of the system seems correct, since it does not contain too many sections. The evaluation phase yielded pertinent information to improve the interface of the system.

However, due Covid-19 restrictions, it was not possible to perform tests at the building. Thus, the first evaluation was carried out with the low-fidelity prototype. Usability tests were executed, with people who satisfied the pre-defined user profile, certain tasks were assigned to them, observers took note of users' interaction with the application. The tests were aimed to trial the memorability, navigability and accessibility of the design, the results provided qualitative and quantitative data that allowed to make improvements to the prototype under development. Figure 1, shows the low-fidelity interfaces of the application.

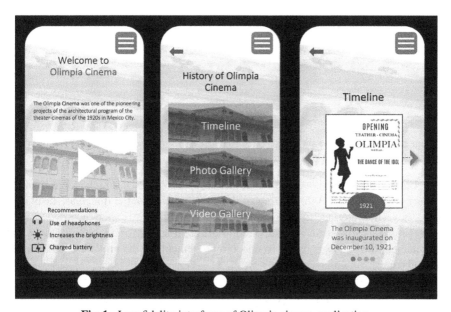

**Fig. 1.** Low fidelity interfaces of Olimpia cinema application.

In fact, one of the main targets of the project was to develop a user-friendly application, in order to accomplish that it was necessary to observe how fluid and effective the navigability was and if the icons were easily recognized and located by users.

Currently, we are working on providing different types of evaluation based on the categories provided in [11], from which we determined 4 different types of evaluation: a) Type of user perception, b) Performance improvement of task execution, c) Multi-user collaboration, d) Usability and experience. Metrics and heuristics are being developed for the evaluation of this type of applications based on augmented reality.

Here, Fig. 2 represents the navigation map, where Augmented Reality is indicated by number 3, this screen presents the loading bar; in 3.1 the active camera is shown;

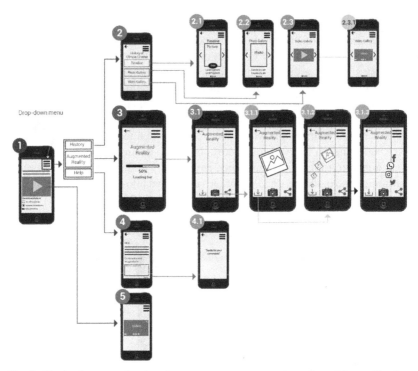

Drop-down menu

**Fig. 2.** Navigation map showing the routes to access to each section of the application.

in 3.1.1 the option of taking a selfie that includes AR objects is simulated and, finally, in screens 3.1.2 and 3.1.3 the options to download and share the image are displayed, Fig. 3, shows the interface to access to the Augmented Reality experience.

Consequently, four tests were applied to different users, from which valuable data was obtained, the data was useful to make improvements to the prototype, some of the obtained data is shown in Table 1.

**Table 1.**  Data collected from usability tests.

| Suggestion | Problem | Improvement |
|---|---|---|
| Change the icons of *recommendations* section | Users thought they were buttons | Change of the graphic form of icons in *recommendations* section |
| Make improvements to the appearance of buttons in *history* section | Only one user was not sure if the elements he saw were buttons | Adding labels to buttons |

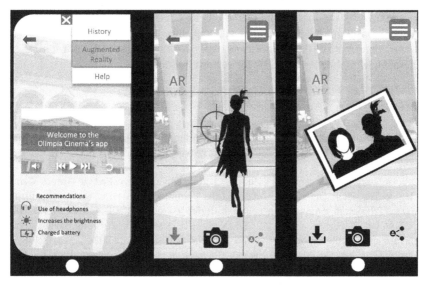

**Fig. 3.** Images of the interface to access to the Augmented Reality experience of Olimpia Cinema application.

## 3 Discussion

Day by day, the immersion of technology in society is greater. This also influences the ways in which culture and history are part of this new era. New types of interactions with digital content are emerging. In this research, we show how multimedia historical information through a mobile device allows visitors to play an active role in their visit to a historical place [12]. Creating new types of experiences and learnings that before could be difficult to imagine, today are possible through tangible interfaces (Interaction with virtual information through physical objects), Graphical User Interfaces (GUI), Interaction based on sensors or interfaces multimodal [13], all of them offer us a wide range of possibilities to create an immersion of the user and that, based on knowledge, they reflect on the spaces that surround them, in order to generate a link with the place and its history.

It is necessary to carry out new evaluation metrics to provide new heuristics to help improve user experiences in these types of applications [11]. The metrics for this project, the more it progresses, are closer and closer to the qualitative nature, since the impact that technology may have to increase interest in these spaces will be reflected in non-measurable ways. It is hoped that this project will help preserve the memory of Mexico City and that more inhabitants value its history.

## 4 Conclusions

This paper shows a prototype with a generic content structure for the dissemination of information about historical places considered as cultural heritage, which have lost recognition, due to the fact that they are in multiple contexts that make them go unnoticed or be unknown by the inhabitants of the cities. This research seeks to show how an Augmented Reality mobile application can contribute to generate interest in citizens to know and appropriate of their culture and history. As well as serving as a starting point to generate new mobile applications for various buildings.

## References

1. United Nations Educational, Scientific and Cultural Organization (UNESCO). Historic Downtown Mexico City and Xochimilco. https://whc.unesco.org/en/list/412. Accessed 6 Jun 2021
2. Official Diary, Decree declaring a Zone of Historic Monuments called the Historic Center of Mexico City, DOF. Graphic Workshops of the Nation, Mexico. http://www.mener.inah.gob.mx/archivos/cnmh_decreto_zmh_centro_historico_cd_de_mex.pdf. Accessed 6 Jun 2021
3. CONACULTA, Historic Center of CDMX, Tourist Destination, 2010, https://www.cultura.gob.mx/turismocultural/destino_mes/cd_mexico/. Accessed 8 Jun 2021
4. Martín, G., Reyes, A.: Management and conservation of the built cultural heritage. An approach to the valorization of the historic center of the city of Mérida. In: BAR International Series. BAR Publishing, England (2017).
5. Galatis, P., Gavalas, D., Kasapakis, V., Pantziou, G., Zaroliagis, C.: Mobile augmented reality guides in cultural heritage. In: Proceedings of the 8th EAI International Conference on Mobile Computing, Applications and Services, Cambridge, Great Britain, pp. 11–19 (2016)
6. Alkhamisi, A., Mostafa, M.: Rise of augmented reality: current and future application areas. Int. J. Internet Distrib. Syst. 1, 25–34 (2013)
7. Ibáñez, M., Portillo, A., Cabada, R., Barrón, M.: Impact of augmented reality technology on academic achievement and motivation of students from public and private Mexican schools. A case study in a middle-school geometry course. Comput. Educ. 145, 103734 (2020)
8. Koutromanos, G., Pittara, T., Tripoulas, C.: "Clavis Aurea": an augmented reality game for the teaching of local history. Eur. J. Eng. Res. Sci. Spec. Issue (EJERS) (2020). CIE, p. 1. https://doi.org/10.24018/ejers.2020.0.CIE.2310
9. CDMX 200 places, Olimpia Cinema. https://www.cdmx200lugares.com/cine-olimpia/#.YLl 8kOuZK9Y. Accessed 3 Jun 2021
10. La Jornada: The legendary Olimpia Cinema disappears, a new cultural crime, https://www.jornada.com.mx/2002/07/24/02an1cul.php?printver=1. Accessed 02 Jun 2021
11. Tiefenbacher, P., Lehment, N.H., Rigoll, G.: Augmented reality evaluation: a concept utilizing virtual reality. In: Shumaker, R., Lackey, S. (eds.) VAMR 2014. LNCS, vol. 8525, pp. 226–236. Springer, Cham (2014). https://doi.org/10.1007/978-3-319-07458-0_22
12. Armanno, G., Bottino, A., Martina, A.: SkyLineDroid: an outdoor mobile augmented reality application for virtual heritage. In: Proceedings International Conference on Cultural Heritage and Tourism, pp. 91–96. Recent Researches in Engineering Mechanics, Urban & Naval Transportation and Tourism (2012)
13. Kassahun, M., Champion, E.: A comparison of immersive realities and interaction methods: cultural learning in virtual heritage. Front. Robot. AI 6, 1–14 (2019)

# Digital Representation of Virtual Reality Environments of Gothic Choirs Using Photogrammetric 3D Models: Monasteries of Yuste and Nájera

Carles Pàmies[✉], Isidro Navarro, Alberto Sánchez Riera, and Ernest Redondo

Escola Superior d'Arquitectura de Barcelona ETSAB – Universitat Politécnica de Catalunya
UPC, Avinguda Diagonal, 649, 08028 Barcelona, Spain
carles.pamies.sauret@upc.edu

**Abstract.** Digital capture of real environments requires a series of techniques that brings together photogrammetry and 3D modelling to create Virtual Reality environment (VRE). In the specific case of the Gothic choirs, the capturing process requires a concrete systematization of all the areas through overlapping series of pictures of multiple sculpted details to avoid areas the complex environment of the church in which the stalls are located. Yuste and Nájera not covered or poorly lit areas. The complex environment of the church in which the stalls are located needs systematic and comprehensive planning approach to get operational data for its representation. This paper reports on the project to digitize the Yuste and Nájera monasteries which have been created using high resolution pictures and graphical documentation to complete disappeared areas. The work suggests that complete sequences from many different angles and distances should be performed from general shots to series of details by very repetitive overlapping. It contributes to create multiple control points and, therefore, an effective and accurate point cloud to be processed for the conservation and enhancement of the cultural heritage.

**Keywords:** Photogrammetry · Gotic art · 3D models · Virtual Reality · Monastery · Chorus · Heritage · UX

## 1 Introduction

### 1.1 Heritage Digitalization

The preservation of Cultural heritage through digital technology [1] has evolved to the present day in the form of the creation of 3D models [2] to produce complete, detailed, and photorealistic documentation. Geometric as well as chromatic aspects, work techniques, state of preservation, etc., are documented using digitization processes that can be saved and used on different platforms and utilities.

In order to get an accurate and effective 3D model a specific process must be carried out: [3] data processing and saving, 3D data archiving and management, 3D data visualization and dissemination, 3D data replication and reproduction.

C. Stephanidis et al. (Eds.): HCII 2021, CCIS 1499, pp. 331–338, 2021.
https://doi.org/10.1007/978-3-030-90179-0_43

## 1.2  Objectives

The main project objectives are: (a) Digitization of specific closed coral environments in precise detail, for the creation of virtual reality environments. (b) capture an accurate High dense point Cloud by means of photographs and overlapping of the elements carved in the maximum detail, for use in different LOD (levels of detail) [4]. (c) Multiple formats data exportation to be used on different platforms and programs [5].

The creation process of complex digitizations of the coral environments is presented for. (a) Neat documentation of the carved elements; (b) the consultation and study; (c) storage of the data in favor of the preservation of the environments; (d) comparison between the various sets; (e) follow-up the study of the chorus condition in time; (f) restoration work support, and digital and physical reconstruction and integration purposes.

## 1.3  Study Area

This work focusses on two unusual Gothic Choir stalls: those of the monasteries of Yuste and Nájera located on top of the choir, at the base of the nave of the church [6–9]. The Gothic choir stalls in the Cathedrals were normally located in the centre of the nave, opposite the altar, although many of them suffered damages (from conflicts, fires, etc.). Choirs on high, frequent in monastic churches, are not very numerous and have barely survived for that period.

**Fig. 1.**  General views of Monastery of Yuste Choir and Monastery of Najera Choir

YUSTE: Relocated in the high choir, its stalls after the confiscations in 1835–1840 were dismantled, divided and moved to the parishes of Cuacos (30 low chairs and 7 high chairs) and Garganta de la Olla (19 high chairs) [7]. In the restoration of 1968, it was recovered and placed in its current location (Fig. 1) [6].

NÁJERA: Originally it consisted of fifty chairs in both the high and low choirs (Fig. 1). At present, after the exclaustration, confiscations in 1835–40, the Carlist wars, etc., and until the restoration that took place between 1908 and 1912, 36 high chairs and 27 low chairs are preserved [9].

# 2   Methodology

The two works in the monasteries of Yuste and Nájera are intended to be: exhaustive in millimetre detail of the carvings. Its virtual reconstruction allows to visualize the choral environments in their original site in the nave of the church, to contextualize their location and to facilitate VRE immersion. Thus, Geometric as well as chromatic aspects, in turn testimony of materials, work techniques, state of preservation, etc., are documented using photogrammetry techniques. It facilitates spatial understanding of the liturgical space in the church, and the coral element and its parts.

Specific Documentation about choral environments, their construction, functions, development over time, iconography, location, etc. [10] has been considered to complete missed information in a thorough and exhaustive way.

## 2.1   Image Acquisition

The constant overlapping in shot series is crucial for optimal results [13]. In this case, due to poorly lit areas, very long sequences were taken of adjacent and overlapping photos up to 80% to minimize errors and produce continuity in images and shared contexts and for proper alignment in digital processing. The photos with underexposed areas have been subsequently treated in brightness and contrast one by one to obtain the maximum details, which is essential in 3D processing.

The manual camera settings used, with very low ISO 100 and long exposures (up to 15 s) obeys the premise of obtaining maximum detail. LED lighting lamps were used to neutralise dim areas and to equalise areas receiving direct natural light.

Index of images taken per day of work:

**Yuste Monastery**
Day 1: 1,420 photographs (Fig. 2):
Superimposed generals at different distances, general sequences in relation to the nave of the church and the altar, general sequences low choir and high choir, central lectern sequences, church nave sequences and general ceiling and surroundings, sequences high choir panels, sequences various bass choir, sequences central lectern, sequences 180° bass choir backrests panels, general sequences choral set.

Day 2: 1,405 photographs:
High choir backrest panels sequences, high choir misericordias sequence, high choir backrest panels sequence, ground sequences, low choir misericordias sequences, low choir misericordias sequences, low choir armrests 180° sequences, high choir floor sequences, Sequences 180° high choir misericordias, sequences 180° high choir armrest, general sequences in relation to church nave, general sequences of choir, sequences in the church nav.

**Nájera Monastery.**
Day 1: 1,139 photographs (Fig. 2):
Superimposed generals at different distances, general ceiling and intone of the church, general floors, high choir generals, high choir sequences at medium distance, high

relief sequences, high choir backrest panels sequences, Sequences 180° misericords high chorus, sequences 180° armrest high chorus.

Day 2: 1.153 photographs:
Sequences 180° high choir armrest, high choir floor sequences, entrance door sequences, sequences grilles and floor in relation to the nave of the church, sequences statue king sancho, sequences upper cresting, low seats sequences, sequences low chorus misericords, sequences low chorus armrests.

Day 3: 574 photographs + 546 church environments:
Sequences low choir armrests, sequences low choir dorsal panels, general sequences in relation to the nave of the church, sequences in the nave of the church, sequences in the chapels of the tombs of kings.

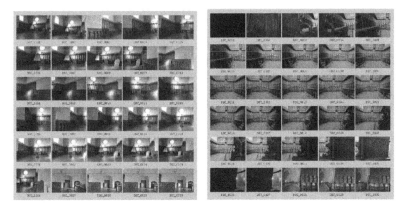

**Fig. 2.** Beginning sequences of general choir and high Chorus of Yuste and Nájera

## 2.2  Texturized Model Generation

Alignment of overlapping image sequences is needed for point cloud calculation. A three-dimensional mesh was created. It includes colorization and texturization of the environment for the creation of the 3D virtual environment.

Generation through Reality Capture software of a Point Cloud. The program uses global alignment of the sequences taken and makes a global aligned point cloud, integrating the sequences of 180° photos into it (Fig. 3).

**Fig. 3.** Overlapping general sequences and 180° sequences of back panels in Yuste with results

## 2.3  Creation of Virtual Reality Environment

When the point cloud is usable polygonal model can be generated from it (Fig. 4). Models are rendered in different formats for different uses and processed in different softwares afterwards: .XYZ (point cloud, .FBX (mesh) and .OBJ (mesh), along with textured images (.PNG and .JPEG) in 8K and 16K.

**Fig. 4.**  Point Cloud creation of Monasterio de Nájera

## 2.4  Validation and Accuracy

Photographs are taken with real tape measure in several stalls (Fig. 5) for precise and comparative millimetre references. This allows a scalable approach to the real measures of the environment and thus the convenient full-scale reconstructions in virtual applications in the future [14].

**Fig. 5.**  Example of measure reference in Yuste

## 3  Results

Two high resolution virtual models were obtained. These allow complete virtual reconstruction of scenarios for different purposes: study, comparison, virtual uses in different devices, projections [15, 16, 17].

a. Monastery of Yuste: It consists of 61 stalls, 31 high and 30 low. Each stall has a misericord and two armrests. The backrest change from narrow friezes carved in the high ashlar and complete panels in the lower ashlar. POINT CLOUD: Generated by a total of 2,480 photos.

b. Monastery of Nájera: It consists of 63 stalls, 36 high and 27 low. Each stall has a misericord and two armrests. The backrest change, in the upper ones there is Gothic tracery and narrow friezes carved at the bottom. In the lower row there would be complete panels with figures of saints, although only 3 of the 30 remain. POINT CLOUD: Generated by a total of 2,628 photos.

## 4   Conclusions

The use of long sequences of overlapping photos (overlapping) is very useful to fit the different alignments of control points. The subsequent retouching of the shots manually one by one with underexposed areas for the visualization of the elements in darkness is advisable. It seems to be essential for the correct alignment of the series of photos.

The complexity of the sculpted reliefs of each chair demands that photographs should be taken around 180° degrees of each piece (misericords, armrests and back panels and friezes), for which the individual reliefs must be perfectly reflected in the global point cloud of the coral ensemble and must be able to be identified and joined by control points. This assembly of multiple sockets of each piece is facilitated if the general sockets of the stalls are made in medium detail and the processing software identifies the parts to add the sockets in 180°. With this the degree of detail is amplified to a few millimeters and a set is assembled with hundreds of 180° shots in conjunction with the general set shots. The resulting point cloud is very dense and involves a few thousand photos and a resulting 3D model of great size.

The 3D documentation in detail should be a source of heritage field and its availability will play a vital role in future studies of Art and environments.

The uses of large models in virtual reality programs present management problems, and some Levels of Detail (LODs) are used to manage them. In this work, two models of great detail and large size were obtained as a basis to reduce resolution and size later. This makes necessary to use a computer with higher performance to move these large size models.

In this work we have shown the multidimensional process of digital capture to obtain two 3D environments of monastic Gothic choir stalls, and some notes and questions to consider for future similar works.

The uses that are intended for the models created are: Preservation and archive of coral environments, interactive 3D, Virtual Reality and Augmented Reality.

**Acknowledgements.** This research was supported by the National Program of Research, Development and Innovation aimed to the Society Challenges with the references BIA2016-77464-C2-1-R &amp; BIA2016-77464-C2-2-R, both of the National Plan for Scientific Research, Development and Technological Innovation 2013–2016, Government of Spain, titled "Gamificación para la enseñanza del diseño urbano y la integración en ella de la participación ciudadana

(ArchGAME4CITY)", &amp; "Diseño Gamificado de visualización 3D con sistemas de realidad virtual para el estudio de la mejora de competencias motivacionales, sociales y espaciales del usuario (EduGAME4CITY)" .(AEI/FEDER, UE).

## References

1. Bedford, J.: Photogrammetric Applications for Cultural Heritage: Guidance for Good Practice. Historic England, UK (2017)
2. Tucci, G., Bonora, V., Conti, A., Fiorini, L.: High-quality 3D models and their use in a cultural heritage conservation project. In: 2017 26th International CIPA Symposium on International Archives of the Photogrammetry, Remote Sensing and Spatial Information Sciences, Ottawa, Canada, 28 August–01 September 2017, vol. XLII-2/W5 (2017)
3. Pavlidis, G., Koutsoudis, A., Arnaoutoglou, F., Tsioukas, V., Chamzas, C.: Methods for 3D digitization of cultural heritage. J. Cult. Herit. **8**(1), 93–98 (2007)
4. Ogleby, C.: Handbook of Heritage Photogrammetry. Australian Government Publishing Service, Canberra (1985)
5. .Callieri, M., Ranzuglia, G., Dellepiane, M., Cignoni, P., Scopigno, R.: Meshlab as a complete open tool for the integration of photos and colour with high-resolution 3D geometry data. In: Proceedings of the 40th Conference in Computer Applications and Quantitative Methods in Archaeology, CAA 2012, pp. 406–416 (2012)
6. Serradilla Martín, C.: La sillería del Coro del Monasterio de Yuste. Asociación Cultural Amigos de la Vera, Spain (1993)
7. Perla De Las Parras, A., Victoria, M., Caba, S.: El Monasterio de San Jerónimo de Yuste Facultad de geografía e Historia – Departamento de Historia del Arte UNED Universidad Nacional de Educación a Distancia (España). Escuela Internacional de Doctorado. Programa de Doctorado en Historia e Historia del Arte y Territorio (2018)
8. Guadan y Gil, I.: Ensayo sobre la sillería del coro alto de Monasterio de Santa María la Real de Nájera. Instituto de Estudios Riojanos, Logroño (1961)
9. García Prado, J.: Los coros alto y bajo de Santa María La Real de Nájera (La Rioja). Logroño, Spain (1993)
10. Kraus, D., Kraus, H.: The Gothic Choirstalls of Spain. Kegan Paul, Cop. 1986, London, Routledge (1989)
11. Mateo Gómez, I.: Temas profanos en la escultura gótica española. Las sillerías de coro (1979)
12. Block, E.C.: Corpus of Medieval Misericords, Iberia (n.d.). ISBN 9782503514994
13. Hellman, T., Lahti, M.: Photogrammetric 3D modeling for virtual reality (pdf). SeAMK School of Technology (2018)
14. Han, J., Shen, S.: Scalable point cloud meshing for image-based large-scale 3D modelling. Visual Computing for Industry, Biomedicine, and Art (2019)
15. Bekele, M.K., et al.: A survey of augmented, virtual, and mixed reality for cultural heritage. J. Comput. Cult. Heritage **11**(2), 1–36 (2018)
16. Redondo, E., et al.: Game4city. Gamification for citizens through the use of virtual reality made available to the masses. Viability study in two public events. In: Zaphiris, P., Ioannou, A. (eds.) HCII 2020. LNCS, vol. 12206, pp. 315–332. Springer, Cham (2020). https://doi.org/10.1007/978-3-030-50506-6_23
17. Fernández-Palacios, B.J., Morabito, D., Remondino, F.: Access to complex reality-based 3D models using virtual reality solutions. J. Cult. Heritage **23**, 40–48 (2017)

# Visualization of Patterns and Impressions in YOSAKOI Costumes

Yuka Takahashi$^{(\boxtimes)}$ and Namgyu Kang

Future University Hakodate, 116-2 Kamedanakano, Hakodate 0418655, Hokkaido, Japan
{b1017010,kang}@fun.ac.jp

**Abstract.** YOSAKOI is a very famous festival held in Sapporo, Hokkaido. Since the costume used in the YOSAKOI require originality of expression, each time's costume is different from the others. So, the dancers themselves are often involved in the production of costumes for their team. However, it is not easy to share vague costume patterns when the dancers determine patterns and create costumes with other dancers. And the determining pattern takes a lot of time also. Therefore, in this study, we focused on the costume patterns used in YOSAKOI and conducted experiments to visualize the relationship between patterns and impressions. We performed the SD method and Factor analysis using 12 types of paired adjectives in the experiment, with ten patterns as impression evaluation stimuli. As a result of Factor analysis, we could extract the following three factors: "Luxury feeling," "Powerful feeling," and "Casual feeling." We could also visualize the ten patterns based on the average of the factor scores and the significant difference of each pattern, the impressions of patterns. This visualized information becomes a standard to understand each costume pattern. This standard helps the dancers understand the various costume patterns and sympathy with others to determine a final costume pattern for the YOSAKOI festival on the co-creation process.

**Keywords:** YOSAKOI · Costume · Patterns

## 1   Introduction

The YOSAKOI Soran Festival (after this called "YOSAKOI") is held in Sapporo City in Japan and has has become a new tradition of early summer in Hokkaido.

Many dance teams compete with performance with an unforgettable dance on YOSAKOI. The judging criteria of the competition are "whether the dance performance has originality" and "whether the dance performance brings excitement and energy to the viewers" [1].

Therefore, many dancers themselves participate in the creation process, named co-creation process, of costume for YOSAKOI to satisfy the originality criterion.

In the co-creation process to create a new costume for YOSAKOI, the dancers themselves select patterns and colors based on the repeated communication with others, whether the impression of the chosen costume matches that of the performance YOSAKOI.

© Springer Nature Switzerland AG 2021
C. Stephanidis et al. (Eds.): HCII 2021, CCIS 1499, pp. 339–346, 2021.
https://doi.org/10.1007/978-3-030-90179-0_44

This process needs much effort to build an open relationship to share each opinion and discuss with others. However, there are many problems cases where the images of each other differ during this co-creation process. For example, in a dancer team's costume-making process, a dancer suggests that the dancer team select a costume pattern with a 'Modern' look. However, the image of 'Modern' is different for each dancer of the dance team. That means it is difficult to share a standard image of what kind of costume pattern the other person has in mind. As a result, they need a lot of time for discussion in the creation costume process, which increases the burden on the dancers. When the dancers determine the color and pattern of costume for YOSAKOI with empathy with others only quickly, there can concentrate on developing their dance performance for the YOSAKOI competition.

That means it is necessary to clarify and visualize the impression above costume patterns or colors associated with the ambiguous image words used during discussions in the co-creation process. However, only a few papers envision the relationship between patterns and image words used in dance costumes. From this background, we focus on a costume pattern for YOSAKOI in this study. Therefore, this study aims to clarify and visualize the relationship between image words and YOSAKOI costume patterns. The result of this research helps the co-creation process to determine a pattern for YOSAKOI.

**Fig. 1.** Examples of various costume patterns on YOSAKOI festival

There is Inoue's research about 'Color Kansei Modeling System,' as a related study. According to the research, when 'designers' and 'clients' participate together in the design process, it isn't easy to recognize and share common Kansei as a specific form. Because there are many ambiguities due to the expression of a design, it differs depending on each individual's Kansei (= sensibility). In other words, it isn't easy to understand the Kansei of the co-producers and the target user's Kansei mutually, so there is a possibility of misinterpreting the concept. As a result, they spend more than necessary time in the preparatory stage in the co-creating process, such as reconciling the co-creators opinions and deciding on the concept. Therefore, Inoue proposed a system that promotes communication among co-creators by visualizing and expressing to color the ambiguous Kansei.

However, there are some researches related to color in the co-creation process, only a few researches related to patterns. Moreover, there are not any approaches to costume patterns in the co-creation process. That is why we focus on the costume patterns for YOSAKOI and will attempt to construct a system based on this study's results.

## 2  Methods

We experimented with clarifying the relationship between image words and costume patterns for YOSAKOI for the co-creation process.

### 2.1  Selecting a Pattern

Firstly, we selected 30 patterns based on the book, named Japanese style and beautiful material [2] with some experimental collaborators. All of them have experience participated in the YOSAKOI as a dancer. The author, named Takahashi, has participated in the YOSAKOI as a dancer for three years also. Next, we selected only ten final patterns for the experimental collaborators with the experimental collaborators to not lose objectivity (Fig. 1). Because too many patterns become a burden to a participant to evaluate with 12 evaluation items. They selected the eight patterns as the costume patterns used in YOSAKOI a lot. We added the two patterns, which were consisted of the only straight line. These two line patterns had been used many times in other researches about evaluating Patterns. And we changed all the colorful patterns into black and white because the influence of color is considered in evaluating visual impressions of patterns [3, 4]. This study focused on only the patterns without color elements. Figure 2 shows the selected ten Patterns.

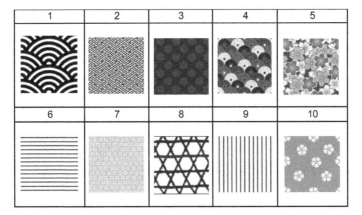

**Fig. 2.**  Ten patterns

### 2.2  Impressionistic Evaluation

Each participant evaluated the ten costume patterns using the following 12 evaluation items of the SD method; "Pure - Dirty", "Pretty - Ugly", "Mild - Violent", "Cheerful - Bovine", "Natural - Artificial", "Peaceful - Clear", "Fancy - Quite", "Elegant - Inelegant", "Dynamic - Static", "Modern – Traditional", "Gentle - Immodest", and "Noble - Vulgar."

These 12 evaluation adjectives were extracted from the IRI image scale as related research [5] with the seven experimental collaborators. The SD method clarifies and visualizes the vague impression against an object.

All of the 12 items had five evaluation scales. For example, "very pure,"-"pure,"-"neither pure nor dirty,"-"dirty," and "very dirty."

Fifty-four university students participated in this evaluation experiment. This evaluation experiment was conducted from October 3 to 7, 2020.

## 3  Analysis and Discussion

### 3.1  Results of Factor Analysis

The results of the impression evaluation using the SD method were analyzed by Factor analysis.

**Table 1.** Result of factor analysis

| Adjective | | Factor 1 | Factor 2 | Factor 3 |
|---|---|---|---|---|
| Gentle | Immodest | 0.867 | -0.104 | -0.026 |
| Noble | Vulgar | 0.772 | 0.025 | -0.116 |
| Pure | Dirty | 0.564 | 0.039 | 0.096 |
| Elegant | Inelegant | 0.511 | 0.079 | 0.224 |
| Fancy | Quite | -0.039 | 0.899 | 0.048 |
| Dynamic | Static | -0.26 | 0.697 | -0.060 |
| Peaceful | Clear | -0.023 | -0.025 | 0.747 |
| Natural | Artificial | 0.031 | 0.096 | 0.640 |
| Cheerful | Bovine | -0.121 | -0.071 | 0.425 |
| Contribution ratio | | 0.216 | 0.148 | 0.137 |
| Cumulative contribution ratio | | 0.216 | 0.364 | 0.501 |

We extracted a total of nine adjective-pair items with factor loadings of 0.4 or higher for factors with eigenvalues of 1 or higher. After that, we adopted the following three factors based on the magnitude of the initial eigenvalues and the Attenuation status (Table 1). The first factor had a strong relationship with the evaluation items of "Gentle," "Noble," "Pure," and "Elegant." Based on these extracted adjectives, we interpreted the first factor as "Luxury feeling." The second factor has a strong relationship with the evaluation items of "Fancy" and "Dynamic." Based on these extracted adjectives, we interpreted the second factor as "Powerful feeling." Finally, the third factor had a strong relationship with the evaluation items of "Peaceful," "Natural," and "Cheerful." Based on these extracted adjectives, we interpreted the second factor as "Casual feeling."

## 3.2   Mean of Factor Scores for Each Pattern and Significance Difference Results

The ten patterns were arranged based on the order of each pattern's factor scores. Figure 3, 4 and 5 show the results of the significant differences in each costume pattern.

The highest factor score of "Luxury feeling" was pattern 4, followed by patterns 5 and 10 (Fig. 3). All of these three were patterns with flowers. That means the "Luxury feeling" is more likely to be perceived when flowers are arranged in an orderly fashion. The lowest factor scores of "Luxury feeling" were pattern 8, 9, and 6. From this result, costume patterns formed by straight lines are less likely to evoke a "Luxury feeling" due to their simple structure.

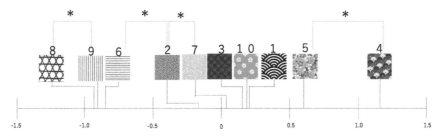

**Fig. 3.** The order of the "Luxury feeling."

The highest factor score of "Powerful feeling" was pattern 4 and followed by pattern 5, in which many flowers were densely packed (Fig. 4). Patterns 4 and 5 with densely packed flowers were ranked lower than pattern 10 with fewer blankly packed flowers.

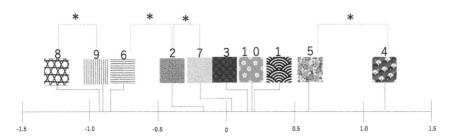

**Fig. 4.** The order of the "Powerful feeling."

This result means even if a flower is used in a costume pattern, it is easier to feel a "Powerful feeling" if there are fewer blank areas. The lowest factor scores of "Powerful feeling" were patterns 6 and followed by pattern 9. That means a simple costume pattern formed by only straight lines is unlikely to produce the "Powerful feeling" identical to the result of the "Luxury feeling."

The highest factor score of "Casual' feeling" was pattern 10 and followed by patterns 5 and 4 (Fig. 5). This result shows the patterns with flowers tend to give the "Casual' feeling" also. The lowest factor score of "Casual' feeling" was pattern 2 and followed patterns 9, 6, and 8.

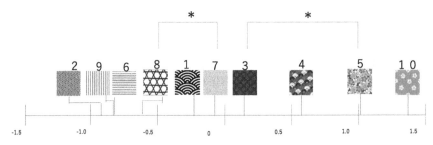

**Fig. 5.** The order of the "Casual feeling."

Figures 6 and 7 show the distribution map with these three factors' scores. If there is a visualized costume pattern information using multiple impressions like this distribution map in the co-creation process to determine a costume pattern for YOSAKOI, it will work as a common standard material based on many dancers themselves when many dancers discuss and determine a costume pattern for YOSAKOI.

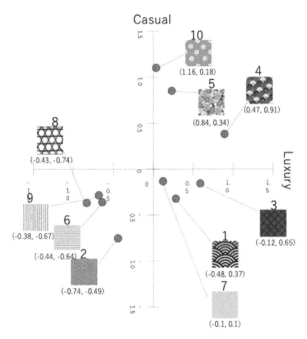

**Fig. 6.** The graph of "Luxury feeling" and "Casual feeling"

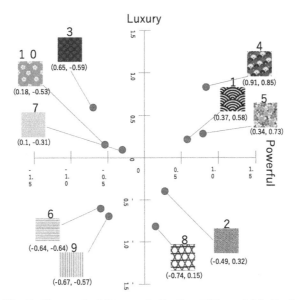

**Fig. 7.** The graph of "Luxury feeling" and "Powerful feeling"

## 4  Conclusion

In this study, we extracted the following three keywords, "Luxury," "Dynamism," and "Casual," by evaluating the impression from only ten patterns for YOSAKOI, considering the participants' burden in the evaluation experiment. However, these three keywords may work as common standards when many dancers discuss a costume pattern for the next TOSAKOI festival even though these ten patterns cannot cover all costume patterns for YOSAKOI. In other words, when the dancers determine a costume pattern for the YOSAKOI festival based on the discussion with other dancers, this standard will be a start line for the debate. Moreover, this standard helps the dancers understand the various costume patterns and sympathy with others to determine a final costume pattern for the YOSAKOI festival on co-creation process. That means if we gather more costume patterns as many as possible and make a database with the collected various costume patterns.

We will experiment on how the dancers evaluate these visualized standards for their co-create process in the future. And we will try to create a database of YOSAKOI costume patterns by accumulating data through additional experiments using various costume patterns. We will also try to apply the database to the construction of a system that supports pattern determination.

## References

1. What is the YOSAKOI Soran Festival? https://app.yosakoi-soran.jp/about.html - english. Accessed 8 Feb 2021
2. Inoue, T., Tazaki, Y., Kato, T.: Collaborative Design Support System Using KANSEI Visualization. J. Jpn. Soc. Kansei Eng. **9**(2), 329–334 (2010)

3. Tamura, Y.: Japanese style and beautiful material. Gijutsu-Hyohron Co., Ltd., Japan, MA (1992)
4. Qing, H., Motoko, Y., Morikawa, A.: Verification of the influence of pleating on visual impression of check patterns by using paper models. J. Text. Prod. Consumption Sci. **49**, 49–64 (2008)
5. Akira, N., Hashimoto, R., Kato, Y.: Psychological and physiological influences of presentation methods and colors of clothes on wearer. J. Jpn. Res. Assoc. Text. End-Uses **48**, 853–862 (2007)
6. Baek, C.-H., Park, S.-O., Kim, H.-S.: The analysis of emotion adjective for LED light colors by using Kobayashi scale and I.R.I scale. J. Korean Inst. Illum. Electr. Installation Eng. **25**(10), 1–13 (2011)

# From Text to Image: Image Application and Design Transformation of Traditional Cultural IP Resources – A Case Study of the Classic of Mountains and Seas

Jie Zhou[✉] and Jingyi Cui

East China University of Science and Technology, Shanghai 200237, China

**Abstract.** Traditional culture needs to be re-disseminated via visual design to achieve enhanced value, particularly in the era of popular new media communication and crossover cooperation. There is much important text in historical books and records that contains abundant historical and humanistic tradition and values. However, due to its professional nature in terms of literal expression and knowledge background, such extremely valuable historical text only circulates in a limited academic community. In fact, such text could serve as excellent materials for cultural mining in the era of new media communication. In this Article, the author takes the example of The Classic of Mountains and Sees whose text exerts profound influence on description of mystical images in literary works through the ages. After going through the main processes i.e. close reading of text, encapsulation of the theme, innovative design and crossover cooperation, the author completed the transition from text to images, from academic level to arts, from theories to practice, hoping to create a research approach and paradigm for image conversion of traditional culture.

**Keywords:** From text to images · The classic of mountains and seas · Cross-media design

## 1 Introduction

The Classic of Mountains and Seas, which was written from the middle and late Warring States to the early and middle of Han Dynasty, can be regarded as the originator of Chinese fantasy books. It is most widely known for its fairy tale and the image of gods and beasts. Compared with God and man, the description of supernatural animals in the Classic of Mountains and Seas is filled with romanticism and imagination. The supernatural images are mostly composed of human body, fish body and snake body, which are usually endowed with the ability to change nature. The fantastic ideas and humanistic wonders in the book provide powerful creative inspiration for later generations. As the first piece of ancient Chinese mythology, the Classic of Mountains and Seas plays an important role. Exploring the aesthetic value of gods and beasts is also a basic problem that must be confronted in design research.

C. Stephanidis et al. (Eds.): HCII 2021, CCIS 1499, pp. 347–355, 2021.
https://doi.org/10.1007/978-3-030-90179-0_45

## 2  Aesthetic Characteristics of Image Writing in the Classic of Mountains and Seas

### 2.1  The Ferocious Beauty of Grotesque Images

The images of gods and beasts in Book of Mountains and Seas are mostly endowed with natural abilities or attributes that human beings do not have. The harsh living environment made the ancestors want to obtain more powerful power, so they hope to have the teeth and eyes of wild animals through compassionate witchcraft, so as to acquire sharper sense of smell and vision. So they will gain the ability of animals, integrated with the characteristics of their own fantasy, to create a supernatural image. Take the Queen Mother of the West as an example. According to the Book of Mountains and Seas, the Queen Mother of the West has fluffy hair, jade jewelry, tiger teeth and leopard tail. The Queen Mother of the West lives in the cave and likes howling. There are three bluebirds on her side that usually forage for her. She is in Kunlun Mountain, responsible for heaven disaster, the five elements of the murderous spirits. In the ancient matriarchal society, the image of Queen Mother of the West is more like a female leader. Combining her with the animals with distinctive properties, it manifests the primitive worship of the clan.

In the case of the bronze ware, the ferocious decoration is a kind of historical progress and the embodiment of human's desire for stronger power. Its mystery and terror are just combined with this irresistible historical force. In addition, it also displays the aesthetic concept that early human beings began to express.

### 2.2  The Beauty of Reincarnation in the Cycle of Life and Death

Death and reincarnation run through almost every national myth. Probing into the value and extinction of life is an eternal topic of mankind. The Classic of Mountains and Seas breaks the boundaries between species and integrates human beings with everything else in the world. "Shanhaijing Dahuangxijing" records the story of Zhuan Xu's resurrection from death: "there is a fish dying, named Yufu. Zhuan Xu recovered after his death. When the wind blows from the north, the sky is a big water spring, and the snake turns into a fish, it is a fish-woman. Zhuan Xu was revived after his death. Although Zhuan Xu died, he could be reborn in another form, and his life was extended [1]. In this way, there is no longer a clear boundary between survival and death, and the exchange of information between species reflects the primitive ancestors' simple and wonderful yearning for life.

Furthermore, these gods are skilled at fighting against nature and forces, and they have heroic tragic beauty. For example, Nu Wa is submerged in the East Sea and turns into a Jingwei bird, while Kua Fu dies of thirst and becomes Deng Lin These images indicate that life is a struggle, and death is a persistence, which suggests that the primitive ancestors are indomitable in the face of nature and powerful hostile forces. The ancestors added this discussion of the meaning of life to the fantasy mythological world.

### 2.3  The Aesthetic Consciousness of Reverence for Nature

As an ancient book reflecting the life of the primitive ancestors, people transfer the spirit of life struggle to gods and beasts, expecting to come to the happiness and resist disasters. In this article, there is a beast named Zhu Jiuyin, who is a snake with a human face. When he closes his eyes, night will fall, and when he opens his eyes, the sky will be bright. He doesn't need to eat, sleep, and can command the wind and rain. He seems to have the occult power to control the light of heaven and earth. Most of the gods in the Classic of Mountains and Seas are the incarnations of the seasons of mountains, rivers, wind and moon. While the ancestors venerated them, they also expressed their reverence for the unknown forces. In ancient sacrificial activities, people gradually entered a state of illusory indulgence by toasting, roaring, waving and jumping. Crazy dancing and devout praying were willing to communicate with the gods. The real world before us is blurred into the void, creating the illusion of gods and beasts.

The Classic of Mountains and Seas not only has the aesthetic characteristics of gods mentioned above in image and concept, but also has its own characteristics in language and text writing. These obscure languages also hinder the prevalence of book in modern society.

## 3  The Disadvantages of the Classic of Mountains and Seas in Modern Communication

### 3.1  Language Patterns Affect Offspring

The language of the Classic of Mountains and Seas not only contains the language characteristics of the book, but also includes some more historical vocabulary. The varied artistic techniques in the book are the spiritual aspiration and beautiful fantasy of people in different eras. Many of the later generations involved in the description of this kind of image, most of them used the Classic of Mountains and Seas as the template. For instance, Zhouli, fengshenzhuan in Ming Dynasty and Liaozhai Zhiyi in Qing Dynasty can be explored.

### 3.2  Obscure Words

Nevertheless, in terms of writing style, there are great differences between the Classic of Mountains and Seas and modern Chinese. First of all, a large number of rare words are employed, and the readers do not know the pronunciation of the words themselves, nor do they comprehend their meaning, which is one of the direct causes of the obstruction in modern communication, such as "quality" and "quality". [2] Secondly, from the perspective of writing, there are few characters in sentence pattern, many of them are omitted, and they are concise to the point, so that modern people not know their meaning.

### 3.3  Miraculous Species

Thirdly, the description of strange gods and animals in the Classic of Mountains and Seas seems to be a combination of multiple species in modern times. "There are animals on it, which are like cattle and hedgehog hair. They are called Qiongqi and sound like dogs. They are cannibals [2]". This is a description of Qiongqi, a ferocious animal. Translated into modern Chinese, Qiongqi is a cow like creature with hedgehog like spines. It sounds like a dog barking and feeds on human beings. The description of similar species is beyond the imagination of modern people. Exaggerated description and its mystery will make people think it is preposterous, which greatly restricts the literary investigation of the Classic of Mountains and Seas. Owing to the recondite expression in the text, more audiences have only heard the name of the Classic of Mountains and Seas, and they are very unfamiliar with the content and story, which has caused a lot of inconvenience to the further dissemination of it.

Text-based information transmission has brought visual impairment and reading fatigue to people's reading and comprehension, and it is difficult to construct a complete image only by text. However, if the obscure text is visualized to assist readers' understanding, it will reduce the difficulty of information acquisition and greatly enhance people's interest in reading [3]. When receiving information, the audience is more inclined to accept the information products produced by new media technologies such as sound, film and painting. As a result, based on the mixture of information visualization and text, it is the direction of this paper to transform complex abstract information into clear visual image symbols.

## 4 Ways of Visualization in the Classic of Mountains and Seas

### 4.1 Picture Books

Modern readers are accustomed to time-fragmented fast reading. It is easier to attract young people's attention by combining books with pictures. [4] In 2015, Chen Siyu's illustrations of the Classic of Mountains and Seas sparked a heated discussion. It is to draw black and white lines with a brush, and then color them with red, which not only manifests the elegance and blank of the Oriental painting style, but also includes the boldness and unrestrainedness of Western schools, and the ancient books of the Classic of Mountains and Seas shine brilliantly in modern times. [5] Through the easy- to-understand annotations and the author's own imagination, the picture book depicts the gods and beasts of ancient times, and makes the Classic of Mountains and Seas a popular book.

Based on the Classic of Mountains and Seas, the painter Shanze created the view of mountains and seas. He expressed the image of exotic animals in his heart with the painting method of national style. It is no longer a simple patchwork of lines, but an integration of the contemporary aesthetic, with fierce, flexible or gentle animal images. The composition is changeable and the ideas are unfettered, which thoroughly embodies the aestheticism of the Oriental painting school.

Since the Classic of Mountains and Seas was written in the middle and late Han Dynasty, the reading threshold for modern people is too high. Therefore, by visualizing the text, the abstractness and ambiguity of the text expression are eliminated [6]. As an auxiliary explanation, the text helps modern people and global readers to understand the enchantment of the Classic of Mountains and Seas.

## 4.2  Film and Television

The adaptation of excellent traditional culture IP has become a critical direction of today's films and TV dramas. "Haijing" caught the attention of the audience. In 2016, the Legend of Red Shadow in the Classic of Mountains and Seas attempted to restore the scenes described in the original text. In 2017, "Kunlun Ruins", "Qingqiu", "junjishan", "Jiren" and many archetypes of characters in To the Sky Kingdom originated from this ancient book, and the total broadcast volume of the play exceeded 50 billion. In order to make the setting reasonable and the role image profound, the domestic immortal dramas often draw inspiration from the Classic of Mountains and Seas, and take the gods, men and beasts as the main characters to shoot.

There are not only TV dramas, but also movies. The image of Huba, the protagonist in Monster Hunt, is derived from the "six- legged human face" in Classic of Mountains and Seas. Meanwhile, the world outlook of "coexistence of human and God" in the film is also influenced by the Classic of Mountains and Seas. This kind of mythological concept has been deeply embedded in Chinese traditional culture in the Classic of Mountains and Seas. There are elements of the Classic of Mountains and Seas in The Legend of Zu and di Renjie's Dragon King directed by Tsui Hark; the archetypes of Pigsy and Monk Sha in the Journey to the West directly copy the bare-eyed pig demon and henggong fish in the Classic of Mountains and Seas.

The Classic of Mountains and Seas not only provides huge excellent resources for domestic cinemas, but also is often referenced by foreign screenwriters. In the second trailer of Fantastic Beasts and Where to Find Them, there exists a Chinese exotic animal. J.K. Rowling explains that this exotic animal is called Ruwu, which is inspired by the Classic of Mountains and Seas. The method of film and television provides a convenient way to spread and highlight the value of the classic text. Through the visual form, the text and audio-visual symbols are combined, so that the ancient text can be rejuvenated in the Internet era (Figs. 1 and 2).

**Fig. 1.** Painting by Chen Siyu in the Classic of Mountains and Seas by Bai Di SHAOHAO

**Fig. 2.** Chen Siyu's painting in the Classic of Mountains and Seas by Nine Tailed Fox

### 4.3 Games

Popular IP game is also a common means at present. Many of the characters in Netease's national version RPG Shendu Nocturnal Journey are from the Classic of Mountains and Seas, while Kuiba, Baize, Putuo, Jiren and other characters in Classic of Mountains and Seas also appear in Guofeng puzzle solving hand tour Huazhen Miaobi Qianshan. In addition to the image of reference, there is the misappropriation of the world outlook of the Classic of Mountains and Seas. For instance, many games emphasize the significance of Kunlun Mountain. Kunlun Mountain is one of the major schools in the ghost of a beautiful girl. The people are upright, brave and strong. The description of Kunlun in Treacherous Waters Online and Chinese Paladin Three is mostly justicial, enormous and powerful.

Many of the scenes of fairyland in Southern Xinjiang, Northern Xinjiang and overseas are related to the description in the Classic of Mountains and Seas. For example, there are many poisonous insects in Southern Xinjiang in Novoland: Eagle Flag; Penglai Island in Chinese Paladin Three is an immortal island surrounded by water; Qingqiu in Shanhai Jinghua is the home of fox demon, which is basically consistent with the description in the book.

In addition to providing a large number of original images and scene elements, many games also choose to incorporate them. Netease further excavates the cultural heritage of the Classic of Mountains and Seas in the end of "World 3" and "World hand travel" and "dream back to the mountain sea" and "exotic mountain sea". It displays the infinite possibility of the game as a new digital medium, and combines with traditional dialogue and reality. The team not only takes the mysterious turtle, cangyun and other foreign animals recorded in the Classic of Mountains and Seas as the blueprint, but also creates a new game in the game law. In other words, the world IP version of the Classic of Mountains and Seas is a profound brand upgrade, and also a dialogue between innovative and high-quality content and users. The Honor of Kings also refers to the images of the beasts in the Classic of Mountains and Seas when designing hero skin, such as the white skin, the gluttonous skin of real person Tai Yi, the Zhu long skin of Cao Cao, Mi Yue's heavy and bright skin and the strange skin of pawy. According to the characteristics of different heroes and the imagination of the beast in the Sutra, the game brings a variety of game experiences to the players. Besides entertainment, it can also stimulate the interest of the players in this ancient book.

There are many other games named "Shanhaijing" as the game name, such as "mountain and sea classics OL", "Legend of mountain and sea classics", "great wasteland mountain and sea classics", etc. The operation of these games is different, but it is not difficult to see that the Classic of Mountains and Seas has become another big game IP after Journey to the West" and "Romance of Three Kingdoms", which also illustrates the feasibility and necessity of gamification IP of the Classic of Mountains and Seas.

### 4.4 Linkage and Derivative Products

In addition to the cross-border cooperation in the above fields, there are also many real industries cooperating with the Classic of Mountains and Seas to launch a series of limited edition to obtain more commercial value. For example, the Chinese women's clothing brand "goblin's pocket" launched "punk Mountains and Seas Classic", which opened the door of traditional culture in a fashion way, and employed the traditional fairy tales for reference to the dressing thinking, forming a unique brand design (Fig. 3).

**Fig. 3.** Official flagship store of Peak

Moreover, the sports shoes "peak" and "the Classic of Mountains and Seas" jointly launched the Taiji joint brand of the Classic of Mountains and Seas, including HuJiao, Luwu, Xuru, Xuangui and Hou. They all come from the supernatural beasts in the "Shanhaijing" and are combined with the tide shoes, bringing great freshness to the younger generation. In particular, in recent years, the more prevailing the trend of national style is, the products that can combine with traditional culture will be better and win more people's interest.

The emerging customizable Guochao cosmetics brand also released the Classic of Mountains and Seas series products at the time of girl culture in 2019. The product names are inspired by the Classic of Mountains and Seas, such as "flying west at night", "bashanyan language", "beimingyouyu" and "Dongshan Rift Valley". According to different colors, they are also named "ink", "kongsang", "fishseed", "chaos" and so on, which give ordinary people a lot of inspiration. The color make-up products of our company give us more profound meaning. Mac launched a limited number of Chinese style Shanhaijing Series in 2018, taking the myth of ancient Chinese Shanhaijing as the theme concept, integrating the design of Chinese style elements such as cloud pattern and tassel, displaying the beauty of the combination of modern make-up and oriental ancient charm. From the perspective of consumers' response, the joint name with Shanhaijing really makes these products more attractive. In addition to the use value, it also brings more collection value and commercial benefits to the brand (Fig. 4).

From virtual to reality, from clothing, food, housing and accommodation to entertainment, it can be seen that the IP of the Classic of Mountains and Seas has been increasingly integrated into daily life. Through various visual manifestations of the Classic of Mountains and Seas, the audience gradually understands the characteristics and fascination of the Classic of Mountains and Seas.

**Fig. 4.** Girlcult * The Classic of the Great Wilderness series eye shadow plate Taobao @Girlcult official flagship store

## 5   Conversion Mode from Text to Image

The traditional culture IP represented by the Classic of Mountains and Seas needs to enter the field of communication and display through modern design vocabulary and new media. In this paper, we need to complete the transformation from text to image and achieve the closed-loop from basic research to practical application through the five main links of text close reading, cultural mining, art design, communication and acceptance. Text close reading and cultural mining are the important foundation to determine the success of visualization (Figs. 5 and 6).

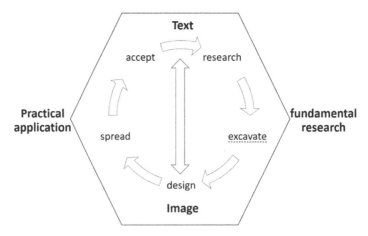

**Fig. 5.**  Text to image conversion path

**Fig. 6.** Painting by Jingyi Cui, Images of fox, Bifang, Jingwei, Fuzhu in The Classic of The Mountains and Seas

# References

1. Lu, L.: On the image of gods in The Classic of Mountains and Seas and its aesthetic implication. Liaoning Normal University, Shenyang (2013)
2. Ke, Y.: Collation and annotation of The Classic of Mountains and Seas. Shanghai Ancient Books Publishing House, Shanghai (1980)
3. Tianyi, Z.: Research on the relationship between text and map in Shanhaijing. Nanjing University, Nanjing (2015)
4. Rong, G.: The visual expression of the strange animal image in The Classic of Mountains and Seas in modern illustration design. Shenyang Normal University, Shenyang (2018)
5. Di, X.: Analysis and application practice of ancient and modern monsters in Shanhaijing. Shaanxi Normal University, Shaanxi (2016)
6. Zhou, W., Xu, D.: The application and advantages of dynamic illustration in illustration design. In: MEICI 2018. Intelligent Systems Research, vol. 163 (2018)

# Social Computing

# Social Media in Politic: Political Campaign on United States Election 2020 Between Donald Trump and Joe Biden

Paisal Akbar[1]($\boxtimes$) ⓘ, Bambang Irawan[2] ⓘ, Mohammad Taufik[2] ⓘ,
Achmad Nurmandi[1] ⓘ, and Suswanta[1] ⓘ

[1] Universitas Muhammadiyah Yogyakarta, JL. Brawijaya, Kasihan,
Bantul 55183, Yogyakarta, Indonesia
[2] Universitas Mulawarman, Jl. Muara Muntai Kampus, Samarinda 75411,
Gunung Kelua, Indonesia

**Abstract.** This research analyzes social media Twitter as a candidate campaign tool in the 2020 United States presidential election. Social media accounts studied include Republican candidate Donald Trump and Democratic candidate Joe Biden. The campaign issues seen in this research are political issues and racial issues. Twitter is one of the most used social media platforms. The number of Twitter users in the United States reaches 68.7 million and is the most significant number of users worldwide. This illustrates Twitter's strategic role in shaping a new communication model for disseminating information in the United States. This study uses the Qualitative Data Software Analysis (QDSA) method with the NVIVO tool. Nvivo is an analytical tool that reads text and content on Twitter accounts (Kaefer et al., 2015). This study shows that Twitter as a campaign tool has a character that is influenced by the type of content and intensity generated from the account of each candidate. On Donald Trump's account, we find political issues that characterize Twitter activity, such as the hashtags #MAGA, #VOTE, #SCOTUS, and #Obamagate. Race problems were not found. Joe Biden's account found several tweets related to political issues tagged with multiple hashtags, namely #DemConvention, #DemDebate, and #BidenTownHall. Some hashtags can be categorized in case of race, such as #NationalBlackVoterDay, # WomenEqualityDay, and #BlackHistoryMonth. Apart from that, the themes and sentiments that the account generates are also discussed.

**Keywords:** Social media · Political campaigns · US elections

## 1 Introduction

The stages of the general election 2020 for the President of the United States have held, based on the electoral votes collected, showing the victory of the 2020 General Election was obtained by the Joe Biden-Kamala Harris pair defeating incumbent presidential candidate Donald Trump-Mike Pence [1]. The difference between the two teams of candidates in the 2020 United States general election is more than 7 million votes; the

© Springer Nature Switzerland AG 2021
C. Stephanidis et al. (Eds.): HCII 2021, CCIS 1499, pp. 359–367, 2021.
https://doi.org/10.1007/978-3-030-90179-0_46

Donald Trump-Mike Pence pair got 74,210,828 votes while the Joe Biden-Kamala Harris pair won with 81,264,673 votes [2].

Based on the Cook Political Report data, the total number of votes that have counted has reached 158.4 million votes [3]. The electoral vote acquisition of each candidate also shows the same thing, Joe Biden-Kamala Harris, whom the Democrat party promoted, has won with 306 electoral votes. In comparison, the Republican pair Donald Trump-Mike Pence only got 232 electoral votes [2]. With 306 electoral votes that Joe Biden-Kamala Harris has pocketed, the minimum electoral vote fulfilled to win the United States General Election, requiring a minimum of 270 electoral votes.

The course of the 59th United States general election in 2020 was held amid the world health disaster of the Covid-19 pandemic. The implementation of this general election also experienced various technical obstacles during the United States presidential election stages. The campaign stage is one of the most critical steps in the general election process. In this stage of the campaign, candidates can inform voters about the vision and mission they carry, and vice versa, voters, can get to know the candidates better through the vision and mission they convey.

However, the general election campaign this time feels different when compared to the US general election in 2016 before, faced with the Covid-19 pandemic situation, the campaign pattern that used to tend to be face-to-face with the number of sympathizers who are present can be hundreds or even thousands of people in one place now, can no longer be done. The pandemic situation has encouraged campaigns not to be carried out massively in public spaces openly. This has made online campaign patterns increasingly popular and effectively reach voters [4].

The trend of increasing use of the internet in the United States election campaign began in 2008 when the US presidential candidate Barack Obama used the website massively as a medium for his online campaign. On this website, Barack Obama introduced the various visions and missions he wanted to build for the United States. This breakthrough was responded to well by US internet users, who then led Barack Obama to victory in the 2008 United States general election [5]. The same is right in the subsequent United States presidential elections in 2012 and 2016 [6, 7].

The use of websites as media for campaign information today has shifted to the use of social media, which is a form of development of web 2.0 technology [4]; social media gives users the freedom to build open communication networks and discussion forums that can be bridging communication [8], also between the government and its people [9]. The increasing growth of social media users has a broad impact on human life [10].

Social media consider to provide improvements in information dissemination effectiveness [11, 12]; it can also give the public freedom to express the current situation. Widayanti (2015) states that social media's role and function in disseminating information can provide a broader understanding of information and better reach users. This is because social media has become part of modern society's lifestyle in supporting various activities [13]. Even social media today has a strong influence on political and social life, where activities that occur in social media can directly influence policymaking [14].

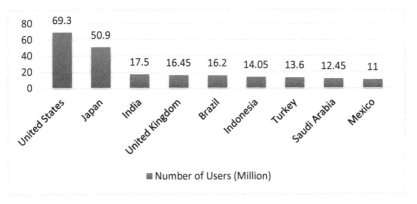

**Fig. 1.** The leading countries by number of Twitter users as of January 2021.

Twitter is one of the most loved social media platforms today [15]. Figure 1 shows that the United States is the country with the most Twitter users globally, with a total of 69.3 million users. This then illustrates the strategic role of Twitter as a medium that can form a new communication model in disseminating information in the United States [16]. The use of social media as a communication medium, with the various types of information presented, will influence the speed at which data received and the level of influence it generates [17, 18], and this can positively affect the election results [19].

Campaigns carried out through social media can provide information, influence public opinion more effectively, and build political communication and political participation between candidates and the public [20]. Besides, campaigns on social media can also make it easy for candidates to maximize the campaign program's influence that will run. For this reason, in this study, the author wants to examine the analysis of social media twitter as the campaign media for Donald Trump and Joe Biden in the 2020 United States Presidential Election. The extent to which each candidate voiced political and racial issues in the US Presidential election of 2020.

## 2 Research Methods

This study uses content analysis on the Twitter accounts of Donald Trump and Joe Biden. Data collection was carried out on December 10, 2020, exactly seven days after the voting for the 59th United States Presidential election, namely on December 3, 2020. This research used the Qualitative Data Software Analysis (QDSA) method with the Nvivo 12 Plus. Nvivo 12 Plus is an analytical tool that reads text and content on Twitter accounts [21]. Data retrieval was done using the NCapture feature, one of the Nvivo 12 plus software tools, directly linked to the Google Chrome software. The data sources and the amount of data generated from the NCapture process can see in Table 1.

**Table 1.** Data source and amount of data.

| Account | Tweet | | Retweet | |
|---|---|---|---|---|
| | Number of references | Percent | Number of references | Percent |
| @realDonaldTrump | 1992 | 62% | 1225 | 38% |
| JoeBiden | 3008 | 94% | 209 | 6% |

## 3  Findings and Discussion

### 3.1  Tweet Theme on Twitter Account

The public space available on social media has described as a space for new democratic deliberations, the desire of social media users to engage in political dialogues around political participation in general elections, information gathering, and active involvement in responding to emerging policies shows the existence of the role of social media. As an information space for political elites, its strategic role cannot be denied [22–24]. Along with Donald Trump and Joe Biden's massive use of social media Twitter during the United States presidential election campaign, the tweets and retweets that the candidates have created generate many data. The data for tweets and retweets are then grouped by NVivo 12 Plus software using automatic coding by identifying themes generated by available tweet and retweet data. The articles generated by each account can see in the following image.

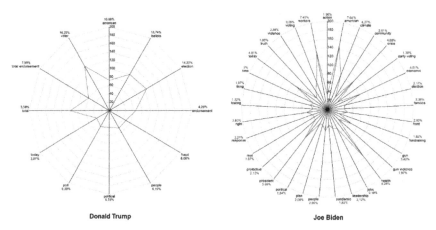

Donald Trump                    Joe Biden

**Fig. 2.** Tweet theme from the Presidential Candidate Account.

Figure 2 above shows the themes generated from using social media as campaign media, which are processed through automatic coding using NVivo 12 Plus. Each of these accounts makes some differences; if we look at Donald Trump's Twitter account, there are only 12 themes that appear, meanwhile in Joe Biden's Twitter account, there are more themes that occur up to 33 themes. The attention of each candidate to an issue that is the focus during the campaign period can also see from the various themes that appear in each candidate's account, in Donald Trump's statement the theme of Voter (16.22%), Election (14.22%), and Ballots (13.74%) were the top three themes that came to the attention of Donald Trump during the election period. Meanwhile, the three highest themes that came to Joe Biden's attention during the election period were Health (8.24%), American (7.64%), and Workers (7.45%). Borah (2016) reveals that social media activities in convincing voters produce a tendency of diction that appears in the content of Republican candidates using more articulation of fear. In the range of candidates from the Democratic Party, more use diction of humor and enthusiasm. This is the character as valid in the themes generated by the respective accounts of candidates Donald Trump and Joe Biden during the election period.

## 3.2  Campaign Issues and Twitter Account Sentiment

Candidates' activities on social media are closely related to the achievement of future election results [26, 27]. Social media provides a space for candidates to be able to compare themselves by describing themselves personally through the various campaign issues they convey [28]. In Donald Trump and Joe Biden's Twitter accounts, various political and racial campaign issues are found, categorized through the use of each candidate's hashtag during tweet and retweet activity on their accounts. The campaign issues can see in the following (Table 2).

**Table 2.** Campaign issues.

| Donald Trump (@realDonaldTrump) | | | |
|---|---|---|---|
| Political issues | | Race issues | |
| Hashtag | Coverage | Hashtag | Coverage |
| #MAGA | 3,20% | x | x |
| #VOTE | 0,34% | x | x |
| #SCOTUS | 0,22% | x | x |
| #Obamagate | 0,19% | x | x |
| Joe Biden (@JoeBiden) | | | |
| Political issues | | Race issues | |
| Hashtag | Coverage | Hashtag | Coverage |
| #DemConvention | 1,34% | #NationalBlackVoterDay | 0,06% |
| #DemDebate | 1,27% | #WomenEqualityDay | 0,06% |
| #BidenTownHall | 0,31% | #BlackHistoryMonth | 0,03% |
| #SOULSaturday | 0,22% | #BlackWomenEqualPayDay | 0,03% |

Donald Trump's account shows the use of the hashtag #MAGA (Make America Great Again) as one of the highest defining hashtags of political issues raised by Donald Trump during the election period. Furthermore, hashtags representing other political issues are character by several hashtags, namely #VOTE, #SCOTUS, and #Obamagate. Meanwhile, during the election campaign, the use of hashtags to characterize Donald Trump's racial issues was found the election period was no Unlike Donald Trump. The campaign issue activities presented by Joe Biden have covered political issues and race issues. Political issues character by using the hashtags #DemConvention, #DemDebate, BidenTownHall, and #SOULSaturday. Meanwhile, race issues are characterized by the hashtags #NationalBlackVoterDay, #WomenEqualityDay, #BlackHistoryMonth, and #BlackWomenEqualPayDay.

In addition to campaign issues, the author has also categorized the tweet and retweet data obtained from each candidate's accounts by looking at tweets' sentiment and retweets delivered by Donald Trump and Joe Biden. We are using the QDSA method of Nvivo 12 plus software, sentiments generated through automatic coding of sentiment identification. The automated coding of these sentiments can see in the following table.

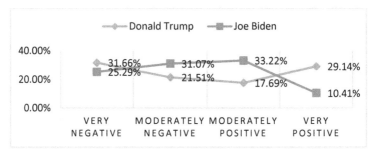

**Fig. 3.** Tweet and Retweet sentiment.

The graph in Fig. 3 above shows that Donald Trump has the advantage of two sentiments, namely very negative sentiment (31.66%) and very positive sentiment (29.14%). Meanwhile, Joe Biden has the edge in two other sentiments: a pretty negative sentiment (31.07%) and a pretty positive sentiment (33.22%). The tendency of each candidate's content sentiment on their Twitter account formed from the diction and retweet of the tweets they generated during the 2020 United States Presidential election. Buccoliero et al. (2020) said Twitter had become one of the most critical campaign communication channels through the intensity of tweets and retweets carried out and coupled with the diction of the correct information an influence on the results of future elections. Besides, politicians, campaigners, and political activists have the opportunity to give their thoughts to the public and get adequate space for dialogue with supporters and the general public through social media, especially in this case, Twitter [28–30].

Enli (2017), in his research on Twitter social media campaigns in the 2016 United States Presidential election, found that Democratic Party candidates put forward campaign strategies with a professional approach inbuilt political communication. Meanwhile, Republican candidates tend to use a campaign strategy with a de-professionalization process that even leads to amateurism as a counter-trend in the present political touch. This then felt repeated when we saw the sentiment generated from the tweets and retweets of each Republican candidate Donald Trump and Democratic candidate Joe Biden in the 2020 United States Presidential election. In his tweets and retweets, Donald Trump uses very negative sentiment and very positive sentiment in responding to various kinds of present issues. In contrast, Joe Biden, on the contrary, tends to be more careful in delivering tweets and retweets with quite negative and quite positive sentiments.

## 4 Conclusion

Social media in political campaigns has become a necessity and is an effective means of smoothing the campaign process and producing tangible results. In the 2020 United States General Election implementation, then-candidate Donald Trump's account showed the theme Voter, Election, and Ballots to be the three highest themes that came to Donald Trump's attention during the election period. Meanwhile, the three highest themes that came to Joe Biden's attention during the election period were Health, American, and Workers. Furthermore, in campaign issues and racial issues, Donald Trump shows the use of the hashtags #MAGA (Make America Great Again), #VOTE, #SCOTUS, and #Obamagate. Meanwhile, on race, the use of hashtags to characterize Donald Trump's racial issues during the election period was not found. Unlike Donald Trump, the campaign issue activities presented by Joe Biden have covered political issues and racial issues. Political issues character by the hashtags #DemConvention, #DemDebate, BidenTownHall, and #SOULSaturday. on race issues characterized by the hashtags #NationalBlackVoterDay, #WomenEqualityDay, #BlackHistoryMonth, and #BlackWomenEqualPayDay.

## References

1. Berty, T.T.S.: Hasil Pilpres AS 2020 Versi AP: Joe Biden Menang 290, Donald Trump 214. Liputan6.com (2020). https://www.liputan6.com/global/read/4402780/hasil-pilpres-as-2020-versi-ap-joe-biden-menang-290-donald-trump-214. Accessed 04 Jan 2020
2. Waller, A.: The electoral college explained. The New York Times (2021). https://www.nytimes.com/article/the-electoral-college.html. Accessed 07 Jan 2021
3. Iswara, A.J.: Hasil Pilpres AS, Selisih Joe Biden atas Trump Melebar Jadi 7 Juta Lebih Suara. Kompas.com (2020). https://www.kompas.com/global/read/2020/12/05/140358970/hasil-pilpres-as-selisih-joe-biden-atas-trump-melebar-jadi-7-juta-lebih
4. Papakyriakopoulos, O., Serrano, J.C.M., Hegelich, S.: Political communication on social media: a tale of hyperactive users and bias in recommender systems. Online Soc. Netw. Media 15 (2020). https://doi.org/10.1016/j.osnem.2019.100058
5. Petre, E.A.: Encouraging identification with the larger campaign narrative: grassroots organizing texts in Barack Obama's 2008 presidential campaign. Commun. Q. 66(3), 283–307 (2017). https://doi.org/10.1080/01463373.2017.1378242
6. Gerodimos, R., Justinussen, J.: Obama's 2012 Facebook campaign: political communication in the age of the like button. J. Inf. Technol. Polit. 12(2), 113–132 (2015). https://doi.org/10.1080/19331681.2014.982266
7. Denton, R.E. (ed.): The 2016 US Presidential Campaign. PCC, Springer, Cham (2017). https://doi.org/10.1007/978-3-319-52599-0

8. Purnomo, E.P., et al.: How public transportation use social media platform during Covid-19: study on Jakarta public transportations' Twitter accounts? Webology **18**(1), 1–19 (2021). https://doi.org/10.14704/WEB/V18I1/WEB18001

9. Botta, A., De Donato, W., Persico, V., Pescapé, A.: Integration of cloud computing and internet of things: a survey. Futur. Gener. Comput. Syst. **56**, 684–700 (2016). https://doi.org/10.1016/j.future.2015.09.021

10. Driss, O.B., Mellouli, S., Trabelsi, Z.: From citizens to government policy-makers: social media data analysis. Gov. Inf. Q. **36**(3), 560–570 (2019). https://doi.org/10.1016/j.giq.2019.05.002

11. Widayanti, R.: Pemanfaatan Media Sosial Untuk Penyebaran Informasi (2015)

12. Yoo, E., Rand, W., Eftekhar, M., Rabinovich, E.: Evaluating information diffusion speed and its determinants in social media networks during humanitarian crises. J. Oper. Manag. **45**, 123–133 (2016). https://doi.org/10.1016/j.jom.2016.05.007

13. Monggilo, Z.M.: Kajian Literatur Tentang Tipologi Perilaku Berinternet Generasi Muda Indonesia. J. ILMU Komun. **13**(1), 31 (2016). https://doi.org/10.24002/jik.v13i1.599

14. Batara, E., Nurmandi, A., Warsito, T., Pribadi, U.: Are government employees adopting local e-government transformation?: the need for having the right attitude, facilitating conditions and performance expectations. Transform. Gov. People Process Policy **11**(4), 612–638 (2017). https://doi.org/10.1108/TG-09-2017-0056

15. Statistic Brain Research Institute: Pengguna Twitter di Indonesia (2014). https://www.statisticbrain.com/

16. Kreis, R.: The 'tweet politics' of president Trump. J. Lang. Polit. **16**(4), 607–618 (2017). https://doi.org/10.1075/jlp.17032.kre

17. DePaula, N., Dincelli, E., Harrison, T.M.: Toward a typology of government social media communication: democratic goals, symbolic acts and self-presentation. Gov. Inf. Q. **35**(1), 98–108 (2018). https://doi.org/10.1016/j.giq.2017.10.003

18. Ebbers, W.E., Van De Wijngaert, L.A.L.: Paper beats ping: on the effect of an increasing separation of notification and content due to digitization of government communication. Gov. Inf. Q. **37**(1), 1–8 (2019). https://doi.org/10.1016/j.giq.2019.101396

19. Bello, B.S., Inuwa-dutse, I., Heckel, R.: Social Media Campaign Strategies: Analysis of the 2019 Nigerian Elections (October 2019)

20. Stieglitz, S., Dang-Xuan, L.: Social media and political communication: a social media analytics framework. Soc. Netw. Anal. Min. **3**(4), 1277–1291 (2012). https://doi.org/10.1007/s13278-012-0079-3

21. Kaefer, F., Roper, J., Sinha, P.: A software-assisted qualitative content analysis of news articles: example and reflections. Forum Qual. Sozialforsch **16**(2) (2015). https://doi.org/10.17169/fqs-16.2.2123

22. Hendriks, C.M., Lees-Marshment, J.: Political leaders and public engagement: the hidden world of informal elite-citizen interaction. Polit. Stud. **67**(3), 597–617 (2019). https://doi.org/10.1177/0032321718791370

23. Skoric, M.M., Zhu, Q., Goh, D., Pang, N.: Social media and citizen engagement : a meta-analytic review. New Media Soc. **19**(9), 1817–1839 (2016). https://doi.org/10.1177/1461444815616221

24. Vitak, J., Zube, P., Smock, A., Carr, C.T., Ellison, N., Lampe, C.: It's complicated: Facebook users' political participation in the 2008 election. Cyberpsychol. Behav. Soc. Netw. **14**(3), 107–114 (2011). https://doi.org/10.1089/cyber.2009.0226

25. Borah, P.: Political Facebook use: Campaign strategies used in 2008 and 2012 presidential elections. J. Inf. Technol. Polit. **13**(4), 326–338 (2016). https://doi.org/10.1080/19331681.2016.1163519

26. DiGrazia, J., McKelvey, K., Bollen, J., Rojas, F.: More tweets, more votes: social media as a quantitative indicator of political behavior. PLoS ONE **8**(11), 1–5 (2013). https://doi.org/10.1371/journal.pone.0079449

27. Kruikemeier, S.: How political candidates use Twitter and the impact on votes. Comput. Hum. Behav. **34**, 131–139 (2014). https://doi.org/10.1016/j.chb.2014.01.025

28. Petruca, I.: Personal branding through social media. Int. J. Commun. Res. **6**(4), 389–392 (2015). https://doi.org/10.4018/978-1-4666-9593-1.les4

29. Buccoliero, L., Bellio, E., Crestini, G., Arkoudas, A.: Twitter and politics: evidence from the US presidential elections 2016. J. Mark. Commun. **26**(1), 88–114 (2020). https://doi.org/10.1080/13527266.2018.1504228

30. Sessions, L.F.: How offline gatherings affect online communities when virtual community members 'meetup.' Inf. Commun. Soc. **13**(3), 375–395 (2010). https://doi.org/10.1080/13691180903468954

31. Enli, G.: Twitter as arena for the authentic outsider: exploring the social media campaigns of Trump and Clinton in the 2016 US presidential election. Eur. J. Commun. **32**(1), 50–61 (2017). https://doi.org/10.1177/0267323116682802

# Exploring the Effect of Activity Intervention on Reducing Social Media Use: Lessons Learned in a Field Study

Ju-Ling Ko[1]([⊠]), Chieh Yuan[1]([⊠]), Billy Malherbe[2], Cheng-Han Yang[1], and Pei-Yi Kuo[1]([⊠])

[1] Institute of Service Science, National Tsing Hua University, Hsinchu, Taiwan
{patty.ko,chieh.yuan,pykuo}@iss.nthu.edu.tw
[2] International Master of Business Administration, National Tsing Hua University, Hsinchu, Taiwan
s109077446@m109.nthu.edu.tw

**Abstract.** Social media addiction has become a serious problem with more than half of teenage users finding it hard to tackle. Prior research has used varying exercise and social activities to solve phone addiction issues. In this paper, we examine how activity intervention helped reduce participants' social media usage time. Through a two-week field study followed by interviews, participants were asked to engage in one exercise (e.g., stretching) or social (e.g., talking to friends) activity per day. A chatbot prompted participants with daily activity two times every day as reminders. In general, participants across groups all built a sense of time awareness after our intervention. We discussed potential factors influencing the effectiveness of our intervention, and proposed several directions for future researchers who would like to design similar activity intervention to reduce social media use time.

**Keywords:** Social media addiction · Activity intervention · Time awareness

## 1 Introduction

With excessive mobile phone use, the number of social media platform users has increased over time. However, the phenomenon has been reported to bring people negative health and social consequences. One of them is social media addiction. It has been found that social media addiction could result in the decrease of physical interaction [1]. Recent statistics have shown that 51% of social media users aged 18 to 24 said it would be hard to give up social media [5], leading to the addiction. Research has suggested the effectiveness of using exercise and social activity interventions to tackle smartphone addiction [2, 4]. These interventions have the potential to help reduce social media usage. However, limited research was conducted using activity intervention to tackle social media addiction, except a few studies involving interventions with exercise and social support activities. To address this, we conducted a field study with college students self-identified as social media addicts by using two different kinds of activity

C. Stephanidis et al. (Eds.): HCII 2021, CCIS 1499, pp. 368–374, 2021.
https://doi.org/10.1007/978-3-030-90179-0_47

intervention techniques to explore the impact of activity intervention on social media addiction and the potential factors influencing the effectiveness of this intervention.

## 2    Related Work

### 2.1    Social Media Addiction

The use of social media is particular popular among younger generations, who are eager to be noticed by others. The overuse of social media resulted in addiction issues in our society nowadays, and that the excessive use of mobile phones can cause negative social effects [1]. According to [6], behavioral addictions are defined as a psychological dependence on repetitive behaviors which typically impair normal functioning and can easily be observed by most people. Current studies have confirmed that the potential of using exercise interventions to treat smartphone addiction (e.g., basketball, dancing, cycling) [5]. However, existing research mainly uses "exercise" intervention for phone addition issue.

### 2.2    The Effect of Social and Exercise Activities on Phone Addiction

In order to solve the problem of social media addiction and to reduce the time on using social media, we used the method of activity intervention. It is proved that exercise intervention has a positive effect on reducing smartphone addiction [3, 4]. Participants tend to agree that being reminded of their usage habits, or being aware that they are being monitored would discourage them from using their phones [1]. Besides, former research developed intervention mechanisms to direct users' attention away from their phones and towards their physical social space [1]. Participants reacted positively to the intervention mechanism designed to discourage phone interactions during social situations. It is confirmed that activity intervention can help users reflect on their social media usage, and possibly decrease their time spending on social media. However, the mechanism developed in prior research (i.e., sending participants more discouragement messages when they use more phone) was applied mainly to tackle phone addiction issue instead of on social media addiction per se [1]. Thus, we aim to investigate the impact of activity intervention on reducing social media usage.

## 3    Methods

We first conducted an online pre-screening survey with 41 college students. In the survey, we asked participants their average daily usage time of social media, the most frequently used time period of a day, the habit of usage, and the influence of addiction on their life to identify those who perceive themselves as social media addicts, and want to decrease their usage time. Then, we conducted a two-week field study with a total of 16 college students to examine how our activity intervention helped reduce their social media use time. The age of the participants ranged from 20 to 27 (mean age = 23, SD = 1.72). We divided our participants into three groups - groups 1, 2, and 3. Participants in group 1 were the control group - they were only asked to report their daily screen usage time daily without performing any activity. Participants in group 2 received one exercise activity per day during the first week and then one social interaction activity per day during the second week. The order was inverted for participants in group 3 to examine if order effect of activity types had an effect on their activity completion and social media use time.

We developed a chatbot called SMA Coach (Social Media Addiction Coach) using Chatfuel to deliver the activity to participants during the study. Participants were asked to choose two periods of time in a day that they are usually on social media. During these two periods of time, participants received activity prompts sent by the chatbot (Fig. 1). If they did not like the default activity, they had a chance to choose an activity they preferred to perform each time. The activities included two categories: exercise activities (e.g., yoga, push-up, squat) and physical social interaction activities (e.g., talking to someone, taking a selfie with a friend, leaving a hand-writing message for your roommate). After participants completed each activity, they were asked to upload a photo or short video to prove they completed particular activities. At the end of the second week, all participants shared their feelings and reactions toward the activity prompts as well as their social media usage situation in a post-study online survey. We interviewed 9 out of 16 participants to further understand their feelings toward our activity intervention approach, including how their feelings and behaviors changed during the study. We chose these nine participants because they have indicated particular opinions and suggestions toward the effectiveness of our intervention in the post-study survey.

**Fig. 1.** Screenshots of social (left) and exercise (right) activities delivered via the chatbot.

## 4   Results

We collected both quantitative and qualitative data in this study. Quantitative data includes screenshots of mobile screen time use shared by participants per day for two weeks. Qualitative data include the activity completion photos uploaded by participants, the post-study online survey data with 16 participants and interviews with 9 participants. Quantitative data provided a descriptive overview on how participants' reactions and behaviors developed over the course of two weeks. Our goal was not to validate the extent of behavioral changes throughout the study as our sample size was not large enough to observe statistical effects. Our focus lies in examining how participants reacted to our activity intervention, and how this influenced their perception and behavior related to social media use.

### 4.1 Reactions Toward Different Activity Prompts in the Intervention

The activities in our experiment were divided into two types - exercise and social interaction. During our interview, one participant mentioned that our activity intervention helped her reduce social media use time, but indicated the duration of our activity (10 min) was too short. Most participants preferred social interaction activities over exercise ones (*"I like social activities more. I feel a sense of control on screen time usage when I was with someone else."-P15*). Interestingly, there was only one participant who preferred exercise activities over social ones as she found it hard to find friends to interact with for our activities (*"I usually do exercise activities for more than 30 min. Yet I don't like social activities because it's hard for me to find someone for interaction"-P07*). Besides, six participants suggested having more diverse activities to choose from, and that some mentioned it would be better that activities are not related to mobile phones (e.g., chat with friends physically) as it could potentially trigger their desire to use their phones.

### 4.2 Reactions Toward Notification Timing

We sent participants two activity reminders every day based on their most active time periods using social media specified at the beginning of the experiment. When participants forgot to click the unlock button, the chatbot reminded them every ten minutes for an hour until they clicked on the button to view the activity content. Our post-study interview data indicated that three participants mentioned there were too many reminders, and hoped that the interval of the reminders could be longer (*"I felt like the chatbot reminded me every 5 min once."-P15*). In addition, our interview data suggested that the timings of the activities sent influenced participants' activity completion situation. The most common scenario was "wrong timings of activities sent", as participants were not informed at the beginning of the study that they would be prompted for activity at their chosen social media use time daily. Although doing so helped observe participants' natural behaviors and reactions, it caused them some inconvenience for activity completion. (*"I didn't know the activities would be sent on the time we picked at the beginning of the study. It turned out that I always received activities before going to bed when I can't really do anything."-P16*).

### 4.3 Awareness Toward Time

The quantitative data did not show statistically significant differences regarding the average social media use times between week 1 and week 2 for participants who received activity prompts in our experimental groups (groups 2 and 3) (Table 1). This was the same regardless of the average social media use time during weekday or over weekend. However, six participants mentioned that they started to realize how long they used social media on their phones after seeing the information from the screenshots every day. Although participants did not have a significant change on their social media usage time, they did have an increased awareness toward time ("*After the experiment, I still go back to see my screen time and try to occupy myself with other things to reduce my usage time.*"-*P04*), which led to the reduction of usage time in some cases.

**Table 1.** Independent samples T-test statistical results

|  | Between groups 1 & 2 | Between groups 1 & 3 | Between groups 2 & 3 |
|---|---|---|---|
| Average social media use times | $t(9) = -1.30, p = 0.15$ | $t(8) = -1.58, p = 0.10$ | $t(9) = 0.70, p = 0.41$ |

## 5   Discussion

### 5.1   Effectiveness of Activity Prompts in the Intervention

Prior research [4] has suggested that there are significant positive effects of exercise interventions on reducing smartphone addiction. However, exercise activities did not work as expected in our field study. This may be due to the following reasons. First, the duration of our experiment lasted for two weeks. More research is needed to further understand the ideal time duration for exercise intervention to take effect on people to reduce their time using social media. Second, we realized the intensity level of exercise activities could play a role in intervention outcomes. Prior research seems adopting more vigorous exercise activities such as basketball, dancing, and cycling [3], whereas the activities in our experiment leaned toward mild exercise such as yoga, stretch, and eye-moving. As limited research examines the effect of performing exercise activities on outcomes of reducing addiction, we chose mild exercises as most participants indicated using social media prior to regular bedtime. Regardless, we believe more research is needed to identify the best times to perform certain intensity levels of exercise to help people reduce their social media use. Third, our experiment asked participants to perform exercise activities individually. Future researchers interested in creating similar intervention can consider prompting participants to do so in group form, as done in prior work [3]. Furthermore, our qualitative data suggested that most participants in our study preferred social activities over exercise ones. It might be because exercise interventions were relatively more time-consuming, and they felt easier and more comfortable to find others doing something for social activities. They even did several social activities like chatting with friends longer than the regular time duration indicated in our activity prompts (i.e., 10 min).

## 5.2  Effectiveness of Notification Timing

We found that the frequency of push notifications had an influence on participants' activity completion. Participants in general felt there were too many reminders. In addition, timings of activity delivery had an impact on activity completion. A few participants just finished taking a bath and laid on the bed when receiving exercise activity, while a few mentioned they had no one else beside them when receiving social activities. These situations prevented them from successfully completing the activity at times. One potential way to improve this limitation is to allow users to deliberately choose the type of activities and the times for receiving push notifications, as well as customize the reminder frequency in advance.

## 5.3  Time Awareness

Even though the activity intervention did not have a statistically significant effect on participants who received exercise/social activities in our experimental groups (groups 2 and 3), participants from both control and experimental groups built a sense of time awareness through seeing screenshots of their daily screen time use. Participants developed two types of behavior to reduce their usage time after building a sense of awareness. Based on our qualitative data, six participants deliberately did something to change their behavior. Some participants tried removing environmental temptations such as going to dinner or toilet without bringing their phones, and some participants changed their habits like going to bed earlier.

## 6  Limitations, Conclusion and Future Work

There are four limitations in our study. First, we currently have 5 exercise and 5 social activities to be completed individually in our intervention. We hope to add 9 more activities which can be done individually or cooperatively with others to increase activity diversity. Second, we tracked the social media usage time on mobile phones. We hope to extend tracking screen time across platforms and devices by using screen monitor software to automate the tracking process. Third, the current interaction between participants and our chatbot is monotonous. In the future, we intend to personalize our chatbot with more personality such as having a humorous or positive tone, sending encouraging words, showing statistical feedback of performance to participants, and so on. Lastly, our experiment lasted two weeks. We plan to recruit more participants, and conduct the experiment for a longer period of time.

**Acknowledgements.** We particularly thank participants in our study, and to the anonymous reviewers for their helpful inputs. This work was supported by the Ministry of Science and Technology in Taiwan (MOST grant 109-2221-E-007-063-MY3). Any opinions or recommendations expressed in this material are those of the author(s) and do not necessarily reflect the views of the MOST.

# References

1. Eddie, T., Ye, J., Stevenson, G.: Are our mobile phones driving us apart? Divert attention from mobile phones back to physical conversation! In: Proceedings of the 17th International Conference on Human-Computer Interaction with Mobile Devices and Services Adjunct, pp. 1082–1087 (August 2015)
2. Herrero Olaizola, J.B., Torres, A.V., Vivas, P., Urueña, A.: Smartphone addiction and social support: a three-year longitudinal study. Psychosoc. Interv. **28**, 111–118 (2019)
3. Kim, H.: Exercise rehabilitation for smartphone addiction. J. Exerc. Rehabil. **9**(6), 500–505 (2013)
4. Liu, S., Xiao, T., Yang, L., Loprinzi, P.D.: Exercise as an alternative approach for treating smartphone addiction: a systematic review and meta-analysis of random controlled trials. Int. J. Environ. Res. Pub. Health **16**(20), 3912 (2019)
5. Pew Research Center: Share of U.S. adults using social media, including Facebook, is mostly unchanged since 2018 (2019)
6. Serenko, A., Turel, O.: Directing technology addiction research in information systems: part I. Understanding behavioral addictions. ACM SIGMIS Database DATABASE Adv. Inf. Syst. **51**(3), 81–96 (2020)

# Social Media as Tools of Disaster Mitigation, Studies on Natural Disasters in Indonesia

Danang Kurniawan[1]([✉]) [iD], Arissy Jorgi Sutan[1,2] [iD], Achmad Nurmandi[3] [iD], Mohammad Jafar Loilatu[1] [iD], and Salahudin[3] [iD]

[1] Government Affairs and Administration, Jusuf Kalla School of Government, Universitas Muhammadiyah, Yogyakarta, Indonesia
[2] Master Government Affairs and Administration, Universitas Muhammadiyah, Yogyakarta, Indonesia
[3] Departement of Governmental Studies, Universitas Muhammadiyah, Malang, Indonesia
salahudinmsi@umm.ac.id

**Abstract.** This research tries to seek the social media role as communication media in disaster management. Since the beginning of 2021, Indonesia has been affected by various disasters. In January, floods occurred in South Kalimantan, an earthquake in West Sulawesi, a landslide in Sumedang, an airplane crash around Kepulauan Seribu Regency, and volcano eruptions in Mounts Semeru and Merapi. On social media, those disasters became a trending topic on Twitter. This research used a qualitative approach and Q-DAS (Qualitative Data Analysis Software). This research found that Twitter could spread information regarding disaster mitigation through hashtags. Also, Twitter helped report updates, distribute supplies, inform requests for help and coordination, and criticize the government. In the coordination aspect of the five disasters, plane crashes, landslides and volcanic eruptions would attract volunteers, while floods, earthquakes and landslides would collect donations. The empathy aspect dominated the parameters of understanding different perspectives, with three disasters, landslides, earthquakes, and floods.

**Keywords:** Social media · Mitigation · Natural disaster · Indonesia

## 1 Introduction

An emergency information system is essential to integrity communication to support operational disaster management [1, 2]. Social media implement communication integrity [3]. Disasters can attract attention and deliver the global and local perspective at the same time. Social media allows information distribution quickly and reduces an emergency on public reaction [4].

Social media's disaster management roles include sending out alerts, identifying critical needs, and considering emergency management countermeasures interventions [5, 6]. Social media platforms like Twitter have over 500 million users globally and may assist the disaster mitigation steps [5, 7]. Twitter spreads temporal trends through hashtags, mentions, and retweets to allow humanitarian actors to understand the effectiveness

© Springer Nature Switzerland AG 2021
C. Stephanidis et al. (Eds.): HCII 2021, CCIS 1499, pp. 375–382, 2021.
https://doi.org/10.1007/978-3-030-90179-0_48

of their preparedness communication on social media, monitor risks and disasters, and build community preparedness networks [8, 9].

As a platform for communication on disaster mitigation, social media has a critical role in countries with high disaster risks, including Indonesia. It belongs to the ring of fire, causing high volcano activities [10]. Table 1 below contains a list of disasters during January 2021.

**Table 1.**  List of disasters on January 2021

| Disaster | Location | Time |
|---|---|---|
| Flooding | City of Manado | 16 January 2021 |
| | Province of South Kalimantan | 09 January 2021 |
| Landslide | Region of Sumedang | 09 January 2021 |
| | City of Manado | 16 January 2021 |
| Gempa Bumi | Region of Mamuju | 14 January 2021 |
| | Region of Majene | 14 January 2021 |
| Erupsi Gunung Api | Mount Semeru, Region of Lumajang | 16 January 2021 |
| | Mount Merapi, Province of DIY | 28 January 2021 |

Source: https://www.bnpb.go.id/.

This situation needs collaboration and coordination cross-institution to reports for response times and avoids duplication of mitigation tasks [11]. Social media plays an essential role in raising awareness and coordinating relief efforts, such as during the catastrophic floods in India [12]. This research focuses on social media Twitter's role in disaster mitigation and looking at the differences in communication messages conveyed from each disaster type. This research's limitation was Twitter when the disaster took place on January 2021 in Indonesia.

## 2  Literature Review

Disaster management has various levels and stages. As a part of information and communication technology (ICT), social media promote disaster management by effectively using society's participation [13]. Social media as a source of data giving the option to collect the data in disaster research [14]. Microblogging platforms, such as Twitter during natural disasters and emergencies, reveal Twitter data's usefulness for some of the most helpful disaster-response tasks [15].

Social media developed disaster mitigation when an earthquake happened in China. [16]. The information aspect is essential to support disaster management to reduce the victim's disaster rate [17]. Social media helps update the data and information regarding the disaster, minimalize the misleading information and situation, distribute supplies, request assistance, coordinate the help, and criticize the government.

# 3   Method

This research conducted a study on how Indonesians used Twitter as a disaster mitigation response. This research used a qualitative approach applying descriptive to deliver the result and values on the social media content intends for disaster management. This research also used Q-DAS (Qualitative Data Analysis Software) to analyze social media data and Nvivo 12Plus to analyze the content and social media data. The data was based on hashtags trendings during five disasters in January 2021 in Indonesia. The steps taken to retrieve hashtags from Twitter are shown in Fig. 1.

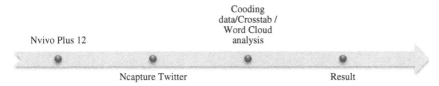

**Fig. 1.**  Twitter hashtags data

The researchers analyzed the data using two thoughtful analyses, graphical analysis to determine relevant content in social media using disaster mitigation and word cloud analysis to explore the main issues.

## 3.1   Result and Discussion

In January 2021, five disasters happened in Indonesia. They were a Sriwijaya Air airplane crash, an earthquake in Mamuju and Majene, a flood in South Kalimantan, a landslide in Sumedang, and volcano eruptions in Merapi and Semeru. The data collection results from five types of disasters in Indonesia based on trending hashtags on Twitter are presented in Table 2.

**Table 2.**  Hashtags and various disaster

| Types of disaster | Locations | Hashtags |
|---|---|---|
| Flood | Manado | #BanjirKalsel |
|  | South Kalimantan | #Kalselbanjir<br>#PrayforKalSel |
| Landslide | Sumedang | #LongsorSumedang<br>#PrayForSumedang |
| Earthquake | Mamuju | #gempamajene |
|  | Majene | #gempamamuju<br>#gempasulbar<br>#PrayforSulbar |

(*continued*)

Table 2. (continued)

| Types of disaster | Locations | Hashtags |
|---|---|---|
| Volcano Eruption | Semeru Mountain | #GunungSemeru |
| | Merapi Mountain | #Merapi<br>#MerapiSiaga |
| Airplane Crash | Kepualan Seribu | #SJ182<br>#SriwijayaAirSJ182 |

The hashtags were categorized based on the types of disasters and locations. Nvivo Plus1 helped the analysis and determined five indicators: coordination aspect, empathy aspect, recovery aspect and information update.

### 3.2  Disaster Information

**Airplane Crash.** In January 2021, Sriwijaya Air crashed in Kepulauan Seriubu, and social media responded to this tragedy using #SJ182 dan #SriwijayaAirSJ182 hashtags. The analysis can be seen in the figure below.

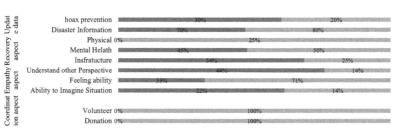

The social media response in the disaster that the Sriwijaya Air plane crashed into the Thousand Islands sea, Saturday (9/1/2021) was informed by the hashtags #SJ182 and #Sriwi-jayaAirSJ182, dominating the coordinating role related to volunteers by achieving a score (100%). The empath aspect shows that feeling ability has the highest percentage (71%) of the other empath aspects. Meanwhile, in the recovery aspect mitigation, the three parameters are dominated by infrastructure improvements (54%). Social media responses also showed social empathy with a percentage (44%). Finally, on updating data, the role of social media is very high (70%). There is another role for social media to prevent hoax news related to disaster data.

**Floods in South Kalimantan.** Floods in South Kalimantan were indicated by three hashtags: #BanjirKalsel #Kalselbanjir #PrayforKalSel. The mitigation was different compared to the airplane crash.

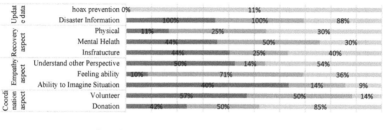

 ■ #BanjirKalsel    ■ #Kalselbanjir    ■ #PrayforKalSel

In response to South Kalimantan's floods, the coordination aspect is the highest for donations, with a percentage of 85%. A donation is a form of public empathy for the victims. The recovery aspect's mitigation shows that mental health recovery has the highest percentage of 50% from the infrastructure and physical aspects, where the public provides support for disaster victims. Finally, social media's role in data updating shows the highest percentage with 100%, dissemination of disaster information, and 11% related to hoax prevention.

**Earthquake in Mamuju and Majene.** The information mitigation conveyed through social media is regarding earthquakes. The overall information is the closest to the occurrence of a disaster with a percentage of 100%. The highest aspect of coordination in mitigation is support for donations, with a percentage of 88%. The social media expression related to the highest empathy aspect in other perspective is 80%. As for mitigation information related to the recovery aspect, the highest portion is in the physical aspect by 77%.

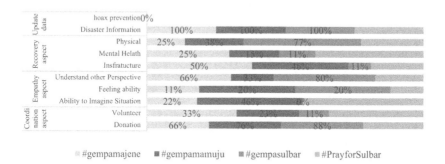

 ■ #gempamajene    ■ #gempamamuju    ■ #gempasulbar    ■ #PrayforSulbar

**Landslide in Sumedang.** Landslides in Sumedang Regency, as a whole, the update information was responded to quickly. One of them is the coordination aspect through donations.

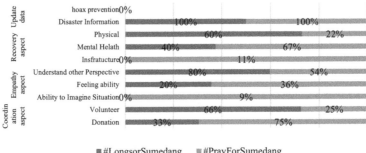

According to the figure above, the mitigation information on the coordination aspect related to donations is 75%. Then, related to social expression, the empathy aspect is the highest, with 80%. Mental health indicators have the highest portion, with 67% related to the recovery aspect. The updated data on the Sumedang landslide case shows a percentage of 100% in disseminating disaster information.

**Volcano Eruptions in Merapi and Merbabu Mountains.** Information on the disaster mitigation of Merapi and Merbabu eruptions on social media shows that the coordination and recovery aspects are the highest by 100%. The coordination aspect is prioritized related to the provision of volunteers who become assistance for evacuation. Then, the empathy aspect has a percentage of 100%. Whereas in the role of disaster, data information has a percentage of 67%, while the media's role can prevent hoaxes by 33%.

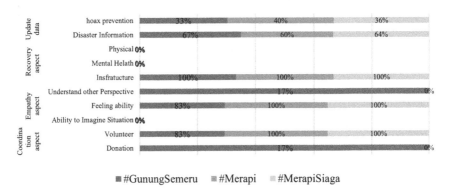

Each disaster has different mitigation aspects on social media. In the case of floods, landslides and earthquakes, the coordination regarding the donations is high, influenced by public empathy for the victims. Besides, social media's role plays an essential role in providing information on disaster data updates in reconstructing prevention's responsiveness. On the other side, the narration spread domination using hashtags like #gunung-merapi, #banjirkalsel, and a single word like 'donation' and the time such as January, February 2021, and 2020.

## 4 Conclusion

Coordination, empathy, recovery, and data update aspects define the social media's roles in disaster mitigation. Each type of disaster has different disaster mitigation on social media. However, overall there are also similarities. Plane crashes, landslides and volcanic activities attract volunteers. Floods, earthquakes and also landslides tend to attract supply requests. Empathy aspects dominate the parameters and understand another perspective, with three disasters: landslides, earthquakes, and floods. Volcano activities and plane crashes tend to belong to sensory, where the netizens can get the victim's perspectives as part of sympathy and empathy. As for the recovery aspect, the dominant one is mental health, with three cases of disasters: landslides, floods, plane crashes. Most netizens would support victims and their families. Lastly, all disaster cases on social media are displayed as disaster information, proving social media can be used as a platform for sharing information in real-time.

## References

1. Anparasan, A., Lejeune, M., Columbia, D.: Analyzing the response to epidemics : concept of evidence-based Haddon matrix. J. Humanit. Logist. Supply Chain Manage. **7**(3), 266–283 (2017). https://doi.org/10.1108/JHLSCM-06-2017-0023
2. Hernantes, J., Maraña, P., Gimenez, R., Sarriegi, J.M., Labaka, L.: Towards resilient cities: a maturity model for operationalizing resilience. Cities **84**, 96–103 (2019). https://doi.org/10.1016/j.cities.2018.07.010
3. Adam, N.R., Shafiq, B., Staffin, R.: Spatial computing and social media in the context of disaster management. IEEE Intell. Syst. **27**(6), 90–97 (2012). https://doi.org/10.1109/MIS.2012.113
4. Panagiotopoulos, P., Barnett, J., Bigdeli, A.Z., Sams, S.: Social media in emergency management: Twitter as a tool for communicating risks to the public. Technol. Forecast. Soc. Change **111**, 86–96 (2016). https://doi.org/10.1016/j.techfore.2016.06.010
5. Carley, K.M., Malik, M., Landwehr, P.M., Pfeffer, J., Kowalchuck, M.: Crowd sourcing disaster management: the complex nature of Twitter usage in Padang Indonesia. Saf. Sci. **90**, 48–61 (2016). https://doi.org/10.1016/j.ssci.2016.04.002

6. Fry, J., Binner, J.M.: Elementary modelling and behavioural analysis for emergency evacu-ations using social media. Eur. J. Oper. Res. **249**(3), 1014–1023 (2016). https://doi.org/10.1016/j.ejor.2015.05.049
7. Rogers, E.B., Rose, J.: A critical exploration of women's gendered experiences in outdoor leadership. J. Exp. Educ. **42**(1), 37–50 (2019). https://doi.org/10.1177/1053825918820710
8. Bosley, J.C., et al.: Decoding twitter: surveillance and trends for cardiac arrest and resusci-tation communication. Resuscitation **84**(2), 206–212 (2013). https://doi.org/10.1016/j.resuscitation.2012.10.017
9. Anson, S., Watson, H., Wadhwa, K., Metz, K.: Analysing social media data for disaster preparedness: understanding the opportunities and barriers faced by humanitarian actors. Int. J. Disaster Risk Reduct. **21**, 131–139 (2017). https://doi.org/10.1016/j.ijdrr.2016.11.014
10. Havet, N., Bayart, C., Bonnel, P.: Why do Gender differences in daily mobility behaviours persist among workers? Transp. Res. Part A Policy Pract. **145**, 34–48 (2021). https://doi.org/10.1016/j.tra.2020.12.016
11. Che, H.W., et al.: PRAISE-HK: a personalized real-time air quality informatics system for citizen participation in exposure and health risk management. Sustain. Cities Soc. **54**, 101986 (2020). https://doi.org/10.1016/j.scs.2019.101986
12. Haddad, L., Aouachria, Z., Haddad, D.: How to use hydrogen in a new strategy to mitigate urban air pollution and preserve human health. Int. J. Sustain. Dev. Plan. **15**(7), 1007–1015 (2020). https://doi.org/10.18280/IJSDP.150705
13. Gobin-Rahimbux, B., et al.: A systematic literature review on ICT architectures for smart Mauritian local council. Transforming Gov. People Process Policy **14**(2), 261–281 (2020). https://doi.org/10.1108/TG-07-2019-0062
14. Varga, B., Tettamanti, T., Kulcsár, B., Qu, X.: Public transport trajectory planning with prob-abilistic guarantees. Transp. Res. Part B Methodol. **139**, 81–101 (2020). https://doi.org/10.1016/j.trb.2020.06.005
15. Olfindo, R.: Transport accessibility, residential satisfaction, and moving intention in a context of limited travel mode choice. Transp. Res. Part A Policy Pract. **145**, 153–166 (2021). https://doi.org/10.1016/j.tra.2021.01.012
16. Karami, A., Shah, V., Vaezi, R., Bansal, A.: Twitter speaks: A case of national disaster situational awareness. J. Inf. Sci. **46**(3), 313–324 (2020). https://doi.org/10.1177/0165551519828620
17. Dias, M.C.D.A., et al.: Vulnerability index related to populations at-risk for landslides in the Brazilian Early Warning System (BEWS). Int. J. Disast. Risk Reduction **49**, 101742 (2020). https://doi.org/10.1016/j.ijdrr.2020.101742

We represent the tree path as `path`, which contains attributes for the index location in the tree, `path.`*addr*, and the branch siblings, `path.`*S* necessary to calculate the Merkle root.

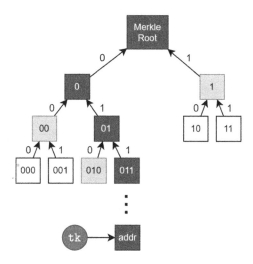

**Fig. 1.** Sparse Merkle tree.

## 3.2 Distributed Anonymous Payment

First, distributed anonymous payment (DAP) schemes allow an entity to prove they have an electronically minted coin, `cm`, without actually revealing the coin. The proof also requires the entity to provide knowledge of an associated, yet untraceable, serial number, `sn`, to prevent an entity from double-spending.

DAP schemes have the important property of retaining the minted coin as a valid leaf value in the Merkle Tree. Unlike Bitcoin, they do not have the luxury of maintaining an unspent transaction object (UTXO) inventory. To do so requires identifying spent coins, which DAP schemes do not reveal. Therefore, we must evaluate the Merkle tree size appropriate to support the life of the blockchain.

## 3.3 zk-SNARKs

The proof of knowledge in [33] uses zero-knowledge Succinct Non-Interactive Arguments of Knowledge (zk-SNARK) proofs from [13]. zk-SNARKs provide an efficient proof construct and verification mechanism. Our proof demonstrates the knowledge of a `cm` ∈ `CMList` without revealing `cm`, which equates to an anonymous user proving, "I have a valid token, but to ensure my anonymity, I am not going to tell you which token."

At its core, a zk-SNARK equates to demonstrating knowledge of a well-formed polynomial, $p(x)$, such that $h(x)t(x) = p(x)$, where $t(x)$ is a target polynomial available to the ledger, and $h(x)$ is derived by the prover as $h(x) = p(x)/t(x)$. The prover constructs the polynomial, $p(x)$, through an algebraic circuit available on the ledger which has been translated from code representing the Merkle Tree proof of knowledge. The prover samples some arbitrarily chosen secret $s$, such that $h(s)t(s) = p(s)$. To ensure the integrity of the target polynomial and sampled value, $s$, all operations are performed using homomorphic encryption with generator, $g$, such that $(g^{h(s)})^{t(s)} = g^{p(s)}$.

The process for non-interactive proof and verification consists of the following steps:

1. **Multi-Party Setup** - A multi-party setup protocol occurs to produce the public parameters, **pp**, which includes the homomorphic encryption of the powers of $x$ in the secret polynomial of dimension, $d$ for secret, $s$. Thus, the proving key consists of the powers necessary to compute the secret polynomial, the target polynomial, and sampled values to ensure zero knowledge of the secret polynomial. An initial setup requires multiple parties with strong zero-knowledge guarantees [14]. The keys used for proving and verification are referred to as the *common reference string*.
2. **Algebraic Circuit** - A program to construct the zero-knowledge proof converts to an algebraic circuit by flattening the program into a series of expressions in the form $x = y\mathbf{op}z$, which form the so-called circuit wires. Ultimately, these form the basis of the secret polynomial coefficients. In our case, the circuit consists of the Merkle Tree proof of inclusion.
3. **Proof** - An entity constructs a proof of knowledge demonstrating they have a valid token in the Merkle tree using both the public parameters and algebraic circuit. The proof is non-interactive because the prover does not need to exchange keys to produce the proof statement. Zero-knowledge comes through a key sampled by the prover, which conceals the secret polynomial.
4. **Verification** - Verification is performed in the chaincode of the ledger to ensure the construction of the secret polynomial in addition to the public inputs to the circuit is valid.

Besides the original works in zk-SNARKs, the papers [11,31] provide good tutorials on the process.

## 4     Distributed Ledger for Threat Sharing

Distributed ledgers provide transactional integrity for large and diverse communities. In its most well-known cryptocurrency implementations, distributed ledgers supply a high assurance system for transacting digital goods such as Bitcoin. Our scheme considers human work as the exchanged commodity for cybersecurity threat sharing. The work of threat identification and attribution involves costly human labor to identify artifacts, piece together the adversarial objective, and tie cyber observables to malware campaigns and threat actors.

Entities receive value through more actionable intelligence and an improved understanding of cyber risk.

The use of a distributed ledger for cybersecurity work is not without precedent. [34] proposes the use of economic incentives to incentivize secure data sharing. Also, in many ways, a marketplace for threat information can be compared to software bug bounty programs where companies wishing to fix software vulnerabilities before an adversary exploits them monetize the work of finding vulnerabilities [5]. However, with cyber threats, the work production comes from entities wishing to protect their systems better.

We propose a distributed ledger in which any participating entity submits monetized threat intelligence work in the form of structured work queries as transactions on the ledger. Entities requesting work do so through anonymous credentials using a web application tied to a peer entity on the distributed ledger. Participants use the same web application to search for information about a given threat. The ledger does not record searches as transactions.

## 4.1  Distributed Ledger Network

This section proposes a permissioned blockchain network architecture to support the exchange of threat intelligence between participating entities. Our implementation for threat sharing uses a permissioned blockchain. These differ from public blockchains by requiring authenticated access and eliminating the need for proof-of-work or proof-of-stake consensus. Chaincode is a set of smart contracts installed by participating entities and serves as the blockchain's central service rather than the currency transaction object. With cryptocurrency, smart contracts are a service of the blockchain, but with permissioned blockchains, the blockchain is a service of the smart contract.

Also, cryptocurrencies overcome almost all trust boundaries, but this is not always desirable, especially with CTI. Instead, we use the permissioned blockchain to overcome trust boundaries existing between organizations.

Figure 2 shows an example blockchain network in where the shaded area represents elements required by the blockchain and users involved in CTI access the network outside of the shaded area. Fundamentally, the blockchain includes a group of entities, referred to as peers, who have consensus on the chaincode execution and maintain a copy of both the blockchain and the current state database of chaincode assets (or objects).

Peers join the network either initially or through peer consensus. The collective peers comprise the distributed system's nodes, and they participate in the validation of new blocks and storage of the data. However, with permissioned blockchains, peers also provide the service of user interaction with the blockchain network.

An organization does not need to be a peer of the blockchain to participate in the service. Instead, peers provide credentialing services through their certificate authority. Users of other organizations are then permitted to execute chaincode transactions through peer applications.

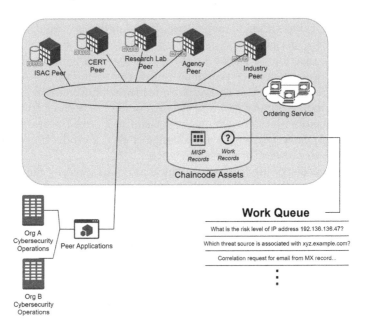

**Fig. 2.** Threat ledger network.

In the example shown in Fig. 2, the peers include organizations typically involved in threat sharing, such as government agencies, CERTs, ISACs, and research labs. These organizations have the incentive and resources to install and maintain the peer service needed for threat sharing. If a private entity wanted to participate in the network, they would only need to obtain credentials from a peer and use a published web application, thus, significantly lowering the bar of complexity for threat exchange participation.

The network also requires an ordering service. Blocks of transactions get added to the blockchain through the ordering service. Consistent with the execute-order-validate consensus approach described in [10], peers will first simulate the execution of proposed transactions before sending them to the ordering service. The ordering service then packages valid transactions into the next block and sends them to all network peers.

### 4.2   Chaincode Assets

The network's chaincode centers on CTI reports commonly exchanged between organizations. We choose to use the standard MISP format [37]. Other CTI taxonomies include STIX [12], and the Common Cyber Threat Framework [6], but the MISP format is extensible and concentrates on the threat report instead of the observable artifacts. By aggregating artifacts into event reports, we can more easily form a high-level representation of the CTI report's value.

# STellaR – A Stationary Telepresence Counselling System for Collaborative Work on Paper Documents

Matti Laak[1]([✉]), Anne-Kathrin Schmitz[2], Dominic Becking[1], Udo Seelmeyer[1], Philipp Waag[1], and Marc Weinhardt[2]

[1] Fachhochschule Bielefeld, Bielefeld, Germany
mlaak1@fh-bielefeld.de
[2] Universität Trier, Trier, Germany

**Abstract.** This paper gives an overview of the ongoing project STellaR – A stationary telepresence counselling system for collaborative work on paper documents. The system consists of dedicated rooms for video counselling, which clients can use to connect to a remotely located counselor without requiring any knowledge about computers or the internet. STellaR rooms are equipped with a large monitor, high quality microphone, camera, and sound system, which represent the counselor in life size.

The system enables a collaborative work on paper documents, that are still widely used in e.g., debt counselling. These documents are scanned and transmitted to the counselor. Through the use of projectors, the counselor can point, mark and annotate the paper documents. Furthermore, the digitized paper documents are archived in a block chain. This enables to track their states of editing over several counselling sessions.

We describe the developments on the system that have already taken place, as well as planned, future work.

**Keywords:** Telepresence · Videoconference · Digital counselling

## 1 Introduction

The recent outbreak of the corona virus has made telepresence systems more important than ever [1]. But even before the covid pandemic the need to move counselling from face to face to online services was present [2–4]. Online counselling services make it easier for clients to connect to a counsellor, without the need to travel.

But these services are not accessible to everyone. In a recent study [5], only 36% of German citizens stated, that they could set up a videoconference. Not everyone in need of

This research and development project is funded by the German Federal Ministry of Education and Research (BMBF) within the funding program "Forschung an Fachhochschulen" (13FH034SX8). The project is in cooperation with Bundesarbeitsgemeinschaft der Freien Wohlfahrtspflege (BAGFW) e.V., Deutscher Caritasverband e.V. and AWO Unterbezirk Hagen-Märkischer Kreis.

© Springer Nature Switzerland AG 2021
C. Stephanidis et al. (Eds.): HCII 2021, CCIS 1499, pp. 383–389, 2021.
https://doi.org/10.1007/978-3-030-90179-0_49

counselling has the necessary hardware, such as high-resolution cameras, microphones or high-speed internet access to partake in a good quality videoconference [7]. For effective counselling, the counsellor needs to be able to understand and see the client clearly, so that they can focus on the consultation and the clients body language. Technical difficulties may make it unnecessarily hard or even impossible to perform a counselling session.

Most counselling practice in Germany still uses paper documents sometimes abundantly so. In debt counselling, for example, the clients often bring folders full of documents such as receipts, letters, contracts, or forms. To work on these documents collaboratively via the internet, these need to be digitized. This process requires hardware like scanners not everyone has access to. Additionally, this process is time consuming and may be too difficult for certain users.

In order to solve these problems, we propose the "Stationary Telepresence system for Rural areas" ("STellaR").

## 2    Equipment and Methods

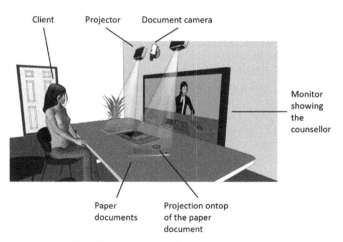

**Fig. 1.** Visualization of a STellaR room. Two projectors are placed left and right of the document camera. The Monitor is placed opposite of the client.

The STellaR system consists of several telepresence rooms (see Fig. 1), which the clients can easily reach to partake in a counselling session. These rooms will be located in nearby public institutions, like libraries or city halls. The rooms and the equipment are designed so that the clients do not need to operate any technology. The counselling session in a stellar room is designed to mirror the in-person session closely. To achieve this, the rooms are equipped with a large 4k monitor showing the counsellor in life-size. The monitor is placed on the wall behind a table. A chair for the client is placed in front of the table so that the counsellor appears to be sitting on the other side of the table. Utilizing high quality microphones and loudspeakers the counsellors voice sounds as if they were present using spatial sound distribution and ambient sound. The clients can place their paper documents on the desk. These documents will be automatically scanned, digitized and made available for the counsellor using high resolution document cameras. The counsellor then can edit, annotate, mark, and point on the digital twin of the document. These gestures and annotations will be projected on the real paper documents with the help of two projectors in the STellaR room. This enables collaborative work on a paper document and its digital twin at the same time at different locations.

The digitization of the documents also makes it possible to archive the documents and the change history using a blockchain. This way changes can be tracked over several sessions spanning the whole counselling process.

At the time of writing, we are building a test environment. In the first step, we will evaluate videoconferencing using our system with the focus on immersion and usability. In later steps the document digitization will be implemented and tested, followed by hard- and software for the collaborative work on paper documents.

Development of the system will take place in 3 phases. In the beginning of each phase the specific requirements of said phase are evaluated. First within our research group and thereafter with counsellors of our cooperation partners. Working closely with our target audience, we hope to develop a useful tool, that fits the needs of the users. In upcoming steps, we will test our so far developed software with students. After that we will further evaluate our software with actual counsellors and their clients. This approach will be repeated for every phase of our project.

## 2.1 Phase 1 – Immersive Videoconference

In phase one all components which are necessary for immersive videoconferencing have been chosen, assembled and connected. This includes all the needed hardware, such as monitor, laptop, microphone, camera and software. At the time of writing the first phase has almost been finished.

### Hardware

To provide an immersive experience the video and audio quality must be excellent. Our goal is to provide the client a counselling situation, that reassembles the face-to-face session as closely as possible. At the same time we have to bear in mind that for further distribution and implementation the hardware components should be picked from standard retail quality stock. High-end or experimental hardware would not be available to social welfare organizations providing counselling.

To present video to the client, the STellaR room is equipped with a 4k 65″ monitor with a 60 Hz refresh rate. Video is captured of both participants by a 4k capable camera that has a built-in microphone. Lifelike audio playback is provided by a 5.1 surround sound system that has a dedicated subwoofer. A stable internet connection with at least 10 Mbps is needed to guarantee good video and audio streams.

The workspace of the counsellor might not have enough space for a dedicated room for STellaR. Because of this the counsellors are equipped with a camera and microphone combination, a laptop, as well as a sound system. This enables them to expand their existing workplace with the necessary hardware to partake in a STellaR meeting.

**Software**

To send audio and video between the counsellor and client, we have chosen the open-source videoconferencing tool "Jitsi[1]". The software supports video calls between multiple participants but in our case the calls will be between two participants – the counsellor and the client. Jitsi handles calls with 2 participants through a peer-to-peer connection. A server is only needed to establish a connection and authenticate the participants. After that, the traffic will be routed between the two participants directly and not through the server.

Our Jitsi instance is configured so that every STellaR room has its own virtual Jitsi room. As soon as the laptop in the STellaR room is turned on, it will automatically open the web browser and login to its virtual room. This way on the counsellor's side they only need to open our Jitsi website and connect to the STellaR room of their choosing. All rooms will be secured by a password. This enables multiple counsellors from different organizations access to the STellaR rooms.

### 2.2 Phase 2 – Document Recognition

In the upcoming phase 2 a document recognition system will be developed. To achieve this a document camera will be installed in the STellaR room. The camera will be placed above the desk of the client, so that it can overlook the whole desk. Documents placed on the desk will then be scanned and send to the counsellor.

As for the software side, "tesseract[2]" is a likely candidate for optical character recognition. Good performance as well as an open-source approach make tesseract a good fit for our project [7]. Jitsi already has an infrastructure in place to send and receive documents. It must be evaluated if we can utilize the existing implementation or if it must be modified to fit our needs.

Handwritten text, that has already been filled in by the client also needs to be transmitted to the counsellor. Recognition of handwritten text has been thoroughly researched [7–10]. It has to be evaluated what approach is best for our use-case.

### 2.3 Phase 3 – Document Augmentation and Persistence

Phase 3 starts with the development of the necessary parts to visualize markings from the counsellor. This includes the installation of two projectors in the STellaR room. These will be used to project onto the paper documents of the client. To prevent shadows, that might be casted by objects on the table, we use two projectors. This way the projections comes from two sources [11].

It must be evaluated what kind of projections are useful for collaborative work on paper documents. Possible are simple pointing visualizations, like arrows, or dots. Other forms of text marking include highlighting, underlining or circling in. Also, text to be

---

[1] https://jitsi.org/, last accessed 11.06.2021.

[2] https://opensource.google/projects/tesseract, last accessed 11.06.2021.

filled in into blank spots of the forms are possibly beneficial for our case [12]. In order to find out what gestures might be useful, interviews with counsellors will be conducted. After that these gestures and annotations will be implemented and evaluated.

The second part of phase 3 consist of document persistence. The scanned paper document will be digitally archived. Their editing state can then be tracked over several consulting sessions. The system will be based on a block-chain [13, 14].

# 3   Evaluation

As already mentioned, we try to work as closely as possible with our target audience. This Co-Creation approach means, that in every step of our process, we also evaluate the software with said users. Since we are now on Phase one, we are currently working on the evaluation of the videoconferencing software.

To evaluate our teleconferencing tool we recently developed a questionnaire to assess (among other aspects[3]) the impact and degree of immersion during the counselling session. Our working hypothesis is that our system will lead to a substantially higher degree of immersion than other forms of online counselling.

The first step of this evaluation process was to find or develop a questionnaire suited for our needs. Since most questionnaires used to evaluate (online) counselling are more focused on counselling techniques, than we need them to be and questionnaires on immersion were mostly found concerning video games, most items used were newly developed. Regarding immersion, the ITQ Items by Witmer and Singer (1998) were used as an example [15].

There are eight items about the experience of immersion (as seen in Table 1) in the questionnaire. Items 1–7.1 are to be answered on a Likert scale. The last two items are open questions. By conducting a first trial run of said items with University students of social pedagogy (who were simulating a "regular" online counselling session), we were not only able to validate the items, but also to collect data to compare to the results of our trial run with the STellaR tool (also with University Students as attendees).

Both questionnaires include items about the affinity to digital devices and technology in general of the user, to see if this correlates with the impact of immersion observed during the counselling session.

The trial runs will be videographed, the students will get the questionnaire (slightly adjusted to the situation) and there will be critical incidents interviews afterwards about what went well and what still needs improvement before moving on.

These trial runs with Students will help us to test and evaluate the software in a 'safe' environment before our cooperating counsellors work with it. Since they will use it (even during our evaluation) with their clients, we want to make sure everything works fine. After evaluating the STellaR tool with Students, we will be able to continue with evaluations in the field.

---

[3] Other aspects include for example: use of digital media, questions about the room in general (clients only), technical difficulties during the session as well as socio-demographic data of participants.

For our field study, the questionnaire is given to the counsellor as well as the client (with slight changes concerning usability e.g.) – a step further to user-centered design. The session will also be videographed, so we can retrace errors if needed.

After the development has been completed, we will test with counsellors and their clients to evaluate our system. After that we will start approaching phase 2, which we hope will be at the end of 2021.

## 4    Conclusion

What we would like to achieve with STellaR, is to develop a video counselling software that serves the needs of counsellors as well as clients who, for various reasons, cannot or do not want to use online counselling or in person counselling. Along the 3 Phases of our work process feedback from users and evaluation are key. The next steps in Phase 1 will be both evaluations with students and in the field, as well as training our cooperating counsellors on how to work with our software. We are planning to wrap up Phase 1 by the end of the year, so we can focus on Phase 2.

## Appendix

**Table 1.** Items from the questionnaire concerning immersion.

| |
|---|
| 1.  I was able to adjust to the situation in front of the monitor well |
| 2.  The video counselling felt natural |
| 3.  Concerning the video image, I felt like I was actually sitting across from the other person |
| 4.  Concerning the audio, I felt like I was actually sitting across from the other person |
| 5.  I was able to focus on the conversation well |
| 6.  During the conversation I forgot that I was sitting in front of a monitor |
| 7.1 The STellaR Video Counselling felt different than a conversation with both people in one room |
| 7.2 If 7.1 is answered with yes: Can you tell us more about |

# References

1. Sadler, M.: COVID-19 Software Industry Statistics. https://www.trustradius.com/vendor-blog/covid-19-software-industry-data-and-statistics. Accessed 08 Jun 2021
2. Drda-Kühn, K., Hahner, R., Schlenk, E.: Mit smartphone, tablet und Sozialen Medien – Online-Beratung und -Therapie für die Generation der "Digital Natives". e-beratungsjournal.net **14**(1), 27–37 (2018)
3. Engelhardt, E. M., Reindl, R.: Blended counseling – beratungsform der zukunft? Resonanzen. E-J. für biopsychosoziale Dialoge in Psychotherapie, Supervision und Beratung, 4(2), 130–144 (2016)
4. Reindl, R.: Zum Stand der Onlineberatung in Zeiten der Digitalisierung. e-beratungsjournal.net **14**(1), 16–26 (2018)
5. D 21-Digital-Index 2020/2021, Initiative D21. https://initiatived21.de/app/uploads/2021/02/d21-digital-index-2020_2021.pdf#page=28, p. 26. Accessed 08 Jun 2021
6. D 21-Digital-Index 2020/2021, Initiative D21, https://initiatived21.de/app/uploads/2021/02/d21-digital-index-2020_2021.pdf#page=12, p. 10. Accessed 08 Jun 2021
7. Dome, S., Sathe, A.P.: Optical charater recognition using tesseract and classification. In: 2021 International Conference on Emerging Smart Computing and Informatics (ESCI), pp. 153–158 (2021)
8. Nathan, K.S., Beigi, H.S.M., Subrahmonia, J., Clary, G.J., Maruyama, H.: Real-time on-line unconstrained handwriting recognition using statistical methods. In: International Conference on Acoustics, Speech, and Signal Processing 1995, vol. 4, pp. 2619–2622 (1995)
9. Zimmermann, M., Chappelier, J., Bunke, H.: Offline grammar-based recognition of handwritten sentences. IEEE Trans. Pattern Anal. Mach. Intell. **28**(5), 818–821 (2006)
10. Simard, P.Y., Steinkraus, D., Platt, J.C.: Best practices for convolutional neural networks applied to visual document analysis. In: Proceedings of the 7th International Conference on Document Analysis and Recognition 2003, pp. 958–963 (2003)
11. Sukthankar, R., Cham, T.-J., Sukthankar, G.: Dynamic shadow elimination for multi-projector displays. In: Proceedings of the 2001 IEEE Computer Society Conference on Computer Vision and Pattern Recognition, CVPR 2001, p. II (2001)
12. Nagabhushan, P., Hannane, R., Elboushaki, A., Javed, M.: Automatic removal of handwritten annotations from between-text-lines and inside-text-line regions of a printed text document. Procedia Comput. Sci. **45**, 205–214 (2015)
13. Abid, G., Aslam, B., Rizwan, M., Ahmad, F., Sattar, M.U.: Block-chain - security advancement in medical sector for sharing medical records. In: 2019 International Conference on Innovative Computing (ICIC) (2019)
14. Christo, M.S., Anigo Merjora, A., Partha Sarathy, G., Priyanka, C., Raj Kumari, M.: An efficient data security in medical report using block chain technology. In: 2019 International Conference on Communication and Signal Processing (ICCSP), pp. 0606–0610 (2019)
15. Witmer, B.G., Singer, M.J.: Measuring presence in virtual environments: a presence questionnaire. Presence **7**(8), 225–240 (1998)

# Why Audiences Donate Money to Content Creators? A Uses and Gratifications Perspective

Lili Liu, Jiujiu Jiang[(⊠)], Shanjiao Ren, and Linwei Hu

College of Economics and Management, Nanjing University of Aeronautics and Astronautics,
Nanjing, China
{llili85,joy9971}@nuaa.edu.cn

**Abstract.** In the "We Media" era, any online user could act as a content creator, by uploading self-made texts, photos, audios and videos. In order to motivate the content creators' contribution, many online platforms allow audiences to support content creators with cash donation or virtual currency donation. This study aims to explore the antecedents of consumers' donation to content creators. Drawing on Uses and Gratifications theory, this study identifies and empirically investigates the impact of six antecedents on audiences' intention to donate, including enjoyment, escapism, social interaction, social identity, content quality, and content quantity. Data were collected from 133 respondents and analyzed with SmartPLS 3.2.9. The results indicate that enjoyment, social interaction, content quality, and content quantity positively affect users' intention to donate money, while escapism and social identity have no significant impact on donation intention. Potential theoretical and practical contributions are discussed.

**Keywords:** Uses and gratifications theory · Hedonic satisfaction · Social satisfaction · Utilitarian satisfaction · Donation intention

## 1 Introduction

In the "We Media" era, any online user could act as a content creator, by uploading self-made texts, photos, audios and videos [32]. In order to motivate content creators' contribution (e.g., the creators upload self-made content more frequently), many online platforms allow the audiences to support content creators with cash donation or virtual currency donation [21]. In Mainland China, the qidian.com (a fan-fiction novel website) firstly launched the donation function in June 2009. Later in August 2014, one of the most popular social media Sina Weibo added the donation function, while its rival WeChat released a beta version with donation function in March 2015. After that, almost all the well-known social media websites in China officially implemented the donation feature, such as Zhihu.com and Douban.com. In addition, video and audio websites are favored by the donation function as well. For instance, a famous uploader on bilibili (one of the famous video website in Mainland China), has received donations from almost 100,000 audiences within nine years, and more than 50 uploaders has been donated by more than 10,000 audiences.

© Springer Nature Switzerland AG 2021
C. Stephanidis et al. (Eds.): HCII 2021, CCIS 1499, pp. 390–398, 2021.
https://doi.org/10.1007/978-3-030-90179-0_50

Donation is a way for users to express their appreciation for works and their authors by giving virtual gold coins, virtual gifts or cash [33]. After watching a video, an audience in happy state might donate the author with a certain amount of virtual currency [17]. Implementing donation function attracts initial content creators to settle in and encourages their contribution of original content, which in turn enhance the impact of the websites. Meanwhile, content creators are able to earn additional revenue by uploading self-made content. Although adding donation function is beneficial for both content creators and websites, researchers has found that audiences' intention to donate is very weak [24]. For instance, Lian's research indicates that online novel readers have low willingness to donate money [23]. Therefore, it is important to identify the determinants of audiences' intention to donate money to content creators.

Drawing on Uses and Gratifications theory, this study empirically investigates the impact of six antecedents on users' donation intention: enjoyment and escapism as hedonic satisfaction, social interaction and social identity as social satisfaction, content quality and content quantity as utilitarian satisfaction.

## 2  Uses and Gratifications Theory

We adopt Uses and Gratifications theory (U&G theory) to investigate audiences' intention to donate in this study. According to U&G theory, audiences actively choose and use media based on their needs. Motivated by their needs, their choice and use of media will also be affected, leading to their affective, cognitive and behavioral outcomes [3, 19]. U&G theory has been widely applied in traditional media studies, such as broadcasting [26], newspapers [9] and television [2]. In recent years, U&G theory has been increasingly applied to IS studies to test users' behaviors in social media environments, such as WeChat [11], Twitter [8], and Facebook [25]. In conclusion, U&G theory provides a nomological framework without a predefined set of concepts [20].

Li et al. [22] has extended U & G theory by identifying three use-related satisfaction (hedonic satisfaction, utilitarian satisfaction, and social satisfaction) to examine the continuous intention towards social network games. Consuming online content not only meet audiences' entertainment and information needs, thus provides hedonic and utilitarian satisfaction [3], but also provides a channel for audiences to social and build relationships with others, hence generates social satisfaction. Therefore, following Li et al.'s research, we develop a contextualized research model which identifies three use-related satisfactions as antecedents of individuals' donation behavior, including hedonic satisfaction, utilitarian satisfaction, and social satisfaction.

## 3  Research Model and Hypotheses

The research model is shown in Fig. 1. We assume that hedonic satisfaction (enjoyment and escapism), social satisfaction (social interaction and social identity) and utilitarian satisfaction (content quality and quantity) are critical factors that affect audiences' donation intention.

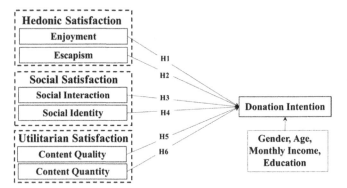

**Fig. 1.** Research model

### 3.1 Hedonic Satisfaction

In marketing discipline, hedonic factors comprises both imagination, such as escapism, and emotional response, such as enjoyment [16]. While consuming online content, audiences are able to generate hedonic satisfaction if they feel enjoyable [13] or they can escape from reality [7]. Prior research identifies perceived enjoyment as the main hedonic motivation for individuals' initial acceptance [22]. Audiences can have fun by browsing online content [13]. For example, on bilibili, users can watch various diverting posts from personal and public accounts, such as short videos, pictures and articles. The more entertaining the users feel, the more likely they would like to donate to content creators. Thus, we assume:

**H1.** Enjoyment positively affects the donation intention.

Escapism reflects escaping from unpleasant realities or stressful problems [16]. According to Hirschman, E. et al. [15], escapism is another important factor in satisfying individual hedonic needs and obtaining hedonic satisfaction, when using hedonic products and services. When people encounter troubles in the real world, and feel depressed, they turn to social media for comfort. Browsing the output from content creators (e.g., videos) is an easy and efficient way to help them escape from reality. Therefore, we hypothize:

**H2.** Escapism positively affects the donation intention.

### 3.2 Social Satisfaction

In this study, social satisfaction is captured by two factors: social interaction and social identity [22]. Social interaction is the critical reason that motivates people to use social media, which provides users with social gratification. Users communicate with each other in social media on a wide array of topics [1]. Users may be more willing to donate when they realize that the social interaction give them the chance to confide themselves and build friendships with others, making them feel more socially satisfied [29]. For example, on the Chinese novel website jinjiang (www.jjwxc.net), readers can donate to the authors they like, correspondingly, the author will express his/her appreciation in return by displaying a donor list publicly. Therefore, we propose:

**H3.** Social interaction positively affects the donation intention.

Social identity refers to a person's definition of who he or she is, including personal attributes and attributes shared with others, According to SIT (Social Identity Theory), people tend to classify themselves and others into various social categories, such as gender or race [30]. Usually people who like the same kind of works have more or less the same characteristics, and they seek the same emotional support from the works. Social identity mainly comes from group membership or qualification. People who strive to pursue or maintain a positive social identity in order to enhance their self-esteem are more likely to donate [5]. We thus hypothesize:

**H4.** Social identity positively affects the donation intention.

### 3.3 Utilitarian Satisfaction

Consumers may consume the same products or services with different goals, for example, for their own pleasure (a hedonic goal) or to achieve some higher level purpose (a utilitarian goal) [4]. Utilitarian satisfaction is evaluated by content quality [10] and content quantity [28]. Internet users are able to obtain information anytime, anywhere. While users' lives are flooded with various forms of information, their requirements for the quality of information are simultaneously increasing [12]. Content with higher quality are more likely to be viewed and read. Hence, we propose:

**H5.** Content quality positively affects the donation intention.

Content quantity refers to the richness of the intellectual aspects covered by the work [28]. Content quantity indicates whether the content is sufficiently interesting and attractive [18]. Tons of content (e.g., YouTube content, from inspiring speeches to music videos to honey badgers) attract more users to spend more time to browse, who are more probably to donate money when they become addicted. Based on the above inferences, we assume:

**H6.** Content quantity positively affects the donation intention.

## 4 Research Methodology

### 4.1 Measurements

The proposed research model was tested empirically with data collected via an online survey. When preparing the questionnaire, we adjusted the existing measurement scales to fit the research background of the project, and used a Likert Seven-level scale to measure all items, ranging from 1 (strongly disagree) to 7 (strongly agree). Items for donation intention were adapted from A.merchant et al. (2010) [27]; items for enjoyment were adapted from Ghani, J. A., & Deshpande, S. P. (1994) [13]; items for escapism were adapted from Colwell, J. (2007) [7]; items for social interaction were adapted from Papacharissi and Z (2002) [29] and Lee et al. (2012) [20]; items for social identity were adapted from Rob Bauer et al. (2015) [3]; items for content quality and content quantity were adapted from Floridi, Luciano. (2013) [10] and Nikolaos Korfiatis et al. (2012) [28].

## 4.2  Data Collection

Questionnaire was developed on the Sojump Platform (a Chinese survey website). Invitation link was distributed to users of representative content platforms, including novel websites such as qidian.com and zongheng.com, SNSs such as WeChat, Sina Weibo and Zhihu.com, video platforms such as bilibili.com and Tik Tok, and audio websites such as Himalaya FM and NetEase cloud music.

We obtained 133 valid and completed responses. Table 1 presents demographic information of the respondents. Majority of the respondents were between 18 and 25 years old (78.95%) and held Bachelor's degree (79.70%).

**Table 1.**  Respondent demographics.

| Item | Category | Frequency | Percentage (%) |
|------|----------|-----------|----------------|
| Gender | Male | 57 | 42.86 |
| | Female | 76 | 57.14 |
| Age | Under 18 | 12 | 9.02 |
| | 18–25 | 105 | 78.95 |
| | 26–35 | 6 | 4.51 |
| | 36–45 | 5 | 3.76 |
| | Above 45 | 5 | 3.76 |
| Monthly Income | Below 1000 yuan | 31 | 23.31 |
| | 1000–3000 yuan | 77 | 57.89 |
| | 3001–5000 yuan | 15 | 11.28 |
| | 5001–8000 yuan | 6 | 4.51 |
| | Above 8000 yuan | 4 | 3.01 |
| Education | High school and below | 13 | 9.77 |
| | Associate's Degree | 10 | 7.52 |

*(continued)*

**Table 1.** (*continued*)

| Item | Category | Frequency | Percentage (%) |
|---|---|---|---|
| | Bachelor's degree | 106 | 79.70 |
| | Master's degree | 3 | 2.26 |
| | Doctor's degree and above | 1 | 0.75 |

### 4.3 Data Analyses and Results

We tested the measurement model and structural model respectively, using SmartPLS 3.2.9. Reliability and validity of the measurement model were examined using SmartPLS 3.2.9. The Cronbach's alphas and the factor loadings of all the items were greater than 0.70, signifying good reliability of the research model. The composite reliabilities (CR) were all above 0.70, and the average variance extracted (AVE) values were all greater than 0.50, exhibiting good convergent validity [6, 31]. The explanatory rate of cumulative variance after rotation is 69.9% (higher than 50%), indicating that information can be extracted effectively [14].

Results of the regression analysis of the structural model were shown in Fig. 2, in which enjoyment ($\beta = 0.266$, $p < 0.01$), social interaction ($\beta = 0.189$, $p < 0.05$), content quality ($\beta = 0.385$, $p < 0.001$), and content quantity ($\beta = 0.166$, $p < 0.05$) were positively associated with donation intention. However, escapism and social identity had no significant impact on donation intention. Hence, H1, H3, H5, and H6 were supported. Besides, among the control variables, monthly income significantly influenced donation intention ($\beta = 0.23$, $p < 0.001$).

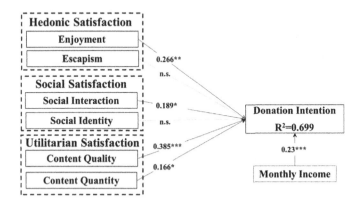

**Fig. 2.** Structural model

## 5   Contribution

This study investigates the antecedents of consumers' donation to content creators. The results of this study confirm that enjoyment, social interaction, content quality and content quantity are positively correlated with donation intention, while escapism and social identity have no significant effect on users' donation intention. It is worth noting that in the control variable, monthly income positively associates with users' donation intention. Many audiences turn to content platforms for comfort from unpleasant realities and the stresses of life, but it doesn't incentivize users to donate money to content creators. On the contrary, users pay more attention to their acquisition of emotional values, such as whether they could be entertained and obtain joy. As a result, escapism has no significant effect on users' intention to donate. In addition, users donate more out of appreciation for the utilitarian value they received from the content, rather than gaining social identity from consuming it. Therefore, we failed to find significant relation between social identity and users' donation intention.

This study is one of the earliest empirical studies that applied the U&G theory to investigate users' donate behavior in online content consumption, aiming to identify and verify the antedate causes of consumers' donation to content creators. In practice, findings of this study provide useful enlightenment for content creators: more than 60% of users have donated to content creators, and entertaining content that induces high enjoyment is more likely to be donated. Content creators can focus more on how much fun their content brings to users. Besides, if content creators are highly responsible and interact with audiences more frequently, users would be more willing to donate money to their works. Last but not least, the rich and comprehensive content arouses users' donation intention. Therefore, content creators should be devoted to producing larger amount of content with high quality.

**Acknowledgements.** This study was supported by the Fundamental Research Funds for the Central Universities No. NR2021003 awarded to the first author; this study was also supported by the Fundamental Research Funds for the Central Universities: No. 2019EC08 awarded to the second author and the Creative Studio of Electronic Commerce in Nanjing University of Aeronautics and Astronautics.

## References

1. Animesh, A., Pinsonneault, A., Yang, S.B., Oh, W.: An odyssey into virtual worlds: exploring the impacts of technological and spatial environments on intention to purchase virtual products. MIS Q. **35**(3), 789–810 (2011)
2. Babrow, A.S.: Student motives for watching soap operas. J. Broadcast. Electron. Media **31**(3), 309–321 (1987)
3. Bauer, R., Smeets, P.: Social identification and investment decisions. J. Econ. Behav. Organ. **117**, 121–134 (2015)
4. Botti, S., Mcgill, A.: The locus of choice: personal causality and satisfaction with hedonic and utilitarian decisions. J. Consum. Res. **37**, 1065 (2011)
5. Cheung, C.M.K., Liu, I.L.B., Lee, M.K.O.: How online social interactions influence customer information contribution behavior in online social shopping communities: a social learning theory perspective. J. Am. Soc. Inf. Sci. **66**(12), 2511–2521 (2015)

6. Chin, W.W.: The partial least squares approach to structural equation modelling. In: Marcoulides, G.A. (ed.) Modern Business Research Methods, pp. 295–336 (1998)
7. Colwell, J.: Needs met through computer game play among adolescents. Personality Individ. Differ. **43**(8), 2072–2082 (2007)
8. Coursaris, C.K., Jieun, S., Van, O.W., Younghwa, Y.: Disentangling Twitter's adoption and use (dis)continuance: a theoretical and empirical amalgamation of uses and gratifications and diffusion of innovations. AIS Trans Hum. Comput. Interact. **5**(1), 57–83 (2013)
9. Elliott, W.R., Rosenberg, W.L.: The 1985 Philadelphia newspaper strike: a uses and gratifications study. J. Q. **64**(4), 679–687 (1987)
10. Floridi, L.: Information quality. Philos. Technol. **26**(1), 1–6 (2013)
11. Gan, C., Li, H.: Understanding the effects of gratifications on the continuance intention to use WeChat in China: a perspective on uses and gratifications. Comput. Hum. Behav. **78**, 306–315 (2018)
12. Gao, S.: On the impact of mobile reading payment on information dissemination: a case study of WeChat reading reward function. Lantai World **2017**(21), 81–84 (2017)
13. Ghani, J.A., Deshpande, S.P.: Task characteristics and the experience of optimal flow in human-computer interaction. J. Psychol. **12**(4), 1143–1168 (1994)
14. Hair, J.F., Black, W.C., Babin, B.J., Anderson, R.E.: Multivariate Data Analysis, 7th edn. Pearson (2009)
15. Hirschman, E., Holbrook, M.: Hedonic consumption: emerging concepts, methods and propositions. J. Market. **46**, 92–101 (1982)
16. Holsapple, C., Wu, J.: User acceptance of virtual worlds: the hedonic framework. ACM SIGMIS Database **38**(4), 86–89 (2007)
17. Jiang, S.Z., Lin, J.M.: Three consumption behaviors of online novel readers. Novel Rev. **2018**(06), 137–146 (2018)
18. Kang, Y.S., Yong, J.K.: Do visitors' interest level and perceived quantity of web page content matter in shaping the attitude toward a web site? Decis. Support Syst. **42**(2), 1187–1202 (2007)
19. Kashif, M., Sarifuddin, S., Hassan, A.: Charity donation: intentions and behavior. Mark. Intell. Plan. **33**(1), 90–102 (2015)
20. Lee, J., Lee, M., Choi, I.H.: Social network games uncovered: motivations and their attitudinal and behavioral outcomes. Cyberpsychol. Behav. Soc. Netw. **15**(12), 643–648 (2012)
21. Lee, S.E., Choi, M., Kim, S.: They pay for a reason! The determinants of fan's instant sponsorship for content creators. Telematics Inform. **45**, 101–286 (2019)
22. Li, H., Liu, Y., Xu, X., Heikkila, J., Van der Heijden, H.: Modelling hedonic is continuance through the uses and gratifications theory: an empirical study in online games. Comput. Hum. Behav. **48**, 261–272 (2015)
23. Lian, S.P.: Research on the willingness of young readers to reward online literature. Pr World **2019**(07), 48–51 (2019)
24. Liu, L.: Motivating user-generated content contribution with voluntary donation to content creators. In: Nah, F.-H., Siau, K. (eds.) HCII 2019. LNCS, vol. 11589, pp. 221–230. Springer, Cham (2019). https://doi.org/10.1007/978-3-030-22338-0_18
25. Malik, A., Dhir, A., Nieminen, M.: Uses and gratifications of digital photo sharing on Facebook. Telematics Inform. **33**(1), 129–138 (2016)
26. Mendelsohn, H.: Listening to radio. In: Dexter, L.A., White, D.M. (eds.) People, Society, and Mass Communication, pp. 239–249 (1964)
27. Merchant, A., Ford, J.B., Sargeant, A.: Charitable organizations' storytelling influence on donors' emotions and intentions. J. Bus. Res. **63**(7), 754–762 (2010)
28. Korfiatis, N., García-Bariocanal, E., Sánchez-Alonso, S.: Evaluating content quality and helpfulness of online product reviews: the interplay of review helpfulness vs. review content. Electron. Commer. Res. Appl. **11**(3), 205–217 (2012)

29. Papacharissi, Z.: The self online: The utility of personal home pages. J. Broadcast. Electron. Media **46**(3), 346–368 (2002)
30. Tafel, H., Turner, C.: The social identity theory of intergroup behavior, 2nd edn. In: Worchel, S., Austin, W.G. (eds.) Psychology of Intergroup Relations, pp. 7–24 (1985)
31. Tenenhaus, M., Vinzi, V.E., Chatelin, Y.-M., Lauro, C.: PLS path modelling. Comput. Stat. Data Anal. **48**(1), 159–205 (2005)
32. Wang, C.L., Zhang, Y., Ye, L.R., Nguyen, D.D.: Subscription to fee-based online services: what makes consumer pay for online content. J. Electron. Commer. Res. **6**(4), 304 (2005)
33. Zhang, C., Wu, S.Q., Chang, S., Tian, J., Ding, Y.: Research on the "reward" mode applied to self-publishing platforms. Sci. Publishing **2015**(06), 134–139 (2015)

# Social Media and Social Movements: Using Social Media on Omnibus Law Job Creation Bill Protest in Indonesia and Anti Extradition Law Amendment Bill Movement in Hongkong

Arissy Jorgi Sutan[1]([✉]) [iD], Achmad Nurmandi[1] [iD], and Salahudin[2] [iD]

[1] Department of Government Affairs and Administration, Universitas Muhammadiyah Yogyakarta, Yogyakarta, Indonesia
arissy.jorgi.psc20@mail.umy.ac.id, nurmandi_achmad@umy.ac.id
[2] Department of Governmental Studies, Universitas Muhammadiyah Malang, Malang, Indonesia

**Abstract.** Social media has become a part of social life, social movement and protest like in Indonesia and Hongkong. This research aims to explore the social media role in Indonesia and Hongkong Protest's social movement case. This research used qualitative research and using Q-DAS (Qualitative Data Analysis Software). This research found 1) Social media users in Indonesia and Hongkong used the platform to protest towards the government policies with the nodes referring to actor and resistant contents. 2) There appeared to be a relation between Indonesia and Hongkong. However, in Indonesia's social media, Omnibus Law was more vital than Hongkong with a limit score of 0,5 higher than Hongkong with 0. This research also had limitations 1) the content and relation without knowing the popular word spread in social media; 2) the focus only based on social media data. The researchers recommend using famous words spread in social media and digital media.

**Keywords:** Social media · Social movements · Protest

## 1 Introduction

Social media has become part of social interaction and has seen alternative media to interact and discuss without limiting a country region [1]. It also plays an essential role in social movement and activism as a media platform [2]. In 2019, 2020, and 2021, there were at least three biggest protests in Asia. Two of them were in Indonesia and Hongkong. This research aims to determine the social media roles on Omnibus Law Protest Movements in Indonesia and Anti Extradition Law Amendment Bill Movement in Hongkong.

Social media can positively and negatively impact society, like mobilizing and organizing the society [2]; social media also gives society a chance to express their voice [3], share contents and discuss the social issue [4]. Social media can accommodate social

© Springer Nature Switzerland AG 2021
C. Stephanidis et al. (Eds.): HCII 2021, CCIS 1499, pp. 399–406, 2021.
https://doi.org/10.1007/978-3-030-90179-0_51

movement or provide the society in three ways: (1) As the platform to provide alternative information; (2) A platform to gain political will in society; and (3) A platform to increase the opposition forces to mobilize [5].

Many previous studies focused on how social media took part in the political phenomena. This research used Twitter to look deeper into the protests. Social media offers fresh information that conventional media like newspapers or television cannot provide, and the users can still interact without limit and face-to-face [6, 7]. This study seeks to answer two questions:

Q1. How do social media content and trends define social movements in Indonesia and Hong Kong?
Q2. How are the hashtags in the social movement cases in Indonesia and Hongkong related?

## 2  Literature Review

### 2.1  Social Media Sees as Platform of Social Movement

As a platform, social media can provide the netizen to raise a voice, discuss the social issue, and even coordinate the movement participant [8]. Social media can give some new perspective to the society about how communities shape and collect the identities to counter the social-political issue [9, 10]. A netizen in social media can use various features like using hashtags, posts, comments and shares, for example. Social movement narration can spread faster using hashtags like #BlackLivesMatters case, giving the social community more tolerant [11, 12]. Social media is more flexible to make their original content and can share it easily, connecting all users to discuss the social problems [13].

Social media can attract citizens' quality and quantity to participate in social and public issues [14]. Social media such as Facebook, Twitter, and blogs gain social attention and become a social movement like in the United States, Egypt, and Chile [15]. The social movement also needs a follow-up action or social movement sustainability. Without real action, the movement will only become clicktivism or slacktivism because the protestor rules out movements' action and sustainability [16].

### Social Movements on Reality

Social movements use various media to express what they want, using slogans to attract citizens to be aware of the social issues [17]. The social movement in this era uses social media to protest and starts to leave traditional ways due to its irrelevance value on social life [18, 19]. Activists take the opportunity to express their voices and protect the values, like an umbrella protecting the local identity value beneath it [20]. Like in Arab spring movements, the fear, anger, outrage turned into better hope for humanity because of social media [21]. This study focuses on social media's role in the social movement and protest case in Indonesia and Hongkong.

# 3   Method

This research implemented a qualitative approach and drove the research to explore the data and value. This research used Q-DAS (Qualitative Data Analysis Software) to analyze the social media data and Nvivo 12Plus to help the analysis. The researchers also used descriptive ways to deliver the research value and result. The data used in analytical parts were hashtags based on two cases: the protest movements of Omnibus Law in Indonesia and the anti-extramental Law Amendment Bill Movement in Hongkong. The hashtags descriptions are shown in Table 1.

**Table 1.**  Description of the Hashtags.

| Hashtags | Description |
| --- | --- |
| *Omnibus Law Case* | |
| #CabutOmnibusLaw | Promoting the Omnibus Law Job Creation Bill rejection |
| #DPRRIKhianatiRakyat | Showing that society did not trust the house representative |
| #GagalkanRUUCiptaKerja | Rejecting Omnibus Law Job Creation Bill |
| #KebenaranMilikPenguasa | Showing a satire from the activist that the government only spoke the truth |
| #MahasiswaBergerak | Showing that college students' participation in the protest movements |
| #MosiTidakPercaya | Showing that society did not trust the governments regarding Omnibus Law |
| #RakyatBukanMusuhNegara | Providing that civil society was not the enemy for the chaos happening |
| *Anti Extradition Law* | |
| #FreeHongKong | Showing the voice of Hongkong people to reject the extradition law amendment |
| #HongKongers | Showing the identity of the Hongkong People proud to be the citizen of Hongkong |
| #HongKongProtest | Showing the protest movement to reject the extradition law amendment |
| #save12hkyouth | Showing empathy to the 12 Hongkong youth that became a victim |
| #StandWithHK | Showing the support and empathy to the Hongkong Protest |
| #Stand With HongKong | Showing the support and empathy to the Hongkong Protest |

The analysis parts used two thoughtful analyses. Chart analysis explored the relevant content from the social media regarding the two cases, and Cluster analysis determined the hashtags.

## 4  Result and Discussion

This section defined the protests on the OmnibusLaw job creation bill in Indonesia and the anti-extradition Law Amendment Bill Movement in Hongkong, using chart analysis to explore the content tendency in social media. Cluster analysis was also used to determine the hashtags relation.

### 4.1  Omnibus Law Case Indonesia

This analysis used charts to determine the tendency of social media to reject the Omnibus Law Job creation Bill policy, using four nodes such as "Mahasiswa" or college students, "Pemerintah" or government, "Polisi" or police, and "Rakyat" or society". The analyses are in Fig. 1 and Table 2.

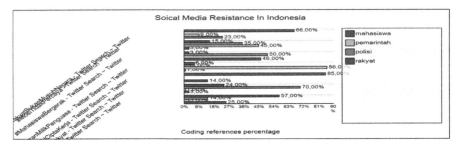

**Fig. 1.** Social media content resistance of Omnibuslaw Job Creation Bill

**Table 2.** Social media content resistance of Omnibuslaw Job Creation Bill

| Hashtags | mahasiswa | pemerintah | polisi | rakyat | Total |
|---|---|---|---|---|---|
| #CabutOmnibusLaw | 25% | 3,57% | 14,29% | 57,14% | 100% |
| #DPRRIKhianatiRakyat | 3,7% | 1,65% | 70,37% | 24,28% | 100% |
| #GagalkanRUUCiptaKerja | 14,29% | 0% | 0% | 85,71% | 100% |
| #KebenaranMilikPenguasa | 1,65% | 86,78% | 4,96% | 6,61% | 100% |
| #MahasiswaBergerak | 46,07% | 0,23% | 50,21% | 3,49% | 100% |
| #MosiTidakPercaya | 3,91% | 45,83% | 35,2% | 15,06% | 100% |
| #RakyatBukanMusuhNegara | 23,53% | 9,35% | 0,97% | 66,16% | 100% |
| **Total** | 23,46% | 22,24% | 37,68% | 16,62% | 100% |

The data provides four dominant content on social media regarding the Omnibus Law Job Creation Bill such as "Mahasiswa" or college students, "Pemerintah" or government, "Polisi" or police, and "Rakyat" or society." On "Mahasiswa", the highest score is #MahasiswaBergerak with 46,07%. The second place is #RakyatBukanMusuhNegara, with a score of 23,53%. The third place is #CabutOmnibusLaw, with a score of 25%.

On "Pemerintah", the highest is #KebenaranMilikPenguasa with 86,78%. The second place is #MosiTidakPercaya, with 45,83%. The third place is #RakyatBukanMusuhNegara, with a 9,35%. On "Polisi," the hashtag is #DPRRIKhianatiRakyat with 70,37%. The second place is #MahasiswaBergerak, with 50,21%. The third place is #MosiTidakPercaya, with 35,2%. On "Masyarakat," the highest is #GagalkanRUUCiptaKerja, with 85,71%. The second place is #RakyatBukanMusuhNegara, with 66,16%. The third place is #CabutOmnibusLaw, with 57,14%. The dominant talks is the word of "polisi" (police) with 37,68%. The second is "Mahasiswa" (college student), with 23,46%. The third place is "pemerintah" (government), with 22,24%. The last is "Masyarakat" (civil society), with 16,62%.

Cluster analysis processed the hashtags in social media, as shown in Fig. 2 and Table 3.

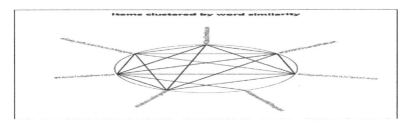

**Fig. 2.** The relationship between social media (hashtags) and Omnibus Law Indonesia rejection

**Table 3.** Top 5 Social media (hashtags) regarding Omnibus Law Indonesia rejection

| Hashtags A | Hashtags B | Pearson correlation coefficient |
|---|---|---|
| #MosiTidakPercaya | #CabutOmnibusLaw | 0,7133 |
| #MosiTidakPercaya | #GagalkanRUUCiptaKerja | 0,708409 |
| #MosiTidakPercaya | #DPRRIKhianatiRakyat | 0,696188 |
| #MahasiswaBergerak | #DPRRIKhianatiRakyat | 0,656569 |
| #GagalkanRUUCiptaKerja | #DPRRIKhianatiRakyat | 0,640077 |

This research used a lower limit of 0,5 and an upper limit of 1 point as a scale. The highest reach is the relation of #MosiTidakPercaya, and #CabutOmnibusLaw, with a score of 0,7133. The second place is #MosiTidakPercaya and #GagalkanRUUCiptaKerja with a score of 0,708409. The third place is #MosiTidakPercaya and #DPRRIKhianatiRakyat with 0,696188. The fourth place is #MahasiswaBergerak, and #DPRRIKhianatiRakyat is in fifth place with 0,65659. #GagalkanRUUCiptaKerja and #DPRRIKhianatiRakyat are in the last place with 0,640077.

## 4.2 Anti Extradition Law in Hongkong

Chart analysis was used to explore the content tendency in social media, and cluster analysis was also used to determine the hashtags relation. Chart analysis is explained in Table 4 and Fig. 3.

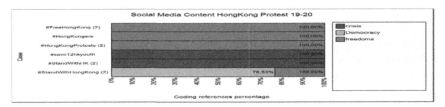

**Fig. 3.** The social media content of Hongkong Protest 19–20

**Table 4.** The social media content of Hongkong Protest 19–20

| Hashtags | Crisis | Democracy | freedoms | Total |
|---|---|---|---|---|
| #FreeHongKong | 0% | 0% | 100% | 100% |
| #HongKongers | 0% | 0% | 100% | 100% |
| #HongKongProtests | 0% | 0% | 100% | 100% |
| #save12hkyouth | 100% | 0% | 0% | 100% |
| #StandWithHK | 100% | 0% | 0% | 100% |
| #StandWithHongKong | 0,14% | 75,9% | 23,97% | 100% |
| Total | 23,37% | 56,8% | 19,83% | 100% |

Three nodes such as "Crisis", "Democracy", and "Freedom" were used in the Hongkong protest case, unlike Indonesia's case. The Hongkong case was more concentrated on a few hashtags. The "Crisis" nodes with 100% have three hashtags such as #save12hkyouth, #StandWithHK and #StandWithHongKong with 0,14%. The highest "Democracy" nodes are #StandWithHongKong with 75,9%, and the other is 0%. The "Freedom" nodes have three hashtags with 100%, such as #FreeHongKong, #HongKongers and #HongKongProtest. The analysis is explained in Fig. 4 and Table 5.

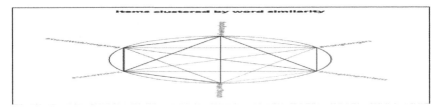

**Fig. 4.** The relationship between social media and hashtags regarding the Hongkong protest case

**Table 5.** Top 5 Social media relation of Hongkong Protest 19–20

| Hashtags A | Hashtags B | Pearson correlation coefficient |
| --- | --- | --- |
| #StandWithHongKong | #FreeHongKong | 0,650795 |
| #StandWithHK | #save12hkyouth | 0,636376 |
| #StandWithHongKong | #StandWithHK | 0,50603 |
| #StandWithHK | #FreeHongKong | 0,439756 |
| #HongKongProtests | #FreeHongKong | 0,43252 |

There was an average relation using 0 points (Lower) and 1 point (Upper) limits. The highest is #StandWithHongKong and #FreeHongKong with 0,650795. The second is #StandWithHK and #save12hkyouth with 0,636376. The third is #StandWithHongKong and #StandWithHK 0,50603. #StandWithHK and #FreeHongKong are in fourth place with 0,439756, while #HongKongProtests and #FreeHongKong are in fifth place 0,43252.

## 5   Conclusion

From the analysis, some conclusions can be drawn: 1) Social media in the Indonesia and Hongkong protests were used as a platform to object to the government policy with the nodes referring to actors and narration of resistance; 2) There appeared to be a relation between Indonesia and Hongkong. However, in Indonesia's social media, Omnibus Law was more vital than Hongkong with a limit score of 0,5 higher than Hongkong with 0. This research also had limitations 1) the content and relation without knowing the popular word spread in social media; 2) the focus only based on social media data.

## References

1. Miladi, N.: Social media and social change. Dig. Middle East Stud. **25**(1), 36–51 (2016). https://doi.org/10.1111/dome.12082
2. McCabe, A., Harris, K.: Theorizing social media and activism: where is community development? Community Dev. J. 1–20 (2020). https://doi.org/10.1093/cdj/bsz024
3. Burke, B.R., Şen, A.F.: Social media choices and uses: comparing Turkish and American young-adults' social media activism. Palgrave Commun. **4**(1) (2018). https://doi.org/10.1057/s41599-018-0090-z
4. Korn, J.U., Kneese, T.: Guest editors introduction: feminist approaches to social media research: history, activism, and values. Fem. Media Stud. **15**(4), 707–710 (2015). https://doi.org/10.1080/14680777.2015.1053713
5. Bui, T.H.: The influence of social media in Vietnam's elite politics. J. Curr. Southeast Asian Aff. **35**(2), 89–111 (2016). https://doi.org/10.1177/186810341603500204
6. Murthy, D.: Introduction to social media, activism, and organizations. Soc. Media Soc. **4**(1) (2018). https://doi.org/10.1177/2056305117750716

7. Murthy, D.: Comparative process-oriented research using social media and historical text. Social. Res. Online (2019). https://doi.org/10.1177/1360780417731272
8. Ozturkcan, S., Kasap, N., Cevik, M., Zaman, T.: An analysis of the Gezi Park social movement tweets. Aslib J. Inf. Manag. **69**(4), 426–440 (2017). https://doi.org/10.1108/AJIM-03-2017-0064
9. Kou, Y., Kow, Y.M., Gui, X., Cheng, W.: One Social movement, two social media sites: a comparative study of public discourses. Comput. Support. Coop. Work CSCW Int J **26**(4–6), 807–836 (2017). https://doi.org/10.1007/s10606-017-9284-y
10. Burgess, J., Marwick, A., Poell, T., Poell, T., van Dijck, J.: Social media and new protest movements. SAGE Handb. Soc. Media 546–561 (2017). https://doi.org/10.4135/978147398 4066.n31
11. Gready, P., Robins, S.: Rethinking civil society and transitional justice: lessons from social movements and "new" civil society. Int. J. Hum. Rights **21**(7), 956–975 (2017). https://doi.org/10.1080/13642987.2017.1313237
12. Zhang, H.: The influence of the ongoing COVID-19 pandemic on family violence in China. J. Fam. Violence (2020). https://doi.org/10.1007/s10896-020-00196-8
13. Lee, F.L.F., Chen, H.T., Chan, M.: Social media use and university students' participation in a large-scale protest campaign: the case of Hong Kong's Umbrella Movement. Telemat. Informatics **34**(2), 457–469 (2017). https://doi.org/10.1016/j.tele.2016.08.005
14. Jost, J.T., et al.: How social media facilitates political protest: information, motivation, and social networks. Polit. Psychol. **39**(3), 85–118 (2018). https://doi.org/10.1111/pops.12478
15. Zhu, Q., Skoric, M., Shen, F.: I shield myself from thee: selective avoidance on social media during political protests. Polit. Commun. **34**(1), 112–131 (2017). https://doi.org/10.1080/105 84609.2016.1222471
16. Specht, D., Ros-Tonen, M.A.F.: Gold, power, protest: digital and social media and protests against large-scale mining projects in Colombia. New Media Soc. **19**(12), 1907–1926 (2017). https://doi.org/10.1177/1461444816644567
17. Gukurume, S.: #ThisFlag and #ThisGown cyber protests in zimbabwe: reclaiming political space. Afr. J. Stud. **38**(2), 49–70 (2017). https://doi.org/10.1080/23743670.2017.1354052
18. Lee, F.L.F.: Internet alternative media, movement experience, and radicalism: the case of post-Umbrella Movement Hong Kong. Soc. Mov. Stud. **17**(2), 219–233 (2018). https://doi.org/10.1080/14742837.2017.1404448
19. Lee, F.L.F., Chan, J.M.: Digital media activities and mode of participation in a protest campaign: a study of the Umbrella Movement. Inf. Commun. Soc. **19**(1), 4–22 (2016). https://doi.org/10.1080/1369118X.2015.1093530
20. Dong, T., Liang, C., He, X.: Social media and internet public events. Telemat. Inform. **34**(3), 726–739 (2017). https://doi.org/10.1016/j.tele.2016.05.024
21. Wang, Y.: Local identity in a global city: Hong Kong localist movement on social media. Crit. Stud. Media Commun. **36**(5), 419–433 (2019). https://doi.org/10.1080/15295036.2019.165 2837

# The Message Is Unclear: Evaluating Disinformation in Anti-Vaccine Communities

Alicia J.W. Takaoka(✉)

University of Hawai'i at Hilo, Hilo, USA
ajwilson@hawaii.edu

**Abstract.** Vaccine hesitancy and speculation are persistent throughout the history of health care. This study employs situated awareness to evaluated the impact information has on decision-making. A set of frequently circulated documents called Vaccine Guide presents information from vaccine inserts, court cases, and other documents. This Guide is widely circulated in anti-vaccine communities on Facebook. A survey was conducted among university college students in order to evaluate claims about vaccine schedules and examine highlighted passages in this collection of documents and to determine how these passages impact information interpretation and personal health literacy from a situated awareness theory perspective.

**Keywords:** Anti-vaccine community · Situation awareness · Health information literacy · Vaccine schedule · Disinformation

In some groups, like anti-vaxxer groups, misinformation and disinformation about vaccines may be taken at face value because either the group or the person sharing the story are viewed as trusted sources of information in the group. However, the decision to trust a source is related to the skills and knowledge one possesses in identifying the ethos of a source and other related skills of information literacy. Vaccine Guide (Guide), housed at vaccine.guide, is a database available to anyone with the link. The guide was updated in October 2019, and the entire database can now be downloaded for free; however, only the first three sections were publicly available without a paywall. In its entirety, the current version of the Guide is over 1600 pages. Select information on each page is highlighted. This information, when read out of context, seems to reinforce the position of anti-vaccination groups that all vaccines are harmful. This study employs a mixed methods approach to evaluate the interpretations of highlighted content in the guide on its own and with context. This study uses the vaccine schedules, theories of situated awareness and disinformation, and a survey to evaluate information interpretation as presented in the Vaccine Guide.

© Springer Nature Switzerland AG 2021
C. Stephanidis et al. (Eds.): HCII 2021, CCIS 1499, pp. 407–413, 2021.
https://doi.org/10.1007/978-3-030-90179-0_52

# 1    Background

Knowing that vaccine hesitancy is persistent through history allows for the exploration of several areas related to this study. First, an overview of disinformation is discussed to evaluate whether or not the information in the Vaccine Guide can be categorized as disinformation. Next, situated awareness theory is introduced. Finally, personal health literacy is employed to understand how people apply information related to health and vaccines.

## 1.1    Disinformation

To understand what disinformation is, information and misinformation must be examined. Fox [7] describes information carried in many ways. By focusing on sentences, Fox examines the distinctions between conveying and containing information in order to contrast information and misinformation and the processes of informing and misinforming. The distinction, to Fox, is in the message's content and how it is conveyed. Misinformation is then categorized as non-factual or outdated when compared to information, which is factual and whose purpose is to "convey meaning by what is contained" (p. 12). Misinformation has since become a vast area of research in information sciences and other fields [6,8,9].

Some researchers believe that disinformation, while starting as a type of misinformation, is becoming separate and distinct. Fallis [3,4] notes that "we need to be able to distinguish disinformation from other forms of misinformation" (p. 136) as exposure to disinformation is becoming more prevalent in media. Rubin [13] articulates the distinction as intent. Misinformation is not intentionally misleading. Examining the information in Vaccine Guide identified the highlighted sentences as cherry-picked. In some instances, highlighted information ignores key context cues in preceding and following sentences and paragraphs that explain why the highlighted passage is in contrast to the surrounding information. As a result, it is hypothesized that *Information highlighted in Vaccine Guide is intentionally misleading, so it can be classified as disinformation.*

## 1.2    Situated Awareness Theory

Situated awareness is defined as viewing and experiencing events in time and space. This includes observing the environment, their meaning, and how they might change in the future [2]. In computer science, situated awareness is often found in literature about social media spaces [14].

When reflecting on disinformation about vaccines, the consequences affect individuals to entire communities. Ahmed et al. express that understanding the mental model of a situation, one can easily preent disinformation that will be accepted as reality [1]. The following hypothesis was developed from situated awareness theory: *The highlighted information in Vaccine Guide documents is designed to impact interpretations about vaccines and vaccine efficacy.*

## 1.3    Personal Health Literacy

Personal health literacy is the ability to find information and apply it to make informed health-related decisions and actions for themselves and others [10, 12]. Health literacy is growing field that evaluates how people across generations search for, access, and apply health information both in educational settings and beyond.

Anti-Vaccine research in online spaces is a growing and robust area, and disinformation relating to vaccines contribute negatively to people's willingness to get vaccines as well as contribute to creating a general distrust in health institutions. As pointed out in Featherstone and Zhang's [5] research on reactions to vaccine misinformation, retractions of disinformation do not stop the spread of the misinformation, and people still make personal health decisions based on these false, retracted studies. From the literature on personal health information and disinformation, the following hypothesis was created: *Survey respondents will select different valence for highlighted information and highlighted information when it is situated in context.* As a result of this body of literature, the study was designed to evaluate information in and out of context through close reading and by evaluating respondent interpretation.

## 2    Methods

This case study employed mixed methods to evaluate types of data shared in anti-vaccine closed groups on Facebook. Of those documents housed in Vaccine Guide, Sects. 1, 2, 3, certain parts of information are highlighted. Those highlighted pieces of information were copied into a spreadsheet, and context words—those preceding and following the highlighted information—were copied to adjoining column to determine if the context changes the meaning of the highlighted information. Close reading was employed to determine changes in meaning using the surrounding text.

The highlighted text of 10 documents were selected at random. They were compiled into a survey evaluating their valence and meaning without context and then again with context. The valence for each text was calculated by assigning a score to the valence and comparing the changes in scores before and after reading the contextual information. Nine out of ten highlighted pieces of information implied meaning in contrast to the contextual information in the surrounding text.

The survey asked respondents to read the passage, assign valence, and explain why they assigned the valence chosen. Then, the respondents read contextual information and were asked to identify the valence, whether or not the contextual information changed their interpretation, and why or why not this was the case. For eight out of ten questions, valence was selected from a multiple choice response while respondents could write in the post-context valence. Total composite scores of valence were compiled, and the total movement in either the positive or negative direction was calculated. One-Way ANOVA was also calculated.

## 3   Results

The differences in the interpretation of information presented in the Guide in and out of context were interpreted differently, and the valence of 90% of passages changed when context information was provided.

It was hypothesized that *Information highlighted in Vaccine Guide is intentionally misleading, so it can be classified as disinformation.* This hypothesis is true. Each section in the Guide contains vaccine inserts, scholarly articles, and other documents relating to the topic like court cases and fact sheets. Only two documents out of 46 (4.3%) contain any notes for how to interpret the highlighted information. Only 0.08% of the highlighted information included notes. Overall, 46 documents totaling 493 pages were included in Sects. 1, 2, 3. Of those, only 239 highlighted pieces of information were present.

It was hypothesized that *The highlighted information in Vaccine Guide documents is designed to impact interpretations about vaccines and vaccine efficacy.* This hypothesis is true. Across all questions, 76.8% of written interpretations of arguments noted a disparity between information presented in the passage when compared against context information. Some highlighted information only stresses one side of an argument. Table 1 identifies the changes in composite valence information before and after context was added.

**Table 1.** Composite valence before and after context information with the total change in valence.

| Source | Composite before | Composite after | Change |
|---|---|---|---|
| Q1. HR 5546 | −2 | 6 | 9 |
| Q2. Supreme Court Case | −10 | −3 | 7 |
| Q3. Supreme Court Case | −2 | 4 | 7 |
| Q4. Summary of Case | −9 | −2 | 7 |
| Q5. Summary of Case | −6 | −6 | 0 |
| Q6. HRSA | 2 | 4 | 2 |
| Q7. Total compensation | 0 | 1 | 1 |
| Q8. Guiellen-Barre | −11 | −6 | 5 |
| Q9. VAERS is a reporting system | 8 | 6 | −2 |
| Q10. Support VAERS | −11 | −13 | −2 |

It was hypothesized that *Survey respondents will select different valence for highlighted information and highlighted information when it is situated in context.* According to survey respondents, the context information did change the valence in seven out of ten passages with movement in the positive direction. Two passages had movement in the negative direction, and one passage had the same composite valence, which was negative.

The one-way ANOVA on composite scores did not indicate significance; however, Spearman's correlation was run on valence for all variables. Some correlations were identified as shown in Figs. 1 and 2. Correlations are identified in red text, and the positive or negative number indicates that they tend to increase and decrease together. The initial interpretation for Q6, HRSA, had the most correlation with independent variables, while many questions exhibited no correlation. When examining the data for correlations between the interpretations and valence, it seems that valence is more related to the interdependence of question responses than to independent variables. Several factors may have contributed to the results in this case study that may not be repeatable in different settings.

| Age | Q1a | Q1b | Q2a | Q2b | Q3a | Q3b | Q4a | Q4b | Q5a | Q5b | Q6a | Q6b | Q7a | Q7b | Q8a | Q8b | Q9a | Q9b | Q10a | Q10b |
|---|---|---|---|---|---|---|---|---|---|---|---|---|---|---|---|---|---|---|---|---|
| From | 0.12 | -0.08 | -0.35 | 0.04 | 0.04 | -0.01 | 0.16 | 0.14 | -0.04 | 0.04 | 0.25 | -0.20 | 0.14 | -0.19 | 0.49 | 0.18 | -0.16 | 0.06 | 0.38 | 0.34 |
| Live | -0.17 | -0.01 | 0.03 | -0.06 | -0.23 | 0.19 | -0.14 | 0.37 | -0.09 | 0.10 | 0.11 | 0.47 | 0.11 | 0.29 | -0.15 | 0.02 | 0.11 | 0.01 | -0.49 | -0.31 |
| Degree | -0.25 | 0.11 | -0.08 | 0.06 | -0.13 | 0.43 | 0.01 | 0.41 | -0.04 | 0.27 | 0.29 | 0.48 | 0.27 | 0.12 | -0.07 | 0.21 | 0.05 | -0.24 | -0.16 | -0.13 |
| Gender | -0.22 | -0.25 | -0.13 | -0.09 | 0.23 | -0.17 | 0.30 | 0.07 | 0.33 | 0.35 | -0.13 | -0.18 | -0.36 | -0.01 | 0.32 | 0.36 | -0.40 | 0.15 | 0.41 | 0.39 |
| Political Party | -0.12 | -0.01 | -0.03 | 0.10 | 0.30 | 0.05 | 0.14 | -0.18 | 0.12 | 0.20 | -0.06 | -0.28 | 0.00 | -0.22 | -0.21 | -0.29 | 0.24 | 0.08 | 0.16 | -0.09 |
| Trust Government | 0.09 | 0.08 | 0.23 | -0.01 | -0.06 | 0.00 | 0.16 | -0.14 | 0.35 | 0.05 | -0.17 | -0.29 | -0.26 | 0.04 | -0.15 | -0.03 | -0.18 | -0.05 | 0.24 | 0.04 |
| Trust CDC | -0.08 | 0.38 | -0.11 | -0.15 | -0.26 | -0.06 | -0.15 | 0.16 | -0.21 | 0.09 | 0.16 | 0.30 | 0.19 | 0.30 | 0.13 | 0.29 | 0.14 | 0.00 | -0.06 | 0.00 |
| Trust News | 0.03 | 0.38 | -0.04 | 0.08 | -0.28 | 0.21 | 0.08 | -0.07 | -0.19 | -0.04 | 0.11 | 0.12 | 0.14 | -0.12 | -0.05 | 0.16 | -0.09 | -0.25 | 0.01 | -0.10 |
| Trust Vaccines | 0.15 | 0.32 | -0.12 | -0.33 | -0.43 | 0.14 | -0.12 | 0.27 | -0.21 | 0.21 | 0.19 | 0.30 | 0.09 | 0.26 | -0.06 | 0.04 | 0.17 | -0.01 | -0.24 | -0.27 |
| Trust Q | 0.05 | -0.17 | -0.17 | -0.15 | 0.29 | 0.01 | -0.14 | -0.15 | -0.19 | -0.10 | 0.15 | -0.02 | 0.24 | -0.27 | -0.34 | -0.27 | 0.13 | 0.24 | -0.30 | -0.23 |
| Is Covid real | 0.37 | 0.01 | 0.45 | 0.09 | -0.39 | -0.21 | 0.23 | 0.31 | 0.08 | 0.10 | -0.15 | 0.05 | 0.00 | 0.32 | 0.20 | 0.21 | -0.30 | -0.01 | -0.18 | -0.14 |
| Groups | -0.04 | 0.09 | 0.21 | -0.06 | -0.03 | 0.35 | -0.12 | 0.24 | -0.08 | 0.20 | 0.03 | 0.39 | 0.36 | 0.31 | -0.16 | 0.22 | 0.13 | -0.22 | -0.32 | -0.19 |
| Vaccine Injured | 0.06 | -0.34 | 0.20 | -0.18 | 0.04 | -0.08 | -0.07 | 0.01 | 0.04 | 0.05 | -0.05 | -0.09 | 0.25 | 0.20 | -0.34 | -0.31 | 0.44 | 0.31 | -0.24 | -0.25 |

**Fig. 1.** Spearman's correlations between dependent and independent variables

| Between | Q1a | Q1b | Q2a | Q2b | Q3a | Q3b | Q4a | Q4b | Q5a | Q5b | Q6a | Q6b | Q7a | Q7b | Q8a | Q8b | Q9a | Q9b | Q10a | Q10b |
|---|---|---|---|---|---|---|---|---|---|---|---|---|---|---|---|---|---|---|---|---|
| Q1a | -0.15 | 0.13 | 0.24 | 0.42 | 0.19 | -0.14 | -0.01 | -0.33 | 0.01 | 0.00 | -0.40 | -0.34 | -0.20 | -0.20 | 0.21 | -0.01 | -0.11 | 0.11 | 0.25 | 0.12 |
| Q1b | 1.00 | -0.30 | 0.21 | 0.12 | -0.16 | -0.30 | 0.38 | 0.12 | -0.05 | -0.28 | 0.02 | -0.33 | -0.17 | 0.16 | 0.03 | -0.34 | -0.30 | 0.21 | -0.09 | -0.01 |
| Q2a | -0.30 | 1.00 | 0.02 | 0.19 | -0.27 | 0.14 | -0.21 | -0.16 | -0.20 | 0.08 | -0.05 | 0.13 | 0.00 | -0.02 | 0.06 | 0.13 | 0.20 | -0.39 | 0.22 | 0.02 |
| Q2b | 0.21 | 0.02 | 1.00 | 0.25 | -0.02 | -0.24 | -0.17 | -0.34 | -0.16 | -0.04 | -0.28 | -0.08 | 0.00 | 0.14 | -0.35 | 0.07 | -0.03 | 0.25 | -0.21 | -0.34 |
| Q3a | 0.12 | 0.19 | 0.25 | 1.00 | -0.04 | -0.05 | 0.00 | -0.17 | -0.15 | 0.10 | -0.06 | -0.17 | 0.12 | -0.28 | 0.20 | 0.11 | 0.15 | 0.06 | 0.35 | 0.08 |
| Q3b | -0.16 | -0.27 | -0.02 | -0.04 | 1.00 | 0.01 | -0.06 | -0.16 | 0.20 | 0.04 | -0.51 | -0.42 | -0.01 | -0.08 | -0.10 | -0.19 | 0.07 | 0.06 | -0.08 | 0.05 |
| Q4a | -0.30 | 0.14 | -0.24 | -0.05 | 0.01 | 1.00 | -0.23 | 0.51 | 0.24 | 0.28 | 0.22 | 0.49 | 0.33 | 0.26 | -0.18 | 0.24 | 0.24 | -0.52 | -0.20 | -0.22 |
| Q4b | 0.38 | -0.21 | -0.17 | 0.00 | -0.06 | -0.23 | 1.00 | 0.42 | 0.40 | 0.20 | 0.11 | -0.14 | -0.23 | 0.10 | 0.08 | -0.07 | -0.33 | 0.01 | 0.09 | 0.15 |
| Q5a | 0.12 | -0.16 | -0.34 | -0.17 | -0.16 | 0.51 | 0.42 | 1.00 | 0.31 | 0.24 | 0.28 | 0.48 | 0.09 | 0.61 | -0.06 | 0.24 | -0.06 | -0.24 | -0.36 | -0.13 |
| Q5b | -0.05 | -0.20 | -0.16 | -0.15 | 0.20 | 0.24 | 0.40 | 0.31 | 1.00 | 0.38 | -0.17 | -0.14 | -0.14 | 0.00 | -0.01 | -0.10 | -0.19 | -0.10 | 0.03 | -0.09 |
| Q6a | -0.28 | 0.08 | -0.04 | 0.10 | 0.04 | 0.28 | 0.20 | 0.41 | 0.38 | 1.00 | -0.07 | 0.33 | 0.10 | 0.14 | 0.00 | 0.33 | -0.07 | 0.07 | 0.00 | -0.10 |
| Q6b | 0.02 | -0.05 | -0.28 | -0.06 | -0.51 | 0.22 | 0.11 | 0.28 | -0.17 | -0.07 | 1.00 | 0.52 | 0.26 | 0.00 | -0.16 | 0.14 | 0.21 | -0.04 | 0.11 | 0.02 |
| Q7a | -0.33 | 0.13 | -0.08 | -0.17 | -0.42 | 0.49 | -0.14 | 0.48 | -0.14 | 0.33 | 0.52 | 1.00 | 0.23 | 0.41 | -0.19 | 0.46 | 0.12 | -0.26 | -0.34 | -0.17 |
| Q7b | -0.17 | 0.00 | 0.00 | 0.12 | -0.01 | 0.33 | -0.23 | 0.09 | -0.14 | 0.10 | 0.26 | 0.23 | 1.00 | 0.00 | 0.21 | 0.30 | -0.10 | -0.17 | -0.12 |  |
| Q8a | 0.16 | -0.02 | 0.14 | -0.28 | -0.08 | 0.26 | 0.10 | 0.61 | 0.00 | 0.14 | 0.00 | 0.41 | -0.11 | 1.00 | -0.19 | 0.15 | -0.04 | -0.11 | -0.34 | 0.05 |
| Q8b | 0.03 | 0.06 | -0.35 | 0.20 | -0.10 | -0.18 | -0.06 | -0.06 | -0.01 | 0.00 | -0.16 | -0.19 | 0.00 | -0.19 | 1.00 | 0.29 | -0.45 | -0.35 | 0.59 | 0.72 |
| Q9a | -0.34 | 0.13 | 0.07 | 0.11 | -0.19 | 0.24 | -0.07 | 0.24 | -0.10 | 0.33 | 0.14 | 0.46 | 0.21 | 0.15 | 0.29 | 1.00 | -0.35 | -0.12 | 0.06 | 0.09 |
| Q9b | -0.30 | 0.20 | -0.03 | 0.15 | 0.07 | 0.24 | -0.33 | -0.06 | -0.19 | 0.14 | 0.10 | 0.12 | 0.30 | -0.04 | -0.45 | -0.35 | 1.00 | 0.24 | -0.09 | -0.27 |
| Q10a | 0.21 | -0.39 | 0.25 | 0.06 | 0.06 | -0.52 | 0.01 | -0.24 | -0.10 | 0.07 | -0.04 | -0.26 | -0.10 | -0.11 | -0.18 | -0.12 | -0.04 | 1.00 | -0.02 | -0.15 |
| Q10b | -0.09 | 0.22 | -0.21 | 0.35 | -0.08 | -0.20 | 0.09 | -0.36 | 0.03 | 0.00 | 0.11 | -0.34 | -0.17 | -0.34 | 0.59 | 0.06 | -0.09 | -0.02 | 1.00 | 0.76 |
|  | -0.01 | 0.02 | -0.34 | 0.08 | 0.05 | -0.22 | 0.15 | -0.13 | -0.09 | -0.10 | 0.02 | -0.17 | -0.12 | 0.05 | 0.72 | 0.09 | -0.27 | -0.15 | 0.76 | 1.00 |

**Fig. 2.** Spearman's correlations among dependent variables only

# 4  Discussion

This case study examining two data sets using comparison and a survey was disseminated to science majors at a small, rural, liberal arts university. As such, the results may not be producible. However, through nationwide dissemination for data collection, a more accurate perspective of how people interpret and apply health information about vaccines may be identified. Some minor adjustments are including a question about whether or not the respondent would take the COVID-19 vaccine. Also in the national edition, the same metrics for gathering valence in the initial passages should be identical after reading the context information. The ability to select from a list rather than to write in interpretations will limit confusion when analyzing the data.

The two participants whose responses were excluded did not indicate any level of reading comprehension with responses ranging from okay to yes and no. There is a lot of reading in this survey, and it is possible that other answers were disingenuous as well. Sample passage responses will be provided for the initial interpretation and follow up interpretations with an optional space for respondents to write in their own interpretation of passages. In addition, the explanation for their choice will remain. This was meaningful to understanding the incorrect valence type (yes/no instead of positive/neutral/negative) entered by respondents for their interpretations of passages after the surrounding text was added.

One interesting revelation from the survey data is that the survey respondents could not properly identify credible news sources, so information literacy my be an issue contributing to the collection of data gathered. According to Media Bias/Fact Check [11], several sources listed are mixed, questionable, and conspiracy/pseudo-news. Those include Fox (questionable), Spirit Science (conspiracy/pseudo), Al Jazeera, CNN, Buzzfeed, and MSNBC (mixed). At least one of these sites were identified by 65% of respondents. Unnamed sources like podcasts and YouTube channels, were identified by 7.7% of respondents, and 7.7% acknowledged that no matter the source, bias is present. It is clear from this study that more research on information literacy is necessary to evaluate how people identify news, good sources of information, and how to adapt that information in their lives and health.

Finally, the only person who indicated they highly trust QAnon was an excluded. Respondent 17 indicated a high trust in vaccines and was the only person to indicate their membership in the Green Party. In the future, this survey should be shared with Anons in order to get representation of their thoughts and feelings in order to further disentangle their trust in vaccines and personal health information literacy.

## 5   Conclusion

The growing body of literature about vaccines, particularly about anti-vax communities ranges from the sources of information to the types of information shared in the community. This study has taken some frequently-shared information and examined it for accuracy and interpretation. The most interesting identified feature is that most people do not read things carefully, even when pressed. It does not matter whether or not disinformation is presented if readers have drawn their conclusions before reading or skip reading altogether.

# References

1. Ahmad, A., Webb, J., Desouza, K.C., Boorman, J.: Strategically-motivated advanced persistent threat: definition, process, tactics and a disinformation model of counterattack. Comput. Secur. **86**, 402–418 (2019)
2. Endsley, M.R. Designing for Situation Awareness: An Approach to User-Centered Design. CRC Press, Boca Raton (2016)
3. Fallis, D.: What is disinformation? Library trends **63**(3), 401–426 (2015)
4. Fallis, D.: The varieties of disinformation. In: Floridi, L., Illari, P. (eds.) The Philosophy of Information Quality. SL, vol. 358, pp. 135–161. Springer, Cham (2014). https://doi.org/10.1007/978-3-319-07121-3_8
5. Featherstone, J.D., Zhang, J.: Feeling angry: the effects of vaccine misinformation and refutational messages on negative emotions and vaccination attitude. J. Health Commun. 1–11 (2020)
6. Fetzer, J.H.: Disinformation: the use of false information. Minds Mach. **14**(2), 231–240 (2004)
7. Fox, C.: Information and misinformation. An investigation of the notions of information, misinformation, informing, and misinforming (1983)
8. Grimes, D.R.: Health disinformation & social media: the crucial role of information hygiene in mitigating conspiracy theory and infodemics. EMBO Rep. **21**(11), e51819 (2020). https://doi.org/10.15252/embr.202051819
9. Lemieux, V. and Smith, T.D. Leveraging archival theory to develop a taxonomy of online disinformation. In: 2018 IEEE International Conference on Big Data (Big Data), pp. 4420–4426. IEEE (2018)
10. Leonard, M., Graham, S., Bonacum, D.: The human factor: the critical importance of effective teamwork and communication in providing safe care. BMJ Q. Saf. **13**(suppl 1), i85–i90 (2004)
11. Media Bias/Fact Check. https://mediabiasfactcheck.com. Accessed 15 Feb 2021
12. Riiser, K., Helseth, S., Haraldstad, K., Torbjørnsen, A., Richardsen, K.R.: Adolescents' health literacy, health protective measures, and health-related quality of life during the Covid-19 pandemic. PLoS ONE **15**(8), e0238161 (2020)
13. Rubin, V.L.: Disinformation and misinformation triangle. J. Documentation (2019)
14. Sawhney, N.: Situated awareness spaces: supporting social awareness in everyday life. Awareness Spaces **2**, 1–21 (2000)
15. Takaoka, A.J.W.: Searching for community and safety: evaluating common information shared in online ex-vaxxer communities. In: Meiselwitz, G. (ed.) HCII 2019. LNCS, vol. 11579, pp. 495–513. Springer, Cham (2019). https://doi.org/10.1007/978-3-030-21905-5_39

# Understanding Continuance Usage Intention of Shopping Guide Apps in Social Commerce

Shuo Zhang, Lili Liu(✉), Mingzhu Li, Qianru Tao, Ruoqi Zhang, and Yunguo Xia

College of Economics and Management, Nanjing University of Aeronautics and Astronautics,
Nanjing, China
{zhangshuo,llili85}@nuaa.edu.cn

**Abstract.** Shopping guide Apps emerge as a new type of social commerce tool, which provide accurate personalized recommendation functions that reduce the online shopping risk caused by information asymmetry through information sharing, and achieve the shopping requirements with "lower search cost". Yet our knowledge on shopping guide Apps and users' attitude and behavior is very limited. Drawing on the Information System Success Model and Expectation Confirmation Theory, we develop a research model to investigate how system quality, service quality, information quality and social interaction quality affect shopping guide APP users' satisfaction and continuance usage intention. Data has been collected from 275 respondents and analyzed with SmartPLS 3.2.9. Findings indicate that service, social and social interaction quality positively affect satisfaction, while information, service and system quality positively affect consumers' continuous usage intention. Additionally, satisfaction is an important predictor of the continuance usage intention. Potential theoretical and practical contributions are also discussed.

**Keywords:** Information System Success Model · Expectation Confirmation Theory · Guide APP · Satisfaction · Continuance usage intention

## 1 Introduction

Social e-commerce is growing rapidly and has become one of the most popular derivative models of e-commerce. With the help of social, social e-commerce promotes the purchase and sales of goods through social interaction and user-generated content (UGC), and realizes the iteration and innovation of traditional e-commerce mode [15]. The rapid development of social e-commerce has attracted a large number of businesses to settle in, resulting in a sharp increase in the number of goods, uneven quality of goods, increasing the search cost of users, and making people stuck in the dilemma of decision-making [9]. Therefore, it is important to establish an accurate personalized recommendation mechanism, reduce the online shopping risk caused by information asymmetry through information sharing, and achieve the shopping requirements with "lower search cost". Based on the above needs, shopping guide APPs have emerged, such as China's Little Red Book, Mogujie, and Weitao [20]. Different from traditional e-commerce websites, which

C. Stephanidis et al. (Eds.): HCII 2021, CCIS 1499, pp. 414–421, 2021.
https://doi.org/10.1007/978-3-030-90179-0_53

utilize purposeless advertising information push service, social commerce websites are designed based on the needs of customers and adopt a targeted advertising information push mode to provide valuable shopping guidance [7]. Consumers rely heavily on the collective wisdom of social networks to make a shopping decision, such as reading reviews and seeking recommendations from other consumers, and sharing the shopping experience with others [17]. At the same time, social commerce websites create online communities where consumers are connected and can interact with each other [8]. The social nature of shopping guide Apps enhances users' stickiness, recognition, trust and sense of belonging towards the Apps, as well as their willingness to make purchase decisions based on shopping guide Apps.

However, as a relatively new social commerce product, our knowledge on shopping guide Apps and users' continuance usage intention is very limited. Based on the Information System Success Model (ISS Model) and Expectation Confirmation Theory (ECT), this paper seeks to investigate how system quality, service quality, information quality and social interaction quality affect shopping guide APP satisfaction and users' continuance usage intention.

## 2 Theoretical Background

ISS Model was firstly introduced by DeLone and McLean in 1992, they further improved the model in 2003 [6]. ISS model examines the impact of system quality, service quality and information quality on user satisfaction and intention to use. A number of e-commerce studies have adopted ISS Model to explore user behavior, such as users' continuance usage intention. Expectation Confirmation Theory (ECT) is a representative theory that has been extensively applied to explore users' behavior and their continuance usage intention of information systems [2]. ECT proposes that consumers evaluate whether they are satisfied with the product or service based on the comparison result of pre-purchase expectations and post-purchase performance, their satisfaction and perceived usefulness jointly influence continuance usage intention [25].

Apart from some basic e-commerce website functions (e.g., search engine), shopping guide Apps provides many social-oriented features, including recommendation lists, ratings, tags, comments and user profiles [24]. Berg et al. point out that "social interaction quality" is an important factor in establishing shared emotional connection and user belonging, thus enhancing user cohesion and promoting user participation [1]. Therefore, this study first extends ISS model by incorporating social interaction quality as an additional antecedent, then integrates the extended ISS model with ECT, in order to explore how information quality, system quality, service quality and social interaction quality affect user satisfaction and continuous usage intention of shopping guide APPs.

## 3  Research Models and Hypotheses

The research model is shown in Fig. 1. Corresponding assumptions are discussed in detail as followings.

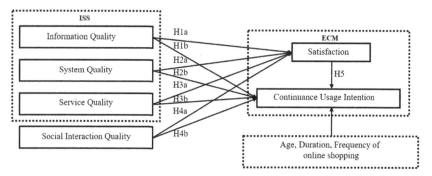

**Fig. 1.** Research model

The information provided by existing social e-commerce sites include note information, product information, user review information and chat information. High quality information should be characterized by timeliness, accuracy and validity [28], in order to reduce the cost, time and effort of information processing [13], thereafter help consumers make better decisions [16]. Previous studies have shown that the improvement of the information quality of social e-commerce could improve consumers' satisfaction, which in turn prompts them to buy repeatedly [34]. Therefore, we assume:

**H1a.** Information quality positively affects satisfaction.
**H1b.** Information quality positively affects users' continuance usage intention.

System quality refers to the technical level reflecting the characteristics of the e-commerce system on the website [18], including the stability of the payment environment, response time, compatibility and security [30]. Nistah et al. prove that some dimensions of system quality (such as ease of use and response time) have significant impacts on customers' satisfaction towards social e-commerce [23], which in turn increase users willingness to continue using the system [32]. Therefore, we assume:

**H2a.** System quality positively affects satisfaction.
**H2b.** System quality positively affect s users' continuance usage intention.

Service quality is defined as "the overall support delivered by the service provider" [6]. Delone and McLean explore service quality from three dimensions: responsiveness, personalization, and continuous optimization [6]. Excellent services enhance service providers' reputation and users' trust toward social commerce platforms [22], thus affect consumers' satisfaction continuance usage intention of on the platform [4]. Thus, we assume:

**H3a.** Service quality positively affects satisfaction.

**H3b.** Service quality positively affects users' continuance usage intention.

By reading reviews and recommendations posted by others, we can better understand products and make better purchase decisions [31]. Existing social e-commerce sites implement functions that support users to share, recommend and discuss products and purchase experiences with each other. McMillan and Chavis argue that the quality of social interaction is a critical factor that encourage users to develop strong sense of community, which promotes users' sense of belonging, satisfaction and continued use intention of the platform [21]. Therefore, we assume:

**H4a.** Social Interaction Quality positively affects satisfaction.

**H4b.** Social Interaction Quality positively affects users' continuance usage intention.

User satisfaction is crucial for the operation of social e-commerce platforms, since compared with retaining existing users, acquiring new users is more expensive (e.g., developing advertising strategies, starting new customers and establishing new accounts) [26]. Brady and Cronin's study shows that some satisfied users may form an intention to continue using, while dissatisfied users may discontinue their use [3].Therefore, we assume:

**H5.** Satisfaction has a positive impact on users' continuance usage intention.

## 4  Research Methodology

### 4.1  Data Collection

An online survey was designed and distributed on a Chinese questionnaire website: Sojump (http://www.sojump.com/). The questionnaire consists of two parts: demographic information questions and measurements items of the variables in the research model. All measurement items were adapted from previous research and have been modified to suit our research context. Items of information quality, system quality, service quality and satisfaction and continuance usage intention were adapted from William and Ephraim [6], Barbara and Peter [33], Gefen et.al [12], while items of social quality were derived from Bhattacherjee [2] and Lankton et al.'s research [19]. A seven-point Likert scale, ranging from "Strongly Disagree" (1) to "Strongly Agree" (7) was used to design the survey. Questionnaire was sent to shopping guide APP users from October 10, 2020 to October 15, 2020. A total of 275 valid responses were collected. 60.73% of respondents aged between 21 and 40. Besides, 57.45% respondents had a bachelor's degree or above. Most apps had been used for more than half a year. Detailed demographic information was shown in Table 1.

**Table 1.** Demographics

| Item | Options | Frequency | Percentage(%) |
|---|---|---|---|
| Age | ≤20 | 36 | 13.09 |
| | 21–30 | 98 | 35.64 |
| | 31–40 | 69 | 25.09 |
| | 41–50 | 56 | 20.36 |
| | ≥50 | 16 | 5.82 |
| Education background | Ph.D | 9 | 3.27 |
| | Postgraduate (Master) | 30 | 10.91 |
| | Undergraduate (Bachelor) | 119 | 43.27 |
| | High School | 76 | 27.64 |
| | Junior high school and below | 41 | 14.91 |
| Online shopping Frequency | Once in a month | 53 | 19.27 |
| | Once a week | 88 | 32.00 |
| | 2 or 3 times a week | 94 | 34.18 |
| | 4 or 5 times a week | 32 | 11.64 |
| | Almost every day | 8 | 2.91 |
| Duration of app use | Half a year and below | 13 | 4.73 |
| | 6 months–1 year | 86 | 31.27 |
| | 1 year–2 years | 77 | 28.00 |
| | 2 years–3 years | 48 | 17.45 |
| | 3 years and above | 51 | 18.55 |

## 4.2  Data Analyses

A two-step method was used to analyze model [5] and SmartPLS3.2.9 was used to analyze data [29]. First, we test the reliability and validity of the measurement model. In general, the reliability of all latent models can be evaluated by four index values: (1) Reliability was evaluated by composite reliability and Cronbach's α value. The composite reliability values of this study ranged from 0.926 to 0.940, both higher than the recommended value of 0.70 [14]; (2) Internal consistency was verified by checking Cronbach's α values, which were all greater than 0.881, exceeding the 0.70 threshold [11]; (3) The average extraction variable of all indexes was between 0.797 and 0.836, which all exceeded the acceptable value of 0.5 [14]. The composite reliability (CR) and average extraction variable (AVE) together explained the interpretation dimension reliability of the model; (4) The factor load coefficients of all variables were between 0.874 and 0.920, greater than the standard value of 0.7 [14]. The comprehensive evaluation from the above four aspects confirmed that our measurement model has high reliability, good stability and reliability. According to Fornell and Larcker [11], the AVE square root of each constructs was greater than the correlation between any pair of corresponding constructs, indicating sufficient discriminant validity.

We then tested the structural model and hypothesis. As shown in Fig. 2, satisfaction was positively affected by service quality, social quality and system quality ($\beta = 0.376$, $t = 2.861$; $\beta = 0.203$, $t = 3.414$; $\beta = 0.242$, $t = 3.835$), H2a, H3a and H4a were thus supported, and continued use intention was also positively impacted by information quality, service quality and system quality ($\beta = 0.194$, $t = 2.145$; $\beta = 0.249$, $t = 2.076$; $\beta = 0.049$, $t = 2.296$), thus supposing H1b, H2b and H3b. In addition, satisfaction was an important predictor of the continuance usage intention ($\beta = 0.192$, $t = 2.030$), the H5 was therefore supported. In addition, 61.1% variance of satisfaction and 56.0% variance of intention of continuous use were explained, which were higher than Falk's and Miller's 10% recommended value [10], indicating that the model has a high degree of fit and strong predictive ability.

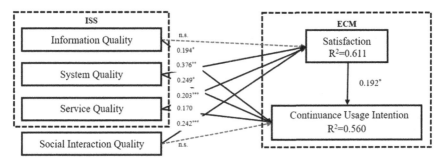

**Fig. 2.** Structural model

## 5 Conclusions

Using mobile phones to shop online has generate more and more popularity [27]. As a rapidly developing product, we know little on consumers of shopping guide APPs, such as the influencing factors of consumers' continuance usage intention. Based on the ISS Model and ECT, this study identifies and verifies how four critical factors affect consumers' satisfaction and continuance usage intention. Findings indicate that system quality, service quality and social interaction quality positively affect the satisfaction of the products, while information quality, service quality and system quality positively affect the consumers' continuous usage intention. Stable systems, high-quality services and healthy social interaction can improve consumer satisfaction with shopping guide APPs. Moreover, satisfaction has a positive role in promoting the continuous usage intention.

Theoretically, our study is one of the first that verifies the applicability of ISS model in explaining consumers' continuance usage intention of shopping guide APPs, which extends our knowledge on social commerce. Practically, this study provides important implications for social commerce market in China. Managers should focus on all of the factors in our research model to encourage their users' continuance usage intention. There are several limitations in this study. First, we focus on domestic social app, foreign social apps were not considered in the discussion. The factors influencing the continuous usage intention of APP in China and abroad may be different, so our research cannot reflect a wider range of situations. Secondly, the factors we summarized and selected are limited. Further research is suggested to consider additional important factors to extend current study.

**Acknowledgment.** This study was supported by the Fundamental Research Funds for the Central Universities No. NR2021003 awarded to the second author; this study was also supported by the Fundamental Research Funds for the Central Universities: No. 2021EC09 awarded to the first author and the Creative Studio of Electronic Commerce in Nanjing University of Aeronautics and Astronautics.

# References

1. Berg, P.V.D., Sharmeen, F., Weijs-Perrée, M.: On the subjective quality of social Interactions: Influence of neighborhood walkability, social cohesion and mobility choices. Transp. Res. Part A: Policy Pract. **106**, 309–319 (2017)
2. Bhattacherjee, A. Understanding information systems continuance: an expectation-confirmation model. MIS Q. **25**, 351–370 (2001)
3. Brady, M.K., Cronin, J.J.: Some new thoughts on conceptualizing perceived service quality: a hierarchical approach. J. Mark. **65**, 34–49 (2001)
4. Caruana, A.: Service loyalty the effects of service quality and the mediating role of customer satisfaction. Eur. J. Mark. **36**, 811–828 (2002)
5. Chin, W.W., Marcolin, B.L., Newsted, P.R.: A partial least squares latent variable modeling approach for measuring interaction effects: results from a Monte Carlo simulation study and an electronic-mail emotion/adoption study. Inf. Syst. Res. **14**, 189–217 (2003)
6. Delone, W.H., McLean, E.R.: The DeLone and McLean model of information systems success: a ten-year update. J. Manag. Inf. Syst. **19**, 9–30 (2003)
7. Demons, E.K.: The complex problem of monetizing virtual electronic social networks. Decis. Support Syst. **48**, 46–56 (2010)
8. Dennis, C., Morgan, A., Wright, L.T., Jayawardhena, C.: The influences of social e-shopping in enhancing young women's online shopping behaviour. J. Customer Behav. **9**, 151–174 (2010)
9. Esmaeili, L., Mardani, S., Golpayegani, S.A.H., Madar, Z.Z.: A novel tourism recommender system in the context of social commerce. Expert Syst. Appl. **149** (2020). Article no. 113301
10. Falk, R.F., Miller, N.B.: A Primer for Soft Modeling. University of Akron Press (1992). https://psycnet.apa.org/record/1992-98610-000
11. Fornell, C., Larcker, D.F.: Evaluating structural equation models with unobservable variables and measurement error. J. Market. Res. **18**, 39–50 (1981)
12. Gefen, D.: Customer loyalty in e-commerce. J. Assoc. Inf. Syst. **3**, 27–51 (2002)
13. Gu, B., Konana, P., Rajagopalan, B., Chen, H.-W.M.: Competition among virtual communities and user valuation: the case of investing-related communities. Inf. Syst. Res. **18**, 68–85 (2007)
14. Hair Jr, J.F., Black, W.C., Babin, B.J., Anderson, R.E., Tatham, R.L.: Multivariate Data Analysis. Auflage, Upper Saddle River (2006). https://scholar.google.com.hk/scholar?hl=zh-CN&as_sdt=0%2C5&q=+Multivariate+Data+Analysis.+Auflage%2C+Upper+Saddle+River+&btnG=

15. Hajli, N.: Social commerce constructs and consumer's intention to buy. **35**, 183–191 (2015)
16. Kim, M.J., Chung, N., Lee, C.-K., Preis, M.W.: Dual-route of persuasive communications in mobile tourism shopping. Telematics Inf. **33**, 293–308 (2016)
17. Kozinets, R.V., Hemetsberger, A., Schau, H.J.: The wisdom of consumer crowds collective innovation in the age of networked marketing. J. Macromark. **28**, 339–354 (2008)
18. Kuan, H.-H., Bock, G.-W., Vathanophas, V.: Comparing the effects of website quality on customer initial purchase and continued purchase at e-commerce websites. Behav. Inf. Technol. **27**, 3–16 (2008)
19. Lankton, N.K., McKnight, D.H., Thatcher, J.B.: The moderating effects of privacy restrictiveness and experience on trusting beliefs and habit: an empirical test of intention to continue using a social networking website. IEEE Trans. Eng. Manag. **59**, 654–665 (2012)
20. Liu, X., Oda, T.: The effects of sharing behavior and trust on consumer purchase intention in Chinese social commerce contexts. J. Soc. Sci. Humanit. **2**, 77–82 (2020)
21. McMillan, D.W., Chavis, D.M.: Sense of community: a definition and theory. J. Community Psychol. **14**, 6–23 (1986)
22. Nasser, M.A., Islam, R., Zainal Abidin, I.S., Azam, M., Prabhakar, A.C.: Analysis of e-service quality through online shopping. Res. J. Bus. Manag. **9**, 422–442 (2015)
23. Nistah, N.M., Sura, S., Lee, O: Applied Mechanics and Materials, vol. 892, pp. 258–265, Trans Tech Publications (2019)
24. Olbrich, R., Holsing, C.: Modeling consumer purchasing behavior in social shopping communities with clickstream data. Int. J. Electron. Commer. **16**, 15–40 (2011)
25. Oliver, R.L.: A cognitive model of the antecedents and consequences of satisfaction decisions. J. Mark. Res. **17**, 460–469 (1980)
26. Parthasarathy, M., Bhattacherjee, A.: Understanding post-adoption behavior in the context of online services. Inf. Syst. Res. **9**, 362–379 (1998)
27. Patel, V., Das, K., Chatterjee, R., Shukla, Y.: Does the interface quality of mobile shopping apps affect purchase intention? An empirical study. Australas. Market. J. (AMJ) **28**, 300–309 (2020)
28. Rieh, S.Y.: Judgment of information quality and cognitive authority in the Web. J. Am. Soc. Inf. Sci. **53**, 145–161 (2010)
29. Ringle, C.M., Wende, S., Becker, J.-M.: SmartPLS 3 (2015). www.smartpls.com
30. Seddon, P.B.: A respecification and extension of the DeLone and McLean model of IS success. Inf. Syst. Res. **8**, 240–253 (1997)
31. Suraworachet, W., Premsiri, S., Cooharojananone, N.: In: 2012 IEEE/IPSJ 12th International Symposium on Applications and the Internet, pp. 245–250. (IEEE)
32. Tajuddin, R.A., Baharudin, M., Hoon, T.S.: System quality and its influence on students' learning satisfaction in UiTM Shah Alam. Proc. Soc. Behav. Sci. **90**, 677–685 (2013)
33. Wixom, B.H., Todd, P.A.: A theoretical integration of user satisfaction and technology acceptance. Inf. Syst. Res. **16**, 85–102 (2005)
34. Yu-Wei, C., Ping-Yu, H., Qing-Miao, Y.: Integration of online and offline channels: a view of O2O commerce. Internet Res. **28**, 926–945 (2018)

# Design Case Studies

# Optimizing the Information of Sport Graphics in the Major League Baseball

Chih-Yung Chen and Meng-Cong Zheng$^{(\boxtimes)}$

Department of Industrial Design, National Taipei University of Technology, No. 1, Sec. 3, Zhongxiao E. Rd. Da'an Dist, Taipei 10608, Taiwan

**Abstract.** Baseball statistics are one of the biggest concerns of baseball fans. This information allows viewers to look at the game from a different perspective. With the development of broadcast technology, complex statistics and information are increasing. The purpose of this study was to investigate the effects of baseball mirror information on audience enjoyment and cognitive load, as well as users' preference and evaluation of the information. This study analyzed 11 regional broadcast networks of Major League Baseball (MLB) and selected the three most-watched networks (AT&T, Fox, and NBC) as experimental samples. Each sample assigned to 10 subjects, and a total were 30 subjects joined this study. The task consisted of three parts: watching baseball clips on different screens, questionnaires, and semi-structured interviews. After viewing the clips, we asked the subjects about their perceptions of the clip. Completed the 7-point Likert Scale questionnaire, which was composed of NASA-TLX and the Measure of Enjoyment and Meaningfulness. Another scale was to examined involvement with baseball fans. Subjects with low-involved baseball spectators (2.86) had a low understanding of the content than people with high-involved baseball spectators (5.06). Enjoyment was positively correlated with meaningfulness and com-prehension (P = .003). 86% of respondents said that visual information helps to facilitate the viewing experience. This study found that users' preferences for viewing information could be a reference for interface design of future broadcast events and improve the spectator's watching experience.

**Keywords:** Sport broadcasting · Graphics · Baseball · User experience

## 1 Introduction

Statistics are a crucial part of sports broadcast, and it also shows more variation in content [1]. Baseball is a sport known for accumulating data, and statistics have always been an essential element of the game. Baseball broadcasts can assist the audience in reviewing previous events and understanding the game's current situation. Still, the graphics data and information are also the communication medium between fans after the game. However, the graphic's complexity and the audience's cognitive load need to be taken into account. Many technologies make statistics more graphic and more frequent to enhance the audience's experience [2]. As a result, the picture elements become more

© Springer Nature Switzerland AG 2021
C. Stephanidis et al. (Eds.): HCII 2021, CCIS 1499, pp. 425–432, 2021.
https://doi.org/10.1007/978-3-030-90179-0_54

and more complex, and a lot of data makes it difficult for fans to enjoy the fun of the game [3]. Some viewers choose to watch the infographics, while others choose to allocate less attention to them or ignore them entirely [4].

Previous studies have focused on the types of data used in broadcast events. Few have discussed how different levels of fans view the broadcast interface and how graphics' deployment during the game might affect the audience experience or impact. Ensure that the game is accessible to a broader audience and that beginner baseball fans are not prevented from enjoying the game. Subsequent experiments will be conducted to investigate users' understanding of information and cognitive load. Evaluate the certification graphics design feasibility to provide future relevant design references, thus providing a good spectator experience.

## 2   Methods

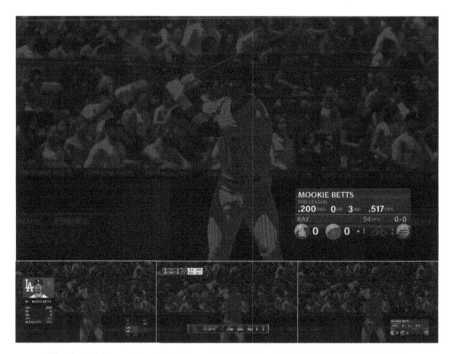

**Fig. 1.** MLB graphics simulation. Under left to right: FOX, NBC and AT&T.

This study want understands the difference between the baseball on-screen graphic, and this study chose the most-watched television baseball broadcast interfaces to discuss. We look at regional network ratings through Forbes [4]. This study selected the highest ratings and total ratings of a single channel, set the top three tracks that received the most attention on TV, namely FOX, NBC, and AT&T, coded their content in MLB, and finally simulated the interface presentation of the three graphics in the game (Fig. 1). In each version, the audio and visual effects outside the interface are the same to reduce hearing and other factors. In this study, the following experiments will be carried out with the baseball game without the announcer's commentary. This study simulates three versions of baseball broadcast graphics, FOX, NBC, and AT&T, which provide information and statistical data about players and games. The usual shows the game's score and status, and the historical data will appear when the hitter enters the field. The timing of the graphic in all versions is consistent. The participants were randomly asked to watch one of three sets of screens. The video of a simulated baseball game showed as much as possible what would happen in an inning. The clips were 10 min long and included batting up, walks, strikeouts, fly-out, hit, and home runs.

### 2.1  Participants

This study recruited 30 participants from a sports community. All the participants had experience watching baseball, and 8 of them were members of a baseball team.

### 2.2  Procedures

First, participants were asked to fill out the Baseball Experience and Baseball spectator involvement Scale to distinguish the high and low involvement of baseball fans and ensure that the number of high and low high involved baseball spectators between each group was the same. Subjects were randomly selected from one of the three groups and watched with a projector. The participants can make comments at any time while watching the film. During the process, a recording is used to record the comments of the participants. At the end of the video, a brief report of the competition content is made again. Participants then filled out the NASA Task Load Index (NASA-TLX) to assess the user's burden when viewing the graphics, and a short questionnaire related to the viewing experience was filled out, which included a scale measuring Enjoyment and Meaningfulness (6 items), as well as the level of understanding of the whole game. At the end of the experiment, we ranked the existing MLB graphics according to their preferences. We used semi-structured interviews to understand how users viewed and understood the broadcast screen and their views on current MLB information.

## 3  Results

Thirty participants, including 13 women and 17 men, completed the study. The participants ranged in age from 16 to 41, with an average age of 20. This study used the seven-point Likert scale to score the Baseball spectator involvement Scale. The overall average was 3.96, A score of more than 3.5 is high-involved baseball spectators. The average of fans with high-scored spectator involvement participants was 5.06, and the standard of fans with low-involved baseball spectators was 2.86.

**Table 1.** The results of NASA Task cognitive load in each group.

| Regional network | High-involved | Low-involved |
|---|---|---|
| NBC | 66.4 | 49.07 |
| FOX | 41.87 | 47.09 |
| AT&T | 44.87 | 51.64 |
| Average | 50.71 | 49.27 |

There were five high involved baseball spectators and five low involved baseball spectators in each of the three baseball graphics groups (Table 1). The results showed that the cognitive load from high to low was NBC (M = 49.98, SD = 22.53), high participation fans (65.4), and low involved baseball spectators (49.07), respectively. AT&T (M = 48.23, SD = 23.60) low involved baseball spectators (44.87), low involved baseball spectators (51.6); FOX (M = 44.48, SD = 21.53) low involved baseball spectators (41.87) and low involved baseball spectators (47.09). Results Univariate analysis of variance (ANOVA) showed no statistically significant effect between each group of graphics and cognitive load.

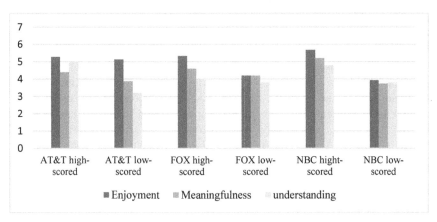

**Fig. 2.** Enjoyment meaningfulness and understanding scores of different films watched at different levels.

The level of Baseball spectator involvement significantly influenced the Enjoyment, Meaningfulness, and understanding of the game (See Fig. 2). Those with high-involved baseball spectators were more likely to enjoy the game than those with low-involved baseball spectators (F = 9.891, P = 0.004, P < 0.01), and those with high-involved baseball spectators were more likely to understand the game (F = 9.891, P = 0.024, P < 0.05) and feel the game was more meaningful (F = 4.336, P = 0.047, P < 0.05).

In terms of enjoyment, AT&T had the highest overall average score (5.2), followed by NBC (4.8) and Fox (4.87), and NBC had the highest overall average score (4.3) in terms of understanding the game, followed by AT&T (4.1) and Fox (3.9). High-involved baseball spectators were able to understand the game better from AT&T's graphics, but the AT&T graphics also made it harder for low-involved baseball spectators to understand the game (Table 2).

**Table 2.** Evaluate the percentage of content in the game.

| Fans' comment's classification | All the spectators (44) | High-involved spectators (29) | Low-involved spectators (15) |
|---|---|---|---|
| Game observation | 19 (43.1%) | 12 (41.3%) | 7 (46.6%) |
| Player/team appraisal | 14 (31.8%) | 10 (34.4%) | 4 (26.6%) |
| Personal passion | 6 (13.6%) | 4 (13.8%) | 2 (13.3%) |
| Statistical information | 2 (4.5%) | 2 (6.8%) | 0 (0%) |
| Game decision-maker | 1 (2.2%) | 1 (3.4%) | 0 (0%) |
| Peripheral subjects | 2 (4.5%) | 0 (0%) | 2 (13.3%) |

A total of 44 comments about the game were collected during the experiment, including 29 comments from fans with high-involved baseball spectators and 15 comments from fans with low-involved baseball spectators. According to Qiyu Zhi et al. 's survey of fans' comments [6], while watching sports events, all comments are classified into six themes: Player/Team Appraisal, Game Observation, personal enthusiasm, statistical information, Personal Passion, and game decision-makers. 43.1% of the comments were Game Observation, 31.8% were comments about Player/Team Appraisal, 13.6% were comments about Personal Passion, and a few contained Statistical Information (4.5%), Peripheral Subjects (4.5%), and game decision-makers (2.2%).

In terms of preference, the participants ranked the top three in order of personal preference for the 11 on-screen graphics they used in the 2020MLB season, with the first one getting 3 points, the second one getting 2 points, and the third one getting 1 point. The results show that Fox (31) is the most popular interface among the respondents, followed by SNY (24) and NBC (22). high-involved baseball spectators prefer to rank NBC (16), Fox (13), and AT&T (13), while low-involved baseball spectators prefer to rank Fox (18), SNY (14), and TBS (11). From the interviews, this study obtained 57 comments about the advantages and disadvantages of 11 MLB on-screen graphics, and the presentation mode of on-screen graphics in users' minds was summarized.

## 4  Discussion

The results showed that the level of participation impacted the experience of watching the game, with participants with high-involved baseball spectators enjoying the game more than those with low-involved baseball spectators. High-involved baseball spectators commented more than low engagement fans. Although the percentage of content posted didn't differ significantly, high-involved baseball spectators were more likely to get deeper insights from the interface and supplementary information. For example, judging pitches by their speed and placement, one of the high-involved baseball specta-tors noted that "the pitcher has a lot of loose control, a good pitch, a slider, and a straight ball, a good speed on the straight ball, but he can't get the ball in, and the batter hits the ball very hard." "And try to imagine what might have happened," If the first baseman hadn't let go, it would have been a double play. "Fans who were less engaged were more likely to report seeing situations such as" the pitcher had bad control of the ball and didn't throw it into the strike zone.""And" Catch and kill." However, the participants in each group are watching the same content because of fans' high participation who have more experience and knowledge of baseball. Part of the data presented to the low involvement of fans does not understand. Physical data information may lead to watching the object experience caused by the difference between the gap. It is difficult between the different ethnic groups to enjoy the pleasure of watching sports [3].

NBC provided the most information on hitters, averaging nine items. NBC scored highest on enjoyment and Meaningfulness for high-involved baseball spectators but higher on cognitive load than the other groups. More information means a lot of data in a short time. Three out of five high-involved baseball spectators who watched NBC said they watched the news, but the abbreviations made it more difficult for them to understand what it meant. On the low-involved baseball spectator's side, they were not affected by the amount of information, with 12 low-involved baseball spectators saying they did not understand most of the data represented and usually scanned but did not try to understand it.

AT&T's graphics provides information about pitch location and makes it easier for participants to judge pitches. Participants in AT&T's high-involved group said that "sometimes I judge pitches first and then review my judgment to see if it is correct, which is how I feel when I am the umpire." The scoring points provided a way to look back, with the more experienced group scoring 5 points on the seven-scale of understanding the game.

FOX is participants ranked the be fond of graphics; eight subjects are graphics ranked the first. In comments, of which five for comment on aesthetic feeling, thought FOX graphic style is concise and order information. The rest of the three said FOX evaluation data presentation, data of leader would have different colors, the graphic below would make players hit the historical information, and compare players showed how recent games.

The subjects' preference rankings were more likely to separate the hitters' informa-tion from the score bug. This arrangement effectively indicated to the audience that when the camera was on the hitter, the data is nearby. Although information integration can reduce screen blocking, respondents can see players and game information in a small range. It takes some time to adapt, making it more time for the subjects to read for the first time.

In recent years MLB has used Statcast (Fig. 3), and respondents rated the technology as helpful for watching games in the future. Twenty-six of the 30 participants expected to see more of the same way Statcast presented its data, with the graph showing them what representation meant quickly, such as the percentage of hitters, the percentage where even low-engagement fans could see the ball, and the movement of defensive formations observed by more experienced fans. Twenty subjects are given when playback the ball

**Fig. 3.** MLB often appears in graphics techniques.

track of positive comments, "trajectory let me more see, placement of the ball," "can see the size of the ball drop how many" and "to review how lost, know to which position, what results caused by" nine subjects further show that hope to see more pitcher and the hitter between data, such as virtual combat zone (virtual strike zone) and pitcher pitches using percentage, such data can make they can predict the game process, such as "can predict what the next could throw the ball," "Hot spots are good, we know where he can't handle them," and "if you have pitchers, you can imagine how you throw them, what kind of hitters you're facing, what kind of pitches you're going to strike out.".

Previous studies have shown that statistical data can improve the experience of watching sports broadcasts. Still, it is not helpful for viewers with low-involved baseball spectators, as low-involved baseball spectators may not use the data due to the viewers' different backgrounds and experiences.

## 5   Conclusions

This study has found that fans with different levels of involvement have different feelings when watching baseball games, and the same information will have other effects due to experience. Consistent with previous findings, non-native speakers had more difficulty interpreting abbreviations in data [7]. The more data abbreviations are used, the more time and cognitive load it takes for the high-involved baseball spectators. Low-involved baseball spectators don't have much data to use, rarely mentioning the data to comment on the game. In post-experiment interviews, they said they preferred to see data presented using graphics, not just words. In terms of on-screen graphic design, the arrangement of baseball information affects the subjects' time to judge the information. The on-screen graphic of information integration can effectively reduce the space. Still, obviously from the perspective of preference ranking, it is not the ideal arrangement for the subjects, and the combined information is not easy to read. This study will continue to explore how to provide viewers with more intuitive visual effects to more easily explain the baseball game through an intuitive on-screen graphic during the process of watching the game.

## References

1. Hesse, B.: Evolution and utility of graphics containing statistics in NCAA championship broadcasts (1986–2016) (2018)
2. Ráthonyi, G., Müller, A., Rathonyi-Odor, K.: How digital technologies are changing sport?. APSTRACT: Appl. Stud. Agribus. Commer. **12.1033–2019–3296**, 89–96 (2018)
3. Gantz, W., Lewis, N.: Sports on traditional and newer digital media: Is there really a fight for fans? Television New Media **15.8**, 760–768 (2014)
4. Isaacowitz, D.M., Wadlinger, H.A., Goren, D., Wilson, H.R.: Is there an age-related positivity effect in visual attention? A comparison of two methodologies. Emotion **6**(3), 511 (2006)
5. Early Regional Sports Network TV Ratings and Ad Sales for MLB Are Up Compared With 2019 (2020). https://www.forbes.com/sites/maurybrown/2020/08/06/early-regional-sports-network-tv-ratings-and-ad-sales-for-mlb-are-up-compared-to-2019/?sh=5fa3a6403441
6. Zhi, Q., et al.: GameViews: understanding and supporting data-driven sports storytelling. In: Proceedings of the CHI Conference on Human Factors in Computing Systems (2019)
7. Tuggle, G.A.: Baseball box scores: Helpful statistics or sports hieroglyphics? Newsp. Res. J. **21**(3), 2–13 (2000)

# Web Interface for Power Grid Database

Sujan Devkota[1], Pedro G. Lind[1,2,3(✉)], and Norun Christine Sanderson[1]

[1] Department of Computer Science, OsloMet – Oslo Metropolitan University,
P.O. Box 4 St. Olavs plass, 0130 Oslo, Norway
[2] ORCA – OsloMet Research Center for AI, Pilestredet 52, 0166 Oslo, Norway
[3] NordSTAR – Nordic Center for Sustainable and Trustworthy AI Research,
Pilestredet 52, 0166 Oslo, Norway

**Abstract.** Different stakeholders of the electric power grid sector need data for their research and decision-making tasks. However, the power grid field lacks an accessible and easy-to-use system that contains openly available data sources that is open to use for everyone. In this study we propose a prototype of an accessible and usable web interface for power grid databases, following the user-centered design (UCD) methodology and using different qualitative research methods and research methods from human-computer interaction (HCI). The prototype is gradually developed through an iterative approach, where we identify user requirements and test it for its accessibility and usability from the perspective of the stakeholders. Finally, we discuss possible future work to further extend this study and to make the software prototype more effective.

**Keywords:** Accessibility and usability · User centered design · Power grid data

## 1 Introduction

In this interdisciplinary study, we aim at solving a problem in the power grid sector by accessing the problem as human computer interaction (HCI) designers. We develop an accessible and usable web interface for the different stakeholders of the power grid sector. The electric power grid is one of the most essential and complex infrastructures of modern society, including different sources of energy, some of them conventional and some other renewable, the wires that connect the sources to the place of consumption and distribution facilities. As the need of electricity is increasing, the power grid systems will continue to become larger, more complex and interconnected [1]. The increased use of renewable sources of energy is also contributing to this complexity [2].

There are several stakeholders of the power grid sector [3], such as grid operators, academic researchers, homeowners, power coordinators, economists, environmentalists, sociologists, information technology companies, governments, and policy makers. All these stakeholders need power grid related data in their respective fields. For example, the academic researchers and engineers need data to carry out their experiments such as developing, testing and validating their

© Springer Nature Switzerland AG 2021
C. Stephanidis et al. (Eds.): HCII 2021, CCIS 1499, pp. 433–440, 2021.
https://doi.org/10.1007/978-3-030-90179-0_55

models. Power grid coordinators want to include multiple sources of renewable sources to the grid and generate new product and service ideas. And policy makers can use historical reports to make future policies about the energy transfer. However, there are several issues related to accessing power grid data, some of these have been pointed out in the literature [2,4–6].

In this paper, we address the problem of easily accessing power grid data from the perspective of the stakeholders. To this end, we develop a software prototype which is an accessible and usable web interface for power grid database. We start in Sect. 2, describing the methodology followed in this study. In Sect. 3, the different stages of the prototype development process are described. The prototype, its limitations, and the development procedure are discussed in Sect. 4, which also highlights the main conclusions and briefly points possible future directions for improving the interface.

## 2    Research Methodology and Methods

The research methodology used in this study is the user-centered design (UCD) [7]. UCD was selected because it has been claimed as a methodology to develop a usable solution with improved user satisfaction, increased productivity, and less training and support cost [8]. UCD suggests, by principle, the active involvement of users throughout the design process, in order to understand them and their requirements. Moreover, UCD also enables to develop, evaluate, and improve the design in an iterative manner [9], including a set of well-defined processes for understanding and analyzing the needs, implementing them in a design solution, and evaluating the design solution [10].

In what concerns specific methods, the prototype has been implemented using a combination of a qualitative approach for user research and other HCI methods. An overview of the process can be seen in the flowchart diagram of Fig. 1.

To understand the users and their requirements, we used survey methods [11] and interview methods [12]. We combined the interviews with ethnographic observation [12]. Qualitative analysis of survey data, was done using coding [13] and paper prototyping for creating a low fidelity prototype so that the evaluation could be done early in the development process [14]. In addition, a user persona was developed to inform the design team about the users' goals, expectations, and frustrations during software prototyping, as well as to inform the experts about the end-users during heuristic evaluation [12]. In addition, methods such as automated testing [15], heuristic testing [16], and discounted user testing [17] were utilized to perform usability testing and to get feedback from users multiple times during the development process.

## 3    Prototype Development

The developed prototype has a back end and a front end. The back end incorporates the sources of power grid data into a database, which is served to the front

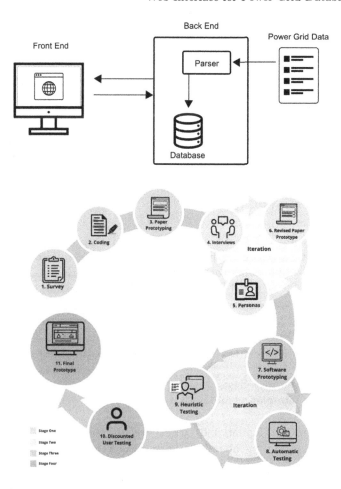

**Fig. 1.** (Top) Overview of the prototype of an interface of power grid data. (Bottom) Overview of the prototype development process.

end via *REST API*. Figure 1 (top) shows an overview of both back- and front-end of the prototype. The prototype was developed in four stages, following an iterative approach, illustrated in Fig. 1 (bottom).

**Stage 1: Survey and Paper Prototype.** In the first stage, we collected data through an online survey and then created a quick paper prototype based on the analyzed data. A brief literature review of the power grid field informed the formulation of relevant questions. The online survey was created in the platform *Nettskjema*[1] and was sent to different stakeholders from research and engineering

---

[1] *Nettskjema* is a tool for designing and conducting online surveys, developed and operated by the University Information Technology Center at the University of Oslo in Norway. Available at https://nettskjema.no/.

fields related to power grids. The survey resulted in 11 valid submissions, from which the majority were from academic researchers.

The participants reported that finding necessary data related to power grid is difficult, and that a website where one can search for power grid data from all available sources would be helpful. Based on the participants' input and literature discussing the problems of power grid data, we created an interactive paper prototype using the tool *Balsamiq*.

The prototype consisted of two pages, a home page and a results page. The home page had a form with fields for entering the following search parameters: type of data, range of dates, and location, in addition to a button to initiate the search. The results page displayed the search results, as well as options to preview and download the results.

**Stage 2: Interviews, Personas, and Revised Paper Prototype.** In the second stage, interviews and ethnographic observations were conducted using the online video conferencing tools *Zoom* and *Skype*. During the interview, the participants were invited to share their screen and demonstrate how they search for power grid data. In this way it was possible to understand the context of use. The questions covered amongst others the users' experiences with similar systems, their challenges, motivations, and goals related to searching for power grid data. The participants were also asked to review the paper prototype from stage one.

The input of the interviews was then used to create a persona. Since only two persons were interviewed and both were academic researchers, we only made one persona.

The prototype was updated by incorporating the relevant feedback from interviews and persona. In the revised prototype, a text field for entering search keywords was added to the home page, replacing the fields for date and location, and on the results page, the preview and download buttons were removed.

**Stage 3: Implementation of the Software Prototype, Automated Testing, and Heuristic Testing.** In the third stage, a software prototype was developed and tested using the automatic and manual (expert) heuristic testing methods. The software prototype consists of a back end and a front end. The back end serves data to the font end using *REST API* and was developed using *Strapi*[2], a tool which allows quick creation of a powerful back end system. The front end of the web application was developed using the tool *ReactJs*, and implements the home page and the results page from the revised paper prototype. In addition, the design system *Primer* was used to create the user interface (UI) to make the components look uniform across the application.

We performed automated testing for compliance to *WCAG 2.1* [18], during all the prototype development process, using the *Wave* and *Lighthouse* extensions

---

[2] *Strapi* is a free and open-source tool to create content management systems and easily build APIs for accessing the content. Available at https://github.com/strapi/strapi.

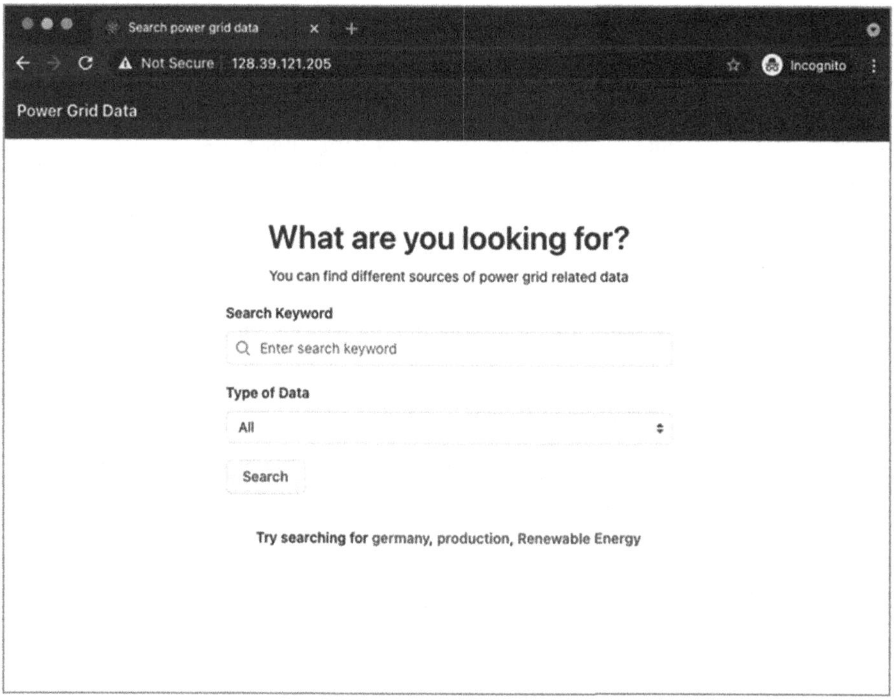

**Fig. 2.** Final software prototype.

for *Google Chrome* browsers. Manual heuristic testing of the software prototype was done with the help of a group of experts using Nielsen's heuristics for evaluation [19]. Five experts participated in this stage, evaluating the prototype. Their input was collected using an online form in *Nettskjema*, and the reported problems aggregated and used for revising the software prototype.

**Stage 4: Discounted User Testing and the Final Prototype.** In the final stage, we tested the prototype with actual end users using discounted testing [20]. Three participants participated in this stage. Two of the participants gave their feedback to a facilitator in sessions online (in *Zoom*) or in person, while the third participant gave input via an online form in *Nettskjema*, without a facilitator. The first two participants were also asked to express their thoughts, applying therefore the think-aloud method [21], while testing the prototype.

During the testing sessions, the facilitator noted any issues detected when observing the participants' screen while they were using the prototype. The participants expressed that an application like the one presented for testing would be helpful and that they would use such an application should the full version be released in the future. They also gave some ideas for additional features and future work. The final prototype is shown in Fig. 2.

## 4   Discussion and Conclusions

In this paper, we have described the process of development of an accessible and usable web interface for searching for power grid data from multiple sources. We used the UCD methodology involving multiple methods performed in an iterative way to develop the prototype.

The results of this study indicate that, even without any prior knowledge of the power grid domain, UCD can help the design team develop a usable solution for the given problem. As indicated by the principles of UCD, including users from the very beginning and multiple times in the design process using methods such as surveys, interviews and usability testing had a positive impact on the end results.

The challenges we faced with the difficult access and availability of stakeholders, were mitigated by using methods such as ethnographic observation, thinking out aloud and unstructured informal communication with the participants. Paper prototyping was found to be effective for quick development and evaluation of design ideas. Furthermore, heuristic testing and discounted user testing helped to carry out multiple usability tests at a low budget, enabling multiple iterations in the prototype development. We, therefore, corroborate Nielsen's claim that discounted methods is a good choice for projects with limited resources [17].

The issues found in the expert heuristic testing procedure were mainly user interface-related problems, while issues discovered by the actual end-users during discounted testing were primarily domain-specific problems, which confirms findings from previous studies, such as Ref. [22].

Limitations to this study include the number of participants and that participants only represented one group of stakeholders. It can therefore be argued that the prototype developed in this study meets only the needs of academic researchers. However, some literature suggests that meeting all the needs of one persona creates better results than aiming at meeting a few needs of all personas [23].

In conclusion, the results and experiences from this study can contribute to the existing knowledge on developing usable and accessible domain-specific search web-interfaces using UCD and HCI methods, in addition to providing a software prototype solution for power grid databases that can be further developed.

Future work includes evaluating the prototype for usability with other stakeholder groups. Moreover, our stand-point enable to proceed with improvements to the effectiveness of the solution, for example by adding new functionalities such as filter options to narrow or expand the search, options to save or share research results, solutions for automatically adding new sources and update existing sources, and possibilities for including different types of metadata for power grids, such as *readme*-files, column headings, and location information. Other improvements for future work could for example include identifying what data will be the most relevant to save in the back end and ranking the results so the most relevant results appear at the top.

# References

1. Amin, M., Stringer, J.: The electric power grid: today and tomorrow. MRS Bull. **33**(4), 399–407 (2008)
2. Medjroubi, W., Müller, U.P., Scharf, M., Matke, C., Kleinhans, D.: Open data in power grid modelling: new approaches towards transparent grid models. Energy Rep. **3**, 14–21 (2017)
3. Obinna, U., Joore, P., Wauben, L., Reinders, A.: Insights from stakeholders of five residential smart grid pilot projects in the Netherlands. Smart Grid Renew. Energy **7**(1), 1–15 (2016)
4. Wiese, F., Bökenkamp, G., Wingenbach, C., Hohmeyer, O.: An open source energy system simulation model as an instrument for public participation in the development of strategies for a sustainable future. Wiley Interdisc. Revi. Energy Environ. **3**(5), 490–504 (2014)
5. Hutcheon, N., Bialek, J.W.: Updated and validated power flow model of the main continental European transmission network. In: 2013 IEEE Grenoble Conference, pp 1–5. IEEE (2013)
6. Zhou, Q.: Cross-border congestion management in the electricity market. Ph.D. thesis, Durham University (2003)
7. ISO/TC 159/SC 4: Ergonomics of human-system interaction. Standard, ISO/TC 159/SC 4 - SECRETARIAT, London, UK (2000)
8. ISO I (1999) 13407: Human-centred design processes for interactive systems. ISO, Geneva
9. Mao, J.Y., Vredenburg, K., Smith, P.W., Carey, T.: The state of user-centered design practice. Commun. ACM **48**(3), 105–109 (2005)
10. Henry, S.L.: Just ask: integrating accessibility throughout design. Lulu.com (2007)
11. Lazar, J., Feng, J.H., Hochheiser, H.: Surveys, Chap. 5, 2nd edn. In: Lazar, J., Feng, J.H., Hochheiser, H. (eds.) Research Methods in Human Computer Interaction, pp 105–133. Morgan Kaufmann, Boston (2017). https://doi.org/10.1016/B978-0-12-805390-4.00005-4. http://www.sciencedirect.com/science/article/pii/B9780128053904000054
12. Cooper, A., Reimann, R., Cronin, D., Noessel, C.: About Face: The Essentials of Interaction Design. Wiley (2014)
13. Lazar, J., Feng, J., Hochheiser, H.: Iintroduction to HCI research. In: Research Methods in Human Computer Interaction (2017)
14. Rudd, J., Stern, K., Isensee, S.: Low vs. high-fidelity prototyping debate. Interactions **3**(1), 76–85 (1996)
15. Lazar, J., Feng, J.H., Hochheiser, H.: Automated data collection methods, chap. 12, 2nd edn. In: Lazar, J., Feng, J.H., Hochheiser, H. (eds.) Research Methods in Human Computer Interaction, pp 329–368. Morgan Kaufmann, Boston (2017). https://doi.org/10.1016/B978-0-12-805390-4.00012-1. http://www.sciencedirect.com/science/article/pii/B9780128053904000121
16. Nielsen, J., Molich, R.: Heuristic evaluation of user interfaces. In: Proceedings of the SIGCHI Conference on Human Factors in Computing Systems, pp 249–256 (1990)
17. Nielsen, J.: Discount usability: 20 years. Jakob Nielsen's Alertbox (2009). http://www.useit.com/alertbox/discount-usability.html. Accessed 23 Jan 2012
18. Connor, J.O., Cooper, M., Kirkpatrick, A., Campbell, A.: Web content accessibility guidelines (WCAG) 2.1. W3C recommendation, W3C (2018). https://www.w3.org/TR/2018/REC-WCAG21-20180605/

19. Nielsen, J.: Enhancing the explanatory power of usability heuristics. In: Proceedings of the SIGCHI Conference on Human Factors in Computing Systems, pp. 152–158 (1994)
20. Nielsen, J.: Discount usability for the web: Article by Jakob Nielsen (1997). https://www.nngroup.com/articles/web-discount-usability/
21. Nielsen, J.: Think aloud: the #1 usability tool. Erişim adresi (2012). https://www.nngroup.com/articles/thinking-aloud-the-1-usability-tool
22. Hassan, M.M., Tukiainen, M., Qureshi, A.N.: (Un) discounted usability: evaluating low-budget educational technology projects with dual-personae evaluators. In: Proceedings of the 2019 8th International Conference on Software and Information Engineering, pp 253–258 (2019)
23. Miaskiewicz, T., Kozar, K.A.: Personas and user-centered design: how can personas benefit product design processes? Des. Stud. **32**(5), 417–430 (2011)

# HyperSCADA: A Codification Framework for Improving SCADA System User Experience Design

Jiachun Du[⊠], Hanyue Duan, Nan Zhao, and Ruihang Tian

IoT Department, Alibaba Cloud, Hangzhou, China
jiachun.djc@alibaba-inc.com

**Abstract.** SCADA is widely used in machine monitoring. However, most of those practices focus on the function ability rather than usability. We promoted a codification framework called HyperSCADA for SCADA systems' user experience design. This framework helps SCADA developers structure their device data, modularize different data in widgets, organize widgets' layout and make a new web-based SCADA with better user experience. We integrated this framework in a low-code application builder called IoT Studio and validated it. Users provide positive feedbacks for new SCADAs.

**Keywords:** SCADA · Cloud · User experience framework · Codification

## 1 Background

Began in early 1950s, SCADA (Supervisory Control and Data Acquisition) is a type of visualization and control systems in industrial application field. SCADA systems are widely used by factories and companies to monitor machine status, control and maintain efficiency, and send data for appropriate decisions [1, 6]. As the internet of things (IoT) industry grows, more and more SCADA systems are integrated in cloud-based structured to communicate with other data services.

However, most of those practices focus on the function ability rather than usability. There are few discussions on improving user experience of SCADA systems in IoT age [11, 12]. Compared with traditional SCADA systems, a cloud-base IoT SCADA system has some new features which leads to different user experiences:

1. Most of the human-machine interactions are on browsers. Browser enables compatibility of different operation systems while it limits interactions in keyboard & mouse.
2. Web browsers has been developed for more than 30 years. Users have already had a certain mindset in using web applications (like clicking on/off button with abstract layout). But it is quite different from SCADA systems (which still use physical layout to describe a button).

3. Cloud-base systems often require compatibility for multi-screens such as laptops, mobiles and pads. Most of traditional SCADA systems do not take it into consideration when designing.

As a result, it is necessary to integrate user experience framework of internet applications to SCADAs. In this process we were hampered by some IoT features:

1. It is often for a certain device to have more than 100 sensor data points. It will cost considerable time if visualizing them step by step.
2. Some SCADA design styles are old-fashion and lack of usability consideration.
3. IoT contexts are highly customized and many IoT companies do not have UX team.

In other words, they don't have the ability to improve the design of a specific SCADA. For solving these problems, we need an efficient way to systematically improve the usability of IoT SCADA systems. Noticing that many IoT platforms are trying to structure things data for better storage [13]. We consider following the method of things structural language to standardize and code SCADA UX would be a breakpoint.

## 2  HyperSCADA Framework - Codification UX in SCADA

We promote a codification framework called HyperSCADA for SCADA systems' user experience design. This framework helps SCADA developers structure their device data, modularize different data in widgets, organize widgets' layout and make a new web-based SCADA with better user experience. We integrate this framework in a low-code application builder called IoT Studio (Fig. 1).

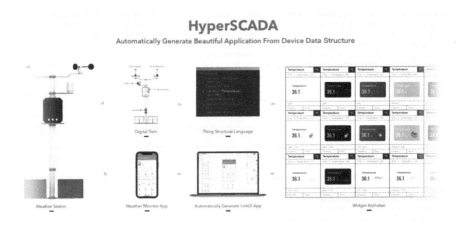

**Fig. 1.** HyperSCADA framework and its implementation.

As the figure above shows, HyperSCADA indicates how to automatically generate beautiful application from device data structure. It takes 6 steps to finish the loop:

1. Deploy a real device in physical environment with certain sensors and reactors, such as a weather station with anemometer, wind vane, thermometer and rain gauge.
2. Connect the device to IoT platform to build a digital twin.
3. Organize data in a certain thing structural language.
4. Match certain property to a certain widget based on the codification UI alphabet. All widgets will combine together into a new UI data structure.
5. Automatically render UI widgets in low-code application builder based on the UI Data structure.
6. Publish the SCADA to access data from device on multi-screens (Fig. 2).

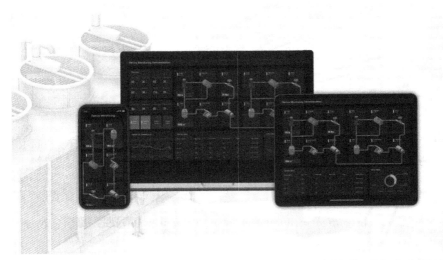

**Fig. 2.** A showcase of multi-screen HAVC (Heating Ventilating and Air Conditioning) SCADA with HyperSCADA framework.

Compared with traditional SCADA production, HyperSCADA has 4 advantages:

1. Hierarchical information allows end users acquire better insights for IoT devices.
2. Relating device data with low-code application builder components decreases 90% SCADA develop time.
3. Widget-based data visualization adapts to screens with different resolutions.
4. Design system help SCADA improve its layouts with iterations.

## 3    Case Study

We applied this framework in SCADAs for city environment, village water pollution, HAVC (Heating Ventilating and Air Conditioning) and manufacture environment (Fig. 3).

**Fig. 3.** Showcases of projects empowered by HyperSCADA framework.

For validating if it improved user experience we interviewed a few users of our IoT platform and got the following feedbacks:

*"These SCADAs update my impression on HMI screens! It would definitly benefit our business!"*

*"It helps me a lot with the HAVC design. Our loves it and we could rapidly deliver our solutions."*

*"Our clients will not leave time for us to design and develop a better SCADA. Your framework could help us decrease develop cost and get better result!The most difficult part would now be defining the device data structure."*

Generally, Users provide positive feedbacks for new SCADAs. A hierarchical and aesthetic graphical user interface would help them better access device information. Also, they highly appreciated the rapid design process in low-code application builder for helping project delivery faster. On the other hand, their concerns happened in the pre-processing part such as applying thing structural language rather than their traditional data structure for all their devices.

## 4   Conclusion and Future Work

SCADA is widely used in machine monitoring. However, most of those practices focus on the function ability rather than usability. We promoted a codification framework called HyperSCADA for SCADA systems' user experience design. This framework helps SCADA developers structure their device data, modularize different data in widgets, organize widgets' layout and make a new web-based SCADA with better user experience. We integrated this framework in a low-code application builder called IoT Studio and validated it. Users provide positive feedbacks for new SCADAs.

The next step would be expanding the codification alphabet and add complex data structure to describe device typology and spatial relations. Also, there would be more researches on improving and validating the user experience of generated SCADA user interfaces in different industries.

# References

1. What is SCADA? (n.d.). Retrieved 15 March 2021. https://www.inductiveautomation.com/resources/article/what-is-scada
2. Janak, J., Schulzrinne, H.: Framework for rapid prototyping of distributed IoT applications powered by WebRTC. In: 2016 Principles, Systems and Applications of IP Telecommunications (IPTComm), pp. 1–7. IEEE, October 2016
3. Datta, S.K., Bonnet, C.: Easing iot application development through datatweet framework. In: 2016 IEEE 3rd World Forum on Internet of Things (WF-IoT), pp. 430–435. IEEE, December 2016
4. Hoarcǎ, I.C., Bizon, N., Enescu, F.M.: The design of the graphical interface for the SCADA system on an industrial platform. In: 2020 12th International Conference on Electronics, Computers and Artificial Intelligence (ECAI), pp. 1–6. IEEE, June 2020
5. Dognini, A.: Field trial user experience including visualization systems (2019)
6. Daneels, A., Salter, W.: What is SCADA? (1999)
7. Hu, W., et al.: Plug-in free web-based 3-D interactive laboratory for control engineering education. IEEE Trans. Industr. Electron. **64**(5), 3808–3818 (2016)
8. Grgić, K., Špeh, I., Heđi, I.: A web-based IoT solution for monitoring data using MQTT protocol. In: 2016 international conference on smart systems and technologies (SST), pp. 249–253. IEEE, October 2016
9. Kao, K.C., Chieng, W.H., Jeng, S.L.: Design and development of an IoT-based web application for an intelligent remote SCADA system. In: IOP Conference Series: Materials Science and Engineering, vol. 323, no. 1, p. 012025, IOP Publishing, March 2018
10. Serikul, P., Nakpong, N., Nakjuatong, N.: Smart farm monitoring via the Blynk IoT platform: case study: humidity monitoring and data recording. In: 2018 16th International Conference on ICT and Knowledge Engineering (ICT&KE), pp. 1–6. IEEE, November 2018
11. Burkimsher, P.C.: Jcop experience with a commercial scada product, pvss. In: Proceedings of the ICALEPCS, October 2003
12. Soete, N., Claeys, A., Hoedt, S., Mahy, B., Cottyn, J.: Towards mixed reality in SCADA applications. IFAC-PapersOnLine **48**(3), 2417–2422 (2015)
13. Ullah, M., Nardelli, P.H., Wolff, A., Smolander, K.: Twenty-one key factors to choose an iot platform: Theoretical framework and its applications. IEEE Internet Things J. **7**(10), 10111–10119 (2020)

# Study on Optimal Design of Dynamic Information Display - a Case Study of Taipei Metro

Hsin-An Huang and Meng-Cong Zheng$^{(\boxtimes)}$

Department of Industrial Design, National Taipei University of Technology, No.1, Sec. 3, Zhongxiao E. Rd. 10608, Taipei 10608, Taiwan

**Abstract.** This study aims to figure out the feasibility of the current information transfer approach to the passengers and clarify the accuracy of information when passing to the passengers. This study focused on Taipei metro's information board and aimed to analyze the information's accuracy and feasibility and understand if the information is legible to the subject with their reviews. This study conducted several investigations, including: 1. Record the behavior and process of drawing; 2. Experiment with static image and motion video; 3. Survey research of Likert scale, usability test, semantic difference, and mental load; 4. Semi-structured interview. This study helps to understand the ease of using the Taipei Metro information display and explore the factors and behavioral differences that affect users' search for information. This study found that: 1. The presentation of the background color of the information block; 2. Specification of information arrangement and number; 3. Identify two trains going to different destinations; 4. The status indication of train information; 5. The dynamic switching effect of different information, all of the above, will affect the reading comprehension of the test participants in searching for information. We will analyze the experimental results and summarize the user requirements to provide suggestions for future design optimization.

**Keywords:** Train information · Information display · Taipei metro · Usability

## 1 Introduction

From Taipei Rapid Transit Corporation's website as of 2020 [1], Taipei Metro's total annual traffic volume has reached about 700 million passengers, and the demand for operation is increasing year by year. People are beginning to expect high-quality information from Taipei Metro. An excellent visual display can be easily read and pleasing to the user [2].

The LCD display in front of the platform is a common way to deliver information to passengers waiting for trains, providing them with a wide range of information such as train arrival information, city promotion activities, and popular lifestyle information. LCD displays can deliver complex information content with high visibility and intelligibility [3]. According to the 2020 Taipei MRT passenger characteristics survey, the leading consumer group aged between 20 and 49 accounts for about 75.4%, bringing

C. Stephanidis et al. (Eds.): HCII 2021, CCIS 1499, pp. 446–453, 2021.
https://doi.org/10.1007/978-3-030-90179-0_57

many people and highlighting the value of advertising. In addition, according to a survey of advertising media, the volume of advertisements in Taiwan's foreign media accounts for 7.6% of the total volume of media advertisements, which is a steadily developing advertising media, providing a large amount of exposure for various types of ads, but also causing advertisements to occupy a large amount of space. In an era of rapid technological development and a large amount of information, users focus on the efficiency, accuracy, and convenience of information access, so the most important thing to consider in designing the interface is the level of user awareness [4]. Since the Train Information Display is a one-way information delivery interface, users will judge and act based on the interface's elements, labels, and layout. In addition to considering readability and visual aesthetics, the layout must also have auxiliary functions to enhance reading comprehension so that users can clearly obtain the correct information from the layout [5]. When designing the interface, we should think of "people" as the starting point and need to understand the user's behavior, needs, experience, and the influence of the environment, to achieve the ideal results with the least amount of thinking and behavior. According to the user's needs, the message is designed to be displayed to make people feel trusted, safe, and convenient [6].

This study uses the Taipei Metro Information Dynamic Display as an experimental object to investigate the passenger's demand for information and how to use visual design elements to convey train information to users effectively. We understand users' actual needs and usage status through task experiments and interviews and summarize their design points to design an information interface that meets their expectations.

## 2   Method

This study, the Taipei Metro information display interface was used as the target object to compile the factors that affect the viewer's search for information from the viewer's perspective. A task experiment was conducted. The test participants were 32 people, 16 men and 16 women, aged 20 to 55, who had taken the Taipei Metro. The test participants were divided into high and low experience groups to investigate the Taipei Metro information display differences between the two groups (Fig. 1).

The experiment is divided into two stages, and the first stage is to view five sets of the static image, the experimental task to explore the content, respectively: 1. In a region within the background information block is the same color, will be misjudged as the same kind of information; 2. For the block sorting of information, it is considered complex and diverse; 3. In a large information block, the amount of information affects the time it takes to search for information; 4. The symbols are presented so that it is difficult to help identify two trains going to different destinations;5. In "Train Information," the content of the information displayed will affect determining the train's inbound status. The second stage is to watch two motion videos, the experimental task to explore the content, respectively: 1. two different information blocks of information, when the switch in action, will affect the reading information; 2. There are two kinds of information in a partnership to do the switching, which will affect the reading information; 3. When the three blocks of information within the area, the language is switched individually, which will affect the reading information; 4. The "Time Information" block has three background colors changing, which will affect the reading information.

The test process is divided into five stages: 1. The test participants are asked to fill out basic information and experience related to riding the Taipei Metro; 2. Conduct the experimental task explanation and ask the test participants to watch the screen according to the situation task; 3. The experiment includes drawing questions that record the subject's behavior and performance in drawing, and each job is completed with an agreement scale; 4. After completing the task's two phases, the post-experimental questionnaire, SUS, Attrack-Diff questionnaire, mental load questionnaire, and information items on display were ranked in order of importance; 5. Finally, a semi-structured interview was conducted to understand the test participants ' problems with the Taipei MRT display interface design and to provide a reference for future design optimization.

**Fig. 1.** Taipei Metro information display interface

## 3    Results

**Table 1.** Experimental task code

| Code | Experimental task |
| --- | --- |
| S1 | Static Image - Task 1 |
| S2 | Static Image - Task 2 |
| S3 | Static Image - Task 3 |
| S4 | Static Image - Task 4 |
| S5 | Static Image - Task 5 |
| M1 | Motion Video - Task 1 |
| M1 | Motion Video - Task 2 |
| M1 | Motion Video - Task 3 |
| M1 | Motion Video - Task 4 |

The results of the 9-item agreement scale in this study found that more than half of the respondents thought that the current design of the Taipei Metro's display screen interface would affect the search for information, and the proportion of those who agreed and strongly agreed was higher than those who generally, disagreed, and strongly disagreed. Among them, the percentages were more elevated in tasks S1, S2, S4, S5, and M1, where they agreed and strongly agreed with 75%, 87.5%, 87.5%, 75%, and 81.3%, respectively. (Table 1 and Fig. 2).

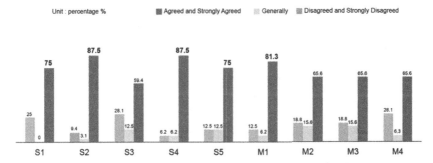

**Fig. 2.** Comparison of the level of agreement of the tasks

Task S1 misjudges the level of agreement when the background color of the information blocks is all the same. In the background of the information block, two classes of "Train Information" will only appear in blue, while the other "Time Information" will switch between blue, red, and orange. Twenty-four respondents indicated that this would affect the interpretation of the information because when all three pieces of information were blue, it was thought that they might all be "train information" messages. (Fig. 3).

**Fig. 3.** Task S1 - Interface comparison

Task S2 is how the different blocks of information are arranged, which is considered the level of consent for complexity and diversity. In the interface, "Train Information," "Advertisement," and "Time Information" are arranged in three different ways. Twenty-eight respondents said that the arrangement of information was complicated and diverse. There was no consistent arrangement and number of "train information" and "advertisements, " making their vision confusing when looking for information. (Fig. 4).

**Fig. 4.** Task S2 - Interface comparison

Task S4 is a symbolic representation that can hardly help to identify the level of agreement between the two trains. There are two forms of "station number" symbols:

white letters on a blue background for terminal trains and blue letters on a white background for sub-terminal trains. Twenty-eight respondents indicated that they could not distinguish which train was the terminal station or the sub-terminal station by the symbols' difference and suggested that the signs were not easy to understand when viewing them. It would be easier to distinguish them in words. (Fig. 5).

**Fig. 5.** Task S4 - Interface comparison

Task S5 is the content of the information displayed in "Train Information," which affects the level of agreement to identify this train's inbound status. In the train information, there are three stages of "Approach Time": the first is the time the train is approaching the station, the second is a text indicating that the train is approaching the station, and the third is a blank indicates that the train is approaching the station. Twenty-four respondents said that it was not easy to understand the train's inbound status with a blank display in the third stage of the ground, and most of them thought that the display might be faulty or delayed. (Fig. 6).

**Fig. 6.** Task S5 - Interface comparison

Task M1 is a task that affects the level of agreement of reading when the contents of two different information blocks are switched between each other. The content of the information in the "large information block" and the "small information block" will switch between each other, and the information in the block will be "train information" and "advertisement." Twenty-six respondents indicated that switching the position of the two types of information would affect their vision in searching for information and that the information was not displayed in a fixed position and needed to be moved in their vision. (Fig. 7).

All 32 participants completed the SUS Ease of Use Evaluation Form. According to [7], the unacceptable score is 0 to 50, 51 to 70 is the acceptable range, and the excellent content must be higher than 71. The average SUS score higher than 68 means higher than average. In this study, the ease of use scores was plotted in a color chart (Table 2). The average SUS score for the high-experience group is 51.3, which is barely acceptable,

**Fig. 7.** Task M1 - Interface comparison

while the average score for the low-experience group is 40.3, which is unacceptable. Therefore, subsequent interface optimization is required to enhance the usability of the display.

**Table 2.** SUS scores.

| | | | | | | | | | | | | | | | | | |
|---|---|---|---|---|---|---|---|---|---|---|---|---|---|---|---|---|---|
| High experience users | H1 | H2 | H3 | H4 | H5 | H6 | H7 | H8 | H9 | H10 | H11 | H12 | H13 | H14 | H15 | H16 | Total Average |
| SUS | 57.5 | 35 | 37.5 | 42.5 | 30 | 70 | 40 | 67.5 | 62.5 | 60 | 70 | 67.5 | 57.5 | 32.5 | 37.5 | 52.5 | **51.3** |
| Low experience users | L1 | L2 | L3 | L4 | L5 | L6 | L7 | L8 | L9 | L10 | H11 | L12 | L13 | L14 | L15 | L16 | Total Average |
| SUS | 25 | 27.5 | 52.5 | 17.5 | 42.5 | 47.5 | 47.5 | 52.5 | 42.5 | 60 | 30 | 32.5 | 32.5 | 37.5 | 65 | 32.5 | **40.3** |

# 4   Discussion

In this study, respondents were divided into two groups based on their riding the Taipei Metro: those with high-experience and those with low-experience. High-experience group live in Taipei City and New Taipei City and take the MRT more than one day a week; Low-experience group live in counties other than Taipei City and New Taipei City and have not taken the Taipei MRT for at least one month. From the percentages of agreeing and strongly agree in the above table, it can be seen that there is a difference between the high and low experience groups of task S1, S4, and M1. (Fig. 8).

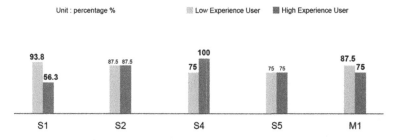

**Fig. 8.** High and low experience group - comparison of the level of agreement of the tasks

In Task S1, 56.3% and 93.8% of the high-experience group and low-experience group agreed, respectively. From the interview, the high-experience group said that the background color of the "Time Information" block had three colors switching, which was confusing. However, as a frequent rider, I can still recognize the position of "Time Information" on the screen because it is mainly read in text when searching for information. The low-experience group said they were not familiar with the arrangement of the messages on the screen, so they were easily influenced by the background color when looking for information and mistook the blue background color for "train information." Color can express the difference, variation, and classification of visual elements. Appropriate use of color helps to identify and enhance reading [8].

In Task S4, the high and low experience group's agreement level was 100% and 75%, respectively. From the interviews, it was found that the high-experience user said that they would read the text messages directly to know which train to take in a short period. The low-experience user said they would first look at the MRT route map on the platform to identify the trains at the terminal and sub-terminal stations. Both groups said they ignored the fact that there are two forms of the "station number" symbol and that they did not understand its meaning as a distinction between the two trains.

In Task M1, the high-experience group's agreement level and the low-experience groups were 75% and 87.5%, respectively. From the interviews, the high-experience group said they could understand that the incoming train would switch from a small block to a large information block, which would help to read the train information clearly. Still, while the animation switched, the eyes would need to shift the focus again and find the search complicated. The low-experience group said that they are used to searching for train information in the form of running lights, and the information display is presented in a fixed position, so they are not accustomed to it compared to the MRT's animation switching, and they cannot understand it in a short time. However, in the behavior and performance of drawing, it was found that 62.5% of the high-experience user could draw the correct switching steps. In comparison, only 31.3% of the low-experience user could draw it correctly and could know the way of dynamic switching. The high-experience user could understand more than the low-experience user. (Fig. 9).

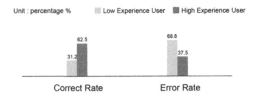

**Fig. 9.** High and low experience group - comparison of drawing behavior

## 5   Conclusion

This study helps to understand how well users read and understand the display interface of the Taipei Metro. From the interview results, we found that the background color of the "Time Information" block's background color is different from that of the "Train Information" and is presented in a single color, which helps users distinguish it from the others. It is recommended that the "arrangement" and "number" of information in the order of different information blocks can have a consistent specification, which will be more in line with the principle of simplicity. The "text" prompt for identifying two trains going to different destinations makes it easier for users to understand. The "Train Coming Soon" status in the train information can be indicated in text to help you know its position. In the "Train Information" and "Advertisement" information, it is suggested to reduce the animation switching effect, helping users search for information. This study will integrate the suggestions from two groups of riders to optimize the future Taipei MRT display interface design.

## References

1. Taipei Metro Media Advertising Manual (2020).https://www-ws.gov.taipei/Download.ashx?u=LzAwMS9VcGxvYWQvNDA1L2NrZmlsZS8zMTU1M2E4YS00M2NlLTRlZWYtODFiZC1kNmE0OTkzMmE3ODguGRm&n=5Y%2bw5YyX5o236YGL5buj5ZGK5aqS6auU5omL5YaKLTEwOVE0LTExMDAzMTcucGRm&icon=.pdf
2. McCrudden, M.T., Rapp, D.N.: How Visual Displays Affect Cognitive Processing. Educ. Psychol. Rev. **29**(3), 623–639 (2017). https://doi.org/10.1007/s10648-015-9342-2
3. Kiaki, M., Koji, N., Kazuya, A., Hiroshi, H., Tatsuya, T., Kazunori, T.: Development of on-board passenger information display. Hitachi Rev. **63**(10), 672–677 (2014)
4. Hong, M.: Contribution title. In: 9th International Proceedings on Proceedings, pp. 1–2. Publisher, Location (2011)
5. Zilun, H.: The graphic medicine bag shows a case study. National Taiwan University of Science and Technology, Taipei (2010)
6. Godwin, S.R.: electronic on-vehicle passenger information displays (visual and audible). Transp. Res. Board Natl. Res. Counc. **5**, 1–5 (2013)
7. Bangor, A., Kortum, P., Miller, J.: Determining what individual SUS scores mean: adding an adjective rating scale. J. Usability Stud. **4**(3), 114–123 (2009)
8. Snyder, H.L.: Image quality. In: Helander, M. (ed.) Handbook of human-computer interaction, pp. 437–474. Elsevier science publishers, Amsterdam (1988)

# Quality Analysis of Local Government Websites (Study Case DKI Jakarta, Bali, Banten Provinces)

Miftahul Jannah Jalil[1]([✉]) [iD], Achmad Nurmandi[1] [iD], Isnaini Muallidin[1] [iD], Danang Kurniawan[1] [iD], and Salahudin[2] [iD]

[1] Department of Government Affairs and Administration, Jusuf Kalla School of Government, Universitas Muhammadiyah Yogyakarta, Yogyakarta, Indonesia
miftahuljannahjalil97@gmail.com
[2] Department of Government Science, Universitas Muhammadiyah Malang, Indonesia, Tlogomas Street, Tegalgondo, Karang Ploso Malang, Indonesia

**Abstract.** This study aims to determine the quality of local government websites in applying the principles of good governance and to analyze the official social media Twitter accounts of the Regional Government in conveying information to the public. Website quality assessment is measured through four aspects: website features divided into several completeness of general information on local government, geography, maps of areas and resources, regional regulations or policies, and guest books and news. The research object is the official website and Twitter account of the Provincial Governments of DKI Jakarta, Bali, and Banten. Sources of research data through surveys and observations. Website quality assessment is done by giving a score on indicators of features, transparency, accountability, effectiveness, and website efficiency with 40 units of analysis. Meanwhile, Twitter content is analyzed using the Nvivo 12 Plus with the NCapture feature to document and analyze data systematically. The results showed that the overall website of the Provincial Government of DKI Jakarta and Banten has (High Quality) with a score above (70%). The Bali Provincial Government website has the lowest score, with 65% (Low Quality). Meanwhile, Twitter social media for the Provincial Governments of DKI Jakarta and Banten has a high level of information delivery activity. In addition, social media information content as a whole has similarities in public matters. The issues surrounding COVID-19 were discussed on two local government Twitter accounts. The issues discussed by the Bali provincial government tended to be the local government's program for the community. Problems that often develop in these three regional governments have also resulted in increased Twitter account activity.

**Keywords:** E-government · Official website · Transparency · Accountability · Effective · Efficient

## 1 Introduction

Government is an organization whose job is to run the wheels of government. The government's job is to provide good service to the community. To achieve this, the government needs to improve the quality of services to get a response from the community. Because the community is a source of information that can improve government performance. The flow of technology and information development is so rapid that it has become necessary for everyone in the business, education, and government world. Providing information about government operations and facilitating electronic communication with the public, information and communication technology (ICT) promises to increase government transparency, accountability, and public participation. Even based on the results of a national survey by the Ministry of Communication and Information in the form of the 2012 e-Government Rating in Indonesia (PeGI), there are only six local governments out of a total of 497 districts/cities (based on data from the 2012 Directorate General of Autonomy, Ministry of Home Affairs) which are considered successful in implementing e-Government while at the provincial level, 230 e-Government implementations still get poor marks.

Since the issuance of Presidential Instruction No. 3 of 2003 concerning E-Government Development Policy, the government is required to be able to take advantage of advances in Information and Communication Technology (ICT) through the development of e-Government to improve the ability to process, distribute, distribute quality information and services to the public [1]. The Presidential Instruction (Inpres) of the Republic of Indonesia was formed to implement good governance and improve effective and efficient public services, so there is a need for strategic policies in the development of e-government [2]. ICT offers governments in developing countries adequate resources to serve citizens and stakeholders through electronic government strategies or E-Government; the terms e-Government and e-Governance are used widely to represent ICT in the public sector organizations [3]. E-government is defined as delivering information from the government based online via the internet or other means to carry out its duties and functions effectively and efficiently [2]. At the same time, E-Governance is a tool or application that functions as government information technology [4].

The government's effort to improve the quality of service performance is to provide online-based services. So the website is one form of effective information technology development in publications. In addition, the website is a means for the public to access information [5]. In addition to the website, the government also needs public feedback to assess its performance. One way to get feedback from the public is to use social media, where the social media used is Twitter [6]. This study aims to determine the quality of the city government's website. The objects of this research are three official websites and the Twitter of three local governments, namely the provinces of DKI Jakarta, Bali, and Banten. In addition, what distinguishes this research is that previous studies only examined quality measurements based on websites, while this study measured the quality of city government websites from the assessment of the city government's official website and Twitter. This research is aimed at three local governments, namely the provinces of DKI Jakarta, Bali, and Banten. The manuscript's composition in this study includes the title, author's name, address, abstract, introduction, literature review, methods, results, and conclusions.

## 2  Literature Review

### 2.1  Use of Websites in e-government the

Technology in government is known as E-Government, where technology plays a role in facilitating the management of information and services [10]. E-government emerged due to Information and Communication Technology (ICT) development to provide government services to stakeholders [11]. Through today's rapidly evolving world, ICTs enable governments to deliver services more efficiently by facilitating sharing information across the globe. ICT provides access to information such as the internet, digital or wireless networks, and other systems [12]. There are three components of e-government—first, ICT, which includes the internet, web-based applications, devices, and mobile; second, stakeholders and consumers of electronic services. The third is the yield component. These three components can increase the interaction between stakeholders and empower the community through transparent access to information to increase the efficiency and effectiveness of government administration [13].

With the growth of the internet, the government's public service model is gradually changing from the traditional manual method to an online e-government website [14]. E-Government services are usually provided through Web portals developed and managed by the government [15]. Government use of websites can increase transparency, foster trust in government, reduce corruption in the public sector, and strengthen accountability and transparency [16]. Government web portals have different functions. Some of them focus on access to information. Access to integrated and open government and citizen electronic participation transactions is also provided through governmentwide access to data, electronic petitions, electronic consultations, etc. [17]. Through the website, the government can provide services according to the needs of the community. Sometimes people use it to get information and exchange information. Some use it for transactions. Therefore, the government's completeness of service information needs to be considered by the government [15].

### 2.2  Quality Measurement of Government Websites Quality

Government websites play an essential role in building trust and ensuring e-government services and delivery [18]. Several factors affect the quality of e-government websites, including accessibility, usability, content, citizen participation, services, features, security, and privacy [19]. Factual information can also build trust, loyalty, and security for its users [20, 21]. In addition, the right images, fonts, colors, download speed, and link speed when accessed, attractive page designs reflect the identity of government entities [22]. Therefore, an evaluation approach is fundamental to improve the quality of the website [23].

The methods for evaluating and selecting evaluation criteria for websites are different and still need more theoretical justification. Most of the previous approaches focused on the importance of certain main content or set of website results. They use subjective factors, such as ease of access, clarity of text, presentation quality, etc., as performance indexes or use manual survey questionnaires to determine specific ranking indexes for websites, such as accessibility, speed, searchability, and websites. content [24]. Various criteria have been used to assess website quality. Henriksson [25] evaluated e-government websites using a list of criteria: security, privacy, usability, content, and citizen participation. Barnes and Vidgen have also developed an eQual approach to assessing e-government websites [26]. Meanwhile, features, transparency, accountability, effectiveness, and efficiency can also be used to evaluate government websites [27, 28]. Its web-government features should also display an overview, organizational structure, geography, maps, local regulations and policies, news, and guest books [29, 30].

### 2.3 Government Social Media (Twitter Account)

Social media is seen as a means of interaction and provides more opportunities for the public to interact with government functions. Social media today offers significant benefits in shaping society and relationships with the government. Users can easily participate, share, interact, discuss, collaborate, and create content with various platforms such as YouTube, Facebook, WhatsApp, Instagram, Twitter, and others [31]. It is limited to the relationship between policymakers and policymakers and new interactions that can be mutually beneficial through social media [32]. Therefore, in theory, the current use of ICT has given birth to new constructions in government and society [33].

The use of social media in government tends to have a significant impact on improving public services. This increase can encourage public participation. Information on government programs can be conveyed through social media [34]. As one of the social media, the government has used Twitter to convey information quickly, such as disaster preparedness, and get a public response [35, 36]. Through microblogging, a social network, Twitter users can quickly read, respond, and send messages called tweets [37]. Twitter's existence has been widely accepted for providing direct and broad access to many of the latest news operations while still helping to spread incident reporting [38].

## 3  Methods

This research uses qualitative research methods in [9], stating that this approach helps researchers investigate a phenomenon so that it is better understood and used in a limited sense to analyze an event. The focus of this research is the analysis of the city government's website and Twitter account. The city's official Twitter accounts were analyzed using NVivo 12 Plus with the NCapture function to record and analyze information systematically [10]. To be studied and researched carefully and thoroughly [11]. By visiting the City Government website, data were obtained. Website output calculation using an instrument provided by Google, Page Speed Insights. On a percentage scale, website loading speed is rated.

Through evaluation using scoring, the efficiency of three local government websites, namely, DKI Jakarta, Bali, and Banten provinces. Score analysis uses indicators to evaluate policy changes developed in line with the developed objectives and, where appropriate, by weighting indicators deemed more relevant than other indicators [12]. A specific score will be given concerning the analysis of the evaluation scale in calculating the comparative rating [13]. If the information is available/available, will be given a score of 1 if the data is not available/not available, then a 0 will be given if the data is not available/not available.

**The formula for the estimated weight score is as follows:**

$$\text{Score Weight} = \frac{\text{Total website score} \times 100\%}{\text{Total score}}$$

After the weight is obtained, an assessment is carried out according to the following Table 1:

**Table 1.** Score and values

| Score (%) | Features | Transparency | Accountability | Effective | Efficient | Overall Score |
|---|---|---|---|---|---|---|
| 0–25 | Incomplete | Not transparent | Not accountable | Ineffective | Inefficient Inefficient | Not quality |
| 51–75 | Incomplete | Less transparent | Less accountable | Less effective | Less efficient | Low quality |
| 26–50 | Fairly complete | Fairly transparent | Fairly accountable | Fairly effective | Fairly efficient | Average Quality |
| 76–100 | Complete | Transparent | Accountable | Effective | Efficient | High Quality |

Local government website access speed is also calculated using Google Tools, namely Page Speed Insights. Website loading speed is rated on a percentage scale, slow (0%–49%), average (50%–89%), and fast (90%–100%). Meanwhile, Twitter content was analyzed using Nvivo 12 Plus with the NCapture feature to systematically document and analyze the data [40].

## 4   Results

### 4.1   Analysis of the Quality of Local Government Websites

Based on the assessment and research on local government websites, namely, the provinces of DKI Jakarta, Bali, and Banten were assessed by 40 review units. Evaluation is done by giving a score on website features, transparency, accountability, performance, and effectiveness. The convenience of the public in accessing the website needs to be considered by the city and regional governments because the official website has a vital role in communicating or conveying information to the public. Data from Google shows that 53% of people in Indonesia will leave a website that takes more than 3 s to load. The website speed of the three city governments in Central Java can be seen in the following Fig. 1:

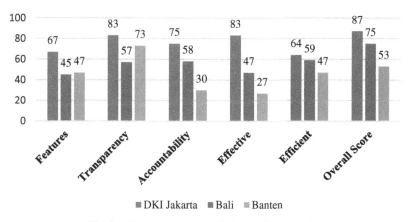

**Fig. 1.** City government website quality score the

The picture above shows the DKI Jakarta Provincial Government website obtaining the highest score with a percentage value of 89%. While the website of the provincial government of Bali, 75%, has the lowest score with a percentage value of 43%. The DKI Jakarta Provincial Government website is in the high-quality category, while the other two provincial government websites are still in the low category.

## 4.2 Use of Local Government Social Media (Twitter Accounts)

Local governments must socialize project and work policies to the community in absolute terms and respond directly. Twitter has been used as a medium for contact and interaction with groups by Banda Aceh, Langsa, Lhokseumawe, Sabang, and Subulussalam. The official Twitter accounts of five city governments in Aceh Province are as follows (Table 2).

**Table 2.** City government twitter account

| No. | Local Government | Twitter Account |
| --- | --- | --- |
| 1 | DKI Jakarta | @DKIJakarta |
| 2 | ProvinceBali Province | @PemprovBali |
| 3 | Banten Province | @banten_prov |

Only DKI Jakarta Province has a blue tick or is checked by Twitter from the three official Twitter of the regional governments studied, namely, DKI Jakarta, Bali, and Banten provinces. Every Tweet from the provincial government provides various information related to the Covid-19 problem and related problems in each of these areas. The results of the NVivo 12 Plus study using Word's cloud function define a publicly known issue. The issues that emerged on the provincial government's Twitter can be seen in Fig. 2.

**Fig. 2.** Twitter Wordcloud for the Regional Governments of DKI Jakarta, Bali, and Banten Provinces

The image above illustrates that the DKI Jakarta provincial government's Twitter discusses a lot about COVID-19. The Bali provincial government itself discusses a lot about the tourism sector. At the same time, the Banten provincial government is more about providing information to the public, namely issues of activities, work programs, and policies in running the wheels of government. Issues that play a role include government-community cooperation, development, education, and religion. Issues that are developing in the provincial government also increase the provincial government's Twitter activity. This increase proves that the government is actively working on various kinds of activities and other activities.

If the activities of the Banda Aceh City Government, Langsa, Lhokseumawe, and Sabang Twitter accounts have been active in the last five years. Only the Subulussalam City Government twitter via @KSubulussalam has a poor activity level or is inactive from 2016 to 2020 with six tweets. This has a terrible impact on the government in increasing public trust in performance and information disclosure in the realization of Good Governance.

## 5    Conclusion

Based on the discussion and debate research findings, the DKI Jakarta Provincial Government's website is included in the high-quality website category, while the Bali and Banten Provincial Government websites are included in the quality website category. Category average quality score. The assessment of the website is not only on its quality but also on the level of access speed. The DKI Jakarta, Bali, and Banten provincial government websites are included in the average speed website category. In addition, Twitter has been used as a medium of information and communication between the city government and the community.

## References

1. Cahyono, T.A., Susanto, T.D.: Acceptance factors and user design of mobile e-government website (Study case e-government website in Indonesia). Procedia Comput. Sci. **161**, 90–98 (2019)

2. DK and Informatics, Blueprint for E-Government Application Systems: For Local Government Institutions, Jakarta (2004)
3. Kanter, C.H., Purnama, A.P.: The role of the manado city government website in supporting the realization of good governance. J. Res. Pemb. commune. Inf.**19**(3) (2015)
4. Masyhur, F.: Performance of the official website of the provincial government in Indonesia official website performance of local government in Indonesia. J. Pekommas **17**(1), 9–14 (2014)
5. Yunita, N.P., Aprianto, R.D.: Current condition of E-government implementation Indonesia: website analysis. In: National Seminar on Information and Communication Technology, pp. 329–336 (2018)
6. Hernikawati, D.: Ministry level website popularity analysis. J. Masy. Telemat. and Inf. **7**(2), 79–88 (2016)
7. Martani, D., Fitriasari, D., Annisa: Financial transparency and performance on websites of district/city governments in Indonesia. In: PESAT Proceedings (Psychology, Economics, Literature, Architecture & Civil Engineering), vol. 5, pp. 70–80 (2013)
8. Sulistiyo, D., Negara, H.P., YFAW: Analysis of the study of standardization of the content of district/city government websites. In: National Seminar on Informatics (SEMNASIF), vol. 1, no. 5 (2008)
9. Sitokdana, M.N.N.: Evaluation of eGovernment implementation on the websites of the city government of Surabaya, Medan, Banjarmasin, Makassar and Jayapura. J. Buana Inform. **6**(4), 289–300 (2015)
10. Muttaqin, M.H., Susanto, T.D.: The Effect of website components on user trust in increasing the interest to use public administration service on E-government website. In: Proc. - 2019 Int. Conf. Comput. Science. Inf. Technol. electr. Eng. COMMITTEE, vol. 1, pp. 30–36 (2019)
11. Kaur, A., Kaur, H.: Exploring E-governance service delivery dimensions: a study of registrar of companies. Indian J. Public Adm. **63**(4), 557–566 (2017)
12. Dutta, A., Devi, M.S., Arora, M.: Census web service architecture for e-governance applications. In: ACM Int. Conf. Proceedings Ser., vol. Part F1280, pp. 1–4 (2017)
13. Cumbie, B.A., Kar, B.: A study of local government website inclusiveness: the gap between E-government concept and practice. Inf. Technol. Dev. **22**(1), 15–35 (2016)
14. Huang, J., Guo, W., Fu, L.: Research on E-government website satisfaction evaluation based on public experience. In: 4th International Conference on Education and Social Development, no. 206–213 (2019)
15. Jiang, Ji: E-government web portal adoption: the effects of service quality. E-Service J. **9**(3), 43 (2014)
16. Porumbescu, G.A.: Linking public sector social media and e-government websites use to trust in government. Gov. inf. Q. **33**(2), 291–304 (2016)
17. Henman, P., Graham, T.: Web portal vs. google for finding government information on the web: From a website-centric approach to a web ecology perspective. Inf. Polity **23**(4), 361–378 (2018)
18. Tan, C.W., Benbasat, I., Cenfetelli, R.T.: Building citizen trust towards e-government services: do high-quality websites matter? In: Proceedings of the 41st Annual Hawaii International Conference on System Sciences (HICSS 2008), p. 217 (2008)
19. Paul, S., Das, S.: Accessibility and usability analysis of Indian e-government websites. Univ. Access Inf. Soc. **19**(4), 949–957 (2019). https://doi.org/10.1007/s10209-019-00704-8
20. Sugandini, D., et al.: Web quality, satisfaction, trust and its effects on government. Int. J. Qual. res. **12**(4), 885–904 (2013)
21. Syaifullah, S., Soemantri, D.O.: Measurement of website quality using the webqual 4.0 method (Case Study: CV. Zamrud Multimedia Network). J. Ilm. Eng. Manage. Sis. Inf., **2**(1), 19–25 (2016)

22. Warjiyono, W., Hellyana, C.M.: Measuring the website quality of the Jagalempeni village government using the webqual 4.0 method. J. Teknol. inf. Comput. Sci. **5**(2), 139 (2018)
23. Abdel-Basset, M., Zhou, Y., Mohamed, M., Chang, V.: A group decision-making framework based on neutrosophic VIKOR approach for e-government website evaluation. J. Intell. Fuzzy System. **34**(6), 4213–4224 (2018)
24. Wu, J., Guo, D.: Measuring E-government performance of provincial government website in China with slacks-based efficiency measurement. Technol. Forecast. Soc. Chang. (2015)
25. Henriksson, A., Yi, Y., Frost, B., Middleton, M.: Evaluation instrument for e-government websites. Electron. Gov. an Int. J. **4**(2), 204–226 (2007)
26. Barnes, S.J., Vidgen, R.T.: Data triangulation and web quality metrics: a case study in e-government. Inf. Manag. **43**(6), 767–777 (2006)
27. Isni, A.R.: Quality analysis of local government websites in west Sesumatra regency. J. Akunt., **6**(3), October 2018
28. Cheisviyanny, C., Helmy, H., Dwita, S.: Analysis of website quality of district/city governments in west Sumatra Province. Simp. Nas. Finance. Country **6**(3), 1087–1104 (2018)
29. Effendi, P.M., Susanto, T.D.: Test of citizens' physical and cognitive on Indonesian e-government website design. Procedia Comput. Sci. **161**, 333–340 (2019)
30. Kurniawan, F., Rakhmawati, N.A., Abadi, A.N., Zuhri, M., Sugiyanto, W.T.: Indonesia local government information completeness on the web. Procedia Comput. Sci. **124**, 21–28 (2017)
31. Cahyono, A.S.: Influence of social media on social change in community in Indonesia. Publiciana **9**(1) (2016)
32. Linders, D.: From e-government to we-government: defining a typology for citizen coproduction in the age of social media. Gov. inf. Q. **29**(4), 446–454 (2012)
33. Gagliardi, D., Misuraca, G., Niglia, F., Pasi, G.: How ICTs shape the relationship between the state and the citizens: exploring new paradigms between civic engagement and social innovation. In: Proceedings of the 52nd Hawaii International Conference on Systems Sciences (2019)
34. Novianti, E., Nugraha, A.R., Komalasari, L., Komariah, K.: Utilization of social media in distribution of government program information (Case Study of the Regional Secretariat of Pangandaran Regency). AL MUNIR J. Komen. and Islamic Broadcasting **11**(1), 48–59 (2020)
35. Chatfield, A.T., Scholl, H.J.J., Brajawidagda, U.: Tsunami early warnings via Twitter in government: Net-savvy citizens' coproduction of time-critical public information services. Gov. inf. Q. **30**(4), 377–386 (2013)
36. Carley, K.M., Malik, M., Landwehr, P.M., Pfeffer, J., Kowalchuck, M.: Crowd sourcing disaster management: the complex nature of Twitter usage in Padang Indonesia. Saf Sci. **90**, 48–61 (2016)
37. Kosasih, I.: The role of Facebook and Twitter social media in building communication (perceptions and motives of social networking society in intercourse). Macy's Gazette. J. Dev. May. Islam **2**(1), 29–42 (2016)
38. Heravi, B.R., Harrower, N.: Twitter journalism in Ireland: sourcing and trust in the age of social media*. Inf. Comm. Soc. **19**(9), 1194–1213 (2016)
39. Dwiyanto, A.: transparency of public services. Yogyakarta: Graha Ilmu (2006)
40. Edwards-Jones, A.: Qualitative data analysis with NVIVO. J. Educ. Teach. **40**(2), 193–195 (2014)

# An Experimental Analysis of Face Anti-spoofing Strategies for Real Time Applications

Aasim Khurshid$^{(\boxtimes)}$ and Ricardo Grunitzki$^{(\boxtimes)}$

Sidia Institute of Science and Technology, Manaus, Brazil
{aasim.khurshid,ricardo.grunitzki}@sidia.com

**Abstract.** Face spoofing is an attack attempt to obtain unauthorized access by using photos, videos, or 3D maps of a user's face. The development of anti-spoofing strategies evolves at the same time as facial authentication technologies. Many methods for preventing such attacks have been proposed recently [1–3], showing excellent results accuracy in fraud detection. However, most of these methods are very efficient in detecting patterns—such as fraud—present a major disadvantage: a high computational cost. This cost directly impacts the user experience of the facial authentication system, since the spoofing verification adds an extra layer of inference by artificial intelligence models, causing a longer waiting time for the authentication system's user. This impact is most noted when the inference is performed on devices with limited computational power, such as mobile, tablets, and edge devices. In this work, we carry out an experimental analysis of the common anti-spoofing strategies considering the trade-off between correctness fraud detection and computational cost, aimed at optimizing the user experience. We also propose to use a fine-tuned Convolutional Neural Network (CNN) with a base network trained on a larger dataset and adds to our analysis.

**Keywords:** Anti-spoofing · Face recognition · Artificial intelligence

## 1 Introduction

Authentication methods such as passwords and barcode readers are easy to design; however, such methods are an easy target for an unauthorized user, mainly because once an unauthorized party has access to the key, it is incredibly challenging to prevent unauthorized access of the system. Recent research on authentication methods is focused on biometrics such as iris, fingerprint, or face recognition to verify the authenticity of the user. Iris and fingerprint authentication systems have been actively researched and tend to be more accurate than older techniques [4]; such techniques, however, require intentional and active

Supported by Sidia Institute of Science and Technology, and Samsung Eletrônica da Amazônia Ltda, under the auspice of the Brazilian informatics law no 8.387/91.

user contact with the device, which might feel unpleasant to the user. Face-based authentication is the most user-friendly and secure method [5], requiring little to no user contact with the device. Face-based authentication, however, is still vulnerable to spoofing, i.e., using photos, videos, or 3D maps of the user to gain unauthorized access [6]. Some systems try to prevent this by acquiring some live face feature, such as yawning [7], but most face-based authentication methods do not provide a built-in anti-spoofing mechanism. In principle, the problem of anti-spoofing is usually treated as an independent problem from face-based authentication.

Different techniques have been proposed in the literature to classify spoofed images of a person, including hardware-based, challenge-response, and software-based anti-spoofing methods. Such strategies present advantages and disadvantages in terms of accuracy in detecting fraud, as well as in terms of running time. Choosing the best face anti-spoofing detection strategy is not a straightforward task, since the trade-off between running time and accuracy in fraud detection must be considered. In this work, we propose a very robust method for detecting face spoofing and compare it to other strategies, taking into consideration the trade-off between fraud detection and time efficiency.

The experimental evaluation is conducted on two well-know datasets for spoofing detection (NUAA [8] and Replay-attack [9]). Experimental results show that state-of-art methods can achieve 99% off accuracy/assertiveness in fraud detection, but costing twice the processing time. The proposed method manages to obtain accuracy as high as other state-of-the-art methods, but providing a reduction in processing cost, improving the user experience.

The rest of this paper is organized as follows. Section 2 presents the related works and compares theoretical aspects that motivated this work. Section 3 explains the important concepts used in the development of the proposed method, which is presented in Sect. 4. Section 5 provides the experimental analysis. Finally, conclusions are drawn in Sect. 6.

## 2   Related Works

Software-based spoofing detection motivated many studies. Pioneer solutions to spoofing detection started with a focus on texture-based methods. Li et al. analyzed frequency distribution to differentiate between live and non-live face images [10]. The authors assumed that the photo image has fewer high-frequency components because of the flat structure of the photo and that the standard deviation of frequency components in the photo image is small because of invariant expressions. These assumptions, however, do not hold for more sophisticated attacks, which include video attacks or 3D map attacks. Anjos et al. created a database and indicated protocols for the evaluation of the spoofing attack solutions [11]. Sun et al. proposed an eye blinking-based face liveness detection [12]; however, the accuracy of the method drops substantially with people using glasses. Furthermore, iris-based liveness detection methods are not practical because it is not uncommon to use sunglasses in outdoor scenarios.

Research on software-based face anti-spoofing was usually based on grayscale image analysis until recently. However, some recent works exploited the color properties as vital visual cues for discriminating spoofed faces from the real ones [5,13]. Boulkenafet et al. proposed a color-based technique that analyses contrast and illumination changes in the captured image or video [5]. Chingovska et al. utilized Local Binary Patterns to analyze face texture to prove liveness [9]; the authors also include alternative LBPs such as transitional LBP, direction-coded LBP, and modified LBP. These LBPs are used as feature vectors and are compared using $X^2$ histogram classification. Also, Khurshid et al. [1] used LBPs and co-occurrence of LBP in YCbCr color space as feature vectors and combine them to train a Support Vector Machine-based classifier. A combination of texture features proved to be effective for anti-spoofing as well. Kim et al. [3] proposed to use Local Speed Patterns (LSP) based on diffusion speed as a feature vector and to train a linear classifier to detect spoofing. The key idea behind this method is that the difference in the surface properties between live and fake faces can be estimated using diffusion speed.

Convolutional Neural Networks (CNN) are also used to face anti-spoofing [14]. Yang et al. trained a CNN with five convolutional (Conv) layers, followed by three fully connected (FC) layers. After learning the CNN, the features from the last connected layer are used to train the SVM classifier. However, to use the full potential of neural network-based solutions, plenty of pre-processed and labeled training data and hardware capabilities. However, this can be improved with transfer learning strategies.

## 3 Fundamental Concepts

This section briefly introduces the two main technical aspects of the proposed method.

### 3.1 Convolutional Neural Network

CNN learns filters automatically for image representation by assigning weights to various aspects of the image and proved to be efficient for image classification problems [15]. Also, CNN requires minimal to no pre-processing to learn filters automatically. However, it requires a larger amount of data for better performance, which also makes the training process time-consuming [16].

### 3.2 Transfer Learning

To overcome the disadvantage of the CNN, transfer learning approaches are adapted recently to decrease the data dependency and faster training of the CNNs [17]. Transfer learning is a technique that allows developers to utilize the pre-trained networks and capitalize on the advantage of their training. Many networks such as GoogelNet [15] are trained with millions of images such as the ones in ImageNet [18]. These networks can be used to generate a more general description of the image and use these weights as a cue for a network designed for a more specific task such as anti-spoofing classification in this work.

## 4   Proposed Method

Mostly face spoofing is performed using printed target faces, displaying videos or masks to the input sensors [3]. The simplest attacks, e.g., using mobile phone displays, can be detected easily using texture analysis because of the artifacts in the image. However, higher-quality spoofed faces are difficult to detect [5]. Some examples of the real and spoofed images from the NUAA database [8] are shown in Fig. 1. Real and spoofed images look very similar, and the task of spoofing detection is not trivial. Interestingly, the luminance distribution is a bit uniform in spoofed images (as shown in the second row of Fig. 1). This behavior can be exploited using CNNs because it starts by detecting low-level features such as edges and contours to more refined features of the image such as the human face. For better efficiency in training and accuracy, we employ a transfer learning strategy by using GoogleNet as a base network [15]. The GoogleNet introduced Inception layers, which allows the network to be more accurate because of its depth, and also fast in training and validation.

**Fig. 1.** Example images from NUAA database [8] (left 2) and replay attack database [9] (right 2); Original images in the first row and spoofed images in the second row

### 4.1   Training

For training, GoogleNet is used as a base network following the same architecture. However, the fully connected layer is updated from 1000 connections to 2 connections layer, which is followed accordingly by the classification output. Furthermore, to customize the model to spoof classification, the weights of only the first two levels of the convolution layers, and pooling layers are fixed (conv1-$7 \times 7$ s2, conv1-ReLU $7 \times 7$, pool1-$3 \times 3$ s2, pool1-norm1, conv2-$3 \times 3$ reduce s1, conv2-ReLU-$3 \times 3$ reduce s1, conv2-$3 \times 3$ reduce s1, conv2-ReLU-$3 \times 3$ reduce s1, conv2-norm2, and pool2-$3 \times 3$ s2). Furthermore, the weights of all the Inception layers are learned using the training dataset.

## 4.2    Classification

The model is created as an end-to-end network such that When a test image is given, it passes through the trained network, which generates features and classifies the image for spoofing detection.

# 5    Experimental Evaluation

Experiments are conducted using Matlab 2019b on a Macbook pro with 2.8 GHz Quad-Core Intel Core i7, 16 GB of RAM, and a macOS operating system. For the quantitative evaluations, the following metrics are used: Attack Presentation Classification Error Rate (APCER), Normal Presentation Classification Error Rate (NPCER), Average Classification Error Rate (ACER), False Positive Rate (FPR), True Positive Rate (TPR), True Negative Rate (TNR) and accuracy. For details on the metrics, we refer to Khurshid et al. [1].

The goal of the anti-spoofing algorithm is to achieve the smallest value of APCER, NPCER, ACER, FPR, and highest TPR, TNR, and accuracy values.

## 5.1    Datasets

For experimental evaluation, the NUAA [8] and Replay-attack databases [9] were used. The NUAA database has 11752 original and spoofed face images from 15 subjects, which are divided into training and test sets. Spoofing attacks are created by printing the photos and taking the photos of these photos to re-capture the image. The Replay-attack database is a 2D face spoofing attack database that contains 1,300 video clips of photo and video attack attempts of 50 clients, under different lighting conditions [9] recorded at 25 fps. The dataset is divided into train, development, and test sets to create and test anti-spoofing algorithms. Some examples from the NUAA database and images generated from videos of replay attack database are shown in Fig. 1. The first row in Fig. 1 shows the originally captured images and the second row shows the spoofed images.

## 5.2    Quantitative Evaluation

In this work, two experimental analyses are conducted to evaluate different aspects of the main methods for facial spoofing detection and compare them to the proposed method. In the first, we assess fraud detection ability from the perspective of different facial spoofing detection model evaluation metrics, such as APCER, NPCER, ACER, FPR, TPR, TNR, and Accuracy. The second analysis, in turn, assesses the method's ability in terms of time efficiency.

**Anti-spoofing Evaluation Metrics.** In this analysis, we evaluate our method and compare its results against the ones yield by the following methods:

- Total variation models for variable lighting face recognition [19];
- Face Liveness Detection from a Single Image with Sparse Low-Rank Bilinear Discriminative Model [8];
- Deep Feature Extraction for Face Liveness Detection [2];
- Face Liveness Detection From a Single Image via Diffusion Speed Model [3]
- Variants of texture feature analysis-based methods: GrayLBP, YLBP (Luminance), CbLBP (Chrominance Blue), CrLBP (Chrominance Red), CoALBP and Combined LBPs [1].

Table 1 presents the results obtained in NUAA dataset. Best results are shown in **bold**, second-best results in *italic*). Each row shows the results of the method indicated in the first column. For APCER, NPCER, ACER, and FPR smallest values indicate the best result. On the other hand, higher values are expected for TPR, TNR, and accuracy. Kim et al. [3] and variants of khurshid et al. [1] performs very closely with the proposed method.

Table 2 shows that the results are very similar in the Replay Attack dataset. The proposed method, CNN combined with SVM [2] and the combined LBP method yield similar results in terms of APCER, FPR, and TNR. The method of Kim et al. [3] performed slightly better than other state-of-the-art methods in terms of accuracy. The simplest method such as Gray LBP performs better than state-of-the-art methods based on accuracy, however, the grayscale LBP method has some APCER, which can allow some frauds. For this reason, robustness against spoofing attacks is achieved by combining LBP histograms of luminance and chrominance components, along with Co-occurrence of LBP. CNN combined with SVM [2] performs well on this dataset, however, it performs badly on the NUAA dataset, which indicates a lack of generality.

**Table 1.** Experimental evaluation of the proposed feature set and comparative methods accuracy on NUAA dataset [8].

| Method | APCER | NPCER | ACER | FPR | TPR | TNR | Accuracy |
|---|---|---|---|---|---|---|---|
| Chen et al. [19] | N/A | N/A | N/A | N/A | N/A | N/A | 0.6844 |
| Tan et al. [8] | 0.2073 | 0.2267 | 0.2170 | 0.2073 | 0.7733 | 0.7927 | 0.7856 |
| Sengur et al. [2] | N/A | N/A | N/A | N/A | N/A | N/A | 0.8809 |
| Kim et al. [3] | N/A | N/A | N/A | N/A | N/A | N/A | 0.9845 |
| GrayLBP [1] | *0.0025* | *0.0033* | *0.0029* | *0.0025* | *0.9967* | *0.9971* | *0.9967* |
| YLBP (Luminance) [1] | 0.0035 | 0.0041 | 0.0038 | 0.0035 | 0.9959 | 0.9967 | 0.9964 |
| CbLBP (Chrominance Blue) [1] | 0.0661 | 0.1132 | 0.0896 | 0.0661 | 0.8868 | 0.9331 | 0.9146 |
| CrLBP (Chrominance Red) [1] | 0.0410 | 0.0725 | 0.0567 | 0.0410 | 0.9275 | 0.9587 | 0.9457 |
| CoALBP [1] | 0.0413 | 0.0879 | 0.0646 | 0.0413 | 0.9121 | 0.9583 | 0.9357 |
| Combined LBPs [1] | **0.0002** | *0.0008* | **0.0005** | **0.0003** | **0.9992** | **0.9995** | **0.9994** |
| Proposed method | 0.0013 | **0.0000** | 0.0007 | 0.0013 | **1.0000** | 0.9987 | **0.9992** |

**Table 2.** Experimental evaluation of the proposed feature set and comparative methods accuracy on Replay-attack database [9].

| Method | APCER | NPCER | ACER | FPR | TPR | TNR | Accuracy |
|---|---|---|---|---|---|---|---|
| sengur et al. [2] | **0.0000** | 0.0071 | 0.0036 | **0.0000** | 0.9929 | **1.0000** | 0.9972 |
| Kim et al. [3] | N/A | N/A | N/A | N/A | N/A | N/A | 0.9434 |
| GrayLBP [1] | *0.0003* | *0.0024* | *0.0014* | *0.0003* | 0.9976 | *0.9997* | 0.9992 |
| YLBP (Luminance) [1] | 0.0003 | 0.0015 | 0.0009 | *0.0003* | *0.9985* | *0.9997* | *0.9994* |
| CbLBP (Chrominance Blue) [1] | 0.0411 | 0.1614 | 0.1013 | 0.0411 | 0.8386 | 0.9589 | 0.9298 |
| CrLBP (Chrominance Red) [1] | 0.0329 | 0.2089 | 0.1209 | 0.0329 | 0.7911 | 0.9671 | 0.9245 |
| CoALBP [1] | 0.0004 | **0.0000** | **0.0002** | 0.0004 | **1.0000** | 0.9996 | **0.9997** |
| Combined LBPs [1] | **0.0000** | 0.0250 | 0.0125 | **0.0000** | 0.9750 | **1.0000** | *0.9939* |
| Proposed method | **0.0000** | 0.1000 | 0.0500 | **0.0000** | 0.9000 | **1.0000** | 0.9610 |

In this experiment, we show that by making use of robust machine learning techniques, as CNN and transfer learning, it is possible to develop very efficient methods for fraud detection. However, the application of such methods in real scenarios needs to take into account the processing cost, which is analyzed in the analysis below.

**Time Efficiency.** This analysis evaluates the time efficiency of methods for face spoofing detection according to the technologies they use in their building. We selected the following methods (according to their characteristics):

- CNN combined to SVM [2];
- Train diffusion speed model [3];
- Texture feature analyses: Combined LBP [1];
- CNN combined to transfer learning: Proposed method.

In Fig. 2, we present the results obtained in the NUAA dataset, by considering the trade-off between fraud detection and time efficiency. As a fraud detection measure, we are considering the accuracy measure, whilst for time efficiency we are considering the frames per second (fps) that the method can execute in one second. The best method is the one that maximizes both the accuracy and the fps it can run. It can be seen that Sengur et al. [2] is the fastest to draw an inference but the margin of error is much higher, Combined LBP [1] have the highest accuracy but it has higher latency. The proposed scheme based on transfer learning provides a better trade-off between inference time and accuracy. The transfer learning approach and Combined LBP method can be effective depending on the scenario it is applied.

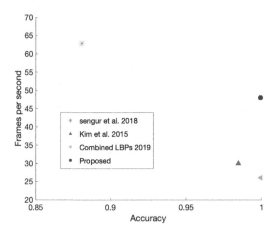

**Fig. 2.** Accuracy vs fps plot at inference of methods conferring accuracy >80%

## 6  Conclusions

In this work, we conduct an experimental analysis of the face anti-spoofing strategies based on their correctness in the spoofing detection and computational cost, to ensure security and a pleasant user experience. In terms of accuracy, fine-tuned transfer learning using CNN and texture-based methods performs close to 99%, at least 20% better than diffusion and sparse models, while 10% better than deep feature detection using independent CNN. Moreover, in terms of time efficiency, CNN based transfer learning approach outperforms comparative methods and may perform at 48 frames per second, while the texture-based method performs at 26 frames per second in our experiments. Therefore, it is safe to say that, for better accuracy, texture-based methods are slightly ahead, however, transfer learning-based approach is less computationally extensive during the inference stage for the anti-spoofing problem.

## References

1. Khurshid, A., Tamayo, S.C., Fernandes, E., Gadelha, M.R., Teofilo, M.: A robust and real-time face anti-spoofing method based on texture feature analysis. In: Stephanidis, C. (ed.) HCII 2019. LNCS, vol. 11786, pp. 484–496. Springer, Cham (2019). https://doi.org/10.1007/978-3-030-30033-3_37
2. Sengur, A., Akhtar, Z., Akbulut, Y., Ekici, S., Budak, U.: Deep feature extraction for face liveness detection. In: 2018 International Conference on Artificial Intelligence and Data Processing (IDAP), pp. 1–4, September 2018
3. Kim, W., Suh, S., Han, J.: Face liveness detection from a single image via diffusion speed model. IEEE Trans. Image Process. 24(8), 2456–2465 (2015)
4. Galbally, J., Marcel, S., Fierrez, J.: Image quality assessment for fake biometric detection: application to iris, fingerprint, and face recognition. IEEE Trans. Image Process. 23(2), 710–724 (2014)

5. Boulkenafet, Z., Komulainen, J., Hadid, A.: Face spoofing detection using colour texture analysis. IEEE Trans. Inf. Forensics Secur. **11**(8), 1818–1830 (2016)
6. Khurshid, A., Scharcanski, J.: Incremental multi-model dictionary learning for face tracking. In: 2018 IEEE International Instrumentation and Measurement Technology Conference (I2MTC), pp. 1–6, May 2018
7. Omidyeganeh, M., et al.: Yawning detection using embedded smart cameras. IEEE Trans. Instrum. Meas. **65**(3), 570–582 (2016)
8. Tan, X., Li, Y., Liu, J., Jiang, L.: Face liveness detection from a single image with sparse low rank bilinear discriminative model. In: Daniilidis, K., Maragos, P., Paragios, N. (eds.) ECCV 2010. LNCS, vol. 6316, pp. 504–517. Springer, Heidelberg (2010). https://doi.org/10.1007/978-3-642-15567-3_37
9. Chingovska, I., Anjos, A., Marcel, S.: On the effectiveness of local binary patterns in face anti-spoofing. In: 2012 BIOSIG-Proceedings of the International Conference of Biometrics Special Interest Group (BIOSIG), pp. 1–7. IEEE (2012)
10. Li, J., Wang, Y., Tan, T., Jain, A.K.: Live face detection based on the analysis of Fourier spectra. In: Biometric Technology for Human Identification, vol. 5404, pp. 296–304. International Society for Optics and Photonics (2004)
11. Anjos, A., Marcel, S.: Counter-measures to photo attacks in face recognition: a public database and a baseline. In: International Joint Conference on Biometrics, pp. 1–7. IEEE (2011)
12. Sun, L., Pan, G., Wu, Z., Lao, S.: Blinking-based live face detection using conditional random fields. In: Lee, S.-W., Li, S.Z. (eds.) ICB 2007. LNCS, vol. 4642, pp. 252–260. Springer, Heidelberg (2007). https://doi.org/10.1007/978-3-540-74549-5_27
13. Wen, D., Han, H., Jain, A.K.: Face spoof detection with image distortion analysis. IEEE Trans. Inf. Forensics Secur. **10**(4), 746–761 (2015)
14. Yang, J., Lei, Z., Li, S.Z.: Learn convolutional neural network for face anti-spoofing. CoRR abs/1408.5601 (2014)
15. Szegedy, C., et al.: Going deeper with convolutions. In: Proceedings of the IEEE Conference on Computer Vision and Pattern Recognition, pp. 1–9 (2015)
16. Karpathy, A., Toderici, G., Shetty, S., Leung, T., Sukthankar, R., Fei-Fei, L.: Large-scale video classification with convolutional neural networks. In: 2014 IEEE Conference on Computer Vision and Pattern Recognition, pp. 1725–1732, June 2014
17. Pan, S.J., Yang, Q.: A survey on transfer learning. IEEE Trans. Knowl. Data Eng. **22**(10), 1345–1359 (2010)
18. Russakovsky, O., et al.: ImageNet large scale visual recognition challenge. Int. J. Comput. Vis. **115**(3), 211–252 (2015). https://doi.org/10.1007/s11263-015-0816-y
19. Chen, T., Yin, W., Zhou, X.S., Comaniciu, D., Huang, T.S.: Total variation models for variable lighting face recognition. IEEE Trans. Pattern Anal. Mach. Intell. **28**(9), 1519–1524 (2006)

# A Meta-analysis of Big Data Security: How the Government Formulates a Model of Public Information and Security Assurance into Big Data

Achmad Nurmandi[1], Danang Kurniawan[1(✉)], Misran[2] ⓘ, and Salahudin[1,2] ⓘ

[1] Jusuf Kalla School of Government, Goverment Affairs and Administration,
Universitas Muhammadiyah Yogyakarta, Yogyakarta, Indonesia
salahudinmsi@umm.ac.id
[2] Goverment Affairs and Administration,
Universitas Muhammadiyah Yogyakarta, Yogyakarta, Indonesia

**Abstract.** This study aims to find a model for guaranteeing the security of big data information using a bibliometric analysis approach. The data of this research are 710 international indexed scientific articles (Scopus) in the form of (Article, Book Chapter and Conference Paper). Data was collected using the keyword ("security information") AND ("assurance big data") and was limited to 2016 to 2020. Bibliometric indicators, such as citations, were used to identify the overall theme structure. The data analysis phase was carried out with the analysis tools of VOSviewer and NVivo Plus 12 software. The use of VOSviewer will map the main theme trends in the research area so that it can find new literature. The main theme mappings are then integrated in the Nvivo Plus12 software analysis tool, to produce large theme visualizations. The results show that the author, institution, and theme keywords infographics that: Research studies on information security and assurance for big data have an increasing trend in the number of articles in the last five years; The study of information security and assurance for big data based on network analysis reveals four important themes of concern to the authors, meaning intelligence, privacy, access, and smart cities. In addition, the Government's big data information security model pays more attention to data security and privacy, public, social, and trends through a cyber physical social system.

**Keywords:** Big data · Security · Assurance · Bibliometric · Policy

## 1 Introduction

Along with the development of the big data era, it is a trend in the world of information. You could say big data is a very large data set which includes various types of data (Chen et al. 2012; Khan et al. 2021). Big Data is becoming a popular word along with how it can store large amounts of data, carry out processing and analysis. It is unavoidable how the impact of this big data on everyday life (Barham and Daim 2018). Big Data has provided

© Springer Nature Switzerland AG 2021
C. Stephanidis et al. (Eds.): HCII 2021, CCIS 1499, pp. 472–479, 2021.
https://doi.org/10.1007/978-3-030-90179-0_60

the opportunity for the government to utilize or identify the importance of big data in determining policy planning (Litchfield et al. 2018; Taylor et al. 2015). Of the many benefits and opportunities, big data can leave several challenges, including technological challenges that can handle this big data, challenges for the skills or expertise of people who will process data so that the available data can become information, useful insights. (Huda 2018).

In the academic world, the term big data refers to the application of information technology to deal with large data problems (Bucher 2012). Such data can come from online activities where users usually upload, retrieve, and store information shared by Internet platforms (Hixon et al. 2012; Omar et al. 2011; Puzziferro 2008). Besides significant data sources, statistical facts are being generated among digital devices such as cell phones, computers, or laptops to extract social networks' value (Arifin and Herman 2017). Then the results of the analysis of the value of social networks based on big data can be used as a useful objective (Huda 2018).

Big data supporting the implementation of a smart city raises problems regarding the operation and data management mechanisms related to how privacy forms protect different data (Huda 2018). Concerns vary along with the intended purpose of using the data, shifting from improving cities' livability and services to advancing surveillance and maintaining citizen control (Van Zoonen 2021). (Viitanen and Kingston 2014) provide a concrete analysis of the problems local governments face when faced with the drive for companies to adopt smart data technologies and big data applications and show how there is a severe risk of following market imperatives, not public policy demands. There are five problems in the operationalization of big data: sources, sharing, security, privacy, and costs (Al Nuaimi et al. 2015; Sayedahmed et al. 2021). Community concerns about privacy: one dimension suggests that people perceive specific data as more private and sensitive than others. Another dimension suggests that everyone's privacy concerns differ according to the purpose of the collected data, contrasting with service objectives and, most crucial, surveillance. (Liu and Terzi 2010). Statistics show that more than 50% of big data projects fail; because it cannot complete and does not offer the desired value.

The ubiquitous collection of data on all urban processes can result in a 'panoptic' city, where "systems that seek to activate more effective modes of government [may] also threaten to choke off the rights to privacy, secrecy, and freedom of expression (Kitchin 2014). This research answers related to significant data privacy security and formulates a model framework. We take a qualitative method approach through a literature review, aiming to find out various distances or findings that have not been found in previous research so that it becomes a comparison material in conducting the latest research. Moreover, formulating a model. Besides, this study develops a framework to explore big data's problem in people's specific privacy in smart cities based on existing research on the issue of people's privacy in general. There are two analyses, first digging information about how the dynamics of research about security city and information assurance for big data in the last ten years. These two studies aim to find the literature's novelty in the study of security and information assurance for big data.

## 2  Methodology

A qualitative literature review study is an appropriate research method chosen to achieve the objectives of this study. The data source of this research is an article that is internationally accredited. Data collection is by searching through a database (https://www. scopus.com/). Scopus is one of the most extensive citations and abstract databases of the review literature, such as scientific journals, books, and conference proceedings (Yue 2012). The Scopus database search used the term or the keyword open access and repository institutions through the search field "Document search." Some data is then analyzed descriptively based on the year of publication, the institution that published it, the country that published it, the name of the journal/publication, the type of document, and the research topic.

Regarding the delivery of research map information, the data is exported in the RIS Export file format. The researchers then exported the data in the (RIS) format. They processed it using VOSviewer to determine the map bibliometric of research development based on the big theme of security and information assurance for big data. This research uses the Nvivo12 Plus software to see the most frequently discussed word frequencies and visualize the relationship between major themes and the latest literature.

## 3  Results and Discussion

### 3.1  Trends in the Development of Research Studies on Security Information Assurance for Big Data

In the development of research in security and information assurance for big data, overall, in the last five years, trends have a growth trend with 100 documents/year. Figure 1 shows the annual trend of publications related to security information assurance for big data. In this study, the data were taken from 2016 to 2020. The total number of data taken in the last five years was 2636. The data for 2016 were 343 documents, 2017 data there were 421 documents, 2018 data there were 514 documents, 2019 data there were 648 documents and last data for 2020 there are 710 articles.

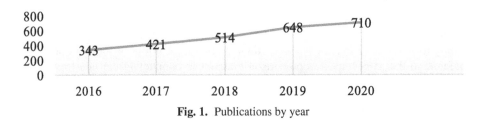

**Fig. 1.**  Publications by year

### 3.2  Visualization of the Research Development Map Network Security Information Assurance for Big Data

Research related to information security assurance for big data can be seen from the visualization mapping results in Fig. 1 above. The network between topics in 2636 documents that have been obtained from the Scopus database was carried out by bibliometric analysis by creating a visualization network, overlay, and density on Vosviewer. A bibliometric network consists of nodes and edges, which indicate the strength of the relationship represented by distance. The closer the distance between the nodes of the nodes, the more significant the correlation between nodes. The topic of security information assurance for big data cannot be separated from security, which is an essential part of big data used to protect and maintain data privacy. Meanwhile, artificial intelligence has a strong relationship with privacy in the collection of big data. The visualization of network title security information assurance for big data can be seen from the VOS viewer analysis results, as shown below (Fig. 2).

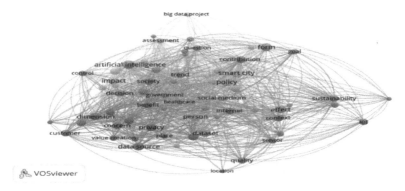

**Fig. 2.** Network by title (Color figure online)

Through keywords, security, information assurance, for big data, zone keywords are connected with keywords artificial intelligence, data sets, databases, social media, information management, big data applications, big data projects, by default VOSviewer (1) forms the entire fill in the title and abstract into 7 clusters. Color of each cluster 1 to 7: red, green, light blue, yellow, purple, orange, dark blue. Can be seen in the table of contents for each cluster below (Table 1):

**Table 1.** Division of Clusters and their items

| | |
|---|---|
| Cluster 1 (14 items) | Adoption, benefit, big data analytic, big data Technology, company, concern, customer, data collection, data source, decision making, dimension, place, privacy, value creation |
| Cluster 2 (14 items) | Acces, big data analysis, significant data research, data science, dataset, government, healthcare, perspective, practioner, public sector, question, security, trend, velocity |
| Cluster 3 (10 items) | Big data application, context, efficiency, internet, IoT, location, quality, sensor, smart, sustainable city, sustainability |

(continued)

**Table 1.** (*continued*)

| Cluster 4 (6 items) | Assessment, big data project, digital transformation, education, experience, expert, impact, nature, smart city, student |
| --- | --- |
| Cluster 5 (8 items) | Artificial intelligence, contribution, control, decision, form, goal, innovation, society |
| Cluster 6 (7 items) | Covid, evaluation, number, person, policy, social medium, social network |
| Cluster 7 (3 items) | Cordination, effect, limitation |

Based on the cluster analysis above, it can be understood that big data and artificial intelligence are widely used in various industries, including the education, health, company, and Government sectors in supporting smart cities. In addition to the manufacturing industry, which has applied artificial intelligence to the production line, many schools have also used a learning outcome assessment system using artificial intelligence (Nasution 2019). As for the government sector in the use of big data, it also uses artificial intelligence to help with tasks.

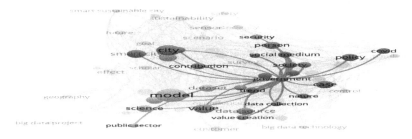

**Fig. 3.** The government in utilizing big data (Color figure online)

The role of big data in the government is used to support smart cities' implementation in improving public services. The availability of data is essential for the government starting from data person, public data, and data on trends in social events (covid), which can help the government formulate policies. Figure 3 shows a data utilization network carried out by the government, which correlates with the security level. Data security is an essential concern for the government in its utilization. On the one hand, data privacy requires data transparency, but on the other hand, privacy is a sensitive issue and is often injured through technological advances.

Privacy relates to a person's data that must be protected. Most of the data used as Big Data obtained directly from consumers is personal data and is very vulnerable to other parties' misused. The use of a person's data must be with the consent of the person concerned if it is to be used by another party. The unwise use of Big Data technology is prone to data privacy issues. Citizen security must be considered, where criminal acts that may arise resulting from disclosing information must be anticipated, especially those that affect the country's stability. So far, artificial intelligence can regulate data or information protection. Various restrictions are used to protect it, including privacy data, IoT, dimensions, sensors, here. We can see artificial intelligence in securing data in Fig. 4 below.

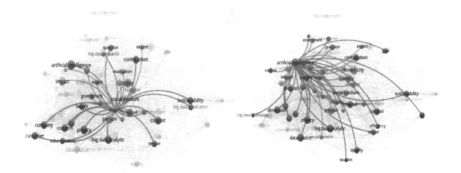

**Fig. 4.** Network security and artificial intelligence network (Color figure online)

### 3.3 The Role of Artificial Intelligence in Data Security and Privacy

In the security information assurance mapping for big data, each node represents a keyword, and each link represents the coincidence of a pair of words. (Lalitha and Radhakrishnamurty 1975). Figure 4 illustrates the network of events with the keywords for AI in data security related to the study of Big network data technology, customer, privacy, dimension, data source. Thus, in the security image, we find strong co-occurrences across sections focused on security privacy, company, big data, social medium, government, and concerns (Fig. 5).

### 3.4 Security Models and the Use of Big Data in the Government Sector

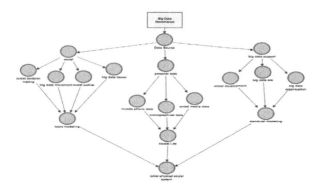

**Fig. 5.** Government big data utilization model

The positive impact of implementing artificial intelligence is reducing waiting times and improving the quality of process or service results (Ririh et al. 2020). However, in some developing countries, artificials face quite a lot of challenges because they reduce the amount of labor absorption, in addition to requiring relatively high investment (Nasution 2019; Ririh et al. 2020). Actors that are the leading players in AI, for example in Indonesia, include multinational companies (such as Google - Alphabet and Facebook), telecommunications companies (such as PT. Telkom Tbk., PT. Telkom Sigma, and PT. XL Axiata Tbk.,), startups (such as Snapcart, Kata.ai, BJtech, Sonar, Nodeflux, Bahasa.ai, AiSensum, and Deligence.ai) and government (such as Incubator). In its development, startups have a strategic role in accelerating the adoption of AI technology in Indonesia. The growth of startups will also attract potential domestic and international talents, which drive the dynamics' AI industry ecosystem. Therefore, startups need to be nurtured and supported by strong actors such as governments and large companies. To support startups AI's growth, the government and large companies can provide infrastructure and superstore facilitation through business and technology incubators (Swara and Zirwan 2018).

## 4   Conclusion

Big data is one of the important factors in the current digitalization era, which can be an important source of information. The government also uses big data as a form of an effort to create efficiency and work effectively in making policies. Three sources of data are used as a reference for the government, including social, personal data, and supporting data. The government has the authority to access data and use it, so the government also guarantees data privacy security. A form of government responsibility in ensuring data privacy security, through innovative development of Artificial Intelligence that can collaborate with private startups.

## References

Al Nuaimi, E., Al Neyadi, H., Mohamed, N., Al-Jaroodi, J.: Applications of big data to smart cities. J. Internet Serv. Appl. 6(1), 1–15 (2015). https://doi.org/10.1186/s13174-015-0041-5
Arifin, F., Herman, T.: The influene of E-Learning. TARBIYA: J. Educ. Muslim Soc.53(9), 45–52 (2017). file:///C:/Users/User/Downloads/fvm939e.pdf
Barham, H., Daim, T.: Identifying critical issues in smart city big data project implementation. In: Proceedings of the 1st ACM/EIGSCC Symposium on Smart Cities and Communities, SCC 2018 (2018). https://doi.org/10.1145/3236461.3241967
Bucher, T.: Want to be on the top? Algorithmic power and the threat of invisibility on Facebook. New Media Soc. 14(7), 1164–1180 (2012). https://doi.org/10.1177/1461444812440159
Chen, H., Chiang, R.H.L., Storey, V.C.: Quarterly36(4), 1165–1188 (2012)
Hixon, E., Buckenmeyer, J., Barczyk, C., Feldman, L., Zamojski, H.: Beyond the early adopters of online instruction: motivating the reluctant majority. Internet High. Educ. 15(2), 102–107 (2012). https://doi.org/10.1016/j.iheduc.2011.11.005
Huda, M.: Paper-Big Data Emerging Technology: Insights into Innovative Environment for Online Learning Re… Big Data Emerging Technology: Insights into Innovative Environment for Online Learning Resources Miftachul Huda Pardimin Atmotiyoso Maragustam Siregar. 13(1), 23 (2018). https://doi.org/10.3991/ijet.v13i01.6990

Khan, H.M., Khan, A., Jabeen, F., Rahman, A.U.: Privacy preserving data aggregation with fault tolerance in fog-enabled smart grids. Sustainable Cities and Society, **64** (2021). https://doi.org/10.1016/j.scs.2020.102522

Kitchin, R.: Big Data, new epistemologies and paradigm shifts. Big Data Soc. **1**(1), 1–12 (2014). https://doi.org/10.1177/2053951714528481

Lalitha, K., Radhakrishnamurty, R.: Response of alanine, tyrosine & leucine aminotransferases to dietary pyridoxine & protein in rat tissues. Indian J. Exp. Biol. **13**(2), 149–152 (1975)

Litchfield, C., Kavanagh, E., Osborne, J., Jones, I.: Social media and the politics of gender, race and identity: the case of Serena Williams. Eur. J. Sport Soc. **15**(2), 154–170 (2018). https://doi.org/10.1080/16138171.2018.1452870

Liu, K., Terzi, E.: A framework for computing the privacy scores of users in online social networks. ACM Trans. Knowl. Discov. Data **5**(1), 1–30 (2010). https://doi.org/10.1145/1870096.1870102

Nasution, M.K.M.: Social network mining: a discussion. J. Phys. Conf. Ser. **1235**(1) (2019). https://doi.org/10.1088/1742-6596/1235/1/012111

Omar, A., Kalulu, D., Alijani, G.: management of innovative E-learning environments. Acad. Educ. Leader. J. **15**(3), 37 (2011)

Puzziferro, M.: Online technologies self-efficacy and self-regulated learning as predictors of final grade and satisfaction in college-level online courses. Int. J. Phytorem. **21**(1), 72–89 (2008). https://doi.org/10.1080/08923640802039024

Ririh, K.R., Laili, N., Wicaksono, A., Tsurayya, S.: Studi Komparasi dan Analisis Swot Pada Implementasi Kecerdasan Buatan (Artificial Intelligence) di Indonesia. Jurnal Teknik Industri, **15**(2), 122–133 (2020). https://ejournal.undip.ac.id/index.php/jgti/article/view/29183

Sayedahmed, H.A.M., Mohamed, E., Hefny, H.A.: Computational intelligence techniques in vehicle to everything networks: a review. In: Hassanien, A.E., Slowik, A., Snášel, V., El-Deeb, H., Tolba, F.M. (eds.) AISI 2020. AISC, vol. 1261, pp. 803–815. Springer, Cham (2021). https://doi.org/10.1007/978-3-030-58669-0_71

Swara, G.Y., Zirwan, A.: Aplikasi Pencarian Barbershop Berbasis Android. Jurnal Teknoif, **6**(2), 74–80 (2018). https://doi.org/10.21063/jtif.2018.v6.2.74-80

Taylor, J.B., Waxman, J.P., Richter, S.J., Shultz, S.J.: Evaluation of the effectiveness of anterior cruciate ligament injury prevention programme training components: a systematic review and meta-analysis. Br. J. Sports Med. **49**(2), 79–87 (2015). https://doi.org/10.1136/bjsports-2013-092358

Zoonen, L.: Performance and participation in the Panopticon: instruments for civic engagement with urban surveillance technologies. In: Jacobs, G., Suojanen, I., Horton, K.E., Bayerl, P.S. (eds.) International Security Management. ASTSA, pp. 243–254. Springer, Cham (2021). https://doi.org/10.1007/978-3-030-42523-4_17

Viitanen, J., Kingston, R.: Smart cities and green growth: outsourcing democratic and environmental resilience to the global technology sector. Environ Plan A **46**(4), 803–819 (2014). https://doi.org/10.1068/a46242

Yue, H.: Mapping the intellectual structure by Co-word: a case of international management science. In: Wang, F.L., Lei, J., Gong, Z., Luo, X. (eds.) WISM 2012. LNCS, vol. 7529, pp. 621–628. Springer, Heidelberg (2012). https://doi.org/10.1007/978-3-642-33469-6_77

# Website Quality Analysis in Three Ministries of Indonesia Study Ministry of Finance, Ministry of Home Affairs, and Ministry of Village

Achmad Nurmandi[1], Ramaini Mei[1]([✉]) [ID], Isnaini Muallidin[1] [ID],
Danang Kurniawan[1] [ID], and Salahudin[2] [ID]

[1] Goverment Affairs and Administration, Jusuf Kalla School of Government,
Universitas Muhammadiyah Yogyakarta, Yogyakarta, Indonesia
[2] Departement of Governmental Studies, Universitas Muhammadiyah Malang, Malang,
Indonesia
salahudinmsi@umm.ac.id

**Abstract.** This study aims to find out how the principles of good governance are applied in Indonesian ministries. This study analyzes the Ministry of Finance, Ministry of Home Affairs, Ministry of Villages, and the Ministry's official Twitter social media accounts. Website quality assessment is based on transparency, accountability, effectiveness, efficiency, and features of the official website. This research is a qualitative descriptive study, using research on the official websites of the Ministry of Finance, Ministry of Home Affairs, and Ministry of Villages. Researchers collect data through surveys and website observations. Website quality assessment is carried out by scoring on the indicators of features, transparency, accountability, effectiveness, and website efficiency. Website quality assessment is carried out by scoring on the indicators of features, transparency, accountability, effectiveness, and efficiency of the website with 50 units of assessment analysis. Meanwhile, Twitter content was analyzed using Nvivo 12 Plus with the NCapture feature to systematically document and analyze data. The results showed that all websites of the Ministry of Finance, Ministry of Home Affairs, and Ministry of Villages had High Quality, with a score above 85.00%. However, the Ministry of Finance website has the lowest score of 30.05 (Low Quality) due to the Interactivity assessment score, navigation system. Then the Twitter content of the three Ministries has provided information to the public and has a reasonably high level of activity.

**Keywords:** Website quality · Social media · Good governance

## 1 Introduction

In this era, technology and information have become a necessity for every individual, business, education, and government. This is based on the development of information and communication technology that is proliferating to obtain information even though it does not know the time, place, region, and country. This convenience can be obtained

© Springer Nature Switzerland AG 2021
C. Stephanidis et al. (Eds.): HCII 2021, CCIS 1499, pp. 480–488, 2021.
https://doi.org/10.1007/978-3-030-90179-0_61

online without any limitations and can be done by everyone but connected to an internet connection. Based on Presidential Instruction No. 3 of 2003, it is stated that the development of e-government in Indonesia is carried out based on government policies so that e-government describes the concept of e-government readiness. It states that e-readiness should be able to get the benefits offered in the ICT sector in a country, especially in terms of policies, infrastructure, and initiatives at the primary level. E-government is no longer an experimental topic but has become a permanent thing in the government process [1]. By providing information about government operations and facilitating electronic communication with members of the public, information and communication technology (ICT) promises to increase government transparency, accountability, and public participation [2].

E-Government can remove restrictions on public services. In particular, improving the quality and effectiveness of public services related to elections, managing and providing various policy information and data from or to all community members. Improving the quality of public services in the government bureaucracy, which is currently known as e-Government, utilizes information technology [3]. The website is one of the e-government products to foster interest and opportunities for the population in providing public services and public input and realizing an open, accountable, and efficient administration. The government can provide various information to public businesses and fellow governments through the website. The website is the source of all the wealth of local government information used to promote the creation and implementation of e-government [4].

Websites with good content, slow access, or inadequate navigation systems. In this case, website builders must realize that the technology owned by the audience is very diverse, from the simplest to the most sophisticated, so that all of them ensure that they can easily access existing websites [5]. This study will discuss the study of the quality of the government's official website and the quality of Twitter content in three ministries in Indonesia. In addition, to look for maps of novelty science in research and literature to become a reference for writers. This is intended to help researchers develop their own may research programs.

## 2  Literature Review

### 2.1  Use of Websites in E-Government

The term e-government is applying the use of technology in government to convey information and provide public services [7]. The emergence of e-government is balanced with ICT (communication and information technology) in the form of services from the government to the public or interested people [8]. The development of technology-based public services has made it easier for the government to provide more efficient services and facilities in general information via the internet, digital networks, wireless or other systems [9]. In the implementation of e-government, there are several related components: first, ICT is closely related to the internet, website applications (desktop), devices, and mobile phones. Second, stakeholders as providers and consumers as users of electronic services. Third, the overall results of the related components. It is hoped that these three components will facilitate interaction between stakeholders in seeking information and transparency to improve the efficiency and effectiveness of government performance [10].

Along with the internet development, what was once a traditional public service has turned into an e-government website [11]. This service is provided through the web, which is managed directly by the government [12]. The existence of this website is intended so that the government can improve service quality, transparency and strengthen government accountability [13]. On the government web, there are different functions, some of which focus on general information. The government is expected to provide services and information through the website to the public. Because this service makes it easier for people to get and exchange information [14], the quality of information and services on the website must be considered to make it easier for users.

## 2.2  Measuring Website Quality

Government plays a vital role in building the quality of the Ministry's website and is responsible for implementing and providing information services [15]. The factors that affect the quality of the website can be seen from the usability, content, accessibility, participation, services, features, and information security of its users [16]. The emergence of the ease of public services aims to build guaranteed trust in users [17]. In addition to features, the access speed is also the main point of an attractive website and page according to the government's identity [18]. Therefore, improving the quality of the website needs to be considered and evaluated at any time [20].

The evaluation process is carried out based on the method and adjusted to the website criteria of each city using in-depth justification with a theoretical approach. Generally, city sites only focus on specific content and results [21]. Hendrickson [22] stated that several things fall into categories to evaluate the quality of an e-government website, such as/: security, privacy, usability, content, and citizen participation [23]. Meanwhile, Barnes and Vidgen use eQual as an approach in assessing websites. The evaluation of the website can also be seen from the features, transparency, accountability, effectiveness, and efficiency [24, 25]. The use of eQual can be seen from the method used by researchers to obtain data from the city's website. From this approach, you can find the value of quality on each website displayed through a graph. However, with this feature on the e-government web, it must display information that includes an overview, structure, location, regional regulations and policies, news, and guest books [26, 27].

## 2.3  Government Social Media: Official Twitter

Technological developments are based on the times from traditional to modern times. The emergence of social media is a web 2.0 concept that has been transformed into a form of e-government [28]. The selection of social media is considered easy in interacting/ and makes it easier for people to communicate directly with the government according to its function [29]. Social media also provides benefits for connecting the government and society, such as discussing, participating, creating content through other social media such as YouTube, Facebook, Instagram, and WhatsApp. All these links between policymakers and new interactions for mutual benefit through social media [31]. Therefore, ICT itself is theoretically good for bringing about construction and engagement between government and society [32]. The emergence of social media has a significant impact on public services, especially in government, so that people can participate. In addition, information can also be channeled through social media [34, 35]. The government uses Twitter as a medium of information that can be accessed and responded to quickly. The public widely accepts twitter because it is easily accessible, the news is up to date, making it easier to provide incident reports.

## 3  Method

This research is a qualitative descriptive study, using the official website of the Ministry of Finance, Ministry of Home Affairs, and Ministry of Villages. Researchers collect data through surveys and website observations. The official website and Twitter account of the local government are shown in Table 1 below.

**Table 1.** Official websites

| Ministry of Indonesia | Official websites | Official twitter |
|---|---|---|
| Ministry of finance | https://www.kemenkeu.go.id | @kemenkeu |
| Ministry of home affairs | https://www.kmendagri.go.id | @kemendagri |
| Ministry of village had high quality | https://www.kMendes.go.id | @kemendesapdtt |

Website quality assessment is carried out by scoring on the indicators of features, transparency, accountability, effectiveness, and website efficiency. Website quality assessment is carried out by scoring on the indicators of features, transparency, accountability, effectiveness, and efficiency of the website with 50 units of assessment analysis. Meanwhile, Twitter content was analyzed using Nvivo 12 Plus with the NCapture feature to systematically document and analyze data. In measuring the quality of this research website using the scoring method. Through this score analysis, it is possible to show the value of policy alternatives by using indicators in the assessment by the objectives and formulations previously. If necessary, there is weighting on indicators considered more important than other indicators [38]. Performance measurement on the website uses the tools available on Google, namely Page speed insight seen from the website's work speed through a percent scale.

$$\text{Score weight} = \frac{\text{Total website scoring results} \times 100\%}{\text{Total score}}$$

After obtaining the weight score, an assessment is carried out according to the following Table 2:

After obtaining the new score weight, it can be examined according to the following table:

**Table 2.** Assessment of page speed insights

| Score | Value |
|---|---|
| 0%–49% | Slow |
| 50%–89% | Average |
| 90%–100% | Quick |

Source: web.dev/performance-scoring.

| Score (%) | Value |
|---|---|
| 0–29 | Poor quality |
| 30–59 | Low quality |
| 60–79 | Quality |
| 80–100 | High quality |

## 4  Results and Discussion

### 4.1  Website Quality Analysis of the Ministry of Finance, Ministry of Home Affairs, and Ministry of Villages

Based on assessments and research on the Ministry of Finance, Ministry of Home Affairs, and Ministry of Villages assessed as many as 50 units of review. Evaluation is done by giving a score on website features, transparency, accountability, effectiveness, and efficiency (Fig. 1). On three ministry websites in Indonesia, the following scores were obtained:

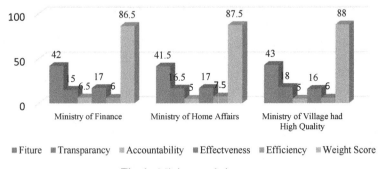

**Fig. 1.** Ministry website score

Based on the picture above, the highest percentage of website ratings is 88%. It is in the quality category on the websites of the Ministry of Villages, Ministry of Home Affairs, and Ministry of Finance. All of them have a good quality website. The difference in the percentage value of each ministry website can be influenced by several aspects of the assessment, such as in the Ministry of Villages, the highest percentage is the quality of its features, 43%. Then for ministry websites with the highest transparency score, the Ministry of Villages is also 18%. Furthermore, the Ministry's website, which has the highest accountability, is at the Ministry of Finance at 6.5. The highest effectiveness scores are the Ministry of Finance and the Ministry of Home Affairs, with 17%. At the same time, the last for the assessment of efficiency aspects with the highest score is the Ministry of Home Affairs at 7.5%.

The emergence of the ease of information through this website has a vital role in society. The ease of finding information wherever we are is a choice of the community compared to before. However, this facility must also be considered by the government. In this era, Twitter has become commonplace among people, especially young people who must have a Twitter account. In addition, use of social media such as Twitter is used for chirping and is used as a medium of information by the government to facilitate interaction with the broader community [33]. Social media such as Twitter allows the government to provide up-to-date and timely information, and the public can also provide direct comments on policies, news, or programs designed by the central government. Several ministries in Indonesia have used Twitter as a public information medium, such as the Ministry of Finance, Ministry of Home Affairs, and Ministry of Villages. The following are the names of the Ministry's Twitter accounts (Fig. 2).

**Fig. 2.** Word cloud twitter ministry of finance, ministry of home affairs, and ministry of villages.

The picture above illustrates that each account has different information regarding developments or news in each Ministry. From Twitter, data analysis is carried out through NCapture to filter out what information is needed. Then the results were analyzed using the NVivo 12 plus application with the Word cloud feature, which explained the most frequently discussed issues on each Twitter account. The following are issues that often arise and develop in the three ministries. The Ministry of Finance is more focused on budget issues, budget implementation than auditing; the Ministry of Home Affairs is more focused on discussing policy and service issues for local, district/city, sub-district, and village governments. At the same time, the Village Ministry is more focused on discussing opportunities, management, development, etc. However, the 3 Ministries have the same issues that are informed to the public, namely economic issues and policies in running the wheels of government. Issues that play a role include cooperation between the three ministries with district/city local governments, sub-district governments, and village governments.

## 5  Conclusion

The conclusion of this research is the study of e-governance readiness through the websites of each Ministry, which is very much needed. The public quality improvement provided by the government has been adjusted to the ease with which the public can obtain the necessary information and data. It is evident from the analysis of website quality data at three ministries that each ministry website has improved the quality of public services in features that will make it easier for the public to find information. The community has participated in providing input, complaints, and suggestions. In this case, improving the quality of the website must also be balanced with social media. Features and information can also be made easier so that people who visit the website do not feel confused when looking for information. For e-governance readiness in each Ministry, it is said to be good because e-government itself has indeed been implemented and is running in every government in Indonesia so that with the existence of e-governance, this readiness can be a benchmark for the government in improving the quality of services in the website sector. The inclusion of the research above is that from the three ministry websites, the highest percentage value is seen from the criteria for the website assessment method. After obtaining the required data, the data is summed up as a whole consisting of features, transparency, accountability, effectiveness, and efficiency.

## References

1. Nugroho, R.A.: A study of e-readiness model analysis in the framework of implementing an e-government study analysis of e-readiness model in the implementation of e-government readiness mode. **1**, 65–78 (2020). https://doi.org/10.17933/.v11i1.171
2. Feeney, M.K., Brown, A.: Are small cities online? Content, ranking, and variation of US municipal websites. Gov. Inf. Q. **34**(1), 62–74 (2017). https://doi.org/10.1016/j.giq.2016.10.005
3. Budhiraja, R., Sachdeva, S.: Readiness Assessment (India) (2002)
4. Basuki, S.: Komunikasi Ilmiah: Dari Surat Pribadi Sampai Majalah. Maj. Ilmu Perpust. dan Inform. **4**(1–2), 11–19 (1989)
5. Muttaqin, M.H., Susanto, T.D.: The effect of website components on user trust in increasing the interest to use public administration service on e-government website. In: Proceeding – 2019 Int. Conf. Comput. Sci. Inf. Technol. Electr. Eng. Committee 2019, vol. 1, pp. 30–36 (2019)
6. Kaur, A., Kaur, H.: Exploring e-governance service delivery dimensions: a study of registrar of companies. Indian J. Public Adm. **63**, 557–566 (2017)
7. Dutta, M.A.A., Devi, M.S.: Census web service architecture for e-governance applications. In: ACMI, Int. Conf. Proceeding Ser, pp. 1–4 (2017)
8. Cumbie, B.A., Kar, B.: A study of local government website inclusiveness: the gap between e-government concept and practice. Inf. Technol. Dev. **22**, 15–35 (2016)
9. Huang, L.F.J., Guo, W.: Research on E-government website satisfaction evaluation based on public experience. In: International Conference on Education and Social Development, pp. 206–213 (2019)
10. Ji, J.: E-government web portal adoption: the effects of service quality. e-Serv. J. **9**(3), 43 (2014)
11. Porumbescu, G.A.: Linking public sector social media and e-government website use to trust in government. Gov. Inf. Q. **33**, 291–304 (2016)

12. Henman, P., Graham, T.: Webportal vs google for finding government information on the web: from a website-centric approach to a web ecology perspective. Inf. Polity **23**, 361–378 (2018)
13. Tan, C.W., Benbasat, I., Cenfetelli, R.T.: Building citizen trust towards e-government services: do high-quality websites matter? In: Proceedings of the 41st Annu. Hawaii Int. Conf. Syst. Sci. (HICSS 2008), p. 217 (2008)
14. Paul, S., Das, S.: Accessibility and usability analysis of Indian e-government websites. Univers. Access Inf. Soc. **19**(4), 949–957 (2019)
15. Sugandini, D., et al.: Web quality, satisfaction, trust and its effects on government. Int. J. Qual. Res. **12**(4), 885–904 (2013)
16. Syaifullah, S., Soemantri, D.O.: Pengukuran Kualitas Website Menggunakan Metode Webqual
17. 4.0 (Studi Kasus, C.V.: Zamrud Multimedia Network) J. Ilm. Rekayasa dan Manaj. Sist. Inf, **2**, pp. 19–25 (2016)
18. Warjiyono, W., Hellyana, C.M.: Pengukuran Kualitas Website Pemerintah Desa Jagalempeni Menggunakan Metode Webqual 4.0. J. Teknol. Inf. dan Ilmu Komput **5**(2), 139 (2018). https://doi.org/10.25126/jtiik.201852666
19. Abdel-Basset, V.C.M., Zhou, Y., Mohamed, M.: A group decision-making framework based on neutrosophic VIKOR approach for e-government website evaluation. J. Intell. Fuzzy Syst. **34**, 4213–4224 (2018)
20. Wu, J., Guo, D.: Measuring e-government performance of provincial government website in China with slacks-based efficiency measurement. Technol. Forecast. Soc. Change **96**, 25–31 (2015)
21. Henriksson, M.M.A., Yi, Y., Frost, B.: Evaluation instrument for e-government websites. Electron. Gov. an Int. J. **4**, 204–226 (2007)
22. Barnes, S.J., Vidgen, R.T.: Data triangulation and web quality metrics: a case study in e-government. Inf. Manag **43**, 767–777 (2006)
23. Isn, A.R.: Analisis kualitas website pemerintah daerah pada kabupaten sesumatera barat. J. Akunt. **6** (2018)
24. Cheisviyanny, S.D.C., Helmy, H.: Analisis kualitas website pemerintah daerah kabupaten/kota di provinsi sumatera barat. Simp. Nas. Keuang. Negara **6**, 1087–1104 (2018)
25. Effendi, P.M., Susanto, T.D.: Test of citizens' physical and cognitive on Indonesian e-government website design. Procedia Comput. Sci. **161**, 333–340 (2019)
26. Kurniawan, W.T.S.F., Rakhmawati, N.A., Abadi, A.N., Zuhri, M.: Indonesia local government information completeness on the web. Procedia Comput. Sci. **124**, 21–28 (2017)
27. Nurmandi, A., et al.: To what extent is social media used in city government policymaking? Case studies in three Asian cities. Public Policy Adm. **17**(4), 600–618 (2018). https://doi.org/10.13165/VPA-18-17-4-08
28. Salahudin, A., Nurmandi, H., Jubba, Z., Qodir, Jainuri, Paryanto: Islamic Political Polarisation on Social Media During the 2019 Presidential Election in Indonesia. Asian Aff. (Lond), **51**(3), 656–671 (2020). https://doi.org/10.1080/03068374.2020.1812929
29. Cahyono, A.S.: Pengaruh media sosial terhadap perubahan sosial masyarakat di Indonesia. Publiciana **9** (2016)
30. Linders, D.: From e-government to we-government: defining a typology for citizen coproduction in the age of social media. Gov. Inf. Q. **29**(4), 446–454 (2012)
31. Gagliardi, G.P.D., Misuraca, G., Niglia, F.: How ICTs shape the relationship between the state and the citizens: exploring new paradigms between civic engagement and social innovation. In: Proceedings of the 52nd Hawaii Int. Conf. Syst. Sci. (2019)
32. Novianti, K.K.E., Nugraha, A.R., Komalasari, L.: Pemanfaatan media sosial dalam penyebaran informasi program pemerintah (Studi Kasus Sekretariat Daerah Kabupaten Pangandaran). AL MUNIR J. Komun. dan Penyiaran Islam **11**, 48–59 (2020)

33. Chatfield, A.T., Scholl, H.J., Brajawidagda, J.: Tsunami early warnings via twitter in govern-ment: net-savvy citizens' coproduction of time-critical public information services. Gov. Inf. Q. **30**, 377–386 (2013)

34. Carley, K.M., Malik, M., Landwehr, P.M., Pfeffer, J., Kowalchuck, M.: Crowd sourcing dis-aster management: the complex nature of twitter usage in Padang Indonesia. Saf. Sci. **90**, 48–61 (2016)

35. Kosasih, I.: Peran media sosial facebook dan twitter dalam membangun komunikasi persepsi dan motifasi masyarakat jejaring sosial dalam Pergaulan. Lembaran Masy. J. Pengemb. Masy. Islam **2**, 29–42 (2016)

36. Heravi, B.R., Harrower, N.: Twitter journalism in Ireland: sourcing and trust in the age of social media. Inf. Commun. Soc. **19**, 1194–1213 (2016)

37. Dwiyanto, A.: Transparansi Pelayanan Publik, Yogyakarta. akuntansi (2012)

# Presentation of a Three-Dimensional Image by Rotating Pepper's Ghost

Ryuichi Shibata[⊠], Wataru Hashimoto, Yasuharu Mizutani, and Satoshi Nishiguchi

Faculty of Information Sciences and Technology, Osaka Institute of Technology, 1-79-1
Kitayama, Hirakata City, Osaka 573-0196, Japan
m1m21a23@st.oit.ac.jp, {wataru.hashimoto,yasuharu.mizutani,
satoshi.nishiguchi}@oit.ac.jp

**Abstract.** In this research, we present a three-dimensional image of a Pepper's Ghost, and simultaneously observed from multiple angles by rotating it. Pepper's Ghost is a technique used to produce aerial images by combining the image reflected on a transparent plate with the background. A three-dimensional image is presented at the center of the rotation by rotating the transparent plate and displaying the image according to its orientation. The proposed system consists of a display placed on its side, transparent plate with a privacy filter attached to it, and motor. The top and bottom of the pyramid-shaped transparent plate, which is often used for the Pepper's Ghost exhibit, are switched to show a three-dimensional image. A PI-controlled motor is used to rotate the transparent plate and facilitate observation from multiple angles by following the images. Because the horizontal viewing angle of Pepper's Ghost exceeds 45 degrees, the image of the neighboring surface will appear to leak when the surfaces are adjacent. Therefore, we used a privacy filter to reduce the leakage of images from neighboring surfaces. We use a 240-fps display as the video playback device and present several images on a rotating the pyramid-shaped transparent plate.

Experimental results indicate a trade-off between the clarity of the 3D image and eye strain depending on the rotation speed.

**Keywords:** Pepper's Ghost · Three-dimensional image · Volumetric display

## 1 Introduction

Volumetric display is an intuitive technique that can display a visual representation of an object in three-dimensional space. This technology has applications in various fields, such as advertising, medicine and entertainment. Therefore, research on display methods has been actively conducted.

In a previous study, Yoshida presented stereoscopic images using multiple projectors [1]. Several projectors were arranged in an annular shape to cast images on a conical screen and represent a stereoscopic image at the center of the cone. Jones et al. [2] proposed a method to present a three-dimensional image using a spinning mirror covered with a holographic diffuser. Yoshida et al. presented a 3D image inside a cube by assembling a lens array and an LCD module into a cubic shape [3].

© Springer Nature Switzerland AG 2021
C. Stephanidis et al. (Eds.): HCII 2021, CCIS 1499, pp. 489–496, 2021.
https://doi.org/10.1007/978-3-030-90179-0_62

In this study, we propose a volumetric display technique based on the concept of Pepper's Ghost. Pepper's Ghost is an illusion technique that was devised by John Pepper in the 19th century, and as shown in Fig. 1, images reflected by a transparent plate appear to be floating. A previous study related to Pepper's Ghost called Pepper's Cone uses a cone reflector to achieve a three-dimensional image [4]. A volumetric display technique based on the concept of Pepper's Ghost and a design of praxinoscope was proposed by Martinez et al., and it used 18 transparent retro-reflective screens to realize a 360° projection configuration [5]. This study differs from the abovementioned studies as it can rotate the Pepper's Ghost (which is visible only from one direction) to present a 3D image that can be simultaneously observed from multiple angles.

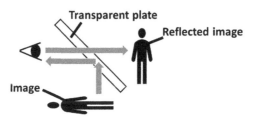

**Fig. 1.** Aerial image generated by Pepper's Ghost.

## 2 Rotating Pepper's Ghost

A Pepper's Ghost is visible to a viewer only when it is observed from the front. However, Pepper's Ghost can be observed from multiple angles by rotating it. It is necessary that the image synchronously follows the rotation of the transparent plate on the vertical axis. However, rotation by a single transparent plate significant flicker. Therefore, we shaped transparent plates into a pyramidal tetrahedron to reduce rotation latency. To reflect the image displayed on the horizontal plane perpendicularly, the transparent plate was tilted by 45 degrees. The pyramidal tetrahedron arrangement is shown in Fig. 2. The left-side of Fig. 2 depicts that the image is reflected by the second transparent plate from the viewpoint, and the reflected image is located outside the pyramid. Additionally, the right-side of the figure shows that the reflected image is located at the center because the image is reflected by the first transparent plate.

When Pepper's Ghost is observed from an oblique direction, the image is not reflected in the correct position. This problem is significantly enhanced when a transparent plate is rotated. To prevent the reflected image from being observed from the front, a privacy filter is used.

**Fig. 2.** Position of the reflect image when the top and bottom of the pyramid are swapped.

## 3   Implementation

As described in Chapter 2, this system is operated using a motor that is controlled through a PC. The images are displayed on a high-speed LCD monitor created in Unity. Figure 3 demonstrates an overview of the device.

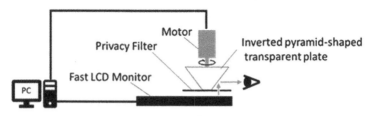

**Fig. 3.** Schematic diagram of the system configuration.

a.   Transparent Plate

The transparent plate used in this study is shown in Fig. 4. Trapezoidal transparent plates were combined to form an inverted pyramid-shaped transparent plate.

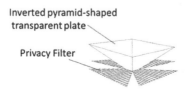

**Fig. 4.** Schematic diagram of an inverted pyramid-shaped transparent plate.

b.   Privacy Filter

Although the transparent plate has an inverted-pyramid shape, the aerial image generated by the Pepper's Ghost has a horizontal viewing angle of greater than 45 degrees. Hence, two images were visible at an angle where only originally one image should appear, as indicated by the red circles on the left side of Fig. 5. This occurred because the transparent plate reflects light-diffusing at a shallow angle from the fast LCD monitor. Therefore, this light diffused at a shallow angle was suppressed using a privacy filter. This ensured that multiple images were not displayed, as shown on the right side in Fig. 5.

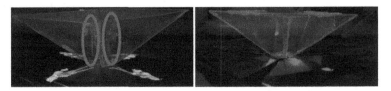

**Fig. 5.** Difference with (right) and without (left) privacy filter.

c.  Rotary Motors and Control Circuits

We matched the speed of the rotating image of the fast LCD monitor and rotation of the transparent plate using a configurable motor controller, which is PI-controlled through a control circuit. The motor controller can prevent the aerial image from shifting away from the center with gradual increase in time and avoid incorrect display of a 3D image. The motor is a TG-85R-SU-4.8-KA, 12 V and uses a control circuit developed by the Sensory Media Laboratory of the Osaka Institute of Technology.

d.  Fast LCD Monitor

We used the Legion Y25-25 fast LCD monitor manufactured by Lenovo. We selected this fast LCD monitor owing to its high refresh rate (240 Hz) compared with that of conventional fast LCD monitors (60 Hz). The refresh rate is defined as the frequency of screen updates. In this research, images are projected under a rotating transparent plate. For example, at an angular velocity of 360 degrees/s, the screen is refreshed every 6 degrees at 60 Hz, while at 240 Hz, the screen is refreshed every 1.5 degrees. Therefore, 3D images can be presented at finer angles.

e.  Creating Images for 3D Images

We created the 3D image shown in Fig. 6 using the Unity game engine. Subsequently, we arranged cameras around the objects to be presented as 3D images, as shown in Fig. 7.

**Fig. 6.**  3D image created in unity.

Next, the images captured by each camera are attached to the 3D object Cube as Render Texture. The image is rotated as shown in Fig. 8(a). Figure 8(b) demonstrates a bird's eye view of the Cube. Pepper's Ghost generates an aerial image by reflecting this image on the inverted pyramid-shaped transparent plate.

**Fig. 7.** Arrangement of cameras around an object.

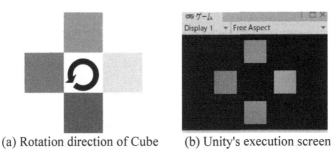

(a) Rotation direction of Cube        (b) Unity's execution screen

**Fig. 8.** Video output to a fast LCD monitor.

f.  Confirmation of the three-dimensional image

Figure 9 is a photograph of the image in Fig. 8 projected onto an inverted pyramid-shaped transparent plate. By changing the shooting position from right to left, the object in the center changes from red to yellow. Therefore, the 3D image was presented accurately.

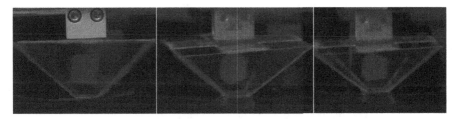

**Fig. 9.** Three-dimensional image captured by changing the viewpoint from left to right.

## 4   User Feedback

### 4.1   Purpose and Methods of the Experiment

This experiment is aimed at investigating the effect of angular velocity on the visibility of 3D images. We will analyze the effects of two angular velocities, 360 degrees per second (one rotation per second) and 720 degrees per second (two rotations per second), using a questionnaire. To prevent order effects from affecting the experiment results, we divided 14 participants into two groups: one group of 7 participants viewing at 360 degrees/s and another group of 7 participants viewing at 720 degrees/s. We orally explained the experimental procedure to the participants before conducting the experiment. Subsequently, the participants answered a four-step questionnaire while viewing the 3D images. The 3D image used in the experiment was a tetrahedral object, as shown in Fig. 6.

## 4.2 Experimental Results

The vertical axis represents the average of the four levels of responses from the subjects. Figure 10 presents the questionnaire results on the flicker of the stereoscopic image. Because both angular velocities exceeded the average value of 2.5 points in four stages, the participant probably observed flicker. Figure 11 shows the questionnaire result regarding whether a color change was observed by looking around and observing the 3D image. We noted a color change because both angular velocities exceeded the average value of 2.5 points in four stages. Figure 12 presents the results of the questionnaire relating to the sharpness of the 3D image. The image was found to be visible because both angular velocities exceeded the average value of 2.5 points in four stages. Figure 13 presents the result of the questionnaire that examined whether asthenopia occurs by looking at the 3D image. The rate of asthenopia at an angular velocity of 360 degrees per second was higher than that at an angular velocity of 720 degrees/s. A t-test was conducted at a significance level of 5%, and the data was proved to be significant.

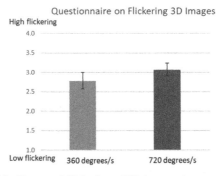

**Fig. 10.** Degree of flickering of 3D images due to rotation.

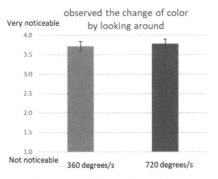

**Fig. 11.** Degree to which participant were able to observe changes in the color of an object by changing their viewpoint.

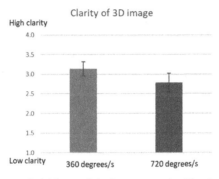

**Fig. 12.** Degree of vividness of the image perceived by the participants.

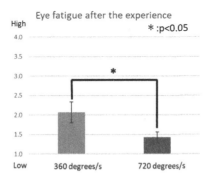

**Fig. 13.** Level of eye strain perceived by the participants.

## 5 Conclusion

We confirmed that a stereoscopic aerial image can be presented by rotating the reflected image generated by Pepper's Ghost. We also confirmed that the perception of sharpness and three-dimensional effect of the image affected the rotation speed. We verified that the color of the surface can be distinguished by representing a cube with different surface colors. However, the problem associated with this method is that the flicker of the rotating image causes asthenopia. Hence, it is crucial to examine the optimal rotation speed through several evaluations because there was a trade-off between the perceived image sharpness and possibility of causing eye strain.

## References

1. Yoshida, S.: fVisiOn: glasses-free tabletop 3D display to provide virtual 3D media naturally alongside real media. In: Proceedings of the SPIE 8384, Three-Dimensional Imaging, Visualization and Display (2012)
2. Jones, A., McDowall, I., Yamada, H., Bolas, M., Debevec, P.: Rendering for an interactive 360° light field display. ACM Trans. Graph. **26**(3), 40–49 (2007)
3. Yoshida, S., Lopez-Gulliver, R., Yano, S., Inoue, N.: A study to realize a box-shaped 3D display: a calibration method to align lens array and display. In: 3DTV-CON 2008, pp. 169–172 (2008)

4. Luo, X., Lawrence, J., M. Seitz, S.: Pepper's Cone: an inexpensive do-it-yourself 3D display. In: UIST 2017 Proceedings of the 30th Annual ACM Symposium on User Interface Software and Technology, October 2017, pp. 623–633 (2017)
5. Martinez, C., et al.: Development of a 360° display based on transparent projection surface: application to a theatrical performance. In: Proceedings of the SPIE 10942, Advances in Display Technologies IX (2019)

# Study on Dynamic Emotional Design Expression in Interface Vision of Digital Media Art

Fei Wang[(✉)]

Beijing Institute of Graphic Communication, No. 1 (band-2) Xinghua Street, Daxing District, Beijing, China

**Abstract.** In the dynamic expression of interface visual design of digital media art, stories can be delivered through dynamic design. These stories are not only about the spatial correlation and functions of objects, but also a kind of consciously flowing aesthetics, which can sublimate interactive design to a new height, and create more natural and flowing interactive experience so that users can feel the emotions that designers want to express. In this paper, dynamic effect design in artistic expression of digital media is taken as a research object to explore the dynamic emotional design expression, including the feedback, friendliness, transition, interest and innovation of the dynamic effect design. Revolving around emotional experience, grabbing of user attention, emotional scenario that triggers emotional response and design practice oriented towards user experience, this paper attempts to improve users' concentration and immersion, thus bringing better dynamic emotional and interactive experience for users.

**Keywords:** Interface vision · Dynamic effect · Interactive experience · Emotional design

## 1  Introduction

As the human society evolves from the digital and information era into the era of artificial intelligence (AI), human needs have been growing to a higher hierarchy, particularly at the emotional and spiritual layer. Only with spiritual satisfaction and psychological recognition can humans obtain enduring happiness in the real sense.

Emotion is the experience of people whether they are satisfied with their needs, which can not only influence the choices made humans to solve problems, but also subconsciously change the cognition system for people to understand the world. People develop the cognition of everything they experience and then endow the everything with the value cognition. Emotion is usually decided by the human needs and expectations. When these needs and expectations are satisfied, people will develop emotions like happiness, pleasure, and excitement, and vice versa.

In the field of product design for the digital media art, emotional design is inevitably reflected in the user experience process, which functions to illustrate the product form, interaction mode and product characteristics, and can bring users psychological cognition, give users satisfaction and pleasure from the perspective of controllable experience,

© Springer Nature Switzerland AG 2021
C. Stephanidis et al. (Eds.): HCII 2021, CCIS 1499, pp. 497–504, 2021.
https://doi.org/10.1007/978-3-030-90179-0_63

participation experience, experience of resonance, and experience of trust, better express the product value, and realize users' psychological expectation.

In order to increase user experience, better satisfy users' needs of emotional experience, and strengthen user engagement and reliance, designers are expected to learn and respond to users' emotional needs from multiple aspects. Only in this way can users' visual and functional experiences be fully satisfied. Meanwhile, this can lay a solid foundation for the exploration of a dynamic effect design that is more consistent with users' interactive emotional experience.

## 2  Emotional Design of Dynamic Effects

Dynamic effect design can deliver stories. Design based on dynamic effects can demonstrate how every element in a product interface is visually connected with each other and gives full play to their role. In this sense, dynamic effect design can lift interactive design to a new height, with more natural experience created to let users experience emotions which designers want to deliver.

It is a human instinct that humans can be easily attracted by moving objects. In contrast to static design, dynamic expression is more novel, vivid, interesting, flexible and interactive. By integrating dynamic design effects into the interface visual design, users' visual experiences can be enriched to not only facilitate the transmission of content, but also promote users' imagination and understanding. In this way, the infinite content is no longer limited to a limited screen, and the intuitive sensory experience achieves infinite extension in senses.

Emotions are originated from intuitive stimulation of senses and long-term life experience. Dynamic emotional design attracts users through dynamic effects, stimulates users' emotional responses, either consciously or subconsciously, satisfy users' current psychological needs, and improve the user experience design process. This suggests an unavoidably close tie between dynamic emotional design and user experience emotional design. Therefore, to satisfy users' emotional and psychological needs and to improve products' user experience constitute two main goals of dynamic effect design.

According to Standards for ISO Platform Design, the ISO user interface is teeming with subtle and exquisitely-made animations, which enhance the attractions and dynamic effects of applications. In the interface visual design, dynamic design delivers not only the spatial correlation and functions between objects, but also a conscious beauty of flowing. The above description seems to give people a notion that dynamic effect is a highly abstruse concept. But after people know more about it and become proficient in using it, everything comes so easy and naturally. With the help of dynamic effects, design is invigorated. Compared with traditional design elements, dynamic effect design after careful consideration can effectively improve the emotional experience for user operations.

## 3  Expression of Dynamic Emotional Design

Dynamic emotional design can arouse users' natural perception and intuitive operation more easily, and help users better understand products so that users' emotional needs can be naturally satisfied. Apart from considering how to recognize product content more conveniently and operate the products more easily, dynamic emotional design lays more emphasis on how users can obtain emotional satisfaction. The emotional needs are driven by users' pursuit of experience. Design expressions can be divided into feedback, friendliness, fun, transition and innovation, from the perspective of dynamic emotional product design.

### 3.1 Feedback Expression of Dynamic Emotional Design

Users' feedback after their use of digital media products, such as mobile media applications, can be divided into the process feedback and the result feedback. In the process of user operations, mobile applications can show users' current operation status through feedback of dynamic effects. This is an example of the process feedback. As to the result feedback, it happens after the end of user operations. Mobile applications can provide a visual status of operation outcomes. In the expression of dynamic design, the result feedback is more common to see than the process feedback. However, both should be demonstrated to users in the visual form, and inform users that the system is interacting with them. This can give users psychological expectation, and stimulate them to participate in actively products' interactive experience.

**Fig. 1.** Feedback dynamic effects of password entry [2]

Feedback is a pleasant hint of dynamic emotional design. Figure 1 is a dynamic effect case of the password entry, which vividly imitates a natural movement of opening eyes and closing eyes. When the passwords are displayed, a pair of eyes are open wide, and it is daytime. When the user chooses to hide the passwords, it is night, and the eyes are shut down. This is a vivid and interesting dynamic effect design for the feedback.

Good feedback can provide encouragements and praises for users, which can create a joyful psychological experience. As to the dynamic effect design for the "like button" in the interface visual design, if the user adds one like, color and shape changes of the button are a result-oriented dynamic effect feedback for the movement of adding one like. People always hope that they can gain recognition after they express something. The result feedback can strengthen the user's confidence, and improve the user's pleasure of product use. Designers can imagine every user as a little child, who have children's natural instinct and need others' praises. To the end, designers can minimize the hints of wrong operations but provide as many praises as possible. Even if the user makes a mistake, designers should try their best to weaken the sense of frustration. For example, after experiencing something or trying something new, users, if failing to gain their desired feedback or finding that the user experience is interrupted, will feel psychological displeased. Hence, dynamic emotional design should strengthen users' sense of achievement in the process of product experience. This can better stimulate their enthusiasm to participate in the interactive experience.

## 3.2  Friendly Expression of Dynamic Emotional Design

Though product visual designers, interactive designers and development designers are all working hard to make products more excellent and satisfactory, bugs and unavoidable problems caused by lack of external conditions, such as failure of refreshing, page errors, and failure of network access, can result in people's declining product experience. Under the condition, it is necessary to introduce dynamic emotional design properly, which can alleviate the unpleasant experience under the above conditions.

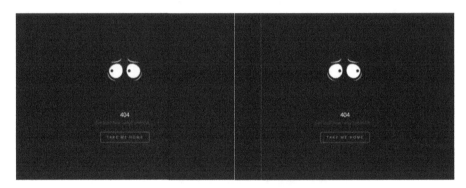

**Fig. 2.**  Friendly dynamic effect of loading failure (404) page [3]

The loading failure (404) page is presented in Fig. 2. The big eyes vividly simulates the real emotional status, including being shivering, frightened, and trembling with fear. When the page is refreshed or the loading fails, the friendly dynamic emotional design is so funny to the user, making the user feel that the error is no longer frustrating. When the product information cannot be immediately presented for some reason, the friendly dynamic effect can help deliver the product status, increase the user's anticipation, mitigate their anxiety, and also weaken unavoidably unpleasant feelings. The user can then use the products in a more pleasant mood not at the sacrifice of the overall usability, ease-to-use, and experience.

## 3.3  Transitional Expression of Dynamic Emotional Design

In the dynamic expression of interface visual design, the basic role of dynamic effects is to demonstrate the transitional status. When the page layout is changed, dynamic effect design will experience a transitional process to subconsciously help users understand changes of the status. The smooth transitional dynamic effect design can strengthen the comfortable user experience. Thereby, users' cognition process will generate an emotional satisfaction with the smooth operation.

The transitional expression of dynamic emotional design can the transition between the navigation content so that dynamic effects can smoothly transition and exchange between different content. Besides, dynamic effects can perfectly explain the correlation between interface elements, and how interface visual changes happen naturally, and expound on how the interaction is realized, namely the connection between the visual layers and elements. In this way, the transitional expression can be reflected.

Dynamic effects can emphasize on some elements in the interface visual design, and clarify the correlation between different elements. A proper transitional dynamic effects can provide some guidance and attract users' attention. Particularly the well-designed transitional dynamic effects can lead users to pay attention to the position that designers want users to notice, highlight the important information for users, and naturally guide users to involve in the interaction.

**Fig. 3.** Transitional dynamic effects for the music player [4]

Dynamic effects can draw users' attention to a specific region or distract them from the current region. A good dynamic effect design can ensure the visual effect of the interface to avoid being awkward and easier for navigation. Take the transitional dynamic effects for the music player for example (see Fig. 3.) It can lead users to pay attention to where a new object appears and disappears, and display how the element function changes from play to pause and then to continue. This can equip users with a direct understanding of the whole case. The transitional change of the rotating disc presents an expectable interactive operation. Users can experience the "immersive" music appreciation atmosphere through the smooth transition.

### 3.4 Interesting Expression of Dynamic Emotional Design

The purpose of emotional design is to create the sense of happiness. To make users happier in using one product is the ultimate realm of the product interface visual design. An interesting dynamic emotional design can create a favorable and vivid first impression, which can successfully draw users' attention, easily generate a resonance between the product and users, make product design more emotional, personalized and unforgettable, and strengthen the product communication and promotion.

An interesting expression of dynamic emotional design means to create unexpected surprises, and to improve the emotional design for user experience on the basis of inter-action. Some trivialities which can easily ignored in life are actually the linchpin to creating favorable user experience. To users, login has been the most common and an unavoidable operation of mobile product use. When users are eager to post their com-ments on a new website or a mobile media app, the appearance of the login window can be annoying.

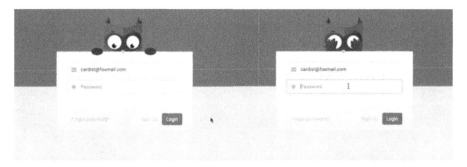

**Fig. 4.** Interesting dynamic effects for password entry upon login [5]

When a user registers an account and enters the passwords for login, the login is actually a highly private operation. So people tend to avoid strangers looking at them when typing in passwords. The password entry interface (see Fig. 4) can effectively protect user's privacy as a physiological instinct by extending the daily habit to the dynamic emotional design of interface. When the user types in passwords, the cute owl above the entry window will automatically cover its eyes. This is a highly interactive logic of dynamic effect design, which can not only tell the user that the system is secure, but also realize a silent interesting interaction with the user. The user can finish the first login pleasantly. In this way, user experience is significantly improved through strengthening of entertainments and vividness and fun of participation. Thereby, a more friendly and fashionable interface visual design effects can be achieved.

### 3.5 Innovative Expression of Dynamic Emotional Design

Sci-fi movies enjoy a large audience, but stories happening in sci-fi movies are usually set against the universe which people have a little knowledge of. When a sci-fi movie is broadcasting, there are only two hours for the audience to understand the stories. An excellent sci-fi movie director focuses on protagonists rather than the distant space, and implants a made-up history of the world into the main line of the story about protagonists. By adhering to the physical rule of the real world and some real physical details which the audience is familiar with, the director ensures the made-up universal to be real. Based on the appeal and reality of the story, the director creates wonderful and forgettable memories for the movie.

Interface visual design is similar to the process of producing a sci-fi movie. Interface visual designers attempt to demonstrate an interactive story on a small screen. The protagonists are interface visual elements in interface visual design. The "made-up world" is the information framework of the interface. But the designer does not have two hours to tell the story. Before users lose their interest and have other puzzlements, the designer just has one second at most to attract users. To the end, the designer should provide attractive frames, interesting dynamic effects and innovative expressions.

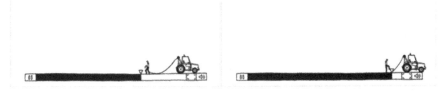

**Fig. 5.** Innovative dynamic effects for the loading page [6]

As shown in Fig. 5, the car cannot go forward, and the protagonist gets off to kick it to help it get started. When the user is waiting, there is a short animation film with vivid and interesting story plots that attracts the user to continue watching it and alleviates the user's anxiety by implanting the pleasure into the user experience. This is also an innovative experience which can not only bring the user surprise, but also demonstrate the product temperament and attitude, and add more fun to the user experience. The user can then get a different perception and experience to better perceive the vigor of the product. Thereby, more and more users will be attracted. Product developers all hope that their products can deliver human care to be more popular. In the design process, it is suggested that some innovative methods can be tried to build the emotional connection between the product and users, which can lead users to experience the story behind the product.

## 4   Conclusions

The role of dynamic emotional design in improving product experience and user engagement in interface visual design is self-evident. It can guide users to effectively focus on certain element on the interface, and indicate the outcome that will be triggered after users' completion of one gesture. Additionally, it can demonstrate the hierarchical and spatial relationship between different elements, alleviate users' anxiety upon waiting, and highlight personalization, sense of novelty and pleasure. So it will be an indispensable element for the current product interface design and interactive design.

Driven by the development of the product-terminal hardware technologies and design languages, the future dynamic design will have more and better design expressions. On the whole, a human-oriented dynamic design is usually a bridge to achieve emotional resonance with users. The ultimate mission is to serve users. Users are eager to gain emotional interaction in the process of product use, which actually reflects the need for product emotional design. Through emotional design, products can better attract users. The dynamic effect design in interface visual design usually resolves around users' experience to better attract users' attention and stimulate their emotional response. In the process of product interface visual design, designers should ensure their user orientation, learn users' aesthetic preferences and emotional experience, and study their behavioral habits and life experience. This can help designers meet users' needs and address their pain spots through their design, and the information carried and expressed by the design can be better accepted by users. Besides, products designed this way will gain users' favor more easily. On that basis, dynamic emotional expressions that can trigger users' emotional resonance can be designed.

# References

1. Normal, D.A.: Design Psychology 3: Emotional Design. CITIC Press Group, Beijing (2015)
2. Dynamic Effect Design. https://dribbble.com/
3. Zcool: https://mobile.zcool.com.cn/work/ZMzkzMzAxMDg=.html. Accessed March 2021
4. Zcool: https://www.zcool.com.cn/work/ZMTI4OTExMTY=.html. Accessed March 2021
5. WEB Backstage Management System Platform Login Page. https://huaban.com/boards/444 05591. Accessed 21 Dec 2020
6. Welfare Daily: http://www.qweixun.com/keji/141482.html. Accessed 16 March 2021
7. Standards for IOS Platform Design. Subparagraph 1.8.
8. Miao, M.: Study on Visual Expression of UI Design Centering on User Experience. Tianjin University of Technology (2017)
9. NetEase Media Design Center: H5 Craftsman Manual: Decryption of H5 Practices. Tsinghua University Publishing House, Beijing (2018)
10. Guo, J.: Applications of emotional design in user experience. Art Appreciat. **10**, 252–253 (2019)

# Research on Furniture Design Based on Parametric Urbanism

Weijia Zhao and Maoqi Xu[✉]

School of Art Design and Media, East China University of Science and Technology, Shanghai 200237, China

**Abstract.** Parameterization is not only a new design style, but also a new design pattern derived from architecture. Parameterization urbanism is the development of parameterization in urban planning, architecture and environment. Parameterized thinking logic enables us to organize and connect the dynamic and complex contemporary society on a new level, which means that the furniture design under the parameterized urbanism should follow some new design methods and principles. This paper expounds the important concepts of parametric and parametric urbanism, and puts forward the key process, significance and principles of furniture design under parametric urbanism. Parametric furniture design is of great significance to design thinking, production and innovation. Parameterized furniture, as an individual in parameterized urbanism, can form a complete urban force field with other urban components such as architecture, environment and products. Under parameterized urbanism, parameterization should become a design paradigm shared among various design fields and produce a whole thinking process logic from concept to manufacturing.

**Keywords:** Parameterization · Parameterized urbanism · Furniture design

## 1 Parameterization

Parameterization is a new design style proposed by Patrik Schumacher. In 2008, he discussed the concept of "parameterization" in the "Dark Side" Salon of the 11th Venice Biennale. In 2009, he published an article named Parametricism as Style-Parametricist Manifesto. In the article, he mentioned that "Parameterism is an another new and great architectural style after postmodernism. Postmodernism and deconstruction have been things of the past, replaced by this fresh, long-term wave of research and innovation...... It provides a new conceptual framework and lays out new goals, new research methods and new values." In fact, parameterization is not only a new design style but also a new design pattern. It represents a new body of knowledge and a new approach in the design discipline.

## 2 From Parameterization to Parameterized Urbanism

### 2.1 Parametric Urbanism

Parameterization originated in the field of architecture, but parameterization is not only a design method, but also a kind of design thinking that can be applied in many fields.

C. Stephanidis et al. (Eds.): HCII 2021, CCIS 1499, pp. 505–512, 2021.
https://doi.org/10.1007/978-3-030-90179-0_64

Parametric Urbanism is a research topic of AADRL, and Schumacher also elaborated on this concept in his article: "Parametric Urbanism refers to the effect of urban internal forces and the direction of force field generated by the change of urban architectural system form". In the process of urban operation and development and evolution, human activities are of vital importance. People with different modes of transportation are constantly circulating, stagnating, gathering and shifting like magnetic lines in the city. In some places, the population is sparse, while in some places, the population is dense. Due to the influence of external and internal factors, people's behavior patterns are different – this is like an urban magnetic field, which can be called urban fluid, as shown in Fig. 1.

**Fig. 1.** Concept extraction of available force field of urban magnetic field

Similar to a force field, a force field model of an urban magnetic field can be extracted and established according to such an urban magnetic field path, as shown in the Fig. 2. Urban space and functional organization are no longer isolated and static, but in a state of "chaos", which is arranged, evolved and moved in an orderly way in a seemingly disorder, and constantly changing and influencing each other.

**Fig. 2.** The urban force field

## 2.2  Necessity of Parametric Furniture Design Under Parametric Urbanism

Under parameterized urbanism, residential buildings, parks, office buildings and other urban buildings are all part of the urban force field, including all kinds of furniture and product design. Furniture should not be seen as an isolated object, but as a part of the material that constitutes the space. Under parameterized urbanism, we need to integrate architectural design, interior design and furniture design to improve the integration of design and form a more organic and integrated world.

# 3 The Key Process of Furniture Design Under Parametric Urbanism

## 3.1 Data of Design Requirement Information

Design requirements are the starting point of design. Furniture design under parameterized urbanism includes people's activities and behaviors, people's requirements for furniture, as well as the requirements of the built environment and the surrounding natural environment. Research and interview on the environment and user groups of furniture can help us to accurately understand the environmental characteristics and user needs, and obtain reliable design information. The digital description of the collected information is very important, because this digital information will be the basis of the formation of furniture.

## 3.2 Establishment of Design Parameter Relationship

After obtaining the information of the data design requirements, it is necessary to distinguish the primary and secondary contradictions in the computer parametric design, find some main factors affecting the design, and establish the relationship between the parameters. For example, to design a seat, its sitting depth and sitting height parameters are the key factors in the design, and the user's body shape, age, height, gender, interior decoration of the building, spatial structure, etc., can be regarded as the parameters that determine the relationship between the sitting depth and sitting height. We need to establish such an understanding of the basic design parameter relationships in order to construct the logic between the parameters.

## 3.3 Establishment of Computer Software Parameter Model

After building the basic design parameter relationship, we also use computer language to build the parameter relationship to generate the furniture form. For example, we can use Grasshopper and other software to establish the morphological parameter model. We can also write our own algorithm to describe the rule system among the parameters and form the model. When we give a certain value to the parameters of the software parameter model, we can get the prototype design. By adjusting the parameter value, we can generate a new version of the prototype design in real time.

## 3.4 Optimization of Prototype Design

So far, we have only solved the main contradiction of furniture design under the parametric urbanism, we still need to let the parameter software continue to carry out the operation instruction, further optimize the design rudiment, achieve the form, the material, the structure, the function coordination, develop the satisfactory design work. From the aspect of form, inspiration can be found from the natural form and the artificial form in the optimization of the prototype design.

**Natural Form.** Nature can always give us infinite inspiration. See Fig. 3. Whether you are looking at birds, flowers, fish, or forest soil, or you are looking at microbes that are invisible to the naked eye, there are many laws of beauty that we can draw from. Through the observation of these natural forms, and then by the designer for abstract extraction, can be further improve the design of the embryonic source of inspiration.

**Fig. 3.** Various natural forms

**Artificial Form.** As shown in Fig. 4, many random phenomena in life often reveal some rules and unity in an uncontrollable way, such as boiling hot water, broken glass, soap foam and smoke. They are not regular basic geometrical bodies, but show an order that can be applied in disorder. Through the abstraction and extraction of these artificial form logic generation relations, it can also become a form source that can be drawn from the optimization scheme of the embryonic form of furniture design.

**Fig. 4.** Soap bubbles and clouds of smoke

### 3.5 Test and Feedback of Design Results

Under parameterized urbanism, furniture design also follows the parameterized design thinking mode and has a complete data logic chain. However, in order to know whether the design results really meet the design requirements, furniture still needs to be tested to test whether it meets the needs of users and responds to the environment and architecture. In terms of testing methods, in addition to allowing users to personally experience testing, they can also conduct testing through parameterized self-testing software and feedback to each link to verify whether the final design results meet the original set parameters.

## 4 The Significance of Furniture Design Under Parametric Urbanism

### 4.1 Connect with Intelligent Manufacturing to Meet the Demand of Mass Production

Furniture design under parameterized urbanism has a more compact and complete logical chain from design to manufacturing. Advanced parameterized digital manufacturing technology can be well connected with production, and the final digital model of furniture can be directly output to two-dimensional or three-dimensional numerical control equipment for molding. With the progress of processing and manufacturing technology, designers can break the shackles between form, material and structure, increase the interest and flexibility of design, and meet people's personalized aesthetic needs at the same time to meet the market demand for mass production.

### 4.2 Exploration of New Materials, New Structures and New Functions

The traditional visual expression is not explicit in expressing the structural logic of the formation process and the production logic of the design object, but this logic becomes explicit in the parameterized design system by intuitively displaying the various parts of the pattern. In the model of parameterized urbanism, such an operating system allows designers to better explore new materials, structures and functions of furniture. As shown in Fig. 5, the design of the Beast is combined with a new manufacturing technology called Variable Energy Design (VPD). Through the VPD, these different colored bricks represent different design attributes. That is, the 3D printing is done according to the performance of the digital material: the continuous bone areas of the shell structure are black, the support structures are gray, and the body pressure areas are supported by a comfortable, soft white part.

**Fig. 5.** Chaise Lounge, Beast

### 4.3 Promote Collaborative Innovation

Under the parametric urbanism, furniture design becomes more interdisciplinary. On the one hand, collaboration between people becomes more efficient and logical, such as collaboration between designers and engineers, collaboration between furniture designers and urban planners and architects; On the other hand, with the advent of the era of AI, the importance of man-machine collaboration is also increasing. With the help of artificial intelligence and big data, designers can informationize design requirements more efficiently. Within the large system of parameterized urbanism, big data can also be used to analyze the results of furniture design, so as to select the optimal solution.

### 4.4 Constructing Systematic Emerging Cities

"Emergence" is a natural phenomenon that often occurs in the objective world and can be understood as an emergent phenomenon, emphasizing that "the whole is greater than the sum of its parts". In fact, like flocks of birds and flocks of fish, the whole parameterized city can be seen as a kind of intelligent cluster that can be explained by emergent theory. Parameterized furniture, as an individual within parameterized urbanism, can form a complete urban force field together with buildings, environment, products and other urban components. Parametric Urbanism focuses on everything from city to architecture, from architecture to interior, from interior to furniture and product design.

### 4.5  Innovation of Design Thinking Mode

It is an innovation of design thinking mode to look at furniture design under parameterized urbanism from a parameterized perspective. Parametric Urbanism is a new urban solution proposed by Schumacher. In fact, it is not only a new design scheme, but also a new parameterized and organic systematic design thinking mode. Under parameterized urbanism, parameterism should become a shared design paradigm among all design fields, generating the overall logic of thinking process from concept to manufacturing.

## 5  Furniture Design Principles Under Parametric Urbanism

### 5.1  Combination with Environment

Under parametric urbanism, the environment within cities and buildings is designed as a dynamic capacity to respond to different usage conditions, such as light, wind direction, sound, terrain, people flow, and so on, and can change configuration to adapt to them. Furniture design under parameterized urbanism is not an independent device, but also parameterized response. When the building responds to the environment, the furniture in the building should also be combined with the environment, and the key parameters of the environment are encoded into the digital language of the computer, which is related to the form design. Through parameterization technology, designers can generate massive results more efficiently than before, and screen out a large number of works that are more closely related to the environment in a short time.

### 5.2  Combination with Architecture

In the modernist architectural theory, furniture is an inseparable part of architecture. The space they co-exist in weaves the net of architecture and furniture as a whole, and space is the common goal of architecture and furniture. Furniture and architecture work together to shape the space in order to break the walls of the building and realize the organic flow of space inside. Under the parameterized urbanism, the architecture follows the rhythm of the city. Furniture, as a part of the architectural space, should also synchronize with the breathing of the building. As shown in Fig. 6, the Moon Sofa designed by famous designer Zaha Hadid features smooth curves and curved forms that make it look comfortable, flexible and elegant. It is obvious that Moon Sofa responds well to architecture and has a strong sense of sculpture.

**Fig. 6.** The moon sofa

## 5.3 Combination with the User

Combined with users of principle stress is actually a early in architecture, urban planning has embody "humanistic care", the parameterized urbanism of furniture design should also be integrated into the humanistic care, efforts to create a kind of people, people and society, science and technology, natural environment and so on each other and harmonious living environment, reveal a person's freedom, equality, dignity, kindness, love, such as good value, thus greatly improve the taste of people's lives. Figure 7 is the "Urban Adapter" for the Urban public seating in Hong Kong designed by Rocker-Lange Architects. This design proposal regards the design of Urban outdoor furniture as a whole, not just providing a single static design, but providing a variety of different solutions that meet specific conditions. In addition to being a seat, it also has some additional functional value, such as being a recycling container, flower basket or charity billboard.

**Fig. 7.** Urban adapter: urban outdoor furniture in Hong Kong

## 5.4 Combination with Material Manufacturing

The rapid development of digital technology and information processing technology harmonizes the relationship between design and manufacturing. Under the parametric design mode, designers can have more space to display than before, and a new design research field arises at the historic moment: Material Manufacturing Design (MFD). By developing the concepts, principles, and patterns of MFD, designers are free to create new, material-related experimental methods of design thinking that were often considered difficult or impossible to achieve before. In today's parametric architecture, we can see a large number of works designed with material manufacturing technology as the structural scale, as shown in Fig. 8. Under parameterized urbanism, furniture design should also break through the shackles among materials, structures and forms to form an organic chaotic complex.

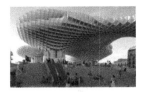

**Fig. 8.** Architectural parametric structure of MFD

## 5.5 Systematic Principles

If the combination of material manufacturing and parametric urbanism is concerned with the internal factors of furniture itself, then the environment, architecture and users are concerned with the external factors. They are not to be seen in isolation, but rather as a harmonious system of interconnections (Fig. 9).

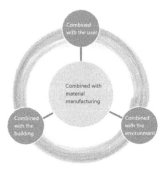

**Fig. 9.** The relationship between furniture design and elements under parameterized urbanism

**User Experience Studies**

# Old-looking yet Usable!: An Investigation of Consumer's Usability Perception of Retro Products

Nektar Ege Altıntoprak[✉] and Wei Wang

Georgia Institute of Technology, Atlanta, GA 30332, USA
naltintoprak3@gatech.edu

**Abstract.** As the market competition increases, brands are trying to come up with strategies that can establish a bond with the users. Using the retro style is rapidly becoming one of these strategies by targeting past emotions however, the perception of the usability of this style hasn't been investigated. The aim of this study is to investigate the user's perception of the product's usability features of retro consumer electronics from the appearance compared to non-retro products. A 5-factor scale was developed to measure the perception of the usability, including aesthetic, durability, reliability, serviceability, and learnability, was applied to 60 people. Paired samples t-tests and ANOVA tests were performed to explore the data. According to the results of the study, the scores of the perception of the usability were not significant between retro and non-retro products. However, retro products have been found to be more durable than non-retro products. In contrast, non-retro products were rated significantly higher for the factor of aesthetic. It was found that the effect of style on the perception of the usability was dependent on the type of the device that retro style didn't have any effect on the perception of usability for toasters while non-retro style was found to be more usable for refrigerators. All statistical tests involving gender or other demographics were not significant.

**Keywords:** Retro design · Consumer electronics design · Perceived usability scale · Product usability · Consumer perception

## 1 Introduction

Retro is designing products or services that utilize the trend and characteristics of the past in newly designed products. The main aim is to combine the past with the present and also give superior functions to the products compared to past designs [1].

Three different retro marketing trends [1] need to be mentioned to highlight the scope of this study. The first category is repro marketing which is reproducing past brands and products. Reproduction of the old Coca-Cola bottles and launching them to the current market can be an example of repro design. The second category is retro design, combining old and new technologies. Crosley Brand produces record players inspired from the past but providing high technological advancements in their design

© Springer Nature Switzerland AG 2021
C. Stephanidis et al. (Eds.): HCII 2021, CCIS 1499, pp. 515–521, 2021.
https://doi.org/10.1007/978-3-030-90179-0_65

which is a good example of retro design. The final category is called retro-repro designs in other words, neo-nostalgia that revives the products that traded on nostalgia to start with. For instance, BMW Mini has already been associated with the retro feeling. In this study, the second category will be the focus.

Even though the term "retro" was coined in the 70s, in recent years this trend became a highly preferred design style in various domains like advertising, industrial design, graphic design, and illustration. One of the reasons proposed by Orth and Gal in 2012 [2] is that products related to the past tend to be a "mood booster" compared to non-nostalgic products.

The aim of this study is to investigate the user's perception of the product's usability features of retro consumer electronics from the appearance compared to non-retro products. The study will focus on their perception of these product's images. Furthermore, participant's demographic information such as age, gender, income, and nationality obtained to understand the relationship between the participant's perception of the product's usability features of retro consumer electronics and their demographic data. Two consumer electronics product categories selected for investigation: fridge and toaster according to their long history and popularity as household items across generations and regions.

## 2 Methodology

The study has two phases. In the first phase, the aim is to identify the retro products and modern style products that can be used for phase two. In this phase, 20 pictures of various products in each category including retro and non-retro presented to 39 participants who have a design related background. Participants asked to select one picture that has the most retro feeling and one picture that has the least retro feeling.

After the product pictures are selected, a two-section online survey is conducted in phase two. The first section, data including age, gender, income, and nationality are obtained. Data obtained to understand the relationship between the participant's perception of the product's usability features of retro consumer electronics and their demographic data. Previously there were studies that investigated the effect of demographic aspects such as gender and age [3] in retro-design trends however, nationality was a new contribution from this study.

In the second section, $2 \times 2$ pictures of retro and non-retro fridges and toasters presented to 60 participants. The aim of this phase was to understand the user's perception of the usability of these products. To measure the subjective usability, researchers have been using scales such as NASA Task Load Index, System Usability Scale [4] or other dedicated scales. For example, a previous study that investigated how fidelity of the software prototypes affects the user perception of usability [5] used four characteristics as measurement criteria: ease of learning, ease of use, the forgiveness of mistakes, and aesthetics. In this study, a 5 determined factors scale (aesthetic, durability, reliability, serviceability, and learnability) was proposed to measure the perception of the usability, which adapted from Nielsen's Attributes of Usability [6], System Usability Scale [7], NASA TLX [8] and CAFEQUE Product Analysis. Participants need to rate these 5 characteristics of four pictures that were previously mentioned by using 5 Point Likert scale in this section.

# 3  Results

## 3.1  Phase 1

Participants (n = 39) from design related backgrounds took the Phase-1 survey (see Fig. 1, Fig. 2). For the retro toaster 22 participants selected the number 4 as the toaster that has the most retro feeling, for non-retro toaster 18 participants selected number 12. For the retro refrigerator, number 9 selected by 19 participants and for the non-retro refrigerator 13 people selected number 18. Hence, these products were used in Phase-2 evaluation.

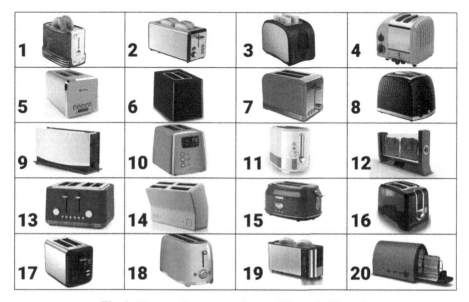

**Fig. 1.** Toasters that presented to participants in Phase-1.

## 3.2  Phase 2

Repeated measures ANOVA has been conducted to understand the effect of style on the perception of usability. Using Pillai's Trace, the main effect of style (retro, non-retro) there was no significant effect on the cumulative perception of the usability score, $V = .01$, $F(1,59) = 0.79$, $p < .05$.

However, the effect of the style for 5 factors of the perception of the usability (aesthetic, durability, reliability, serviceability, learnability), was meaningful which means that style has a significant effect on at least one of these factors, $V = .32$, $F(4,56) = 6.57$, $p < .05$.

In order to look at the effect of style on different factors regardless of device paired samples t-test was conducted. Aesthetic scores of non-retro products (M = 8.15, SD = 1.99) are found to be significantly higher than retro products (M = 6.28, SD = 1.99);

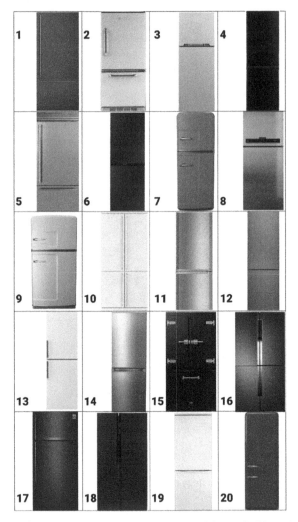

**Fig. 2.** Refrigerators that presented to participants in Phase-1.

t(59) = −5.75, p < 0.000. In contrast, retro products found to be more durable compared to non-retro products; t(59) = 2.84, p < 0.006 (see Fig. 3).

It was found that the effect of style on the perception of the usability was dependent on the type of the device (toaster, refrigerator), $V = .07$, $F(1,59) = 13.35$, $p < .05$. The effect of style on the perception of the usability of the different types of devices was investigated by paired samples t-test. Retro style didn't have any effect on the perception of usability for toasters while non-retro style found to be more usable for refrigerators; t(59) = −3.33, p < 0.001.

All statistical tests involving gender were not significant.

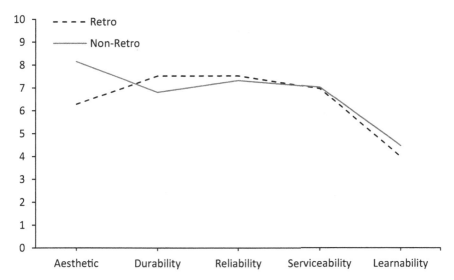

**Fig. 3.** Total perception of usability score for retro and non-retro products.

## 4   Discussion

According to the results, user's perception of usability did not change according to the style of the product. On the other hand, if we investigate the 5 factors individually, even though the user's perception of reliability, serviceability, and learnability did not change according to the style of the product, the same statement can't be mentioned for aesthetic and durability. Users rated the factor of aesthetic lower for retro products than non-retro products while durability is higher for retro products. Hence, it is important for designers to be mindful of their style selection. Even though the retro style is widely used, our findings suggest that participants are visually dissatisfied by retro products compared to non-retro. In contrast, retro style can be used to give a sense of durability. Our participants think that retro products will have less breakdowns, withstand wear, pressure, or damage compared to non-retro products.

Our study suggests that the perception of the usability was dependent on the type of the device. Participants found the non-retro refrigerator more useful than the retro refrigerator while there was no significant difference between retro and non-retro toasters. This outcome should promote designers to be mindful about selecting the design style according to the type of device that they are designing.

The nationality, age, education and income did not provide enough heterogeneity to provide conclusions regarding the effect of style on the user's usability perception.

On the other hand, outcomes suggests that there is no gender difference on the effect of style on the user's usability perception. This outcome contradicts with the study that investigates the difference in attitudes of consumers towards retro products according to their demographic data [3]. In previous study, it was found that there is a significant difference in consumer attitudes based on gender. However, from our study, it shows no difference. Hence, the gender factor should be investigated further.

## 5  Conclusion and Limitations

In this study, the effect of retro style (retro vs. non-retro) on usability perception was evaluated by participants' rating in 5 factors of four pictures of household appliances (retro or non-retro toasters, retro or non-retro refrigerators). Even though the user's perception of usability did not change according to the style of the product, participants found non-retro products more aesthetically pleasing. On the other hand, the perception of the durability was significantly higher for retro products than non-retro.

For the successes of the products, it is important to explore aspects that shape the user's perception of usability [9]. It is important to point out that this trend should be used effectively and consciously to achieve the expected outcomes on the consumer electronics market [10]. This study highlights the importance of the careful usage of design trends by showing the effect of retro design on various usability criteria.

However, several limitations should be noted. The non-retro product selection for refrigerator in Phase-1 had very close outcomes hence the number of products could be increased.

The 5-factor scale (aesthetic, durability, reliability, serviceability, and learnability) that were proposed for this study has been proved effective to measure the perception of the usability with preliminary results. For the future study, more factors can be added to increase the dimensions of the investigations to obtain more accurate usability scores. Another limitation was the inability to provide diversity of demographic data hence, further analysis was not conducted considering these data. Providing the analysis including demographic data will add value to future studies.

Besides the limitations, this investigation of the effect of retro style to the user's perception of the usability of these products provided insightful outcomes for future studies.

## References

1. Brown, S.: Retro-marketing: yesterday's tomorrows, today! Mark. Intell. Plan. **17**(7), 363–376 (1999)
2. Orth, U.R., Gal, S.: Nostalgic brands as mood boosters. J. Brand Manag. **19**(8), 666–679 (2012)
3. Arslan, B., Yetkin, B.O.: Determining the demographic that affect consumer attitudes towards retro products. Nişantaşı Üniversitesi Sosyal Bilimler Dergisi **5**(1), 92–108 (2017)
4. Longo, L.: Subjective usability, mental workload assessments and their impact on objective human performance. In: Bernhaupt, R., Dalvi, G., Joshi, A., Balkrishan, D.K., O'Neill, J., Winckler, M. (eds.) INTERACT 2017. LNCS, vol. 10514, pp. 202–223. Springer, Cham (2017). https://doi.org/10.1007/978-3-319-67684-5_13
5. Wiklund, M.E., Thurrott, C., Dumas, J.S.: Does the fidelity of software prototypes affect the perception of usability? Proc. Hum. Factors Soc. Annu. Meet. **36**(4), 399–403 (1992)
6. Nielsen, J.: "2.2," in Usability Engineering, pp. 26–37. Academic Press, San Diego, California (1993)
7. Bangor, A., Kortum, P.T., Miller, J.T.: An empirical evaluation of the system usability scale. Int. J. Hum. Comput. Interact. **24**(6), 574–594 (2008)

8. Hart, S.G., Staveland, L.E.: Development of NASA-TLX (task load index): results of empirical and theoretical research. Adv. Psychol. Hum. Mental Workload **52**, 139–183 (1988)
9. Flavián, C., Guinalíu, M., Gurrea, R.: The role played by perceived usability, satisfaction and consumer trust on website loyalty. Inf. Manage. **43**(1), 1–14 (2006)
10. Goo, K., Self, J.A., Jeong, Y.: Retrospective automotive design and innovative meaning making the influence of retro design features. Arch. Des. Res. **29**(1), 61 (2016)

# Customer Value Co-creation Behaviors Through Online Interactions in Luxury Hotels: Effect on Customer Loyalty

Zineb Bouchriha[1]([✉]), Sabra Farid[2], and Smail Ouiddad[1]

[1] Research Laboratory in Marketing, Management and Communication,
Hassan First University of Settat, Settat, Morocco
`z.bouchriha@uhp.ac.ma`
[2] Research and Study Laboratory in Quality, Marketing, SME Management and Technology
Transfer, Cadi Ayyad University, Marrakech, Morocco

**Abstract.** The proliferation of information and communication technologies has profoundly changed the way people travel, behave and enjoy experiences. This research aims to examine the influence of interactions in online engagement platforms on tourists' value co-creation behaviors that affect their loyalties. In order to do this, the current study uses a mixed-method approach, including 14 semi-structured interviews, and a 159-respondent survey. The research model was tested using structural equation modeling with SMARTPLS. The results show that tourists' value co-creation behavior is mostly determined by engagement in online platforms, and confirm a significant relationship between value co-creation behavior and loyalty. Our research aims to contribute to the knowledge of value co-creation, and provide managerial implications for tourism and hospitality management.

**Keywords:** Customer value co-creation behaviors · Engagement · Digital experience · Customer loyalty

## 1   Introduction

Over time, the world has been moving steadily into the digital age. The emergence of these technologies has redefined the interactions between tourism service providers and customers, enabling them to exchange information, enhance their creativity, strengthen their problem-solving abilities, and improve the sharing of their consumption experiences, regardless of time, distance, and location [1]. Establishing a focused dialogue with customers and integrating their personal resources with those of organizations characterizes value co-creation [2]. Forcing the application of these technological advances, customer engagement often occurs in online environments [3]. Indeed, customer engagement is essential in the value co-creation process [4]. Actual customer engagement in value co-creation refers to value co-creation behavior (VCCB) that involves customer participation and citizenship behavior [5, 6]. Specifically, VCCB is fundamental in the service sector as it ensures a positive outcome [7].

© Springer Nature Switzerland AG 2021
C. Stephanidis et al. (Eds.): HCII 2021, CCIS 1499, pp. 522–526, 2021.
https://doi.org/10.1007/978-3-030-90179-0_66

The tourism services industry is often impacted by new changes and new forms of online interactions. Indeed, the majority of hotel establishments offer their guests mobile applications that make the experience of staying in hotel wealthier, more relevant and memorable [2]. Several works have focused on value co-creation. It is about improving customer loyalty [8] and boosting customer engagement online [9]. However, very little attention has been paid to studying value co-creation behaviors in an online context [4]. In light of the paucity of research on this issue, authors [10, 11] have recently called for the development of contribution research on value co-creation behavior. Indeed, this research aims to examine the influence of interaction in engagement platforms on value co-creation behavior that affects customer loyalty to hotels.

## 2 Literature Review

### 2.1 Interactions in Online Engagement Platforms and VCCB

Information and communication technologies have become an integral part of our lives and tourism industry isn't an exception [12]. Indeed, technology platforms enhance consumer experiences and strengthen online co-creation activities without limitations of time and distance [1]. Previous research has shown a positive link between online engagement platforms and value co-creation based on Service-Dominant Logic (SDL). Indeed, Buhalis and Foerste [13] provided a mobile marketing framework that implies the use of smart technologies in the tourism industry can engage the customer in the value creation process. In their conceptual article France et al. [14] introduced customer engagement with the brand as a determinant of co-creation behavior. Furthermore, [7] demonstrate that engagement had a significant influence on participatory and citizenship co-creation behavior. This is because companies disseminate their products and services on online platforms to stimulate customer engagement and encourage real participation and information-seeking behaviors [15]. Moreover, the more customers are engaged in the service process, the more they can benefit from service products and share their experiences [16]. As a result, the hypotheses are formulated as follows:

H1.1 The interactions in online engagement platforms impact positively the customer participation behavior.

H1.2 The interactions in online engagement platforms impact positively the customer citizenship behavior.

### 2.2 VCCB and Loyalty

Customer loyalty has for several decades been considered one of the best intangible assets an organization can possess [8]. Therefore, explaining the factors on which this loyalty depends is of definite interest to both researchers and practitioners in the marketing field. Many previous studies have shown that VCCB can lead to positive customer outcomes such as customer loyalty. Indeed, Cossío-Silva et al. [8] show that there is a positive relationship between VCCB and their loyalty levels. VCCB represents the set of customer-initiated interactions that occur between service providers and customers that contribute to value co-creation [14]. Lewin et al. [17] determined that customer participation in services influenced their own perceptions and loyalty, and was beneficial in building customer loyalty in places designed for leisure and entertainment. Lee et al. [18] studied VCCB and determined that customer participation increased their loyalty in leisure sectors. Therefore, Liu and Jo [7] assert that the value co-creation process has a positive influence on loyal members' evaluation of the service because it improves the quality of the service with members' participation behavior and meets members' internal needs through citizenship behavior. The following hypotheses are therefore proposed as follows:

H2.1 The more customer participation behavior engages in, the more they will be loyal to the company.

H2.2 The more customer participation behavior engages in, the more they will be loyal to the company.

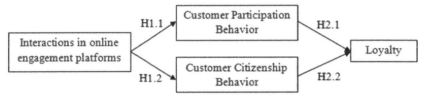

**Fig. 1.** Conceptual framework of this study

## 3 Research Methodology

**Research Methods.** This research consists of a mixed methods approach. Our research philosophy was inspired by the social sciences in terms of triangulation [19]. Indeed, the principle of triangulation implies the combination of qualitative and quantitative approaches to study a given phenomenon and/or behavior, and ensure that the underlying theme is examined in a scientific manner. Therefore, our research mobilized semi-structured interviews with 14 tourists to explore the specifics of value co-creation in the context of tourism accommodation, and a quantitative questionnaire administered online to 159 tourists who stayed in different 4 or 5 star hotels in Morocco and gave their opinions on the co-creation experience in these establishments. A partial least squares structural equation model (PLS-SEM) was used to estimate the structural research model using SMARTPLS software.

**Tourist Participants.** This research collected data from tourists who have recently stayed in 4 or 5 star hotels in Morocco. This category of hotel caters to a mid to high-end, even luxury, customers who speak several languages, have visited several countries, and are willing to pay a higher price for a more personalized experience. This is a target of all ages that travels for several reasons, from a relaxing stay to a professional one, who consumes all the services offered by the hotel and who travels alone as well as in groups. This target generally uses digital channels for communication as well as for purchasing and consumption. However, the majority of these establishments now offer mobile applications that make the experience of a tourist more relevant and interesting, since they allow customers to book online, select rooms and configurations, check-in, check-out, access rooms without keys, have the day's entertainment program, select activities to do, and order room service.

**Study Process.** Semi-structured interviews were conducted to generate additional information about the value co-creation behavior of tourists. First, a sample was used according to our personal knowledge of tourists, who would have, in the last six months frequented a hotel for a tourist stay of at least four days. Second, the researchers followed a snowball method and asked respondents to invite people from their social network who were qualified for this study. This research met the saturation criterion, and interviewed 14 people, between the January 2019 and March 2019. In addition, the conduct of our quantitative fieldwork was established by administering an online questionnaire to tourists who had recently visited Moroccan hotel facilities and experienced value co-creation. The questionnaire frame focused on questions adapted for the VCCB process using a five-point Likert-type agreement scale (1 = strongly disagree to 5 = strongly agree), in addition to descriptive variables for the sample. This questionnaire was pre-tested and recommended by experts who had previously developed the measurement scales for clarity, readability and comprehension. The questionnaire was administered for a first test on Facebook pages created through targeted Facebook/Instagram advertising on Moroccan geographical areas to maximize the response rate. The researchers offered a raffle to win Moroccan gifts for those who responded to the questionnaire. For the final collection, the researchers took the same approach, and continued to alternate Facebook/Instagram advertising options by changing the targeting and insertions, and offered other types of incentives for the targets. The survey was administered to a final sample of 159 usable responses. However, this number is statistically significant as it is above the threshold set by Tabachnick and Fidell (2013). The final data collection was spread over the period from July 2019 through January 2020.

## 4   Discussion and Conclusion

Our research aims to contribute to knowledge about value co-creation, but also by providing managerial implications for tourism and hospitality management. Customers engage in value-creating activities in various ways such as participating for self, creating for self, participating for others, or creating for others. Furthermore, fostering interactions in engagement platforms could result in participation and citizenship co-creation behavior on the part of customers, which would tend to build customer loyalty. This is further enhanced if digital technologies are well integrated into the offer and if the hotel has a powerful digital application. The hotel industry can then take advantage of these practices to optimize spending and improve loyalty behavior. Moreover, these value-creating activities can take place at the pre-consumer, consumer and post-consumer stages. There is clearly considerable potential within the tourism and hospitality industry when adopting a large-scale SDL perspective. For the specific case of Moroccan hoteliers, we see a weakness in technology investments, despite the fact that hotels are well ranked. On the other hand we see that customers are increasingly using digitalized services during the hotel stay, beyond simple booking or payment. There is a need to improve internal digitalization skills to support all facets of the service offering, but also to align with international practices since customers are also becoming more international and expect the same level of offering from hotels ranked at the same level.

# References

1. Dover, Y., Kelman, G.: Emergence of online communities: empirical evidence and theory. PloS one **13**(11), e0205167 (2018)
2. Prahalad, C.K., Ramaswamy, V.: Co-creation experiences: the next practice in value creation. J. Interact. Mark. **18**(3), 5–14 (2004)
3. Bouchriha, Z., Ouiddad, S.: Towards a theoretical clarification of the co-creation experiences in online brand communities. Reinnova **3**(10) (2021)
4. Yen, C.H., Teng, H.Y., Tzeng, J.: C. Innovativeness and customer value co-creation behaviors: mediating role of customer engagement. Int. J. Hospitality Manage. **88**, 102514 (2020)
5. Shamim, A., Ghazali, Z., Albinsson, P.A.: An integrated model of corporate brand experience and customer value co-creation behaviour. Int. J. Retail Distribut. Manage. **44**(2), 139–158 (2016)
6. Yi, Y., Gong, T.: Customer value co-creation behavior: scale development and validation. J. Bus. Res. **66**(9), 1279–1284 (2013)
7. Liu, J., Jo, W.: Value co-creation behaviors and hotel loyalty program member satisfaction based on engagement and involvement: Moderating effect of company support. J. Hosp. Tour. Manag. **43**, 23–31 (2020)
8. Cossío-Silva, F.J., Revilla-Camacho, M.Á., Vega-Vázquez, M., Palacios-Florencio, B.: Value co-creation and customer loyalty. J. Bus. Res. **69**(5), 1621–1625 (2016)
9. Fernandes, T., Remelhe, P.: How to engage customers in co-creation: customers' motivations for collaborative innovation. J. Strateg. Mark. **24**(3–4), 311–326 (2016)
10. Ahn, J., Lee, C.K., Back, K.J., Schmitt, A.: Brand experiential value for creating integrated resort customers' co-creation behavior. Int. J. Hosp. Manag. **81**, 104–112 (2019)
11. Roy, S.K., Balaji, M.S., Soutar, G., Jiang, Y.: The antecedents and consequences of value co-creation behaviors in a hotel setting: a two-country study. Cornell Hospital. Q. **61**(3), 353–368 (2020)
12. Fan, D.X., Hsu, C.H., Lin, B.: Tourists' experiential value co-creation through online social contacts: Customer-dominant logic perspective. J. Bus. Res. **108**, 163–173 (2020)
13. Buhalis, D., Foerste, M.: SoCoMo marketing for travel and tourism: empowering co-creation of value. J. Destin. Mark. Manag. **4**(3), 151–161 (2015)
14. France, C., Merrilees, B., & Miller, D. Customer brand co-creation: a conceptual model. Marketing Intelligence & Planning (2015).
15. Sashi, C.M.: Customer engagement, buyer-seller relationships, and social media. Manage. Decis (2012)
16. Pansari, A., Kumar, V.: Customer engagement: the construct, antecedents, and consequences. J. Acad. Mark. Sci. **45**(3), 294–311 (2016). https://doi.org/10.1007/s11747-016-0485-6
17. Lewin, J., Rajamma, R.K., Paswan, A.K.: Customer loyalty in entertainment venues: the reality TV genre. J. Bus. Res. **2015**(68), 616–622 (2015)
18. Lee, Y.-L., Pan, L.-Y., Hsu, C.-H., Lee, D.-C.: Exploring the sustainability correlation of value co-creation and customer loyalty-a case study of fitness clubs. Sustainability **11**(1), 97 (2018)
19. Jick, T.: Qualitative and quantitative methods: triangulation in action. Qualitative methodology, Beverly Hills (1975)

# Perceptions in Two-Dimensional and Three-Dimensional Aperture Problems

Guang-Dah Chen[1]([⊠]) and Hsiwen Fan[2]

[1] National Taiwan University of Art, New Taipei City 22058, Taiwan
chengd@ntua.edu.tw
[2] Chiba University, Chiba 263-8522, Japan

**Abstract.** The two-dimensional (2D) and three-dimensional (3D) aperture problems are different forms of display in which moving stripes induce illusory perceptions of motion. From the viewpoint of visual psychology, this study applied a psychophysical method to determine the similarities and dissimilarities between the induced motion perceptions caused by the 2D and 3D aperture problems. The results indicate that for the 3D aperture problem, more time is required to induce motion perceptions than is required in the 2D aperture problem. The velocity thresholds of the 2D and 3D aperture problems also revealed that a certain velocity must be reached if induced motion perceptions are to occur, and the perceived motion in both cases appears to be toward the aperture edge that has the most terminal points. Generally, the 2D aperture problem is more effective at causing induced motion perception than the 3D aperture problem.

**Keywords:** Dynamics optical illusion · Perception of movement · Aperture problem

## 1 Introduction

The three-dimensional (3D) barberpole illusion (BPI) is a visual illusion illustrated by the observed versus real motion of stripes on a barber pole, and because it is quite similar to an aperture problem, it has long been treated as one. Hence, the BPI is also known as the 3D aperture problem, as opposed to the normally two-dimensional (2D) aperture problem. The similarity between the 3D and 2D aperture problems is that, once the motion of the stripes on a pole has reached a certain speed, the stripes appear to move toward the direction that has more terminal points, rather than the actual direction. This is named induced motion perception. As for their dissimilarities, they are represented using different forms and their patterns of motion differ.

Studies on visual perception have confirmed that when humans observe an object in 3D space, a stereoscopic image is generated by the brain once it has processed the parallax of the two eyes, which view the object from different positions [1]. The present study employed an experiment to examine the effects of different forms of vision on induced motion perceptions in the 2D and 3D aperture problems. Additionally, similarities and dissimilarities between the induced motion perceptions in the 2D and 3D

© Springer Nature Switzerland AG 2021
C. Stephanidis et al. (Eds.): HCII 2021, CCIS 1499, pp. 527–534, 2021.
https://doi.org/10.1007/978-3-030-90179-0_67

aperture problems were investigated to enrich the theoretical basis of kinetic art and to provide a reference for future studies on illusory motion perception. Specifically, the objectives of this study were as follows: (1) to investigate the relationship between the induced motion perceptions in the 2D and 3D aperture problems according to movement velocity thresholds; (2) to determine whether vision of different dimensions affects the induced motion perceptions in the aperture problem; (3) to investigate the effects of different shapes in the different forms of the aperture problem; and (4) to identify the similarities or dissimilarities between the induced motion perceptions in the 2D and 3D aperture problems.

## 2  Literature Review

### 2.1  Induced Motion Perception in the 2D Aperture Problem

When observing a moving grating through a small aperture, the observer notices that no matter whether the grating is actually exhibiting up-and-down or left-and-right movement, the movement discerned through the aperture is oriented in a consistent direction [2]. Moreover, although the velocity of the grating can be measured, the observer is unable to ascertain the direction in which it is moving; that is, the grating observed through the aperture could be moving in a variety of directions [3–5]. This phenomenon is called aperture problem.

Wallach [3] suggested that when observing a moving grating through apertures of different shapes, the perceived direction of movement is different from the actual direction because the grating appears to be moving toward a direction that has the most terminal points. This illusory motion is similar to the illusion of induced motion perception, and it occurs because the edges of apertures can create different numbers of corresponding points. These points give the brain clear signals of local movement and hence generate the perception that the movement is toward the edge that has the most corresponding points [6, 7].

### 2.2  Induced Motion Perception in the 3D Aperture Problem

The 3D aperture problem is the seemingly upward or downward movement of parallel stripes on a spinning object. The most typical example of this phenomenon is the BPI introduced by Wallach in 1935, which can be observed on the rotating cylindrical sign of an old-style barbershop. The rotation of the cylinder generates the visual effect that the stripes are not rotating but moving vertically upward.

The 3D aperture problem is reliant on the pole's rotation velocity for the generation of induced motion perception; when the rotating velocity exceeds a certain threshold, the stripes appear to be moving toward an edge that has relatively more terminal points, rather than appearing to spin horizontally. Because this induced motion perception toward the direction with more terminal points is the same as the induced motion perception in the 2D aperture problem, the BPI has always been treated as an aperture problem [8], which is why it is also known as the 3D aperture problem.

### 2.3  2D Aperture Problem Versus 3D Aperture Problem

According to the preceding literature review, both the 2D and 3D aperture problems describe ambiguous movements caused by motion that is perceived to proceed toward an edge that has more terminal points. This can intensify the illusory motion of continuous stripes, but it weakens and interferes with the illusory motion of discontinuous stripes or other figure shapes. In the 2D aperture problem the stripes move parallel to the grating, whereas in the 3D aperture problem the stripes spin with the 3D object, yet the moving stripes cause viewers to perceive the same illusory motion. Because visual psychology studies have often asserted that human vision perceives 2D spaces much quicker than 3D spaces, the present study conducted an experiment to investigate the differences, or similarities, between induced motion perceptions in the 2D and 3D aperture problems.

## 3  Methodology

Based on the principles of visual psychology, this study developed an experiment to evaluate induced motion perceptions in the 2D and 3D aperture problems. The experiment consisted of three tasks: (1) task one: motion perception induced using a rectangular aperture and cylindrical helix; (2) task two: motion perceptions induced using an isosceles triangular aperture and conical helix; and (3) task three: motion perceptions induced using a circular aperture and spherical helix. Generally, the experiment observed the relationship between the induced motion perception and velocity threshold by varying the movement velocity in the 2D aperture problem and the rotation velocity in the 3D aperture problem.

### 3.1  Psychophysical Method-Velocity Thresholds

Psychophysical methods were used to measure the velocity thresholds to determine the relationship between stimuli and the sensory system [9]. Once the effect of a stimulus has gradually strengthened to a value that provokes a reaction from the subject, this value is defined as the sensory threshold of the specific stimulation. The minimum value that has to be reached or exceeded to provoke a reaction is the "lower absolute threshold." After exceeding the lower absolute threshold, the stimulation is further intensified to the extent that the subject can no longer detect it: this is deemed the "upper absolute threshold." The range between the lower and upper absolute thresholds is defined as the "velocity threshold." Studies on motion perception have discovered that the smaller the lower absolute threshold, the quicker the illusion occurs, and the greater the upper absolute threshold, the longer the reaction time for illusory motion, and hence the sharper the illusion. The aim of the present experiment was to discern the relationship between the stimulus, which was the rotating velocity, and the sensory reaction, which was the intensity of the motion perception.

### 3.2  Conversion of Rotation Velocity to Translational Velocity

In the present experiment, the 3D aperture problem was investigated by having participants observe a rotating object, whereas the 2D aperture problem was conducted by having participants observe the translation of an image. Therefore, a means of converting rotation velocity to translational velocity had to be devised so that they could be compared.

In the experiment, rotation velocity was measured in revolutions per minute (rpm); hence, rpm/60 would represent revolutions per second, and multiplying rpm/60 by the circumference of the cylinder in the 3D aperture problem would result in the translation per second. For this reason, rotation velocity was converted into translational velocity using the following equation:

$$rpm/60 \times (diameter \times \pi) \tag{1}$$

### 3.3 Participants

The present experiment used non-probability sampling for the recruitment of participants. A total of 30 participants were eventually selected, of whom 15 were male and 15 were female, all between 20 to 30 years of age. Regarding their visual acuity, all of the participants had normal or corrected (glasses or contact lenses) vision.

### 3.4 Experiment Environment, Apparatus and Samples

The experiment was conducted in a laboratory illuminated using 750 lx ceiling fluorescent lamps that do not cause glare or reflections. The participants were seated 1 m from samples.

(1) Digital variable frequency control system: 220 V motor, 0–1300 rpm.
(2) Disc holder: A disc 35 cm in diameter and made of a lightweight aluminum alloy was used to hold a sample in place.
(3) Computer monitor: ACER V243HL LCD monitor (2012, 1920 × 1080 pixels, 60 Hz).

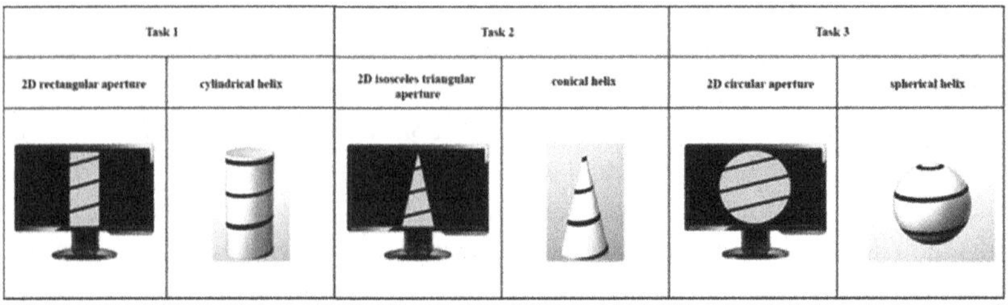

| Task 1 | | Task 2 | | Task 3 | |
|---|---|---|---|---|---|
| 2D rectangular aperture | cylindrical helix | 2D isosceles triangular aperture | conical helix | 2D circular aperture | spherical helix |

**Fig. 1.** Samples used in the experiment

For each of the tasks, the samples consisted of a 2D animation displayed on the monitor and a corresponding physical 3D object (Fig. 1). The areas and volumes of the samples were all determined using geometry. At the observation distance of 1 m, the 3D objects appeared to be 25 cm in height and 11 cm in width; accordingly, the 2D apertures were constructed with length 25 cm. In the 2D animations, the stripes moved at different velocities. Following Chen [9], who investigated the optimal stripe design on a cylindrical helix for generating illusory motion, the stripes in the present experiment were set to be continuous and parallel straight bands 10 mm in width and at a 15° angle to horizontal. The 3D objects were created using 3D printing on models built with SolidWork 2015 to prevent the instrumentation effect of handcrafting [10]. The 2D samples were designed using 3ds Max and Adobe Premiere.

### 3.5  Design of Experiment

The experiment was divided into three tasks, and to prevent the participants experiencing visual fatigue, there was an interval between each session to allow the participants a break. The samples served as the independent variable in the experiment, and each task was performed separately. For each task, the participants were required to watch the animation of the 2D sample and the 3D sample, the spinning of which was powered by a motor. The lower absolute threshold and upper absolute threshold thus measured were the dependent variables in the experiment. Through the upper and lower absolute thresholds, this experiment investigated the relationship between the velocity of the 2D/3D samples and the induced motion perception, as well as the intensity of the induced motion perception. The results of the three tasks were analyzed separately, and then jointly, to determine the influence of different aperture shapes.

## 4  Analysis

### 4.1  Induced Motion Perceptions Caused by the 2D Rectangular Aperture and 3D Cylindrical Helix

The average value of the lower absolute threshold (3.93 rpm) of the 2D rectangular aperture was dramatically smaller than that of the 3D cylindrical helix (62.57 rpm), which indicates that the 2D rectangular aperture induced a motion illusion much more quickly. Additionally, it reveals that with the 2D rectangular aperture, induced motion perception occurred at a very low rotation velocity, which means that the participants were more susceptible to induced motion perception under such circumstances.

The average upper absolute threshold of the 3D cylindrical helix (271.28 rpm) was greater than that of the 2D rectangular aperture (217.20 rpm), suggesting that the motion perception induced by the 3D cylindrical helix lasted longer than that induced by the 2D rectangular aperture. However, because the velocity threshold of the 2D rectangular aperture (213.70 rpm) was greater than that of the 3D cylindrical helix (208.71 rpm), the 2D rectangular aperture was generally more effective at inducing illusory motion than the 3D cylindrical helix, with the illusion also lasting longer.

These results indicated that after reaching a certain rotation velocity, both the 2D rectangular aperture and 3D cylindrical helix could induce illusory motion, which was movement toward the direction with more terminal points. However, the velocity of the illusory motions induced by the 2D rectangular aperture and 3D cylindrical helix varied greatly because of the differences between participants. The perception of a 3D form is not as straightforward as that of a 2D form because it relies on the binocular disparity between an observer's two eyes to create a sense of depth. This explains why different types of visual display directly and indirectly influenced the perceptions of the participants.

### 4.2   Induced Motion Perceptions Caused by the 2D Isosceles Triangular Aperture and 3D Conical Helix

The average value of the lower absolute threshold of the 2D isosceles triangular aperture (3.7 rpm) was much smaller than that of the 3D conical helix (55.63 rpm), which indicates that the 2D isosceles triangular aperture induced an illusory motion much more quickly. It also reveals that with the 2D isosceles triangular aperture, induced motion perception occurred at a very low rotation velocity.

The average upper absolute threshold of the 3D conical helix (244.2 rpm) was greater than that of the 2D isosceles triangular aperture (215.367 rpm), suggesting that the motion perception induced by the 3D conical helix lasted longer than that induced by the 2D isosceles triangular aperture. However, because the velocity threshold of the 2D isosceles triangular aperture (211.669 rpm) was greater than that of the 3D conical helix (188.57 rpm), generally the 2D isosceles triangular aperture had a wider range for the inducing illusory motion than the 3D conical helix, and the illusion also lasted longer. Thus, after reaching a certain rotation velocity, both the 2D isosceles triangular aperture and 3D conical helix induced illusory motion. However, the velocity of the illusory motions induced by the 2D isosceles triangular aperture and 3D conical helix varied greatly for the reason addressed in Sect. 4.1.

### 4.3   Induced Motion Perceptions Caused by the 2D Circular Aperture and 3D Spherical Helix

The average value of the lower absolute threshold of the 2D circular aperture (3.6 rpm) was much smaller than that of the 3D spherical helix (75.63 rpm), which indicates that the 2D circular aperture induced illusory motion much more quickly.

The upper absolute threshold of the 3D spherical helix (185.33 rpm) was particularly close to that of the 2D circular aperture (184.33 rpm). However, the velocity threshold of the 2D circular aperture (180.73 rpm) was greater than that of the 3D spherical helix (109.7 rpm). This suggests that compared with the 3D spherical helix, the 2D circular aperture was more effective at inducing motion perception and this perception persisted over a wider range of velocities.

After reaching a certain rotation velocity, both the 2D circular aperture and 3D spherical helix induced illusory motion, although the velocity of the illusory motions induced by the 2D circular aperture and 3D spherical helix varied for the same reason mentioned previously.

# 5  Discussion

## 5.1  Difference Between the 2D- and 3D-Induced Motion Perceptions

From the results of the three tasks, the lower absolute thresholds of the 2D apertures were found to be relatively low. Thus, the 2D apertures generally induced motion perception at a low velocity. The 3D objects had greater upper absolute thresholds than the 2D apertures, indicating that the motion perceptions induced by these objects lasted longer; however, the 2D apertures had greater velocity thresholds than the 3D objects, which indicated that although the motion perceptions induced by the 2D apertures ended earlier, they also occurred earlier and hence occurred over a wider velocity range, resulting in a greater effectiveness at inducing illusory motion for a longer duration overall. This corroborates other studies that investigated visual perception, which have concluded that the 2D x-y space is easier to visualize than the 3D x-y-z space and hence quicker to perceive. The 3D x-y-z space requires the human brain to perform extra processing to account for the binocular disparity of an observer's two eyes located at different positions to create a sense of depth. Thus, 3D spatial perception can be concluded to require more time to sense induced motion. The findings presented herein also verify that the different visual displays used to present 2D and 3D objects can influence the occurrence of induced motion perceptions and the effects of illusory motions.

## 5.2  Difference in Stripe Patterns

The experiment results suggest that, as indicated from the influence of 2D and 3D displays, the pattern of the stripes on an object (width number of stripes, etc.) can also influence induced motion perception. For the 2D apertures, because the stripes were parallel and equally spaced, four such stripes were selected for observation through different shapes of aperture. The rectangular aperture was formed by lines that were either parallel or perpendicular to each other; hence, the induced motion was a steadily vertical motion heading downward or upward. The isosceles triangular aperture had a tapered shape along its vertical axis; hence, the four stripes appeared to be shrinking as they moved toward the top, or they appeared to be expanding as they moved toward the bottom. Moreover, the edges of the aperture also created the illusion that the stripes were shrinking because they were acquiring more depth. For the circular aperture, widest in the middle, the induced motion made the stripes appear to be expanding and then shrinking.

For the 3D objects, the aspect ratios of the stripes were determined according to the shapes of the objects; a stripe width of 10 mm and angle of 15° to the horizontal were employed. The cylindrical helix, with a constant radius along the vertical axis, had four stripes on it, each the same length and distance. When it was rotated by the motor, the stripes induced the illusory motion that they were moving upward or downward at a steady speed. For the conical helix, which tapered toward the top along its vertical axis, the stripes appeared to become shorter as they moved upward, and their spacing also gradually shortened. There were a total of seven stripes, and as the object was rotated by the motor, the stripes induced the illusion that their movement toward the top was accelerating, which was caused by the shortening stripe length and interval that made the stripes on the upper half of the cone denser than those on the lower half. On the spherical helix, there were only two stripes and the spacing between them was relatively greater than for the other objects. When this shape was rotated by the motor, the stripes induced the illusion that their movement was accelerating toward the top or bottom.

After analyzing the characteristics of the samples, the 2D apertures were found to have equally spaced stripes, which is why they induced stronger motion perceptions, with the stripes moving upwards in a more pronounced manner than those on the 3D objects. As for the 3D objects, Lin (2017) studied the motion perceptions induced by varying helix forms and found that stripe characteristics influence perception of movement velocity. The stripes on the cylindrical helix were equally spaced, unlike those on the conical helix and spherical helix, which induced weaker motion perceptions than the cylindrical helix. Therefore, shape can be concluded to be a factor that strongly influences induced motion perception, and stripes moving at a constant velocity are particularly effective in this regard.

**Acknowledgement.** This study was financially supported by the Research Grant MOST 103–2410-H-224–030 & MOST 104–2410-H-224–027- from Taiwan's Ministry of Science and Technology.

# References

1. Chen, C.H., Wu, W.H., Huang, K.C.: A study of lenticular printing used in military technology practices stereo photography. J. CAGST **2014**, 28–58 (2014)
2. Fisher, N., Zanker, J.M.: The directional tuning of the barber-pole illusion. Perception **30**, 1321–1336 (2001)
3. Wallach, H.: Uber visuell wahrgenommene Bewegungsrichtung. Psychol. Forsch. **20**(1), 325–380 (1935)
4. Marr, D., Ullman, S.: Directional selectivity and its use in early visual processing. Proc. Roy. Soc. London B Biolog. Sci. **211**(1183), 151–180 (1981)
5. Adelson, E.H., Movshon, J.A.: Phenomenal coherence of moving visual patterns. Nature **300**(5892), 523–525 (1982)
6. Lorenceau, J., Shiffrar, M.: The influence of terminators on motion integration across space. Vision. Res. **32**(2), 263–273 (1992)
7. Vallortigara, G., Bressan, P.: Occlusion and the perception of coherent motion. Vision. Res. **31**(11), 1967–1978 (1991)
8. Chen, G.D., Lin, C.W., Fan, H.: Motion perception on column of rotational dynamic illusion in kinetic art. J. Des. **20**(3), 1–19 (2015)
9. Chen, G.D.: The Study of Kinetic Art Dynamic Optical Illusion on Column with Spiral Pattern. National Taiwan Univ. of Science and Technology, Taipei (2008)
10. Guan, S.S.: Design Research Methods. Chuan Hwa Book Co. Ltd, New Taipei (2010)

# A Pilot Study on Navigation for Information Acquisition Using Eye Tracking

Fumiya Inoue[1][(✉)] and Makio Ishihara[2]

[1] Graduate School of Fukuoka Institute of Technology, Fukuoka, Japan
`mfm21102@bene.fit.ac.jp`
[2] Fukuoka Institute of Technology, Fukuoka, Japan
`m-ishihara@fit.ac.jp`

**Abstract.** With the increasing number of opportunities to search for the desired content from a large amount of information, it is required to improve the efficiency of information search. Therefore, we propose a support method for information search using eye movement. In information search, the gaze moves quickly during the search, and the gaze stops when it is judged whether the content is the desired content or something close to it. From this, it was thought that by coloring the stopped part in real time, it would be possible to read back quickly, and it would be easier for the gaze to go to similar contents. A pilot experiment was conducted on four subjects and it was found that the total distance of eye movements and elapsed time to complete information search were shorter and more efficient.

**Keywords:** Eye movements · Information acquisition · Reading comprehension

## 1 Introduction

In recent years, with the spread of information terminals such as smartphones and tablets, there are increasing opportunities to search for the desired content from a large amount of information. Along with this, efficient information search is required. In addition, research on the theme of readability of sentences is also being conducted [1]. However, there are not many systems that support information search in real time. Therefore, in this research, we propose a system that supports information search in real time by using eye-gaze tracking technology. During users search for a desired piece of information, the quick movement of back and forth of gazing happens iteratively for them to organize information of sentences and determine whether the content is the desired one or close to it. Our basic idea to support information search is to help users to organize information of sentences by making the part where gazing stops, conspicuous such as coloring, so that reading back and forth is encouraged to happen smoothly and users could find the desired information quickly.

© Springer Nature Switzerland AG 2021
C. Stephanidis et al. (Eds.): HCII 2021, CCIS 1499, pp. 535–538, 2021.
https://doi.org/10.1007/978-3-030-90179-0_68

## 2    Our Basic Idea for Navigation

Eye movements in reading consist of two types: fixation and saccade. A fixation is a state in which the eye is kept at a point for a certain period of time, and a saccade is a state in which the eye is moving from one point to another at high speed. As regards reading, fixation happens to capture a line of characters and saccade does to move the eyes next. It is known that reading comprehension is performed while repeating fixation and saccade [2]. In this research, we suppose that a period of duration when the user determine whether the content is the desired one or close to it, becomes long if it is. In our proposed method, the part where fixation is kept within a radius of 30 pixels for a time span of 300ms is colored to make it conspicuous so that users could move easily between those candidates for the desired content, resulting in quick access to it.

## 3    Experiment

An experiment was conducted to confirm the effect of the proposed method. The gaze data was acquired using the screen-based eye tracker Tobii Pro Spectrum (Tobii). The size of the display is 23.8 inches and the resolution is 1920 × 1080. Figure 1 shows a scene of the experiment, and Fig. 2 shows a screenshot of the actual colored text obtained from a subject. In the experiment, there were four subjects and they were asked to perform a finding task of the main point of the given document. Six different documents which consist of about 600 characters in Japanese were prepared. Three of them were used for coloring condition and the remaining three for no-coloring condition (control condition). Note that the result depends on the difficulty of documents and coloring parts are different between subjects.

**Fig. 1.** A scene of the experiment

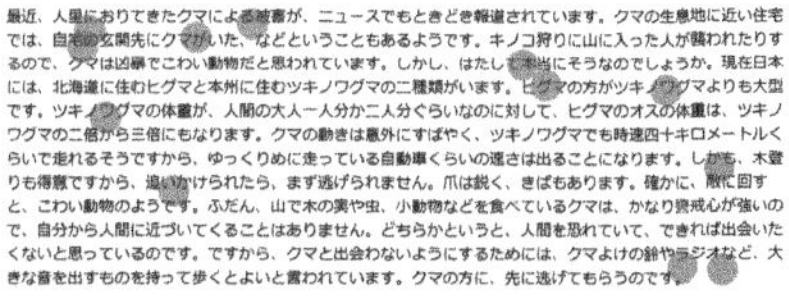

最近、人里におりてきたクマによる被害害が、ニュースでもときどき報道されています。クマの生息地に近い住宅
では、自宅周辺な関先にクマが近いた、などということもあるようです。キノコ狩りに山に入った人が襲われたりす
るので、クマは近隣でこわい動物だと思われています。しかし、はたして本当にそうなのでしょうか。現在日本
には、北海道に住むヒグマと本州に住むツキノワグマの二種類がいます。ヒグマの方がツキノワグマよりも大型
です、ツキノワグマの体重が、人間の大人一人分か二人分ぐらいなのに対して、ヒグマのオスの体重は、ツキノ
ワグマの二倍から三倍にもなります。クマの動きは意外にすばやく、ツキノワグマでも時速四十キロメートルく
らいで走れるそうですから、ゆっくりめに走っている自動車くらいの速さは出ることになります。しかも、木登
りも得意ですから、逃げ切けられたら、まず逃げられません。爪は鋭く、きばもあります。権力に、猛に回す
と、こわい動物のようです、ふだん、山での実や虫、小動物などを食べているクマは、かなり警戒心が強いの
で、自分から人間に近づいてくることはありません。どちらかというと、人間を恐れていて、できれば出会いた
くないと思っているのです。ですから、クマと出会わないようにするためには、クマよけの鈴やラジオなど、大
きな音を出すものを持って歩くとよいと言われています。クマの方に、先に逃げてもらうのです。

**Fig. 2.** A screenshot of one of documents used in the experiment

## 4    Results

The results obtained from the experiment are shown in Fig. 3 and 4. Figure 3 shows the total distance of eye movements in pixels, and Fig. 4 shows the elapsed time to complete the task in milliseconds. First, it can be seen that the total distance of eye movements for coloring is smaller than the one for no coloring. This would indicate that subjects could move the eyes easily between candidates for the main point. Next, the elapsed time for coloring is shorter than the one for no coloring, and it would indicate that reading comprehension is performed efficiently.

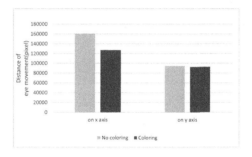

**Fig. 3.** Result of eye movements

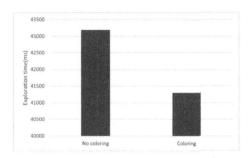

**Fig. 4.** Result of the elapsed time

## 5   Conclusion

For reading comprehension, this study shows that coloring documents shorten both the total distance of eye movements and the elapsed time to find out the main point of the documents, and it is a possible course of action to support reading comprehension. Our future tasks include increasing the number of subjects and evaluating the effect of the proposed method more accurately and qualitatively.

## References

1. Rayner, K., Fischer, M.H., Pollatsek, A.: Unspaced text interferes with both word identification and eye movement control. Vis. Res. **38**, 1129–1144 (1998)
2. Rayner, K., Pollatsek, A.: The psychology of reading, Lawrence Erlbaum associates. Open J. Modern Linguist. **4**(4) (1989)

# A Comparison of Multiple Selections Using Multiple Checkbox Selections and List Boxes

Wasana Leithe[1]([⊠]) and Frode Eika Sandnes[1,2]

[1] Kristiania University College, 0107 Oslo, Norway
frodes@oslomet.no
[2] Oslo Metropolitan University, 0167 Oslo, Norway

**Abstract.** Website forms are commonly used for collecting information from users. Users choose one or more alternatives from a list. However, data input can be time-consuming. We therefore set out to explore which multiple selection method is the fastest and perceived most positively; the ones relying on multiple checkboxes or list boxes. An experiment with 24 participants was conducted involving 20 multiple selection tasks. The result shows that the mean response time to select three options in each question of multiple checkboxes was faster and more positively perceived than multiple list boxes. The results thus suggest that web developers should use multiple checkboxes instead of multiple list boxes.

**Keywords:** Multiple checkbox · Multiple list Box · Interactive form

## 1 Introduction

Many companies and governmental institutions rely on interactive online web forms as the main contact point with its customers and users. Such forms should therefore be carefully designed, as they may impact whether an online transaction succeeds or fails. Users usually visit a website with an intention, which relates to the content of that site, for example, purchasing a product, gathering information, etc. [1].

Most web forms rely on standard html elements such as text fields, radio buttons, dropdown lists, links, and checkboxes [2]. Web form design has been studied extensively within HCI, for example label placement in forms, layout optimization on web forms, the content of the web forms, types of input methods such as form controls, form submission methods, and ways of handling errors in forms [3]. Moreover, html forms comprise as a structured collection of variables which can be conveniently tied to database storage, data retrieval and data display [4].

A checkbox (check box, tick box) is a GUI widget that permits the user to make a binary choice such as a choice between one of two possible mutually exclusive options. For example, the user may have to answer 'yes' (checked) or 'no' (unchecked) on a simple yes/no question [5]. It can make a checkbox in the dropdown list that can pull down or hide options.

A list box is a graphical control element that allows the user to select one or more options from a list contained within a static, multiple-line text box. The user clicks to

C. Stephanidis et al. (Eds.): HCII 2021, CCIS 1499, pp. 539–544, 2021.
https://doi.org/10.1007/978-3-030-90179-0_69

select an option inside the box. When mouse clicks are made in combination with Shift or Ctrl to make multiple selections (or unselect) [6].

Both multiple checkbox selections in the dropdown and multiple list box selections can be used in web form. This study set out to explore the differences between the two in terms of task completion time and perceived preference.

## 2  Related Work

Web forms are the primary medium for user input on the web and are used for a variety of reasons, including registration, e-commerce sales, and security purposes. Sometimes, the process of completing these web forms can be complex [7]. A free-form query mechanism has been proposed where vocabulary is restricted to the keywords commonly used in the grid domain with a tailored matching algorithm [8].

Sometimes web forms have reduced user experience and are inefficient due to page refresh each time the form is submitted. Form validations on both the client-side and server-side may be triggered unnecessarily. It is therefore recommended that web forms should employ more responsive designs using interactive technology such as Ajax [9].

Studies of historical data have revealed how users have made use of regular expressions over time on various websites. Although regular expressions are increasingly being used, their use is highly repetitive; on the most popular websites, only 4% of the regular expressions were unique [10]. Form auto-complete mechanisms can be achieved by exploring the relationship between user inputs. Auto complete may help reduce the prevalence of repeatedly entering the same information by reusing the user's previous inputs [11].

Dropdown menus, which are often used on web page to select items, can also be problematic. Designers use dropdown menus to make better use of web page real-estate. Dropdown menus only allow the available options to be selected, and users are unable to input their own alternatives as with text fields [12].

## 3  Method

A within-groups experiment was designed comprising one independent variable and three dependent variables. The independent variable input type had two levels, namely multiple checkbox selections in the dropdown and multiple list box selections. The time to select the answers, success rate, and subjective preference scores were dependent variables. A total of 24 participants volunteered to complete the experiments. As the study was conducted during the COVID-19 pandemic the participants were acquired through convenience sampling. Experiments were conducted remotely.

Dropdown multiple checkbox selections (see Fig. 1) and multiple list box selections (see Fig. 2) were implemented using HTML5, CSS3, jQuery, and data were collected using a MySQL database. Response time measurements were implemented using JavaScript. The tasks comprised making three selections. For example, if shown pink, gray, red means participants selected pink, gray, and red to get 1 point correct, 0 points otherwise. The tasks had to be completed without breaks. It took several minutes to complete the 20 tasks, comprising 10 multiple checkbox tasks and 10 multiple list box tasks. Moreover, each task had 12 options. Participants were instructed to use either a notebook or a desktop computer. Smartphones and tablet were not allowed to keep the independent variable constant, as touch interaction is quite different to keyboard and mouse interaction. Participation was anonymous as the experiment was conducted in a single session [13].

**Fig. 1.** Dropdown multiple checkbox selection

The dropdown menu had 12 options (see Fig. 1). One point is gained if only "Pink, Gray, Red" are selected. The users click on "Next" to go to the next task. All options were selected when clicking "Select All", and unselected if "Select All" was clicked again. It defaulted to hide options. However, they were shown when the arrow was clicked.

The multiple list box selection had 12 options (see Fig. 2). Options were moved from left to the right list box when the user selected one or more items and clicked on the right double arrow. Ctrl + click was used to select multiple options. Moreover, a double click on a option would move it to the opposite list box. The "Next" buttons were used for moving to the next task.

**Fig. 2.** Multiple list box selection. Selected items appear on the right.

The last question asked participants to voice their subjective preference by responding to "Is it better to use multiple checkbox selections in the dropdown than multiple list box selections?". Participants responded using a 5-point Likert scale (strongly agree, agree, neither agree nor disagree, disagree, and strongly disagree).

**Table 1.** Mean and standard deviation (SD) of the multiple checkbox and multiple list box

|  | Multiple checkbox | Multiple list box |
|---|---|---|
| Mean response time (s) | 9.7 | 10. 7 |
| Std. Deviation response time (s) | 2.5 | 2.2 |
| Success rate (%) | 98% | 96% |

## 4 Result

Descriptive statistics show that multiple checkboxes yielded both shorter response time and higher success rate than multiple list boxes (see Table 1). A t-test reveals that the response time differences were statistically significant ($t(23) = 2.811$, $p = .01$). A Shapiro-Wilks test confirmed that the observation distribution did not deviate from normality.

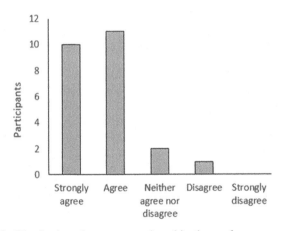

**Fig. 3.** Distribution of responses to the subjective preference question.

The responses to the question about whether multiple checkbox selections in the dropdown is preferable over multiple list boxes revealed a clear agreement with a preference for multiple checkbox selection ($M = 4.25$). None of the participants strongly disagreed and only one participant disagreed, while only 2 participants responded neutrally.

## 5 Discussion

There were differences in response time between the two input types. The hypothesis that multiple checkboxes are more effective than multiple list boxes was supported. Most of the participants managed to select the correct options. They had to click four times with the multiple checkboxes using the dropdown menu; first one clicks to show the dropdown, then three clicks are needed to select the three options.

The participants had varying backgrounds in terms of age, gender, and occupation. Most of the participants did not know, or find out, that it was possible to double click in multiple list boxes. Several participants clicked to select the option, one by one, and then clicked on the triangular arrow (resulting in six clicks to make three selections as opposed to three double clicks). Obviously, the six clicks took longer than four clicks. If they had known about the possibility of double clicking, their response times might have been comparable to, or shorter than, what was observed with multiple checkboxes.

Several participants did not read the instruction and chose their preferred options instead of the instructed answer. One participant thought the task was to click as many times as possible without making selections. Some had never used multiple list boxes before, and they did not understand how it should be used. We did not record the extent to which the controls were correctly used. In some instances, participants only clicked on an option without moving it to the right (only the first step of the two-step process).

## 6  Conclusion

This study explored the differences between drop down menus and list boxes for making multiple selections. An experiment with the 24 participants was conducted to assess differences between the two input mechanisms in terms of task completion time and subjective preference. The results showed that the multiple checkbox approach led to a significantly shorter response time. This input mechanism was also preferred by the participants. The results also show that established conventions such as holding the control button while clicking is not universally known and used by all computer users.

## References

1. Bargas-Avila, J.A., Brenzikofer, O., Roth, S.P., Tuch, A.N., Orsini, S., Opwis, K.: Simple but crucial user interfaces in the World Wide Web: introducing 20 guidelines for usable web form design (2010)
2. Hammoudi, M., Rothermel, G., Tonella, P.: Why do record/replay tests of web applications break?. In: 2016 IEEE International Conference on Software Testing, Verification and Validation (ICST), pp. 180-190. IEEE, USA (2016).
3. Al-Saleh, M., Al-Wabil, A., Al-Attas, E., Al-Abdulkarim, A., Chaurasia, M., Alfaifi, R.: Inline immediate feedback in arabic web forms: an eye tracking study of transactional tasks. In: 2012 International Conference on Innovations in Information Technology (IIT), pp. 333–338. IEEE, United Arab Emirates (2012)
4. Saissi, Y., Zellou, A., Idri, A.: Extraction of relational schema from deep web sources: a form driven approach. In: 2014 Second World Conference on Complex Systems (WCCS), pp. 178–182. IEEE, Morocco (2014)
5. Wikipedia. https://en.wikipedia.org/wiki/Checkbox. Accessed 10 May 2021
6. Wikipedia. https://en.wikipedia.org/wiki/List_box. Accessed 10 May 2021
7. Thompson, S., Torabi, T.: A process improvement approach to improve web form design and usability. In: 18th International Workshop on Database and Expert Systems Applications (DEXA 2007), pp. 570–574. IEEE, Germany (2007)

8. Gupta, C., Govindaraju, M.:. Semantic framework for free-form search of grid resources. In: 2008 IEEE Fourth International Conference on eScience, pp. 454–455. IEEE, Canada (2008)
9. Ying, M., Miller, J.: Refactoring traditional forms into ajax-enabled forms. In: 2011 18th Working Conference on Reverse Engineering, pp. 367–371. IEEE, Ireland (2011)
10. Hodován, R., Herczeg, Z., Kiss, Á.: Regular expressions on the web. In: 2010 12th IEEE International Symposium on Web Systems Evolution (WSE), pp. 29–32. IEEE, Romania (2010)
11. Wang, S., Zou, Y., Upadhyaya, B., Ng, J.: An intelligent framework for auto-filling web forms from different web applications. In: 2013 IEEE Ninth World Congress on Services, pp. 175–179. IEEE, USA (2013)
12. Xiong, Y.: The design of automatically generating drop-down menu on JSP. In: 2012 International Conference on Computer Science and Information Processing (CSIP), pp. 1404–1406. IEEE, China (2012)
13. Sandnes, F.E.: HIDE: short IDs for robust and anonymous linking of users across multiple sessions in small HCI experiments. In: CHI 2021 Conference on Human Factors in Computing Systems Extended Abstracts Proceedings. ACM (2021). https://doi.org/10.1145/3411763.345 1794

# The Influence of Team Workload Demands During a Cyber Defense Exercise on Team Performance

Ricardo G. Lugo[1,2(✉)], Torvald F. Ask[1,2], Stefan Sütterlin[2,3], and Benjamin J. Knox[1,2]

[1] Norwegian University of Science and Technology, Gjøvik, Norway
Ricardo.g.Lugo@ntnu.no
[2] Østfold University College, Halden, Norway
[3] Albstadt-Sigmaringen University, Sigmaringen, Germany

**Abstract.** Cyber defense is dependent on individual functioning as well as teamwork. Research has identified teamwork factors, such as communication and coordination, that increase performance, while more supporting behaviours, i.e. emotional and team support, have shown to inhibit team performance but currently the understanding of impact workloads have on performance is still limited. This study investigated the role of team workload demands on team performance.
**Methods:** Data was collected during the Norwegian Defense Cyber Academy's annual Cyber Defense Exercise. We investigated how team workload demands influenced performance outcomes (Team Effectiveness and Team Dissatisfaction).
**Results:** Teamwork demands, i.e. communication, coordination, and team performance monitoring could predict Team Effectiveness, while Task-team workload demands, i.e. team support, team emotion, and time-share demands could predict Team Dissatisfaction.
**Discussion:** Results support the hypotheses that teamwork demands could predict team effectiveness while task-team demands could predict more negative aspects of team performance and the results are in line with previous research.

Future research in cyber security operations should incorporate team workload demands to assess performance.

**Keywords:** Team workload demands · Team performance · Cyber security

## 1 Introduction

Research has shown that cyber defense is dependent on individual functioning as well as teamwork [1, 2]. Research has identified teamwork factors, such as communication and coordination, that increase performance [1, 3], while more team supporting behaviours, i.e. emotional and team support, have shown to inhibit team performance [3, 4] but currently the understanding of impact workloads have on performance is still limited [4].

Within the military domain, cyber defense operators rely on teamwork since cyber operations are integrated at every level of the military, from soldier assistance on the battlefield to network defense at higher command levels. Multiple operators work in teams

© Springer Nature Switzerland AG 2021
C. Stephanidis et al. (Eds.): HCII 2021, CCIS 1499, pp. 545–549, 2021.
https://doi.org/10.1007/978-3-030-90179-0_70

inside a conventionally hierarchical military structure that reacts to military leadership in their surroundings.

Several characteristics of team functioning have been found as having an impact on performance in studies. Operators must have an understanding and awareness of a) the network, which includes technical aspects and the behaviour of the network; b) the world – how the physical world is affected or may be affected by events in the world including emergent threats and abnormal activities and behaviours; and finally c) the team, where awareness of work (completed, in-progress tasks), processes (demands, needs), and being able to communicate with other inter-agencies to maintain focus [5]. Research has shown that improving team processes that focus on more teamwork aspects (i.e. communication, coordination) increases team functioning and performance, more task-team support behaviours (i.e. team emotional support) leads to more inefficient functioning [6]. But recent findings have shown that the more expertise there is among team members, the less actual communication and coordination behaviours might be shown due to more overlapping and shared situational awareness and mental models between team members, therefore no need for explicit communication [7, 8].

## 1.1 Aims

Based on previous research, we argue that more teamwork behaviours focusing on communication, coordination and performance monitoring will lead to better team effectiveness, while team supporting behaviours focusing on more emotional, time and support processes will cause more dissatisfaction in a team.

## 2 Methods

### 2.1 Participants and Procedure

Data was collected during the Norwegian Defense Cyber Academy's (NDCA) annual Cyber Defense Exercise (CDX). This arena facilitates the opportunity for students to train in tactics, techniques, and procedures for handling various types of cyberattacks. The exercise contributes to improving appreciation for the human and technical competences necessary to establish, manage and defend a military digital information infrastructure under simulated operational conditions. The exercise lasted five days. At the end of the day the participants were asked to assess team workload and performance. A total of 13 cadets participated in the research.

### 2.2 Measurements

The Team Workload Questionnaire (TWLQ) was used to assess the workload demand in team tasks. Items are scored on an 11-point Likert scale (very low – very high) with high scores indicating higher levels of subjective workload. Average scores for team workload performance were computed on the subscales of the two dimensions, the Teamwork component (communication, coordination, team performance monitoring) and Task-Team component (time-share, team emotion, team support). The TWLQ has shown good reliability on all subscales (Cronbach's a > .70) [80] and also for this research (Teamwork Cronbach's a = .847; Task-team Cronbach's a = .624). The TWLQ subscales were used as predictor variables in analyses.

For performance outcomes, two self-reported items were created, Team Effectiveness and Team Dissatisfaction, on a single items 10-point Likert scale (none-very). These two items were then used as dependent variables.

## 2.3  Ethical Considerations

The study conformed to institutional guidelines and was eligible for automatic approval by the Norwegian Social Science Data Services' (NSD) ethical guidelines for experimental studies. Participants gave their informed consent verbally prior to the study and were informed that they could withdraw from participation at any time and without any consequences.

## 2.4  Data Analysis

Statistical analysis was done with JASP version .14.1 [9]. All variables were centered and standardized for analysis. Alpha levels for hypothesis testing were set at the 0.05 level. Multiple linear regressions where each of the TWLQ subscales (Teamwork component; Task-team component) were entered as predictor variables and Team Effectiveness and Team Dissatisfaction were entered as dependent variables.

## 3  Results

Descriptives and correlation for all variables are given in Table 1.

**Table 1.**  Descriptives and correlations ($N = 13$)

|  | M | SD | 1 | 2 | 3 | 4 | 5 | 6 | 7 | 8 |
|---|---|---|---|---|---|---|---|---|---|---|
| Communication | 5.60 | .70 | – | | | | | | | |
| Coordination | 5.16 | .92 | .675** | – | | | | | | |
| TPM | 4.04 | 1.06 | −.114 | .218 | – | | | | | |
| TSD | 4.12 | 1.26 | .187 | .346 | .067 | – | | | | |
| Team emotion | 2.91 | 1.08 | −.320 | .066 | .193 | .177 | – | | | |

*(continued)*

To test the hypothesis that teamwork components will influence team effectiveness, a multiple linear regression was computed.

Teamwork component demands (communication ($\beta = .608$), coordination ($\beta = .224$), team performance monitoring ($\beta = -.149$)) of the TWLQ could predict Team Effectiveness ($R^2 = .632$, $F = 5.16$, $p = .024$).

**Table 1.** (*continued*)

| Team support | 3.86 | 1.24 | −.144 | -.264 | −.050 | .604* | .128 | – | | |
| Team effectiveness | 6.50 | .70 | .776 | .602** | −.170 | .139 | −.098 | −.305 | – | |
| Team dissatisfaction | 2.63 | .67 | −.510* | −.223 | .230 | .158 | .886*** | .322 | −.393 | – |

TWLQ: Team Workload Questionnaire; TPM: Team Performance Monitoring; TSD: Time Share Demands

* p < .05 1-tailed, ** p < .05, *** p < .01

To test the hypothesis that Task-team components will influence team dissatisfaction, a multiple linear regression was computed.

Task-team workload demands (team support ($\beta$ = .328), team emotion ($\beta$ = .878), time-share demands ($\beta$ = −.196)) of the TWLQ could predict Team Dissatisfaction ($R^2$ = .853, $F$ = 17.36, $p$ < .001).

## 4  Discussion

This study investigated the influence of team workload demands on team performance and the results support the hypotheses. Teamwork demands could predict team effectiveness while Task-team demands could predict more negative aspects of team performance and the results are in line with previous research [3, 4, 7].

### 4.1  Limitations

While the study had robust findings, this study only had thirteen participants, too few for any generalizations. The participants also come from the same school and previous research has shown that the officer cadets are similar on many cognitive aspects [3, 10], therefore little variance may occur. Also, the dependent variables were constructed for this exercise and not validated. The results show that one variable in each of the TWLQ subscales could explain most of the variance in team effectiveness (coordination: r = .602) and team dissatisfaction (team emotion: r = .886).

## 5  Conclusion

This research has shown that the TWLQ can assess team effectiveness and dissatisfaction. Future research in cyber security operations should incorporate team workload demands to assess performance by incorporating both micro- and macrocognitive approaches as well as identifying objective outcome variables for performance measurement.

**Funding.**  This study was conducted as part of the Advancing Cyber Defense by Improved Communication of Recognized Cyber Threat Situations (ACDICOM; #302941) project. ACDICOM is funded by the Norwegian Research Council.

# References

1. Champion, M.A., et al. : Team-based cyber defense analysis. In: 2012 IEEE International Multi-Disciplinary Conference on Cognitive Methods in Situation Awareness and Decision Support. IEEE (2012)
2. Granåsen, M., Andersson, D.: Measuring team effectiveness in cyber-defense exercises: a cross-disciplinary case study. Cogn. Technol. Work **18**(1), 121–143 (2015). https://doi.org/10.1007/s10111-015-0350-2
3. Lugo, R.G., Sütterlin, S.: Cyber officer profiles and performance factors. In: Harris, D. (ed.) EPCE 2018. LNCS (LNAI), vol. 10906, pp. 181–190. Springer, Cham (2018). https://doi.org/10.1007/978-3-319-91122-9_16
4. Deline, S., Guillet, L., Rauffet, P., Guérin, C.: Team cognition in a cyber defense context: focus on social support behaviors. Cogn. Technol. Work **23**(1), 51–63 (2019). https://doi.org/10.1007/s10111-019-00614-y
5. Gutzwiller, R.S., Hunt, S.M., Lange, D.S.: A task analysis toward characterizing cyber-cognitive situation awareness (CCSA) in cyber defense analysts. In: 2016 IEEE International Multi-Disciplinary Conference on Cognitive Methods in Situation Awareness and Decision Support (CogSIMA). IEEE (2016)
6. Sellers, J., et al.: Development of the team workload questionnaire (TWLQ). In: Proceedings of the human factors and ergonomics society annual meeting. 2014. SAGE Publications Sage CA: Los Angeles, CA (2014)
7. Buchler, N., et al.: Cyber teaming and role specialization in a cyber security defense competition. Front. Psychol. **9**, 2133 (2018)
8. Buchler, N., et al.: Sociometrics and observational assessment of teaming and leadership in a cyber security defense competition. Comput. Secur. **73**, 114–136 (2018)
9. Goss-Sampson, M.: Statistical analysis in JASP: A guide for students. JASP (2019)
10. Lugo, R.G., et al.: Interoceptive sensitivity as a proxy for emotional intensity and its relationship with perseverative cognition. Psychol. Res. Behav. Manag. **11**, 1 (2018)

# Estimation of Consumer Needs Using Review Data in Hotel Industry

Shin Miyake[1], Kohei Otake[2], Tomofumi Uetake[3], and Takashi Namatame[1(✉)]

[1] Graduate School of Science and Engineering, Chuo University, 1-13-27, Bunkyo-ku, Kasuga, 112-8551, Tokyo, Japan
a15.66cc@g.chuo-u.ac.jp, nama@indsys.chuo-u.ac.jp
[2] Faculty of Science and Engineering, Tokai University, 2-3-23, Minato-ku, Takanawa, 108-8619, Tokyo, Japan
otake@tsc.u-tokai.ac.jp
[3] School of Business Administration, Senshu University, 2-1-1, Tama-ku, Higashimita,Kawasaki 214-8580, Kanagawa, Japan
uetake@isc.senshu-u.ac.jp

**Abstract.** Recently, utilization of word-of-mouth data in business represents an important issue for all companies, and it is necessary to consider a marketing approach using mathematical technology. This study focused on the hotel industry in Japan and attempted to clarify the relationship between services provided by companies and consumer needs for each service in the hotel industry. Concretely, using review data that posted on reservation sites by customers who had previously used the hotel, we obtained the emotional evaluation of consumers for each service by natural language processing. Moreover, using the emotional evaluation of each service and rating score, we constructed the model for each hotel type based on the Random Forest and compared the differences between the important services of the customers. From these results, it became clear that the evaluation criteria differ depending on the needs and the factors that are important for each hotel to improve the service.

**Keywords:** Hotel industry · Review data · Random forest

## 1 Introduction

With the digitalization of product sales channels, consumers who utilize services can reserve, use, and evaluate them through platforms such as websites.

Especially from the consumer voices, from which it is possible to obtain word-of-mouth data, companies can grasp the actual evaluation by customers. The utilization of word-of-mouth data in business represents an important issue for all companies, and it is necessary to consider a marketing approach using mathematical technology [1].

C. Stephanidis et al. (Eds.): HCII 2021, CCIS 1499, pp. 550–557, 2021.
https://doi.org/10.1007/978-3-030-90179-0_71

## 2  Purpose of This Study

The study focused on the hotel industry in Japan and attempted to clarify the relationship between services provided by companies and consumer needs for each service in the hotel industry. Currently, various bookings are done via the Internet; however, these sites do not have only bookings but also display the reviews of actual users [2]. Word-of-mouth information is known to have a significant impact on the booking behavior of other customers. Specifically, we divided the 623 hotels into two groups according to the services provided (i.e., for resorts or for business), and by using 150,622 review texts and evaluation points, we clarified the difference in the relationship between customer needs for services and evaluations.

## 3  Data and Analysis Method

In this study, we analyzed the relationship between service providers and customer needs using hotel reviews (word-of-mouth) and rating scores. These reviews and rating scores were posted on reservation sites by customers who had previously used the hotel (Table 1). We targeted data submitted from January 1, 2016, to January 1, 2020.

**Table 1.** Data description

| Data type | Data details |
| --- | --- |
| Master data in the hotels (total of 623) | A total of 623 hotels offering services at reservation sites.<br>For business: 178 hotels, For resort: 210 hotels<br>· Average evaluation score in the hotels |
| Review data (total of 150,622) | Data about customer who posted the reviews.<br>· Review texts<br>· Evaluation score in the hotels |

Table 2 shows the actual sentences in part of this category. Here, we show the actual text in Japanese and its English translation.

First, we extracted 1000 reviews from all reviews by random sampling and divided them into sentences. Using these parts of sentences, we flagged them for each label of the services provided by the hotel as categories. In particular, we set 11 categories (interior design of room, structure of building, environment around the hotel, landscape, policy, hotel staff, toilets in room, access to hotels, lodging charges, and other guests).

Table 3 shows the number of sentences corresponding to each category.

From the results presented in Table 3, there are many sentences about meals, interior design of room, and hotel staff. On the other hand, there are few sentences on other guests. Using these results, we calculated the feature words for each category.

552 S. Miyake et al.

**Table 2.** Examples of sentences of category

| Category | Examples of review |
|---|---|
| Meals | 朝食時の長蛇の列が残念 (It's a pity that there was a long queue at breakfast.)<br>夕食のバイキングが豪華で良い (It was nice that the dinner buffet was gorgeous.)<br>朝食は品数も多く美味しかった (Breakfast was delicious and there are many items.) |
| Lodging charge | 宿泊代は高すぎると感じた (I felt that the accommodation fee was too expensive.)<br>価格に対し充実したホテル (Contrary to the price, it was a hotel with a lot of things of offer.)<br>部屋は古いが値段は適切 (I felt the room was old, but the price was reasonable.) |

**Table 3.** Number of ssentences in each category

| Category | Number of sentences |
|---|---|
| Meals | 1141 |
| Interior design of room | 1412 |
| Structure of building | 789 |
| Environment around the hotel | 478 |
| Landscape | 223 |
| Policy | 281 |
| Hotel staff | 1012 |
| Toiletries in room | 133 |
| Access to hotel | 410 |
| Lodging charge | 312 |
| Other guests | 62 |

### 3.1 Feature Extract by Natural Language Processing

Using sentences divided by category in the previous subsection, we created documents about service using each label and calculated the feature words in each document by the TF-IDF methods from Eqs. (1)–(3). In this study, we used Mecab, a Japanese morphological analysis engine [3]. Moreover, we focused on nouns whose meanings could be understood by themselves.

$$\text{TFIDF}_{i,j} = tf_{i,j} \times idf_i, \tag{1}$$

$$tf_{i,j} = \frac{n_{i,j}}{\sum_S n_{S,j}}, \tag{2}$$

$$idf_i = \log \frac{D}{\{d : d \in t_i\}},$$ (3)

Where

| | |
|---|---|
| $n_{ij}$ | the frequency of word $i$ in the sentence $j$, |
| $\Sigma_{S} n_{S,j}$ | the frequency of all words in the sentence $j$, |
| $|D|$ | the total number of all sentences, |
| $|\{d : d \in t_i\}|$ | the number of sentences containing word $i$ |

Table 4 shows the results for the characteristic noun words in each category. Here, the upper part of each category shows the original Japanese word, and the lower part shows the English translation.

**Table 4.** Characteristic noun words in each category

| Category | Characteristic noun words (categorical top 5 words) | | | | |
|---|---|---|---|---|---|
| Meals | 食 | 朝 | 朝食 | バイキング | 食事 |
| | Meal | Morning | Breakfast | Buffet | Meal |
| Interior design of room | 広い | お部屋 | 風呂 | 泊 | ベッド |
| | Large | Room | Bath | Stay days | Bed |
| Structure of building | 風呂 | 大 | ホテル | 浴場 | 温泉 |
| | Bath | Big | Hotel | Bathhouse | Hot spring |
| Environment around the hotel | 立地 | 駅 | コンビニ | 便利 | ホテル |
| | Location | Station | Store | Convenient | Hotel |
| Landscape | 眺め | 景色 | 夜景 | 窓 | 高 |
| | View | Landscape | Night view | Window | High |
| Policy | サービス | ホテル | チェック | イン | 朝 |
| | Service | Hotel | Check | In | Morning |
| Hotel staff | 対応 | スタッフ | フロント | ホテル | 親切 |
| | Correspondence | Staff | Front | Hotel | Kindness |
| Toiletries in room | アメニティ | 充実 | アメニティー | 歯ブラシ | 設備 |
| | Amenity | Enrichment | Amenity | Toothbrush | Equipment |
| Access to hotel | 駅 | 便 | 便利 | ホテル | 立地 |
| | Station | Flight | Convenient | Hotel | Location |
| lodging charge | 泊 | 高 | 段 | 料 | ホテル |
| | Stay days | Height | Price | Price | Hotel |
| Other guests | マナー | 国 | 人 | 多い | アジア |
| | Manners | Country | People | Many | Asia |

In the meal category, there were not only words for meal such as "meal" and "buffet," but also, there were many words representing time zones such as "morning." In the interior design of room category, almost all words are related to the room, and in the structure of building category, many words were related to the facilities such as the "bath." In addition, although environment around the hotel category and access to hotel category are similar in that there are words about "location," there are also some words such as means of transportation in the access to hotel category. The results of other categories contain many words that describe each service provided by the hotel. In addition, we calculated the evaluation value for each category of each text by multiplying the TF-IDF values of characteristic noun words and the scores of the adjective emotion value in the polar phrase dictionary (Table 5) [4].

**Table 5.** Emotion value of word in polar phrase dictionary

| Word | | Part of speech | Emotion value | Box-Cox Transformation ($\lambda=-0.22$) |
|---|---|---|---|---|
| 優れる | (Excellent) | Verb | 1 | 17.45354 |
| 良い | (Good) | Adjective | 0.999995 | 17.453405 |
| よろこぶ | (Be delighted) | Verb | 0.999979 | 17.452973 |
| ... | | ... | ... | ... |
| 死ぬ | (Die) | Verb | −0.999999 | −2.546459 |
| 悪い | (Wrong) | Adjective | −1 | −2.54646 |

Using the results pertaining to characteristic words and emotion values, we calculated the evaluation value for the service corresponding to the category in each review. We obtained the score by multiplying the TF-IDF value and the emotion value when there is a relationship between the target words in each category, using the dependency relationship between the feature and emotion words in each review.

In particular, to calculate the score for each category of each review, when multiple words from the same category are included in the review, we use the sum of the results of multiplying the TF-IDF value and the polarity value. From this result, we obtained the emotional evaluation of consumers for each service by each review.

Next, using the evaluation of each service, we clarify how the evaluation of each service affects the entire facility evaluation.

### 3.2 Classification by Random Forest

Using the evaluation of the category of each text, we constructed a model based on the Random Forest [5] to determine whether the rating score for each review is higher or lower than the average rating of each company. Table 6 presents the outline of the discriminant model.

**Table 6.** Objective and explanatory variables used in the discriminant model

| Objective variable | Whether the evaluation score of each review is high compared to the average evaluation of the target hotel |
|---|---|
| Explanatory variable | Scores of each category based on the content of the review |

Here, the number of reviews for resort hotels was 55,382, and the number of reviews for business hotels was 95,240. Table 7 shows the outline of each review depending on the purpose of use. The data in each model were divided into model learning (70%) and evaluation data (30%).

**Table 7.** Outline of each review depending on how to use

| For business model (95,240 data) | Learning data 66,668 data {0: 54%, 1: 46%} <br> Evaluation data 28,572 data {0: 53%, 1: 47%} |
|---|---|
| For resorts model (55,382 data) | Learning data 38,766 data {0: 41%, 1: 59%} <br> Evaluation data 16,616 data {0: 41%, 1: 58%} |

The data to be handled were treated as model training data and model evaluation data.

Furthermore, when training each model, the imbalance of learning data adjusted using the SMOTE method which is an oversampling technique [6].

## 4   Results

The accuracy results of the model learned in each data are presented in Table 8.

**Table 8.** Confusion-Matrix of each model (using evaluation data)

| For Business Model Results | | | | For Resorts Model Results | | | |
|---|---|---|---|---|---|---|---|
| | Predicted Negative | Predicted Positive | | | Predicted Negative | Predicted Positive | |
| Actual Negative | 10331 | 4812 | 15143 | Actual Negative | 4841 | 2031 | 6872 |
| Actual Positive | 4298 | 9131 | 13429 | Actual Positive | 2854 | 6890 | 9744 |
| Accuracy | 0.681 | | | | 0.706 | | |

From the results of Table 8, it can be seen that both models can make predictions with an accuracy of approximately 70%. Both models use data with the number of labels adjusted by the SMOTE method; however when evaluating the model, each model discriminates in unbalanced data.

In addition, Figs. 1 and 2 show the feature variables that are important for discrimination in each model.

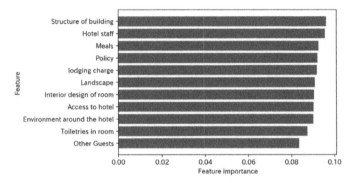

**Fig. 1.** Results of variable importance of random forest in resorts reviews

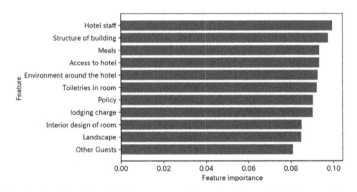

**Fig. 2.** Results of variable importance of random forest in business reviews

From Fig. 1, which shows the results for resorts reviews, it can be seen that customers are highly interested in the quality of each service in the order of building structure, hotel staff, and meals. In addition, it was found that policy, lodging charge, landscape, and interior design of room were assuming the fourth place or lower considering importance.

Furthermore, from Fig. 2, which shows the results for business reviews, it can be seen that customers are highly interested in the quality of each service in the order of hotel staff, structure of building, and meals. The upper level of the variable is similar to the resort results, but services related to staff were more important. Furthermore, it becomes clear that access to hotels, the environment around the hotel, toilets in the room, and policy are important assuming the fourth place or lower.

# 5  Discussion

From the results of the above two models, it can be seen that the customer evaluates the facility based on different needs. In particular, for business use other than tourism, it can be predicted that access and environment around the hotel will be important. From the results of feature importance, it can be seen that access to hotels and the environment around the hotel are more important when evaluating than the results of resort. In contrast, the results showed that policy, lodging change, landscape, and interior design of rooms are important when evaluating the hotel next to the top three features. Compared to the results of business, resort hotel tends to provide unique services, and in fact, some of the characteristic words of landscape category include the unique services such as "view" and "night view," and "enrichment" and "amenity" were included in the characteristic words of interior design of room.

From the results of words about unique services in resort hotels, it can be inferred that the facility service itself is the subject to be evaluated by customer. However, based on the results of business hotels, it can be inferred that points such as convenience for business purposes lead to evaluation in customers.

# 6  Conclusion

In this study, we used the data of hotels as companies that provide services to customers and clarify what kinds of needs exist in customers by words in reviews. In addition, we compared the differences between the important services of customers who gave higher evaluations than the average evaluation of each hotel. From these results, it became clear that the evaluation criteria differ depending on the needs and the factors that are important for each hotel to improve the service.

**Acknowledgement.** This work was supported by JSPS KAKENHI Grant Numbers 19K01945, 21H04600 and 21K13385.

# References

1. Manes, E., Tchetchik, A.: The role of electronic word of mouth in reducing information asymmetry: an empirical investigation of online hotel booking. J. Bus. Res. **85**, 185–196 (2018)
2. Nishikawa, T., Okada, M., Hashimoto, K.: Verification of text preprocessing method in automatic classification of review sentences. In: Proceedings of the 18th Annual meeting of the Association for Natural Language Processing, pp. 246–251 (2012). (in Japanese)
3. MeCab: Yet Another Part-of-Speech and Morphological Analyzer
4. http://taku910.github.io/mecab/. Accessed 25 March 2021
5. Japanese Sentiment Polarity Dictionary (Noun)
6. https://www.nlp.ecei.tohoku.ac.jp/research/open-resources/. Accessed 25 March 2021
7. Breiman, L.: Random forests. Mach. Learn. **45**(1), 5–32 (2001)
8. Fernandez, A., Garcia, S., Herrera, F., Chawla, N.V.: SMOTE: synthetic minority over-sampling technique. J. Artif. Intell. Res. **16**, 321–357 (2002)

# Influence of the Contact Surface Size on the Illusory Movement Induced by Tendon Vibrations

Hiroyuki Ohshima[(⊠)] [iD] and Shigenobu Shimada

Tokyo Metropolitan Industrial Technology Research Institute (TIRI), Sumida-ku, Tokyo 130-0015, Japan
ohshima.hiroyuki@iri-tokyo.jp

**Abstract.** In human limbs, tendon vibration evokes the feeling of illusory movement, which is a kinesthetic sensation experienced in the absence of any actual joint movement. This phenomenon can be effectively used to generate kinesthetic sensation in virtual-reality settings, which can solve a variety of problems. However, its implementation remains limited due to the hitherto-unclear relationship between stimulus and perceptual characteristics. This study is aimed at examining the effects of the size of contact surfaces on the illusory kinesthetics evoked by tendon vibration. Tendons of the biceps brachii in the dominant-side arm of five participants were stimulated for 30 s at 100 Hz and 120 m/s$^2$ by a vibration device. Contact heads of different sizes ($\varphi$5, $\varphi$10, $\varphi$15, and $\varphi$20 mm) were tested on subjects. The shoulder was held stationary on an armrest at a flexion of 90° while the elbow was flexed at 0°—both in the midsagittal plane, with palms facing upwards. After the experiment, participants were asked to take two subjective evaluations based on the visual analog scale, pertaining to the vividness (1: weak, 5: clear) and range of extension of their elbow-joint angle (1: slight, 5: significant). During the illusory motion, both these parameters increased with the size of the contact surface. Thus, we concluded the perceptual characteristics of the illusory movement to be affected by the size of the contact surface.

**Keywords:** Kinesthetic sensation · Sensorimotor system · 3D printing

## 1 Introduction

Inducing vibrations on the tendons in human limbs evokes the illusion of motion, which is kinesthetic sensation experienced without any actual movement of the joint [1]. The underlying mechanism here is that the application of approximately 100 Hz of a vibratory stimulus to a tendon excites the Group Ia [2, 3] and Group II [4] afferent nerve fibers present in skeletal muscle spindles; this leads to them communicating with the central nervous system that the muscle is stretched [5]. This appears to induce a nerve signal corresponding to the perception of joint movement. Prior to our previous work [6, 7], the influence of joint angles on motion illusion was not reported. Since gravitational torque depends on the joint angle, it could influence perceptual parameters such as the

© Springer Nature Switzerland AG 2021
C. Stephanidis et al. (Eds.): HCII 2021, CCIS 1499, pp. 558–563, 2021.
https://doi.org/10.1007/978-3-030-90179-0_72

strength of motion illusion. We compared motion illusion for two different angles of the elbow joint by a subjective assessment of three aspects—strength of illusion, range and velocity of extension [6]—and a quantitative assessment of two other aspects: latency and duration [7]. Results showed the three subjective aspects to be affected by limb position, while the two quantitative aspects were unaffected by joint angle.

**Fig. 1.** Vibration device fixing base and armrest.

Conversely, it is known that the area of contact affects vibrotactile thresholds and is a more important stimulus parameter than the gradient or curvature of displacement [8]— this is called spatial summation. Based on this, we propose the following hypothesis: the size of the contact surface area influences perceptual parameters such as the strength of motion illusion evoked by the vibration of tendons. Our previous studies had used an accelerometer externally attached to the contact-head to record tendon vibrations. This setup, however, makes it difficult to change the size of contact area, which is necessary to test our hypothesis. Hence, we modified the set-up of this study from the design of our previous studies by developing a more convenient method in which an accelerometer was mounted inside a 3D-printed contact head [9], with which we test the hypothesis postulated above.

## 2   Materials and Methods

### 2.1   Participants

Two males (aged 29 and 37 years) and three females (aged 43, 43, and 47 years) volunteered as participants in this study. All of them provided prior written informed consent according to institutional requirements. The experi-mental procedure was approved by the ethics committee of the Tokyo Metropolitan Industrial Technology Research Institute.

### 2.2   Apparatus and Experimental Setup

A palm-sized vibration device (WaveMaker-Mobile, Asahi Seisakusho, Japan) was fastened to a pre-existing fixing base (Fig. 1) [10]. The participant sat in front of the fixing base wearing a protective eye mask and earmuffs (Fig. 2, left). Their arm was positioned on the horizontal armrest, so that their shoulder and elbow were held still at flexions of 90° and 0°, respectively, in the midsagittal plane, with palms facing upwards. The vibrator was positioned over the biceps brachii tendon, just above the elbow.

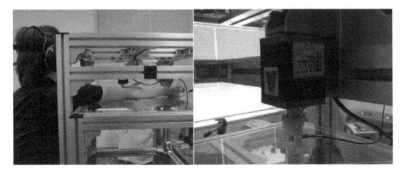

**Fig. 2.** Experimental setup. Left: arm position. Right: vibration device, contact head and accelerometer.

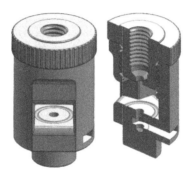

**Fig. 3.** 3D model of the contact head.

The contact head was designed with a hole in its center for fastening a single-axis accelerometer (710-D, EMIC, Japan). Figure 2, right, shows the setup of the vibration device, contact head, and accelerometer. The upper end of the contact head was bolted onto the vibrator (Fig. 3); this contact head was printed with a commercial 3D printer (Objet500 Connex3, Stratasys, USA). Contact heads of different sizes (φ5, φ10, φ15, and φ20 mm) were tested in this experiment (Fig. 4). First, the φ10 mm contact head, whose size was close to that of the biceps brachii tendon, was used, followed by a contact head with the smallest diameter at which no pain was felt—determined to be φ5 mm. The remaining two contact heads, with diameters of φ15 and φ20 mm, were then used in succession. The accelerometer was connected to a PC (VJ27M/C-M, NEC, Japan) through a vibration meter (UV-16, Rion, Japan) and a multifunction I/O Device (USB-6000, National Instruments, USA). LabVIEW 2014 (National Instruments, USA) was used to record the output of the accelerometer.

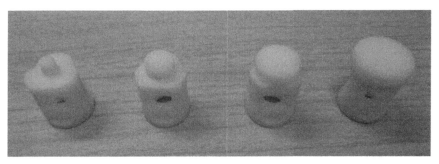

**Fig. 4.** Contact heads with different radii used in the experiment (from left to right: φ5, φ10, φ15, and φ20 mm).

## 2.3  Procedure

Before the experiment, participants were informed that they would experience a sensation of their elbow joint extending, without any actual movement of said joint. In a preliminary experiment, we determined the appropriate amplitude of vibration and anatomical location to consistently elicit the target kinesthetic sensation. The location on the participant's forearm where the stimulus was presented to them was marked on their skin with a felt-tipped marker. The right arm, which was the dominant arm for all five participants, was used.

The biceps brachii tendon of the right arm of all participants was stimulated for 30 s at 100 Hz and 120 m/s$^2$. The accelerations measured by the internal accelerometer were recorded at 1000 Hz and the RMS value of each acceleration was calculated using the following equation:

$$\text{RMS} = \sqrt{\frac{1}{n}\sum\nolimits_{i=1}^{n}(x_i)^2} \tag{1}$$

where $x_i$ is an acceleration sample and $n$ is the total number of samples.

The stimuli were presented in the order of φ10, φ5, φ15, and φ20 mm. After the experiment, participants were asked to take two subjective evaluations based on a five-point visual analog scale, pertaining to the vividness (1: weak, 5: clear) and range of their perceived extension of their elbow-joint angle (1: slight, 5: significant).

## 3  Results

All five participants described consistent sensations of motion. Table 1 shows the vividness and range of extension of the elbow-joint angle as perceived by each of the five participants. In all participants, both parameters increased with the size of the contact surface.

**Table 1.** Subjective evaluation of vividness and range of extension of the elbow-joint angle during tendon vibration for each participant.

| Participant | Vividness | | | | Range of extension of elbow | | | |
|---|---|---|---|---|---|---|---|---|
| | φ10 | φ5 | φ15 | φ20 | φ10 | φ5 | φ15 | φ20 |
| #1 | 3 | 2 | 4 | 5 | 3 | 2 | 4 | 5 |
| #2 | 3 | 3 | 4 | 5 | 3 | 3 | 4 | 5 |
| #3 | 3 | 1 | 4 | 5 | 3 | 1 | 4 | 5 |
| #4 | 3 | 2 | 4 | 5 | 3 | 2 | 4 | 5 |
| #5 | 3 | 2 | 4 | 5 | 2 | 2 | 4 | 5 |

## 4 Discussion and Conclusion

The purpose of this study was to examine the effects of the size of contact surfaces on the illusory kinesthetics evoked by tendon vibrations. Due to the effect of spatial summation, we hypothesized that the size of the contact surface influenced perceptual parameters such as the strength of illusory motion. To verify our hypothesis, contact heads of different sizes (φ5, φ10, φ15, and φ20 mm) were tested on five subjects. After the experiment, participants were asked to take two subjective evaluations based on a five-point visual analog scale, pertaining to the vividness and range of extension of the elbow-joint angle. Results demonstrated that both parameters increased with the area of the contact surface during the illusory motion. Thus, we concluded that the perceptual characteristics of illusory movement are affected by the size of the contact surface.

Existing VR systems require the user to actually move their body, which poses various issues ranging from safety concerns arising from falls and collisions and economic problems that require wide spaces and large-scale equipment, to accessibility issues for users with physical disabilities. The realization of a VR system that does not require the user to actually move their body can make VR safer, more economical, and more accessible. On the other hand, by modulating the proprioceptive sensation—which is related to the posture and movement of the body (primarily the limbs)—it is possible to generate the illusion of motion even in the absence of any actual movement. This phenomenon is called kinesthesia. Kinesthesia is as important as the visual and auditory senses for safety, comfort, and entertainment quality in immersive VR environments. However, since the mechanisms of kinesthesia are not known in as much detail as are those of the audiovisual senses, the presentation methods of kinesthesia, too, have not kept up with those of the visual and auditory senses.

In our previous study, we focused on the joint angle in motion illusion [6, 7], while this study demonstrates the effect of contact-surface area on illusory motion. In our future work, we plan to examine the combined effects of contact-surface area and joint angle in motion illusion. A systematic amalgamation of knowledge on the relationship between vibratory stimulus and motion illusion can enable us to control kinesthesia and perhaps simulate the experience of an Olympian or a Paralympian.

In addition, it can also be a breakthrough to solve the essential problem in motor learning—the transmission of first-person motor sensation—and break away from the conventional trial-and-error method of learning. This is an important step towards establishing a novel motor-learning method based on the first-person motion illusion.

**Acknowledgements.** This work was supported by JSPS KAKENHI Grant Numbers JP19K20105.

# References

1. Goodwin, G.M., McCloskey, D.I., Matthews, P.B.: Proprioceptive illusions induced by muscle vibration: contribution by muscle spindles to perception? Science **175**(4028), 1382–1384 (1972)
2. Burke, D., Hagbarth, K.E., Lofstedt, L., Wallin, B.G.: The responses of human muscle spindle endings to vibration of non-contracting muscles. J. Physiol. **261**(3), 673–693 (1976)
3. Matthews, P.B.: Where does Sherrington's "muscular sense" originate? Muscles, joints, corollary discharges? Annu. Rev. Neurosci. **5**, 189–218 (1982)
4. Bove, M., Nardone, A., Schieppati, M.: Effects of leg muscle tendon vibration on group Ia and group II reflex responses to stance perturbation in humans. J. Physiol. **550**(Pt 2), 617–630 (2003)
5. Vallbo, A.B., Hagbarth, K.E., Torebjörk, H.E., Wallin, B.G.: Somatosensory, proprioceptive, and sympathetic activity in human peripheral nerves. Physiol. Rev. **59**(4), 919–957 (1979)
6. Ohshima, H., Shimada, S.: Does the limb position influence the motion illusion evoked by tendon vibration? In: IEEE Engineering in Medicine and Biology Society, 40th Annual International Conference, Honolulu, ThPoS-22.6 (2018)
7. Ohshima, H., Shimada, S.: The effects of the angle of an elbow joint on the latency and duration when tendon vibration evoke the motion illusion. In: IEEE Engineering in Medicine and Biology Society, 41st Annual International Conference, Berlin, WePOS-34.27 (2019)
8. Verrillo, R.T.: Effect of contactor area on the vibrotactile threshold. J. Acoust. Soc. Am. **35**(12), 1962–1966 (1963)
9. Ohshima, H., Ishido, H., Iwata, Y., Shimada, S.: Development of a quantification method for tendon vibration inducing motion illusion. In: Stephanidis, C., Antona, M. (eds.) HCII 2020. CCIS, vol. 1225, pp. 212–216. Springer, Cham (2020). https://doi.org/10.1007/978-3-030-50729-9_30
10. Ohshima, H., Shimada, S.: Development of a system to quantify the depth of tendon stimulus for the illusion of motion achieved by a vibrator. In: IUPESM World Congress on Medical Physics and Biomedical Engineering, Prague, T10–06 (2018)

# Training and Learning for Long Duration Spaceflight

Terry Rector[1]([⊠]), Curtis Cripe[2]([⊠]), and James Casler[1]

[1] University of North Dakota, Grand Forks, ND, USA
{terry.rector,james.casler}@und.edu
[2] NTL Group, Scottsdale, AZ, USA
ctcripe@att.net

**Abstract.** Living and working in outer space introduces unique physiological, psychological, and psychosocial stressors to the human body. While most stressors are known and well researched, Long Duration Spaceflight creates additional and more worrisome stressors. This paper describes preparation and research plans for a 30-month repeated-measures, cognitive decay, and memory recall study utilizing ten practical space mission tasks performed by 32 astronaut-like subjects in an Isolation, Confined and Extreme (ICE) analogous environment.

**Keywords:** Long Duration Spaceflight (LDSF) · Training · Isolation · Confined and Extreme (ICE) · Analogous environment · Human factors · Human-Machine Interface (HMI)

## 1 Introduction

As NASA plans for deep space and long-duration missions, it has identified a gap in understanding how the personal relations/interactions (family, friends, and colleagues) affect astronauts' behavioral health and performance during missions, including negative behaviors, and in understanding how such behavior may affect other crewmembers. As discussed, there are other stresses to be considered such as space adaptation syndrome (SAS), micro-zero gravity, ionizing radiation exposure, mission time and location, orientation clues and knowledge, noise types and levels, temperatures, workload and schedule, boredom, cultural differences, and types and length of physical fitness activities [1].

As of the time writing this paper, fewer than 600 humans have traveled to space, with fewer than ten remaining in orbit for more than 300 days. Future spaceflight will entail long-duration missions constrained by technical challenges now being methodically investigated. One of the largest concerns is mitigating any effects from high energy radiation, fluid shift due to microgravity, and any damage either may engender in cognitive decay or memory recall [2].

This paper introduces the preparation and research plans for a 30-month repeated-measures, cognitive decay, and memory recall study utilizing ten practical space mission tasks performed by 32 astronaut-like subjects in an Isolation, Confined and Extreme (ICE) analogous environment. The genesis for this research is the expectation that

© Springer Nature Switzerland AG 2021
C. Stephanidis et al. (Eds.): HCII 2021, CCIS 1499, pp. 564–571, 2021.
https://doi.org/10.1007/978-3-030-90179-0_73

Long-Duration Spaceflight (LDSF) crews must operate autonomously requiring real-time access to an estimated double to triple current knowledge content [3]. This increased demand for knowledge creates critical learning and forgetting dilemmas for spaceflight crew members already densely cross-trained in two or more disciplines. With adequate pre- and during-mission training systems, many of the other LDSF stressors can be mitigated. However, detecting changes in the "forgetting curve" and identifying when training is most needed to ensure continued fitness for duty is pivotal for sustained and safe spaceflight [4].

Living and working in outer space introduces unique physiological, psychological, and psychosocial stressors to the human body. While most stressors are known and well researched, LDSF crews will travel well beyond Earth's protective lower orbits, which will create additional and more worrisome stressors. More research is needed into how these stressors can be adequately mitigated. Currently, the best solution is to train, practice, and test for all possible outcomes, recognizing the need for responding to the unknown-unknown possibilities [5].

LDSF alters the structure and function of the human brain. Many spaceflight stressors, including altered gravity, sleep loss, radiation, and isolation and confinement, may dysregulate the brain's structure and microenvironment, leading to an imbalance in the neuronal and glial networks' function and the neurovascular unit [6].

## 2 Background

Training for human spaceflight operations is demanding, costly, and time-consuming, starting with the space agency's use of omnifarious facilities, mock-ups, simulators, and emulators. Before today's lengthy stays aboard the International Space Station (ISS), spaceflight missions remained short enough that the natural forgetting process was not a safety concern. However, NASA's goal of landing humans on Mars by 2030 necessitates two to three times current trained content to prepare astronauts for such missions, increasing the risk of inadequate or latent training potentially inadequate decision making due to delayed or un retrievable memories [7, 8].

The critical component motivating the need for a change in training is anticipated communications latency due to the increased distance between the spacecraft and Earth and the increased speed with which communication signals must travel. Since communications can only travel as fast as the speed of light (approximately 300,000 km or 186,000 mi per second), once the spacecraft proceeds beyond our Moon's orbit (238,900 mi), duplex communications will quickly drop to simplex, increasing to over 40 min (worst case) round-trip from Mars [9, 10].

The communications delay is expected to double or triple the knowledge content needed for the crew to operate autonomously from NASA's Mission Control Center (MCC). The MCC has always monitored and managed the spacecraft and crew's activities but LDSF precludes these MCC functions. The MCC is staffed with decades of perishable experience and knowledge in many different disciplines, including lessons learned from past successes and failures as well as detailed spacecraft and support systems knowledge, some of which cannot be taught [11]. This latency will preclude readily available decision-making support from the MCC. LDSF crews will be the first in space exploration history to operate fully autonomously without MCC oversight [12].

Historically, the MCC has served a pivotal role in monitoring the spacecraft and crew health, anomaly detection, crew tasks scheduling, and decision support 24 h a day, seven days a week. The MCC's role must transfer to LDSF crews and their spacecraft to facilitate future LDSF missions. However, to enable future LDSF crews, most, if not all of the knowledge currently maintained at the MCC must transition to the crew [13, 14].

There is no adequate understanding of how the brain or body will react to being cooped up in a spacecraft with three to five other people traveling to and returning from Mars. Additionally, after arriving at Mars, the crew may spend most of their time together in one or more habitat modules no larger than a large bus or recreational vehicle with minimal opportunity for privacy other than inside a spacesuit exploring the inhospitable Martian landscape. The crews' survival and overall mission success will depend heavily on new technologies, training methods, and refresher training [14].

The commonly accepted and revaluated Ebbinghaus forgetting curve will provide a foundation for test subjects to establish a test baseline (establishing control group) before each mission [15–17]. Test subjects will receive pre-mission training on individual and crew tasks, both simple and complex (estimating ten complete tasks) identified by Stuster [8, 18]. Each subject will be trained using standardized methodologies and allowed to practice acceptable competencies corresponding to the task(s) complexities before testing, to establish a baseline for future comparisons.

As spacecraft crews prepare for LDSF, training must utilize methods and tools that encompass the full training continuum for an exploration mission scenario. Complementing pre-flight training with an adaptive, in-flight training regimen may offer several advantages, including reducing neurocognitive workload burden on the crew and optimizing training content to enhance brain function and provide meaningful work, particularly en route to Mars [19]. A training regimen must keep individual crew and team members motivated and engaged by maintaining brain areas and motor skills areas honed for readiness during post-landing mission requirements [20].

The human brain is a dense, dynamically reconfiguring connectome of multiple network-hub architectures, hosting five commonly accepted frequency bands of oscillating electronic signals [21–24]. As previously learned task performance (critical skills) will undoubtedly diminish over time due to natural forgetting, there is an expectation that adaptive on-board training systems integrated within the spacecraft's systems will be necessary. However, when during the spaceflight journey is the most optimum time for refresher training? How far in advance of a critical mission event such as landing on Mars should refresher training be taken so the crew's performance can be at its peak when most needed? These questions and others both guide and inform this research.

Although the ISS has several different types of on-board training systems, they operate independently ("stovepiped") instead of being collected on a central computer where the combined training effect can be monitored and measured. The stovepiped training systems require space (volume), weight, power, and connectivity independent from other competing on-board systems, using highly limited resources which produce additional noise and heat that must be mitigated. Additionally, each training system has a different human to machine interface (HMI) that requires requiring the trainee to respond differently, thus using additional time and mental resources. For increased effectiveness and efficiency, future training systems should be seamlessly integrated within the spaceflight crew's everyday activities and, where possible and appropriate, should provide some level of release and mental respite from operational activities, thus reducing boredom and monotony [3, 25].

## 3   Problem Statement

Future spaceflight exploration to Mars and beyond will expose human crews to prolonged microgravity, Galactic Cosmic Radiation, and many other stresses while living and working within an ICE environment. These factors are expected to negatively impact the body's central nervous system, cognition, memory, and behavior. This research goal is to enable new technologies needed to mitigate these effects.

Research is needed to comprehensively measure and model human cognitive decay and memory recall limitations in a spaceflight-realistic environment—the purpose of this research opportunity.

## 4   Research Questions

This research project seeks responses to the following questions:

- Q1. By employing an electroencephalogram (EEG) 32-Channel device to detect instances of increased brain activations (frequency and signal strength), can skill retention levels be determined with enough accuracy to maintain a predestined cognitive skill level?
- Q2. Given performance degradation concerns related to the broadly recognized "forgetting curve" model research, can an acceptable degree of degradation be measured to determine when training must be conducted to maintain acceptable proficiency?
- Q3. For a given set of mission tasks, can cognitive performance degradation be detected reliably at levels that permit timely application of refresher training protocols in advance of a future mission event?
- Q4. Can factor(s) or variables affecting (accelerating or decelerating) cognitive skill retention and loss rates be determined, prioritized, and mitigated?
- Q5. Can mission planning and execution be designed to accommodate individual training protocols to fine-tune mental or physical performance training a manner similar to athletic training?
- Q6. Can the cognitive decay rate be used to delineate requirements for on-orbit high fidelity training systems and simulator requirements?

## 5   Methods

This paper introduces a planned 30-month, repeated-measures, ad hoc research study of 32 subjects possessing similar education backgrounds, experiences, skill sets, etc., recruited from the UND's John D. Odegard School of Aerospace Sciences department. The 32 subjects will be evenly divided between an experiment and a control group and then further divided into four, four-person crews (teams), yielding eight teams of four persons. The experiment teams (four teams of four subjects) will live and work for 30 days in the Inflatable Lunar/Mars Analog Habitat (ILMAH) facility simulating LDSF rigors similar to those expected in future Mars exploration missions, including communications delays and no other in-person human contact. The control group (four teams of four subjects) will run concurrently with the isolated (treatment) group) while living everyday lives as UND graduate students and completing the same mission activities outside the habitat environment. The ILMAH serves as an analogous facility mimicking an ICE environment facility, located at the University of North Dakota, Grand Forks, North Dakota. The ILMAH was funded by NASA and is owned and operated by the UND Department of Space Studies Human Spaceflight Laboratory.

Test subjects will receive training in specific tasks, participate in practice sessions, and be tested before each mission starts. Cognitive tasks will have ten levels of difficulty and be designed to imitate spaceflight activities, An average of 320 measurements will be taken during each of the four missions. In addition to individual surveys, questionnaires, observation opportunities, and verbal feedback sessions during testing events, subjects will wear a high-resolution (24-bit) electroencephalogram (EEG) device to record electrical activity produced by the human brain at varying mission times and stress levels. The recorded electrical signals will be post-processed by Matlab®, EEGLab®, eLORETA, NeuroCoach™, and SCCN neuroscience tools to develop a real-time predictive cognitive performance/health profile. Neurophysiological metrics will be used to illustrate neural functional performance changes resulting from changing multiple environmental effects. These metrics will monitor the performance and communication changes from a healthy baseline within and between the brain regions of interest described above.

Researchers will manipulate environmental factors over varying lengths of retention intervals using an operationally realistic LDSF analog to produce each test subject's performance modeling. While many mature training models exist, they generally have not been utilized outside the clinical setting.

Task performance will be observed and measured using EEG recordings while monitoring subjects' knowledge level transitions within the Skill-Rule-Knowledge (SRK) systematic taxonomy [26, 27]. Rasmussen's SRK model will be used to characterize or detect various categories of human behavior, widely applied in many operational environments such as aviation and healthcare.

Objective measurement of task proficiency will focus on the time required for task completion and the number of errors. Test subjects and crews (teams) will also assess their own performance of each task. Individual cognition will be measured by situational awareness, decision-making, and an EEG 32-Channel device as indicated by the time taken to recognize and respond to the emergence of a task or problem and the number of steps (or time) required for a solution.

All EEG measurements will be corrected to individual pre-mission baseline readings seeking variations between individual brains that results in different responses to stimuli as measured by the instrumentation. All research data will undergo a complete statistical analysis, including calculating Pearson's correlation coefficient and subsequent significance testing, *t-tests*, *F-tests*, and repeated measures analysis of variance (ANOVA) over time with subject and control groups comparisons. Pre- and post-test event surveys relevant to the task will be conducted (referred to as the "ICE" or "Control" group) for later comparison and analysis with post-surveys conducted concurrently with de-briefing after the month is concluded [28].

## 6  Analysis Approach

After selection and signing of the consent agreement, all questionnaires and surveys will be administered privately and online using the University-supported QualtricsXM Research Core™ software system accessed by the crew member's Pi-Top-3 laptop computer. Qualtrics is a secure, robust, integrated software suite that interfaces nicely with all essential statistical tools for data reduction and analysis. Should a need arise for hardcopy documents to be added, they will be scanned after completion and stored electronically within the limited access system, then destroyed for privacy.

Research data will be analyzed for significance within the groups, testing differences between mean cognitive psychometric scores over time. This will allow any changes in psychometric responses to be modeled concerning time and predictability. The control group will be the sample of participants for which differences in mean scores can be compared between groups to ascertain whether ICE group participants experience cognitive deficiency due to isolation, confidence, or extreme stressors (as a treatment factor).

## 7  Research Benefits

This experiment is expected to provide high-level considerations for redesigning pre-flight and in-flight training regimens [29, 30]. This offers several advantages, such as reducing the neurocognitive workload burden on the crew and optimizing training content to enhance brain function and provide meaningful work, particularly en route to Mars. [5] A well-designed, planned, and executed training regimen is expected to keep crewmembers motivated and engaged by maintaining brain areas and motor skills areas honed for readiness during post-landing mission requirements [20, 31].

Additionally, discoveries from this research may contribute to defining onboard training systems specifications, given the projected limits in available spacecraft weight, volume, and power. This research will help identify content that should be trained before the spaceflight and content that can be delayed for in-flight training, to reduce potential cognitive overload [7, 33]. New training systems must adapt to the trainee's performance [29, 32].

The broad-reaching significance of these findings may lead to efficient and effective training methodology, systems, and programs to cover the entire mission duration. These findings are expected to impact training applications in other fields such as spaceflight mission control, military and commercial flight crews, surgeons, law enforcement personnel, and other professionals trained to deal with high-risk, complex, and uncertain tasks in highly stressful environments. The next step may be to conduct these same or similar experiments aboard the ISS for continued evaluations and refinement.

# References

1. Stanley, G., Love, R.P.H.: Crew Autonomy for Deep Space Exploration - Lessons from the Antarctic Search for Meteorites (2014)
2. Garrett-Bakelman, F.E., et al.: The NASA twins study: a multidimensional analysis of a year-long human spaceflight. Science, **364**(6436), eaau8650 (2019)
3. Pieters, M.A., Zaal, P.M.T.: Training for long-duration space missions: a literature review into skill retention and generalizability. IFAC PapersOnLine **52**(19), 247–252 (2019)
4. Fisher, J.S., Radvansky, G.A.: Patterns of forgetting. J. Mem. Lang. **102**, 130–141 (2018)
5. Dempsey, D.L., Barshi, I.K.P.: Evidence Report: Risk of Performance Errors Due to Training Deficiencies. Risk Statement: Given that existing training methods and paradigms may inadequately prepare long-duration, autonomous crews to execute their mission, there is a risk that increased flight and ground crew errors and inefficiencies, failed mission and program objectives, and increased crew injuries will occur (2016)
6. Roberts, D.R., et al.: Effects of spaceflight on astronaut brain structure as indicated on MRI. N. Engl. J. Med. **377**(18), 1746–1753 (2017)
7. Dempsey, D.L., Barshi, I.: Applying research-based training principles: towards crew-centered, mission-oriented space flight training. In: Training for a Mars Mission (2019)
8. Stuster, J.W., et al.: Human Exploration of Mars: Preliminary Lists of Crew Tasks (2019)
9. Moore, M., et al.: Simulation Based Investigation of High Latency Space Systems Operations (2017)
10. Rader, S.N., et al.: Human-in-the-loop operations over time delay: lessons learned. In: International Conference on Environmental Systems (ICES). NASA Center for AeroSpace Information (CASI), Vail (2013)
11. Bubeev, A., V.I.G.K.Y.M.S.V.S.G.V.: The Evolution of Methodological Approaches to the Psychological Analysis of the Crew Communications with Mission Control Center (2016)
12. Orgel, C., et al.: Scientific Results and Lessons Learned from an Integrated Crewed Mars Exploration Simulation at the Rio Tinto Mars analogue site (2014)
13. Gershman, B., et al.: Low-latency teleoperations for human exploration and evolvable mars campaign. In: IEEE Aerospace Conference Proceedings (2017)
14. Lupisella, M.L., Bobskill, M.R.: Human Mars Surface Science Operations (2014)
15. Cowan, N., Rachev, N.R.: Merging with the Path not Taken: Wilhelm Wundt's Work as a Precursor to the Embedded-Processes Approach to Memory, Attention, and Consciousness (2018)
16. Murre, J.M., Dros, J.: Replication and analysis of Ebbinghaus' forgetting curve. PLoS One **10**(7), e0120644 (2015)
17. Fuchs, A.H.: Ebbinghaus's Contributions to Psychology After 1885 (1997)
18. Stuster, J., et al.: Generalizable Skills and Knowledge for Exploration Missions - Final Report (2018)
19. Landon, L.B., et al.: Selecting astronauts for long-duration exploration missions: considerations for team performance and functioning. REACH – Rev. Hum. Space Explor. **5**, 33–56 (2017)
20. Fiore, S.M., et al.: Critical Team Cognitive Processes for Long-Duration Exploration Missions. Institute for Simulation and Training, NASA (2015)
21. Kaiser, M.: A tutorial in connectome analysis: topological and spatial features of brain networks. NeuroImage (Orlando, Fla.) **57**(3), 892–907 (2011)
22. Tompson, S.H., et al.: Functional brain network architecture supporting the learning of social networks in humans. NeuroImage (Orlando, Fla.) **210**, 116498 (2020)
23. Zhang, W., et al.: Dynamic reconfiguration of functional topology in human brain networks: from resting to task states. Neural Plast. **2020**, 1–13 (2020)

24. Stam, C.J., van Straaten, E.C.W.: The organization of physiological brain networks. Clin. Neurophysiol. **123**(6), 1067–1087 (2012)
25. Goldberg, J.H.: Training for Long Duration Space Missions (1986)
26. Rasmussen, J.: Skills, rules, and knowledge, signals, signs, and symbols, and other distinctions in human performance models. In: IEEE Transactions on Systems, Man, and Cybernetics, SMC-13, vol. 3, pp. 257–266 (1983)
27. Fleming, E., Pritchett, A.: SRK as a framework for the development of training for effective interaction with multi-level automation. Cogn. Technol. Work **18**(3), 511–528 (2016). https://doi.org/10.1007/s10111-016-0376-0
28. Baguley, T.: Calculating and graphing within-subject confidence intervals for ANOVA. Behav. Res. Methods **44**(1), 158–175 (2012)
29. Kelley, C.R.: What is adaptive training? Hum. Factors **11**(6), 547–556 (1969)
30. O'Keefe, W.: Training Concept for Long Duration Space Mission. NASA (2008)
31. Cuevas, H.M., Schmorrow, D.D.: Exploring Cognitive Readiness in Complex Operational Environments: Advances in Theory and Practice (2012)
32. Gallego-Durán, F.J., Molina-Carmona, R., Llorens-Largo, F.: Measuring the difficulty of activities for adaptive learning. Univ. Access Inf. Soc. **17**(2), 335–348 (2017). https://doi.org/10.1007/s10209-017-0552-x
33. Aidman, E.: Cognitive fitness framework: towards assessing, training and augmenting individual-difference factors underpinning high-performance cognition. Front. Hum. Neurosci. **13**(466), 466–466 (2020)

# Changes of Multiple Object Tracking Performance in a 15 Days' - 6° Head-Down Tilt Bed Rest Experiment

Hongqiang Yu[✉], Ting Jiang, Bingxian Zhou, and Chunhui Wang

National Key Laboratory of Human Factors Engineering, China Astronaut Research and Training Center, Beijing 100094, China

**Abstract.** Human-computer interface (HCI) design should fully consider the basic human visual ability including multiple object tracking (MOT). A MOT test was conducted in a 15 days' - 6° head-down tilt bed rest (HDTBR) experiment to investigate effect of weightlessness environment on MOT performance. During 15 days' HDTBR, subjects were asked to stay in bed and hold the specific postural all the time even when they were being tested, taking meals and relieving themselves. A computer program which lasted for about 25 min to measure the MOT performance was used. MOT performance was represented by the selection accuracy. MRM ANOVA results showed that the main effect of the number of target balls was significant ($P < 0.001$) and the main effect of test time was significant ($P = 0.002$). Back testing of paired test showed that the selection accuracy of 4 target balls ($79.324 \pm 3.147$) was higher than selection accuracy of 5 target balls ($70.918 \pm 3.175$) and selection accuracy of 6 target balls ($66.118 \pm 2.715$) significantly ($P < 0.001$). Also the selection accuracy of 5 target balls was higher than selection accuracy of 6 target balls significantly ($P = 0.002$). The above results means that when the number of tracking targets is from 4 to 6, the smaller the number to be tracked, the higher the tracking performance. In addition, selection accuracy after 13 days' HDTBR ($75.840 \pm 3.113$) was highest than others and was higher than selection accuracy at one day before HDTBR ($68.857 \pm 2.602$) and 3 days' HDTBR ($71.206 \pm 2.351$) significantly ($P = 0.008, P = 0.043$), which means best tracking performance appeared after head down tilt bed rest 13 days in the experiment. The weightlessness environment may improve the performance of MOT by some mechanism.

**Keywords:** Multiple object tracking · Head-down tilt bed rest

## 1 Background

Visual information presentation and acquisition is an important part of human-computer interface (HCI). As is widely recognized, in order to improve the efficiency and security of the HCI system, the design should fully consider the basic human visual ability. Multiple object tracking (MOT) is one of important visual perception ability, which is widely studied and considered to be able to provide design boundary for dynamic interface element such as in area of advertisement and computer games. Since the classical

© Springer Nature Switzerland AG 2021
C. Stephanidis et al. (Eds.): HCII 2021, CCIS 1499, pp. 572–577, 2021.
https://doi.org/10.1007/978-3-030-90179-0_74

MOT testing paradigm was proposed by Pylyshyn and Storm in 1988, a lot of researches were conducted to focus the influencing factors of MOT performance. Most researchers revealed that many factors of human like gender, age and occupation and factors of tracking task like target characteristics (quantity, color, size), move speed, and route will affect MOT performance, while relatively few researchers have focused on the effect of changed environment on human which may also influence MOT performance. The space environment is one of the most special environments, since astronauts in spacecraft or space station will be influenced by weightlessness which is the most typical elements compared to other environments. Considering the limitations that it is impossible to build a real weightlessness environment on the ground, researchers always study changes in human abilities through - 6° head-down tilt bed rest which is considered to simulate the physiological effects of weightlessness well.

In this study, we conducted MOT test in a 15 days' - 6° head-down tilt bed rest experiment to investigate effect of weightlessness environment on multiple object tracking performance.

## 2 Method

### 2.1 Subjects

Seventeen male participants with an average age of 28.06 years (ranging from 24 to 34) participated in this study. The participants were all right-handed. None of the participants suffer from eye diseases except eight of them are myopic and their visual acuity or corrected visual acuity was 1.0 or more. All subjects were gave informed consent prior to their participant in the study and received reward after participation.

### 2.2 Measurements

A computer program which lasted for about 25 min to measure the MOT performance was used. There were fifteen white balls whose diameter was 2°visual angle on the black ground in the program. The number of target balls is four, five or six in three continuous test. In each test, target balls will glitter before all the fifteen balls began to move around in a speed of 1°visual angle per second. Subjects were asked to track the glitter target balls and find them out when the fifteen balls become static after ten seconds moving. There are twenty such trials in each test of different target balls, which means that a complete MOT test last for sixty trials. The number of balls which were tracked correctly was recorded to reflect MOT performance. A Dell P2415Q LCD Monitor was used to present test program (Fig. 1).

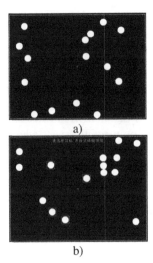

a)

b)

**Fig. 1.** Computer program of MOT test, a) fifteen white balls whose diameter was 2°visual angle on the black ground; b) find 4, 5, or 6 glitter balls out when the fifteen balls become static again.

## 2.3 Procedure

The experiment was conducted in a standard postural changes laboratory. There were enough rotating bed which allowed postural changes to - 6° head-down tilt bed rest. Five MOT tests were conducted for each subject. After understanding the content of the experiment, seventeen subjects completed first round of test in the sitting position state one day before they got in head-down tilt bed. During 15 days' - 6° head-down tilt bed rest, subjects were asked to stay in bed and hold the specific postural all the time even when they were being tested, taking meals and relieving themselves. Professional nurses helped subjects to do aforementioned tasks in different kinds of specific beds. MOT test conducted three times during 15 days' bed rest which conducted in 3, 9 and 13 days after subjects got in head-down tilt bed respectively. After 15 days' head-down tilt bed rest, subjects returned to normal state and completed the fifth MOT test 3 days after the time getting out of head tilt bed in the sitting position just like the first round test. The distance between the eyes and the screen is confirmed before each measurement to ensure that the distance is consistent for each test.

The time point of measurement were shown in Table 1. In order to simplify the illustration later, we use BR−, BR* and BR+ to represent time point of each measurement (BR−*: before bed rest * days; BR*: bed rest * days; BR+ *: after bed rest * days).

**Table 1.** Procedure of the experiment

**Table 1.** Procedure of the experiment

| Time point of measurement | Measurement content | Participant state |
|---|---|---|
| BR-1 | MOT | Sitting |
| Change to - 6° head-down tilt bed rest state | | |
| BR3 | MOT | 6° head-down tilt bed rest |
| BR9 | MOT | 6° head-down tilt bed rest |
| BR13 | MOT | 6° head-down tilt bed rest |
| Return to normal state | | |
| BR+ 3 | MOT | Sitting |

# 3  Results

Data processing and analysis used software IBM SPSS Statistics 25. All difference tests used repeated measurements analysis of variance (MRM ANOVA) and all correlation tests used bilateral Pearson test. Statistical significance was set at $p < 0.05$.

We calculate three kinds of MOT performance data (mean selection accuracy of all twenty trails: $SA_{20all}$, mean selection accuracy of best ten trails: $SA_{10best}$, and mean selection accuracy of middle ten trails: $SA_{10mid}$,) and found there is a strong correlation between any two kinds of performance data (Table 2). Therefore, we used $SA_{10mid}$, which eliminated the effects of accidental bad data and lucky data, to represent MOT performance.

**Table 2.** Correlation between any two kinds of three kinds of MOT performance

| | MOT of 4 target balls | | MOT of 5 target balls | | MOT of 6 target balls | |
|---|---|---|---|---|---|---|
| | $SA_{10mid}$ | $SA_{10best}$ | $SA_{10mid}$ | $SA_{10best}$ | $SA_{10mid}$ | $SA_{10best}$ |
| $SA_{20all}$ | $0.979^{**}$ | $0.940^{**}$ | $0.986^{**}$ | $0.960^{**}$ | $0.984^{**}$ | $0.961^{**}$ |
| $SA_{10mid}$ | | $0.941^{**}$ | | $0.952^{**}$ | | $0.953^{**}$ |

$^{**}$ Significant correlation at 0.01 level.

Each of seventeen subjects performed MOT test five times during the experiment and each test was carried out at different stages of the experiment. Average value of all subjects' SA10mid which represented average performance was presented as shown in Fig. 2.

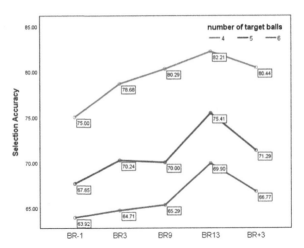

**Fig. 2.** Average value of all subjects' selection accuracy at different stages of the experiment.

The number of target balls (three levels: 4, 5, and 6) and test time (five levels: BR-1, BR3, BR9, and BR13) were taken as two independent variables for MRM ANOVA. The results show that: the main effect of the number of target balls was significant, $F(2,15)$ = 20.505, $\eta^2 = 0.732$, $P < 0.001$; the main effect of test time was significant, $F(4,13)$ = 7.474, $\eta^2 = 0.697$, $P = 0.002$; the interaction between the number of target balls and test time was not significant, $F(8,9) = 0.204$, $\eta^2 = 0.154$, $P = 0.982$.

Back testing of paired test showed that the selection accuracy of 4 target balls (79.324 ± 3.147) was higher than selection accuracy of 5 target balls (70.918 ± 3.175) and selection accuracy of 6 target balls (66.118 ± 2.715) significantly ($P < 0.001$). Also the selection accuracy of 5 target balls was higher than selection accuracy of 6 target balls significantly ($P = 0.002$). The above results means that when the number of tracking targets is from 4 to 6, the smaller the number to be tracked, the higher the tracking performance. In addition, selection accuracy at BR13 (75.840 ± 3.113) was highest than others and was higher than selection accuracy at BR-1 (68.857 ± 2.602) and BR3 (71.206 ± 2.351) significantly ($P = 0.008$, $P = 0.043$), which means best tracking performance appeared after head down tilt bed rest 13 days in the experiment. No significant difference was found in other paired comparisons ($P > 0.05$).

## 4  Discussion

In order to explore the changes of MOT performance under the physiological effect of simulated weightlessness, we took part in a 15 days' - 6° head-down tilt bed rest experiment and conducted three kinds of MOT tests of seventeen subjects at five different time points. Results showed that the more the targets need to be tracked, the worse the tracking performance was. This result is easy to understand and confirmed by many other studies whether in a normal environment or not.

However, what's interesting is that the best performance of MOT was on the 13th day of bed rest, and the change trends of three kinds of MOT tests distinguished by different target number show beautiful consistency. The result was difficult to predict before the experiment, and besides the effect of weightlessness on MOT performance, we try to explain this result from two aspects combined with the specific experimental situation. Firstly, there is training effect in MOT test. Although all subjects took exercise before each formal testing, it seems that the exercise was not enough since upward trend was obviously as time goes on. What's more, the performance of last test was better than the first test though the experimental conditions and subjects' status of the two tests were the same. Secondly, the performance of MOT test may be affected by physical stability. Thomas et al. considered self-motion impairs MOT performance. In our experiment, each subject underwent five times MOT tests. The first and the last tests were took in the sitting position while the second, third and fourth tests were took in bed. When test in the sitting position, subject sit in the chair with head suspended without effective restraint measures which may cause slight shaking of the head and body. The shaking may impaired MOT performance since there was no possibility of shaking when subjects were lying in bed. This possibly explains why the results of the last test were worse than penultimate test despite the learning effect.

## 5  Conclusion

Tracking performance decreased significantly with the increase of the number of tracking targets. Weightlessness effect may have a positive impact on tracking performance considered that tracking performance increased with time increase of subjects stayed in - 6° head-down tilt bed rest postural though it may also cause by learning effect and self-motion.

**Acknowledgments.** This work was supported by the Foundation of National Key Laboratory of Human Factors Engineering (SYFD160051801).

## References

1. Allen, R., McGeorge, P., Pearson, D., Milne, A.B.: Attention and expertise in multiple target tracking. Appl. Cogn. Psychol. **18**(3), 337–347 (2004)
2. Heaton, K.J., Maule, A.L., Maruta, J., Kryskow, E.M., Ghajar, J.: Attention and visual tracking degradation during acute sleep deprivation in a military sample. Aviat. Space Environ. Med. **85**(5), 497–503 (2014)
3. Liu, T.W., Chen, W.F., Liu, C.H., Fu, X.L.: Benefits and costs of uniqueness in multiple object tracking: the role of object complexity. Vision. Res. **66**, 31–38 (2012)
4. Pylyshyn, Z.W., Storm, R.W.: Tracking multiple independent targets: evidence for a parallel tracking mechanism. Spat. Vis. **3**(3), 179–197 (1988)
5. Taibbi, G., Cromwell, R.L., Zanello, S.B., Yarbough, P.O., Vizzeri, G.: Evaluation of ocular outcomes in two 14-day bed rest studies. Invest. Ophthalmol. Vis. Sci. **53**(14), 4903 (2012)
6. Thomas, L.E., Seiffert, A.E.: Self-motion impairs multiple-object tracking. Cognition **117**(1), 80–86 (2010)
7. Thomas, L.E., Seiffert, A.E.: How many objects are you worth? Quantification of the self-motion load on multiple object tracking. Front. Psychol. **2**(245), 1–5 (2011)

# Author Index